Ⓢ1774547

Dictionary of Literary Biography

1 *The American Renaissance in New England,* edited by Joel Myerson (1978)

2 *American Novelists Since World War II,* edited by Jeffrey Helterman and Richard Layman (1978)

3 *Antebellum Writers in New York and the South,* edited by Joel Myerson (1979)

4 *American Writers in Paris, 1920-1939,* edited by Karen Lane Rood (1980)

5 *American Poets Since World War II,* 2 parts, edited by Donald J. Greiner (1980)

6 *American Novelists Since World War II, Second Series,* edited by James E. Kibler Jr. (1980)

7 *Twentieth-Century American Dramatists,* 2 parts, edited by John MacNicholas (1981)

8 *Twentieth-Century American Science-Fiction Writers,* 2 parts, edited by David Cowart and Thomas L. Wymer (1981)

9 *American Novelists, 1910-1945,* 3 parts, edited by James J. Martine (1981)

10 *Modern British Dramatists, 1900-1945,* 2 parts, edited by Stanley Weintraub (1982)

11 *American Humorists, 1800-1950,* 2 parts, edited by Stanley Trachtenberg (1982)

12 *American Realists and Naturalists,* edited by Donald Pizer and Earl N. Harbert (1982)

13 *British Dramatists Since World War II,* 2 parts, edited by Stanley Weintraub (1982)

14 *British Novelists Since 1960,* 2 parts, edited by Jay L. Halio (1983)

15 *British Novelists, 1930-1959,* 2 parts, edited by Bernard Oldsey (1983)

16 *The Beats: Literary Bohemians in Postwar America,* 2 parts, edited by Ann Charters (1983)

17 *Twentieth-Century American Historians,* edited by Clyde N. Wilson (1983)

18 *Victorian Novelists After 1885,* edited by Ira B. Nadel and William E. Fredeman (1983)

19 *British Poets, 1880-1914,* edited by Donald E. Stanford (1983)

20 *British Poets, 1914-1945,* edited by Donald E. Stanford (1983)

21 *Victorian Novelists Before 1885,* edited by Ira B. Nadel and William E. Fredeman (1983)

22 *American Writers for Children, 1900-1960,* edited by John Cech (1983)

23 *American Newspaper Journalists, 1873-1900,* edited by Perry J. Ashley (1983)

24 *American Colonial Writers, 1606-1734,* edited by Emory Elliott (1984)

25 *American Newspaper Journalists, 1901-1925,* edited by Perry J. Ashley (1984)

26 *American Screenwriters,* edited by Robert E. Morsberger, Stephen O. Lesser, and Randall Clark (1984)

27 *Poets of Great Britain and Ireland, 1945-1960,* edited by Vincent B. Sherry Jr. (1984)

28 *Twentieth-Century American-Jewish Fiction Writers,* edited by Daniel Walden (1984)

29 *American Newspaper Journalists, 1926-1950,* edited by Perry J. Ashley (1984)

30 *American Historians, 1607-1865,* edited by Clyde N. Wilson (1984)

31 *American Colonial Writers, 1735-1781,* edited by Emory Elliott (1984)

32 *Victorian Poets Before 1850,* edited by William E. Fredeman and Ira B. Nadel (1984)

33 *Afro-American Fiction Writers After 1955,* edited by Thadious M. Davis and Trudier Harris (1984)

34 *British Novelists, 1890-1929: Traditionalists,* edited by Thomas F. Staley (1985)

35 *Victorian Poets After 1850,* edited by William E. Fredeman and Ira B. Nadel (1985)

36 *British Novelists, 1890-1929: Modernists,* edited by Thomas F. Staley (1985)

37 *American Writers of the Early Republic,* edited by Emory Elliott (1985)

38 *Afro-American Writers After 1955: Dramatists and Prose Writers,* edited by Thadious M. Davis and Trudier Harris (1985)

39 *British Novelists, 1660-1800,* 2 parts, edited by Martin C. Battestin (1985)

40 *Poets of Great Britain and Ireland Since 1960,* 2 parts, edited by Vincent B. Sherry Jr. (1985)

41 *Afro-American Poets Since 1955,* edited by Trudier Harris and Thadious M. Davis (1985)

42 *American Writers for Children Before 1900,* edited by Glenn E. Estes (1985)

43 *American Newspaper Journalists, 1690-1872,* edited by Perry J. Ashley (1986)

44 *American Screenwriters, Second Series,* edited by Randall Clark, Robert E. Morsberger, and Stephen O. Lesser (1986)

45 *American Poets, 1880-1945, First Series,* edited by Peter Quartermain (1986)

46 *American Literary Publishing Houses, 1900-1980: Trade and Paperback,* edited by Peter Dzwonkoski (1986)

47 *American Historians, 1866-1912,* edited by Clyde N. Wilson (1986)

48 *American Poets, 1880-1945, Second Series,* edited by Peter Quartermain (1986)

49 *American Literary Publishing Houses, 1638-1899,* 2 parts, edited by Peter Dzwonkoski (1986)

50 *Afro-American Writers Before the Harlem Renaissance,* edited by Trudier Harris (1986)

51 *Afro-American Writers from the Harlem Renaissance to 1940,* edited by Trudier Harris (1987)

52 *American Writers for Children Since 1960: Fiction,* edited by Glenn E. Estes (1986)

53 *Canadian Writers Since 1960, First Series,* edited by W. H. New (1986)

54 *American Poets, 1880-1945, Third Series,* 2 parts, edited by Peter Quartermain (1987)

55 *Victorian Prose Writers Before 1867,* edited by William B. Thesing (1987)

56 *German Fiction Writers, 1914-1945,* edited by James Hardin (1987)

57 *Victorian Prose Writers After 1867,* edited by William B. Thesing (1987)

58 *Jacobean and Caroline Dramatists,* edited by Fredson Bowers (1987)

59 *American Literary Critics and Scholars, 1800-1850,* edited by John W. Rathbun and Monica M. Grecu (1987)

60 *Canadian Writers Since 1960, Second Series,* edited by W. H. New (1987)

61 *American Writers for Children Since 1960: Poets, Illustrators, and Nonfiction Authors,* edited by Glenn E. Estes (1987)

62 *Elizabethan Dramatists,* edited by Fredson Bowers (1987)

63 *Modern American Critics, 1920-1955,* edited by Gregory S. Jay (1988)

64 *American Literary Critics and Scholars, 1850-1880,* edited by John W. Rathbun and Monica M. Grecu (1988)

65 *French Novelists, 1900-1930,* edited by Catharine Savage Brosman (1988)

66 *German Fiction Writers, 1885-1913,* 2 parts, edited by James Hardin (1988)

67 *Modern American Critics Since 1955,* edited by Gregory S. Jay (1988)

68 *Canadian Writers, 1920-1959, First Series,* edited by W. H. New (1988)

69 *Contemporary German Fiction Writers, First Series,* edited by Wolfgang D. Elfe and James Hardin (1988)

70 *British Mystery Writers, 1860-1919,* edited by Bernard Benstock and Thomas F. Staley (1988)

71 *American Literary Critics and Scholars, 1880-1900,* edited by John W. Rathbun and Monica M. Grecu (1988)

72 *French Novelists, 1930-1960,* edited by Catharine Savage Brosman (1988)

73 *American Magazine Journalists, 1741-1850,* edited by Sam G. Riley (1988)

74 *American Short-Story Writers Before 1880,* edited by Bobby Ellen Kimbel, with the assistance of William E. Grant (1988)

75 *Contemporary German Fiction Writers, Second Series,* edited by Wolfgang D. Elfe and James Hardin (1988)

76 *Afro-American Writers, 1940-1955,* edited by Trudier Harris (1988)

77 *British Mystery Writers, 1920-1939,* edited by Bernard Benstock and Thomas F. Staley (1988)

78 *American Short-Story Writers, 1880-1910,* edited by Bobby Ellen Kimbel, with the assistance of William E. Grant (1988)

79 *American Magazine Journalists, 1850-1900,* edited by Sam G. Riley (1988)

80 *Restoration and Eighteenth-Century Dramatists, First Series,* edited by Paula R. Backscheider (1989)

81 *Austrian Fiction Writers, 1875-1913,* edited by James Hardin and Donald G. Daviau (1989)

82 *Chicano Writers, First Series,* edited by Francisco A. Lomelí and Carl R. Shirley (1989)

83 *French Novelists Since 1960,* edited by Catharine Savage Brosman (1989)

84 *Restoration and Eighteenth-Century Dramatists, Second Series,* edited by Paula R. Backscheider (1989)

85 *Austrian Fiction Writers After 1914,* edited by James Hardin and Donald G. Daviau (1989)

86 *American Short-Story Writers, 1910-1945, First Series,* edited by Bobby Ellen Kimbel (1989)

87 *British Mystery and Thriller Writers Since 1940, First Series,* edited by Bernard Benstock and Thomas F. Staley (1989)

88 *Canadian Writers, 1920-1959, Second Series,* edited by W. H. New (1989)

89 *Restoration and Eighteenth-Century Dramatists, Third Series,* edited by Paula R. Backscheider (1989)

90 *German Writers in the Age of Goethe, 1789-1832,* edited by James Hardin and Christoph E. Schweitzer (1989)

91 *American Magazine Journalists, 1900-1960, First Series,* edited by Sam G. Riley (1990)

92 *Canadian Writers, 1890-1920,* edited by W. H. New (1990)

93 *British Romantic Poets, 1789-1832, First Series,* edited by John R. Greenfield (1990)

94 *German Writers in the Age of Goethe: Sturm und Drang to Classicism,* edited by James Hardin and Christoph E. Schweitzer (1990)

95 *Eighteenth-Century British Poets, First Series,* edited by John Sitter (1990)

96 *British Romantic Poets, 1789-1832, Second Series,* edited by John R. Greenfield (1990)

97 *German Writers from the Enlightenment to Sturm und Drang, 1720-1764,* edited by James Hardin and Christoph E. Schweitzer (1990)

98 *Modern British Essayists, First Series,* edited by Robert Beum (1990)

99 *Canadian Writers Before 1890,* edited by W. H. New (1990)

100 *Modern British Essayists, Second Series,* edited by Robert Beum (1990)

101 *British Prose Writers, 1660-1800, First Series,* edited by Donald T. Siebert (1991)

102 *American Short-Story Writers, 1910-1945, Second Series,* edited by Bobby Ellen Kimbel (1991)

103 *American Literary Biographers, First Series,* edited by Steven Serafin (1991)

104 *British Prose Writers, 1660-1800, Second Series,* edited by Donald T. Siebert (1991)

105 *American Poets Since World War II, Second Series,* edited by R. S. Gwynn (1991)

106 *British Literary Publishing Houses, 1820-1880,* edited by Patricia J. Anderson and Jonathan Rose (1991)

107 *British Romantic Prose Writers, 1789-1832, First Series,* edited by John R. Greenfield (1991)

108 *Twentieth-Century Spanish Poets, First Series,* edited by Michael L. Perna (1991)

109 *Eighteenth-Century British Poets, Second Series,* edited by John Sitter (1991)

110 *British Romantic Prose Writers, 1789-1832, Second Series,* edited by John R. Greenfield (1991)

111 *American Literary Biographers, Second Series,* edited by Steven Serafin (1991)

112 *British Literary Publishing Houses, 1881-1965,* edited by Jonathan Rose and Patricia J. Anderson (1991)

113 *Modern Latin-American Fiction Writers, First Series,* edited by William Luis (1992)

114 *Twentieth-Century Italian Poets, First Series,* edited by Giovanna Wedel De Stasio, Glauco Cambon, and Antonio Illiano (1992)

115 *Medieval Philosophers,* edited by Jeremiah Hackett (1992)

116 *British Romantic Novelists, 1789-1832,* edited by Bradford K. Mudge (1992)

117 *Twentieth-Century Caribbean and Black African Writers, First Series,* edited by Bernth Lindfors and Reinhard Sander (1992)

118 *Twentieth-Century German Dramatists, 1889-1918,* edited by Wolfgang D. Elfe and James Hardin (1992)

119 *Nineteenth-Century French Fiction Writers: Romanticism and Realism, 1800-1860,* edited by Catharine Savage Brosman (1992)

120 *American Poets Since World War II, Third Series,* edited by R. S. Gwynn (1992)

121 *Seventeenth-Century British Nondramatic Poets, First Series,* edited by M. Thomas Hester (1992)

122 *Chicano Writers, Second Series,* edited by Francisco A. Lomelí and Carl R. Shirley (1992)

123 *Nineteenth-Century French Fiction Writers: Naturalism and Beyond, 1860-1900,* edited by Catharine Savage Brosman (1992)

124 *Twentieth-Century German Dramatists, 1919-1992,* edited by Wolfgang D. Elfe and James Hardin (1992)

125 *Twentieth-Century Caribbean and Black African Writers, Second Series,* edited by Bernth Lindfors and Reinhard Sander (1993)

126 *Seventeenth-Century British Nondramatic Poets, Second Series,* edited by M. Thomas Hester (1993)

127 *American Newspaper Publishers, 1950-1990,* edited by Perry J. Ashley (1993)

128 *Twentieth-Century Italian Poets, Second Series,* edited by Giovanna Wedel De Stasio, Glauco Cambon, and Antonio Illiano (1993)

129 *Nineteenth-Century German Writers, 1841-1900,* edited by James Hardin and Siegfried Mews (1993)

130 *American Short-Story Writers Since World War II,* edited by Patrick Meanor (1993)

131 *Seventeenth-Century British Nondramatic Poets, Third Series,* edited by M. Thomas Hester (1993)

132 *Sixteenth-Century British Nondramatic Writers, First Series,* edited by David A. Richardson (1993)

133 *Nineteenth-Century German Writers to 1840,* edited by James Hardin and Siegfried Mews (1993)

134 *Twentieth-Century Spanish Poets, Second Series,* edited by Jerry Phillips Winfield (1994)

135 *British Short-Fiction Writers, 1880-1914: The Realist Tradition,* edited by William B. Thesing (1994)

136 *Sixteenth-Century British Nondramatic Writers, Second Series,* edited by David A. Richardson (1994)

137 *American Magazine Journalists, 1900-1960, Second Series,* edited by Sam G. Riley (1994)

138 *German Writers and Works of the High Middle Ages: 1170-1280,* edited by James Hardin and Will Hasty (1994)

139 *British Short-Fiction Writers, 1945-1980,* edited by Dean Baldwin (1994)

140 *American Book-Collectors and Bibliographers, First Series,* edited by Joseph Rosenblum (1994)

141 *British Children's Writers, 1880-1914,* edited by Laura M. Zaidman (1994)

142 *Eighteenth-Century British Literary Biographers,* edited by Steven Serafin (1994)

143 *American Novelists Since World War II, Third Series,* edited by James R. Giles and Wanda H. Giles (1994)

144 *Nineteenth-Century British Literary Biographers,* edited by Steven Serafin (1994)

145 *Modern Latin-American Fiction Writers, Second Series,* edited by William Luis and Ann González (1994)

146 *Old and Middle English Literature,* edited by Jeffrey Helterman and Jerome Mitchell (1994)

147 *South Slavic Writers Before World War II,* edited by Vasa D. Mihailovich (1994)

148 *German Writers and Works of the Early Middle Ages: 800-1170,* edited by Will Hasty and James Hardin (1994)

149 *Late Nineteenth- and Early Twentieth-Century British Literary Biographers,* edited by Steven Serafin (1995)

150 *Early Modern Russian Writers, Late Seventeenth and Eighteenth Centuries,* edited by Marcus C. Levitt (1995)

151 *British Prose Writers of the Early Seventeenth Century,* edited by Clayton D. Lein (1995)

152 *American Novelists Since World War II, Fourth Series,* edited by James R. Giles and Wanda H. Giles (1995)

153 *Late-Victorian and Edwardian British Novelists, First Series,* edited by George M. Johnson (1995)

154 *The British Literary Book Trade, 1700-1820,* edited by James K. Bracken and Joel Silver (1995)

155 *Twentieth-Century British Literary Biographers*, edited by Steven Serafin (1995)

156 *British Short-Fiction Writers, 1880-1914: The Romantic Tradition*, edited by William F. Naufftus (1995)

157 *Twentieth-Century Caribbean and Black African Writers, Third Series*, edited by Bernth Lindfors and Reinhard Sander (1995)

158 *British Reform Writers, 1789-1832*, edited by Gary Kelly and Edd Applegate (1995)

159 *British Short-Fiction Writers, 1800-1880*, edited by John R. Greenfield (1996)

160 *British Children's Writers, 1914-1960*, edited by Donald R. Hettinga and Gary D. Schmidt (1996)

161 *British Children's Writers Since 1960, First Series*, edited by Caroline Hunt (1996)

162 *British Short-Fiction Writers, 1915-1945*, edited by John H. Rogers (1996)

163 *British Children's Writers, 1800-1880*, edited by Meena Khorana (1996)

164 *German Baroque Writers, 1580-1660*, edited by James Hardin (1996)

165 *American Poets Since World War II, Fourth Series*, edited by Joseph Conte (1996)

166 *British Travel Writers, 1837-1875*, edited by Barbara Brothers and Julia Gergits (1996)

167 *Sixteenth-Century British Nondramatic Writers, Third Series*, edited by David A. Richardson (1996)

168 *German Baroque Writers, 1661-1730*, edited by James Hardin (1996)

169 *American Poets Since World War II, Fifth Series*, edited by Joseph Conte (1996)

170 *The British Literary Book Trade, 1475-1700*, edited by James K. Bracken and Joel Silver (1996)

171 *Twentieth-Century American Sportswriters*, edited by Richard Orodenker (1996)

172 *Sixteenth-Century British Nondramatic Writers, Fourth Series*, edited by David A. Richardson (1996)

173 *American Novelists Since World War II, Fifth Series*, edited by James R. Giles and Wanda H. Giles (1996)

174 *British Travel Writers, 1876-1909*, edited by Barbara Brothers and Julia Gergits (1997)

175 *Native American Writers of the United States*, edited by Kenneth M. Roemer (1997)

176 *Ancient Greek Authors*, edited by Ward W. Briggs (1997)

177 *Italian Novelists Since World War II, 1945-1965*, edited by Augustus Pallotta (1997)

178 *British Fantasy and Science-Fiction Writers Before World War I*, edited by Darren Harris-Fain (1997)

179 *German Writers of the Renaissance and Reformation, 1280-1580*, edited by James Hardin and Max Reinhart (1997)

180 *Japanese Fiction Writers, 1868-1945*, edited by Van C. Gessel (1997)

181 *South Slavic Writers Since World War II*, edited by Vasa D. Mihailovich (1997)

182 *Japanese Fiction Writers Since World War II*, edited by Van C. Gessel (1997)

183 *American Travel Writers, 1776-1864*, edited by James J. Schramer and Donald Ross (1997)

184 *Nineteenth-Century British Book-Collectors and Bibliographers*, edited by William Baker and Kenneth Womack (1997)

185 *American Literary Journalists, 1945-1995, First Series*, edited by Arthur J. Kaul (1998)

186 *Nineteenth-Century American Western Writers*, edited by Robert L. Gale (1998)

187 *American Book Collectors and Bibliographers, Second Series*, edited by Joseph Rosenblum (1998)

188 *American Book and Magazine Illustrators to 1920*, edited by Steven E. Smith, Catherine A. Hastedt, and Donald H. Dyal (1998)

189 *American Travel Writers, 1850-1915*, edited by Donald Ross and James J. Schramer (1998)

190 *British Reform Writers, 1832-1914*, edited by Gary Kelly and Edd Applegate (1998)

191 *British Novelists Between the Wars*, edited by George M. Johnson (1998)

192 *French Dramatists, 1789-1914*, edited by Barbara T. Cooper (1998)

193 *American Poets Since World War II, Sixth Series*, edited by Joseph Conte (1998)

194 *British Novelists Since 1960, Second Series*, edited by Merritt Moseley (1998)

195 *British Travel Writers, 1910-1939*, edited by Barbara Brothers and Julia Gergits (1998)

196 *Italian Novelists Since World War II, 1965-1995*, edited by Augustus Pallotta (1999)

197 *Late-Victorian and Edwardian British Novelists, Second Series*, edited by George M. Johnson (1999)

198 *Russian Literature in the Age of Pushkin and Gogol: Prose*, edited by Christine A. Rydel (1999)

199 *Victorian Women Poets*, edited by William B. Thesing (1999)

200 *American Women Prose Writers to 1820*, edited by Carla J. Mulford, with Angela Vietto and Amy E. Winans (1999)

201 *Twentieth-Century British Book Collectors and Bibliographers*, edited by William Baker and Kenneth Womack (1999)

202 *Nineteenth-Century American Fiction Writers*, edited by Kent P. Ljungquist (1999)

203 *Medieval Japanese Writers*, edited by Steven D. Carter (1999)

204 *British Travel Writers, 1940-1997*, edited by Barbara Brothers and Julia M. Gergits (1999)

205 *Russian Literature in the Age of Pushkin and Gogol: Poetry and Drama*, edited by Christine A. Rydel (1999)

206 *Twentieth-Century American Western Writers, First Series*, edited by Richard H. Cracroft (1999)

207 *British Novelists Since 1960, Third Series*, edited by Merritt Moseley (1999)

208 *Literature of the French and Occitan Middle Ages: Eleventh to Fifteenth Centuries*, edited by Deborah Sinnreich-Levi and Ian S. Laurie (1999)

209 *Chicano Writers, Third Series*, edited by Francisco A. Lomelí and Carl R. Shirley (1999)

210 *Ernest Hemingway: A Documentary Volume*, edited by Robert W. Trogdon (1999)

211 *Ancient Roman Writers*, edited by Ward W. Briggs (1999)

212 *Twentieth-Century American Western Writers, Second Series*, edited by Richard H. Cracroft (1999)

213 *Pre-Nineteenth-Century British Book Collectors and Bibliographers*, edited by William Baker and Kenneth Womack (1999)

214 *Twentieth-Century Danish Writers*, edited by Marianne Stecher-Hansen (1999)

215 *Twentieth-Century Eastern European Writers, First Series*, edited by Steven Serafin (1999)

216 *British Poets of the Great War: Brooke, Rosenberg, Thomas. A Documentary Volume*, edited by Patrick Quinn (2000)

Documentary Series

1 *Sherwood Anderson, Willa Cather, John Dos Passos, Theodore Dreiser, F. Scott Fitzgerald, Ernest Hemingway, Sinclair Lewis*, edited by Margaret A. Van Antwerp (1982)

2 *James Gould Cozzens, James T. Farrell, William Faulkner, John O'Hara, John Steinbeck, Thomas Wolfe, Richard Wright*, edited by Margaret A. Van Antwerp (1982)

3 *Saul Bellow, Jack Kerouac, Norman Mailer, Vladimir Nabokov, John Updike, Kurt Vonnegut*, edited by Mary Bruccoli (1983)

4 *Tennessee Williams*, edited by Margaret A. Van Antwerp and Sally Johns (1984)

5 *American Transcendentalists*, edited by Joel Myerson (1988)

6 *Hardboiled Mystery Writers: Raymond Chandler, Dashiell Hammett, Ross Macdonald*, edited by Matthew J. Bruccoli and Richard Layman (1989)

7 *Modern American Poets: James Dickey, Robert Frost, Marianne Moore*, edited by Karen L. Rood (1989)

8 *The Black Aesthetic Movement*, edited by Jeffrey Louis Decker (1991)

9 *American Writers of the Vietnam War: W. D. Ehrhart, Larry Heinemann, Tim O'Brien, Walter McDonald, John M. Del Vecchio*, edited by Ronald Baughman (1991)

10 *The Bloomsbury Group*, edited by Edward L. Bishop (1992)

11 *American Proletarian Culture: The Twenties and The Thirties*, edited by Jon Christian Suggs (1993)

12 *Southern Women Writers: Flannery O'Connor, Katherine Anne Porter, Eudora Welty*, edited by Mary Ann Wimsatt and Karen L. Rood (1994)

13 *The House of Scribner, 1846-1904*, edited by John Delaney (1996)

14 *Four Women Writers for Children, 1868-1918*, edited by Caroline C. Hunt (1996)

15 *American Expatriate Writers: Paris in the Twenties*, edited by Matthew J. Bruccoli and Robert W. Trogdon (1997)

16 *The House of Scribner, 1905-1930*, edited by John Delaney (1997)

17 *The House of Scribner, 1931-1984*, edited by John Delaney (1998)

18 *British Poets of The Great War: Sassoon, Graves, Owen*, edited by Patrick Quinn (1999)

19 *James Dickey*, edited by Judith S. Baughman (1999)

See also DLB 210, 216

Yearbooks

1980 edited by Karen L. Rood, Jean W. Ross, and Richard Ziegfeld (1981)

1981 edited by Karen L. Rood, Jean W. Ross, and Richard Ziegfeld (1982)

1982 edited by Richard Ziegfeld; associate editors: Jean W. Ross and Lynne C. Zeigler (1983)

1983 edited by Mary Bruccoli and Jean W. Ross, associate editor Richard Ziegfeld (1984)

1984 edited by Jean W. Ross (1985)

1985 edited by Jean W. Ross (1986)

1986 edited by J. M. Brook (1987)

1987 edited by J. M. Brook (1988)

1988 edited by J. M. Brook (1989)

1989 edited by J. M. Brook (1990)

1990 edited by James W. Hipp (1991)

1991 edited by James W. Hipp (1992)

1992 edited by James W. Hipp (1993)

1993 edited by James W. Hipp, contributing editor George Garrett (1994)

1994 edited by James W. Hipp, contributing editor George Garrett (1995)

1995 edited by James W. Hipp, contributing editor George Garrett (1996)

1996 edited by Samuel W. Bruce and L. Kay Webster, contributing editor George Garrett (1997)

1997 edited by Matthew J. Bruccoli and George Garrett, with the assistance of L. Kay Webster (1998)

1998 edited by Matthew J. Bruccoli, contributing editor George Garrett, with the assistance of D. W. Thomas (1999)

Concise Series

Concise Dictionary of American Literary Biography, 7 volumes (1988-1999): *The New Consciousness, 1941-1968; Colonization to the American Renaissance, 1640-1865; Realism, Naturalism, and Local Color, 1865-1917; The Twenties, 1917-1929; The Age of Maturity, 1929-1941; Broadening Views, 1968-1988; Supplement: Modern Writers, 1900–1998.*

Concise Dictionary of British Literary Biography, 8 volumes (1991-1992): *Writers of the Middle Ages and Renaissance Before 1660; Writers of the Restoration and Eighteenth Century, 1660-1789; Writers of the Romantic Period, 1789-1832; Victorian Writers, 1832-1890; Late-Victorian and Edwardian Writers, 1890-1914; Modern Writers, 1914-1945; Writers After World War II, 1945-1960; Contemporary Writers, 1960 to Present.*

Concise Dictionary of World Literary Biography, 20 volumes projected (1999-): *Ancient Greek and Roman Writers; German Writers.*

Dictionary of Literary Biography® • Volume Two Hundred Sixteen

British Poets of the Great War: Brooke, Rosenberg, Thomas
A Documentary Volume

Dictionary of Literary Biography® • Volume Two Hundred Sixteen

British Poets of the Great War: Brooke, Rosenberg, Thomas
A Documentary Volume

Edited by
Patrick Quinn
Nene College

A Bruccoli Clark Layman Book
The Gale Group
Detroit • San Francisco • London • Boston • Woodbridge, Conn.

Advisory Board for
DICTIONARY OF LITERARY BIOGRAPHY

John Baker
William Cagle
Patrick O'Connor
George Garrett
Trudier Harris

Matthew J. Bruccoli and Richard Layman, Editorial Directors
C. E. Frazer Clark Jr., Managing Editor
Karen L. Rood, Senior Editor

Printed in the United States of America

The paper used in this publication meets the minimum requirements
of American National Standard for Information Sciences–Permanence
Paper for Printed Library Materials, ANSI Z39.48-1984.∞™

This publication is a creative work fully protected by all applicable copyright laws, as well as by misappropriation, trade secret, unfair competition, and other applicable laws. The authors and editors of this work have added value to the underlying factual material herein through one or more of the following: unique and original selection, coordination, expression, arrangement, and classification of the information.

All rights to this publication will be vigorously defended.

Copyright © 2000 by The Gale Group
27500 Drake Road
Farmington Hills, MI 48331

All rights reserved including the right of reproduction in
whole or in part in any form.

Library of Congress Cataloging-in-Publication Data

British poets of the Great War: Brooke, Rosenberg, Thomas: a documentary volume / edited by
  Patrick Quinn.
    p. cm.–(Dictionary of literary biography: v. 216)
"A Bruccoli Clark Layman book."
Includes bibliographical references and index.
ISBN 0-7876-3125-6 (alk. paper)
1. English poetry–20th century–History and criticism–Sources. 2. World War, 1914–1918–Great Britain–Literature and the war–Sources. 3. Soldiers' writings, English–History and criticism–Sources.
4. Poets, English–20th century–Biography–Sources. 5. War poetry, English–History and criticism–Sources. 6. Soldiers–Great Britain–Biography–Sources. 7. Brooke, Rupert, 1887-1915. 8. Rosenberg, Isaac, 1890-1918. 9. Thomas, Edward, 1878-1917. I. Quinn, Patrick. II. Series.
PR605.W65 B75 1999
821'.91209358–dc21   99–047642

For Trajan:
in whom I am well pleased

Contents

Plan of the Series xiii

Introduction. xv

Permissions xix

Rupert Brooke (1887–1915) 5

Isaac Rosenberg (1890–1918) 101

Edward Thomas (1878–1917) 207

Appendix: Other British Poets
Who Fell in the Great War 301

Index 321

Plan of the Series

... Almost the most prodigious asset of a country, and perhaps its most precious possession, is its native literary product—when that product is fine and noble and enduring.

Mark Twain*

The advisory board, the editors, and the publisher of the *Dictionary of Literary Biography* are joined in endorsing Mark Twain's declaration. The literature of a nation provides an inexhaustible resource of permanent worth. We intend to make literature and its creators better understood and more accessible to students and the reading public, while satisfying the standards of teachers and scholars.

To meet these requirements, *literary biography* has been construed in terms of the author's achievement. The most important thing about a writer is his writing. Accordingly, the entries in *DLB* are career biographies, tracing the development of the author's canon and the evolution of his reputation.

The purpose of *DLB* is not only to provide reliable information in a convenient format but also to place the figures in the larger perspective of literary history and to offer appraisals of their accomplishments by qualified scholars.

The publication plan for *DLB* resulted from two years of preparation. The project was proposed to Bruccoli Clark by Frederick G. Ruffner, president of the Gale Research Company, in November 1975. After specimen entries were prepared and typeset, an advisory board was formed to refine the entry format and develop the series rationale. In meetings held during 1976, the publisher, series editors, and advisory board approved the scheme for a comprehensive biographical dictionary of persons who contributed to North American literature. Editorial work on the first volume began in January 1977, and it was published in 1978. In order to make *DLB* more than a reference tool and to compile volumes that individually have claim to status as literary history, it was decided to organize volumes by topic, period, or genre. Each of these freestanding volumes provides a biographical-bibliographical guide and overview for a particular area of literature. We are convinced that this organization—as opposed to a single alphabet method—constitutes a valuable innovation in the presentation of reference material. The volume plan necessarily requires many decisions for the placement and treatment of authors who might properly be included in two or three volumes. In some instances a major figure will be included in separate volumes, but with different entries emphasizing the aspect of his career appropriate to each volume. Ernest Hemingway, for example, is represented in *American Writers in Paris, 1920-1939* by an entry focusing on his expatriate apprenticeship; he is also in *American Novelists, 1910-1945* with an entry surveying his entire career, as well as in *American Short-Story Writers, 1910-1945, Second Series* with an entry concentrating on his short stories. Each volume includes a cumulative index of the subject authors and articles. Comprehensive indexes to the entire series are planned.

Since 1981 the series has been further augmented by the *DLB Yearbooks,* which update published entries and add new entries to keep the *DLB* current with contemporary activity. There have also been *DLB Documentary Series* volumes which provide biographical and critical source materials for figures whose work is judged to have particular interest for students. One of these companion volumes is devoted entirely to Tennessee Williams.

We define literature as the *intellectual commerce of a nation:* not merely as belles lettres but as that ample and complex process by which ideas are generated, shaped, and transmitted. *DLB* entries are not limited to "creative writers" but extend to other figures who in their time and in their way influenced the mind of a people. Thus the series encompasses historians, journalists, publishers, book collectors, and screenwriters. By this means readers of *DLB* may be aided to perceive literature not as cult scripture in the keeping of intellectual high priests but firmly positioned at the center of a nation's life.

DLB includes the major writers appropriate to each volume and those standing in the ranks behind

---

*From an unpublished section of Mark Twain's autobiography, copyright by the Mark Twain Company

them. Scholarly and critical counsel has been sought in deciding which minor figures to include and how full their entries should be. Wherever possible, useful references are made to figures who do not warrant separate entries.

Each *DLB* volume has an expert volume editor responsible for planning the volume, selecting the figures for inclusion, and assigning the entries. Volume editors are also responsible for preparing, where appropriate, appendices surveying the major periodicals and literary and intellectual movements for their volumes, as well as lists of further readings. Work on the series as a whole is coordinated at the Bruccoli Clark Layman editorial center in Columbia, South Carolina, where the editorial staff is responsible for accuracy and utility of the published volumes.

One feature that distinguishes *DLB* is the illustration policy–its concern with the iconography of literature. Just as an author is influenced by his surroundings, so is the reader's understanding of the author enhanced by a knowledge of his environment. Therefore *DLB* volumes include not only drawings, paintings, and photographs of authors, often depicting them at various stages in their careers, but also illustrations of their families and places where they lived. Title pages are regularly reproduced in facsimile along with dust jackets for modern authors. The dust jackets are a special feature of *DLB* because they often document better than anything else the way in which an author's work was perceived in its own time. Specimens of the writers' manuscripts and letters are included when feasible.

Samuel Johnson rightly decreed that "The chief glory of every people arises from its authors." The purpose of the *Dictionary of Literary Biography* is to compile literary history in the surest way available to us–by accurate and comprehensive treatment of the lives and work of those who contributed to it.

The DLB Advisory Board

Introduction

This volume is the second of two documentary volumes dedicated to British poetry of World War I. It focuses on three English poets who saw action and died in World War I and whose literary accomplishments during the conflict have kept their reputations alive and their works read since that catastrophic event occurred. The entries include representative photographs, manuscripts, military and medical records, interviews, essays, poems, reviews, obituaries, literary assessments, prose excerpts, and personal letters written throughout the writers' lives in order to offer the reader a comprehensive awareness of how the personality of each individual was molded by the conflict that the British still call the "Great War."

The choice of six representative poets for inclusion in the two volumes was not an easy one. The omission of writers such as Julian Grenfell, Charles Sorley, David Jones, Richard Aldington, Edmund Blunden, or Ivor Gurney was made with regret. The decision to include Rupert Brooke, Edward Thomas, Isaac Rosenberg, Siegfried Sassoon, Robert Graves, and Wilfred Owen was made with some trepidation, but their lives and works seemed to be representative of the widest responses to the Great War. All six of the writers represented in the two volumes were in the military service during the war; only two of them managed to survive. Three of the six were less than twenty-five years old when the war started: the oldest, Thomas, was in his mid thirties; the youngest, Graves, had just left Charterhouse School at the age of eighteen. While all of these soldiers had considered writing poetry when the war broke out, only Brooke had an established reputation as a poet. With the encouragement of the American poet Robert Frost, Thomas had only just begun to think about writing verse. Except for Rosenberg, all of these poets experienced the war from the perspective of the officer class: Brooke was in the navy and Thomas in the artillery, while the other three were infantry officers. Two of the writers–Sassoon and Owen–underwent psychiatric care at the same time in Craiglockhart Hospital in Edinburgh, and the two survivors, Graves and Sassoon, were each badly wounded on two separate occasions. Two writers, Sassoon and Rosenberg, came from Jewish backgrounds; Graves had German and Irish blood; Thomas felt an affinity for Wales; and Brooke and Owen were English. Three of the writers attended famous public schools; the other three did not. Three attended university, and three did not. Brooke's death and his war sonnets became synonymous with English patriotism, whereas Sassoon's protest against the prolonging of the war in 1917 became the focus of immense antiwar sentiment.

The materials in this volume present the war experiences of each of these writers and discuss the nature of their poetic responses to what they saw and felt as they prepared for and participated in the Great War. These entries sketch the biographies of the poets in order to reveal how emotionally and psychologically ill prepared they were for what was to be one of the most horrific bloodbaths in modern history.

All the poets of the Great War were influenced by the prevailing attitudes toward poetry in the first fifteen years of the twentieth century. Most of the poets at that time were in revolt from the earnestness and didacticism of Victorian poetry. Not for them were the philosophical speculations on the complexities of existence posed by the long-serving poet laureate Alfred Tennyson; not for them were the sticky questions of religious faith in Matthew Arnold's verse or the psychological probing of Robert Browning's dramatic monologues. Furthermore, these Georgian poets–those who reached their maturity as writers during the reign of George V– also dismissed Edwardian poets such as Alfred Austin and William Watson, writers whose works they felt were too political and full of bombastic jargon. In the preference that Georgian poets had for lyrical romanticism and in the shadow of nervous sensibility that informed their work, they did owe a debt to the "nineties Decadents"; echoes of the works of Ernest Dowson, Lionel Johnson, and even Oscar Wilde can often be heard in their poetry. The soldier poets in this volume all wrote in a style that is conveniently termed *Georgian* by literary historians principally because of *Georgian Poetry* (1911-1922), Edward Marsh's five anthologies of poems. In fact, only the work of Brooke and Rosenberg was published in *Georgian Poetry,* and, had he lived, Thomas would have been a contributor.

What is this Georgian poetic style? What distinguishes a writer as a "Georgian" poet? What do the poets included in Marsh's collection have in common?

The Georgians sought to avoid using archaic diction. Following William Wordsworth's instructions in his "Preface to the Lyrical Ballads" (1800), they were encouraged to use the language of the common people in their poetry. Seldom did they use elevated language for its effect, and they favored the lyrical form rather than the epic and ode forms preferred by the Victorians. The subject matter of the Georgians was seldom concerned with great events or moments; instead, they looked to the commonplace and the everyday for their inspiration. At times the Georgian poets were accused of being too commonplace: Brooke's notorious presentation of a case of seasickness in "A Channel Passage" was criticized for being too graphic.

More often, the Georgians found great pleasure in contemplating the pastoral, and they closely linked their fondness for birds and flowers, which they incorporated throughout their verse, with rich description of the English countryside, which they presented in a somewhat idealized vision of rural England. Their poetry became pantheistic, and the spirit of nature was seen to flow in the Cotswolds, through the Sussex Downs, and across the weald of Kent. English yeoman values were highlighted; the fox hunt, the old English inns, and the autumn harvest were nostalgically linked with past times and childhood memories. The landscape and English life were venerated: the honest Englishman with his warm heart and sense of fair play became the basis of Georgian poetry.

When the war broke out, most of the Georgians refused to acknowledge in their poetry the catastrophe that was raging across the English Channel. For them, war was an abstract concept to be avoided in their poetry, or, if it were discussed, it should celebrate English manly virtues and idealistic goals. After the outbreak of the Great War, it is not surprising that the initial poetry written about it by all the poets in this study was Georgian in form and sentiment.

By 1916, especially after losses on the Somme battlefield, the mawkish sentiments expressed in Georgian poetry were often mocked in the intellectual and philosophical circles of the modernists. Edith Sitwell, a poet in revolt against the plain language and subject matter favored by the Georgians, dismissed Georgian poets as those "who only appeared to be able to write about sheep." Such a reductionist attitude toward a lively literary movement was unjust, and most of the soldier poets were able to use their Georgian poetic grounding with startling effect in contrasting a pastoral, prelapsarian world before the war and the nightmare scenarios they faced daily on the western front. But the Georgian poetic vision dissipated as the war continued to drag on and it became less feasible to write about quiet corners of Gloucestershire, for the ugliness of war had permeated English life and culture. The soldier poets who survived not only changed emotionally and psychologically following their war experiences but also returned home to a changed world in which the light lyrical verses of 1912 seemed entirely out of place—the modernist postwar world of Ezra Pound, Wyndham Lewis, and T. S. Eliot. By the end of the war, the myth of rural England and its singers had nearly disappeared; it was replaced by the cacophony of jazz music and the sound of machinery grinding through forests and glens of rural England.

The Great War changed the face of modern civilization and ushered in what Eliot, through the title of his poem, called "The Waste Land" in 1922. Sheer numbers cannot tell the story of that conflict, which involved nearly every industrialized nation. The casualties, which have been estimated at thirty-seven million people killed or wounded, are incomprehensible. As more-recent wars and crises have demanded our attention, the devastation and ruin in Belgium, France, Italy, Russia, and the Balkan nations have been nearly forgotten, but vestiges of trenches in the Somme or bullet-ridden village churches in rural corners of France or Italy remind us of past events.

While literary critics and twentieth-century historians have been quick to point out that the bucolic milieu of the Edwardian world of 1912 already had been disintegrating before the conflict began, no one doubts that the postwar world of 1919 was far different from that which had existed in 1914. By 1918 two major European dynasties had fallen, and new nation-states had appeared. The United States had emerged as a world leader, and no longer could England and France accept the United States as insignificant. Women throughout the West had tasted freedoms and gained rights that they were not going to give up willingly with the cessation of hostilities. A new political power had arisen in Russia, and the threat of communism became a specter that haunted both Europe and the United States as capitalism was threatened by the "red menace."

It is difficult to believe that any of the soldier poets included in these two documentary volumes might have imagined they were fighting and dying for anything other than the preservation of a way of life that they knew to be British. However, if a particular writer in this volume was seen to be going to war to preserve the quintessential English way of life, that writer was Brooke. Critics have speculated that, had Brooke lived beyond the first eight months of the war, his sentiments would have changed from the nationalistic ones espoused in his five-sonnet series, *"1914"* (1915). But if one judges the evidence in the poet's last letters and his completed poetry, one finds that Brooke still writes as a man fully committed to the English cause and not fluctuating a jot from the jingoistic sentiments he had advocated when the war broke out.

In fact, Brooke wrote the 1914 "War Sonnets" after he had witnessed the disastrous wastage of life and wanton devastation of property in the Antwerp expedition in October 1914. Although his letters show that he was aware of the consequences borne of modern mechanized warfare, he was still writing idealized verse until the last weeks before he died on the Greek island of Skyros, where he and his fellows were preparing for the ill-fated Dardanelles campaign. Perhaps because of his presumed loyalty to the English cause and his great personal appeal (he was judged to be the handsomest man in England by his admiring friends), Brooke's death became a rallying point for patriotic fervor. His death on 23 April, both Saint George's Day and William Shakespeare's birthday, made him a natural icon in the propaganda of the English press. Winston Churchill's stirring obituary in *The Times* (London) ensured not only that Rupert Brooke would have a place in the affections of an already war-weary country looking for models of self-sacrifice but also that his war sonnets would be read over and over on every 11 November. His poetry will always be read where patriotism is encouraged and war glorified in order to unify national consciousness and purpose.

Rosenberg was in many ways the antithesis of Brooke. Whereas Brooke was tall, handsome, and elegant, Rosenberg was short, ungainly, and intense. Whereas Brooke was raised in solid middle-class elegance, Rosenberg grew up in the slums of London. After attending public school, Brooke's education was at the illustrious King's College, Cambridge, where he was admired for his physical beauty and charm in addition to his gifts as a poet. Rosenberg, on the other hand, studied art at the Slade School in London, where his Jewishness and his working-class background made him an outsider. Through the force of his will Rosenberg achieved artistic successes, and his paintings and poetry were brought to the attention of Brooke's patron, Marsh. Although never convinced of Rosenberg's poetic potential, Marsh encouraged Rosenberg's creative talents with both moral and financial support. When the war broke out, Rosenberg was with his sister's family in South Africa, where he was enjoying a decent standard of living for the first time. His initial reaction to the war was negative, but by the middle of 1915 he was back in England trying to find some employment to support his parents and siblings. When he failed to find a decent job, he reluctantly joined the army and was placed in a regiment for undersized men, where he managed somehow to survive the rigors of basic training.

As a private in the army, Rosenberg was denied many of the necessities that a poet requires. He could find paper and pencils only with great difficulty; he lacked the advantages that artistic cross-fertilization with other writers could provide; and he suffered religious persecution, ill health, and psychological problems during his two years on active duty. But still he managed to produce some of the most passionate and original antiwar verse written during the conflict. His experimental linguistic vision offers new glimpses of the battlefields. Almost surrealistic in structure and modernist in tone, Rosenberg's poetry seems at least ten years ahead of its time, and his death in action in April 1918 was a serious loss for English letters.

Edward Thomas was a reluctant hero—a father of three children, a husband to a wife who loved him, and a man who died tragically in France at the age of thirty-nine. In some ways any study of this gentle but disconsolate man leads one to ask why he was fighting in France when he had many opportunities to be safe in England, training artillery officers for the front. It is difficult to believe that Brookean optimism and patriotism made him volunteer for active duty, for Thomas had considered immigrating to the United States as late as 1915 in order to work with Robert Frost, his friend and poetic mentor. Unlike Rosenberg, Thomas was earning enough money during the war by writing literary articles and nonfiction books to have lived through the war as a civilian. Furthermore, to a writer who was a delicate observer of nature, a careful witness of detail, and a lover of the intrinsic magnificence of the Cotswolds and rural Wales, the horrors of the battlefields of France could not have offered much allure. Perhaps what the war offered Thomas was an escape from his responsibility to his family, from the monotonous rigor of producing a steady flow of books, year after year, on subjects that he often disliked. The war brought Thomas closer to the essential simplicity of life and death, and during his last two years of life he demonstrated a maturation and insight that augmented his creativity.

The haunting presence of the Great War is with us in art, in language, in politics, and in the cynicism that pervades much of late-twentieth-century thought. Perhaps the reluctance of many people to see war as the only answer to international disputes, as an inevitable consequence by which one supposedly "superior" civilization prevails over another lesser-endowed one, is the true legacy of those men who fought and died for an insignificant patch of earth on the Somme, at the Dardanelles, or wherever the jingoism and misguided patriotism of 1914 drew men to their deaths. Lest we forget.

NOTES ON SOURCES:

The documents in this volume are from a variety of sources, including the archives at the British Library; The Imperial War Museum, London; the Harry Ransom Humanities Research Center, the University of Texas at Austin; King's College Library, Cambridge; the Cambridge University Library; the English Faculty Library at Battersea Public Library, London; the New York Public Library; the St. John's College Robert Graves Trust of Oxford; the University of Virginia Library; The Lilly Library, Indiana University; the Delyte W. Morris Library, Southern Illinois University, Carbondale; and the Baker Library, Dartmouth College. These institutions hold letters, photos, manuscripts, diaries, and books that offer extensive insights into the lives and works of the three poets. All of these writers have been the subjects of biographies, and the most relevant chronicling of their lives can be found in the "Biographical Studies" rubric of each entry. Critics have made literary analyses of the works of these poets since those works were first published, and these critical studies permit readers to see the literary development in each writer's books. Lists of secondary sources about the works of these writers are provided in the "Critical Studies" sections of each chapter. The location of each document presented in the book is given in the caption or headnote accompanying each item. All the works of poetry and prose by each author are listed chronologically, along with their places of publication, publishers' names, and dates of first publication in England and the United States.

–Patrick Quinn

Acknowledgments

This book was produced by Bruccoli Clark Layman, Inc. Karen L. Rood is senior editor for the *Dictionary of Literary Biography* series. Denis Thomas was the in-house editor.

Production manager is Philip B. Dematteis.

Administrative support was provided by Ann M. Cheschi, Tenesha S. Lee, and Joann Whittaker.

Accountant is Kathy Weston. Accounting assistant is Angi Pleasant.

Copyediting supervisor is Phyllis A. Avant. Senior copyeditor is Thom Harman. The copyediting staff includes Brenda Carol Blanton, James Denton, Worthy B. Evans, Melissa D. Hinton, William Tobias Mathes, Jennifer Reid, and Michelle L. Whitney. Freelance copyeditors were Rebecca Mayo and Jennie Williamson.

Editorial assistant is Margo Dowling.

Editorial trainee is Carol A. Fairman.

Indexing specialist is Alex Snead.

Layout and graphics supervisor is Janet E. Hill. Graphics staff includes Karla Corley Brown and Zoe R. Cook.

Office manager is Kathy Lawler Merlette.

Photography editors are Charles Mims, Scott Nemzek, Alison Smith, and Paul Talbot. Digital photographic copy work was performed by Joseph M. Bruccoli.

SGML supervisor is Cory McNair. The SGML staff includes Tim Bedford, Linda Drake, Frank Graham, and Alex Snead.

Systems manager is Marie L. Parker.

Kimberly Kelly performed data entry.

Typesetting supervisor is Kathleen M. Flanagan. The typesetting staff includes Mark J. McEwan and Patricia Flanagan Salisbury. Freelance typesetter is Delores Plastow.

Walter W. Ross and Steven Gross did library research. They were assisted by the following librarians at the Thomas Cooper Library of the University of South Carolina: Linda Holderfield and the interlibrary-loan staff; reference-department head Virginia Stefanie Buck, Stefanie DuBose, Rebecca Feind, Karen Joseph, Donna Lehman, Charlene Loope, Anthony McKissick, Jean Rhyne, and Kwamine Simpson; circulation-department head Caroline Taylor; and acquisitions-searching supervisor David Haggard.

Permissions

RUPERT BROOKE

TEXT: For permission to quote the letters of Rupert Brooke to Owen O'Malley, St. John Lucas, Francis MacCunn, Frances Darwin, Mrs. Brooke, Katharine Cox, Frances Cornford, Mrs. Chauncey Wells, Leonard Bacon, and Cathleen Nesbitt: King's College Library, Cambridge; and the Rupert Brooke Trust. For permission to use copies of Brooke's poems in manuscript, "The Call," "A Channel Passage," "The Fish," "Libido," "The Old Vicarage, Grantchester," "Clouds," "Tiare Tahiti," and "The Soldier": King's College Library, Cambridge; and the Rupert Brooke Trust. For permission to quote the letters of Brooke to Geoffrey Keynes: Cambridge University Library. For permission to quote Brooke's letter to Erica Cotterill: the Bodleian Library, Oxford University. For permission to quote Brooke's letters to Dudley Ward: British Library, London. For permission to use the copy of *Second Problems Book:* Joseph M. Bruccoli Great War Collection, the University of Virginia Library. For permission to quote excerpts from the critical discussion of Rupert Brooke's "Channel Passage," "The Old Vicarage, Grantchester," "The Soldier," and "Tiare Tahiti": Twayne Publishers, an imprint of Simon and Schuster Macmillan; from *Rupert Brooke* by William E. Laskowski. Copyright © 1984 by Twayne Publishers. For permission to use Noel Olivier's letter to Rupert Brooke: Bloomsbury Publishers. For permission to use the report of Brooke's last day: Peter Miller. For permission to copy the title page of *Poems 1911:* Dartmouth College Library. For permission to quote excerpts from Ronald L. Olesky, "A Poet in the Wild: Rupert Brooke in Manitoba Cottage Country, 1913": *The Beaver.* For permission to quote extracts from the preface to *Friends and Apostles: The Correspondence of Rupert Brooke and James Strachey, 1905–1914,* edited by Keith Hale: Keith Hale. For permission to quote extracts from Clive Bloom, "The Falling House That Never Falls: Rupert Brooke and Literary Taste" in *British Poetry 1900–1950: Aspects of Tradition* (1995), edited by Gary Day and Brian Docherty: St. Martin's Press. For permission to quote from Paul Moeyes, "Georgian Poetry's False Dawn" (July 1991): *Neophilologus.*

PHOTOS: For permission to use photographs of Rupert Brooke and of the manuscripts of letters and poems: King's College Library, Cambridge; and the Rupert Brooke Trust.

ISAAC ROSENBERG

TEXT: For permission to quote from Bernard Bergonzi's *Heroes Twilight:* Carcanet Press, Manchester. For permission to copy Isaac Rosenberg manuscripts: The Imperial War Museum, London. For permission to publish "Reminiscences of Isaac Rosenberg" by Mrs. W. Horvitch: the literary executor of the Isaac Rosenberg Estate. For permission to quote from letters of Isaac Rosenberg to Edward Marsh: The Berg Collection of English and American Literature, The New York Public Library; Astor, Lenox, and Tilden Foundations. For permission to publish extracts from "Isaac Rosenberg 1890–1918" by Dennis Silk: *Judaism.* For permission to quote from Charles Tomlinson's *Isaac Rosenberg of Bristol:* Local Historical Pamphlets, Bristol. For permission to quote from "The 'Trench Poems' of Isaac Rosenberg" by Jack Lindeman: *The Literary Review.* For permission to quote extracts from "Isaac Rosenberg: From Romantic to Classic" by Joseph Cohen: *Tulane Studies in English.*

PHOTOS: For permission to use family photographs, paintings, and manuscripts: the literary executor of the Isaac Rosenberg Estate. For permission to use copies of manuscripts and photographs of Isaac Rosenberg: The Imperial War Museum, London.

EDWARD THOMAS

TEXT: For permission to quote from the letters to Ian MacAlister: the Battersea Public Library. For permission to use quotations from *Edward Thomas: A Portrait* by R. George Thomas (1985): Oxford University Press. For permission to quote W. H. Davies's "Killed in Action": Jonathan Cape. For permission to publish copies of the manuscripts of Thomas's "Home," "This Is No Petty Case of Right or Wrong," "P.H.T.," and "The Long Small Room": the Bodleian Library, Oxford University. For permission to quote from Eleanor Farjeon's *Edward Thomas: The Last Four Years:* David Higham Associates. For permission to quote from *World Without*

End by Helen Thomas: William Heinemann. For permission to quote from Edward Thomas's letters to Robert Frost: Dartmouth College Library. For permission to quote from letters written by Edward Thomas: R. George Thomas. For permission to quote from Andrew Motion's *The Poetry of Edward Thomas:* Routledge and Kegan Paul. For permission to quote from Jeremy Hooker's *Writers in a Landscape:* University of Wales Press. For permission to quote extracts from Stan Smith's "'A Language Not to Be Betrayed': Language, Class and History in the Work of Edward Thomas": *Literature and History*. For permission to quote from Piers Gray's "The Childhood of Edward Thomas": *Critical Quarterly*. For permission to quote from "The 'Poetical Character' of Edward Thomas" by Hugh Underhill: *Essays in Criticism*. For permission to quote extracts from "The Business of the Earth: Edward Thomas and Ecocentrism" by Edna Longley, which appeared in *High and Low Moderns: Literature and Culture, 1889–1939,* edited by Maria DiBattista and Lucy McDiarmid: Oxford University Press.

PHOTOS: For permission to use the photograph of Mr. and Mrs. W. H. Davies: Sylvia Harlow. For permission to use the personal photographs of Edward Thomas and his family: Myfanwy Thomas. For permission to use the photograph of Robert Frost: Dartmouth College Library.

Dictionary of Literary Biography® • Volume Two Hundred Sixteen

British Poets of The Great War: Brooke, Rosenberg, Thomas
A Documentary Volume

Dictionary of Literary Biography: A Documentary Volume

Rupert Brooke
(3 August 1887 – 23 April 1915)

See also the Brooke entry in *DLB 19: British Poets, 1880–1914.*

BOOKS:
The Pyramids (Rugby: Over, 1904);
"The Bastille": A Prize Poem Recited in Rugby School, June 24, 1905, as R. C. B. (Rugby: Lawrence, 1905);
Poems (London: Sidgwick & Jackson, 1911);
"1914": Five Sonnets (London: Sidgwick & Jackson, 1915); enlarged as *1914 and Other Poems* (London: Sidgwick & Jackson, 1915; Garden City, N.Y.: Doubleday, Page, 1915);
The Collected Poems of Rupert Brooke, with an introduction by George Edward Woodberry (New York: John Lane, 1915);
Lithuania: A Drama in One Act (Chicago: Chicago Little Theatre, 1915; London: Sidgwick & Jackson, 1935);
Letters from America (London: Sidgwick & Jackson, 1916; New York: Scribners, 1916);
John Webster and the Elizabethan Drama (London: Sidgwick & Jackson, 1916; New York: John Lane, 1916);
Selected Poems (London: Sidgwick & Jackson, 1917);
The Collected Poems of Rupert Brooke with a Memoir, edited by Sir Edward Marsh (London: Sidgwick & Jackson, 1918); revised as *Rupert Brooke: The Collected Poems* (London: Sidgwick & Jackson, 1942);
Fragments (Hartford, Conn.: Finlay, 1925);
The Complete Poems of Rupert Brooke (London: Sidgwick & Jackson, 1932);
Twenty Poems (London: Sidgwick & Jackson, 1935);
The Poetical Works of Rupert Brooke, edited by Geoffrey Keynes (London: Faber & Faber, 1946); republished as *The Poems of Rupert Brooke,* (New York: Nelson, 1952);
Democracy and the Arts (London: Hart-Davis, 1946);
The Prose of Rupert Brooke (London: Sidgwick & Jackson, 1956);

The Letters of Rupert Brooke, edited by Keynes (London: Faber & Faber, 1968);
The Letters of Rupert Brooke to his Publisher, 1911–1914 (New York: Octagon, 1975);
Friends and Apostles: The Correspondence of Rupert Brooke and James Strachey, 1905–1914, edited by Keith Hale (New Haven: Yale University Press, 1998).

BIBLIOGRAPHY AND CATALOGUE:
Geoffrey Keynes, *A Bibliography of Rupert Brooke* (London: Hart-Davis, 1954);
John Schroder, *Catalogue of Books and Manuscripts by Rupert Brooke Edward Marsh & Christopher Hassall* (Cambridge: Rampant Lion, 1970).

BIOGRAPHICAL STUDIES:
Maurice Browne, *Recollections of Rupert Brooke* (Chicago: Greene, 1927);
Paul Delany, *The Neo-Pagans: Rupert Brooke and the Ordeal of Youth* (New York: Free Press, 1987);
John Drinkwater, *Rupert Brooke: An Essay* (London: Chiswick Press, 1916);
Pippa Harris, *Songs of Love* (London: Bloomsbury, 1991);
Christopher Hassall, *Rupert Brooke: A Biography* (London: Faber & Faber, 1972);
Michael Hastings, *The Handsomest Young Man in England* (London: Joseph, 1967);
John Lehmann, *Rupert Brooke: His Life and Legend* (London: Weidenfeld & Nicolson, 1980);
Sandra Martin and Roger Hall, *Rupert Brooke in Canada* (Toronto: PMA, 1978);
Peter Miller, *The Cross of Skyros* (Rugby: Apex, 1994);
Cathleen Nesbitt, *A Little Love and Good Company* (Owings Mills, Md.: Stemmer House, 1977);
Robert B. Pearsall, *Rupert Brooke: The Man and Poet* (Amsterdam: Rodopi, 1974);

Arthur Stringer, *Red Wine of Youth: A Life of Rupert Brooke* (New York: Bobbs-Merrill, 1948).

CRITICAL STUDIES:
Gary Day and Brian Docherty, eds., *British Poetry 1900–1950: Aspects of Tradition* (New York: St. Martin's Press, 1995);
Walter de la Mare, *Rupert Brooke and the Intellectual Imagination* (London: Sidgwick & Jackson, 1919);
Geoffrey Keynes, ed., *Four Poems* (London: Scolar, 1974);
William E. Laskowski, *Rupert Brooke* (New York: Twayne, 1994);
Timothy Rogers, *Rupert Brooke* (London: Routledge, 1971);
Robert H. Ross, *The Georgian Revolt: Rise and Fall of a Poetic Ideal, 1910–1922* (Carbondale: Southern Illinois University Press, 1965);

Rupert Chawner Brooke was born at Rugby, where his father, William Parker Brooke, was a form master at the famous public school. His mother, Mary Ruth Cotterill Brooke, was a dominant influence throughout his life. Brooke, the second of three sons, was educated initially at a preparatory school near Hillbrow before entering Rugby in September 1901 at the age of fourteen.

Rupert Chawner Brooke at age three (Michael Hastings, The Handsomest Young Man in England, *p. 20*)

Rupert's father, William Parker Brooke, 1903 (Michael Hastings, The Handsomest Young Man in England, *p. 21*)

Brooke, his mother, and his younger brother, Alfred, in fancy dress, 1898 (King's College Library, Cambridge)

At Hillbrow, Brooke became acquainted with Duncan Grant, the future artist, and James Strachey, younger brother of Lytton Strachey. During this pleasant but largely uneventful time at Hillbrow, Brooke also developed an interest in English literature and in drama.

Brooke, third from right, as Portia, in the Hillbrow School production of The Merchant of Venice *in 1900 (Michael Hastings,* The Handsomest Young Man in England, *p. 23)*

Brooke (right) and Alfred at Rugby, 1900 (King's College Library, Cambridge)

Jonathan Rutherford, *Forever England: Reflections on Masculinity and Empire* (London: Lawrence & Wishart, 1997).

ARCHIVES:
Rupert Brooke materials are available at Baker Library, Dartmouth College, Hanover, New Hampshire; the Department of Rare Books, University of Cambridge Library, Cambridge, England; the Department of Manuscripts, British Library, London; and King's College Library, Cambridge, England.

Brooke was considered a good athlete, but recurrent health problems prevented his athletic development. He suffered from a persistent throat inflammation that often sent him to his sickbed and may indicate that his immune system was inherently susceptible to infection. His earliest surviving letter, which was written from his sickbed, notes that the infection caused him to miss both the athletic finals at his school and his public school exams for entering Rugby. In spite of this setback he was accepted by Rugby, and one of his friends there, Geoffrey Keynes, claims that Brooke was popular with his schoolmates. He was passionate about English literature, and his appreciation for the works of William Shakespeare was especially strong for such a young boy.

Brooke's letter to Owen O'Malley parodying Shakespearean English (Geoffrey Keynes, ed., The Letters of Rupert Brooke, *p. 4)*

School Field, Rugby
[1901]

From Ye Oyster to Ye Bug Greeting Child,

Wherefore sendest thou strange manuscripts adorned with divers devices which bring back to the mind thoughts of a time which is past? Also, the manner in which thou inscribest the word "exeat" (which thou hast spelt exiat, O friend) sheweth clearly that thou art of one race with the strange people who inhabit the country (known to some as "the isle of Emerald hue") across the sea: for this people have many strange habits, such as flourishing shillelaghs and other divers things. But I have somewhat whereof I would tell thee. On the 9th day of May the Sports for Athletes were held, and I did win many heats, and when I had finished running 3600 inches (in a heat) a boy by name B. Foote was about 70 inches behind. And on the next day I was ill and unable to compete wherefore my temper was exceeding warm. And the aforesaid Foote did win the 3600 inches Final amidst divers other things in the which perchance I might have gained honour and prizes; wherefore my temper's temperature did increase. And I lay on my bed many days—more or less—and finally I was unable to compete in the Examination of Scholars, wherein one Russell was successful. Wherefore an irritability of marvellous size possessed me—and still possesses me. Also, I have partaken of but 4 games of cricket this century—woe is me.

Forgive my letter being strange in manner. The reason is that much trouble hath unhinged my brain; wherein I resemble Hamlet. And if you gaze closely on my portrait which I have sent you, you will see a wild look in my eyes; denoting insanity.

Farewell

At Rugby, Brooke overcame any difficulties that his father's position as a Master might have presented, and his fellow students accepted the boy as one of the group. He played cricket and rugby for his house and also joined the Rifle Volunteer Corps.

The Rugby Rifle Volunteer Corps, 1904. Brooke is in the front row, fifth from the left (King's College Library, Cambridge).

The Rugby School rugby team, with Brooke in the back row, fourth from the right (King's College Library, Cambridge)

Brooke in his cricket outfit at Rugby School, 1904 (King's College Library, Cambridge)

At the age of sixteen Brooke wrote The Pyramids (1904), a poem for which he won second prize at Rugby and his family paid to have privately printed and distributed. In May that year another young author, St. John Welles Lucas-Lucas, read the poem and, on the basis of its potential, visited Brooke, who was recovering from yet another throat infection. Lucas-Lucas introduced the young poet to the writings of the English Decadent poets, who subsequently inspired his devotion to the writing of Ernest Dowson. Brooke's "Decadent" period lasted for the better part of three years. On Christmas Eve 1904 he was sick again, and as part of his recuperation he and Alfred were sent to Italy, where the climate was milder.

After returning from abroad, Brooke worked diligently on his submission for the Rugby poetry prize, which he won in June 1905 with "The Bastille." His academic performance at Rugby also won him a place at King's College, Cambridge, for the following academic year. During 1906, his last year at Rugby, he participated in the debating society program, where his arguments that the Labour Party should be recognized foreshadowed his political sympathies that were later manifested in his flirtation with the Fabian Society. He also continued to write poetry in the fashion of the Decadents. He left Rugby with regret; the prospect of life at Cambridge, in spite of the freedom from his family that it promised, was not appealing, for Brooke cherished his Rugby friends such as Keynes and the experiences they had shared.

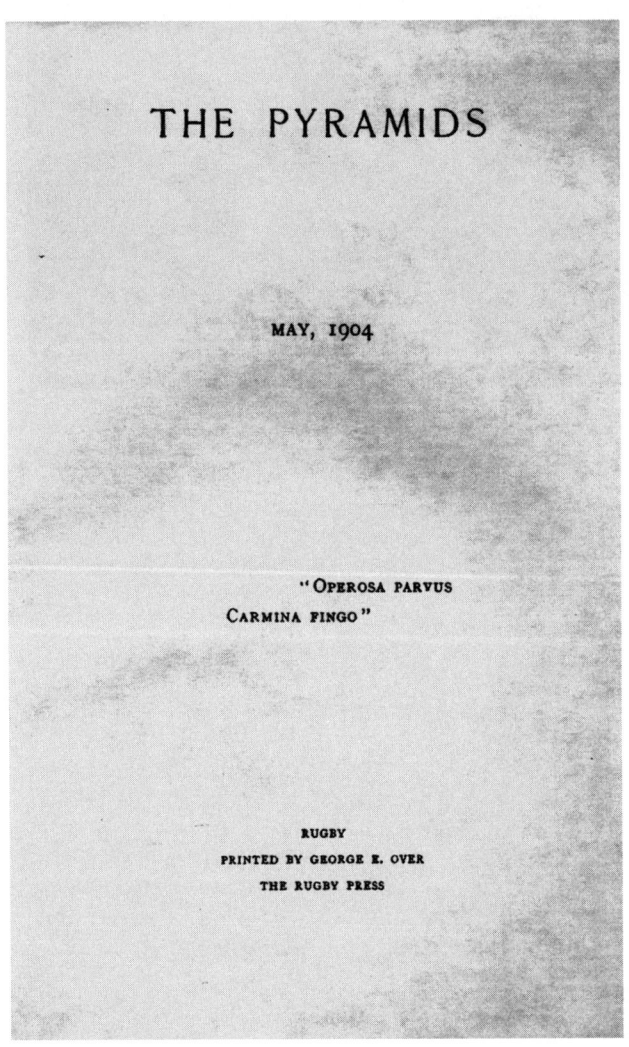

Title page for Brooke's first publication, the poem he submitted for the Rugby School poetry prize. Although he did not win the competition, the poem was privately printed by his family.

Brooke at Rugby, 1905 (King's College Library, Cambridge)

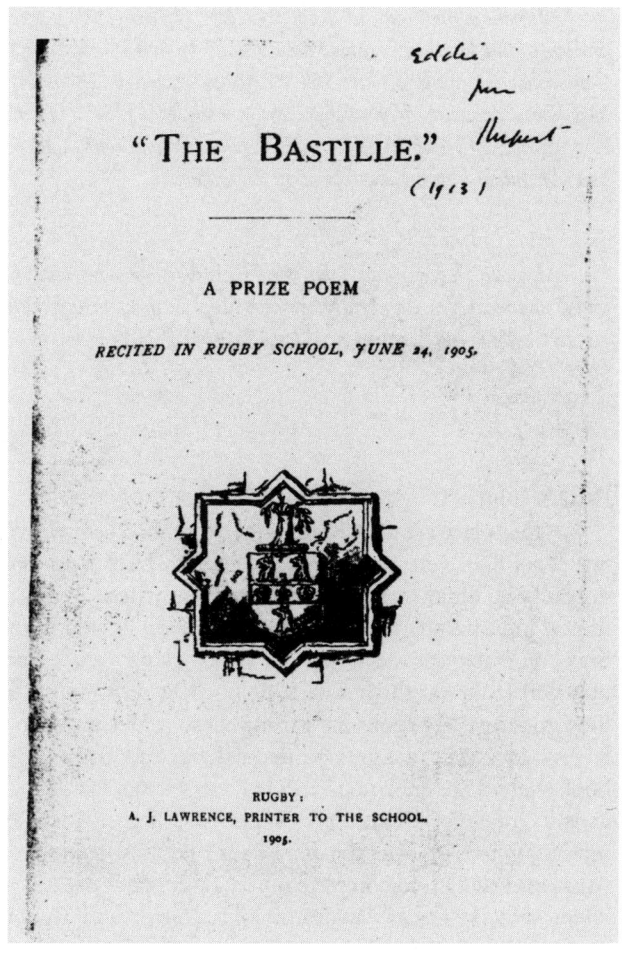

Title page for Brooke's prize-winning poem, "The Bastille," inscribed to Edward Marsh

Geoffrey Keynes, 1906 (Geoffrey Keynes, ed., The Letters of Rupert Brooke, p. 65)

Brooke's letter to Keynes on 10 May 1906, praising Rugby School and exalting his youth (Geoffrey Keynes, ed., The Letters of Rupert Brooke, p. 51)

School Field, Rugby

Dear Geoffrey,
    I shall hurry to get the book you recommend. I am evil not to have written to you before: but I spent the last five days of the holidays in a feverish attempt to write an English Historical Essay. This effort has incapacitated me so much & worked such havoc in my carefully elaborated prose-style, that I dared not write a letter sooner. Even now some lingering harshness and cacophonies betray me. . . .
    The Summer Term has dawned. It is my last, and I weep. The same fantastic things happen, there is that strange throng of young beings, unconscious of all their youth & wonder. Another Spring dies odorously in Summer. . . . But I am quite happy. To be here is wonderful, and suffices. I live in a mist of golden dreams. Afterwards life will come, cold and terrible. At present I am a child. . . .
    I am writing nothing, not even a Hymn to Antinous. I am content to exist. I know now whither the Greek Gods have vanished now-a-days. They are to be found in public schools. Always, in the sunshine, and the Spring, I see them, thinly disguised, rushing over the grass, supple of limb & keen-eyed, young and beautiful. Here is Olympus, and now. I feed on the nectar of Life, from Ganymede's hands and from amidst my young unconscious gods, write to you now, ecstatically.

                                Rupert Brooke

Brooke's first year at King's College (1906–1907) posed problems, and his letters recount the difficulty he had in adjusting to Cambridge and university life. Still, by November 1906 he was occupied with amateur dramatics, with playing the Herald in the Eumenides of Aeschylus. His radiant figure in gold and vivid red and blue made a strong impression on the audience.

Brooke's letter to St. John Welles Lucas-Lucas presenting his initial impressions of Cambridge life and his taste in literature, October 1906 (Geoffrey Keynes, ed., The Letters of Rupert Brooke, pp. 64–65)

King's College, Cambridge

Dear St John,
 This place is rather funny to watch; and a little wearying. It is full of very young people, and my blear eyes look dolefully at them from the lofty window where I sit and moan. Innumerous people I knew on the other side of the Styx come in to see me. They talk vivaciously for three minutes and I stare at them with a dumb politeness, and then they go away. My room is a gaunt yellow wilderness with a few wicked little pictures scattered here and there. The book-shelves are enormous and half empty: but it was rash in you to inquire about books I needed. I had thoughts of sending you a list of all the evil books I really should like. I want, for instance, to complete my set of the three great decadent writers (Oscar Wilde, St John Lucas, and Rupert

Brooke as a cadet officer, Rugby School, 1906 (King's College Library, Cambridge)

King's College Chapel at the time Brooke was at Cambridge (Michael Hastings, The Handsomest Young Man in England, *p. 73)*

Brooke.) Of the last and most infamous of the three I possess most of the works but of the other two I have less. But perhaps these would have a too bad influence on me. I have none of Belloc's ridiculous works; the madder Elizabethans would please me; and if you dare find some of your evil Frenchmen of the more decadent sort they would delight my wicked mind. A complete set of the most infamous of Beardsley's drawings might be purchased for about 50 guineas in Paris and would certainly bring a gleam of faint interest into my wan eye. Of particular authors I might welcome any of Fiona Macleod's poems, or Maeterlinck's, or any fair book illustrated by one of these infamous moderns in whom I delight—such as "Time and the Gods" by Dunsany and Sime—the new one. But you know my disgusting mind. There is a wide field open—if you have time before leaving England. Anyhow, I shouldn't advise you to get anything for me. I have given up reading or writing nice things now. I only read Shaw and write clever verse. It's very easy; and hurts less than writing poetry.

I go to my frugal lunch.

Rupert

Brooke as the Herald in Aeschylus's Eumenides *(King's College Library, Cambridge)*

Excerpt from the review of Eumenides *in* The Cambridge Review, *6 December 1906, p. 137*

The part of the Pythian Prophetess—most difficult because necessarily begun in cold blood, so to speak—was extremely well sustained by Mr J. Brooke. Admirable was his rendering of the reentry of the horrified Pythia after sight of the Furies within the sacred precinct: as also of her description of what she has witnessed within. His impersonation on the later nights showed a marked improvement and advance on that of the opening performance. Mr Alderson, as Hermes, and Mr R. O. Brooke, as the Herald, both acquitted themselves with credit in the minor parts assigned to them, but we regret that it was thought right to impose upon the latter an ossified dignity which kept the spectator on the verge of perpetual laughter.

The Brooke family suffered a tragedy in early 1907, when Brooke's elder brother, Richard, died of pneumonia. Brooke reacted by writing "The Call," a poem that marks an advance in his maturity as a poet despite its awkward use of artificial Decadent imagery. During the rest of that year Brooke began writing highly competent poems, some of which were published in The Cambridge Review.

Brooke's 1907 letter to Francis MacCunn, a school friend, after the death of his brother (Geoffrey Keynes, ed., The Letters of Rupert Brooke, *p. 76)*

My dear Francis,
   Thinking I should see you today or tomorrow, I did not write. But now it is decided that I "go up" this afternoon.
   You have heard of our trouble, or at any rate this paper explains itself. I am very glad to get away before you all return. This sounds rude. But I am feeling terribly despondent and sad, and I feel that I could not face everybody. The only thing was if I could help Father and Mother by staying, but they say not, and I do not think so. And if I stayed I know I should break down.
   There is an instinct to hide in sorrow, and at Cambridge where I know no one properly I can be alone. Therefore I am running away from all you whom I like so much, and one especially. I should only make you unhappy.
   I hope you'll all be gentle to my pater at first. He has had a terrible time, and is very tired and broken by it.
        Yours ever
        Rupert Brooke

The Call.

Out of the nothingness of sleep,
   The slow dreams of Eternity,
There was a thunder on the deep:
   I came, because you called to me.

I broke the night's primaeval bars,
   I dared the old abysmal curse,
And flashed through ranks of frightened stars
   Suddenly on the universe!

The eternal silences were broken;
   Hell became Heaven as I passed.
— What shall I give you as a token,
   A sign that we have met, at last?

I'll break and forge the stars anew,
   Shatter the heavens with a song;
Immortal in my love for you,
   Because I love you, very strong.

Your mouth shall mock the old and wise,
   Your laugh shall fill the world with flame.
I'll write upon the shrinking skies
   The scarlet splendour of your name.

Till Heaven cracks, and Hell thereunder
   Dies in her ultimate mad fire,
And darkness falls, with scornful thunder,
   On dreams of men and men's desire.

Then only in the empty spaces,
   Death, walking very silently,
Shall fear the glory of our faces
   Through all the dark infinity.

So, cloth'd about with perfect love,
   The Eternal End shall find us one,
Alone above the Night, above
   The dust of the dead gods, alone.

Brooke's copy of his poem written at Cambridge (King's College Library, Cambridge)

Throughout 1908 Brooke became more involved with the Fabian Society, and under the influence of Hugh Dalton, another new friend, he became a full member. He also was enjoying the social and cultural life of Cambridge, and by April he was admitted into the elite circle of the Cambridge Apostles, a group of intellectuals who adhered to the moral principles set down in George Edward Moore's Principia Ethica *(1903), in which Moore emphasizes the importance of beautiful objects and of personal relations between individuals. Membership in this society gave Brooke access to some of the leading young thinkers and artists in Cambridge.*

Hugh Dalton, a political theorist whose thinking about socialism influenced Brooke at Cambridge (Michael Hastings, The Handsomest Young Man in England, *p. 80)*

During his years at Cambridge, Brooke continued to pursue his interests in amateur dramatics: he produced a version of John Milton's Comus *(1637), in which he also acted as the Attendant Spirit. The production widened his appreciation not only of the poetry and music of the period but also of the theater. During that production he met Frances Darwin (later Cornford), who described him as a golden-haired Apollo, an epithet for Brooke that became familiar after his death.*

Edward Marsh, Brooke's friend who edited Georgian Poetry, *gives E. J. Dent's account of how staging* Comus *affected the young Cambridge student* (Rupert Brooke: The Collected Poems with a Memoir by Edward Marsh, *[London: Sidgwick & Jackson, 1942], pp. xxxiii–xxxv).*

"It is difficult to criticise *Comus,* or to write the history of its preparation. It had much the same faults and the same merits as *Faustus,* though on a larger scale. Rupert was not a good actor, nor even a good speaker of verse. Yet I feel now that anyone who remembers *Comus,* and remembers it with ever so slight a sense of beauty, will think of Rupert as the central figure of it; and watching rehearsals daily as I did, I felt that, however much his personal beauty might count for, it was his passionate devotion to the spirit of poetry that really gave *Comus* its peculiar and indescribable atmosphere.

"*Comus,* however unimportant to the world at large, did, in fact, mean a great deal for Rupert and his friends. It was the first time that he had had to bear the responsibility of a large undertaking, and he addressed himself to it in the spirit of a scholar. It deepened his sense of poetry, of drama, and of music; it made him develop an ideal continually present in his mind, even in later years, which gave solidity to his group, the ideal of Cambridge, of young Cambridge, as the source from which the most vital movements in literature, art, and drama, were to spring. *Comus* effected an intimate collaboration of all sorts of brains, and it effected especially a co-operation of men and women. Rupert was by no means the only remarkable person in the circle. He had, moreover, a power of making friends with women as well as with men, and although *Comus* was probably a symptom rather than a cause, it was from about that time that joint societies, such as the Heretics and the Fabians, began to make a new influence felt."

Rupert was knocked up by his exertions over *Comus.* He wrote from Rugby to Mrs Cornford (then Miss Frances Darwin): "I went off without even saying good-bye or thank-you to people. My mother (I can plead) packed me up and snatched me here to sleep and recover. I am now convalescent, and can sit up and take a little warm milk-and-Tennyson. I feel a deserter; but I can always adduce the week when the Committee went to the seaside, and I faced the world and Albert's Artistic Temperament alone."

At Cambridge, Brooke initiated many new friendships, including one with Justin Brooke, with whom he founded the Marlowe Dramatic Society, and these early Cambridge friends were important influences on Brooke through the remaining eight years of his life: Jacques Raverat, the painter and writer; Dudley Ward, one of the Socialists who induced Brooke to join the Fabian Society; and Margery Olivier of Newnham College, the daughter of Sir Sydney Olivier, former governor of Jamaica and a Socialist sympathizer.

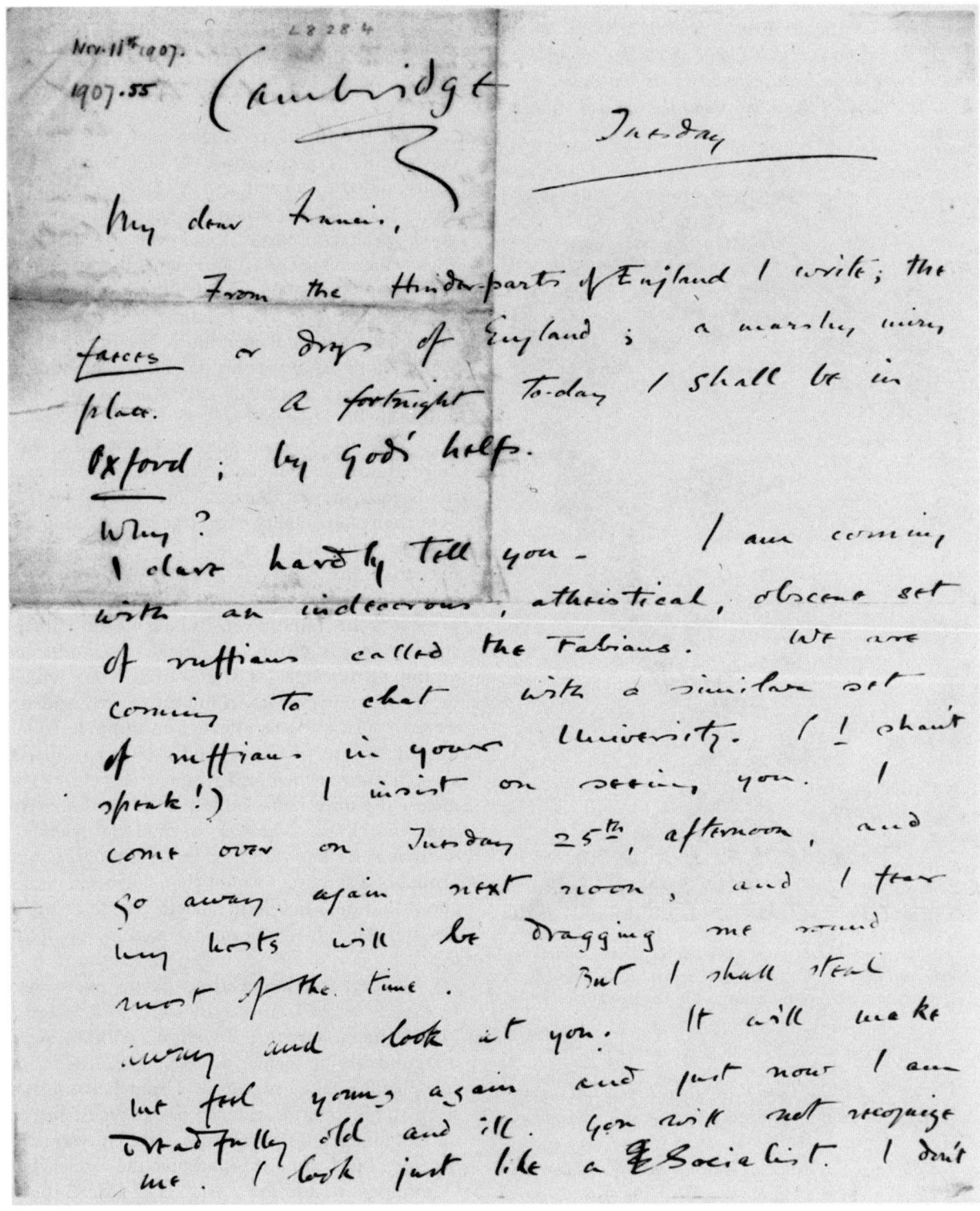

First page of Brooke's letter to Francis MacCunn discussing the Fabian Society, 11 November 1907 (King's College Library, Cambridge)

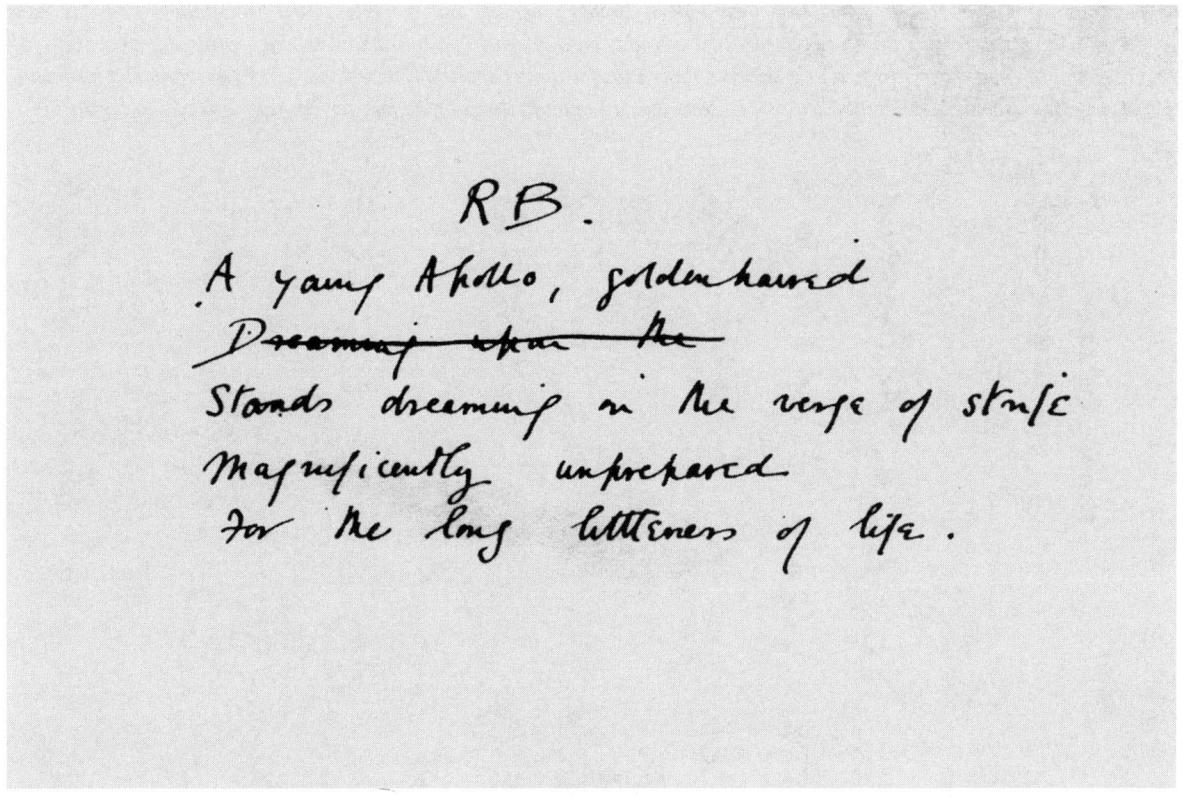

Frances Cornford's description of Brooke after she had worked with him to produce Comus (Michael Hastings, The Handsomest Young Man in England, p.8)

Brooke (far left) at Klosters in Switzerland, December 1908. Noel Olivier is seated at the far right, front row (King's College Library, Cambridge).

These extracurricular activities soon took their toll on Brooke's health, and by July 1908 he collapsed from his exertions. He returned home to Rugby to recuperate. By his twenty-first birthday on 3 August 1908 he had recovered sufficiently to venture to Wales for a meeting of Socialists, and that Christmas he traveled with friends for winter sport to Switzerland, where he again met his friend Margery Olivier and her sister Noel. His physical attraction to Noel was an important reason he had for wishing to travel to the Alps.

Opening pages of Brooke's letter to his mother thanking her for financing his planned trip to Switzerland and listing the people who he believes will be in his group (King's College Library, Cambridge)

In 1909 Brooke met Katherine Cox, a student from Newnham College, and the tensions that developed between the two throughout the following years had serious consequences for Brooke.

Katherine Cox, 1911 (King's College Library, Cambridge)

Also in 1909 Brooke became better acquainted with Marsh, private secretary to Winston Churchill and a man who later, as editor of Georgian Poetry, *helped direct Brooke's literary career. Brooke was disappointed but not surprised when at the end of May he took the Cambridge Classics Tripos exam and attained only a second-class mark, but in spite of this mediocre performance he decided to study English literature in his fourth year. In 1909 he moved from Cambridge and into "The Orchard," a house near the River Granta.*

Brooke's letter to Erica Cotterill describing "The Orchard," July 1909 (Geoffrey Keynes, ed., The Letters of Rupert Brooke, *pp. 172–173)*

The Orchard, Grantchester near Cambridge
Sunday

Well, I've been frightfully busy with work, & that's why I've not written about books. Also it takes such a frightful lot of thinking about. I've been at home for ten days & came here on Friday. It is a lovely village on the river above Cambridge. I'm in a small house, a sort of cottage, with a dear plump weatherbeaten kindly old lady in control. I have a perfectly glorious time, seeing nobody I know day after day. The room I have opens straight out onto a stone verandah covered with creepers, & a little old garden full of old-fashioned flowers & crammed with roses. I work at Shakespere, read, write all day, & now & then wander in the woods or by the river. I bathe every morning & sometimes by moonlight, have all my meals (chiefly fruit) brought to me out of doors, & am as happy as the day's long. I am chiefly sorry for all you people in the world. Every now & then dull bald spectacled people from Cambridge come out & take tea here. I mock them & pour the cream down their necks or roll them in the rosebeds or push them in the river, & they hate me & go away. The world smells of roses. Books? Pah!— however—

Read: *G. E. Moore's Principia Ethica* very slowly & carefully, as you want to think.

Samuel Butler.

The best story ever written is in the July *English Review,* called *Other Kingdom,* by E. M. Forster.

E. M. Forster's novel *A Room with A View,* is very good: lighter than the other things I recommend.

W. H. Hudson's *Green Mansions* ditto.

You've read Yeats' *Ideas of Good & Evil,* I think.

McDougall's *Social Psychology.*

Havelock Ellis, *The New Spirit,* a *little* book. What about Meredith?

Shakespeare's *Anthony & Cleopatra* is very good.

Do be careful about Wells' *First & Last Things.* It is nice: but it *does* encourage inaccurate thinking so.

If you're reading the New Quarterly, as you say, don't miss *Roger Fry* in the April number.

Have you read any Lowes Dickinson? such as *Justice & Liberty: Modern Symposium: Letters from John Chinaman?*

Arnold Bennett's *The Old Wives' Tale* is good: I believe I told you.

I suppose it would do you good to read Congreve's *The Way of the World.*

Rossetti & Browning I hope you will enjoy. Browning's not a very good poet. *Blake* is.

As for people in love with people of the same sex as themselves, I know all about it, & will tell you some time.

Rupert

Oh! Death will find me, long before I tire
    Of watching you, and swing me suddenly
Into the Shade and Loneliness and Mire
    Of the Last Land! There, waiting patiently,
One day, I think, I'll feel a cool wind blowing,
    See a slow light across the Stygian tide,
And hear the Dead about me stir, unknowing,
    And tremble. And I shall know that you have died,

And watch you, a broad-browed and smiling dream,
    Pass, light as ever, through the lightless host,
Quietly ponder, start, and sway, and gleam,
    — Most individual and bewildering ghost! —
And turn, and toss your brown, delightful head
Amusedly, among the ancient Dead.

Final draft of "Sonnet," written in early 1909. The penultimate line may refer to Noel Olivier.

In addition to his busy social life at Cambridge, Brooke stayed politically active and organized Fabian discussions about the repeal of the Poor Law. He worked closely with fellow Fabians Cox and Margery Olivier, whose friendship Brooke cultivated partially for easier access to Olivier's sister, Noel. It is likely that Brooke wrote "In a Wood" as a commentary on his uneven relationship with Noel.

Noel Olivier in Bedales School uniform, 1909 (Michael Hastings, The Handsomest Young Man in England, p. 76)

Poem that suggests the ambiguous nature of Brooke's relationship with Noel Olivier, 1909 (N. G. Royde Smith, ed., The Second Problems Book: Prizes and Proximes from the Westminster Gazette, *1908–1909, pp. 69–70)*

In a Wood

Safe in the magic of my woods
    I lay, and watched the dying light.
Faint in the pale high solitudes,
    And washed with rain and veiled by night,

Silver and blue and green were showing.
    And the dark woods grew darker still;
And birds were hushed; and peace was growing;
    And quietness crept up the hill;

And no wind was blowing . . .

And I knew
That this was the hour of knowing,
And the Night and the Woods and You
Were one together, and I should find
Soon in the silence the hidden key
Of all that had hurt and puzzled me,–
Why You were You, and the Night was kind,
And the Woods were part of the heart of me.

And there I waited breathlessly,
Alone; and slowly the holy three,
The three that I loved, together grew
One, in the hour of knowing,
Night and the Woods and You–

And suddenly,
There was an uproar in my woods,
The noise of a fool in mock distress,
Crashing and laughing and blindly going,

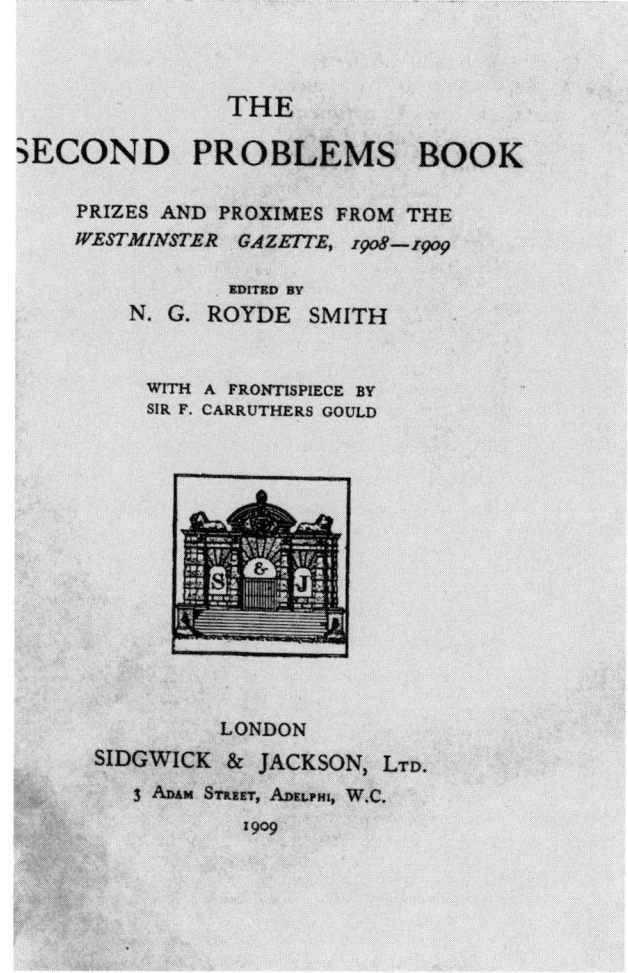

Title page of the collection that includes Brooke's "In a Wood" (Joseph M. Bruccoli Great War Collection, University of Virginia Library)

Of ignorant feet and a swishing dress,
And a Voice profaning the solitudes.

The spell was broken, the key denied me.
And at length your flat clear voice beside me
Mouthed cheerful clear flat platitudes.

You came and quacked beside me in the wood.
You said "The view from here is very good!"
You said "It's nice to be alone a bit!"
And "How the days are drawing out!" you said.
You said "The sunset's pretty isn't it?"
. . . .
My God! I wish–I wish that you were dead!

Critical comment on "A Channel Passage" (William E. Laskowski, Rupert Brooke, *p. 38)*

Another aspect of Brooke's "realism" is its antiromanticism. Brooke proferred this reason as a justification to Marsh when defending his most notorious realistic poem, "A Channel Passage." In it a lover finds himself becoming seasick on a channel ferry and, as a preventive, tries to recall anything, but the only image that comes to mind is that of his lover: "You, you alone could hold my fancy forever!" Such remembrance, however, leaves the speaker with only the choice of "A seasick body, or a you

At the end of the year Brooke returned to Switzerland. On his way home he became ill from eating "green honey," and while he was recovering in Rugby he rewrote "A Channel Passage," a strong attempt at realistic verse that he had first drafted in Switzerland after a rough crossing.

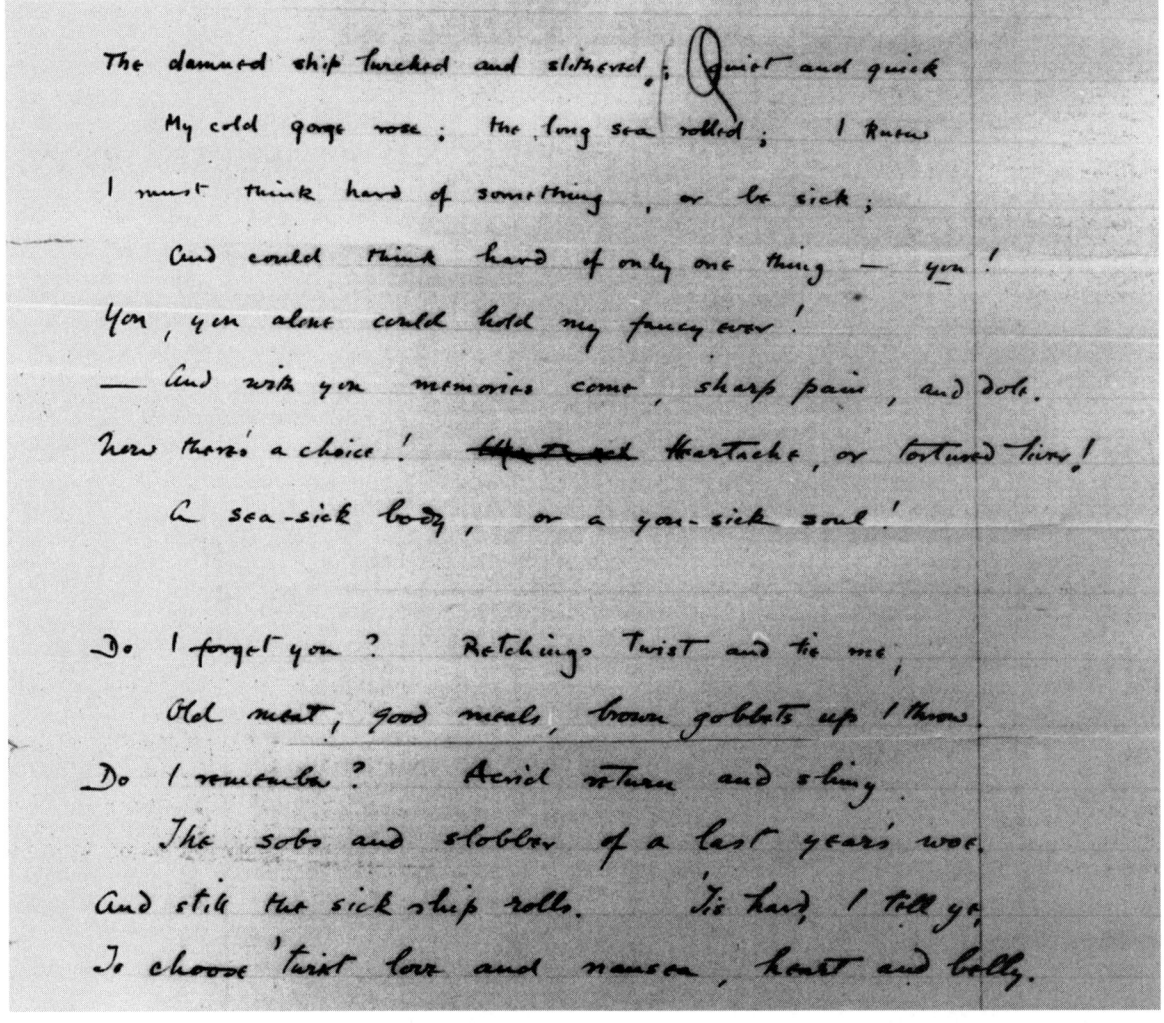

Manuscript copy of "A Channel Passage," 1909 (King's College Library, Cambridge)

sick soul!" Instead of being a prophylactic, his lover's image acts as an emetic, as he is wracked with "The sobs and slobbers of a last year's woe!" and vomits. Many critics have pointed out that the poem is in itself weak, yet one assumes Brooke realized the undercutting effect that the inverted word order of "up I throw" would have. Complaining that such a dose of realism, "the brutality of human emotion," was necessary "after I've beaten vain hands in the rosy mists of poets' experiences," Brooke invoked to Marsh the example of Shakespeare's sonnet 130, "My mistress' eyes are nothing like the sun." Brooke's main reason for writing "Channel Passage" seems to have been to stake out his own territory, independent of Marsh and of whatever other "dew-dabblers" were writing at the time. His most unpleasant unpublished poem, for example, concerns a lover celebrating his beloved's becoming the main course at a cannibal feast (preceding Evelyn Waugh's *Black Mischief* by about 20 years); it was written in a letter from the South Seas to the daughter of the prime minister of England, Violet Asquith. Not for nothing was one of his papers to the Apostles titled "Why Not Try the Other Leg."

Brooke's letter to Dudley Ward, written just before the death of Brooke's father, 24 January 1910 (Geoffrey Keynes, ed., The Letters of Rupert Brooke, p. 217)

School Field, Rugby

This may not get you in time. I hope my telegram found you. I'm sorry. I was fetched from Cambridge this morning by telegram. Father has had a stroke. He is unconscious. We sit with him by turns. It is terrible. His face is twisted half out of recognition: and he lies gurgling and choking and fighting for life. He is much weaker now. Probably he will not last the night. I hope not. It is all terrible for mother.

I wish I could have seen you. I'll write. Send me your German address. I shall be here till you've gone: probably long after. There's only worry ahead—all the settling and keeping mother going, and probably mother and I will have to go on managing the House for ten weeks—the world won't stop for a death. And father, who's strong in a way, may fight it out for—a week? And 54 boys come into the House on Thursday! . . .

My love to Margery and Daphne and so on if you see them—to everyone. I reread the parts of your letter about Noel. Does it cheer me or make it worse? A deathbed is so infinitely far from her. I think she and all of you are dreams I've had. It's so faint. And there's pain everywhere.

Rupert

You and Jacques spend the summer in a Caravan! I will take occasional weeks with you.

Brooke reciting Faustus *to Cambridge friends Dudley Ward and Jacques Raverat (King's College Library, Cambridge)*

The Swiss experience reawakened Brooke's romantic nature, and he wrote several poems including "The One Before the Last," which he sent to his friend Ward in mid January. The romantic mood, however, was quickly dispelled when Brooke's father died suddenly on 24 January 1910. Brooke took over as Deputy Housemaster at Rugby School for the whole of the Lent term.

Manuscript for Brooke's "The One Before the Last," 1910 (Papers of Rupert Brooke, Sotheby Catalogue, 17 December 1979, p. 121)

While remaining at Rugby, Brooke worked on "Puritanism as Represented or Referred to in the Early English Drama up to the Year 1642," a monograph for which he won the Harness Prize later in 1910. His verse was also receiving critical attention, and in April he heard from Henry Nevinson, acting editor of The Nation, that the journal wished to publish several of his poems, but before doing so the editor felt that Brooke should emend several phrases that Nevinson considered too strong for publication. Brooke visited Nevinson to discuss the proposed emendations and to present his own case; eventually The Nation published "The Goddess in the Wood" with minor changes.

Brooke returned to Cambridge for the summer term and worked strenuously on a production of Johann Wolfgang von Goethe's Faustus (1832) for visiting German students. The themes of the dramatic production allowed him to contemplate the transient nature of existence, and sonnets such as "The Life Beyond" convey his metaphysical speculations.

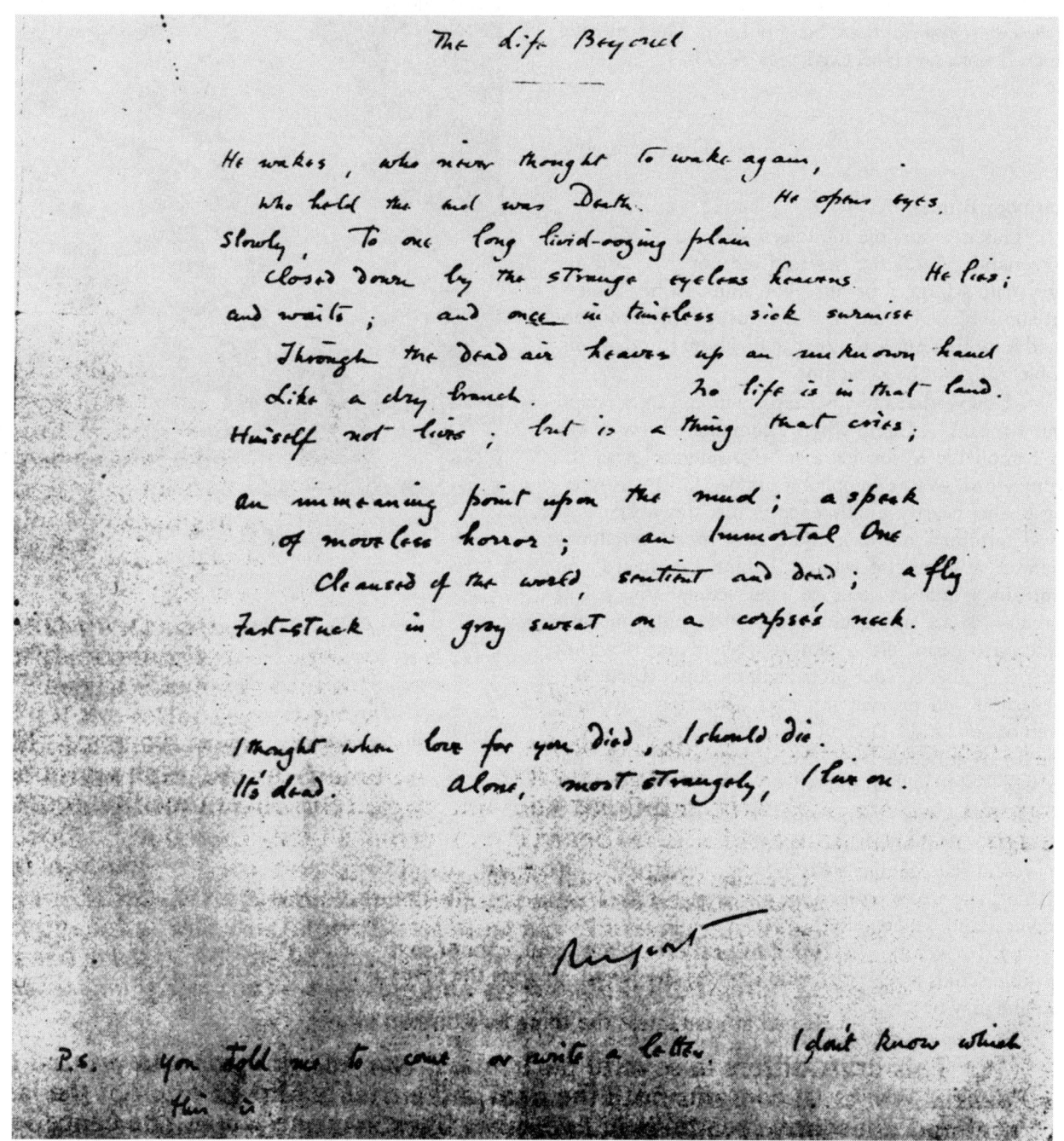

Manuscript for the sonnet written in spring 1910, while Brooke was involved in rehearsals for Faustus (Papers of Rupert Brooke, Sotheby Catalogue, 17 December 1979, p. 123)

In July 1910 Brooke was back with his mother in Rugby, and in early August he went camping with a group of friends on the Beaulieu River, where he succeeded in manipulating seventeen-year-old Noel Olivier into a secret engagement. She realized early on that she did not love Brooke and tried to temper his advances. Her resistance gradually drove him into the arms of the maternal Katherine Cox later that year, and the tensions of this new love relationship are manifest in Brooke's letter to Cox early in 1911.

Letter from Noel Olivier to Brooke stating her indifference to his attentions (Pippa Harris, ed., Song of Love: The Letters of Rupert Brooke and Noel Olivier, *pp. 74–75)*

The Champions

Dear poor Rupert,

    This is a horrible muddle. I seem to be going to Switzerland. My Father has told me not to & you are angry with Margery because you think its her fault & that she schemed it all. And I, as usual am damnably placid & indifferent, & wanting to do about three incompatible things at the same time.

    I believe that now, perhaps, you can understand what I meant at Camp when I complained that I was too compliable & considerate. "Considerate" was the wrong word, so was compliable almost; but I was referring to this beastly indifference in me, this absence of any determination which could help me to do things whatever anyone else wanted. I think I've heard you complain a little in some of your letters; you call it "serenity" & are polite about it as such, but you have muttered occasionally & almost wished that it wasn't quite so apathetic. Your quite right to object. I hate it & feel that it will prevent my ever achieving anything, "even of any kind". Do you remember how "it" lost the train for us at Beaulieu Rd? It has done worse than that tho & probably will do still worse.

    I hope you grasp what I mean. This thing (wretched trait of my character) is entirely responsible for the present state of affairs. Margery is as innocent as—oh anything, she wrote & asked me whether I wanted to go to Switzerland, said it would be nice, & on that I decided to come. For goodness sake don't abuse her anymore, she understands about you as well as Ka or Bryn or anyone! She may be a little less efficient, that's all.

    Your coming down here when we get back from Switzerland & I shall have to entertain you as they try & work.

    I am suddenly summoned to a train. Cabs are bad to write in.

Love from
Noel

Noel Olivier camping along the Beaulieu River (King's College Library, Cambridge)

Paul Moeyes discusses how Brooke's early rebellious poetry gradually evolved into his fervently patriotic war poetry by 1914 in "Georgian Poetry's False Dawn: A Reassessment of Rupert Brooke: His Poetry and Personality," Neophilologus, *75 (July 1991), pp. 456–469.*

Rupert Brooke is regarded as one of the leading lights among the Georgian Poets, the group of poets Edward Marsh anthologised in his five volumes of *Georgian Poetry* (1911–1922). The Georgians have largely been ignored since the moment they went out of fashion in the mid-1920s, mainly because the Modernists labelled them reactionary, but more recent criticism has convincingly shown that they were in fact, like the Modernists, reacting against the late-Victorian Tory imperialist tradition, represented by such poets as Kipling, Newbolt, Henley, Watson, and Noyes. The Georgians resented their patriotism, rhetoric and pomposity, and instead wanted a poetry that dealt with even the humblest of subjects, written in a more natural language, though, unlike the Modernists, they still

Rupert Brooke (reading) during a camping expedition on the Beaulieu River, 1910. Bill Hubback is on the left taking a photograph. On the ground are Brynhild Olivier and Katherine Cox (King's College Library, Cambridge).

believed good poetry could be enjoyed by a large reading audience. The Georgians were, on the whole, Liberal, anti-Victorian, and anti-imperialistic, and from the time the first *Georgian Poetry* anthology was published in 1912, the Georgians were considered an innovative movement, headed by Rupert Brooke.

Even before that time he had made a name for himself as the voice of a new generation: while at Cambridge, he had been the centre of a group of friends called the "Neo-pagans." Previous commentators, however, have already noted that Brooke's paganism "was a wilful, sometimes desperate attempt to escape from his engrained puritanism," and it is indeed noticeable that a religious undercurrent is a constant presence in his poetry. It is surprising, therefore, that Brooke's reputation as a rebel-innovator has never been seriously questioned, the more so since no commentator has been able to explain how an arch-rebel came to write a cycle of fervently patriotic *War Sonnets*. These are the questions, then, that this essay seeks to answer.

It was Brooke's mother, yet another example of that nineteenth century type of fiercely Evangelical, dominating women, who instilled in him the Victorian values that were to burden him for the rest of his life. In his adolescent years he discovered the poets of the Nineties, and their decadence inevitably clashed with his mother's religious upbringing. This is evident in his early poetry, for the most part consisting of decadent pastiches with strongly religious overtones. The earliest poem included in the *Poetical Works* is "God Give" (1903), and two years later he wrote a poem in which, despite the inflated language, he successfully sums up his own post-Victorian dilemma:

> Why are we vexed with yearning? Surely it is
> Enough for us to crouch about the fire
> And laugh the irretrievable hours away,
> Heedless of what may wait us in the gloom,
> The muttering night beyond? Yet though we strive
> So to live in the present and forget,
> Ever the voice returning wakes again
> The old insatiate yearning in our hearts,
> Whispering words incomprehensible,
> Infinity, Eternity, and–God.
> ("Man," ll. 11–20)

In retrospect, this is oddly enough one of his most honest poems, expressing as it does both a concern with fleeting youth and a latent religiosity. Despite its world-weary tone, Brooke was only 17 when he wrote it; what is perhaps most significant about this poem is that it shows what a talented poseur its author is.

The adolescent Brooke seems to have developed a strong need to be loved, and in the letters he wrote in this period he is quite honest about his dishonesty, frankly admitting to his friend Geoffrey Keynes that it is his intention to cultivate a public persona and to be "all things to all men." In combination with his desire to get away from his mother's Evangelical influence and the Classical education he received at Rugby, this accounts for his eagerness to take up fashionable new ideas, thus at the same time reacting against his elders and gaining popularity among his contemporaries. By 1906 Brooke had sufficiently worked out his own creed, and he explained it in a letter to Geoffrey Keynes:

> All art rests on the sexual emotions which are merely the instruments of the Life-force–of Nature–for the propagation of life. That is all we live for, to further Nature's purpose. Sentiment, poetry, romance, religion are but mists of our own fancies, too weak for the great nature-forces of individuality and sexual emotion.

For the moment, then, both the Christian religion and Platonic Love were apparently dead for him. He expressed this new stage in his thinking in two dramatic poems. In "The Vision of the Arch-angels" (December 1906), four archangels carry a small coffin ("where a child must lie") up a steep peak:

> They then from the sheer summit cast, and watched it fall,
> Through unknown glooms, that frail black coffin–and therein
> God's little pitiful Body lying, worn and thin,
> And curled up like some crumpled, lonely flower-petal.

Two years later he returned to this theme in "Failure." The speaker's rebellious mood in the opening lines of this sonnet is reminiscent of a similar defiant mood in the first lines of George Herbert's "The Collar," but in Brooke's poem the blaspheming speaker, incensed by thwarted Love, vows to go up the Golden Stair and curse God on his throne. But on entering the Iron Gate he finds the Kingdom of God deserted, "the glassy pavement" covered in moss, the council-halls dusty, and an "idle wind [blowing] round an empty throne."

When he wrote this poem, Brooke was already the centre of that group of friends Virginia Woolf later dubbed the "Neo-Pagans," a term that may require further explanation. Calling them a "group" is largely misleading, evoking, as it does, a picture similar to that of the Bloomsbury group. But the Neo-pagans were basically no more than some young people who were at Cambridge together, united by friendship and some shared pet-hates, and their ideas, if any, were fashionable rather than heartfelt or original. As Paul Delany puts it:

> When the Neo-pagans came together . . . many ways for the new generation to escape from Victorianism were in the air, but they had no thought of any formal manifesto to found their group on. They were friends of Rupert, and friends of each other, who had a common style of youthful unconventionality, and overlapping links to Bedales, Fabianism, Cambridge and the Simple Life.

Also it is essential to interpret "pagan" as meaning "rustic" rather than "unbeliever" or "non-Christian." Brooke's theory about the "Life-force" might as well be ignored altogether, for in comparison with Bloomsbury's promiscuity the Neo-pagan summer camps had all the libertinism of a Sunday school outing.

Too many people seem to have been taken in by the Brooke persona. This strikingly handsome young man, who proclaimed his belief in the Life-force, Fabianism and the Simple Life was in fact a very insecure romantic with a yearning for a spiritual dimension. For how otherwise can it be explained that in his *Poetical Works* there is only one poem that could be said to be dealing with the "Life-force" ("Lust"), and only one about Fabianism ("Second Best"), whereas the God he buried in "The Vision of the Archangels" is resurrected in such poems as "My Song," "Song of the Children in Heaven" and "The Song of the Pilgrims."

The only real development that is noticeable in his Neo-pagan phase is regressive rather than progressive. Brooke's first poems (1903–06) were heavily influenced by his friendship with the local decadent poet St John Lucas, and as a result of that they are drenched in pessimism and Weltschmerz and filled with lost loves, fading petals and purple kisses. But in the first stage of his "Neo-pagan poetry" (1907–9), when love is still his main subject and he still lacks any firsthand experience of it, Brooke's inspirational sources lie further back in the nineteenth century: Wordsworth, Keats, Meredith and the pre-Raphaelites are now the new, dominating influences.

The nature-mysticism present in "Seaside" and "Pine Trees and the Sky: Evening" is purely Wordsworthian. In the love poems the beloved is now a distant, nymph-like ideal (reminding one of Keats as well as of the renewed interest in chivalry in Victorian art & literature); she is described as a "flower," "white" and "innocent," and with long flowing hair (thus evoking the picture of a pre-Raphaelite "stunner"). And the fact that she is distant and unattainable is essential, as is illustrated by two poems written within a month of each other, in April and May 1909. In "The Voice" the poet is alone "in the magic of my woods" about to reach "the hour of knowing." But then the silence is disturbed by the arrival, on her "ignorant feet," of his flesh-and-blood beloved: "The spell was broken, the key denied me / And at length your flat voice beside me / Mouthed cheerful clear flat platitudes." The exact opposite is described in "Blue Evening," where, again in a sylvan setting, the lover/poet admires an idealised nymph: "A flower in moonlight, she was there / Was rippling down white ways of glamour / Quietly laid on wave and air." The important difference being that in this poem the woman is beyond the poet's reach, only to be admired from a distance.

Further evidence of a Victorian influence can be found in many other poems. In "Day That I Have Loved," the day itself is personified, and the poet carries her "to the shrouded sands / Where lies your waiting boat, by wreaths of the sea's making." The imagery here is purely Tennysonian, either The Lady of Shalott or the Fair Elaine (both very popular subjects in Victorian painting). The setting of his sonnet "Oh! Death will find me," on the other hand, appears at first sight to have been derived from Dante: the poet pictures himself in the Underworld, waiting for his love to arrive from across "the Stygian tide." But it seems more likely that Brooke found this idea (including the "Oh!") in Bridges, the last stanza of whose "Elegy–on a lady whom grief for the death of her betrothed killed" (1890) describes the dead betrothed in a similar situation: "And thou, O lover, that art on the watch / Where, on the banks of the forgetful streams / The pale indifferent ghosts wander." What is obvious is that the world evoked in all these poems is very much like the dream world F. R. Leavis considered characteristic of the nineteenth century.

Brooke entered the second stage of his Neo-pagan phase towards the end of 1909, and it lasted until his nervous breakdown in 1912. It is characterized by a growing desire to escape from reality, culminating in a return to Platonism and, though perhaps less obviously, Christianity. There are two reasons for Brooke's increasing need to get away from reality. By 1909 he began to lose his centre stage position as the Neo-pagans broke up into several courting couples. At the same time Brooke himself felt unable to fall in love, which caused both sexual frustration and jealousy, and when he sought release from his sexual frustration in a homosexual encounter with a Rugby schoolfriend this only filled him with an intense self-disgust.

The intensity of his emotion can be felt in "Jealousy" (1909), in which the speaker addresses a girl who refused him in favour of somebody else. The poem expresses an enormous desire to hurt the girl and console the speaker's damaged pride, and this is achieved by picturing the couple in their decrepit old age:

When all that's fine in man is at an end,
And you, that loved young life and clean, must tend
A foul, sick fumbling dribbling body and old,
When his rare lips hang flabby and can't hold
Slobber

The concern for fleeting youth expressed so vaguely and unconvincingly in the early poems is now juxtaposed with an evocative and horrible image of old age. But the poet is trapped by his own image when in the last line of the poem he realises that she, and by implication he, will be old and "dirty" too....

From 1909–10 onwards, then, Brooke is gradually moving away from Neo-paganism. As a result of the courtships among his friends, his own failing in love and the disgust he felt after his homosexual affair the onetime leader of the Neo-pagans was thrown off his pedestal, and left in a state of emotional upset and insecurity. His major concern in the poetry written at this time is to find a new creed to hold on to and which will exonerate him from any personal failing. More and more this leads him back to his Platonic/Puritan starting-point.

The new creed now gradually emerging in his poetry is a belief in friendship with distinct Platonic and Christian overtones. Brooke shies away from earthly love and its physical aspects, instead "love" changes into a purely spiritual "Love," a Platonic Ideal existing in an eternal realm separate from this world, and therefore unattainable for mortal man. In relation to this Love the poet becomes a worshipper, and Love his God. At the same time the poet celebrates friendship as the only ideal human relationship attainable on earth.

Brooke was desperately in search of peace of mind, and for the moment this creed seems to have helped him find a new equilibrium. It is in this period that he wrote two poems about friendship, "Dining-Room Tea" and "Kindliness." The first poem reveals that Brooke experiences friendship, as he did with "love" in the Neo-pagan phase, with a religious fervour. The speaker in the poem is among friends, and then suddenly experiences a vision of ideal friendship, a brief and yet timeless moment which for him has all the intensity of a religious revelation:

Under a vast and starless sky
I saw the immortal moment lie.
One instant I, an instant, knew
As God knows all.

In the second poem, "Kindliness," Brooke returns to his earlier theme, the fallacy of perfect human love.

But this time he is able to take a more detached view of the subject, which results in a convincing and at times even moving poem. He starts out by reiterating the point that, no matter how perfect love is, the fire of passion cannot last: "the best that either's known / Will change, and wither, and be less / At last, than comfort, or its own / Remembrance." So what to do at that stage, when love has changed to kindliness? The poet suggests suicide, or going separate ways, but then, with a serenity that is new in Brooke, he proposes friendship as another viable alternative, one that enables him to accept the inevitable with quiet resignation:

> Or shall we stay
> Since this is all we've known, content
> In the lean twilight of such day,
> And not remember, not lament?

It is this tone of submission that makes the poem stand out in Brooke's oeuvre. He himself thought it one of his best, possibly for this very reason. For the way love continued to be his main subject, and the passionate and often frantic quality of his writing in this period suggests that he was still emotionally upset.

In his 1968 review of Brooke's *Letters,* Philip Larkin noted that in the period 1909–1912 "Brooke almost obsessively overworked the adjectives 'clean' and 'dirty.'" In his poetry this clean/dirty contrast is only one of the many puritanical good/evil, Heaven/Hell juxtapositions that serve as framework for his writing. His particular obsession is physical love, which he considers both sinful and dirty, and this is juxtaposed with the Platonic "Love" which is like a state of grace, and where the ecstacy is purely spiritual.

Brooke's nature imagery also becomes part of this Heaven/Hell juxtaposition. In an earlier poem, "Paralysis" (1909), the poet is alone in his house in the town, his beloved nymph having left him to return to "the world beyond the town." Lying in his bed, he is tormented by the idea that she will forget him as soon as she is alone with her "hills and heaven." This somewhat literal symbol of a hill or mountain as the closest point to heaven recurs in several other poems. A sonnet describing two happy lovers is called "The Hill," but more interesting is another sonnet, in which Brooke blames Katherine Cox for awakening sexual desires in him, which had been the cause of the emotional upset he was still suffering from. This sonnet is called "The Descent," and in the opening lines the symbolic meaning is explicitly stated: "Because you called, I left the mountain height / Bleak nurse and neighbour to Infinity. . . ."

Brooke's complete collapse occurred towards the end of 1911. After the previous crisis he had sought solace in another creed, adopting friendship as his new ideal, but after his 1912 breakdown there was no attempt to comfort his feelings in new beliefs. The poems he wrote in the period between his breakdown and his departure for America and the Pacific in May 1913 are all purely escapist: as when he wrote "Dining-Room Tea," he needed to calm his nerves and therefore avoided any "disturbing" subjects. Instead he wrote pieces of pure escapism: mostly they are "Songs" (in his letters he had expressed his admiration for the Elizabethan lyricists), and there are only a few longer poems of some interest. The allegorical "The Funeral of Youth: Threnody" again displays Brooke's tendency towards self-dramatisation: among the friends who appear at his Youth's graveside are Friendship ("not a minute older") and Contentment ("who had known Youth as a child"), with Love as the only absentee ("Love had died long ago"). A most remarkable poem is "Mary and Gabriel." This poem marks the culmination of Brooke's puritanical obsession with sex, and in "Mary and Gabriel" he escapes from this physical dirtiness by writing a poem about the Immaculate Conception!

Brooke's belief in love was somewhat restored on Samoa, where he found both sex and solace with a native girl, but the influence this had on his poetry was not altogether a beneficial one. The poems he wrote in the Pacific still deal with a Platonic paradise, the important difference being that Brooke was obviously in much better spirits, and this affected the tone of the poems. Harold Monro said that Brooke was "stimulated to write by the oddness rather than by the intensity of an idea," and the humorous tone already present in "The Old Vicarage, Grantchester," now becomes more pronounced: poems like "Heaven," the self-mocking "The Great Lover," and "Tiare Tahiti" are basically clever jokes. In "Tiare Tahiti" Brooke even mocks his Neo-Platonic creed, saying that in his Platonic heaven there is no possibility for physical love: "And there's an end, I think, of kissing / When our mouths are one with Mouth. . . ."

There is an enormous contrast between the witty poems Brooke wrote during his stay in the South Pacific and the highflown tone of the *War Sonnets* he wrote in November-December 1914. This contrast has never been satisfactorily explained and is in most cases simply ignored. As war poems, they are usually discussed in combination with some of the war poems of Siegfried Sassoon and Wilfred Owen, a comparison which then results in a dismissal of Brooke's poems as blindly patriotic and warlike. But it should never be forgotten that the early war poetry of both Sassoon and Owen is at least as patriotic and warlike. . . .

In September 1914 he confessed in a letter that "I am . . . carried along on the tides of my body, rather helplessly." His mother's religion had never suited him, because he was too active and passionate. But when he took up love as his new religion, his puritanism proved to be enough of an inhibition to prevent him from taking up free love or anything permissive. It is this that explains his desire to marry: he wanted to channel his passions in a socially acceptable way. But after the 1912 breakdown, the idea of having to drop his mask and give himself completely proved too great a stumblingblock, and besides, Brooke's fears of settling down, ending up in a rut and growing old were all too real.

All these points help to explain the appeal the war held for him; it was a temporary escape into the relative safety of camaraderie, a way out from all the choices that had to be taken and the adult responsibilities that had to be accepted. This is the interpretation John Press favours: "[Brooke's] war sonnets can no longer be read as a simple clarion call to arms: they are a desperate attempt by a tormented man to find emotional relief from a morbid self-disgust." But the problem with this view is that one does not get the impression that Brooke was particularly tormented when he wrote the sonnets: the poems written in the Pacific suggest that he had at least partly recovered from his breakdown, and neither the tone of his letters nor that of the sonnets is that of a man in great emotional distress.

A more likely explanation is that, some time before the outbreak of the war, Brooke had entered a new phase. And it was this new focus of attention that was to determine the course of the last part of his life. This new and decisive influence on the tone of Brooke's *War Sonnets* was the social circle he was now moving in.

Towards the end of 1912, Brooke had become a protégé of Edward Marsh, the future editor of the *Georgian Poetry* anthologies and at that time Private Secretary to Winston Churchill, the First Lord of the Admiralty. Marsh introduced Brooke to "Winston" (as Brooke called him in his letters), and at the outbreak of the war he arranged for Brooke to be commissioned in Winston's private army, the Royal Naval Division. But he also introduced Brooke to London's high-society, and by the summer of 1914 Brooke was a frequent guest at the Admiralty and 10 Downing Street. Among his close friends were Lady Eileen Wellesley, daughter of the Duke of Wellington, and Violet Asquith, eldest daughter of the Prime Minister. H. H. Asquith himself was also quite taken with Brooke: in a letter to his confidante Venetia Stanley, he wrote that "it would not be a bad thing if Violet & Rupert Brooke came together". . . The author of the *War Sonnets,* then, has nothing to do with the erstwhile Neo-pagan; rather he is a latter day Soul, a role for which he was ideally suited: handsome, charming, witty and intelligent, and eager to please rather than to probe. Many of his hosts had been leading members of the Souls: Violet's stepmother, Margot Asquith, had been at the centre of the group, in April 1913 Brooke was the guest of the Conservative MP and former Soul George Wyndham, in his day referred to as "the handsomest man of England," and when Enid Bagnold asked Lady Horner about another leading Soul Harry Cust, she was told that "he was the Rupert Brooke of our day."

This is the background against which the *War Sonnets* should be read. Brooke had found a new voice, a voice that went down well with his new friends. As a schoolboy at Rugby in 1905, Brooke had held a talk on modern poetry in which he said that he hated W. E. Henley's patriotism and that reading Kipling was like "reading life by flashes of superb vulgarity." Ten years later Edward Marsh had no problems converting Brooke into an admirer of Kipling's poetry, and the fact is that in the *War Sonnets* the tone is hardly distinguishable from that of the imperialist poets, Henley, Kipling and Sir Henry Newbolt. Brooke's rhetoric in these sonnets is that of an evangelist preaching a new gospel to the masses, though at the same time, as at the beginning of his Neo-pagan phase, he is trying to lose himself in a popular cause: as before, the preaching of the public figure seems primarily intended to take his mind off and divert his own attention from the disturbing problems of the private individual.

This is not to say that the *War Sonnets* are mere propaganda pieces written to boost the numbers of Kitchener's Army. In the opening sonnet especially there are unmistakeable references to his personal problems, but the point is that in adopting the Happy Warrior pose Brooke simply reflected an image that was prevalent in the society in which he now moved. Julian Grenfell, that other epitome of early war enthusiasm and himself the son of a leading Souls hostess, wrote his "Into Battle" from personal experience, whereas Brooke, as in his Neo-pagan phase, was fantasising about his new role rather than describing his deepest feelings and experiences.

The *War Sonnets* are hardly concerned with the war, and not at all with victory. They are about early death, and the desirability of early death, and it is this welcoming of an early death as an escape from growing old that links the *War Sonnets* with his 1909 poem "Menelaeus and Helen." In this poem Brooke suggested that Paris's early death was a blessing in disguise, and this idea recurs in the first of the *War Sonnets*.

The opening poem of the cycle, "Peace," is the most personal of the *War Sonnets* in that it is only in this poem that Brooke refers to what went before. The paradoxical title is particularly revealing, referring as it does to the inner peace Brooke thought he had re-found in the year war broke out in Europe. Since it was no more than an escape and had done nothing to actually solve any of his problems, it also indicates an element of self-deception Brooke seems not to have been aware of.

"Peace" opens with a thanksgiving to the Christian God he had abjured in his Neo-pagan period: "Now God be thanked, Who has matched us with His hour / And caught our youth, and wakened us from sleeping." Brooke returns to his God as a repentant sinner, welcoming war as a baptism, a possibility to cut loose from the immediate past, including his love-worship, and redeem himself.

The "sick-hearts" and "half-men" could well be a reference to his hated enemy Lytton Strachey, like other "Bloomsberries" a conscientious objector, but the most revealing line is of course "the little emptiness of love," followed by the equally telling "Oh!, we, who have known shame, we have found release there." The last line of "Peace" introduces Death as a young man's "worst friend and enemy," and the desirability of a heroic Death is the subject of the following three sonnets. Whereas the rhetorical "we" in the first sonnet was but the faintest disguise for Brooke's own voice, the "we" in these poems does seem to refer to the young soldiers in general. But there is a sudden departure from this plural form in the last four lines of "Safety," where after four separate references to "we" Brooke reverts to the first person singular to repeat his main theme: "And if these poor limbs die, safest of all."

The third sonnet continues the theme of the cleansing effect of wars, welcoming the return of such Platonic ideals as Honour, Nobleness and Holiness, and referring in passing to old age as "that unhoped for serene." This unlikely-to-be-enjoyed serene old age is juxtaposed in the fourth sonnet with the desirability of early death, which is described as an "unbroken glory," since it preserves the soldiers' eternal youth.

The last and perhaps most famous sonnet of the sequence, "The Soldier," introduces an imperialist note that puts Brooke on a par with Henley and Newbolt. The poem reads as the imperialist's answer to Thomas Hardy's bleak "Drummer Hodge," but on a more personal level it also seems an attempt by the poet to reconcile himself with death. In February 1915 Prime Minister Asquith reported to his friend that "Rupert Brooke is quite convinced that he will not return alive." In the event he did not return at all, and was buried on the isle of Skyros. It is impossible to say if he indeed thought he would die, or if this was all part of the new role of a romantic hero he had adopted.

Thinking of Brooke as the leader of the Neo-pagans is to misunderstand him completely: holding court at Grantchester was never a role that suited him, still adhering as he was to Christian morality as well as lacking in the necessary qualities of leadership. It was his last role, that of the poet laureate of the young English upper classes, that suited him best. In this capacity he created an imaginary portrait of an idealised self, the Happy Warrior of the *War Sonnets,* and found that it was a portrait that appealed to a whole generation. By that time he had completely distanced himself from his Cambridge past, both as a Neo-pagan and as a Cambridge Apostle and follower of G. E. Moore's philosophy, which held that one had to base one's judgement "strictly on the exercise of reason, each man his own severest judge in his own case."

It is this basic insincerity and lack of depth that make his poetry ultimately disappointing. Even more so since his unmistakable craftsmanship and popularity would have enabled him to make a far more important and lasting contribution to that much maligned new school of Georgian Poetry.

Brooke is a transitional figure, entering a new age for which he was not prepared. It was the following generation, led in America by the young F. Scott Fitzgerald and the Flappers, and in England by Evelyn Waugh and the Bright Young Things, that succeeded where Brooke failed: cutting loose from the past, rejecting all responsibilities and flouting nineteenth-century morality, they enjoyed life to the full and gathered as many rosebuds as they could.

Brooke never succeeded in breaking away from the nineteenth century, and that must have been a contributory factor in his failing to fulfil his promise as a talented and innovative young poet. It is a subject he avoids in his correspondence, but in one of his last letters, written to one of his closest friends, he gives up all pretence and frankly admits that "the realization of failure makes me unpleasantly melancholy."

It was a letter only to be opened in the event of his death.

Brooke's letter to Katherine Cox expressing the confusion that he felt in being attracted to her, 5 January 1911 (Geoffrey Keynes, ed., The Letters of Rupert Brooke, *p. 269)*

24 Bilton Road, Rugby

. . . We drifted away, I all the time too (somehow) lost and shy and perplexed ever quite to seize a chance of saying one or two things that I was on fire to say. I wanted passionately to know that you were painless and vacuously cheery. All yesterday and today (though–do you find it–half a day and eighty miles are all time and space for the veils they hang between oneself and one's yester-self) I'm red and sick with anger at myself for my devilry and degradation and stupidity. I hate myself because I wickedly and unnecessarily hurt you several times. (I don't mean that I'm sorry for my own sake–for all that happened; or that I'm an atom changed from what I said and suggested. That stands.) But I hurt you, I hurt you, Ka, for a bit, unforgiveably and filthily and infamously; and I can't bear it; I was wild to do anything everything in the world to *undo* the hurt, or blot it out (but what could I do? I waved my arm in the bookshop at thirty books–but that'ld have meant nothing. And I couldn't, as I wanted, take hold of you and put mouth hard to mouth, for you had somehow put that aside, and it would have confused other issues, and–I daredn't.) Oh, tell me that you're unhurt, for I hurt you in *such* a way, and I was mean and selfish, and you're, I think, one of the most clear and most splendid people in the world.

Rupert

I go to the Champions on Monday or Tuesday, perhaps; not for the week-end.

Brooke campaigned vigorously for the election of the Labour Party during late autumn 1910. However, when the Liberal Party emerged victorious, Brooke felt that many Fabian causes would be implemented by the sympathetic Asquith government. He placed political concerns aside and concentrated on winning a Cambridge fellowship, learning German, and researching the works of John Webster, the Elizabethan playwright.

Early in 1911 Brooke left for Munich, where he stayed for three months and where he was lonely in spite of his active social life. During this period in Germany he wrote one of his more important and successful poems, "The Fish."

Brooke's letter to Frances Cornford expressing his loneliness in Germany, February 1911 (Geoffrey Keynes, ed., The Letters of Rupert Brooke, *pp. 278-279)*

Pension Bellevue, Munich

The worst of solitude–or the best–is, that one begins poking at one's own soul, examining it, cutting the soft and rotten parts away. And where's one to stop? Have you ever had, at lunch or dinner, an overripe pear or apple, and, determined to make the best of it, gone on slicing off the squashy bits? You may imagine me, in Munchen at a German lunch with Life, discussing hard, and cutting away at the bad parts of the dessert. "Oh," says Life, courteous as ever, "I'm sure you've got a bad Soul there. Please don't go on with it! Leave it, and take another! I'm so sorry!" But, knowing I've taken the last, and polite anyhow, "Oh no, please!" I say, scraping away, "it's really all right. It's only a little gone, here and there–on the outside.... There's plenty that's quite good. I'm quite enjoying it. You always have such delightful Souls! ..." And after a minute, when there's a circle of messy brown round my plate, and in the centre a rather woebegone brown-white thin shapeless scrap, the centre of the thing, Life breaks in again, seeing my plight, "Oh, but you can't touch any of that! It's bad right through! I'm sure Something must have Got Into it! Let me ring for another! There is sure to be some in the Larder...." But it won't do, you know. So I rather ruefully reply "Ye-s-s, I'm afraid it *is* impossible. But I won't have another, thanks. I don't really want one at all. I only took it out of mere greed ... and to have something to do. Thank you, I've had quite enough. Such excellent meat and pudding! I've done splendidly.... But to go on with our conversation. About Literature–you were saying, I think...?" and so the incident's at an end.

Dear! dear! it's very trying being ever so exalted one day & ever so desperate the next–this self-knowledge (*why* did that old fool class it with Self-reverence and Self-control? They're rarely seen together)! But so one lives in Munich....

Rupert

Geoffrey Keynes discusses the background of "The Fish" in his Four Poems *(London: Scolar, 1974)*

"The Fish," a favourite among Brooke's less slanted poems, has no undertones of war on prettiness, primness, the absurdities of love, or loss of youth. A few years later he wrote another fish poem, satirizing the conventional view of God and Heaven through the thoughts of a fish. The present poem is a brilliantly clever fantasy, attempting to get inside the skin of a fish by making a picture of the strange world in which it lives with its clouded consciousness, but with the least possible tinge of anthropomorphism.

It was written in March 1911, while Brooke was spending three months in Munich to learn German and observe the habits and culture of the bourgeoisie. In March he had had an adventure at a Carnival or *Bacchus-Fest* with a Dutch sculptress ("A round damp young sculptress, a bit like Lord Rosebery to look on") which had ended with his suddenly becoming "quite coldly aware of my position in the Universe." The feeling, he said, was mutual and at five in the morning "we very solemnly and pathetically kissed each other on our quiet intellectual lips and hugged a space and so parted." On 25 April Brooke reported in a letter to Eddie Marsh that "I spent two months over a poem that describes the feelings of a fish in the metre of *L'Allegro*. It was meant to be a lyric, but has turned into a work of 70 lines with a moral end. It is quite unintelligible." He

The Fish.

In a cool curving world he lies
And ripples with dark ecstasies.
The kind luxurious lapse and steel
Shapes all his universe to feel
And know and be; the clinging stream
Closes his memory, glooms his dream,
Who lips the roots o' the shore, and glides
Superb on unreturning tides.
Those silent waters weave for him
A fluctuant mutable world and dim,
Where wavering masses bulge and gape
Mysterious, and shape to shape
Dies momently through whorl and hollow,
And form and line and solid follow
Solid and line and form to dream
Fantastic down the eternal stream;
An obscure world, a shifting world,
Bulbous, or pulled to thin, or curled
Or serpentine, or driving arrows,
Or serene slidings, or March narrows.
There slipping wave and shore are one,
And weed and mud. No ray of sun,
But glow to glow fades down the deep,
(As dream to unknown dream in sleep);
Shaken translucency illumes
The hyaline of drifting glooms;

Manuscript for the poem Brooke wrote in Germany, 1911 (King's College Library, Cambridge)

The strange soft-handed depth subdues
Drowned colour there, but black to hues,
As Death to living, decomposes,
— Red darkness of the heart of roses,
Blue brilliant from dead starless skies,
And gold that lies behind the eyes,
The unknown unnamable sightless white
That is the essential flame of night,
Lustreless purple, hooded green,
The myriad hues that lie between
Darkness and darkness! . . .
                          And all; one
Gentle, embracing, quiet, dim,
The world he rests in, world he knows,
Perpetual curving. Only, — grows
An eddy in that ordered falling
A knowledge from the gloom, a calling
Weed in the wave, gleam in the mud —
The dark fire leaps along his blood;
Dateless and deathless, blind and still
The intricate impulse works its will;
His woven world drops back; and he,
Sans providence, sans memory,
Unconscious and directly driven,
Fades to some dark sufficient Heaven.

O world of lips, O world of laughter,

Where hope is fleet and thought flies after,
Of lights in the clear night, of cries
That drift along the wave and rise
Into [...] the yielding stars above,
You know the hands, the eyes of love!
The strife of limbs, the sightless clinging,
The infinite distance, and the singing
Blown by the wind, a flame of sound,
The gleam, the flowers, and vast around
The horizon, and the heights above —
You know the sigh, the song of love!

But there the night is close, and there
Darkness is cold and strange and bare;
And the secret deeps are whisperless;
And rhythm is all deliciousness;
And joy is in the throbbing tide,
Whose intricate fingers beat and glide
In felt bewildering harmonies
Of trembling touch; and music is
The exquisite knocking of the blood.
Space is no more, under the mud;
His bliss is older than the sun.
Silent and straight the waters run.
The lights, the cries, the willows dim,
And the dark tide are one with him.

was in fact probing the consciousness of a fellow creature to determine its place in the universe, using all his command of verbal ingenuity to describe and fix the deliquescent fishy underworld.

Brooke's biographer, Christopher Hassall, remarked in the course of describing the later poem, "Grantchester," that "The Fish" shows that he had already mastered the craft of octosyllables. "It was becoming his characteristic measure, as it was of Andrew Marvell, whom in many other ways and on a smaller scale, Brooke resembles. If in a literary guessing game, confronted with

> Annihilating all that's made
> To a green thought in a green shade

some player should answer 'Brooke,' he would lose a mark, and perhaps the game, but he would be no fool." The comparison seems just.

In the penultimate division of the poem Brooke contrasted briefly the bright but transitory world of human love. *But there,* for the fish,

> the night is close, and there
> Darkness is cold and strange and bare;
> And the secret deeps are whisperless;
> And rhythm is all deliciousness;
> And joy is in the throbbing tide,
> Whose intricate fingers beat and glide
> In felt bewildering harmonies
> Of trembling touch;

The poem is a *tour-de-force* and completely successful.

Brooke moved on from Munich to Vienna and then to Florence, and by mid May he returned to Cambridgeshire to live in his new lodgings, The Old Vicarage at Grantchester. By July he was working on his dissertation about John Webster and the Elizabethan dramatists, a work that he intended to submit in competition for a fellowship at King's College.

*Christopher Hassall's description of Brooke's new lodgings, the Old Vicarage, at Grantchester (*Rupert Brooke: A Biography, *pp. 263–264)*

The Old Vicarage was a long, ramshackle, three-storied house of red brick, with attics and dormer windows in a high roof; at the back was a veranda, sagging in places, and canopied all along with Virginia creeper, and a profuse, overgrown, sweet-smelling garden with random trees, mostly ancient chestnuts, enclosing the demesne; a lawn ending in long grass, giant trees, and briars on the river bank where the water flowed four feet deep; and here and there stray relics of the nineteenth century—on the lawn a cement sundial in the form of a book lying open on a lectern, a cement basin with a fountain in the centre, and the sham Gothic ruin in a far corner, overlong with branches; and to one side stood Mr. Neeve's orderly beehives, concealed among the thickets. A five-barred gate, hooked back among the bushes, stood at one corner of the gravelled approach, giving access from the road; the whole property was shut in by trees entangled with ivy, and the nearness of the river filled the air with the smell of dampness. Brooke rented three rooms; at the top of his part of the stairs there was a low wicket gate, for his bedroom had been a nursery, and he would tell how on going up late at night it was almost as if the ghosts of Victorian children

Brooke working in the garden of the Old Vicarage (King's College Library, Cambridge)

plucked at his sleeve; beneath it was the livingroom, a round table in the centre littered with books and letters, and a glass door with yellow panes of art nouveau design which, he said, gave him the illusion of sunshine on a wet day, shadowed by strands of creeper from the veranda roof beyond, led out onto the lawn. The branches of an old box-tree also darkened his garden window.

At the same time Brooke was doing his research about Webster, he was assembling the contents of his first book of collected poems for Sidgwick and Jackson. Primarily because of the impious language and subject matter of what the publisher called Brooke's "unpleasant" or "ugly" poems such as "Lust" and "A Channel Passage," this collection caused problems between the author and the publishing house. However, the disagreements were resolved when Brooke made some compromises, such as changing the title of "Lust" to "Libido."

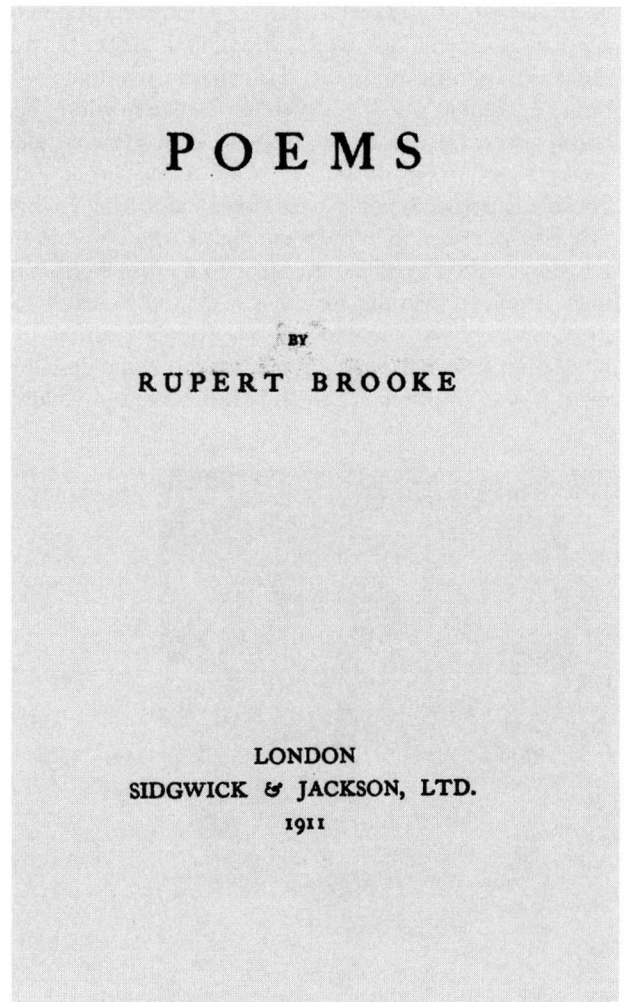

Title page for the first trade edition of Brooke's verse

The highly favorable review of Poems *in the* Times Literary Supplement, *29 August 1912*

Mr. Rupert Brooke's swagger and brutality we are inclined to take much more leniently; they are so obviously boyish. His disgusting sonnet on love and seasickness ought never to have been printed, but we are tempted to like him for it. Most people pass through some such strange nausea as this on their stormy way from romance to reality, and its expression affects one in the same as might an ebullition of temper in a healthy child. But the child must be healthy. Mr. Brooke is thoroughly healthy, and something more. We can endure his "showing off" in this and some other such outbursts, because here is clearly a rich nature—sensuous, eager, brave—fighting eagerly towards the truth. And already Mr. Brooke can show now and then an almost uncanny accomplishment. "The Fish" is as cleverly written as could be:—

> In a cool curving world he lies
> And ripples with dark ecstasies,
> The kind luxurious lapse and steal
> Shapes all his universe to feel
> And know and be; the clinging stream
> Closes his memory, glooms his dream,
> Who lips the roots o' the shore, and glides
> Superb on unreturning tides.

But only the whole poem can exhibit Mr. Brooke's power over words and sounds. A more convenient example of the average of his work is the irregular sonnet "The Hill":—

> Breathless, we flung us on the windy hill,
>   Laughed in the sun, and kissed the lovely grass.
> You said, "Through glory and ecstasy we pass;
> Wind, sun, and earth remain, the birds sing still,
> When we are old, are old . . ." "And when we die
>   All's over that is ours; and life burns on
> Through other lovers, other lips," said I,
>   –"Heart of my heart, our heaven is now, is won!"

> "We are Earth's best, that learnt her lesson here.
>   Life is our cry. We have kept the faith!" we said;
>   "We shall go down with unreluctant tread
> Rose-crowned into the darkness!" . . . Proud we were,
> And laughed, that had such brave true things to say.
> –And then you suddenly cried, and turned away.

We shall watch Mr. Brooke's development with high hopes; but he must remember that swagger and brutality are no more poetry than an unripe pear is fruit.

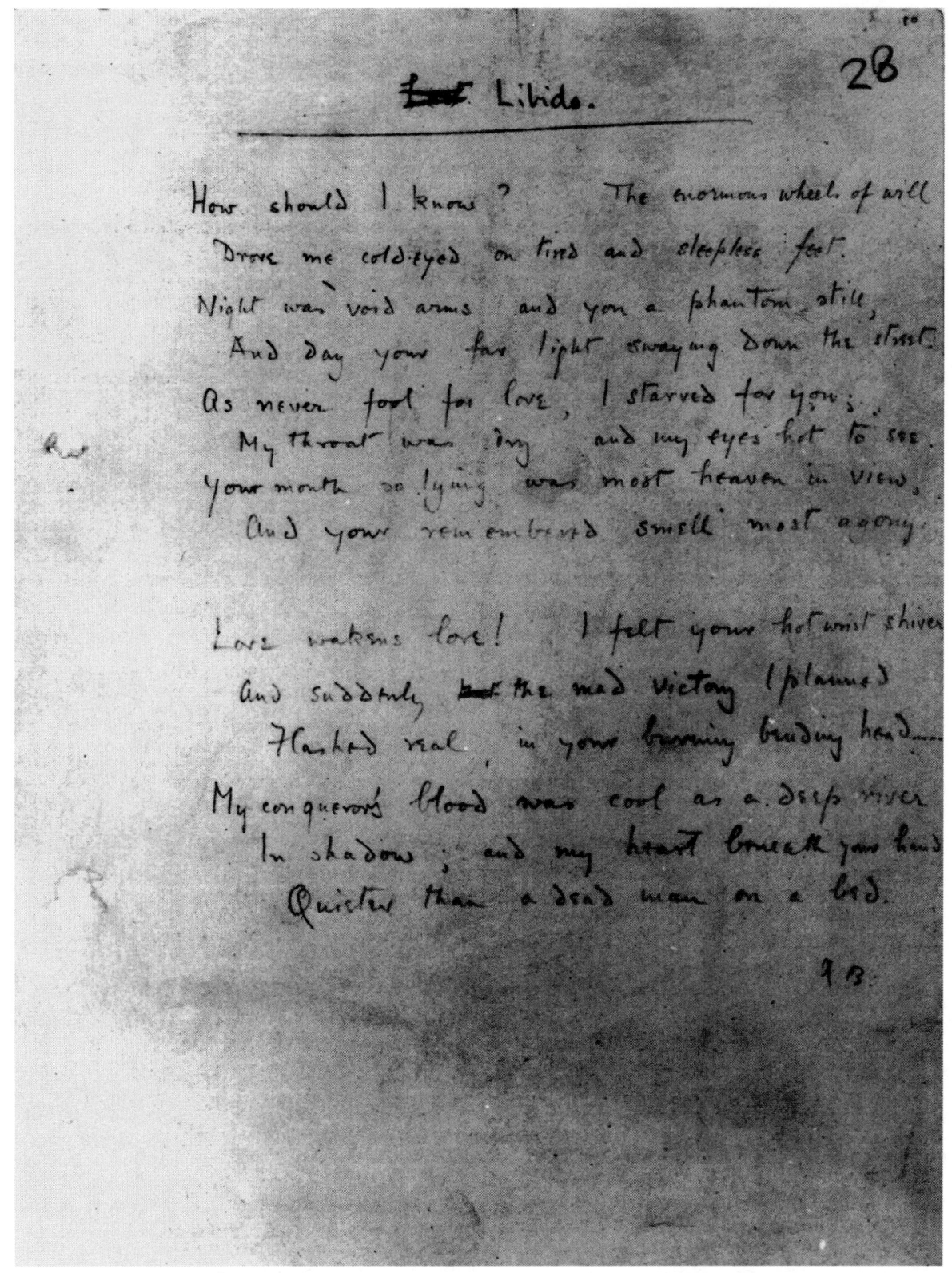

Manuscript of "Libido" with the title altered from "Lust" (King's College Library, Cambridge)

Brooke eventually went to Munich, where Cox joined him. The two lived together until she divulged that she had been seeing Henry Lamb during Brooke's recuperation in Cannes, a revelation that made Brooke melancholy and upset him. He and Cox then returned to England, where at one moment Brooke would write affectionate love letters to Cox and at another he would display complete indifference to her. It was paradoxical that Cox was at this time falling in love with him.

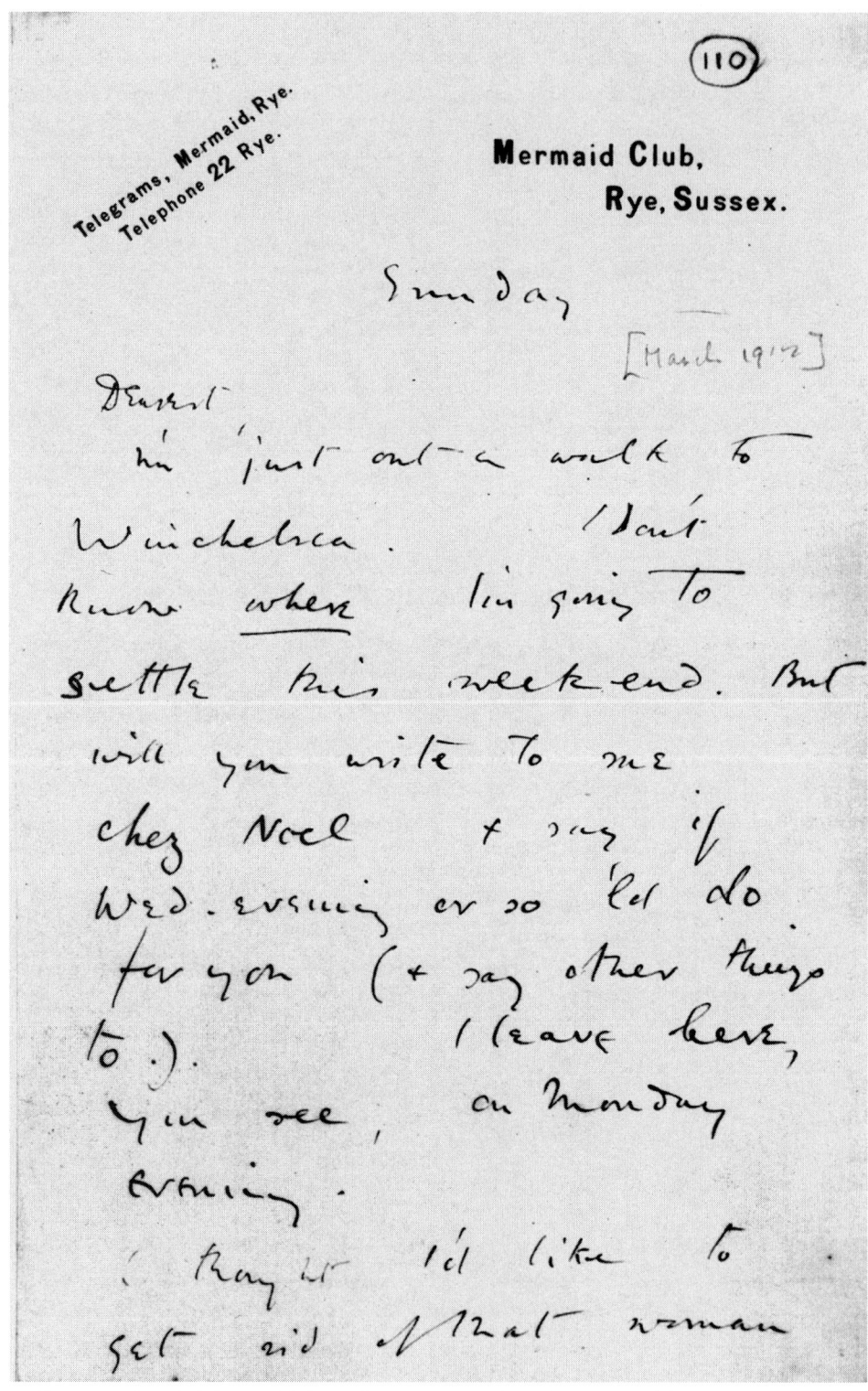

First page of Brooke's letter to Katherine Cox declaring his love, March 1912 (King's College, Cambridge)

Throughout October 1911, Brooke had been working on his dissertation at the British Museum, and he completed it on 20 December. Worn and tense through the Christmas season, he planned to visit his friends at Lulworth for a reading party during the New Year holiday. Throughout 1911 his affection for Katherine Cox had grown, and his desire for physical intimacy with her appeared to be increasing—as was hers for Henry Lamb, the painter who was to join her at Lulworth. Brooke had decided to break off his secret engagement to Noel Olivier in mid December, and he was in a highly emotional state by the time he arrived at Lulworth.

His emotional distress peaked during those opening days of 1912 when Cox announced that she was in love with Lamb. In response to this declaration Brooke offered to marry her, but she refused him. The stress of the situation brought Brooke near to a nervous breakdown. After consulting a nerve specialist in London, he was sent to Cannes in the south of France to join his mother for a rest cure.

Excerpt from Brooke's letter to Cox, written from Cannes, January 1912 (Geoffrey Keynes, ed., The Letters of Rupert Brooke, *pp. 336–337)*

Saturday evening.

I posted a beastly letter to you this morning. Since, I've been thinking and looking at you. I see better how feeble and silly and mean I am. And how fine in your slow way, you. I'm sorry if my letter worried and hurt you, Ka dear. I'm just writing for half an hour this evening to put myself in a better light.

You have been so wonderfully nice, your presence has been so cool and happy to me, these weeks when I've been a devil to you—I'm ingratitude, dirty, dirty, dirty—

One changes so, if one's ill and on a rainy Riviera. Two nights ago I had (after a German consultation with Evelyn) a Hot Bath. I was so radiant, getting out of it. I almost rushed to you. I looked at myself, drying, in the glass, and I thought my body was very beautiful and strong, and that I was keeping it and making it splendid for you. And I knew that if I rested a night on your breasts, and then caught fire from you, my mind and heart too would be able to give you a million things that only I in the world knew of and could give. I was so happy. I was happy thinking of Munich. I thought of the whole of Ka, inside and out. I was so happy.

And then at other times I lie and *ache* to twist my thoughts onto Shakespeare, a poem—anything; and they always go back to the blackness, till I can't bear it and from thinking of suicide then, think of it immediate, to cut the thing clear and set you free from a fool.

Eh, I *do* want your presence, you know, to keep me fine and sane, just now.

But tonight I *know* I shall get to Munich. I can see the Ranee [Brooke's mother] thinks she's going to keep a hand on me for a month or six weeks. But I give her ten days at the outside. I shall have to be beastly to her, I suppose. . . .

A quarter of an hour to dinner. . . .

". . . with a sort of fero-defiance (My dear, I don't know), he is often, as in–and–and–, ineffectively ugly and unpleasant. And once or twice he is merely nasty. . . . He dares to be a Daniel (?), however, and it is enormously to his credit that he has managed to stagger free from convention. But if he is content with the merely surface freedom of speech and manner; if he is content with his present Puritan ignorance of passion and his own body, and pursues the phantom of sensation, his power of concentration will gradually leave him, he will stagger back into the conventional fold, and eventually, sick of 'mad magenta minutes,' be received into some great hospital (Rome?) for men's souls. . . ." He may, on the other hand, it appears, turn out a Poet. There's a lot more; Yes. It's what a gentleman in the *Observer* thinks about

Your lover
Rupert

In April 1912 Brooke learned that he had failed to obtain the fellowship for which he had applied at King's College. In May he left for Germany, where Cox followed him for ten days and where, during this trip, Brooke wrote his well-known poem, "The Old Vicarage, Grantchester," while sitting in a Berlin café. In spite of Cox's increasing devotion to him, Brooke never regained his former love for her, and their relationship continued to degenerate.

Excerpt from the letter to Dudley Ward about Brooke's lack of feeling for Katherine Cox, May 1912 (Geoffrey Keynes, ed., The Letters of Rupert Brooke, *pp. 378–379)*

Things have, in almost every way, been entirely for the best. Ka's been slightly tired at times; but I've regulated her life so damn well, and forbidden her to do so much, that that's pretty well gone. She's enjoyed herself a lot; and found her feelings—physical and mental—were sixty (her figure) times livelier than she thought they'd be. And she has climbed down a lot about Lamb. Tonight she said she didn't feel much interest in him now. She still says she doesn't think him a beast and that she'll always have immense affection for him. . . . So she says that even if she and I don't marry, she'll almost certainly have nothing to do with him—beyond occasionally seeing him. But—though she's wiser—I think of course, she'd get trapped fairly soon, on those terms. But she'd promise never to see him again, she says, if we married. And I'm pretty sure she'll marry me, if I want.

The crux is that that absolutely dead feeling I had when I was in Berlin before she came, hasn't vanished. I was afraid, beforehand, I might—when I saw her—be dragged down into that helpless tortured sort of love for her I had all the first part of the year, and had just crept out of. The opposite. I remain dead. I care practically nothing for any person in the world. I've anxiety, and a sort of affection, for Ka—But I don't really care. I've no feeling for anybody at all—except the uneasy ghosts of the immense reverence and rather steadfast love for Noel, and a knowledge that Noel is the finest thing I've ever seen in the world, and Ka—isn't. But that doesn't come to much.

So—that's the fix I'm in at present. Time may clear things a lot, and waken them. From Neu-Strelitz we're going a week's walking, probably. After that we may or may not continue together, just now: things being as they are. I've sometimes a wish I could take the last step—exact a promise she'd not *see* the man again—and then go off and sleep in some unknown place for six weeks.

But next week, walking'll be great for both.
Love to A. M. and the gondolier—with love
Rupert

"The Old Vicarage, Grantchester" (The Collected Poems of Rupert Brooke with a Memoir, *pp. 33-37*)

Just now the lilac is in bloom,
All before my little room;
And in my flowerbeds, I think,
Smile the carnation and the pink;
And down the borders, well I know,
The poppy and the pansy blow . . .
Oh! there the chestnuts, summer through,
Beside the river make for you
A tunnel of green gloom, and deep
Deeply above; and green and deep
The stream mysterious glides beneath,
Green as a dream and deep as death.—
Oh, damn! I know it! and I know
How the May fields all golden show,
And when the day is young and sweet,
Gild gloriously the bare feet
That run to bathe . . .
Du lieber Gott!

Here am I, sweating, sick and hot,
And there the shadowed waters fresh
Lean up to embrace the naked flesh.
Temperamentvoll German Jews
Drink beer around; and *there* the dews
Are soft beneath a morn of gold.
Here tulips bloom as they are told;
Unkempt about those hedges blows
An English unofficial rose;
And there the unregulated sun
Slopes down to rest when day is done,
And wakes a vague unpunctual star
A slippered Hesper; and there are
Meads towards Haslingfield and Coton
Where *das Betreten*'s not *verboten*.

εἴθε γενοίμην . . . would I were
In Grantchester, in Grantchester!—
Some, it may be, can get in touch
With Nature there or Earth, or such.
And clever modern men have seen
A Faun a-peeping through the green,
And felt the Classics were not dead,
To glimpse a Naiad's reedy head,
Or hear the Goat-foot piping low: . . .
But these are things I do not know.
I only know that you may lie
Day-long and watch the Cambridge sky,
And, flower-lulled in sleepy grass,
Hear the cool lapse of hours pass,
Until the centuries blend and blur
In Grantchester, in Grantchester. . . .
Still in the dawnlit waters cool
His ghostly Lordship swims his pool,
And tries the strokes, essays the tricks,
Long learnt on Hellespont, or Styx;
Dan Chaucer hears his river still
Chatter beneath a phantom mill;
Tennyson notes, with studious eye,
How Cambridge waters hurry by . . .
And in that garden, black and white
Creep whispers through the grass all night;
And spectral dance, before the dawn,
A hundred Vicars down the lawn;
Curates, long dust, will come and go
On lissom, clerical, printless toe;
And oft between the boughs is seen
The sly shade of a Rural Dean . . .
Till, at a shiver in the skies,
Vanishing with Satanic cries,
The prim ecclesiastic rout
Leaves but a startled sleeper-out,
Grey heavens, the first bird's drowsy calls,
The falling house that never falls.

God! I will pack, and take a train,
And get me to England once again!
For England's the one land, I know,
Where men with Splendid Hearts may go;
And Cambridgeshire, of all England,
The shire for Men who Understand;
And of *that* district I prefer
The lovely hamlet Grantchester.

For Cambridge people rarely smile,
Being urban, squat, and packed with guile;
And Royston men in the far South
Are black and fierce and strange of mouth;
At Over they fling oaths at one,
And worse than oaths at Trumpington,
And Ditton girls are mean and dirty,
And there's none in Harston under thirty,
And folks in Shelford and those parts
Have twisted lips and twisted hearts,
And Barton men make cockney rhymes,
And Coton's full of nameless crimes,
And things are done you'd not believe
At Madingley on Christmas Eve.
Strong men have run for miles and miles
When one from Cherry Hinton smiles;
Strong men have blanched and shot their wives
Rather than send them to St. Ives;
Strong men have cried like babes, bydam,
To hear what happened at Babraham.
But Grantchester! ah, Grantchester!
There's peace and holy quiet there,
Great clouds along pacific skies,
And men and women with straight eyes,
Lithe children lovelier than a dream,
A bosky wood, a slumbrous stream,
And little kindly winds that creep
Round twilight corners, half asleep.
In Grantchester their skins are white,
They bathe by day, they bathe by night;
The women there do all they ought;
The men observe the Rules of Thought.
They love the Good; they worship Truth;
They laugh uproariously in youth;
(And when they get to feeling old,
They up and shoot themselves, I'm told) . . .

Ah God! to see the branches stir
Across the moon at Grantchester!
To smell the thrilling-sweet and rotten
Unforgettable, unforgotten
River smell, and bear the breeze
Sobbing in the little trees.
Say, do the elm-clumps greatly stand,
Still guardians of that holy land?
The chestnut shade, in reverend dream,
The yet unacademic stream?
Is dawn a secret shy and cold
Anadyomene, silver-gold?
And sunset still a golden sea
From Haslingfield to Madingley?
And after, ere the night is born,
Do hares come out about the corn?

Oh, is the water sweet and cool
Gentle and brown, above the pool?
And laughs the immortal river still
Under the mill? Under the mill?
Say, is there Beauty yet to find?
And Certainty? and Quiet kind?
Deep meadows yet, for to forget
The lies, and truths, and pain? . . . oh! yet
Stands the Church clock at ten to three?
And is there honey still for tea?

Geoffrey Keynes's background notes concerning "The Old Vicarage, Grantchester" (Keynes, ed., Four Poems*)*

The village of Grantchester is accessible by an easy journey in a canoe up the river Granta from Cambridge or by half-an-hour's walk through the Grantchester water-meadows. Brooke had stayed in lodgings at The Orchard, close to the tea-gardens, for periods in 1910 and for a short time at the Old Vicarage on the bank of the river. Early in 1911 he was for some weeks in Germany and when he returned to England in May he established himself at once in the Old Vicarage, deciding to adopt this as his permanent headquarters. Much of the work for his Fellowship thesis on John Webster was done in the house and his friends, so often entertained there, came to identify the place so intimately with his presence that it tended to efface all memories of other places where he had lived. . . .

A description of the surroundings which I contributed to the *Biography* will help to explain the references in the poem entitled "The Old Vicarage, Grantchester." The day at the Old Vicarage often began betimes, "for a crisp early morning was the best time to bathe. You went out of the garden into the lane where the thick white dust shifted and slipped under the sandshoes, over the bridge in front of Grantchester Mill, across a meadow still sopping wet with dew and into the river above Byron's Poole, to bathe naked in the dark water smelling of mint and mud. The water was held up above the Pool by a dam with grey sluice-gates marking the site of Chaucer's Mill at 'Trompyngtoun,' as described at the beginning of the Reeve's Tale. At the dam was the gathering place of deep waiting water, where you plunged in for the bath. Below was the Pool, from which a placid reach of the Granta moved away northwards by yellow flags and trees bordering the farmlands of the Trumpington Hall estate. From a point above the bathing-place flowed the lea leading to the Grantchester Mill (burnt down in 1928), the water gushing out, cold and swirling, from beneath it into the Grantchester pool, broad and deep—to one side a meadow, to the other the tremendous chestnuts on the edge of the Old Vicarage garden. A short distance below the garden the two streams, from Byron's Pool and Grantchester Mill, united; then, to the north, the prospect opened out, and over there, between the willows and across a flatness of intervening fields, were the distant pinnacles of King's."

Fair copy for "The Sentimental Exile," later titled "The Old Vicarage, Grantchester," written in 1912. The last two lines are among his best known (King's College Library, Cambridge).

With Nature there, or Larks, or such.
And clever modern men have seen
A Faun a-peeping through the green,
And felt the Classics were not dead,
To glimpse a Naiad's reedy head,
Or hear the Goat-foot piping low:......
But these are things I do not know.
I only know that you may lie
Daylong and watch the Cambridge sky,
And, flower-lulled in sleepy grass,
Hear the cool lapse of hours pass,
Until the centuries blend and blur
In Grantchester, in Grantchester......
Still in the dawnlit waters cool
His ghostly Lordship swims his pool,
And tries the strokes, essays the tricks,
Long learnt on Hellespont, or Styx.
Dan Chaucer hears his river still
Chatter beneath a phantom mill.
Tennyson notes, with studious eye,
How Cambridge waters hurry by......
And in that garden, black and white,
Creep whispers through the grass all night;
And spectral dance, before the dawn,
A hundred Vicars down the lawn;
Curates, long dust, will come and go
On lissom, clerical, printless toe;
And oft between the boughs is seen
The sly shade of a Rural Dean ......
Till, at a shiver in the skies,
Vanishing with Satanic cries,
The prim ecclesiastic rout
Leaves but a startled sleeper-out,
Grey heavens, the first birds' drowsy calls,
The falling house that never falls.

God! I will pack, and take a train,

"And get me to England once again!
For England's the one land, I know,
Where men with Splendid Hearts may go;
And Cambridgeshire, of all England,
The shire for Men who Understand;
And of that district I prefer
The lovely hamlet, Grantchester.

For Cambridge people rarely smile,
Being urban, squat, and packed with guile;
And Royston men in the far south
Are black and fierce and strange of mouth;
At Over they fling oaths at one,
And worse than oaths at Trumpington,
And Ditton girls are mean and dirty,
And there's none in Harston under thirty,
And folks in Shelford and those parts
Have twisted lips and twisted hearts,
And Barton men make cockney rhymes,
And Coton's full of nameless crimes,
And things are done you'd not believe
At Madingley on Christmas Eve.
Strong men have run for miles and miles,
When one from Cherry Hinton smiles;
Strong men have blanched, and shot their wives,
Rather than send them to St Ives;
Strong men have cried like babes, bydam,
To hear what happened at Babraham.
But Grantchester! ah, Grantchester!
There's peace and holy quiet there,
Great clouds along pacific skies,
And men and women with straight eyes,
Lithe children lovelier than a dream,
A bosky wood, a slumbrous stream,
And little kindly winds that creep
Round twilight corners, half asleep.
In Grantchester their skins are white,

They bathe by day, they bathe by night.
The women there do all they ought;
The men observe the Rules of Thought.
They love the Good; they worship Truth;
They laugh uproariously in youth;
(And when they get to feeling old,
They up and shoot themselves, I'm told.).....

— Ah, God! To see the branches stir
Across the moon at Grantchester!
To smell the thrilling-sweet and rotten
Unforgettable, unforgotten,
River-smell, and hear the breeze
Sobbing in the little trees.
Say, do the elm-clumps greatly stand
Still guardians of that holy land?
The chestnuts shade, in reverend dream,
The yet unacademic stream?
Is dawn a secret shy and cold
Anadyomene, silver-gold?
And sunset still a golden sea
From Haslingfield to Madingley?
And after, ere the night is born,
Do hares come out about the corn?
Oh, is the water sweet and cool,
Gentle and brown, above the pool?
And laughs the immortal river still
Under the mill, under the mill?
Say, is there Beauty yet to find?
And Certainty? and Quiet kind?
Deep meadows yet, for to forget
The lies, and truths, and pain?..... oh! yet
Stands the church clock at ten to three?
And is there honey still for tea?
R. B.

des Westens. Berlin. May. 1912.

When Brooke was again in Germany in the following year, his Grantchester home was constantly in his mind, as many references in his letters show, and on an unknown date in May he wrote his most famous poem, "Grantchester," while sitting in the Café des Westens in Berlin. This long nostalgic fantasy seems to have been thrown off without much preliminary thought and he later referred to it, in a letter to Eddie Marsh, as "this hurried stuff." To another correspondent he called it "a long lanky lax-limbed set of verses"; yet there is no doubt that the picture he conjured up came from his heart.

The early stages of the poem were scribbled on four small sheets of paper. That which I judge to be the first one used has the word *Umbrageous* writ large at the top and underlined. It was the memory of the trees and greenery surrounding the house that immediately caught his fancy, though in fact the word was not used in the poem. . . .

These preliminary thoughts snatched from the air show well how his mind was working. The other side of the sheet has the heading *The Sentimental Exile* immediately followed by the first six lines of the poem in a form never afterwards changed; then come a number of lines from later parts of the poem with but few alterations. Many of the lines are numbered to indicate their final ordering.

On the other three sheets of the first draft are written the remaining lines of the poem, not always in their final positions, but with few variations from the fair copy. Written sideways in the margin of one sheet are four lines, difficult to read and afterwards discarded.

For the rest, the first draft was copied with few verbal changes of any importance–though it is worth noting that the penultimate line was written: *Stands the church clock at half past three?* and was changed back to the accepted version in the fair copy.

The poem was first printed in the King's College magazine *Basileon,* June 1912, under the title taken from the fair copy: "Fragments from a Poem to be Entitled 'The Sentimental Exile.'" It next appeared in *The Poetry Review,* vol. i, no. ii, November 1912, with the title altered to: "The Old Vicarage, Grantchester," which has remained the accepted form.

Analysis of "The Old Vicarage, Grantchester" (William E. Laskowski, Rupert Brooke, *pp. 48–51)*

The path Brooke's politics took toward a more conventional patriotism and idea of order can be seen in what is undoubtedly his most famous (or notorious) poem outside of "The Soldier": "The Old Vicarage, Grantchester." It has inspired extreme reactions from both ends of the political spectrum. For some it is the ideal expression of Georgian bucolics; Denis Cheason has written and illustrated a book about the eponymous house and all the villages and locales mentioned in the poem. For a later socialist like George Orwell, it "is nothing but an enormous gush of country sentiment, a sort of accumulated vomit from a stomach stuffed with place-names"; on its poetic merits it "is something worse than worthless." The problem with both views is that they result from not having read the poem carefully enough. One wants to blame Marsh for much of this misreading, since it was he who persuaded Brooke to change its title from "Fragments of a Poem" to be entitled "The Sentimental Exile," its title when it was first published in the King's College magazine *Basileon* in June of 1912. Yet even such a clue to the poem's multiple ironies has not prevented a critic from missing its self-deprecating point: "But was it," Alan Read asks, "really 'sentimental?'" The answer is that parts of it undoubtedly are, and Brooke's giving it that title is both an admission and an avowal; he will show how such sentimentality can be justified.

Even so harsh a Brooke critic as Samuel Hynes concedes that "Brooke managed in this poem to sustain a tension of attitudes that is missing from his other work." Brooke does this by shifts of tone and perspective that are unusual in his poetry. Most of his poems are short (his favorite form is the sonnet) and strive for and often achieve what Edgar Allan Poe called "totality of effect." "Grantchester" veers around what Bernard Bergonzi has called "a kind of switchback irregularity of tone, alternately satirizing the Cambridge landscape (and by implication the poet) and idealizing it." This "irregularity" would have been much easier for the poem's readers to assess had it kept its original title. Faced with "Grantchester" by itself (or accompanied by at most "The Soldier") in an anthology, readers cannot see that the first lines of the poem–"Just now the lilac is in bloom, / All before my little room" are, even for Brooke, uncharacteristically fey, self-consciously "Georgian" in the most pejorative sense of the term, and a weakness to which much Georgian poetry, as Brooke well knew, was all too often prone. The speaker is wallowing in a self-indulgent sentimentality. The ellipsis in the first stanza marks the first subtle shift in tone as the speaker wants his desires to be taken more seriously, and the images now begin to recall those of Marvell:

> A tunnel of green gloom, and sleep
> Deeply above; and green and deep
> The stream mysterious glides beneath,
> Green as a dream and deep as death.

Immediately the mood is shattered by the speaker's "– Oh, damn! I know it!" But when he remembers "the day" that "gild[s] gloriously the bare feet," he has slipped into rhetoric again.

The second stanza describes the scene around the Café des Westens in Berlin, where the speaker is recalling the English countryside. It includes the unfortunate but characteristic lines about *"Temperamentvoll* German Jews." Juxtaposed against the disciplined German tulips are the perhaps most successfully realized lines of the poem, as far as its tone is concerned. "Unkempt about those hedges blows / An English unofficial rose." The theme of comfortable English disorganization is continued in the image of "the vague unpunctual star, / A slippered Hesper." It is interesting to note how much Brooke had changed in the year since he'd last visited Germany. He had written to two different correspondents the year before that the Germans were "soft," and to Noel Olivier he explained that, as he was telling the Germans that town life was superior, "Thoughts of English Nature lovers creep into my mind. Oh, it is so easy and so troublesome to love Nature–that way." Perhaps some of that feeling against oversimplified nature lovers entered into the third stanza of the poem, when the speaker refers to "clever modern men" in England who "have seen / A Faun a-peeping through the green . . . glimpse a Naiad's reedy head, / Or hear the Goatfoot piping low," a possible veiled reference to the short fiction of another Kingsman, E. M. Forster. The subsequent ellipsis leads to another delicate shift of tone: the lines "flower-lulled in sleepy grass, / Hear the cool lapse of hours pass" are meant to be taken seriously, and the next ellipsis leads into a literary time machine, from which the reader can glimpse Byron ("his ghostly Lordship"), Chaucer, and Tennyson. The feathery satire of these lines leads into the images that so offended Edmund Gosse: a nocturnal vision of "A hundred Vicars down the lawn" and "The sly shade of a Rural Dean" who are dispelled by the dawn, "Vanishing with Satanic cries." Brooke could not resist a few more thrusts against religion and refused to remove the offending lines.

The fourth stanza, which begins with the knowingly overhearty "For England's the one land, I know, / Where men with Splendid Hearts may go," contains the beginning of that catalog of place-names which has caused the poem to be both praised and vilified. The humor, or lack of it, in the litany of exaggerated faults of neighboring locales is in the end a matter of personal taste, and a lack of sympathy for Brooke's humor has probably led to the greatest reactions against the poem. The deliberate caricature of the perfection of the place when the speaker again speaks of Grantchester, "A bosky wood, a slumbrous stream, / And little kindly winds that creep / Round twilight corners, half asleep," shows that the speaker is still being self-consciously sentimental. The next lines contain what is perhaps Brooke's last semi-balanced view of the Apostles, the gentle humor of

The men observe the Rules of Thought,
They love the Good; they worship Truth;
They laugh uproariously in youth;
(And when they get to feeling old,
They up and shoot themselves, I'm told). . . .

This leads into the last and trickiest section of the poem, as far as tone is concerned. Its whole series of questions is a mix of the serious and the ironic. The diction at times approaches the mock-heroic ("ere the night is born") and sometimes is serious and archly overprecious in the same sentence:

To smell the thrilling-sweet and rotten
Unforgettable, unforgotten
River-smell, and hear the breeze
Sobbing in the little trees.

The realistic description in the word *rotten,* hearkening back to the smell of leaves in "In January," clashes with the pathetic fallacy of the "sobbing" breeze. The questions near the end of the poem come close to the personal anguish that in part prompted the poem, and do not quite fit in with the half-serious, half-flip philosophical questions that precede them:

Say, is there Beauty yet to find?
And Certainty? and Quiet kind?
Deep meadows yet, for to forget
The lies, the truth, and the pain?

Even the use of the dialect phrase "for to" (which functions in Brooke's poetry as a colloquial deflator of rhetoric, as in his poem "It's Not Going to Happen Again") cannot hide the dropping of the mask in the line referring to all Brooke felt had happened to him–"lies, truth, and pain"–since Lulworth.

Thus, the very last lines of the poem, probably the most well known, assume an air of not what Michael Hastings has called "intolerable smugness" but desperation: "Oh! yet / Stands the Church clock at ten to three? / And is there honey still for tea?" The reader who assumes the poem has only one tone, that of the Georgian version of "emotion recollected in tranquillity," will miss much of the poem's point. Modern readers have been taught that ambiguity in meaning is admirable; ambiguity in tone uncomfortable. The main weakness of "Grantchester" is that the tones are not successfully welded together, and in the last section, the tone is at times impossible to pin down precisely. The

Dividing his time between Germany and England, Brooke started work on his one-act play, Lithuania *(1915)*, and continued to write poetry between bouts of depression. As 1912 ended, he became more and more concerned with literary matters. In Poetry Review *he defended the work of Georgian poet Lascelles Abercrombie against the Modernist criticism of Ezra Pound. Brooke also took an interest in Marsh's projected first volume of* Georgian Poetry (1911–1912), *which included five of Brooke's poems.*

In December 1912 Brooke met Cathleen Nesbitt, a young actress who was playing Perdita in The Winter's Tale *at the Savoy Theatre in London. Throughout the rest of his life she assumed the role of emotional supporter that Noel Olivier and then Katherine Cox had held. At the start of 1913 Brooke wrote to Edward Marsh to ask if he might bring Nesbitt as his companion to a dinner party. Their growing intimacy, which this request betokened, gave Brooke the opportunity to begin new friendships and interests, as well as to disengage himself gradually from many of his older relationships.*

Title page for the influential collection of poetry, first published in 1912, that includes five poems by Brooke

Cathleen Nesbitt in the play Quality Street, *1913 (Geoffrey Keynes, ed.,* The Letters of Rupert Brooke*)*

problem probably arises because Brooke was essentially an accretive artist; most of his longer works are composed of sections joined together: the chapters in *John Webster and the Elizabethan Dramatists,* the articles that make up *Letters from America.* For all his dreams of being a dramatist, the only play he wrote was one act long. Even some of his longer letters were composed in bits and pieces, a few paragraphs here, some sentences there, over a period of days. As "Grantchester" came to be reprinted, Marsh wanted Brooke to rework it, and Brooke replied, "I fear it's too old for revising. If a couplet or two could be taken out of the last part & shoved in elsewhere, it'd improve the balance. . . . I fear it'll have to remain its misbegotten self." Brooke dimly perceived that the problem was in the last section, but perhaps if he had attempted to correct the problem the poem would have lost its edge of desperation and have become truly "intolerably smug."

Excerpt from Brooke's letter to Cathleen Nesbitt recounting his life at Cambridge and telling her how much he misses her, 20 March 1913 (Geoffrey Keynes, ed., The Letters of Rupert Brooke, *pp. 433–434)*

24 Bilton Road, Rugby

. . . It was a very nice letter you wrote me. Yourself comes out through the fall of the sentences. One hears the tone–and the silly Irish accent you sometimes put on, you know.

Lord, Lord!

I was in Cambridge last night–I really got admitted at length, not having a dinner with you to put it off for! I dined solemnly with very old white-haired men at one end of a vast dimly-lit hall, afterwards drank port somnolently in the common-room, with the College silver and seventeenth-century portraits and a sixteenth-century fireplace and fifteenth-century ideas. The perfect don, I. You'll hardly recognize me, when we blessedly next meet.

I'm going to stay here till I'm entirely sound again. My fever's left me with a cough. Oh the weather at Cambridge was Spring–wonderful. And I wanted to be out, walking, taking you with me. Your account of your walk fired me with a mad hunger for the country, and with a devasting fire of jealousy against the man who was with you. Damn him! What good deed did he ever do to be rewarded by hours and hours of your company on the Surrey hills? What deed *could* any one do good enough?

But that other people should see your face turning and changing hour by hour, wonderfully, and I not be there. Nash's Magazine (my only reading) is but a makeshift. Woman, I will *not* have you blaspheming. You have done it in two letters. If you don't know that you're the most beautiful thing in the world, either you're imbecile, or else, something's wrong with your mirror. But I refuse to let you deny it, impiously. If you try, I shall kill you. Your beauty–it's only the insensate poverty of the English language and the feebleness of my imagination that prevent me describing it you. Helen and Deirdre–evoking names can only document it. How can one catch and preserve and pin down a living thing? Is it an insane chance that your features and attributes all happened to meet?

"So may your mighty amazing beauty move
Envy in all women, and in all men, love."

His spirits elevated, Brooke concentrated on his literary endeavors: he contributed to various literary periodicals, including Blue Review *and* Poetry and Drama, *and with fellow poets Abercrombie, Wilfred Gibson, and John Drinkwater he planned a new periodical,* New Numbers, *which began publication in 1914. At this time Brooke also began seriously to contemplate organizing a tour of North America and the South Seas. Marsh introduced him into the political circle of Prime Minister Herbert Asquith, and these new acquaintances and projects distanced Brooke further from his old life.*

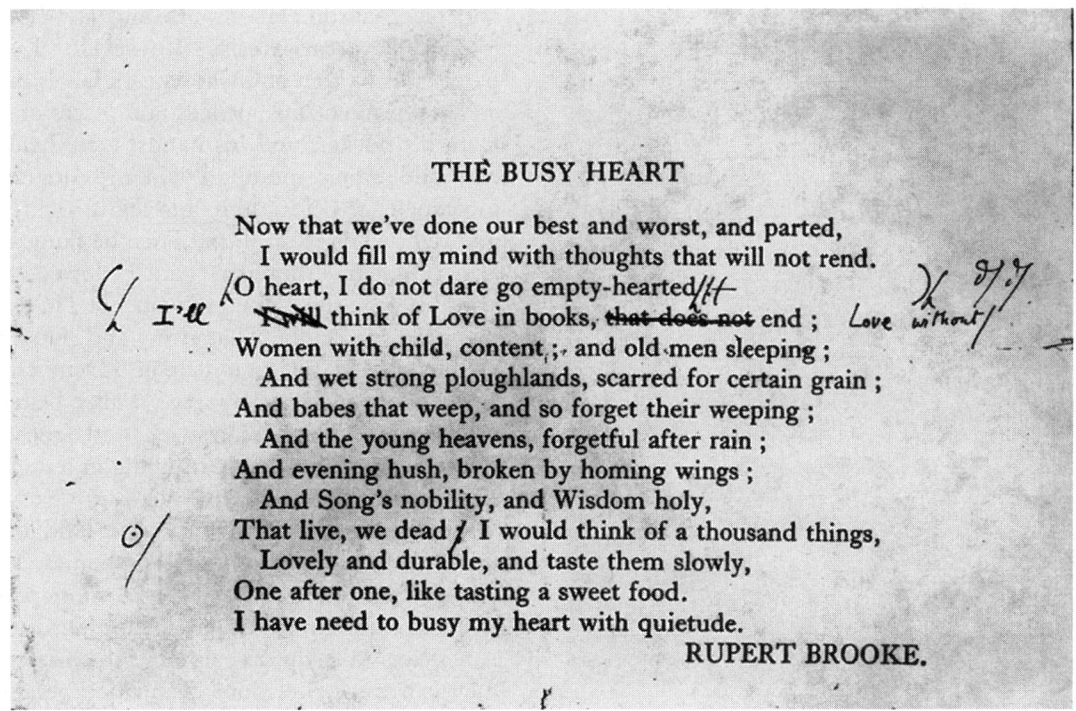

Brooke's revisions in "The Busy Heart" after it was published in Blue Review *(Special Collections, Dartmouth College Library)*

(That's old Donne.)

But there aren't any words, most radiant. I can only measure it by its result—as one records the light of the sun on photographic paper, or the rain of all the heavens in a little water-gauge. There have been evenings when two or three hours of you left me as if I'd run ten miles, panting, knees trembling, and entirely exhausted. That's your damned face. Do you understand that?

. . . Good-night.

I have no doubt I shall dream of you as usual—"How can a woman live with such a face?"

Do not blaspheme. It offends me—a worshipper.

Rupert

On 8 March 1913 Brooke finally succeeded in winning a fellowship at King's College for the following academic year, and with the security that this position promised to provide, he turned his thoughts to travel. There is little doubt that escaping his emotional entanglement with Cox was also part of his motive for travel, and when the Westminster Gazette *agreed to publish and pay for a report of his experiences in America, he was determined to leave England. After spending some time with his mother in Rugby, Brooke left for a tour on 21 May.*

One of a series of photographs taken of Brooke at Schell's studio, 1913
(King's College Library, Cambridge)

Brooke's experiences in North America were eventually published in Letters from America *(1916), with a preface by Henry James. These letters express Brooke's loneliness and his bewilderment about the customs and values of North Americans, in addition to his intense appreciation of the wilder parts of Canada, especially the George Lake region of Manitoba.*

*Excerpts from Brooke's "New York" (*Letters from America, *pp. 7–8, 10–12, 17–18)*

In five things America excels modern England—fish, architecture, jokes, drinks, and children's clothes. There may be others. Of these, I am certain. The jokes and drinks, which curiously resemble each other, are the best. There is a cheerful violence about them; they take their respective kingdoms by storm. All the lesser things one has heard turn out to be delightfully true. The first hour in America proves them. People here talk with an American accent; their teeth are inlaid with gold; the mouths of car conductors move slowly, slowly, with an oblique oval motion, for they are chewing; pavements are "sidewalks." It is all true. . . . But there were other things one expected, though in no precise form. What, for instance, would it be like, the feeling of whatever democracy America has secured?

I landed, rather forlorn, that first morning on the immense covered wharf where the Customs mysteries were to be celebrated. The place was dominated by a large, dirty, vociferous man, coatless, in a black shirt and black apron. His mouth and jaw were huge; he looked like a caricaturist's Roosevelt. "Express Company" was written on his forehead; labels of a thousand colours, printed slips, pencils and pieces of string, hung from his pockets and his hands, were held behind his ears and in his mouth. I laid my situation and my incompetence before him, and learnt right where to go and right when to go there. Then he flung a vast, dingy arm round my shoulders, and bellowed, "We'll have your baggage right along to your hotel in two hours." It was a lie, but kindly. That grimy and generous embrace left me startled, but an initiate into Democracy. . . .

The American by race walks better than we; more freely, with a taking swing, and almost with grace. How much of this is due to living in a democracy and how much to wearing no braces, it is very difficult to determine. But certainly it is the land of belts, and therefore of more loosely moving bodies. This, and the loosely-cut trousers, make a figure more presentable, at a distance, than most urban civilizations turn out. Also, Americans take their coats off, which is sensible; and they can do it the more beautifully because they are belted, and not braced. They take their coats off anywhere and anywhen, and somehow it strikes the visitor as the most symbolic thing about them. They have not yet thought of discarding collars; but they are unashamedly shirt-sleeved. Any sculptor, seeking to figure this Republic in stone, must carve, in future, a young man in shirtsleeves, open-faced, pleasant, and rather vulgar, straw hat on the back of his head, his trousers full and sloppy, his coat over his arm. The motto written beneath will be, of course, "This is some country." The philosophic gazer on such a monument might get some way towards understanding the making of the Panama Canal, that exploit that no European nation could have carried out. . . .

I slipped from my car up about Fortieth Street, the region where the theatres and restaurants are, the "roaring forties." Broadway here might be the offspring of Shaftesbury Avenue and Leicester Square, with, somehow, some of Fleet Street also in its ancestry. I passed two men on the sidewalk, their hats on the back of their heads, arguing fiercely. One had slightly long hair. The other looked the more truculent, and was saying to him, intensely, "See here! We con-tracted with you to supply us with sonnets at five dollars per sonnet—". . . .

Fifth Avenue is handsome, the handsomest street imaginable. It is what the streets of German cities try to be. The buildings are large, square, "imposing," built with the solidity of opulence. The street, as a whole, has a character and an air of achievement. "Whatever else may be doubted or denied, American civilization has produced this." One feels rich and safe as one walks. Back in Broadway, New York dropped her mask, and began to betray herself once again. A little crowd, expressionless, intent, and volatile, before a small shop, drew me. In the shop-window was a young man, pleasant-faced, a little conscious, and a little bored, dressed very lightly in what might have been a runner's costume. He was bowing, twisting, and posturing in a slow rhythm. From time to time he would put a large card on a little stand in the corner. The cards bore various legends. He would display a card that said, "THIS UNDERWEAR DOES NOT IMPEDE THE MOVEMENT OF THE BODY IN ANY DIRECTION." Then he moved his body in every direction, from position to position, probable or improbable, and was not impeded. With a terrible dumb patience, he turned the next card: "IT GIVES WITH THE BODY IN VIOLENT EXERCISING." The young man leapt suddenly, lunged, smote imaginary balls, belaboured invisible opponents, ran with immense speed but no progress, was thrown to earth by the Prince of the Air, kicked, struggled, then bounded to his feet again. But all this without a word. "IT ENABLES YOU TO KEEP COOL WHILE EXERCISING." The young

Title page of the volume originally published in the United States (John Schroder, Catalogue of Books and Manuscripts by Rupert Brooke Edward Marsh & Christopher Hassall, p. 22)

man exercised, and yet was cool. He did this, I discovered later, for many hours a day. . . .

Through Broadway the dingily glittering tide spreads itself over the sands of "amusement." Theatres and "movies" are aglare. Cars shriek down the street; the Elevated train clangs and curves perilously overhead; newsboys wail the baseball news; wits cry their obscure challenges to one another, "I should worry!" or "She's some Daisy!" or "Goodnight, Nurse!" In houses off the streets around children are being born, lovers are kissing, people are dying. Above, in the midst of those coruscating divinities, sits one older and greater than any. Most colossal of all, it flashes momently out, a woman's head, all flame against the darkness. It is beautiful, passionless, in its simplicity and conventional presentation queerly like an archaic Greek or early Egyptian figure. Queen of the night behind, and of the gods around, and of the city below—here, if at all, you think, may one find the answer to the riddle. Her ostensible message, burning in the firmament beside her, is that we should buy pepsin chewing-gum. But there is

Page from Brooke's letter to Cathleen Nesbitt detailing his experiences in the Canadian wilderness, 1 and 3 August 1913 (Geoffrey Keynes, ed., The Letters of Rupert Brooke, *pp. 495–497)*

On 7 October, Brooke left the United States and sailed to Hawaii, with plans to visit Samoa, Fiji, and Tahiti. His affections were won by the Pacific islanders, whom he described as wonderful people—beautiful, strong, and hospitable. By Christmas 1913 he had reached New Zealand, where he was treated for an infected foot before setting off to Tahiti. His Pacific voyage inspired several new poems, such as "The Clouds" and "One Day," which also reveal his desire to expunge painful memories of Kathleen Cox and Noel Olivier.

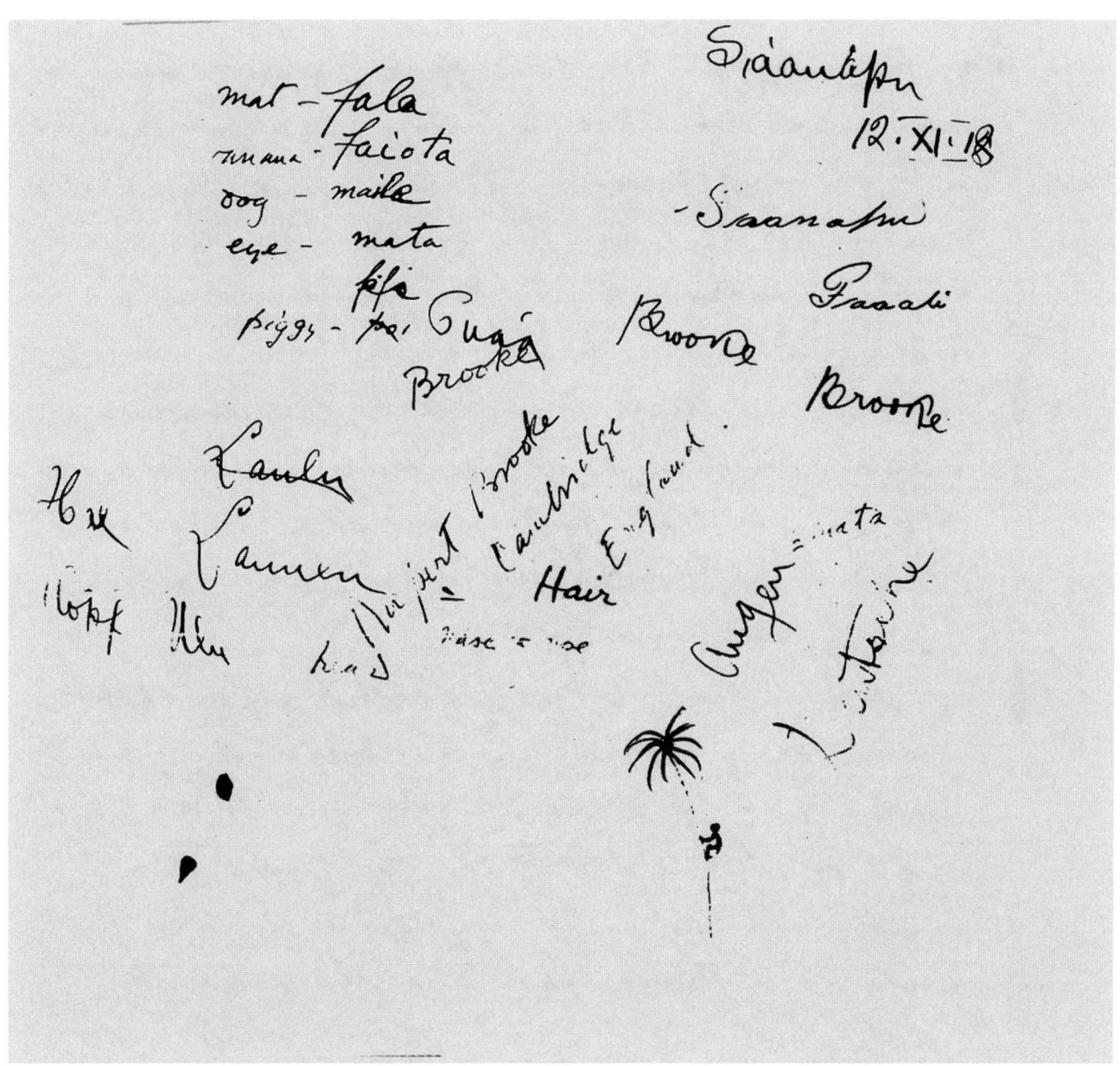

Brooke's lists of words in Tahitian and their English equivalents, with his sketch of an islander climbing a coconut tree (Papers of Rupert Brooke, Sotheby Catalogue, 17 December 1979, p. 141)

First page of Edward Marsh's transcription of Brooke's letter to Cathleen Nesbitt discussing his stay in Fiji and her acting career, 17 December 1913 (Geoffrey Keynes, ed., The Letters of Rupert Brooke, *pp. 550–554)*

Clouds.

Down the blue night the unending columns press
In noiseless tumult, break and wave and flow,
Now tread the far South, or lift rounds of snow
Up to the white moon's hidden loveliness.
Some pause in their grave wandering comradeless,
And turn with profound gesture vague and slow,
As who pray good for the world, but know
Their benediction empty as they bless.

They say that the Dead die not, but remain
Near to the rich heirs of their grief and mirth.
I think they ride the calm mid-heaven, as these,
In wise majestic melancholy train,
And watch the moon, and the still-raging seas,
And men, coming and going on the earth.

The Pacific. October 1913

R.B.

Manuscript for Brooke's "Clouds" (King's College Library, Cambridge)

Brooke being carried across a stream by his Fijian servant, Abel (King's College Library, Cambridge)

By the middle of January 1914 Brooke was in Tahiti, which he described as "the most ideal place on earth." He stayed there for more than three months and derived great satisfaction from his experiences. This visit allowed him to return to the imagined Eden of his childhood, and he also met Taatamata, a Tahitian woman who became his lover. Brooke enjoyed the sexual freedom of Tahitian society and compared it favorably with the complicated sexual mores of English society.

Taatamata, Brooke's Tahitian lover who provided the inspiration for his poem "Tiare Tahiti" (King's College Library, Cambridge)

The combination of perfect weather with his physical activity and youthful energy combined to stir Brooke's imagination and inspired some of his more effective poetry, including what may be his finest poem, "Tiare Tahiti." But in April he left his paradise and sailed for San Francisco and the United States on his way back to England.

First page of Brooke's letter to Cathleen Nesbitt announcing his decision to remain on Tahiti for a few months but failing to mention Taatamata, 7 February 1914 (King's College Library, Cambridge)

Tiare Tahiti

Mamua, when our laughter ends,
And hearts and bodies, brown as white,
Are dust about the doors of friends,
Or scent ablowing down the night,
Then, oh! then, the wise agree,
Comes our immortality.
Mamua, there waits a land
Hard for us to understand.
Out of time, beyond the sun,
All are one in Paradise,
You and Pupure are one,
And Taü, and the ungainly wise.
There the Eternals are, and there
The Good, the Lovely, and the True,
And Types, whose earthly copies were
The foolish broken things we knew;
There is the Face, whose ghosts we are;
The real, the never-setting Star;
And the Flower, of which we love
Faint and fading shadows here;
Never a tear, but only Grief;
Dance, but not the limbs that move;
Songs in Song shall disappear;
Instead of lovers, Love shall be;
For hearts, Immutability.
And there, on the Ideal Reef,
Thunders the Everlasting Sea!

And my laughter, and my pain,

Manuscript for the poem addressed to Taatamata (King's College Library, Cambridge)

Shall home to the Eternal Brain.
And all lovely things, they say,
Meet in ~~Time to~~ Loveliness again;
— Miri's laugh, Teïpo's feet,
And the hands of Matua,
Stars and sunlight there shall meet,
Coral's hues and rainbows there,
And Teüra's braided hair;
And with the starred tiare's white,
And white birds in the dark ravine,
And flamboyants ablaze at night,
And jewels, and evenings after green,
And dawns of pearl and gold and red,
— Mamua, your lovelier head!
And there'll no more be one who dreams
Beneath the ferns, of crumbling stuff,
Eyes of illusion, mouth that seems,
All time-entangled human love.
And you'll no longer swing and sway
Divinely down the scented shade,
Where feet to Ambulation fade,
And moons are lost in endless Day.
How shall we wind these wreaths of ours,
Where there are neither heads nor flowers?
Oh, Heaven's Heaven! — but will be missing
The palms, and sunlight, and the south;
And there's an end, I think, of kissing,
When our mouths are one with Mouth........

Taü here, Mamua,
Crown the hair, and come away!
Hear the calling of the moon,

And the whispering scents that stray
About the idle warm lagoon.
Hasten, hand in human hand,
Down the dark, the flowered way,
Along the whiteness of the sand,
And in the water's soft caress,
Wash the mind of foolishness,
Mamua, until the day.
Spend the glittering moonlight there
Pursuing down the soundless deep
Limbs that gleam and shadowy hair,
Or floating lazy, half-asleep.
Dive and double and follow after,
Snare in flowers, and kiss, and call,
With lips that fade, and human laughter,
And faces individual,
Well this side of Paradise! . . . . .
There's little comfort in the wise.

~~Matira~~. Papeete.   R.B.
February 1914.

more, not to be given in words, ineffable. Suddenly, when she has surveyed mankind, she closes her left eye. Three times she winks, and then vanishes. No ordinary winks these, but portentous, terrifyingly steady, obliterating a great tract of the sky. Hour by hour she does this, night by night, year by year. That enigmatic obscuration of light, that answer that is no answer, is, perhaps, the first thing in this world that a child born near here will see, and the last that a dying man will have to take for a message to the curious dead. She is immortal. Men have worshipped her as Isis and as Ashtaroth, as Venus, as Cybele, Mother of the Gods, and as Mary. There is a statue of her by the steps of the British Museum. Here, above the fantastic civilization she observes, she has no name. She is older than the skyscrapers amongst which she sits; and one, certainly, of her eyelids is a trifle weary. And the only answer to our cries, the only comment upon our cities, is that divine stare, the wink, once, twice, thrice. And then darkness.

Discussion of "Tiare Tahiti" by William E. Laskowski (Rupert Brooke, *pp. 55-56*)

Many critics have pointed out how Brooke's best poem about his experiences in the South Seas, "Tiare Tahiti," represents a step forward. At its start the poem treats characteristic themes, as the speaker tells his beloved that when they die they will become "dust about the doors of friends, / Or scent a-blowing down the night"; the bodies are no longer for Brooke the habitation of corruption. The paradise they shall enter is Platonic, where "the Eternals are": "The Good, the Lovely, and the True, / And Types," and "instead of lovers, Love shall be; / For hearts, Immutability." In a line that looks forward semi-seriously to "The Soldier," the speaker declares that "my laughter, and my pain, / Shall home to the Eternal Brain"; so far "Tiare Tahiti" contains few surprises. But in the second long section, the speaker begins to describe how physical objects shall be subsumed into what he has called in the first section "the Eternals": a laugh, feet, hands, braided hair, a head–all connected with the Polynesian names of their owners. He catalogs the visual aspects of nature that will be there as well: the colors of coral, rainbows, birds, sunsets and sunrises. Most important is the figure who will be absent from this scene, the former speaker in Brooke's poetry, who was consumed with the dooms of chronological passion: "one who dreams . . . of crumbling stuff, / Eyes of illusion, mouth that seems, / All time-entangled human love." If all these things subsided into the ideal, the speaker asks, then how can the lovers worship each other? "How shall we wind these wreaths of ours, / Where there are neither heads nor flowers?" Significantly, the speaker here, unlike in "Retrospect," allows his own head to be garlanded as well, because the passion is mutual.

Thus, the last section begins with the command to his beloved to "Crown the hair, and come away!" In a line reminiscent of W. H. Auden's acceptance of mortal frailty in "Lullaby" ("Human on my faithless arm"), the speaker tells Mamua to "Hasten, hand in human hand, / Down the dark, the flowered way." The image of dark floral places, which before had been separated from the speaker by space ("Grantchester") and time ("Retrospect"), is here accepted and experienced. As Delancy has pointed out, the image of water in "Tiare Tahiti"–its "soft caress"–represents a transformation from its formerly absolutive function in Brooke's poetry (and letters). Its use also shows that the speaker has become one with the world of "The Fish": "Pursuing down the soundless deep / Limbs that gleam and shadowy hair." No longer is there "the strife of limbs"; indeed, the lovers are able to bring the world of color and individuality into the formless depths. The last litany shows that the speaker has embraced what has formerly been mistrusted in Brooke's poetry: "lips that fade, and human laughter, / And faces individual, / Well this side of Paradise!" While this is a crucial progression in Brooke's development, it ultimately proved to be a dead end, for he compartmentalized his experience in the South Seas as rigidly as he did other areas of his life, and he did not live long enough to reintegrate them into his life when he returned to England.

Maurice Browne's account of Brooke's visit to America and voyage back to England, spring 1914 (Recollections of Rupert Brooke *[Chicago: A. Greene, 1927], pp. 11-44*)

Brooke and I had been chasing each other for two years across two continents before we finally met. For two previous years, mutual friends had plagued us with mutual tales. In London, in the summer of 1913, I had seen his photograph for the first time: the beauty of the man–I repeat the abysmal mythopoeic phrase: the beauty of the man–astounded me; when I asked who it was, I got heartily damned for my "American" provincialism. At last, early in 1914, coming down to the Chicago Little Theatre one morning, I found a note which he had scribbled there an hour or so before:

Dear Mr. Browne,
My friend Harold Monro,–who claims some relationship with you,–and also Eileen Allenby and other

people, told me when I passed through Chicago to give you various messages of affection—Are you too busy to receive them? I'm staying at the Auditorium Hotel for a few days—

> Yours sincerely
> Rupert Brooke

I telephoned him at once; the Auditorium Hotel is next door to the Fine Arts Building, where the Chicago Little Theatre used to be; and a minute later he was in the theatre.

At the moment of our meeting I happened to be standing on my head, no unusual position for a theatre-manager. The humanity of my position—which, in relation to Brooke has not noticeably changed and is now not likely to—appealed to his sense of fitness in mortal affairs, especially as my mother-in-law, an elderly, white-haired and austere lady, immediately threw her arms around his neck. He promptly kissed my wife, and five minutes later the four of us were marching arm-in-arm down Michigan Avenue to drink beer.

My memory of the next ten days is a riotous blur of all-night talks, club sandwiches, dawns over Lake Michigan, and innumerable "steins." Brooke continued staying at the Auditorium (which he detested), but spent virtually all his time at our theatre—where Mme. Borgny Hammer was then playing *Hedda Gabler*—and at our studio a few blocks south, which overlooked the lake. There he showed us his South Sea treasures and told us of his Gauguin find. I have beside me as I write several chains of tiny South Sea shells which he gave to Miss Van Volkenburg together with a copy of Belloc's *Four Men;* the latter he knew almost by heart. The three of us would sit up night after night in our studio, talking, singing folk-songs, reading poetry, surging across the tiny room, like happy healthy children. On three successive mornings we saw the sun rise. . . .

One night I remember with peculiar vividness. I had telegraphed Arthur Ficke to tear himself from his desk in Davenport (where he then pretended to be practicing law), bribing—as is customary—the ascetic attorney with promises of poetry, beer and Brooke. He came, saw and fell. The Johnsonian literary editor of the *Chicago Evening Post,* Llewellyn Jones, that true and disinterested friend of poets, was there with his rectitude, brave platitudes, and sturdy brain; several members of the Chicago Little Theatre Company drifted in after their performance; and, among others who came and went, I remember a woman who was at that time a public librarian in Chicago, one who has given the best years of her life to unobtrusive kindliness and the service of beauty in others, to whom Brooke took an immediate liking: and a lost dog with bad teeth named D—.

D— had descended on us from the unknown, as, periodically, lost dogs did in those days, from Arizona and Saskatchewan and the parts about Podunk, for free drinks, a meal or two, and the few dollars they could beg—or occasionally steal—from the theatre's till: one of those lost dogs is in an American prison today—shamefully enough, and the shame is not his—for being an I. W. W.; another, a confessed till-robber, is today a man of affairs on Broadway and operates, with the connivance of the police, a sensationally successful bootlegging-joint in Greenwich Village. Brooke disliked D— as vigorously, and treated him as kindly, as any of us, but he would not read poetry in his presence. So eventually D— departed, with others who had come to gape, and the night began. Ficke has celebrated it in his sonnet:

PORTRAIT OF RUPERT BROOKE

> One night the last we were to have of you—
> High up above the city's giant roar
> We sat around you on the studio floor—
> Since chairs were lame or stony or too few—
> And as you read, and the low music grew,
> In exquisite tendrils twining the heart's core,
> All the conjecture we had felt before
> Flashed into torch-flame, and at last we knew.
>
> And Maurice, who in silence long has hidden
> A voice like yours, became a wreck of joy,
> To inarticulate ecstasies beguiled.
> And you, as from some secret world now bidden
> To make return, stared up, and like a boy
> Blushed suddenly, and looked at us, and smiled.

What the poems were which Brooke read that particular night I have, of course, no recollection (in the course of those ten days we made him read us almost everything he had written, including *Lithuania* and all the South Sea poems, then still in manuscript), but I can vividly see him sitting on the floor—his favourite position—with his knees hunched up, his arms round them, and his back against a wardrobe, blushing—with unfeigned pleasure, not embarrassment—when any of us became peculiarly inarticulate over some special loveliness. Ficke (despite his sonnet: poets are notoriously untruthful) sat in a decrepit rocker, the only chair we boasted, with his long legs infernally in the way, while the rest of us sprawled over the two cots, a table, a packing-case, and what other furniture the room afforded. Brooke read well—much better, of course, than the average professional reader or actor reads poetry—quietly and shyly, with little tone-variation, dwelling slightly on significant vowel-sounds and emphasizing rhyme and rhythm: reading, in fact, as a good lyric poet always reads good lyric poetry, taking care of the sound and letting the sense take care of itself. Occasionally one of us would fall foul of something which another had written—for both Ficke and I read some of our things that night—and the virulence of our mutual criticism made, I learned later, those who were unused to hearing craftsmen discuss each other's work believe that we did not mean what we said.

Brooke had the poet's passion for doing and seeing everything—he even suffered (not gladly) to be thrown as a lion to the Christians at one of those Sunday afternoon receptions in the Chicago Little Theatre, which delighted our guests so incomprehensibly and so comprehensibly terrified their hosts—and one day, when the strange odour which periodically descends on Chicago from the west was borne in upon him, he snuffed eagerly and departed for the stock-yards. We were all hoping that we might arrange to cross the Atlantic together, so Miss Van Volkenburg and I, eager to go east with him from Chicago, dilated on the smell, and superlative squalor of Gary. But the rumour of Pittsburgh had reached his ears: even our thrilling account of the infinitely superior monstrosity of middle-western industrial prostitution failed to convince him—he was extraordinarily pig-headed—and, a day or two later, he set his face vitriolically toward Eastern Steel, to study the Feudal System. . . .

A few days later he wrote, on New Willard Hotel stationery, from a somewhat different habitation:

[Washington, DC]
Sunday
May 10 1914

Dear Browne,

I'm leaving this place on Thursday, sooner than I expected, and my ticket seems to compel me to cut out Philadelphia, and other places by the way. So I may be able to get away from these shores sooner than I thought. It would be extraordinarily pleasant for *me,* if I knew there was going to be a couple of people one could exchange ideas with on the boat . . . *Your* view of the situation isn't my affair. But, if you answer, by return, on a card, giving the name and date of sailing of your boat, you'll be running the RISK of me coming on her (especially if she's Atlantic Transport). Don't say you weren't warned.

Isn't it typical of America that the *Auditorium* porter checked all my luggage to Washington, Pennsylvania? Now, if I'd been in England, my luggage wouldn't have gone a thousand miles in the opposite direction. But if it *had,* I should never have seen it again. Whereas, this being America, it has been located and is to arrive here tomorrow. A nation of kindly dreamers.

Urana!
Rupert Brooke

. . . The next letter is from New York, from the Hotel McAlpin:

Monday [May 25, 1914]

Dear Browne,

I'll rub along with the gods till Thursday. I'll meet you then. If I miss you: this is where I am: God help me. I don't know your taste in hotels. Mine corresponds with Mr. Arnold Bennett's. But this is rather cheaper than the Auditorium—

Hutchinson, who has a distressingly modern mania for photographing the soul instead of the body, has sent me a lovely reproduction of a beautiful middle aged woman playing a piano, thinking of the Ewigkeit, in profile, facing the dawn.

"Is that the mouth that touched Tahitian lips, And drained the topless tankards of Berlin?"

No: no! I have not changed so much. I returned the infamy with a jeer.

One thing, if you have time to think. Do you stock or does Chicago, *Georgian Poetry*? If so, will you buy and bring me two copies. New York has run out of them.

Y. . .
RB

We did reach New York on Thursday; but Brooke had rushed off somewhere for a last American supper, and, as we had an engagement that evening with Mrs. Havelock Ellis, who had been the Little Theatre's guest in Chicago a short time previously, during our production of some of her plays, the three of us did not foregather till the following morning at breakfast. . . .

Just before the *Philadelphia* sailed, Miss Van Volkenburg wrote in her diary-letter home: "Rupert Brooke is looking very fit and Rupertish, and is carrying a straw hat, an overcoat, Hutchinson's photographs, some magazines, books and a writing-case! His arrival on board created a *succés de scandale*. Thus are we English made! . . ."

Miss Van Volkenburg's diary-letters home tell the story of the voyage.

June 2

It has been a *wonderful* day, a Mediterranean day: the water deep blue with a carpet of silver gauze and the sky like Dorothy Fuller's eyes—clearly enigmatical. . . . The sun has sunk in an absolutely cloudless sky: a steamer has passed on the horizon: we have seen some more porpoises: and, there being nothing else to see, we have come in for our regular evening occupation [*three-handed bridge*.] Last evening there was a dance, but, needless to say, we didn't participate. There are two young sisters on board, whom Mr. Brooke has named Mimi and Fifi; they are probably about twenty and twenty-two, but they wear their hair in loose curls down their backs, have their skirts to their shoe tops and their eyes on every man in sight—several hundreds. The younger—Mimi—is quite the most luscious little sweetmeat I've yet seen; last evening, as Don and I were sitting demurely on a bench looking at the moon, I heard her tones raised in a weakly protesting "Oh George!" We turned and saw George silhouetted against that decent self-respecting moonlight in a torrid embrace which lasted until Don and I got bored and went to bed.— Mr. Brooke is having sighs and eyes cast at him; even a married woman took a snapshot of him today, because he has "such a noble head." A young girl two tables down from us gazes at him, awestruck and beautifully melancholy. When I told him of her adoration, he remarked "How dull." How we women suffer!

June 3

A nasty, ducky, day—cold, drizzly, and very windy. . . . We have been gazing on maps of London, and I find them more bewildering than ever. . . .

Mr. Brooke told me a conversation that he had overheard in the library today; at least he vowed he had and pointed out the alleged conversationalists. A sad-looking English officer was sitting at a table sorting papers, when he was joined by a loquacious lady who asked him where he was going and why; importuned sufficiently, he told her that he was going home to England on account of the death of his little son, who had run through a French window and cut his throat so severely that he had bled to death; instantly and sympathetically the lady responded: "I know just how you feel, because I lost a large diamond ring two weeks ago."— I'm scribbling hurriedly, for in a moment I am going to hear three immortal sonnets written respectively by Maurice Browne, Rupert Brooke and Ronald Hargreave, to *bouts rimés;* they were composed between the hours of five and six fifteen, and, every time I approached the trio, someone would look up and say "sssh!" solemnly, so now I await the result. . . .

June 4

This has been another grey and rather windy day; stormy and a bit misty—not enough for the foghorn, thank goodness, and not too cold to sit on deck. We—Mr. Brooke and I—installed ourselves in our corner, while Don went off to his writing. We sit facing the stern with our backs haughtily turned to the rest of our fellow-passengers, who wander past and eye Mr. Brooke with elaborate carelessness. He was in fine form, telling stories of the great and near-great for about three hours, with just the slightest touch of frosty snobbishness. I grew so interested in watching him that at times I forgot to listen. When he finished a story, he would set his eyes ahead until the queer little cast came in one of them, run his fingers through his hair with ferocious energy, pause, grasp his nose between his thumb and forefinger, tweak it gently two or three times (you know that "quirky" way of his), stop, pull his Jaeger blanket high around his head (leaving none of it to protect his legs), and start on some fresh recollection. He told me a delightful story about Henry James, which ran something like this: Mr. James, coming out of a Bond Street bookshop in an abstracted mood, ran into a most aristocratic lady about to enter her victoria; shocked at his awkwardness, he began an apology, but, as a simple I beg your pardon failed to express his exact shade of feeling, he leapt on the step of the carriage as it moved off and began again; his second attempt proving no better than his first, he clung to the step and tried once more; his third attempt was no more fruitful; so he rode on, clinging to the carriage-door with one hand, holding his hat in the other, with his coattails streaming in the breeze. As they reached the Marble Arch, he formed a perfect sentence of nine lines, asked permission to descend, and departed. . . .

We have relaxed our frigid exclusiveness in favour of two charming young girls from New York, Ethel and Frances P–; even Don likes them, and I caught a sudden glimmer in both his and Mr. Brooke's eyes, when Ethel quoted *The Crock of Gold.* . . . As we began our evening ritual tonight, I looked up, saw three girls' faces at the library porthole, and heard one of them say wistfully, as she gazed at Mr. B., "Do they always play three-handed?"

. . . We have finished our evening bridge and will soon take our turn around the deck and then go to bed. The Olympic passed us in all her glory this morning about eight; she would be sharply defined for a moment, then the mist would slowly drop over her and leave only a dim mass against the sky. . . .

We expect to reach Plymouth about 6:30 tomorrow evening. . . . "Eddie" Marsh, a friend of Mr. Brooke's and Eileen Allenby's, has just sent Mr. Brooke a marconigram (!) asking the three of us to dine with him and Eileen at his flat tomorrow night, but we, of course, wouldn't get there in any case, and poor Mr. Brooke can't: he is *rather* distressed!

June 5

It is about 10:45 of our last morning on board: always a sad day when it's been a good voyage; this has—except for my back. . . . By the way, the mattresses in our berths, which I thought were feather, are air: we were in our cabin with Mr. Brooke, and the steward, who was fixing it, suddenly turned to him and said: "These ere-mattresses! Yeh cawnt get henny hair hintoo em. Hi doan mean the air yer ead, Hi mean the hair uv the hatmosphere." Mr. Brooke behaved nobly, but Don precipitately vanished.

Our table steward has nearly sent the three of us into hysterics—he's tall and square, his hair is black and square, so are his eyes, and he smiles bewilderedly when we go off into meaningless paroxysms of laughter. The other day Don said, "I'll have pineapple fritters and queen's cake, please." The steward paused, opened his mouth, closed it, and then gasped horrifiedly, "One's cold—an' the other's 'ot, sir!" Whereat Don and Mr. Brooke exploded, and the steward departed in wounded dignity to bring the queen's cake and the pineapple fritters. . . .

We're almost in. Land was sighted a long time ago, and we can smell new-mown hay! Mr. Brooke is leaning over the taffrail, sniffing ecstatically. A few moments ago, as I was standing there beside him, suddenly we heard an awful noise behind us; our heads turned sharply— and click went kodak, amid laughter and apologetic smiles. A little later a woman came up to the three of us, and rather embarrassedly asked who we were; we rather embarrassedly replied, "Brooke"; whereupon she said that she was asking for a friend of hers, "who simply *had* to know, for we looked *quite* the most interesting people on board, and *wouldn't* talk to anyone else and seemed to have such a good time." We assured her that we did—and were! . . .

Here's a "threnody" for Mr. Hargreave that Mr. Brooke has just written; the steward came up and solemnly gave Mr. B. a note from Mr. H., in which he (Mr. H.) said that he was so ashamed of his sonnet that he had jumped overboard.

I. M. R. H.   June 5–1914

The world's great painter-soul, whom we deplore,
Loved California much, but music more.
His verse—but hush! the poor man's dead and gone.
What Fili lost the mermaidens have won.

June 6, dawn

We're on land—blessed blessed land. We saw Mr. Brooke off about Midnight—in wild spirits; we're to meet him in town next week. . . .

For two or three days after landing, the mere fact of being home, in England, breathing deep breaths of English air, was an ecstasy obliterating thought. Brooke rushed up to London and on to his mother's house at Rugby; my mother drove Miss Van Volkenburg and myself to Dartmoor to eat Devonshire cream; thence to Exeter and Salisbury, where we listened to many-century-old antiphonies and trod many-century-old lawns: and on to Stonehenge, where at nightfall among the haunted pillars we watched for the tragic shape of Tess. We reached London early the following week, to find a letter from Brooke waiting for us:

24 Bilton Road   Sunday [*June 7, 1914*]
Rugby

Dear Browne,

Marsh had already got tickets for me and him for the Ballet on *Thursday*. So I am coming up to Town on Wednesday or Thursday. I suppose you'll very likely be going to the Ballet that night. But wherever you are, you'll be free at 11:15 p.m. For that's when our supper party at Marsh's begins. Eileen's coming—who else, I don't yet know. Millions of lovely people. For further particulars, I refer you to Eileen, (who is nice, though old and ugly.) Leave news of your whereabouts with her or the Poetry Bookshop, if you haven't time to write.

(By the way, any letters from Germany, about the German theatrical things, astonishingly waiting for you at the P. B. will be by my command. But there'll likely be none.)

Go to Boris Godunov
    Go to Whitechapel
        Go to Prinz Igor
            Go to Hell
                Britanically
                    R B

At the bottom of this letter is a pen and ink drawing, rather in the style of Mr. Wells' illustrations to his own novels, of a Union jack *rampant*. . . .

Brooke, Marsh and Lascelles Abercrombie met Miss Van Volkenburg and myself for dinner on Friday evening at Simpson's. Abercrombie—a small, dark, shy man, with spectacles and straight slightly greasy-looking hair—wore, I remember, a queer little green hat which tipped up preposterously in front: his intellectual power, the power of one of the best brains in England, lying unobviously, under it, like Bolshevism under Bond Street in 1914. He and I knew each other rather well "by proxy and correspondence," but had not met personally before; nor, I learn from the *Memoir*. . . , had Abercrombie and Brooke: they saw each other that day for the first time; yet, although Brooke and I had spoken of Abercrombie and his work many times, it never occurred to me, until the *Memoir* was in my hands, that they were not old friends: Brooke's genius for friendship had nothing in common with the hypotheses of time and place.

After dinner Marsh left us, and, picking up Gibson (and, I think, Monro) on our way, we went again to the Ballet, where we sat (in the gallery, of course) directly behind Lennox Robinson, for the second night that week finding ourselves, by the grace of Celtic or Slavonic gods, next to this gentle maker of plays. The magic of the Russians left us all too thrilled and happy for bed, and once more we adjourned to Marsh's till dawn.

It may have been that night, it may have been another—my memory of those days in London in that summer of 1914 is a phantasmagoria of music and talk and color and dance and "lovely people," and, though Miss Van Volkenburg's diary-letters are dithyrambic, they do not always give details of dates; if Brooke went back to Rugby next day, as I think he did, it must have been on that night—that he and Abercrombie and Monro and Gibson talked metaphysics at each other and me in Marsh's rooms the night through: Marsh, discreetly, had gone to bed when we came in. Brooke's grasp and handling of intellectual abstractions was much more than unusual, but he was a child in the philosophical hands of Abercrombie, perhaps the most compelling, conversationally, of contemporary British metaphysicians: Brooke did not nibble at the edges of life, but Abercrombie bit clean and straight at the core. I suppose there was no happier group of men in London that night, none with greater capacity for happiness or exercising it more keenly, and, at the same time, no group more aware of the tragic foundations of happiness. While we were young men (our average age could hardly have exceeded 32), none of us—and certainly not Brooke, though he was the youngest—took any of the young man's romantic pleasure in the contemplation of human misery: actuality was actual to us all. It is true that later, as will be told in its time, the great and all-too-actual tidal-wave of human misery swept Brooke and myself apart; but most would say that it was I whom that wave wrecked: nor would I care to contradict them; nor do I think that, even then, his romanticism—as some have called it—was other than youth hurt past bearing by a cataclysm past understanding. The sane and fundamental strength of character in him, his tragic grasp of life, discount, in my judgment, the opinion of those who hold that his best work had been done.

. . . [A]fter our return, a day or two later, to my mother's house at Eastbourne, there was a letter, full of European plans for us, from Brooke:

24 Bilton Road   Tuesday evening
Rugby   [*June 16, 1914*]

Dear Browne,

. . . I *shall* be in town by Thursday afternoon; so if you're fortunately deferring departure till Friday, I'll yet be at the train with roses and tears. If you *are* staying till then, send a card to me at Marsh's—

If not—we shall meet again: either in this world, or in the next world, or in America. If in this world, we will drink and argue, and your wife shall write us some of her delightful *bout-rimé* sonnets. If in the next world—why, I've little hope of drink, but there'll surely be argument; and whether there are *bouts-rimés* or not—the wise disagree. But we can plan superb light effects with a Fortuny apparatus in the Empyrean, and God himself will work innumerable dimmers for us, and never a hitch.

I had fun in Chicago, on the Atlantic, and in London. I hope you did. When you're safe in Italy, and at peace, send me a card saying what good things Europe showed you. Love to you both— Farewell, lebwohl, talefa, χαίρετε, valete—

                                       Rupert

We postponed our departure from England for another twenty-four hours. Brooke rejoined us in London on Thursday afternoon; the three of us and Miss Allenby had dinner together that evening and talked far into the night. By the time we were "safe in Italy," peace had left the world.

By June, Brooke was home with his mother. He then left for Gloucestershire to assist William Gibson with the next issue of New Numbers, *which included Brooke's South Sea poems. In his memoir* The Weald of Youth *(1942), poet Siegfried Sassoon recalls having met Brooke for breakfast following Brooke's return from the South Seas.*

Breakfast was already well under way when I became aware that Rupert Brooke had entered the room. He had slipped in unnoticed, for the door was behind me and my attention was being held by Davies, whose eyes had an expression of childlike nobility. I looked up, and he was at my elbow, composedly awaiting the jubilant "Welcome home, from, foreign parts!" with which his friend Davies greeted him. Eddie then introduced me to him; he shook hands rather shyly. From the first I got the impression that the great Rupert Brooke was quite a modest chap after all.

At this date it is perhaps unnecessary to describe what he looked like. He was wearing an open-necked blue shirt and old grey flannel trousers, with sandals on bare feet, and hadn't bothered to brush his brown-gold hair, which was, I thought, just a shade longer than it need have been. Seen in the full light as he sat beside the window, his eyes were a living blue and his face was still sunburnt from outdoor life on a Pacific Island....

My glimpse of him a couple of days before had been nearer my preconceived notion, for he had been, neatly dressed in conventional clothes and had looked, if anything, a little over satisfied with himself. Was it his way of speaking which now seemed vaguely associated with something in my own experience? Groping for the clue, I got it at last. Absurdly enough, it was nothing more than the word Cambridge. Why had I forgotten to connect him with Cambridge, when there was that brilliant Grantchester poem of his which I knew so well? I had known too that he'd gone up to King's in my last term at Clare, and had sometimes wondered how often I'd walked past him in the street. Anyhow, wasn't he still rather the same sort of highly intelligent young man my brother Hamo used to go rock-climbing with in Wales before he went to his engineering job in the Argentine? And those sandals (were they Tahitian, I wondered), didn't they somehow suggest certain young men—and young women also—of whom my mother was wont to remark that she did wish they wouldn't dress in that sloppily artistic way and talk silly Fabian Socialism?...

Soon afterwards Davies departed, and I was alone with Rupert Brooke for about half-an-hour. Some way removed from me, he sat by a window serenely observing the trees of Gray's Inn gardens. From time to time his eyes met mine, but it was with a clouded though

Siegfried Sassoon

direct regard. I was conscious that his even-toned voice was tolerant rather than communicative, and that his manner had become gravely submissive to the continuing presence of a stranger. He may have been shy, but I am afraid he was also a little bored with me. We agreed that Davies was an excellent poet and a most likeable man. I then asked him a few clumsy questions about his travels. His replies were reserved, and unilluminating. One fragment of our talk which I remember clearly was—as such recoveries often are—wholly to my disadvantage. "What were the white people like in the places you stayed at in the tropics?" I had asked. ("The tropics" sounded somehow inept, but it was too late to correct myself now!)

"Some of them," he said, "were rather like composite characters out of Conrad and Kipling." Hoping that it would go down well, I made a disparaging remark about Kipling's poetry being terribly tub-thumping stuff.

"But not always, surely," he answered; and then let me off easily by adding, "I used to think rather the same myself until Eddie made me read Cities and Thrones and Powers. There aren't many better modern poems than that, you know."

I could only admit that I had never read it.

And yet, if I'd been more at my ease, I might have saved my credit by telling him that I knew by heart the first eight lines, which I really loved of Kipling's "Neither the harps nor the crowns amused, nor the cherubs' dove-winged races." After that it seemed safer not to mention poetry any more. It would be comforting if I could record that I expressed some admiration for his work—if I had said, for instance, how delightful I thought his Grantchester poem. But I didn't. I was, indeed, reduced to informing him of the uninspiring fact that we'd been at Cambridge together for a term—the autumn one of 1906. Yes, that was his first term there, he replied, and he'd acted in the Greek play—the Eumenides it was—as the Herald. This was something I'd entirely forgotten, though it came back to me vividly now. For the Herald had been such a striking figure that everybody in Cambridge had talked about him. But I didn't mystify him by exclaiming "So I had seen you before!" I merely thought how odd it was that I had never connected the Herald in his gorgeous red and gold with the young poet whose work had since then startled and attracted me.

During that singular encounter it was his kindness, I think, which impressed me, and the almost meditative deliberation of his voice. His movements, too, so restful, so controlled, and so unaffected. But beyond that was my assured perception that I was in the presence of one on whom had been conferred all the invisible attributes of a poet. To this his radiant good looks seemed subsidiary. Here, I might well have thought—had my divinations been expressible—was a being singled out for some transplendent performance, some enshrined achievement. That I believe, was the effect he made on many of those who met him as I did, and on all who fully understood the strength and sweetness of his nature.

Brooke was in Rugby when war was declared. His patriotism, which had been increasing during his absence from England, was fired by threats of a German onslaught, and about this time he drafted an article that presented his earliest reflections on the outbreak of war. This article, "An Unusual Young Man," was published in The New Statesman *(29 August 1914).*

Some say the Declaration of War threw us into a primitive abyss of hatred and the lust for blood. Others declare that we behaved very well. I do not know. I only know the thoughts that flowed through the mind of a friend of mine when he heard the news. My friend—I shall make no endeavour to excuse him—is a normal, even ordinary man, wholly English, twenty-four years old, active and given to music. By a chance he was ignorant of the events of the world during the last days of July. He was camping with some friends in a remote part of Cornwall, and had gone on, with a companion, for a four-days' sail. So it wasn't till they beached her again that they heard. A youth ran down to them with a telegram: "We're at war with Germany. We've joined France and Russia."

My friend ate and drank, and then climbed a hill of gorse, and sat alone, looking at the sea. His mind full of confused images, and the sense of strain. In answer to the word "Germany" a train of vague thoughts dragged across his brain. The pompous middle-class vulgarity of the buildings of Berlin; the wide and restful beauty of Munich; the taste of beer; innumerable quiet, glittering cafés; the *Ring;* the swish of evening air in the face, as one *skis* down past the pines; a certain angle of the eyes in the face; long nights of drinking, and singing, and laughter; the admirable beauty of German wives and mothers; certain friends; some tunes; the quiet length of evening over the Starnberger-See. Between him and the Cornish sea he saw quite clearly an April morning on a lake south of Berlin, the grey water slipping past his little boat, and a peasant-woman, suddenly revealed against apple-blossom, hanging up blue and scarlet garments to dry in the sun. Children played about her; and she sang as she worked. And he remembered a night in Munich spent with a students' *Kneipe.* From eight to one they had continually emptied immense jugs of beer, and smoked, and sung English and German songs in profound chorus. And when the party broke up he found himself arm-in-arm with the president, who was a vast Jew, and with an Apollonian youth called Leo Diringer, who said he was a poet. There was also a fourth man, of whom he could remember no detail. Together, walking with ferocious care down the middle of the street, they had swayed through Schwabing seeking an open café. Café Benz was closed, but further up there was a little place still lighted, inhabited by one waiter, innumerable chairs and tables piled on each other for the night, and a row of chessboards, in front of which sat a little bald, bearded man in dress-clothes, waiting. The little man seemed to them infinitely pathetic. Four against one, they played him at chess, and were beaten. They bowed, and passed into the night. Leo Diringer recited a sonnet, and slept suddenly at the foot of a lamppost. The Jew's heavy-lidded eyes shone with a final flicker of caution, and he turned homeward resolutely, to the last not wholly drunk. My friend had wandered to his lodgings, in an infinite peace. He could not remember what had happened to the fourth man. . . .

A thousand little figures tumbled through his mind. But they no longer brought with them that air of comfortable kindliness which Germany had always signified for him. Something in him kept urging, "You must hate these things, find evil in them." There was that half-conscious agony of breaking a mental habit, painting out a mass of associations, which he had felt in ceasing to believe in a religion, or, more acutely, after quarrelling with a friend. He knew that was absurd. The picture came to him of encountering the Jew, or Diringer, or old Wolf, or little Streckmann, the pianist, in a raid on the East Coast, or on the Continent, slashing at them in a stagey, dimly imagined battle. Ridiculous. He vaguely imagined a series of heroic feats, vast enterprise, and the applause of crowds.

From that egotism he was awakened to a different one, by the thought that this day meant war and the change of all things he knew. He realized, with increasing resentment, that music would be neglected. And he wouldn't be able, for example, to camp out. He might have to volunteer for military training and service. Some of his friends would be killed. The Russian ballet wouldn't return. His own relationship with A–, a girl he intermittently adored, would be changed. Absurd, but inevitable; because–he scarcely worded it to himself–he and she and everyone else were going to be different. His mind fluttered irascibly to escape from this thought, but still came back to it, like a tethered bird. Then he became calmer, and wandered out for a time into fantasy.

A cloud over the sun woke him to consciousness of his own thoughts; and he found, with perplexity, that they were continually recurring to two periods of his life, the days after the death of his mother, and the time of his first deep estrangement from one he loved. After a bit he understood this. Now, as then, his mind had been completely divided into two parts: the upper running about aimlessly from one half relevant thought to another, the lower unconscious half labouring with some profound and unknowable change. This feeling of ignorant helplessness linked him with those past crises. His consciousness was like the light scurry of waves at full tide, when the deeper waters are pausing and gathering and turning home. Something was growing in his heart, and he couldn't tell what. But as he thought "England and Germany" the word "England" seemed to flash like a line of foam. With a sudden tightening of his heart, he realized that there might be a raid on the English coast. He didn't imagine any possibility of it succeeding, but only of enemies and warfare on English soil. The idea sickened him. He was immensely surprised to perceive that the actual earth of England held for him a quality which he found in A–, and in a friend's honour, and scarcely anywhere else, a quality which, if he'd ever been sentimental enough to use the word, he'd have called "holiness." His astonishment grew as the full flood of "England" swept over him from thought to thought. He felt the triumphant helplessness of a lover. Grey, uneven little fields, and small, ancient hedges rushed before him, wild flowers, elms and beeches, gentleness, sedate houses of red brick, proudly unassuming, a countryside of rambling hills and friendly copses. He seemed to be raised high, looking down on a landscape compounded of the western view from the Cotswolds, and the Weald, and the high land in Wiltshire, and the Midlands seen from the hills above Prince's Risborough. And all this to the accompaniment of tunes heard long ago, an intolerable number of them being hymns. There was, in his mind, a confused multitude of faces, to most of which he could not put a name. At one moment he was on an Atlantic liner, sick for home, making Plymouth at nightfall; and at another, diving into a little rocky pool through which the Teign flows, north of Bovey; and again, waking, stiff with dew, to see the dawn come up over Royston plain. And continually he seemed to see the set of a mouth he knew to be his mother's, and A–'s face, and, inexplicably, the face of an old man he had once passed in a Warwickshire village. To his great disgust, the most commonplace sentiments found utterance in him. At the same time he was extraordinarily happy.

Gripped like many of his compatriots by the prospect of war, Brooke first tried to find work as a war correspondent for a newspaper and then as an administrative officer with the government. Eventually he succeeded in joining the Royal Naval Division as a sub-lieutenant and, along with his old school friend Denis Browne, served with the Anson Battalion in evacuating Antwerp.

Brooke's letter to Cathleen Nesbitt recounting his military experience in Antwerp, 17 October 1914 (Geoffrey Keynes, ed., The Letters of Rupert Brooke, *pp. 622–625)*

5 Raymond Buildings
Gray's Inn

Dearest child,

I've been very evil and idle in not writing to you. Indeed, I've been extremely slack and sleepy these last few days. I think it was the reaction after the excitement. Also caught *conjunctivitis,* alias pinkeye, in some of the foul places we slept in: and my eyes have been swollen, red, unlovely, exuding thick plum-tree gum, and very painful. I *hope* they're getting better. I did adumbrate, in myself, a project for dashing up to Ilkley? Today. But my cold and my eyes constrained me to stay lazily and fuggily here, with a conversation with Masefield as poor recompense, and hourly lotions instead of the chrism of your kisses. I've my eye on Folkestone. I think—by hook or crook—I'll see you for an hour then; and tell you a few of all my marvellous tales, and refresh myself for my next glimpse (far enough off!) of death. It's only a fortnight ago! . . . We were pulled out of bed at 5 a.m. on the Sunday, and told that we started at 9. We marched down to Dover, highly excited, only knowing that we were bound for Dunkirk, and supposing that we'd stay there quietly, training, for a month. Old ladies waved handkerchiefs, young ladies gave us apples, and old men and children cheered, and we cheered back, and I felt very elderly and sombre and full of thoughts of how human life was like a flash between darknesses, and that *x* per cent of those who cheered would be blown into another world within a few months; and they all seemed to me so innocent and patriotic and noble, and my eyes grew round and tear-stained.

But by the quay we halted for hours, while the goods were being shipped, in a street composed of public-houses: so there was a nice busy time for all of us, keeping the men out of them.

We sailed that night, and lay off Dunkirk next morning, waiting for the tide: spent the afternoon unloading; and then sat in a great empty shed, a quarter of a mile long, waiting for orders. After dark the senior officers rushed round and informed us that we were going to Antwerp, that our train was sure to be attacked, and that if we got through we'd have to sit in trenches till we were wiped out. So we all sat under lights writing last letters: a very tragic and amusing affair. My dear, it did bring home to me how very futile and unfinished life was. I felt so angry. I had to imagine, supposing I was killed. There was nothing but a vague gesture of goodbye to you and my mother and a friend or two. I seemed so remote and barren and stupid. I seemed to have missed everything. Knowing you shone out as the only thing worth having. . . . Men kept coming up and asking things. One said "Please, Sir, I've a bit o' money on me. It's not much to me: but it'd

Sub-lieutenant Brooke with his mother, September 1914 (Michael Hastings, The Handsomest Young Man in England, *p. 173)*

be a lot to my wife: we've got fourteen children: and supposing anything happened to me, I wouldn't like them bloody Germans to get hold of it." What should he do? We arranged he should give it for the time to the parson. . . . We *weren't* attacked that night in the train. So we got out at Antwerp, and marched through the streets, and everyone cheered and flung themselves on us and gave us apples and chocolate and flags and kisses, and cried *Vivent les Anglais* and "Heep! Heep! Heep!"

We got out to a place called *Vieux Dieu* (or something like it), passing refugees and Belgian soldiers by millions. Every mile the noises got louder, immense explosions and detonations. We stopped in the town square in Vieux Dieu; five or six thousand British troops, a lot of Belgians, guns going through, transport waggons, motor-cyclists, orderlies on horses, staff-officers, and the rest. An extraordinary and thrilling confusion. As it grew dark the thunders increased, and the sky was lit by extraordinary glares. We were all given entrenching tools. Everyone looked worried. Suddenly our battalion was marched round the corner out of the din through an old gate in the immense, wild, garden of a recently-deserted villa chateau. There we had to sleep. The rather dirty and wild-looking sailors trudged over lawns, through orchards and across pleasaunces. Little pools glimmered through the trees, and deserted fountains: and round corners one saw, faintly, occasional Cupids and Venuses—a scattered company of rather bad statues—gleaming quietly. The sailors dug their latrines in the various rose-gardens and lay down to sleep—but it was bitter cold—under the shrubs. It seemed infinitely peaceful and remote. I was officer on guard till the middle of the night. Then I lay down on the floor of a bedroom for a decent night's sleep. But by 2 the shells had got unpleasantly near. A big one (I'm told) burst above the garden: but too high to do damage. And some message came. So up we got—frozen and sleepy—and toiled off through the night. By dawn we got into trenches, very good ones, and relieved Belgians.

Sweetheart, this is *very* dull. And it doesn't really reflect any state of mind. For when I think back on it, my mind is filled with various disconnected images and feelings. And, if I could tell you those fully, you *might* find it wonderful—or at least queer. There's the excitement in the trenches—we weren't attacked seriously in our part—with people losing their heads and fussing and snapping. It's queer to see the people who *do* break under the strain of danger and responsibility. It's always the rotten ones. Highly sensitive people don't, queerly enough. "Nuts," do. I was relieved to find I was incredibly brave! I don't know how I should behave if shrapnel was bursting on me and knocking the men round me to pieces. But for risks and nerves and fatigue I was all right. That's cheering.

And there's the empty blue sky and the peaceful village and country scenery, and nothing of war to see except occasional bursts of white smoke, very lazy and quiet, in the distance. But to hear, incessant thunder, shaking buildings and ground and you and everything; and, above, recurrent wailings, very shrill and queer, like lost souls, crossing and recrossing in the emptiness—nothing to be seen. Once or twice a lovely glittering aeroplane, very high up, would go over us; and then the shrapnel would be turned on it, and a dozen quiet little curls of white smoke would appear round the creature—the whole thing like a German woodcut, very quaint and graceful and unreal. Eh, but the retreat drowned all those impressions. At 6:30 on the second evening the forts away on our left had been smashed and the Belgians had run away (probably) and the Council of War in Antwerp had decided that we'd have to get out. So we stole away from the trenches, across half Antwerp, over the Scheldt, and finally entrained in the last train left, at 7.30 next morning, thirty miles away. We had one hour's sleep, from 2 to 3, in a wet field: and we very nearly walked into a German ambush. It was rather a miracle we got away. But the march through those deserted suburbs, mile on mile, with never a living being, except one rather ferocious looking sailor, stealing sulkily along. The sky was lit by burning villages and houses; and after a bit we got to the land by the river, where the Belgians had let all the petrol out of the tanks and fired it. Rivers and seas of flame leaping up hundreds of feet, crowned by black smoke that covered the entire heavens. It lit up houses wrecked by shells, dead horses, demolished railway stations, engines that had been taken up with their lines and signals, and all twisted round and pulled out, as a bad child spoils a toy. And there we joined the refugees, with all their goods on barrows and carts, in a double line, moving forwards about a hundred yards an hour, white and drawn and beyond emotion. The glare was like hell. We passed on, out of that, across a pontoon bridge, built on boats. Two German spies tried to blow it up while we were on it. They were caught and shot. We went on through the dark. The refugees and motor-buses and transport and Belgian troops grew thicker. After about a thousand years it was dawn. The motor-buses indicated that we were bound for Hammersmith and Fleet Street and such places, and might be allowed to see *Potash and Perlmutter*. Women gave us apples.

My dear, I've a million things to tell you. We'll meet at Folkestone or in London. Are you glorious as ever? I so want to be with you. I finish this at Camp. We're all training ourselves again.

Goodbye, dear love
Rupert

Brooke spent most of October and November training for war, during which time he wrote the drafts of the first three "War Sonnets."

Brooke's letter to Leonard Bacon explaining why England had to fight Germany, 11 November 1914 (Geoffrey Keynes, ed., The Letters of Rupert Brooke, *pp. 631-632)*

Anson Battalion
R.N.D.

Dear Bacon,
    It was a pleasure to get your letter: and more than a pleasure to know that you're all with us. The muses have fled to America, and are to be interned in that (technically) neutral country, I'm told, for the period of the war. Don't keep them forever. I've forgotten them—for this. I've been in the Naval Division for some two months: went through Antwerp: and am training for further service. Where will that be—Cyprus? the Kiel Canal? the Rhine? Ypres?—and when, next week? next month? next year? No one knows. Anyway, it'll be good work, I hope: and (with the horror) fun.

    It seems a most damnably long time since I saw that quiet garden off Piedmont Avenue. All my friends, but a few, are training or serving. One or two have been killed. Others wounded, and are going back. The best Greek scholar of the younger generation at Cambridge, Cornford, is a musketry instructor at Aldershot. Among my fellow officers are one of the best young English pianists, and a brilliant young composer. Gilbert Murray gets up every morning to line a hedgerow, gun in hand, before dawn. What a world! Yet I'm still half ashamed of England, when I hear of the holocaust of the young poets, painters and scholars of France and Belgium—and Germany.

    It hurts me, this war. Because I was fond of Germany. There are such good things in her, and I'd always hoped she'd get away from Prussia and the oligarchy in time. If it had been a mere war between us and them I'd have hated fighting. But I'm glad to be doing it for Belgium. That's what breaks the heart to see and hear of. I marched through Antwerp, deserted, shelled, and burning, one night, and saw ruined houses, dead men and horses: and railway-trains with their lines taken up and twisted and flung down as if a child had been playing with a toy. And the whole heaven and earth was lit up by the glare from the great lakes and rivers of burning petrol, hills and spires of flame. That was like Hell, a Dantesque Hell, terrible. But there—and later—I saw what was a truer Hell. Hundreds of thousands of refugees, their goods on barrows and handcarts and perambulators and waggons, moving with infinite slowness out into the night, two unending lines of them, the old men mostly weeping, the women with hard white drawn faces, the children playing or crying or sleeping. That's what Belgium is now: the country where three civilians have been killed to every one soldier. That damnable policy of "frightfulness" succeeded for a time. When it was decided to evacuate Antwerp, all of that population of half a million, save a few thousands, fled. I don't think they really had any need to. The Germans have behaved fairly well in the big cities. But the policy of bullying had been carried out well. And half a million people preferred homelessness and the chance of starvation, to the certainty of German rule. It's queer to think one has been a witness of one of the greatest crimes of history. Has ever nation been treated like that? And how can such a stain be wiped out?

    Well, we're doing our best. Give us what prayers or cheers you can. It's a great life, fighting, while it lasts. The eye grows clearer and the heart. But it's a bloody thing, half the youth of Europe blown through pain to nothingness, in the incessant mechanical slaughter of these modern battles. I can only marvel at human endurance. Come and see us all when it's all over. Love to the Wells' and to you both.

"The Soldier," the last of the five poems in Brooke's series known as "War Sonnets" (The Collected Poems of Rupert Brooke with a Memoir, *p. 9*)

> If I should die, think only this of me:
>   That there's some corner of a foreign field
> That is forever England. There shall be
>   In that rich earth a richer dust concealed;
> A dust whom England bore, shaped, made aware,
>   Gave, once, her flowers to love, her ways to roam,
> A body of England's, breathing English air,
>   Washed by the rivers, blest by suns of home.
>
> And think, this heart, all evil shed away,
>   A pulse in the eternal mind, no less,
> Gives somewhere back the thoughts by England given;
>   Her sights and sounds; dreams happy as her day;
>   And laughter, learnt of friends; and gentleness,
>   In hearts at peace, under an English heaven.

Discussion of "The Soldier" by William E. Laskowski (Rupert Brooke, *pp. 61-62*)

"The Soldier" is Brooke's most famous, the poem inscribed by Eric Gill on his memorial in Rugby chapel, the poem by which Brooke can most easily be identified

Manuscript for one of Brooke's "War Sonnets," the opening lines of which became the best-known English-language poem of the Great War (King's College Library, Cambridge) to people who do not otherwise know his name. Its most famous image, "some corner of a foreign field / That is forever England," has been exhaustively analyzed and even called a symbol of economic imperialism. More insightfully, the image's origin has been traced to one of Brooke's favorite books, Belloc's *The Four Men*, whose last chapter contains a poem establishing this sentiment: "One with our random fields we grow . . . He does not die that can bequeath / Some influence to the land he knows . . . He does not die, but still remains / Substantiate with his darling plains." Brooke may have repeated the sentiment, but he vastly improved the rhetoric of the utterance. In an uncanny irony for a poem written in 1911, Belloc's poem also contains an allusion to no-man's land. The use of this phrase by both Belloc and those who fought on the Western front reveals one reason why "The Soldier" became so popular: death had become so anonymous (this war originated the memorials to the unknown soldier), and the struggle for a small piece of territory so seemingly meaningless, that any means that could personalize and localize sacrifice were seized on. The image of the afterlife in "The Soldier" that Dean Inge criticized in his sermon—"a pulse in the eternal mind"—is a continuation of the tentative substitutes for the afterlife that Brooke had been exploring in his recent poetry. Adorned with dreams, laughter, and gentleness, this afterlife is in a sense a regression to the safe and sterile Platonic paradises of Brooke's earlier work. The heaven for which Brooke had been searching so long, now called specifically English, has washed clean the sin and pain of Peace ("all evil shed away"), and the "hearts at peace" in the last line of the poem fulfill the promise of the title of the first poem. War, not the political revolution of "The Bastille," will remove guilt and sin.

The Hood Battalion remained at Blandford through February 1915. By 8 March, Brooke's ship, the Grantully Castle, *was anchored off Malta, where the officers were waiting to join Winston Churchill's ill-fated second-front offensive at Gallipoli in the Dardanelles. On 11 March the ship arrived at the Greek island of Lemnos. Brooke appears to have known that the odds of surviving the battle were not good.*

Through the influence of high political acquaintances such as Herbert Asquith and Churchill in December 1914 Brooke was transferred to the Hood Battalion in Dorset, where he wrote the last two of his "War Sonnets" on active duty. All five of these sonnets were published in New Numbers *in December 1914. At the end of the year Brooke was enjoying leave in London.*

Officers of the Hood Battalion in December 1914. Brooke is in the second row, second from left (King's College Library, Cambridge).

Indeed, his letter on 17 March to Dudley Ward reveals that Brooke anticipated his own death: on the envelope he wrote, "If I die to be sent to Dudley Ward," whom Brooke instructed how to dispose of his letters in the event of his death (Geoffrey Keynes, ed., The Letters of Rupert Brooke, *p. 671).*

       S.S. "Grantully Castle"
          Lemnos

My dear Dudley,

You'll already have done a few jobs for me. Here are some more.

My private papers and letters I'm leaving to my mother, and when she dies, to Ka.

But I want you, now–I've told my mother–to go through my letters (they're mostly together, but some scattered) and *destroy* all those from (a) Elizabeth van Rysselberghe. These are signed E. v. R.: and in a handwriting you'll pick out easily, once you've seen it. They'll begin in the beginning of 1909 or 1910, my first visit to Munich, and be rather rare except in one or two bunches.

(b) Lady Eileen Wellesley: also in a handwriting you'll recognize quickly, and generally signed Eileen. They date from last July on.

If other people, Ka, for instance, agitate to have letters destroyed, why, you're the person to do it. I don't much care what goes. . . .

Indeed, why keep anything? Well, I might turn out to be eminent and biographiable. If so, let them know the poor truths. Rather pathetic this.

Brooke's letter to his mother from Egypt telling of his illness and run-down physical condition, 5 April 1915 (Geoffrey Keynes, ed., The Letters of Rupert Brooke, *pp. 675–676)*

Dear Mother,

Here we still are: though not for long, perhaps. It's not been a bad time in some ways: but on the days

A week later the Grantully Castle *sailed into the Dardanelles and back out before returning to Lemnos. It then sailed for Port Said, Egypt, where it arrived on 28 March. Brooke took leave time to explore Cairo and to visit the Pyramids with friends of Arthur Asquith.*

Brooke is at the far right with this group visiting the Pyramids (King's College Library, Cambridge).

when there's a bit of a sandstorm, life is almost insupportable. I went down with a slight touch of sunstroke a few days ago. Nothing bad, but enough to make me feel pretty miserable, for a little. Patrick Shaw Stewart had it a day or two, before me, and now we're both lying in a quiet hotel bedroom, having moved away from Camp. We shall stay here a few days: to get quite well. We ought to be all right in time for any work. It began with a racking headache, sickness and incessant diarrhoea. Feeding on arrowroot has brought the diarrhoea under a good deal: and my temperature and headache have vanished. So I'm well on the way to recovery. So is Shaw Stewart. A good many of the men have had the same. The glare is awful here.

The first day I was sick—before I got out of camp—was the day when our new G.O.C. in Chief [Sir Ian Hamilton]—you'll know who that is—reviewed us. I'd met him once or twice in London. He came to see me after the review and talked for a bit. He offered me a sort of galloper-aide-de-camp job on his staff: but I shan't take it. Anyhow, not now, not till this present job's over. Afterwards, if I've had enough of the regimental officer's work, I might like it. But I'm very happy where I am. I'm with quite a good lot of fellows.

I'm sending you a little old small glass bottle I picked up in a bazaar. It's *supposed,* I think, to be an old Egyptian tear-bottle, found in a tomb. But I imagine it's really very recently manufactured. Still it's amusing; and if you clean out the inside with a little warm water, it might look nice, and hold scent.

I was going to write to Alfred to say it was still open to him to come into the R.N.D. when he liked, if he could work the transfer. But I got today a letter from Dent, dated March 12, saying he heard Alfred was off to France that day. I suppose I shall hear if that's so.

The posts are odd. I got a letter from Eddie, March 17 or 18, a *Nation,* March 8, from you and this from Dent. I think most intermediate letters are somewhere else: waiting to be sent on. They'll catch us up some time.

The pyjamas and handkerchiefs arrived, safe though battered, and the cover much torn; many thanks.

By the time Brooke returned to camp his health was weakening. He was visited on 2 April by the commander in chief, General Sir Ian Hamilton, who offered him a staff appointment at Naval Headquarters aboard the Queen Elizabeth, *but Brooke declined. Physically worn by dysentery and a lip infection caused by an insect bite, he rejoined his ship in time for its departure for Lemnos on 10 April. The voyage gave him a chance to recover some strength.*

When the ship arrived, the harbor was full, and the Queen Elizabeth *was forced to sail to Trebuki Bay on the southern tip of the island of Skyros, where it docked on the evening of 17 April. The next day Brooke received long-overdue mail, which included a letter from Edward Marsh with an article from* The Times *about an Easter sermon that Dean Inge had delivered at St. Paul's. In his sermon the clergyman had quoted and praised Brooke's "The Soldier," as the article on 5 April 1915 reports.*

Dean Inge At St. Paul's
Spirit of the Martyr-Patriot

Dean Inge preached at St. Paul's Cathedral in the morning. He was suffering from a severe cold, and his sermon was rather brief in consequence. When the Dean entered the pulpit a man in the congregation rose to his feet and began a loud harangue protesting against the war. He was quickly conducted outside the Cathedral. The Dean took his text from Isaiah xxvi., v. 19:— "Thy dead shall live; my dead bodies shall arise. Awake and sing, ye that dwell in the dust, for thy dew is as the dew of lights, and the earth shall cast forth the dead."

There were thousands of English parents, and young widows, and young orphans, who on this Easter Day were thinking of the hastily made graves in a foreign land, where their dearest are sleeping. When the day of peace and restored safety dawned for England, as please God it would before very long, what of them? Would they be left out of it? Was their day over and done, while the struggle was still undecided and the victory uncertain? How could God refuse them the happiness they so well earned, of sharing in our rejoicing over the peace?

He had just read a beautiful little poem on this subject, a sonnet by a young writer who would, he ventured to think, take rank with our great poets—so potent was a time of trouble to evoke genius which might otherwise have slumbered. A young soldier spoke thus:

[He reads "The Soldier"]

The enthusiasm of a pure and elevated patriotism, free from hate, bitterness, and fear, had never found a nobler expression. And yet it fell somewhat short of Isaiah's vision and still more of the Christian hope. It was a worthy thought that the dust out of which the happy warrior's body was once compacted was consecrated for ever by the cause for which he died. Yet was there not a tinge of materialism in such an idea? The spirit of heroism and self-sacrifice knew no restrictions of this kind. When it had once shown itself in action, it became part of the whole world's spiritual wealth. The earth was a better place because such things had been done in it. The spirit of the martyr-patriot was everywhere near, where there was a man to say, "This is how I should like to live and die." And a Christian would hardly be quite content to think of the brave man's soul living on only as "a pulse in the eternal mind." The Christian hope of immortality was not impersonal.

Military training continued on Skyros, and after an exhausting field day on 20 April, Brooke, who had never recovered fully from the illnesses that he had suffered in Egypt, went to bed feeling unwell, thinking that some wine he had drunk had made his lip swollen. The next day his temperature rose considerably, and his body was wracked with pain. Because of the congenital weaknesses of his immune system, his resistance to infection was dangerously low. The doctors on the ship decided that the seriousness of his condition required that he be transferred to the French hospital ship, the Duguay-Trouin, *but this move came too late. Shortly after Brooke arrived there he died at 4:46 P.M., 23 April 1915.*

Report of Brooke's last day (Peter Miller, The Cross of Skyros, *p. 10)*

The scene is recorded by J. Perdriel-Vaissieres, one of the personnel of the hospital ship. "They have brought on a stretcher a man who is ill of some malady . . . his face is bloodless, he gazes with large blue eyes which have still a good deal of life in them; he has an eruption on the lip," and then—barely 24 hours later—"Never did face seem paler on the bed of death. Is it because of that black mark on the lip? Or is it that the Eastern light beats more pitilessly on the skin of this man from the North? Everybody is silent."

He was barely conscious and virtually already dying by the time he was received on board the hospital ship.

*In a memoir of Brooke, Edward Marsh includes a narrative of the poet's death that was sent to him by Denis Browne, Brooke's fellow soldier (*Rupert Brooke: The Collected Poems with a Memoir, *pp. cli–clv).*

Next morning he was much worse; the swelling had increased, and a consultation was held. The diagnosis was acute blood-poisoning, and all hope was given up. It was decided to move him to the French hospital-ship *Duguay-Trouin* which happened to be at Scyros. When he was told this, his one anxiety was lest he should have difficulty in rejoining his battalion. They reassured him, and he seemed to be content. Soon afterwards he became comatose; and there does not seem to have been any moment when he can have realised that he was dying. The rest of the story shall be told in the words of the letter which Denis Browne wrote me on the 25th from the transport.

> In less than half an hour we had carried him down into a pinnace and taken him straight aboard the *Duguay-Trouin*. They put him in the best cabin, on the sundeck. Everything was very roomy and comfortable; they had every modern appliance and the surgeons did all that they possibly could. Oc and I left him about 6 when we could do nothing more, and went to the *Franconia*, where we sent a wireless message to the Admiralty. Next morning Oc and I went over to see what we could do, and found him much weaker. There was nothing to be done, as he was quite unconscious and they were busy trying all the devices they could think of to give him ease. Not that he was suffering, for he was barely conscious all Thursday (he just said 'Hallo' when I went to lift him out into the pinnace), and on Friday he was not conscious at all up to the very last, and felt no pain whatever. At 2 the head surgeon told me he was sinking. Oc went off to see about arrangements, and I sat with Rupert. At 4 o'clock he became weaker, and at 4.46 he died, with the sun shining all round his cabin, and the cool sea-breeze blowing through the door and the shaded windows. No one could have wished a quieter or a calmer end than in that lovely bay, shielded by the mountains and fragrant with sage and thyme.
>
> We buried him the same evening in an olive grove where he had sat with us on Tuesday—one of the loveliest places on this earth, with grey-green olives round him, one weeping above his head; the ground covered with flowering sage, bluish-grey, and smelling more delicious than any flower I know. The path up to it from the sea is narrow and difficult and very stony; it runs by the bed of a dried-up torrent. We had to post men with lamps every twenty yards to guide the bearers. He was carried up from the boat by his A Company petty officers, and it was with enormous difficulty that they got the coffin up the narrow way. The journey of a mile took two hours. It was not till 11 that I saw them coming (I had gone up to choose the place, and with Freyberg and Charles Lister I turned the sods of his grave; we had some of his platoon to dig). First came one of his men carrying a great white wooden cross with his name painted on it in black; then the firing party, commanded by Patrick; and then the coffin, followed by our officers, and General Paris and one or two others of the Brigade. Think of it all under a clouded moon, with the three mountains around and behind us, and those divine scents everywhere. We lined his

grave with all the flowers we could find, and Quilter set a wreath of olive on the coffin. The funeral service was very simply said by the Chaplain, and after the Last Post the little lamplit procession went once again down the narrow path to the sea.

>   Freyberg, Oc, I, Charles and Cleg [Kelly] stayed behind and covered the grave with great pieces of white marble which were lying everywhere about. Of the cross at the head you know; it was the large one that headed the procession. . . . At his feet was a small wooden cross sent by his platoon. We could not see the grave again, as we sailed from Scyros next morning at 6.

The same friend wrote to Mrs. Brooke: "No words of mine can tell you the sorrow of those whom he has left behind him here. No one of us knew him without loving him, whether they knew him for ten years, as I did, or for a couple of months as others. His brother officers and his men mourn him very deeply. But those who knew him chiefly as a poet of the rarest gifts, the brightest genius, know that the loss is not only yours and ours, but the world's. And beyond his genius there was that infinitely lovable soul, that stainless heart whose earthly death can only be the beginning of a true immortality.

"To his friends Rupert stood for something so much purer, greater, and nobler than ordinary men that his loss seems more explicable than theirs. He has gone to where he came from; but if anyone left the world richer by passing through it, it was he."

Text of Winston Churchill's tribute published in The Times *(London), 26 April 1915*

Rupert Brooke is dead. A telegram from the Admiral at Lemnos tells us that this life has closed at the moment when it seemed to have reached its springtime. A voice had become audible, a note had been struck, more true, more thrilling, more able to do justice to the nobility of our youth in arms engaged in this present war, than any other—more able to express their thoughts of self-surrender, and with a power to carry comfort to those who watch them so intently from afar. The voice has been swiftly stilled. Only the echoes and the memory remain; but they will linger.

During the last few months of his life, months of preparation in gallant comradeship and open air, the poet-soldier told with all the simple force of genius the sorrow of youth about to die, and the sure triumphant consolations of a sincere and valiant spirit. He expected to die: he was willing to die for the dear England whose beauty and majesty he knew: and he advanced towards the brink in perfect serenity, with absolute conviction of the rightness of his country's cause and a heart devoid of hate for fellow-men.

The thoughts to which he gave expression in the very few incomparable war sonnets which he has left behind will be shared by many thousands of young men moving resolutely and blithely forward in this, the hardest, the cruellest, and the least-rewarded of all the wars that men have fought. They are a whole history and revelation of Rupert Brooke himself. Joyous, fearless, versatile, deeply instructed, with classic symmetry of mind and body, ruled by high undoubting purpose, he was all that one would wish England's noblest sons to be in the days when no sacrifice but the most precious is acceptable, and the most precious is that which is most freely proffered.

Obituary by Lascelles Abercrombie for Brooke in the Morning Post, *27 April 1915 (Michael Hastings,* The Handsomest Young Man in England, *p. 185)*

The news, which has been privately received, of the death of Rupert Brooke, as the result of a sunstroke, at Lemnos (he was serving as a sublieutenant in the Royal Naval Division), will be lamented by all true lovers of English literature. Not since Sir Philip Sidney's heroic death have we lost such a gallant and joyous type of the poet-soldier. He was at Rugby, where his father (who might well have been the "Young Brooke" of "Tom Brown's School Days") was a master. Not only did he win a prize in 1905 for a poem on "The Bastille," which was fine, fluent stuff, but he also played both cricket and football for the School and took a keen interest in other athletic sports. Indeed, when, a year ago, the necessity of a true poem of the *funera nefunera* of the modern Prize Ring was being discussed by certain cultured connoisseurs of the "sweet science," his name was at once mentioned as that of the only young poet who could do justice to the subject, and it was unanimously decided to take him to the next big fight. He was then travelling in Canada and the United States and sending home delightful prose-pictures of the multitudinous life in the vast demi-Englands of the West—he enjoyed it all joyously, but loved his Motherland too well ever to be deeply intrigued by the lavish beauties of any mistress-land afar. In 1913 he was elected to a Fellowship at King's College, Cambridge, where he had taken the classical tripos. Then came the war, when he sought and obtained a commission in the Hood Battalion of the Royal Naval Division. He was in the futile, foolish Expedition to Antwerp, and, after continuing his training at Blandford Camp sailed on the last day of

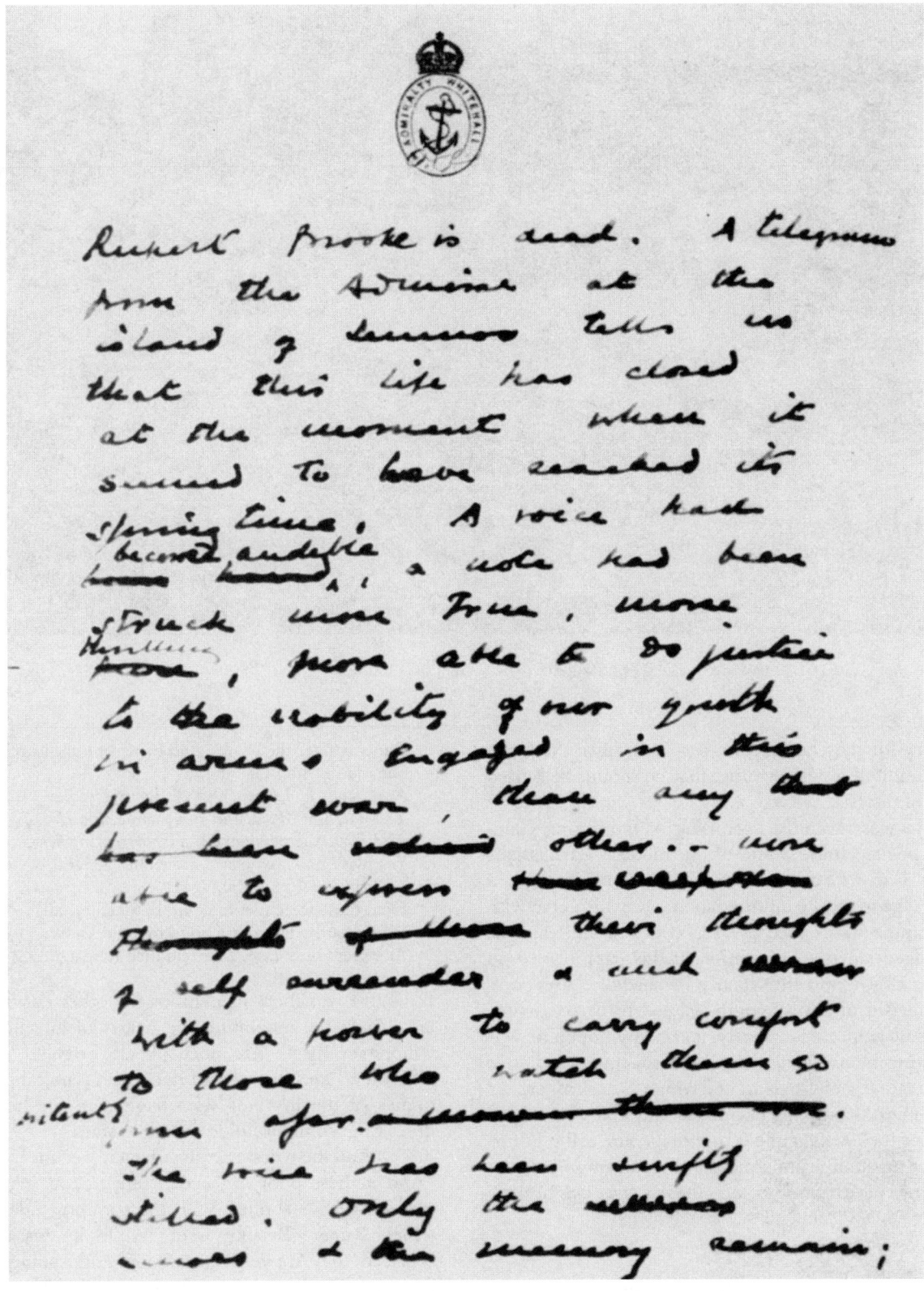

First page of Winston Churchill's draft of his tribute to Brooke (Christopher Hassall, A Biography of Edward Marsh, p. 417)

Brooke's grave on Skyros (Geoffrey Keynes, ed., The Letters of Rupert Brooke, *p. 673)*

February for the Dardanelles. It is well, since the Gods loved him and he died young, that he should be buried in one of the Isles of Greece.

He was the most promising of the young Cambridge poets. Unlike some of the modern Parnassians (James Elroy Flecker, for example, who was also a Cambridge man), he did not labour over his verse with the file; indeed, his poetry was as effortless and eager as the winged songs of springtide. In his later play (you cannot call it work) the "dainty melancholy" and rootless cynicism of happy youth seemed to be departing. He was no minor poet, surely, and many hoped he was destined to reconcile in himself the old traditional style of lyric poetry in England (of which Dr. Bridges, his master-in-art, is a living exemplar) and that which is so much for the needs of the future that some call it Futurism. Let us quote from a piece in his transition manner a few lines which may serve as the *ave atque vale* of their author:

> Beauty was there,
> Pale in her black; dry-eyed; she stood alone.
> Poor maz'd *Imagination; Fancy* wild;
> Ardour, the sunlight on his greying hair
> Contentment, who had known *Youth* as a child
> And never seen him since. And *Spring* came too,
> Dancing over the tombs, and brought him flowers–
> She did not stay for long.
> And *Truth,* and *Grace,* and all the merry crew,
> The laughing *Winds* and *Rivers,* and little *Hours;*
> And *Hope,* the dewy-eyed; and sorrowing *Song;*–
> Yes, with much woe and mourning general,
> At dead *Youth's* funeral,
> Even these were met once more together, all,
> Who rest the fair and living *Youth* did know;
> All except only *Love. Love* had died long ago.

But Love was there in Lemnos the other day none the less. And she, inhabiting the hearts of all who loved, will never forget her poet-soldier. England also will remember, keeping ever in her secret remembrance the names of the myriads who have died for her as the quiet English night holds the silent stars.

"And the worst friend and enemy is but Death" . . . "And if these poor limbs die, safest of all." So ended two of the five sonnets with the common title "1914," which Rupert Brooke wrote while he was training between the Antwerp expedition and sailing for the Aegean. These sonnets are incomparably the finest utterance of English poetry concerning the Great War. We knew the splendid promise of Rupert Brooke's earlier poetry: these sonnets are the brief perfection of his achievement. They are much more than that: they are among the few supreme utterances of English patriotism. It was natural, perhaps, that they should leave all else that has been written about the war so far behind. It is not so much that they are the work of a talent scarcely, in its own way, to be equalled today; it was much more that they were the work of a poet who had for his material the feeling that he was giving up everything to fight for England—the feeling, I think, that he was giving his life for England. Reading these five sonnets now, it seems as if he had in them written his own epitaph. I believe he thought so himself; a few words he said in my last talk with him makes me believe that— now. At any rate, the history of literature, so full of Fate's exquisite ironies, has nothing more poignantly ironic, and nothing at the same time more beautifully appropriate, than the publication of Rupert Brooke's noble sonnet-sequence, "1914," a few swift weeks before the death they had imagined, and had already made lovely. Each one of these five sonnets faces in a quiet exultation, the thought of death, of death for England, and understands, as seldom even English poetry has understood, the unspeakable beauty of the thought. . . .

This—this music, this beauty, this courage—was Rupert Brooke. But it is, we may be sure, his immortality. It is not yet tolerable to speak of personal loss. The name seemed to stand for a magical vitality that must be safe—safe! yes, "and if these poor limbs die, safest of all!" What poetry has lost in him cannot be judged by anyone who has not read those last sonnets, now his farewell to England and the world. I am not underrating the rest of his work. There was an intellectual keenness and brightness in it, a fire of imagery and (in the best sense) wit, the like of which had not been known, or known only in snatches, in our literature, since the best days of the later Elizabethans. And it was all penetrated by a mastering passion, the most elemental of all passions, the passion for life. "I have been so great a lover," he cries, and artfully leads us on to think he means the usual passion of a young poet's career. But it is just life he loves, and not in any abstract sense, but all the infinite little familiar details of life, catalogued with delighted jest. This was profoundly sincere: no one ever loved life more wholly or more minutely. And he celebrated his love exquisitely, often unforgettably, through all his earlier poetry, getting a further intensity from a long sojourn in the South Seas. But this passion for life had never had seriously to fight for its rights and joys. Like all great lovers of life, he had pleased himself with the thought of death and after death; not insincerely by any means, but simply because this gave a finer relish to the sense of being alive. Platonism, which offers delightful games for such subtle wit as his, he especially liked to play with.

It was one more element in the life of here and now, the life of mortal thought and sense and spirit, infinitely varying and by him infinitely loved. And then came 1914; and his passion for life had suddenly to face the thought of voluntary death. But there was no struggle; for instantly the passion for life became one with the will to die—and now it has become death itself. But first Rupert Brooke had told the world once more how the passion for beautiful life may reach its highest passion and most radiant beauty when it is the determination to die.

After his death Brooke became a martyr for the English cause, and his war poems, lavishly praised, became templates for much patriotic verse, as tributes to him reveal. The Cambridge Review *eulogized him as a representative of the best that the university produced. Henry James saw him as a representative of youth and vitality, and* Putnam's Magazine, *a popular literary journal, saw him as a victim of war, a young Apollo silenced too quickly.*

Tribute to Brooke in The Cambridge Review *(5 May 1915, p. 287)*

When it is so hard for us to write at all, it is very hard to write what is true. But Rupert Brooke would not have wished us to write about him anything else. That is why I am going to say that it was not his beauty, about which so much is being said, that mattered to us, nor his verse, though it gave us pleasure, and showed the promise of so much good; but something in himself, the real Rupert, only half expressed in his writing, not fully developed, I think, even in the friend we knew. Though it is not easy, we owe it to him not to comfort ourselves by letting our thoughts dwell on a mythical person who was not Rupert, and whose loss is therefore easier to bear. We must not, as he wrote, "praise all the bad about him, and hush all the good away."

He was kind and unaffected. But he was not miraculously unselfish, nor indifferent to his popularity. The fact that in small things he sometimes seemed to choose the pleasant second-best, and, as he himself realised, rather eagerly to accept the little successes which he could so easily win, should make us appreciate not less, but more, the rightness and the goodness of his larger choices. He was very sensitive to praise, and it would be wrong to say that he was always wisely praised. But he was sensible enough and strong enough to take flattery, in the long run, for what it was worth; and he valued the affection that was critical, not flattering. At Rugby, which he always loved, he was happy and successful in games as well as in the rest of the life and work of the school. At Cambridge he found that other pursuits were, now, for him, more important than games, and that English literature was now, for him, more important than the ancient classics. He has convinced us all that he was right. It hurt him, I know, to disappoint those who were hoping for his more immediate academic success. The work which he did at Rugby when, for a short time, he took charge of his father's house, showed how successful he might have been as a schoolmaster if his choice had been different.

Because he was human he enjoyed his popularity. The quality which won it was, I think, his power of liking people, and making them feel, because he liked them all, not only at their ease with him, but also happy and friendly to one another. His company had this effect at home, and in his rooms at King's, in his garden at Grantchester, in London, and, I feel sure, wherever he went in Germany and in America. Certainly the most varied people used to delight in it, and he, for his part, was delighted when some of the incongruous persons he liked, unexpectedly also liked one another. He would laugh at his friends and would sometimes treat their most cherished enthusiasms as amusing, if harmless foibles; but he had not the power, possessed by some people who matter less, of making you seem small and dull. His society was, in fact, in the good sense, comfortable. He loved children, and when he treated his grownup friends as rather absurd, but very nice, children, they would have had to be very absurd indeed to resent it. It must have been very hard to be pompous or priggish in his company. He was himself, in some ways, like a child, very frank and simple; generally knowing what he wanted, and, if he could see it, taking it; but also, where his affections were concerned, most loyal and devoted; suffering acutely in the few great troubles that came to him, but generally confident and happy; above all, delighting, and making other people share his delight, in a great number of different things.

Among the things which gave him pleasure in his undergraduate days were the societies to which he belonged. The Carbonari, I think, he founded; a society which, in spite of its terrifying name, was very friendly. The paper and the talk which followed it at the one meeting to which, as an elderly person, I was allowed admission, were frank and amusing, but my chief memory is of the cheerful kindliness of the members. Three of them have given their lives in the war. Then there were the Fabians, whom he sometimes entertained to a frugal supper of bread and cheese and beer in his rooms, and to whom he never tired of teaching the importance of poets and artists in the good society which is to be built up by our children. His advice to the state was very practical. Since poets and artists matter, and since they need time for development, we, who are not the poets and the artists, ought to organise the material requisites, bread and cheese and leisure, for those who seem to show the promise of good work. He believed that you do not improve a poet by starving and neglecting him; and one good way of showing that we remember him would be to remember also that it is our duty to buy as well as read the works of the poets who are still writing. He was an enthusiastic member of the Marlowe Society, and some readers will be glad to be reminded of the performances in which he took a part. His actual role was generally small, but he always contributed much to the happiness of the rehearsals and the success of the performance.

Many will remember how they first saw him as the Herald in the *Eumenides,* December 1906. In November, 1907, he played Mephistopheles in *Dr Faustus,* and I think he took the same part in a parody subsequently produced at the A.D.C. In June 1908, he was Major Kildare in the A.D.C. performance of *His Excellency the Governor,* and in July he was the Attendant Spirit in *Comus.* He also took part, I think, in *Epicoene* (1909), and *King Richard II* (1910), and he danced in the Cambridge production of the *Magic Flute* (December 1911).

But it was chiefly because he made so many friends that he lived so full a life at Cambridge, as in the later days at Grantchester and elsewhere. He succeeded, even, in breaking through the barrier which so unfortunately for sound education cuts off the University in general from the society of Newnham and of Girton. Here also he used sometimes to be criticised, but, of course, he was right.

All the time he was working hard at the books which for him most mattered, making himself a good critic and a good writer. At school he had twice written prize poems, on the Pyramids in 1904, and on the Bastille in 1905. It is not creditable to the Cambridge examiners that he competed without success for the Chancellor's English medal. The poem was good, and was unhappily destroyed. Having obtained the Charles Oldham Shakespeare scholarship in 1909, he devoted himself to the Elizabethans, and particularly to Webster. The dissertation which brought him his Fellowship at King's in 1911 showed the very rare combination of a fresh and appreciative mind with an exactness and an intimate knowledge of detail which must have surprised those people who think that poets are idlers. Those who had a right to an opinion expected him to give a new impulse and inspiration to English criticism.

As to his poetry, it is hoped that the *Cambridge Review* may presently be able to publish an appreciation by a writer better qualified to speak of it than I. I will only venture to say that the charm of the simpler poems in which he seemed to catch the vividness and beauty of youth, and the splendid courage of the 1914 sonnets, appeared to me to show the promise of a much finer achievement. Some of his earlier poems have been thought harsh and rather cruel. These did not seem to me to express his personality as a whole; he was, indeed, disgusted with things that are really disgusting; and he had the courage and the honesty to say so. Those who criticised should read the scathing words with which, in his dissertation, he rebuked the modern impertinence of offering regrets or apologies for the outspokenness of the Elizabethans; when he exaggerates what is unpleasant, he is often, I think, protesting against prudery. But the poems which seem to me most expressive of his own temperament are pleasant, like his kindness. His last poems are inspired by a heroic sacrifice and love of English men and things. Had he lived, he would have given us, with deepened experience, something deeper and better still. For he loved also the Germans, against whom he felt that he was fighting in a good cause. He would have fought, when the time came, with the same high courage, against vindictiveness, for kindness, and reason, and freedom.

*Edward Thomas's tribute to Brooke (*The English Review, *20 [June 1915], pp. 325–328)*

Rupert Brooke

On April 23rd the poet Rupert Brooke died of sunstroke at Lemnos in his twenty-eighth year. He was a second lieutenant in the Royal Naval Division, on his way to the fighting in the Dardanelles. No poet of his age was so much esteemed and admired, or was watched more hopefully. His work could not be taken soberly, whether you like it or not. It was full of the thought, the aspiration, the indignation of youth; full of the praise of youth. Many people knew the man or the reputation of his personal charm. Wherever he went he made friends, well-wishers, admirers, adorers. He was himself a friendly man, with humour and good humour added. Successful in many fields—he played in the eleven and the fifteen for Rugby school; he won a fellowship at King's College, Cambridge; he was celebrated as a golden young Apollo, in Mrs. Cornford's phrase—

"Magnificently unprepared
For the long littleness of life,"—

his attractiveness included modesty and simplicity. He stretched himself out, drew his fingers through his waved, fair hair, laughed, talked indolently, and admired as much as he was admired. No one that knew him could easily separate him from his poetry: not that they were the same, but that the two inextricably mingled and helped one another. He was tall, broad, and easy in his movements. Either he stooped, or he thrust his his head forward unusually much to look at you with his steady, blue eyes. His clear, rosy skin helped to give him the look of a great girl. The papers nearly all said something about his "beauty," his good looks, his "glamour"; one said that he was one of the handsomest Englishmen of our time. And just before he died it happened that one of his last-published sonnets was quoted in St. Paul's Cathedral by the Dean:–

"If I should die, think only this of me:
That there's some corner of a foreign field
That is for ever England. There shall be
In that rich earth a richer dust concealed;
A dust whom England bore, shaped, made aware,
Gave, once, her flowers to love, her ways to roam,
A body of England's, breathing English air,
Washed by the rivers, blest by suns of home.

"And think, this heart, all evil shed away,
A pulse in the eternal mind, no less
Gives somewhere back the thoughts by England given;
Her sights and sounds; dreams happy as her day;
And laughter, learnt of friends; and gentleness,
In hearts at peace, under an English heaven."

So, instantly he took his share of the fame that comes to young poets dying conspicuously and unexpectedly, but not unprophesied by themselves.

In his lifetime he was not widely known for his one book, *Poems* (1911), the essays on Donne and John Webster published in *Poetry and Drama,* and the poems published in the same quarterly, in *Georgian Poetry,* in the four parts of *New Numbers,* and here and there in the newspapers.

His poems had referred a good deal to death, long before the war began. He was so eager for enjoyment and performance worthy of a very lofty conception of life and youth, that death, and old age, and the end of love, could not but confront him prodigiously. He varied between a Shelleyan eagerness and a Shelleyan despair. It was characteristic of him to apply the Shelleyan epithet "swift" to a girl's hair. Sometimes it seemed to him he could not love; sometimes that so great was his love it would endure in his dust and haunt the mean lovers of later years:–

"In that instant they shall learn
The shattering ecstasy of our fire,
And the weak passionless hearts will burn

And faint in that amazing glow,
Until the darkness close above;
And they will know—poor fools, they'll know!–
One moment, what it is to love."

He wrote a threnody for the "Funeral of Youth," where "fussy Joy, Passion, grown portly, something middle-aged," and "Ardour, the sunlight on his greying hair," were among the mourners; but not Love—"Love had died long ago." Like Shelley, he was metaphysical. One of his poems was the result of an effort to look at the world, another to see God, like a fish; while a third spoke of the cold life of the herring, but ended:—

"He has his hour, he has his hour."

The "eternal instant," the "immortal moment," troubled his mind. He was discontented with its rareness, and even in the midst of one such moment, before exclaiming—

"Heart of my heart, our heaven is now, is won!"

he must yet remember—

"Through glory and ecstasy we pass;
Wind, sun, and earth remain, the birds sing still,
When we are old, are old...."

Yet he would turn from metaphysical Platonising to very substantial enumeration of the things he loved:—

"So, for their sakes I loved, ere I go hence,
And the high cause of love's magnificence,
And to keep loyalties young, I'll write those names
Golden for ever, eagles, crying flames,
And set them as a banner, that men may know,
To dare the generations, burn, and blow
Out on the wind of Time, shining and streaming...."

The list includes tea-cups and peeled sticks as well as rainbows.

He celebrated the beauty and quiet of Grantchester, near Cambridge, and in a Berlin café thought of the honey for tea there. He was not going to stop short at youth any more than at vegetarianism, or walking barefoot in the dust, or bathing in the winter in the Cam. He was beginning not only to enjoy things as mortals do, but perhaps to be content to do so. It had long been true of him what he said of Donne: that "humour was always at his command. It was part of his realism, especially in the bulk of his work, his poems dealing with love." He turned to—

"Lips that fade, and human laughter,
And faces individual,
Well this side of Paradise...."

and remarked—

"There's little comfort in the wise."

He did not attain the "Shelleyan altitude where words have various radiance rather than meaning," but perhaps no poet better expressed the aspiration towards it and all the unfulfilled eagerness of ambitious self-conscious youth. His promise is more generally spoken of, but it was a rare and considerable achievement to have expressed and suggested in so many ways the promise of youth.

When the war came to Europe, apparently a minor peace came to his heart, not with imagined "love's magnificence," but ridding him of "all the little emptiness of love," in a new life of which he wrote:—

"Oh! we, who have known shame, we have found release there,
Where there's no ill, no grief, but sleep has mending,
Naught broken save this body, lost but breath;
Nothing to shake the laughing heart's long peace there
But only agony, and that has ending;
And the worst friend and enemy is but Death."

He felt safe, "and if these poor limbs die, safest of all." His reputation is safe: it was never greater than now, when he stands out clearly against that immense, dark background, an Apollo not afraid of the worst of life.

Henry James's assessment of Brooke the poet and Brooke the man (Preface to Brooke's Letters from America, *pp. xii–xiii)*

Rupert Brooke, young, happy, radiant, extraordinarily endowed and irresistibly attaching, virtually met a soldier's death, met it in the stress of action and the all but immediate presence of the enemy; but he is before us as a new, a confounding and superseding example altogether, an unprecedented image, formed to resist erosion by time or vulgarisation by reference, of quickened possibilities, finer ones than ever before, in the stuff poets may be noted as made of. With twenty reasons fixing the interest and the charm that will henceforth abide in his name and constitute, as we may say, his legend, he submits all helplessly to one in particular which is, for appreciation, the least personal to him or inseparable from him, and he does this because, while he is still in the highest degree the distinguished faculty and quality, we happen to feel him even more markedly and significantly "modern." This is why I speak of the mixture of his elements as new, feeling that it governs his example, put by it in a light which nothing else could have equally contributed—so that Byron, for instance, who startled his contemporaries by taking for granted scarce one

Posthumous appraisal of Brooke published in Putnam's Magazine *(Milton Bronner,* Rupert Brooke: A Postscript, Summer 1916, *pp. 54–58)*

Henry James

A little group of literary undertaker's men gathers round the tomb of a young poet, earnestly mournful, respectful, prudent and red-nosed. . . .

So spoke a poet not long ago concerning those who assembled to eulogise one of their number who had just departed into the great beyond. These are bitter words. It is conceivable that others than professional mourners may gather by the bier of the dead, to pay their last respects, to offer genuine and unselfish tribute to the work of him who has preceded them. And for those who love English poetry and care greatly for its future, there could be no more serious loss than the untimely taking off of Rupert Brooke, who promised to be a veritable Prince Rupert among the newer singers. Happily for us, his career, though short, was not marked solely by mere promise. There was performance, too. There were definite gifts that one is fain to believe will assure him at least a niche in our literature.

As one looks back now, he seems among those fated from the beginning. He was so avid of life and love and, yet, always so conscious of death. He sought to cram his career with sensations before the great silence put an end to things forever. He joyed in all beautiful objects, calling himself a great lover, his emotion being keyed to highest pitch just because of the premonition whose shadow never left his heart. He hurried from one experience to another—from university to the feverish delights of London town; from the world-centre to the dream-languor of the South Sea Islands; from those faery lands of the lotos-eaters to the strenuous, terrible scenes of the world war, finding death in the torrid sun of the Dardanelles in the service of his country. He is gone and his fresh, clear, young voice is silenced, stilled just when there was every prospect that his accents would not fall on deaf ears.

It seems but yesterday that his occasional verses, contributed to the magazines, were gathered in a little book of eighty-eight pages. It was but yesterday that one English reviewer spoke of him as an *enfant terrible*. And that, in some respects, he remained to the end. He was a vexation to those appraisers who are never happy unless they can label a man as belonging to this or that school. Brooke defied such classification. He refused to be ticketed. He was by turns mystic, amatory, realistic, sardonic, nature-loving, reverent, agnostic, charming, and coarse. His variety was bewildering. His book was full of sur-

of the articles that formed their comfortable faith and by revelling in almost everything that made them idiots if he himself was to figure as a child of truth, looks to us, by any such measure, comparatively plated over with the impenetrable rococo of his own day. I speak, I hasten to add, not of Byron's volume, his flood and his fortune, but of his really having quarrelled with the temper and the accent of his age still more where they might have helped him to expression than where he but flew in their face. He hugged his pomp, whereas our unspeakably fortunate young poet of to-day, linked like him also, for consecration of the final romance, with the isles of Greece, took for his own the whole of the poetic consciousness he was born to, and moved about in it as a stripped young swimmer might have kept splashing through blue water and coming up at any point that friendliness and fancy, with every prejudice shed, might determine. Rupert expressed us *all*, at the highest tide of our actuality, and was a creature of a freedom restricted only by that condition of his blinding youth, which we accept on the whole with gratitude and relief—given that I qualify the condition as dazzling even to himself. How can it therefore not be interesting to see a little what the wondrous modern in him consisted of?

prises, and he was never dull. So modern in so many ways, he held aloof from the new schools of poets who made weird experiments in matter and manner. He had little sympathy with that class of verse-men who might well have said with the poet in Gil Blas:

> If this sonnet is hardly intelligible, so much the better, my friend. For sonnets, odes and the other poems which aim at the sublime, the simple and the natural are not adapted; all their merit lies in obscurity; it is enough if the poet thinks he understands himself....
> There are five or six of its bold innovators who have undertaken to change the language from white to black.

... Brooke was torn between two moods. His reason told him there was no hereafter, that death ended all, that the faiths of men were subject to pity or for laughter, but not for belief. On the contrary . . . we see what his heart would fain believe,—that death is not the end, that there is another life, that there is some fuller state of being. As representative of his agnostic mood consider this sonnet on "Mutability," contributed to *New Numbers*:

> They say there's a high windless world and strange,
>   Out of the wash of days and temporal tide,
>   Where Faith and Good, Wisdom and Truth abide,
> *Aeterna corpora,* subject to no change.
>
> There the sure suns of these pale shadows move;
>   There stand the immortal ensigns of our war;
>   Our melting flesh fixed Beauty there, a star,
> And perishing hearts, imperishable Love....
>
> Dear, we know only that we sigh, kiss, smile;
>   Each kiss lasts but the kissing; and grief goes over;
>   Love has no habitation but the heart.
> Poor straws! on the dark flood we catch awhile,
> Cling, and are borne into the night apart.
> The laugh dies with the lips, Love with the lover.

But it must not be thought that Brooke was always thus solemn. He did not always descant upon grave matters. As broad satirist, as laughing philosopher, as confirmed pagan, hear him also in *New Numbers* discourse upon heaven from the standpoint of a fish, a creature whose world he was fond of portraying in highly imaginative and original verse:

> Fish say, they have their Stream and Pond,
> But is there anything Beyond?
> This life cannot be All, they swear,
> For how unpleasant if it were!
> One may not doubt that, somehow, Good
> Shall come of Water and of Mud;
> And, sure, the reverent eye must see
> A Purpose in Liquidity.
> We darkly know, by Faith we cry,
> The future is not Wholly Dry.
> Mud unto mud!—Death eddies near—
> Not here the appointed End, not here!
> But somewhere, beyond Space and Time,
> Is wetter water, slimier slime!
> And there (they trust) there swimmeth One
> Who swam ere rivers were begun,
> Immense, of fishy form and mind,
> Squamous, omnipotent, and kind;
> And under that Almighty Fin,
> The littlest fish may enter in.

Brooke's moods were protean and it would be easy to make quotation after quotation to prove it. There were occasions when he produced nothing but dewy beauty as in the verses in which he gave a vision of his sweetheart's sleep, with nature keeping vigil over her; or those tender stanzas in which he sang of the day he had loved; or the song in which his sorrow was assuaged by a sight of the pine trees against the evening sky. There was a unique touch in his love poetry. He dreamed of the day he and his dear one will have mouldered into dust arid then of that other day, long after, when one atom of that dust which was his and another that was hers, would meet and dance in the sunshine in some old garden where another young pair were enacting the same love-play. Thus far the verses moved with beauty. But from this point on they mounted higher and higher with a splendour and passion that took us back to an earlier day than this, when great singers sang of great things, greatly:

> Then in some garden hushed from wind,
>   Warm in a sunset's afterglow,
> The lovers in the flowers will find
>   A sweet and strange unquiet grow
>
> Upon the peace; and, past desiring,
>   So high a beauty in the air,
> And such a light, and such a quiring,
>   And such a radiant ecstasy there,
>
> They'll know not if it's fire, or dew,
>   Or but of earth, or in the height,
> Singing, or flame, or scent, or hue,
>   Or two that pass, in light, to light,
>
> Out of the garden, higher, higher....
>   But in that instant they shall learn
> The shattering ecstasy of our fire,
>   And the weak passionless hearts will burn
>
> And faint in that amazing glow,
>   Until the darkness close above;
> And they will know—poor fools, they'll know!—
>   One moment, what it is to love.

To the lover and nature-worshipper there is a mood in which fear and mastery enter and Brooke possesses the faculty of presenting this, too, in a few swift lines. For instance, he is climbing a hill, dreaming of one who is very dear to him, and all suddenly it comes to him she is dead, comes, to him through the strange and unaccountable thrill in the dusk:

> Gold is my heart, and the world's golden,
>   And one peak tipped with light;
> And the air lies still about the hill
>   With the first fear of night;
>
> Till mystery down the soundless valley
>   Thunders, and dark is here;
> And the winds blows, and the light goes,
>   And the night is full of fear.

The Baudelaire strain in Brooke is shown in such ghastly, such brutal, such charnel-house things as "Dead Men's Love" and "Jealousy." Time and again he applied his realism and his satire, none too dainty, in a display of his hatred of German manners, German ways, and German sentimentalism, while in "A Channel Passage," a poem of sea-sickliness he quite forgot the canons of good taste. "Menelaus and Helen" consists of two striking sonnets. In one he tells the old story of how Menelaus, at the taking of Troy, succumbed once more to Helen's beauty. In the second sonnet, Brooke, with ruthless realism, showed himself a student of the terrible ballades of Villon:

> So for the poet. How should he behold
> That journey home, the long connubial years?
> He does not tell you how white Helen bears
> Child on legitimate child, becomes a scold,
> Haggard with virtue, Menelaus bold
>   Waxed garrulous, and sacked a hundred Troys
>   'Twixt noon and supper. And her golden voice
>   Got shrill as he grew deafer. And both were old.
> . . . .
> So Menclaus nagged; and Helen cried;
> And Paris slept on by Scamander side.

It seemed surely that Brooke's next book must take him to the parting of the ways. If he cultivated his very great ability to write beautiful lyrics and sonnets, he would take a high place in the literature of his country. If he perversely gave rein to his tricksy desire at times for the coarse, the nastily realistic, the cheaply satirical, his would be a case of rich powers wasted, of unusual abilities lost to the abiding things of song.

But he never came to the cross-roads of his career. A seal was put upon him all suddenly. The call of his country rang in his ears. In his poet's vision he beheld where Englishmen

> – poured out the red
> Sweet wine of youth,

as he himself phrased it. And he heeded England's call for her youngest and bravest and best. He did it with his eyes open and with no delusions. His mood resembled that of the fated beings in a Greek tragedy. Like them, he knew his doom was upon him. He knew he was sacrificing life and all its sweets to whatever gods might be. He did not expect to come back. He did not believe he would survive. Gone forever were light loves and wandering in pleasant faraway places. There was nothing left, save to pronounce the elegy of those departing—and then to depart.

And so it was. One of his last legacies was a series of five wartime sonnets, notable riot only for their premonition of the end, but also for their beauty, their ability to touch the heart, their lofty patriotism.

In order to "protect" Brooke's personal reputation, his literary executors used many strategies to sustain his golden-haired Apollo myth. Keith Hale discusses these in his preface to the letters he has collected in Friends and Apostles: The Correspondence of Rupert Brooke and James Strachey, 1905–1914 *(New Haven: Yale University Press, 1998, pp. ix–xiii).*

The Berg Collection of the New York Public Library purchased the complete set of correspondence between the English poet Rupert Brooke (1887–1915) and his close friend, the primary English translator of Freud, James Strachey (1887–1967), in November 1967 from Alix Strachey, James's widow. The collection also included a small number of letters from Brooke to James's brother Lytton.

The letters were obtained on condition that no one would have access to them for ten years without Alix Strachey's permission. In addition, the Brooke Trust sent a letter to Berg curator Lola L. Szladits on 19 December 1969 to say that after the ten-year period the Brooke Estate would be unlikely to grant permission for publication. Although Paul Levy, James Strachey's literary trustee, was subsequently given permission to edit the correspondence (he later abandoned the project), the letters have remained unpublished for more than eighty years.

When Brooke died of blood poisoning on his way to fight the Turkish forces at Gallipoli, his friends in England were quick to turn him into a national hero—a patriotic symbol of the many young men of England who were going to war. That Brooke had recently published five sonnets glorifying patriotic sacrifice did much to promote his legend. That his friends included

British troops on the beach at Gallipoli. Brooke was en route to the Dardanelles at the time of his death (J. M. Winter, The Experience of World War I *[New York: Oxford University Press, 1989]).*

Winston Churchill, Anthony Asquith and General Ian Hamilton did even more. Churchill capitalized on Brooke's "most precious" and "most freely proffered" sacrifice, painting a portrait of Brooke as an eager defender of nation and honour willing to give up his life for England.

Brooke has since been known as a "war poet," although he saw no action during the war and completed only five poems on the subject. This classification has done his reputation serious injury, for his war sonnets seem misguided and maudlin when compared with the verse of his fellow soldier poets. Although Siegfried Sassoon and others were writing the same type of sentimental poetry as Brooke in the early days of the war, they were fortunate enough to live long enough to provide a more realistic correction to their early verse. Brooke never had that chance. His war poems have often been used by critics as a foil against which Owen and Sassoon's later war poems are favourably compared.

Whatever one thinks of Brooke's poetry, it is difficult to dispute Bernard Bergonzi's claim that "of all the myths which dominated the English consciousness during the Great War the greatest, and the most enduring, is that which enshrines the name and memory of Rupert Brooke." Bergonzi says Brooke's life "will never lack some kind of archetypal quality, if only because he was such a perfect symbol of the doomed aspirations of Liberal England: a figure from an unwritten, or suppressed, novel by his friend, E. M. Forster." Samuel Hynes has echoed Bergonzi, saying the story of Brooke's life and death "becomes an obituary of a class and a generation that was destroyed in the war" (*Occasions* 151). He is correct: Rupert Brooke was a man of his time—just not the man they thought he was.

Indeed, to maintain the patriotic legend during and after the war, Brooke's biography had to be altered beyond recognition. And it was. When Brooke Trustee Geoffrey Keynes edited and published his collection of Brooke's letters, he deleted much of the evidence that would have proven that Brooke the man was not the same as Brooke the legend. Keynes edited the letters heavily. . . . The correspondence from his editor at Faber and Faber is full of exasperated enquiries of "Why delete?" and "Why bowdlerize this?" To give but one example, Keynes deleted this passage from Brooke's 30 November 1908 letter to Erica Cotterill: "Do you understand about loving people of the same sex? It is the question people here discuss most, in all its aspects. And of course most of the sensible people would permit it." In selecting the letters to be published, Keynes in particular refused to includes those between Brooke and James Strachey, saying they would appear in print "over my dead body" (Rogers, *Brooke* 6). Keynes's refusal to allow the Brooke-Strachey letters into print was undoubtedly due to the strong homosexual current running through the correspondence. Even at Rugby, Keynes had tried to moderate that side of Brooke, complaining of his "decadent" posings, and expressing his disapproval of Brooke's flirtation with Michael Sadleir. To his credit, Keynes did publish, with few omissions, many of Brooke's letters to him about the poet's adolescent romances. But he was reluctant to print anything the adult Brooke had to say on the subject, and he tried to prevent others from writing on the subject as well.

While working on his 1948 biography of Brooke, *Red Wine of Youth*, Arthur Stringer advanced the view that Brooke was homosexual. When Keynes received word of Stringer's conclusion, he wrote to him to rebut the idea, adding that he hoped Stringer would not allow his book "to be even remotely coloured by the idea that Rupert was in any way abnormal" (10 June 1947). But the idea of Brooke being homosexual became an increasingly touchy subject for Keynes from this time forward. Robin Skelton added to Keynes's concern by writing to him some time later: "my generation and all succeeding generations will continue to regard Rupert as a plaster-cast Apollo with homosexual tendencies, as an effete and decadent boy with a gift for sentimentalising reality: that is what my colleagues and my students think" (4 December 1955). Skelton blamed Edward Marsh's *Memoir* of Brooke for this perception and went on to suggest that Keynes's forthcoming edition of Brooke's letters would certainly correct it. Just a month after receiving Skelton's letter, Keynes wrote to Cathleen Nesbitt: "The letters should effectively dispose of the widespread belief (particularly, I believe, in America) that Rupert was 'queer'" (14 January 1956).

Keynes was not the only friend of Brooke who had been upset by Marsh's memoir. James Strachey and many others were concerned that the book had damaged Brooke's reputation. To a large extent, Marsh presents Brooke through Brooke's own words, often by quoting from his letters. Unfortunately, when he is not quoting, Marsh is gushing. Critics also felt that Marsh's quotations from Brooke and his friends did not tell the whole story. Virginia Woolf, herself a longtime friend of Brooke, reviewed the *Memoir* anonymously for the *Times Literary Supplement*, noting that "it is evident that his friends have not cared to publish the more intimate passages in his letters to them. Inevitably, too, they have not been willing to tell the public the informal things by which they remember him best" (*TLS* 8 August 1918). She was more to the point in a letter to Brooke's friend Katherine Cox written five days after the review appeared:

> It seemed useless to pitch into Eddy [Marsh]. James [Strachey] meant to try, but gave it up. I think it was one of the most repulsive biographies I've ever read. . . . He contrived to make the letters as superficial and affected as his own account of Rupert. We're now suggesting that James should write something for us to print. He's sending us the letters to look at. (*Question* 267–8)

The letters Woolf refers to in her letter to Cox, obviously, are those Brooke had written to Strachey. It is unclear whether she ever saw them, but Strachey did approach C. K. Ogden, editor of the *Cambridge Magazine*, in July 1918 about the possibility of reviewing Marsh's *Memoir*. "I knew him better than many people," Strachey writes, "and it would give me a good deal of pleasure to try and explain what he was really like. . . . If I wrote it would be something rather scandalous." Whatever Ogden's response, Strachey did not write a review.

Years later, in 1948, Leonard Woolf addressed the problem when discussing his wife's letters with Vita Sackville-West: "The difficulty is that the really personal letters are unpublishable and it seems to me that if one publishes only the impersonal ones, one gives a totally false impression of the character. This was certainly the case with the first volume of Rupert Brooke's letters which were published" (L. Woolf, *Letters* 488).

Geoffrey Keynes called Marsh's *Memoir* "an elegantly written trifle" (*Gates* 164) and complained that

> Brooke's unmanly physical beauty was often taken as an indication that he was probably a homosexual and therefore to be despised. . . . [I]t had, of course, been far from Marsh's intention to produce any such impression. He had been deeply attached to Rupert, as he was to many young men, but lived himself in a sexual no-man's-land whose equivocal aura pervaded the memoir and contributed to the Brooke "legend." Mrs. Brooke had probably sensed this even though she might not have been able to put it into words, and was quite right to feel that the pretty sketch should never have been printed. (165)

. . . the *Memoir* never had a chance because of the constraints placed on Marsh by Mrs. Brooke. She is at least partially responsible for the two omissions David Garnett complained of in a letter to his mother:

> James—who knew him better than anyone else . . . is silent—he is mentioned once as having been on a walking tour with him—Noel [Olivier] is of course not mentioned. I am amazed at the underlying assumption of the authors.

That is: We like our boys to wear their hair rather long–to dabble in Socialism, to dabble in "decadence" . . . to fancy they really care about ethics–but all the time we know they are SOUND: SOUND TO THE CORE.

When the time comes they'll go off heroically and forget their wild oats and die in a Greek island and then we can wallow in sentiment . . . but the wild oats of Mr Marsh are really the important things in life. Rupert even though he did go to the bad some time before his death at one time cared about the important things and was able to understand them.

Strachey eventually approached a Cambridge publisher concerning the possibility of writing something–which would have included publishing some of Brooke's letters to him–to "set the record straight." His reasons for eventually abandoning the idea no doubt included the realization that the Brooke Trustees, not he, owned the rights to Brooke's half of the correspondence, and Geoffrey Keynes had made it quite clear that he would never allow publication. Strachey may have decided as well that the letters should eventually be published in their entirety, after those individuals mentioned unfavourably within them were no longer alive to be wounded by their appearance in print. The letters themselves testify, in any case, that both Brooke and Strachey, while writing them, fully expected them one day to be published.

Strachey was Brooke's best friend for longer than any other person, and of Brooke's surviving letters more were addressed to Strachey than to any correspondent other than his own mother. The letters to Strachey cannot provide a completely accurate portrait of Brooke–since he was so intent on showing different sides of himself to different people, none of his letters can. But these letters are among Brooke's most important precisely because they more than any others show the side of Brooke that his early executors tried so hard to suppress.

In reassessing Brooke's reputation as a modernist poet in "The Falling House That Never Falls: Rupert Brooke and Literary Taste," Clive Bloom discusses how the writer's reputation has suffered at the hands of the academic community (Gary Day and Brian Docherty, eds., British Poetry 1900–1950: Aspects of Tradition, *pp. 37–47).*

"Rupert Brooke's poetry remains a firm favourite with readers and listeners alike": such might be the opinion of the popular poetry radio programmes broadcast by BBC Radio 4 or, perhaps, the comments in the introduction to yet another anthology of the slim collected works (with a selection of letters added for good measure). Brooke's reputation, which is at stake here, has never rested on anything other than quicksand. The "worth" or quality of his poetic ability becomes, as has rarely been the case with any but Dylan Thomas, subordinated to a quasi-biographical determinism in which the poetry itself plays little part. It is ironic yet it can be said that the value of Brooke's reputation is independent of the very work he did to secure that reputation.

As a "firm favourite," Brooke is damned as a lower-grade Kiplingesque populist by the academic community whose fare consists of the modernists and those the modernists chose to applaud. Meanwhile Brooke is relegated to the outer corridors of fame, conversing posthumously with the likes of both Ella Wheeler Wilcox and Longfellow. In such a way, Brooke is left to those whose poetic taste is untrained except by personal predisposition and whose "love" of poetry consists of enjoying a large chunk of meaning laced with a keen disregard for free verse. Brooke's Georgianism is damned both by those who dislike it (academics) and those who applaud it ("untrained" amateurs). To like Brooke is a form of eccentricity, peculiar to the English upper middle classes, akin to that dilettantism which would prefer an elderberry wine to a vintage claret.

Having safely relegated Brooke's poetry to the realm of amateur taste, professional opinion can comfortably exist on the acceptable fare of modernism and pre- or post-modernist tendencies. This, I contend, has little to do with the merit or otherwise of particular writers, it is much more to do with the history of academic predisposition.

What might a typical poetry course look like? Most poetry courses would include Yeats and Eliot in their survey, they could then choose other rankers: Auden, Spender, MacNeice, and then, perhaps Larkin, Hughes and Heaney. At this point a loss of nerve would set in. They might have some Hardy, as a token of changes in poetic taste, but Kipling could be added only for the sake of debunking. Owen would represent war (*all* war). Plath, whose poetic abilities are not as great as claimed, would be included for the sake of form, and because she also represents a type of obligatory tokenism in British poetry courses despite being an American. Finally, new writing, where it was possible to include it, would consist of "fringe" writers, writers found outside the "canon," in order to appease students who dislike upper-middle-class-white-male-Oxbridge-educated-types and who need a dose of proletarian consciousness. The lecturer might turn gratefully to the very anthologies that inevitably prove pretty conclusively that the best poetry written in Britain in the last hundred years came from the very poets whose gender and education are now so out of fashion.

Although the canon of the literary great among novelists has been radically challenged, such a challenge to the canon of acceptable poets has not. Recent tastes masquerade as valid professional judgements, and female poets who indulge in four-letter words are acceptable primarily because the establishment (from which they come, to which they belong, and against which they intend no harm) can provide the very *fake* radical oppositional voices that half-educated students think are relevant. This amounts to a case of the emperor's new clothes. Alternative traditions and attitudes are always acceptable but not ever at the expense of the *full* and complex *real* history of poetry in this country.

Georgianism is the expression of British poetry in the twentieth century and yet modernism, with its primarily American base (Amy Lowell, H. D., Eliot, Pound and company) has taken the Georgians' place and stepped across the shadow they throw in order to obscure them. Which is simply to say that before we look for alternative new voices we must *recuperate* what has been lost and re-evaluate its relevance. This is *not* a question of the quality of the poetry produced—such is not the point. What is at stake is the very idea of poetry as having a real lived material history which one must explore. The names on such a "lost" list are Housman, Brooke, de la Mare, Masefield, Graves, Hughes, Thomas (Edward and Dylan) and many others. The influence extends through much of the poetry of the First World War and that of the Second World War as well as to Larkin and the so-called postmodernism attributed to those anthologised in the *Penguin Book of Contemporary Verse* edited by Blake Morrison and Andrew Motion in 1982.

Let me repeat, this is not a question of the quality of the works produced but a simple form of justice to poetic history and its grounding in material history. The work of feminist publishing houses has recuperated much of the "lost" in women's writing and this we must do for poetry. Most of the poets I have listed have never been out of print, so the books are readily available; what is missing is the breaking out from methods of constructing poetic histories which circle around T. S. Eliot, however massive his influence. The other still voice in the poetic history of Britain in the modern age is the voice exemplified in Brooke. And this voice, as we shall see, has much more in common with the modernism of Eliot than is usually accepted by those only concerned with Brooke's association with the Georgian anthologies. The equation lacks its constituent parts, for the work of Ezra Pound and T. S. Eliot must be seen in conjunction, in Britain, with the work of Rupert Brooke and Edward Marsh. Such was the complex parallelism of influence that lead to the "English" modernism of Virginia Woolf and the horticultural design interests of her friend Vita Sackville-West. Indeed, hostility to Georgianism did not come from the major modernists, however much they wished to carve out a path for themselves. What existed was rather, on the one hand a techno-futuristic modernism whose interests were urban and functional, and on the other a ruralist modernism whose interests were countrified and decorative. The two strands were *not* incompatible in modernism's heyday but have been pronounced incompatible only retrospectively. The latter type of Georgianism has become out of fashion, stranded in a Laura Ashley whimsicality, whereas the former has gained strength as the *only* form of modernism acceptable.

What must be said is that Brooke's poetry, more than much of that of his contemporaries, *is* modern in the terms of either of these two types of modernistic approach. Why then does Brooke exist only as a "reputation" and as a marker and yet Eliot exist as a full-blown poet whose work is studied?

Before looking for an answer to the question just set, we must pause to answer a real problem in literary history. If we are to recuperate historical writers who are rarely read, at what point do we stop? The ideological inconsistency of the canon of fiction as the Leavises (husband and wife) constructed it was undermined by those whose egalitarianism mistook popular for better. If the canon was to be taught, then so were Agatha Christie, Dorothy L. Sayers, Baroness Orczy and Mills and Boon. This, all in the name of relevance. Relevance to what? If to an idea of quality, then the list just given hardly dents even the shadow of the Leavises' Desert Island selection. If relevant only to history, then the questions posed by art and the formal conditions governing aesthetics would of necessity collapse. What happened was that the barriers did collapse and everything became acceptable, for the discovery of Kate Chopin or Alice Walker we have paid with the study of such dross as feminist science fiction and lesbian detective tales.

And yet this was not a real emancipation of lost, forgotten or half-remembered relevant texts, but a partial recuperation of what is now actually only fashionable but which disguises that fashionableness with an appeal to an unwritten agenda that suggests some texts are higher than others on the "worthiness" scale. Any real recuperation, however, must also include the *unacceptable*, that which is racist, sexist, imperialist, ageist, rightist and elitist, and this is a hard pill to swallow. We long ago learned to turn away from the anti-semitic, misogynistic and religious T. S. Eliot in order to understand both his contribution to culture's understanding of itself (alienation) and his contribution to literary form (style). In some ways we have stripped Eliot of content in order to salvage his achievement.

It is the very opposite with Brooke–if only he'd not written those war sonnets! Brooke's contribution to formal practice (style) is relegated to a secondary position whilst stripped from a content highlighted for its naivety and gross nationalist romance. In Eliot's case we recuperate his verse and in Brooke's damn it with a classic double standard.

Let me pull some arguments together after this long digression, before returning to the question of Brooke's position in literary history. First, "academics" (except in a form of tokenism) have not found an alternative poetic tradition to the one usually offered in courses. However, within those courses a radical suppression has occurred that has distorted poetic history by an act of omission. In general literary courses the idea of the canon has only been undermined by an inclusiveness so wide as to be meaningless. Hence two things have been lost: the first is a sense of what art is and what it does. These are formal questions reserved for the realm of aesthetic analysis. The second is a sense of real history at work in the formal properties of the text and from which the text emerges as a type of *dialogue* with its culture. By widening choice in courses, the Leavises are not answered on any of their points (however right or wrong), they are merely *overrun*. By avoiding the forces of real historical process, the questions proper to the study of art (its discipline) do not even get approached. Brooke is a particular victim.

One must acknowledge that the forces that allowed Brooke to become a brilliant and urbane stylist (his class background, education, expectations etc.) also made much of what he said difficult to swallow. What too many people do is chuck out the baby with the bathwater: we must have the poet as a totality if he is to be seen and understood as a poet *qua* poet and if his poetry is to have any independent value.

People rarely die on cue. Brooke's glory and his tragedy is that he died "on cue" in 1915. Unlike Owen (a poet technically of a lesser stature but able to put into words the horror of the war), Brooke's "final" words were patriotic and, apparently jingoistic. Owen's hatred of war quite correctly gained the limelight once the war had finished but, in doing so, distorted the importance of Brooke's artistic (formal) achievement, which was "suppressed" in favour of works whose content spoke of suffering banality.

Once dead, Brooke as the golden boy became the mythic tool of those who need heroes and hero worship. Brooke stood for an attitude which canonised him, his generation and his era and at the same time delivered his poetry over to non-professional advocacy. Parallel with the canonisation of Brooke by imperialist conservatives such as Winston Churchill, was the suppression of Brooke by the rising oppositional forces within Cambridge academics.

It was now indeed that in Cambridge, modern English literature made its appearance as an object of study for those released from the rigours of war and disillusioned by establishment (classical?) values. I. A. Richards's *Principles of Literary Criticism* became the standard text for what one did when studying literature. Such study was required to be seen to be impersonal and scientific and rigorous: as a former psychologist, Richards saw literature as a branch of communication and the study of literature as a branch of communication study (a behavioural process originating in neurology). This whole pseudoscientific procedure was needed to give the fledgling study of modern literature a real base, but its origin lay not in the human sciences such as psychology or sociology but actually in T. S. Eliot's essay "Tradition and the Individual Talent." This aesthetic base was predicated on the idea of impersonality and of art as a cultural artefact. Richards's work is deeply indebted to Eliot's functionalist approach, which, whatever else it did, would, through the pedagogy of Richards, force all poetry to conform to modernist canons of taste. Richards's version of scientific enquiry was ultimately a procedure based on an aesthetic of modernist taste. In such a process the romantic personality cult of Brooke could only fare badly at the hands of the professionals.

At the same time, the "*Scrutiny* Group" around F. R. and Q. D. Leavis were in an embattled position not only against the establishment in Cambridge but also against the philistines of "Golders Green" (see Eliot's "A Cooking Egg"). Although they were not interested in Brooke *per se,* his reputation does badly under the attacks on the reading habits of Cambridge dons (an attack led by Queenie Leavis). Donnish taste, it seems, was in the same lamentable condition as that of the philistine public. Brooke, it turned out, was liked by both readerships. In Q. D. Leavis's "The Case of Miss Dorothy Sayers" she trounces Sayers and those academics whose lack of judgement supports the latter's way of writing. In the essay, Leavis identifies those shelves kept for show in a don's house and those where the books are actually read and enjoyed. On *these shelves* all that is second-rate and "easy" is collected, including the work of Brooke. . . .

While Leavis and his wife acted as the opposition to Richards, Richards actually saw himself as a force for radical change in the gentleman's club of Cambridge. Of course, *both* Richards and the Leavis group felt themselves to be outside the establishment of Cambridge. How implicated in the establishment appeared

Allied troops at Steele's Post, Gallipoli, 3 May 1915 (Jay Winter and Blaine Baggett, The Great War and the Shaping of the 20th Century *[New York: Penguin, 1996])*

Brooke and how loved by uninformed opinion! For Richards, whose work relied on Eliot's aesthetics, Brooke was outside the pale, because he was apparently an unregenerated romantic whose work did not conform to the aesthetic paradigm (clinically exact) of T. S. Eliot. For F. R. Leavis and his wife, Brooke's work belonged to those who *think* they are educated but who fail the acid test of culture (as defined by them and based firmly in the aesthetic of Eliot's seminal essay).

In such a way, and devoid of professional advocacy, Brooke's work fell foul of the very academic prejudice needed to launch modern literary studies in the first place. A preeminent modern writer, Brooke became a nowhere figure stranded helplessly at ten to three one sunny afternoon in Grantchester in 1912. For generations of English students modernism *was* English literature and T. S. Eliot was English poetry. Indeed, somehow one couldn't even study Brooke "objectively" for his very emotionalism got in the way of the intellectual force of the argument; T. S. Eliot had convinced academics to convince themselves that poetry was a branch of philosophy or politics or theology.

The attack on the establishment by Richards and Leavis was doubly compounded when the New Left alliance in the 1960s and 1970s attacked Richards and Leavis themselves for being the voice of conservatism. In this attack, Brooke, imperialism, conservatism, liberal-humanist consensus were all crudely lumped together.

Those who supported Leavis were branded "Leavisites," and the discipline of English letters as it had existed from 1917 to the mid-seventies began to fall apart. In this, Brooke became a casualty yet again–this time through association with perceptions about Leavis's conservatism–that very conservatism that had attacked Brooke years before!

On the Left, another story emerged. For the Left, a proper Marxist aesthetic has always been a problem, and an answer that allows for art has never really been successful. While historical materialism very adequately answers questions of cultural production and reception, it has no proper answer to questions about "quality," "value," and "importance." In a very basic sense, for Marxism, because all literature reveals the contradictions in social forces, the very best literature simply papers over the contradictions with greater skill. To such a Marxist view, the one levelled at Brooke, the work of art is always *faulty,* its perfection a deceptive bourgeois device to hide the contradictory tensions latent in society. In this view all art is *failure*. To Leavisite humanism the Brookian poetic is a failure because it says nothing true about the eternality of human values, whereas to the Marxist it is a failure because it says too much. On one count Brooke fails the quality test, on the other the test of being too obviously historical: a product of an imperialist elitist establishment. Curiously, the Leavis approach is the "properly" formal examination as the Marxist would have to invoke outside criteria and then apply a *moral* caveat.

Thus has Brooke's reputation fared in scholarly debate–our loss of nerve over the empire and over our role in the world contributed to a worried condemnation of Brooke as representative of all we wished *not* to remember in the last hundred or so years.

For poets this was otherwise. By the 1940s modernism had lost its hold in Britain, Eliot was discredited because of his return to the church, Auden had scurried off to the United States when war broke out, Pound was in Fascist Italy, Yeats was dead. British poets, under the pressure of the War (and later Suez, with the introspective period that followed), rediscovered the Georgianism "lost" previously. Yet the Georgianism they discovered was not that of Brooke but rather an emotionalised romantic ruralist poetry that appealed to "ordinary folk" and which avoided the harsh, cynical and urbane note struck by Brooke. Rather than Brooke, we get a version of the world by a latter-day Edward Thomas or W. H. Davies.

The "parochiality" actively sought by Larkin or the later Liverpool poets is quite against the grain of a parochial/lyrical content in Brooke, which is always at a distance from the metropolitan-international voice he employs. Quite simply, Brooke has more in common with T. S. Eliot than with Larkin and has more the tone of e. e. cummings or Noel Coward than that of Dylan Thomas.

> It's the very first word that poor Juliet heard
>   From her Romeo, over the Styx;
> And the Roman will tell Cleopatra in hell
>   When she starts her immortal old tricks;
> What Paris was tellin' for goodbye to Helen
>   When he bundled her into the train–
> Oh, it's not going to happen again, old girl,
>   It's not going to happen again.
>   ("It's not going to Happen Again")

Georgianism is not a movement, despite any argument to the contrary–rather it describes another current in the modern movement sometimes parallel to and sometimes intermixed with imagism, vorticism and futurism. Despite the fact that many see Georgia poetry as a tag-end Victorianism, it is (again, despite its adherence to rhyme, metre and traditional content) a full branch of *modern* poetry. Note here, indeed, how Eliot himself adheres to strict metres and traditional rhyme.

If the tag "Georgian" is dropped for a moment, then Brooke emerges as a modern writer with the concerns, both aesthetic and historical, of those who are known as modernists. His work is at once dextrous, urbane, metropolitan, "free," distanced and ironic; his subject matter, modern life and experience. As a modern, his work also reveals the prejudice and posturing of that group of people at that time, and this cannot be ignored.

I do not intend in this essay to explore the importance of Brooke to the British version of the modernist movement or to attempt to prove in detail the relationship between modernist theory and Brooke's techniques. It must suffice that Brooke needs to be read with the same critical apparatus as T. S. Eliot and judged accordingly. Here, I reiterate that the question of quality is a separate issue and that I am only concerned to show that if a certain procedure is followed then Eliot and Brooke emerge as stablemates.

As a modernist, Brooke's best work compares more than favourably with that of Ezra Pound, and his work with Edward Marsh is every bit as distinguished as Pound's achievement with *Poetry*. What Brooke adds is a dimension rarely present in the functionalist performances of the imagists. In "Grantchester" (whose influence in terms of "tone" on "The Waste Land" is rarely acknowledged) Brooke proves himself both a highly serious modernist and a Hogarthian humourist. His wit is founded on an attitude both distanced and yet comfortable. Brooke is both alienated and dispossessed, yet the seriousness of the meditation is only possible via the satiric panorama he puts before us.

Humour is a rarity in the modernist movement yet it goes with the urbane and sophisticated tone we expect of some aspects of modernism: those of Noel Coward, P. G. Wodehouse, Irving Berlin or Cole Porter. "Grantchester" is, in this sense, a supremely cool and controlled poem, with its roots in Alexander Pope rather than Wordsworth and with its message drawn from money, continental travel and speed. At every point that "Grantchester" has a Browningesque nostalgia it is undercut by a satiric distaste for the object of that nostalgia. Parochial in its subject matter yet international in its style, "Grantchester" is the "other" of "The Waste Land" and should be read by the discerning as a prefiguring and a commentary on Eliot's work. Brooke's work is almost the epic of the English character, both comic and yet, because comic, also true.

Brooke's achievement in the war sonnets, "1914 Sonnets I–V," is to provide a language the totality of which transcends its literal meaning. His phrasing displays a control of language which does not allow the musicality of that phrasing to be reduced to the banal jingoism of passions which hardly can have been felt by Brooke! Eliot "proved" that sincerity was an unnecessary criterion in poetic appreciation. Whilst Brooke's message appears "hot" and sincere, his control is as cool as a modernist's martini. The clean lines of the functional swimmer predominate. If we are embarrassed by nationalism we need not be embarrassed by the skill of the maker.

This might be special pleading on behalf of Brooke, but the message of modernism is the message of internal coherence. Purpose (moral integrity) had been replaced by organisation (aesthetic integrity), and the sonnets measure up to this criterion. The *skill* of the artist must be seen as integral to the message and the message as integral to the aesthetic (poetic) strategy of the poet in his culture. In such a way, Brooke can be seen as working complex emotional issues through a control of literary technical skills against which the overt antiwar messages of Owen appear dull and repetitive.

Brooke's oeuvre is slight, his reputation problematic, his future doubtful, yet despite all this it is necessary that he take his place as an important writer, whose main contributions to the history of British poetry, though slim, are probably the equal of the best of Eliot or Yeats and whose work demands to be read through the criteria of modernism and not relegated to the trashcan marked "Georgian."

For its part, Georgianism, which Brooke did so much to aid, is to be seen as a type of modernism rather than an outworn, outmoded, Victorianism finally defeated by the harsh *reality* of war.

I have described how Brooke's reputation has been caught between the rock of professional enquiry and the hard place of amateur enthusiasm. It may be that, as I suspect, Brooke's world was irrecoverably lost and will always be irrecoverably lost somewhere in our own "Edwardian" mental space, and the half-life he suffers will continue much as before. But in a world intent on recuperating the lost to challenge the accepted, it is time we revisited the half-forgotten not merely for the sake of the historical record but also because we must, in the end, care about the value of art. In both these areas, Brooke deserves more than just a passing mention.

Isaac Rosenberg

(25 November 1890 – 1 April 1918)

See also the Rosenberg entry in *DLB 20: British Poets, 1914-1945.*

BOOKS:
Night and Day (London: Narodiczky, 1912);
Youth (London: Narodiczky, 1915);
Moses: A Play (London: Paragon, 1916);
Poems, edited by Gordon Bottomley (London: Heinemann, 1922);
The Collected Works of Isaac Rosenberg: Poetry, Prose, Letters and Some Drawings, edited by Bottomley and Denys Harding (London: Chatto & Windus, 1937);
Collected Poems, edited by Bottomley and Harding (London: Chatto & Windus, 1949; New York: Schocken, 1949);
The Collected Works of Isaac Rosenberg: Poetry, Prose, Letters, Paintings, and Drawings, edited by Ian Parsons (London: Chatto & Windus, 1979; New York: Oxford University Press, 1979).

CATALOGUES:
Isaac Rosenberg, 1890-1918: A Catalogue of an Exhibition Held at Leeds University, May-June 1959, Together with the Text of Unpublished Material, edited by Jon Silken and Maurice de Sausmarez (Leeds, West Yorkshire, U.K.: University of Leeds & Partridge Press, 1959);
Isaac Rosenberg, 1890-1918: A Poet and Painter of the First World War; Catalogue of an Exhibition at the National Book League (London: National Book League, 1975).

BIOGRAPHICAL STUDIES:
Joseph Cohen, *Journey to the Trenches: The Life of Isaac Rosenberg, 1890-1918* (London: Robson, 1975; New York: Basic, 1975);
Jean Lilliard, *Isaac Rosenberg: The Half Used Life* (London: Gollancz, 1975);
Charles Tomlinson, *Isaac Rosenberg of Bristol* (Bristol, U.K.: Bristol Branch of the Historical Association, 1982);

Jean Moorcroft Wilson, *Isaac Rosenberg: Poet and Painter* (London: Cecil Woolf, 1975).

CRITICAL STUDIES:
Bernard Bergonzi, *Heroes' Twilight: A Study of the Literature of The Great War,* third edition (Manchester, U.K.: Carcanet, 1996);
Paul Fussell, *The Great War and Modern Memory* (New York & London: Oxford University Press, 1975);
Desmond Graham, *The Truth of War: Owen, Blunden, Rosenberg* (Manchester, U.K.: Carcanet, 1984);
John H. Johnstone, *English Poetry of the First World War* (Princeton: Princeton University Press, 1965).

ARCHIVES:
Isaac Rosenberg materials are held in the Berg Collection at the New York Public Library, New York; the Department of Manuscripts at the British Library, London; the Eton School Library, Eton; and the Imperial War Museum, London.

Discussion of Rosenberg's early family life in Bristol, the years in which poverty shaped what became his artistic vision (Charles Tomlinson, Isaac Rosenberg of Bristol*)*

Isaac Rosenberg of Bristol. To say that now is to arouse less surprise than it would have done a few years ago. When, in 1960, D. S. R. Welland wrote a book on Rosenberg's more famous contemporary Wilfred Owen, he mentioned Rosenberg en passant but had him transplanted to London, as though that were the place for a writer to be born. Despite the so-called *Complete Works* of 1937, published the better part of twenty years after Rosenberg's death, and despite a *Collected Poems* of 1949, this Jewish poet-painter was slow to attract widespread critical attention, let alone that sort of popular acknowledgement which ensured repeated printings of the poetry of Owen.

Within specialist circles he was, of course, being written about. Then suddenly and unexpectedly in

Isaac Rosenberg was born to Lithuanian immigrants Barnard and Anna Davidov Rosenberg in Bristol on 25 November 1890. He was their second child, their firstborn son.

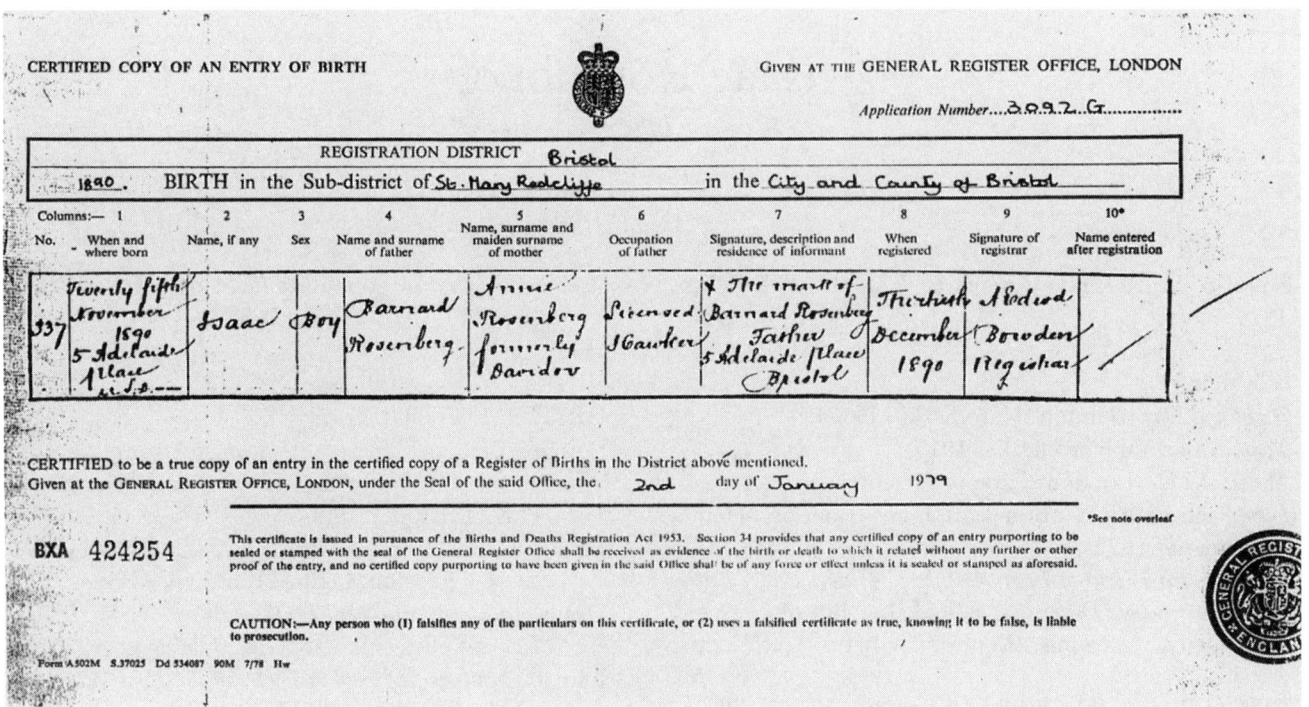

Isaac Rosenberg's birth certificate, 1890, designating his father's occupation as a "licensed hawker" (Isaac Rosenberg Estate)

Rosenberg as a baby with his parents, Barnard and Anna, and his sister Minnie in 1891 (Isaac Rosenberg Estate)

When Rosenberg was seven, his parents and their five children moved to Stepney in London. Barnard Rosenberg was an itinerant peddler, and the impoverished family was aided by various Jewish charitable organizations and the local Jewish community. According to Rosenberg's biographers, the deprivation that the poet experienced in his early life contributed to his artistic outlook and to his fragile health, which included a lung ailment that developed after the move to London.

Rosenberg as a young boy with his siblings (Isaac Rosenberg Estate)

1975 appeared—not one, but three biographies of our poet. These are very informative books and Joseph Cohen's *Journey to the Trenches* is perhaps the best of them. It brought forth, in the pages of *The Times Literary Supplement,* the following pithy letter from one of our poets:

> Sir,— Joseph Cohen calls the marriage of Isaac Rosenberg's parents "disastrous." But it produced Isaac Rosenberg.
>
> C. H. Sisson.

In all these biographies Bristol is still giving trouble, in so far as none of the three writers seems to know the city very intimately, and all of them offer a different place of birth. Cohen has young Rosenberg see the light of day at 5 Victoria Square, Jean Moorcroft Wilson chooses Adelaide Place but is coy about the number, Jean Liddiard says 5 Adelaide Road. The truth of the matter seems to be that on November 25, 1890, Isaac Rosenberg was born at 5 Adelaide Place near St. Mary Redcliffe. You will not find the house today. In an as yet unpublished article, Dr. Diana Collecott, a graduate of our university, tells us of the area that only the Nelson Arms pub on Clarence Road survives after successive extensions of Mardon and Hall's printing works, bombs and council redevelopment. A plaque affixed to Mardon's wall would now offer a welcome, if long over-due, tribute to Rosenberg's memory there.

Before glancing briefly at his life and in more detail at his poetry, . . . a final bibliographical fact needs to be noted. In 1979 Ian Parsons, shortly before he died, finished editing for Chatto and Windus the definitive *Collected Works of Isaac Rosenberg,* a splendid compilation which gives us not only poems, essays and letters, but reproduces all the extant paintings and drawings of Rosenberg, and very fine they are. . . .

Isaac Rosenberg's father, Barnett, a Lithuanian Jew, had fled from Russia to avoid military service. He arrived in England in either 1887 or 1888, and was joined—in Bristol—by his wife and their first child, a baby daughter. Some nine years later, with an increasing family, they moved to London. Ian Parsons sums up this phase compactly. . . . "They found," he says, "a refuge in England from persecution, but not from poverty. What saved them and is an abiding testimony to the generosity of their co-religionists, was the practical help which they received from the charitable organisations set up by their predecessors in the flight from oppression, some of whom, by their gifts and their industry, had become affluent citizens. Barnett Rosenberg tried his hand at all sorts of jobs, unsuccessfully, and ended up as an itinerant pedlar, earning very little. His wife took in washing and did needlework for neighbours, in order to keep the family going. But in those early London days, and for many years to come, poverty bordering on destitution was their lot. This needs to be said, for poverty was a basic ingredient of Rosenberg's childhood and youth, and it not only helped to mould his character but influenced his whole life, and more especially his development as a creative artist."

There is a passage in the letters of the great modern German poet, Rainer Maria Rilke, which takes us to the heart of Rosenberg's concern as a writer–namely how to make meaningful a life that, on the surface, seems only one of privation, discord and disaster. Rilke is writing at a point in his own life when his deepest sufferings have released some of his greatest poetry, and this is what he says: "Nobody's position in the world is such that it might not come to be of particular benefit to his soul.... And I must confess that, whenever I have been compelled to share in the destiny of another, what, above all, seemed to me important and urgent was this: to help the afflicted person to recognise the peculiar and special conditions of his distress–an act which, every time, is not so much one of consolation as of ... enrichment." This is surely a salutary sentiment for us in the midst of comfortable moanings, self-pityings and imaginary ills–and, indeed, in the midst of real ills, ills that refuse simply to go away. For these are "the peculiar and special conditions of our distress" (as Rilke puts it), that refuse to be tranquillised and so robbed of meaning and real content.

This is where the poetry of Rosenberg is so nutrifying, and where it is so different from the war poetry of Wilfred Owen. Owen's poetry seems to be saying to us, "This ought never to have happened," whereas Rosenberg's is a poetry which attempts to realise new potentiality in life by saying: "This *is* and I accept the fact." There comes to mind his most famous letter: "I will not leave a corner of my consciousness covered up, but saturate myself with the strange and extraordinary new conditions of this life [in the war]," and: "I believe however hard one's lot is one ought to try and accommodate oneself to the conditions; and except in a case of purely physical pain, I think it can be done.... I endeavour to waste nothing."

Rosenberg's endeavour arises directly, then, out of having been born in poverty to a Bristol Jewish family. He was one of six children. After living in two other nearby slum-dwellings (in Victoria Square, Temple, and in Harford Street, Cathay), the family moves when he is seven to the East End of London where hardships are still unremitting. "You mustn't forget," he says to one of his correspondents, "the circumstances I have been brought up in, the little education I have had. Nobody ever told me what to read, or ever put poetry in my way." At fourteen, in 1904, he is taken from school and apprenticed to an engraving firm. He goes, in 1907, to evening art classes and in 1911 actually finds patrons to send him to the Slade School of Art. Quarrels with one of these patrons ensue; neither poetry nor painting brings any material gain; in 1914 he is thought to be suffering from tuberculosis and the Jewish Educational Aid Society pays his passage to South Africa where he stays with his sister Minnie. The period in South Africa ends and he is shortly afterwards in the army and, before long, in action, having joined up in order to acquire an allowance for his mother. Ian Parsons puts the matter succinctly, thus: "At the end of October 1915 he went to Whitehall and joined up, being posted immediately to Bury St. Edmunds, where, because he was such a very small, slight man he was drafted into the so-called "Bantam" battalion of the Suffolk Regiment. Thereafter he was increasingly deprived of the opportunity and the wherewithal to paint, and once he had crossed to France at the beginning of June 1916, they ceased altogether." But "I endeavour to waste nothing," he had written, and his attention now turns wholeheartedly to poetry.

We catch in his earliest letters a hint of that harmony which may be won even in the hardest circumstances. The hint comes in his mention of music–a theme the poems increasingly pursue. "To most people life is a musical instrument," he writes, "on which they are unable to play, but in the musician's hands it becomes a living thing." And again, confessing that he hasn't had the opportunity to know anything about music: "Once I heard Schubert's Unfinished Symphony at the band; and—well, I was in heaven ... it was articulate feeling. The inexpressible in poetry, in painting, was there expressed." This notion of music as "articulate feeling" and life as an instrument that one learns to play, was to be worked out in the poems, worked out in confronting a life that was apparently mostly discord and was to end in early death at the age of 28. The problem was, on what terms could this life be accepted and rendered meaningful? "It is all experience," he writes in 1911, "but, good God! it is *all* experience and nothing else." One is reminded of Keats' letters and of his memorable phrase about life as "a continual struggle against the suffocation of accidents."

The history of Rosenberg's struggle goes back to his first long poem, *Night and Day* of 1912, written when Rosenberg, having experienced years of poverty, was coming to recognise "the peculiar and special conditions of his distress," to recur to Rilke's phrase. What *Night and Day* deals with–very immaturely as yet, and with echoes of Swinburne, Rossetti, *Omar Khayyám,* the Bible–is the unconditional acceptance of fate. One of the outcomes of this acceptance, once it is achieved, appears in what Rosenberg represents in his work by the symbol of music. Music seems to stand in Rosenberg's poetry for a kind of attitude of mind which can hear, as it were, the true melody of its own being and to which it had previously been deaf because insufficiently alive. This hearing of unearthly music occurs where the conditions of one's fate are fully responded to, and it is associated with a new access of inner power–the kind of power that in the play *Moses,* of 1916, is necessary to release the Jews from their spiritual bondage in Egypt. So Rosenberg's acceptance of fate isn't merely a passive thing, a lying down to be walked over, or a stoical pose: it is the condition that makes lived life possible and that gives it its unpremeditated music.

About *Night and Day* of 1912 and the remarkable volume *Youth* of 1915, I shall be brief, since these predate the maturer poetry of *Moses* (1916) and the subsequent "Trench Poems," as an earlier edition entitled the war poetry. What's striking about both *Night and Day* and *Youth* is the way they go straight to the centre of Rosenberg's mature interests. *Youth* he so structured as to build up to and end with an impressive poem, "God Made Blind," where fate and what may be won from fate is the abiding question. *Night and Day* had already explored (uncouthly as yet) the symbol of music, as the poet, watched by the stars—"the steadfast eyes of fate," Rosenberg calls them—labours for insight and the insights come in the form of music, in four songs which are the four climaxes of the poem. This prentice work shows in embryo the dual nature of Rosenberg's attitude—acceptance, yet advance—a discovery of the real dimension of life through acceptance, a discovery of what he calls here "the strange wine / Of some large knowledge." Then at the very end of *Night and Day* the silence of the stars is broken, and the poem closes with a token of this "large knowledge"—the song of the evening star.

Let us . . . look ahead to poems of 1915–16, where fate and music recur and where we are made to experience, side by side with the need for acceptance, the pain of fate and the fear of wasted potentiality. Take "First Fruit":

> I did not pluck at all,
> And I am sorry now.
> The garden is not barred,
> But the boughs are heavy with snow,
> The flake-blossoms thickly fall,
> And the hid roots sigh, "How long will our flowers be marred?"
>
> Strange as a bird were dumb,
> Strange as a hueless leaf.
> As one deaf hungers to hear
> Or gazes without belief,
> The fruit yearned "fingers, come."
> O, shut hands, be empty another year.

"I did not pluck at all": life had offered fruit and they hadn't been noticed, hadn't been accepted. This is a poem of unrealised potentiality, a potentiality that now can only be waited for and seized upon when and if it is offered again. It is by way of being a self-reproach—"I did not pluck at all": failure to be alive to the present hour had impoverished that hour. The life we don't live is impoverished life:

> Strange as a bird were dumb,
> Strange as a hueless leaf.
> As one deaf hungers to hear.

That verb *hear* is the recurrent verb in Rosenberg. At the end of *Night and Day* he *hears* the evening star; in *Moses* music makes itself *heard* as Moses embraces his destiny, and Rosenberg's use of the verb "to hear" reinforces that sense we get in his work of a dimension we are likely to miss in life because we are deaf to the undertones of reality. Moses lives in fear of uncreative silence, of "Virgin silences waiting a breaking voice." In an earlier poem, "A Girl's Thoughts," a girl resists her fate, clings regressively to her simpler, known self which, as she says, "strives to shut out what it hears, / The founts of being, murmuring." These variations on the verb "to hear" provide Rosenberg with a highly suggestive gamut of expression, covering the symbolic possibilities from the sudden impingement of sounds unnoticed to the full harmonic utterance of music. What he does with this gamut I hope to make clear in looking at Rosenberg's pervasive theme of destiny.

A poem from the fragments of *Moses,* called "Chagrin," communicates the naked feeling of what it means to be fated. It does so by the use of the image of Absalom, David's son, caught by his hair in the branches of a tree. This condition of being so caught seems to apply to the whole universe, to that of matter and that of thought. This existential fact is contemplated in all its fearfulness and at the moment of release at the end of the poem, when for a time we seem freed, suddenly we are caught back onto the boughs:

> CHAGRIN
> Caught still as Absalom,
> Surely the air hangs
> From the swayless cloud-boughs,
> Like hair of Absalom
> Caught and hanging still.
>
> From the imagined weight
> Of spaces in a sky
> Of mute chagrin, my thoughts
> Hang like branch-clung hair
> To trunks of silence swung,
> With the choked soul weighing down
> Into thick emptiness.
> Christ! end this hanging death,
> For endlessness hangs therefrom.
>
> Invisibly—branches break
> From invisible trees—
> The cloud-woods where we rush,
> Our eyes holding so much,
> Which we must ride dim ages round
> Ere the hands (we dream) can touch,
> We ride, we ride, before the morning

> The secret roots of the sun to tread,
> And suddenly
> We are lifted of all we know
> And hang from implacable boughs.

When the *Moses* volume appeared, Rosenberg had been in the army a year, exchanging a period of respite from poverty and near poverty–the period spent in South Africa–for the horrors of the Western front:

> We ride, we ride, before the morning
> The secret roots of the sun to tread,
> And suddenly
> We are lifted of all we know
> And hang from implacable boughs.

But there was something else beside the implacable boughs for Rosenberg and that was those "secret roots of the sun." (These roots of the sun, by the way, though spelt like tree-roots, seem to be a pun on the other sort of route.) If "to hear" is his most significant verb, the word "root" is the noun we find repeatedly throughout his poems. The phrase in "Chagrin" "the secret roots of the sun" is already a quotation from an earlier poem called "At Night," and it's to reappear yet again, this phrase, in different guises–first of all in *Moses* when Moses is talking about the static, priest-ridden world of ancient Egypt and opposes to it his own sense of a wider destiny:

> I have a trouble in my mind for largeness,
> Rough-hearted, shaggy, which your grave ardours lack.
> Here is the quarry quiet for me to hew,
> Here are the springs, primeval elements,
> The roots' hid secrecy, old source of race,
> Unreasoned reason of the savage instinct.

Moses' aim is to put the Jews back into contact with "the roots' hid secrecy" and to bring them wider possibilities for life by breaking out of the civic mould of the Egyptians in which their potentialities have hardened. He realises that to do so is to release the "Unreasoned reason of the savage instinct," and that this primal root energy is necessary but that in itself it is insufficient; and Rosenberg defines the insufficiency by placing side by side with the image of the *root* the image of *music:* Moses goes on,

> I'd shape one impulse thro' the contraries
> Of vain ambitious men, selfish and callous,
> And frail life drifters, reticent, delicate.
> Litheness thread bulk; a nation's harmony.

The music image–"a nation's harmony"–is defined and consolidated further as, still speaking of the Jewish slaves, Moses draws towards the conclusion of his speech:

> These are not lame, nor bent awry, but placeless
> With the rust and stagnant. All that's low I'll charm;
> Barbaric love sweeten to tenderness.
> Cunning run into wisdom, craft turn to skill.
> Their meanness threaded right and sensibly
> Change to a prudence, envied and not sneered.
> Their hugeness be a driving wedge to a thing,
> Ineffable and useable, as near
> Solidity as human life can be.
> So grandly fashion these rude elements
> Into some newer nature, a consciousness
> Like naked light seizing the all-eyed soul . . .

The passage grows out of that primitive "Unreasoned reason of the savage instinct" to an image of full consciousness: "the all-eyed soul." Its craggy plunging energy mimes this growth as it moves from term to term. Each term in the passage, that is "rough . . . new, and will have no tailor" (to quote Rosenberg)–namely bulk, barbaric love, hugeness–all these are poised against a humanising, subtilizing counterpart, against litheness and tenderness. Similarly, the fallen elements of the Jewish slaves–cunning, craft, meanness–are juxtaposed by wisdom, skill, prudence. The terms balance out into the word *solidity* near the close with its sense of physical rootedness, combining with the spiritual insight of "a consciousness / Like naked light seizing the all-eyed soul."

This conception of ordered human potentialities, coming at the play's climax, is focused upon the significance of partaking of a meaningful destiny by the act of choice. Moses chooses to break with the static, destinyless Egyptian world of priests and forms. He must move forward to the unknown and the unlived, though the play itself ends in his arrest and on the words "or die." Behind the play, of course, are the tensions and fears of Rosenberg's own existence–"I endeavour to waste nothing." He, too, like Moses, had "a trouble in [his] mind for largeness," and one notes in the letters his impatience with the constricted form-bound world of contemporary England and its material certainties. Its mental horizons were represented by Horatio Bottomley's popular magazine, *John Bull,* and the campaign waged there in mock puritan horror to secure the banning of D. H. Lawrence's novel, *The Rainbow*–is this the kind of book you would have your daughters read?

At first Rosenberg had seen the war as a welcome end to that narrow world of British commercialism whose spirit he recognised in the Cape Town of 1914, the passageways to the souls of its inhabitants "dreadfully clogged up" as he wrote–"gold dust, diamond dust, stocks and shares, and heaven knows what other flinty muck." Rosenberg shared with so many others of his generation their contempt for British mercantilism, and he shared with them, too, the apocalyptic sense that

English civilisation, like other civilisations that had failed and disappeared, was now doomed to extinction. He broods on the spiritual somnolence of England in "A worm fed on the heart of Corinth":

> A worm fed on the heart of Corinth,
> Babylon and Rome:
> Not Paris raped tall Helen,
> But this incestuous worm,
> Who lured her vivid beauty
> To his amorphous sleep.
> England! famous as Helen
> Is thy betrothal sung
> To him the shadowless,
> More amorous than Solomon.

Would the war, perhaps, renovate England with its cleansing fire? Might it not sweep clean the human mind of dead forms, might its demands not restore to men spiritual energies they had ignored? In his poetry he asked of the "crimson curse" of war to "Give back this universe / Its pristine bloom." This romantic hopefulness, like Rainer Maria Rilke's hopefulness when he (on the other side) wrote his five hymns to the war, was not lasting, but it didn't turn to its usual alternative, romantic despair, or to Owen's pity or Lawrence's angry rejection. War, like the destiny of Moses in Egypt, meant for Rosenberg the necessity of exposing more of himself, of living and growing with tragic awareness. He tried to see in war, as one of his earliest critics, D. W. Harding, has said, "a significance for life as such, rather than seeing only its convulsion of the human life he knew." He tried, in his poetry, Harding goes on, to define "the living effort called forth by war." In short, this is the discipline that Rilke speaks of—the need to "recognize the peculiar and special conditions of [one's] distress" by the refusal to simplify these in one's consciousness. In the letters the result is the astonishing impersonality of Rosenberg's descriptions of his own sufferings in the trenches. In the poems he ranges from humane detachment through stark realism to heroic acceptance....

His sense of "shrieking iron and flame / Hurled through still heavens" is intensified in "Dead Man's Dump," his most extended war poem, where he comes closest to Owen....

> The wheels lurched over sprawled dead
> But pained them not, though their bones crunched,
> Their shut mouths made no moan.
> They lie there huddled, friend and foeman,
> Man born of man, and born of woman,
> And shells go crying over them
> From night till night and now.
>
> . . . .
>
> What fierce imaginings their dark souls lit?
> Earth! Have they gone into you!
> Somewhere they must have gone,
> And flung on your hard back
> Is their souls' sack
> Emptied of God-ancestralled essences.
> Who hurled them out? Who hurled?
>
> None saw their spirits' shadow shake the grass,
> Or stood aside for the half used life to pass
> Out of those doomed nostrils and the doomed mouth,
> When the swift iron burning bee
> Drained the wild honey of their youth....

... Owen doesn't have this sense of the numinous, of "God-ancestralled essences." When Rosenberg speaks of waste, as Owen does, in that phrase about the "half-used life," ... he does so against the background we've been looking at—the background of his desire to accept fate in its totality. He's aware of the waste, but unlike Owen, he can go on to contemplate a further possibility than waste in war—the possibility of that living effort called forth by it, as Harding says. In the first version of "Dead Man's Dump," Rosenberg asks what sort of men death takes up in war—what can be said about this "half used life" at the point of death:

> Dark Earth! Dark Heaven! swinging in chemic smoke,
> What dead are born when you kiss each soundless soul
> With lightning and thunder from your mined heart
> Which man's self dug, and his blind fingers loosed?

Perhaps the word "soundless"— if we recall Rosenberg's use of the verb "to hear"—is meant to imply not merely that the souls were stunned into silence by the noise of battle but that the souls lacked the significant music that Rosenberg finds in an achieved destiny. At all events the question—"What dead are born when you kiss each soundless soul?" is never answered. Instead the poem continues:

> A man's brains splattered on
> A stretcher-bearer's face;
> His shook shoulders slipped their load,
> But when they bent to look again
> The drowning soul was sunk too deep
> For human tenderness.
>
> They left this dead with the older dead,
> Stretched at the cross roads.

The half-used life is left at that, "joined," as Rosenberg says, "to the great sunk silences," wasted. Yet we have the sense at the back of the poem—and this is where Rosenberg is least like Owen—that the waste was not merely that of human life but the waste of death. Rosenberg seems to be implying that, had there been possible among these half-used lives the open readiness for the music of destiny, the half-used life could have achieved a heightened spiritual power, an intensity which would have been beyond pity because having no need for it. This is a conception which an essentially humanistic poet like Wilfred Owen never entertained—the waste of a death as well as the waste of a life. And, indeed, for Rosenberg it was not a conception easily contemplated. He attempted its full and painful contemplation in what he thought of as his finest poem, "Daughters of War."

He wrote from France shortly before his death: "It has taken me about a year to write." He has, he says, "striven hard to get that sense of the inexorableness the human (or inhuman) side of war has." In "Daughters of War," Rosenberg imagines Amazon-like figures in the beyond, resembling the Valkyries, who receive the released spirits of the slain earth-men as their lovers:

> Space beats the ruddy freedom of their limbs—
> Their naked dances with man's spirit naked
> By the root side of the tree of life,
> (The underside of things
> And shut from earth's profoundest eyes).

The ubiquitous image of the root is there again in "the root side of the tree of life" and with the force of the poem behind it, that image attempts to unite Rosenberg's idea of the life fed from the deepest energies with the death died in the possession of that full-fed life. What is inexorable in life has to be faced by the individual if he wishes to attain that dimension, if he wishes to be the lover of the daughters of war in the poem and not merely the good citizen, the man bounded by the social rut as were the Jewish slaves in their Egyptian captivity.

How successful is "Daughters of War"? It was clearly a very important poem for Rosenberg, important for what it represented in terms of sheer spiritual effort. . . . I wonder . . . whether the kind of thing it is trying to do is not, perhaps, more impressive than the final product—whether the spiritual effort did not go into the sheer fact of contemplating and preparing oneself for the full death rather than into the art of the poem about the full death, the full death that (Rosenberg tells us) gives the earth-men "new hearing" as they drink its "sound." What weakens the poem itself is its purple diction. Good and bad are so closely entwined in it, it's difficult to disentangle them:

> I saw in prophetic gleams
> These mighty daughters in their dances
> Beckon each soul aghast from its crimson corpse
> To mix in their glittering dances.

> I heard the mighty daughters' giant sighs
> In sleepless passion for the sons of valour,
> And envy of the days of flesh
> Barring their love with mortal boughs across—
> The mortal boughs—the mortal tree of life.

Even there, with the bits of Blake and the crimson corpses, one can see the attempt to articulate an interesting and central idea of Rosenberg's: "And envy of the days of flesh / Barring their love with mortal boughs across. . . ." The mortal tree of life wants protection from the full death—it resists a possible dimension; it wants to protect the dying from the weight of their death as, in a sense, Wilfred Owen did. "This book is not about heroes," Owen had said of *his* poems. But Rosenberg's book is very much about heroes, or rather about the possibility of heroism—heroism, note, not patriotism. If the possibility is not poetically achieved in "Daughters of War," the attempt at any rate was a highly important one. Something closer to achievement occurs in a more modest poem like "Returning we hear the larks." It brings back once more our theme of music, in describing a return to camp in the thick of war and symbolising the terrible and vulnerable beauty of experience in a song that is heard while its source is unseen:

> Sombre the night is.
> And though we have our lives, we know
> What sinister threat lurks there.
>
> Dragging these anguished limbs, we only know
> This poison-blasted track opens on our camp—
> On a little safe sleep.
>
> But hark!—joy—joy—strange joy.
> Lo! heights of night ringing with unseen larks.
> Music showering our upturned list'ning faces.
>
> Death could drop from the dark
> As easily as song—
> But song only dropped,
> Like a blind man's dreams on the sand
> By dangerous tides,
> Like a girl's dark hair for she dreams no ruin lies there,
> Or her kisses where a serpent hides.

The ideal behind Rosenberg's poems comes close to Nietzsche's definition of the Dionysiac spirit in *The Birth of Tragedy*—"The affirmative answer to life, even in its strangest and hardest problems; the will to life, rejoicing . . . at its own inexhaustible nature." But to guard against the rhetoric, the stoical fanfares in the face of a meaningless universe that Nietzsche usually sounds off, one can say also that the spirit of Rosenberg's poetry is profoundly Bibli-

Rosenberg began his schooling in a grim section of the London slums at St. Paul's, where he managed to learn basic writing and numerical skills. Even as child he loved writing and drawing, and these talents were encouraged when he moved to the Baker Street School, where he was often left alone to practice drawing. At the age of eleven he had one of his paintings, Caxton and Edward IV, *displayed at a children's exhibition.*

One of Rosenberg's earliest surviving paintings, 1901 (Isaac Rosenberg Estate)

cal, with its sense of the need to hallow life by spiritual effort and of the need to accept the destiny of suffering ordained by transcendent powers. He was still working at this conception in his unfinished play "The Unicorn," a play variously about the impingement of the unknown into the lives of ordinary people, into a humdrum marriage, and also about the symbolic unicorn uprooting, destroying, that all may begin anew. I want to draw towards a close, with the description from the first draft of the play, "The Amulet," of the arrival of the unknown in the shape of a storm and a strange man to Saul, whose marriage is failing and who has ceased to live the full spiritual life. His cart is stuck in the mud and out of the storm which has scattered the human certainties of his life he hears the unpremeditated music of the unknown. The landscape in which all this occurs, with its rain and mud, clearly recalls the western front. . . .

"The Unicorn" was never finished. It is merely a series of drafts. Writing from the trenches in 1916, Rosenberg speaks of the skin that must grow "round and through a poet's ideas if they are to be presented whole" and he adds: "If you are not free, you can only, when the ideas come hot, seize them with the skin in tatters, raw, crude, in some parts beautiful, in others monstrous." This very much describes the effect of many of his poems, a fact which makes him so difficult a writer to assess. One critic, David Daiches, goes so far as to suggest that Rosenberg's survival might have changed the entire course of modern English poetry, that he might have inaugurated a new romanticism distinct from the metaphysical strain of T. S. Eliot. But such claims, of course, one can only leave in the area of speculation, tempting as they are.

Rosenberg . . . was in a very fundamental sense a religious poet. He feels that the demands made upon him are transcendent ones. Indeed we should be grateful to Isaac Rosenberg that, in an increasingly humanist world, he awakes us to the awareness of the barrenness of that world if it no longer lies open to what exceeds the merely human and the merely civic vision of life.

In 1902 Rosenberg began to attend special afternoon classes at the Stepney Green Art School, where he developed his nascent artistic techniques and skills. His artistic endeavors were not limited to painting and drawing: he won a certificate of merit for essay writing in 1904, and he enjoyed reading and writing poetry. His earliest extant poem, "Ode to David's Harp," Zionist in intent and Byronic in meter and form, was written about this time.

"Ode to David's Harp," 1905 (Ian Parsons, ed., The Collected Works of Isaac Rosenberg, *p. 2*)

> Awake! ye joyful strains, awake!
> In silence sleep no more;
> Disperse the gloom that ever lies
> O'er Judah's barren shore.
> Where are the hands that strung thee
> With tender touch and true?
> Those hands are silenced too.
>
> The harp that faster caused to beat
> The heart that throbbed for war,
> The harp that melancholy calmed,
> Lies mute on Judah's shore.
> One chord awake—one strain prolong
> To wake the zeal in Israel's breast;
> Oh sacred lyre, once more, how long?
> 'Tis vain, alas! in silence rest.
>
> Many a minstrel fame's elated
> Envies thee thy harp of fame,
> Harp of David—monarch minstrel,
> Bravely—bravely, keep thy name.
> Ay! every ear that listen'd,
> Was charmed—was thrilled—was bound.
> Every eye with moisture glisten'd
> Thrilling to the harp's sweet sound.
>
> Hark! the harp is pouring
> Notes of burning fire,
> And each soul o'erpowering,
> Melts the rousing ire.
> Fiercer—shriller—wilder far
> Than the iron notes of war,
> Accents sweet and echoes sweeter,
> Minstrel—minstrel, steeds fly fleeter
>
> Spurred on by thy magic strains
> Tell me not the harp lies sleeping,
> Set not thus my heart aweeping,
> In the muse's fairy dwelling
> There thy magic notes are swelling.
> But for list'ning mortals' ear
> Vainly wait, ye will not hear.
> So clearly, sweet—so plaintive sad
> More tender tone no harper had.
> O! when again shall Israel see
> A harp so toned with melody?

Throughout his poetic career Rosenberg felt a strong sense of his Jewish background and often wrote from a Jewish perspective, as Diana Collecott notes in her chapter about him in The Jewish East End, 1840–1939 *(London: The Jewish Historical Society, 1981, pp. 270–274)*

Isaac Rosenberg (1890–1918):
A Cross-Cultural Case-Study

. . . Rosenberg's father fled from his native Lithuania to escape conscription into the Russian army. He . . . had been a rabbinical student in Russia and disdained manual work; he continued the pattern of the *stetl,* traveling as a peddlar in the West Country, while his wife eked out the family income as best she could. At one time she kept a sweet-shop, at others she hawked her embroidery around the richer houses of North London. One of her clients there, Mrs. Amschewitz, was among Isaac's first encouragers: her own son J. H. Amschewitz was also destined for the Slade and his portrait of Rosenberg at the age of twenty-one hung for some time in Jews' College.

Rosenberg's parents spoke the *mame loshen* and had minimal English. The father was literate in both Yiddish and Hebrew, but Isaac seems to have rejected both languages early on in favour of English. When sent to Hebrew classes after school, he spent his time drawing. His father's gift of an English Bible containing both Testaments tacitly acknowledged this recalcitrance. Thus, although he must have been familiar with the rhythms of liturgical Hebrew, he acquired his knowledge of the Bible through the medium of Shakespeare's English. This deeply informed the language of his own poetry. By the time he was twenty, his Yiddish was so limited that he asked [Joseph] Leftwich to translate some of his poems for the benefit of his father. His letters from the Front were interpreted for his parents by one of his sisters. In these and other writings we encounter verbal wit, self-mockery, liveliness and subtlety, yet in actual encounters Rosenberg was often hesitant and tongue-tied. His biographers attribute this to an introverted personality, but something must be due to his limited experience of oral English. The hero of his verse-drama *Moses* has a "halt tongue" and can be seen as an archetype of the artist. Articulation is one symptom of the new-found power that enables him to rebel against the Egyptians, and in the development of Rosenberg's art, Moses' speeches represent a new power of expression.

According to Laurence Binyon, Rosenberg's poetry came in "clotted gushes and spasms" and the resourcefulness of his written English sometimes suggests the "locked brain" of the spastic child. Expression is difficult, fought for, but extremely original. For instance, the poem entitled "Expression" grapples with the mystery of meaning, and celebrates in its very syllables the act of articulation:

Can this be caught and caged?
Wings can be clipt
Of eagles, the sun's gaudy measure gauged,
But no sense dipt

In the mystery of sense:
The troubled throng
Of words break out like smother'd fire through dense
And smouldering wrong.

That energetic cluster "troubled throng" should, of course, be followed by the singular verb "breaks," and this is just the kind of pedantic detail which would lead to criticisms of "blindness or carelessness" . . . but the plurality of words is the dominant idea here, leading into that vivid metaphor of smothered fire which would, if fanned, break *out* and *through* in many places. Commenting on this aspect of Rosenberg's use of language, D. W. Harding, has argued that it gave him a compression "totally unlike the compression of acute conversation," and suggested that rather than illustrating his ideas by writing, Rosenberg "reached them through writing." This notion that writing itself, as opposed to speech, played a central role in Rosenberg's poetic practice, is an interesting one, and may well reflect his linguistic situation.

Language is still the least considered aspect of Rosenberg's art, and it may well be that, in ways we do not fully understand, he turned the apparent disadvantage of his Yiddish background to advantage. In other respects, this background had special and unexpected strengths. Though the poverty of Rosenberg's parents dogged him to his end, they gave him access to a rich vein of intellectual, cultural and political experience. This cosmopolitan inheritance extended his own response to the realities that he had to live (and die) with. His letters reveal that his parents were "Tolstoyians," and that his father was familiar with Jewish writers such as Heinrich Heine. Writing to his mother from the Front, he noted Trotsky's rise to power and remarked "I hope our Russian cousins are happy now"; as Jon Silkin has pointed out, there is here a radical as well as an ethnic sense—a sense of what it means to be a Jew, and also to be a member of an international working class.

Such a sense was strongly developed in the East End immigrants of Rosenberg's generation by Rudolf Rocker's Anarchists' Club, which in 1906 was established in Jubilee Street where the Rosenberg family was living. In 1907, it was the scene of the Russian Social Democratic Labour Party's Congress, attended by Lenin, Stalin, Trotsky and Gorky, and Lenin continued to be a visitor during his exile. William Fishman has given a vivid account of the activities of the Club, which served as a social and educational centre as well as a political one. One of its functions was to make available European and English culture to the Yiddish-speaking community: Rocker himself, a fluent Yiddish-speaker, gave evening courses on Shakespeare. Joseph Leftwich attributes a part of his own intellectual formation to the Anarchists' Club, which he frequented with Rosenberg before the 1914 War, and where they often met Yiddish poets together. . . .

The Rosenbergs' move to London failed to secure Isaac a Jewish education, but it did put him in the way of other opportunities, firstly in the immediate neighbourhood of Stepney and Whitechapel and secondly in the capital itself. From St Paul's School, Wellclose Square, the boy was moved in 1899 to the Baker Street Elementary School, where the headmaster recognized his talent for drawing and arranged for him to attend extra art classes at the local Craft School, which occupied a handsome house on Stepney Green. At about the same time (1902–4) Isaac's elder sister Minnie, seeking guidance for his writing, took him to see Morley Dainow, one of the Yiddish assistants at the Whitechapel Public Library. It is very likely that Dainow encouraged Rosenberg's reading of the English Romantic poets and also suggested that he write on Jewish themes; if so, he was a key person in the young artist's cross-culturation.

The importance of the Whitechapel Library continued throughout Rosenberg's adolescence. It was a source of books and reproductions, where he could read Blake, Donne and Whitman and glut himself on the Pre-Raphaelites. Moreover it was a warm and quiet place to work, outside the crowded home, when the only alternative was the street. Mark Wayner remembered his dismay, one Yom Kippur when all good Jews

Family financial problems forced Rosenberg to leave school at the end of 1904, but his family attempted to find him a job using his artistic talent. With the help of an influential London Jewish family, Rosenberg was apprenticed to art publisher Carl Hentschel, through whom he was to learn platemaking and engraving. To compensate for the physical drudgery and mental boredom during the apprenticeship, Rosenberg read and wrote poetry. One of his poems from this time is "Fleet Street," a study of London life that reveals his discontent.

Manuscript for a poem written during Rosenberg's apprenticeship as an engraver (Imperial War Museum, London) were in the Synagogue, on meeting Rosenberg hurrying to the library to get a poem down.

Around 1911, Leftwich's circle would spend whole evenings in the upper reading room, and the Librarian of the time, Mr. Bogdon, recalls their obsession with Shelley. This implies a cultural ambivalence which would not have been lost on Rosenberg and his friends, for Shelley was both poet and reformer, and *their* closet romanticism would be interspersed with meetings of the Whitechapel and Stepney Young Socialists' League, and evenings at the Anarchists' Club or Toynbee Hall.

By the time Rosenberg was caught up in this energetic cultural environment, he had entered an apprenticeship with Carl Hentschel's in Fleet Street, to learn photo-etching. The work was wretched for him and as a Shelleyan he hated being confined to it "when my days are full of vigour and my hands and soul craving for self-expression." A limited channel for self-expression offered itself in evening-classes at the Birkbeck College Art School in Chancery Lane. Here he learnt the traditional academic practice of copying master-works, and it was while copying at the National Gallery that Rosenberg, met Mrs. Delissa Joseph who, with two other well-to-do Jewish ladies, sponsored his entry to London University's Slade School in 1911. Thus, for Rosenberg, the City of London was a stepping-stone between the local institutions of the East End and the national institutions of the West End. And thus, in spite of his poverty, the cultural resources of the capital opened to him. He introduced himself, as an aspiring artist and writer, to Laurence Binyon, Keeper of Prints and Drawings at the British Museum; he was introduced to Ezra Pound, the impresario of Imagism, and Edward Marsh, the patron of the Georgians, at the Café Royal. He saw important exhibitions at the Tate and other London galleries, and showed his own paintings at the New English Art Club and, in 1914, in Bomberg's Jewish Section of the Twentieth Century Art Show at the Whitechapel Art Gallery.

Eventually Rosenberg met other artistic people congregating at the Whitechapel Library & Art Gallery, where they enjoyed the cultural activities. There Rosenberg studied the paintings of Dante Gabriel Rossetti, William Hogarth, and Sir Joshua Reynolds. By the time he was seventeen, Rosenberg struck up friendships with future painters Mark Gertler, Mark Weiner, and David Bomberg. The same year he began attending evening classes at Birkbeck College, where he won the 1908 Mason Prize for nude studies and the 1909 Pocock Prize for a nude in oils. When he completed his studies in 1911, he wrote to Winifreda Seaton, a schoolmistress friend, about his thoughts for the future.

Rosenberg's copy of Madonna and Child *(John Silken and Maurice de Sausmarcz, eds.,* Isaac Rosenberg, 1890–1918: A Catalogue*)*

Rosenberg's letter to Winifreda Seaton lamenting his frustrations with his life and work, circa 1911 (Ian Parsons, ed., The Collected Works of Isaac Rosenberg, *pp. 180–181)*

It is horrible to think that all these hours, when my days are full of vigour and my hands and soul craving for self-expression, I am bound, chained to this fiendish mangling-machine, without hope and almost desire of deliverance, and the days of youth go by . . . I have tried to make some sort of self-adjustment to circumstances by saying, 'It is all *experience;* but, good God! it is *all* experience, and nothing else. . . . I really would like to take up painting seriously; I think I might do something at that; but poetry—I despair of ever writing excellent poetry. I can't look at things in the simple, large way that great poets do. My mind is so cramped and dulled and fevered, there is no consistency of purpose, no oneness of aim; the very fibres are torn apart, and application deadened by the fiendish persistence of the coil of circumstance.

Rosenberg at about age twenty, while studying art at Birkbeck College (Isaac Rosenberg Estate)

After Rosenberg left Hentschel, he was determined to dedicate his life to artistic pursuits, but he had no income and was doubtful about how to achieve his aspirations. One afternoon while he was sitting in the National Gallery copying Antonio Allegri da Correggio's Venus, Cupid, and Mercury, he was "discovered" by Lily Delissa Joseph, an Anglo-Jewish patron of the arts. Rosenberg re-created this discovery in "Rudolph," a short story, a year later.

"Rudolph," April 1911 (Ian Parsons, ed., The Collected Works of Isaac Rosenberg, *pp. 276–283*)

Poor Rudolph! He was an artist and a dreamer—that is, one whose delight in the beauty of life was an effective obstacle to the achievement of the joy of living; whose desire to refine and elevate mankind seemed to breed in mankind a reciprocal desire to elevate him to a higher and still higher–garret. Though a nearer view of heaven and though a poet, he would have preferred a less lofty dwelling place to preserve, what he

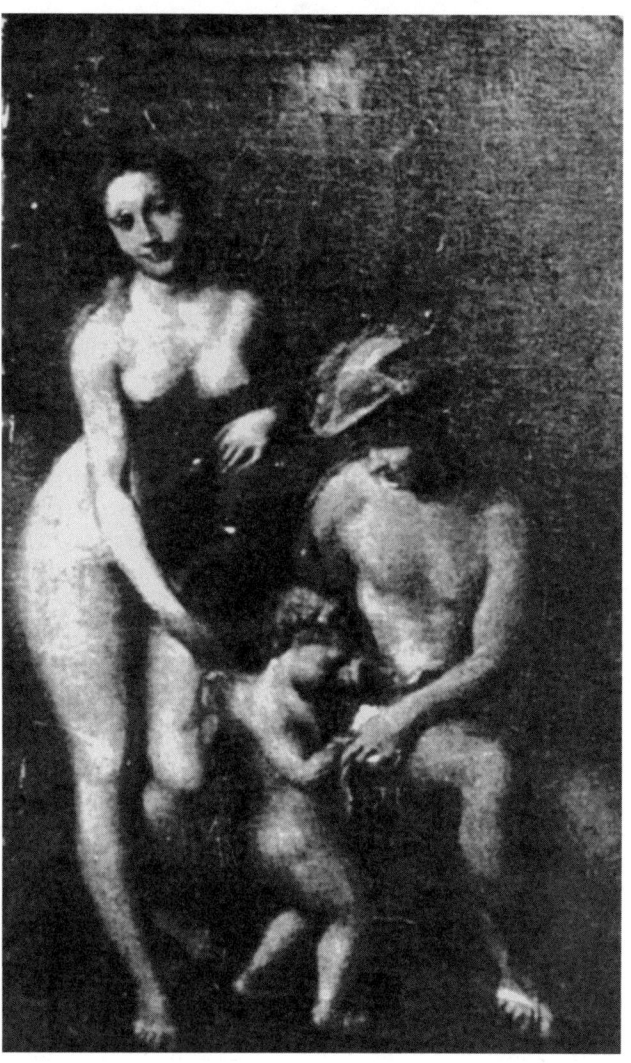

Rosenberg's copy of Correggio's Venus, Cupid, and Mercury, *circa 1911 (Jon Silken and Maurice de Sausmarcz, eds.,* Isaac Rosenberg, 1890–1918: A Catalogue*)*

facetiously termed his ancestor's remains, from the chill November weather–but so it was. In this garret, in the dim waning light God could see day by day the titanic wrestlings of genius against the exigencies of circumstances, the throbbings of a sensitive organism, touched to emotion at the subtlest changes of the face of nature; the keen delight simply in endeavour, the worship and awe of genius before the altar of genius. But day after day of unrequited endeavour, of struggle and privation, brought depression, and in the heaviness of his spirit the futility of existence was made manifest to him. Often inspiration was dead within, and all his aspirations and ideals seemed to mock at his hollow yearning. In his social and spiritual isolation, in his utter desolation he felt as if he was God's castaway, out of harmony with the universe, a blot upon the scheme of humanity.

Opening page of Rosenberg's manuscript for "Rudolph" (Imperial War Museum, London)

Life appeared so chaotic, so haphazard, so apathetic–O! it was miserable. He–a spark struck from God's anvil, he–who could clasp the Heavens with his spirit–to whom Beauty had revealed herself in all her radiance–and to what end? What purpose was there in such wasted striving–and supposing success did come would it be sufficient recompense for the wasted life and youth, the starved years–the hopelessness of the barren Now?

In one of these moods he strayed to the National Gallery. It was Students' Day, and he wandered round without being able to concentrate himself on his old loves and longings, till at length he sat down on a seat brooding and revolving "the fragments of the broken years. . . ." He was awakened from his reverie by hearing a feminine voice saying "O! please don't rise, oblige me." He looked up and saw a lady at an easel gazing intently at him and painting.

"I am painting the interior and you just happen to fit in well, I won't be many minutes," she called out to him.

"O! certainly," murmured Rudolph, "as long as you like." She was a pleasant faced lady of about thirty five, rosy and buoyant, and he wondered what her work would be like. He thought what a strange thing Art was, life was. Around were the masters, to whom Art was life, and life meant Art. Here were the dilettanti to whom Art was a necessity as an alternative to the boredom of doing nothing; an important item in the ingredients that go to make up culture.

She was soon finished and asked Rudolph to see it, which he accordingly did, and was and expressed himself greatly struck by the result.

"Dutch in idea and influence and yet exceedingly modern," he told her.

She assented, and then in a tone of defiant confession "Do you know I think Van Eyck the greatest artist that ever lived. I adore him because he makes the commonplace so delightfully precious."

"I think a picture should be something more," protested Rudolph. "Van Eyck is interesting to me just as a pool reflecting the clouds is interesting, or a landscape seen through a mirror. But it is only a faithful transcript of what we see. My ideal of a picture is to paint what we cannot see. To create, to imagine. To make tangible and real a figment of the brain. To transport the spectator into other worlds where beauty is the only reality. Rossetti is my ideal."

She smiled, amused at his enthusiasm.

"But why go out of the world for beauty when we can find beauty in it?"

"I admit an artist with imagination might make a most exquisite picture out of what may seem most uncompromising in nature. But it is his imagination, his refinement of sentiment that only uses the object itself as a basis to give expression to his vision. Why then were we given the creative faculty? What, if not this, is the meaning of God?"

The lady laughed. "I have a nephew who used to think like you, until he saw Degas, and now he raves over the beauty of ugliness. He said to me, 'We are all idealists when we are young. We begin in the clouds and as we are slipping away from existence we come nearer to existence in thought and feeling. We are born with wings but we find our feet are safest.' Perhaps you have heard of him, Leonard Harris, the poet."

"Leonard Harris! he could never have said that," exclaimed Rudolph, and added: "Though the expression sounds his. Surely Heaven hasn't got too bright for him."

"Anyway that's how he talks now. Do you know him?" she asked.

"No, but I should very much like to," he replied eagerly.

"Well, I shall talk to him about you. Are you an artist?" she questioned. "You certainly have the artistic spirit."

"I am unfortunately."

"Why unfortunately? It is a golden gift."

"A golden gift; but I could not exchange it for a pair of shoe laces if I wanted to. Unless one has the golden means the gift is only one of misery."

"You are young to be a pessimist."

"I am not old enough to be an optimist. When I have experienced occasion for optimism I will be one."

She looked concerned. "Dear, dear, you are young to talk like that. I think that if one has the golden means, and everything made smooth for him, one does not try so much; that is why the geniuses are always those who have had great difficulties to contend against."

He smiled bitterly. "When one has to think of responsibilities, when one has to think strenuously how to manage to subsist, so much thought, so much energy is necessarily taken from creative work. It might widen experience and develop a precocious mental maturity, of thought and worldliness, it might even make one's work more poignant and intense, but I am sure the final result is loss, technical incompleteness, morbidness and the evidence of tumult and conflict."

"Well, it may be so," she admitted half doubtingly. "But you must see my nephew on those matters. I will talk to him and leave you his address in case you'd care to write to him."

"I'd write this moment. I too am a poet."

"Yes! How nice. Well, send your poems. I myself am not very poetical in my tastes. In any case you'll hear from me, as I cannot let a sinner so young go on sinning," she said smilingly as she bade him goodbye.

"Then I shall owe my good fortune to my wickedness. The way of the world, Madam."

Some time after this Rudolph received a letter from Leonard Harris, to whom he had sent his poems, inviting him to dine with him the following evening. Rudolph immediately wrote back accepting the invita-

Rosenberg about the time he graduated from Birkbeck College in 1911 (Isaac Rosenberg Estate)

tion, and in the elation caused by the turn fortune seemed to be taking with him, rushed off to communicate the wonderful intelligence to a friend.

"And you've accepted the invitation?" his friend asked sceptically.

Rudolph looked at him. "Why–I never waited to finish reading the letter before I answered."

His friend shook his head pityingly. "You simple Simon. Do you know what a wealthy supper is? Evening dresses, immaculate shirt fronts, diamond pins, and sparkling patent boots. If you don't look as if you'd just stepped out of a fashion plate you're a pariah, you'll be trampled on, pulverised. And probably the whole family will be there. You haven't even got an ordinary dress. Why, I'd sooner think of dropping through a chimney pot than going."

Rudolph rubbed his cheek, perplexed; this view of the case had never presented itself to him.

"Then what shall I do?" he questioned disconsolately. "Can't you suggest something in my dire extremity? Go I must; even if it's in this," pointing to his transparent alpaca which had the appearance of a Turkish carpet, for he had used it as it palette once or twice by mistake.

"Good God! If you can pretend that you mistook the invitation for one to a fancy-dress ball it might work. But I'll tell you what. My landlady, who as you know is very sweet on me, possesses a husband, who possesses an evening dress, which God knows what he uses for, unless it's to hide a hole in the wall which they want no one to see; for I've lived there two years and that suit has never shifted. It's in a state of remarkable preservation except for some green paint spots on the shoulder little Madge dropped on [it] when the house was being repaired; but that wouldn't notice in the evening. She'll lend it me if I say it's for myself."

"Dave, you've saved me. Thou art indeed a friend in need. But you must have a swell landlord."

"He seems to have some mysterious connections with 'igh society, from what I can make out from his missis. I rarely see him."

Next day Dave brought the prize round. He had succeeded in borrowing it without much difficulty, but with a caution from the landlady to be careful, as it was a particular favourite of her ole man's, being the one in which he had captivated and conquered his Mary Ann, it being so precious that he would not wear it but look at it only to remind him of their honey days.

The suit was laid out, and Rudolph proceeded to make his entrance into the uniform of a gentleman, into which he completely disappeared. When gradually his limbs one by one emerged from its recesses, and he had managed to extricate his head from the vacuity, he desired to know Dave's unbiased impression as to its decorative qualities. After careful examination from all points of view, Dave delivered judgment to the effect that he thought its decorative qualities immense, but that one was inclined to lose sight of the object it was intended to decorate.

"Do you really think it is slightly too big?" queried Rudolph anxiously; "I feel somehow I am lost in it. But don't you think it will make me look bigger?"

"It might, if one could see you, but I think we can do it with pins. I expect it'll look a little creasy but it won't notice at night."

"And these green spots, are they noticeable?"

"O! they won't notice at night."

"And now, the shirt front. Didn't she have one?"

"Well, he couldn't keep the shirt front for two years. Possibly he might if he had foreseen this emergency. I don't know what to suggest unless we buy one. We may get one at the pawnbroker's shop. You might even exchange your alpaca for one, these stains won't notice in this light."

Thus arrayed in swallow-tail and shirt front, enveloped by his friend's overcoat, with his portfolio under his arm, and the inevitable sombrero on his head, the transformed Rudolph set out on his way to Harris. This was just the opportunity he desired; now he would assert himself. For one night the evening dress was his, for one night would he revel in the privileges it meant. He felt transformed, transfigured; and in his sense of power he mentally pictured society as a beautiful lady, deferential and smiling, showering flowers and delights. . . . These thoughts were counteracted by a sudden inrush of natural shyness; of embarrassment; and he suddenly felt bewildered and mute in the presence of this beautiful creature. While he listened to her mellifluous voice, masculine voices seemed to respond in rich tones, and elegant forms of perfect ease made him appear to shrink—shrink but unable to escape. "St John's Wood," he heard the conductor call, and he rushed out just in time. He soon found the house and rang. The servant after inquiring his name asked him to follow and announced him. A young man came out, shook hands and pulled him in. After the preliminaries of introduction and the inevitable weather discussion, Rudolph undid his portfolio and arranged his drawings round the room, then stood by to explain and elucidate where elucidation was necessary, which was not seldom; for he painted on the principle that the art of painting was the art of leaving out, and the pleasure in beholding a picture was the pleasure of finding out. Where he had not left out the whole picture, sometimes it was successful. After he had inculcated Harris with a sense of the sacred supremacy of his principles and proved his principles without justifying his pictures, and bewildered and mystified him into acceptance of his creed with a suspicion of its results, Harris found breath to ejaculate, "I should say you take more trouble in defending your pictures than in painting them." "Yes!" flashed Rudolph. "A religion may be the conception of a moment but it takes ages to spread. Propaganda is a necessary evil."

At supper, Mrs Harris asked Rudolph whether his father had literary or artistic propensities. Rudolph smiled, "The only deviation into artistic endeavour I have ever seen my father make was when he, in a frenzy of inspiration, turned and decorated my left eye most beautifully in blue and black (which decorative effect, unfortunately, I was not in a condition to appreciate, not being able to see it), and he accompanied that extraordinary feat with a fervour of exuberant flowery language. The most complete combination of poetry and painting I have ever experienced. But otherwise our genealogical tree has not many blossoms of genius. I am the first to scandalise the family with a difference. They consider it perfectly immoral to talk and think unlike them—and—well what can I do—they show their sense of superiority by being ashamed of me!"

"Perfectly atrocious," broke in young Harris. "But as I am rather interested in heredity I am curious to know whether you acquired your taste for art and literature after or before your father's (private or public) exhibition of his skill."

"Oh! domestic exhibition. I had always practised it to some extent. I wanted to do a sketch of Romeo and Juliet. I got my father to pose for Romeo, and the servant girl for Juliet. When it was finished my mother came across it and of course thought I had sketched my father kissing the servant girl as I had seen it. Well, I have told you the consequences. It was a practical demonstration of his abhorrence for realism—and preference for decoration. I have altered my style since."

"A sure proof," gravely asserted Harris, smothering laughter, "that the genius of the child is sprung from seed in the parent."

Rudolph assented. "But my father also had mature qualifications which have descended to me. I have inherited from him a remarkable genius for taciturnity and an amazing facility for forgetting things. Just now I am exercising the latter to exorcise the former."

The plates clattered with the laughter: under its cover Miss Lily said sweetly to Rudolph "Len says you also write."

"I am afraid I must plead guilty."

He almost flushed, while young Harris said "You should see his verses, mother, he writes beautifully."

"Which do you prefer, writing or drawing?" inquired Mrs. Harris.

"Drawing when I must write, writing when I must draw," replied Rudolph becoming flippant.

"Then you never enjoy either, as you must do what you don't want to do: I condole with you!" sympathised Harris with mock pathos on his face.

"No need!" retorted Rudolph. "I enjoy my disappointment and laugh at myself."

From this glimpse of Rudolph we might surmise he was one of those superficial wits who are like bottles of soda-water just being opened, and never open their mouths but to fizzle like a chinese cracker. This apparent superficiality was the natural consequence of a super-selfconsciousness, a desire not to frustrate expectation, and a lack of sustaining inspiration to keep up with desire. Constructively and inherently he was serious, because he was an enthusiast—and because he was an enthusiast the comic in his nature would run riot once begun. Wit is the flash of the knit brows of a refined intellect, capped by the smile of achievement. Superficiality is the easy snatch at wit when the knit brows refuse to work, and in him the comic always strove to snatch: sometimes happy, sometimes not.

Brought up as he had been: socially isolated, but living in spiritual communion with the great minds of all the ages, he had developed a morbid introspection in all that related to himself, and a persistent frivolousness in relations with others; a dark book for his bedside and a gaudy one for the street. The development of temperament had bred a disassociation from the general run of the people he came in contact with, that almost rendered him inarticulate when circumstances placed him amongst those of more affinity to himself, from disuse of the ordinary faculties and facilities of conversation. Naturally these circumstances would be such where his vanity suggested he had a reputation to sustain, and he would be perpetually on the strain to say something clever. He was totally lacking in the logic of what might be called common sense, but had a whimsical sort of logic of his own which was amusing till it became too clever, and then—patience was a crime.

Now although Rudolph was in the conversational mood, and felt that in the small talk of the table he was acquitting himself well, he was not wholly at his ease. Some of the pins of his evening dress had come out and he had a feeling of general discomfort, and that they were all looking at him and eyeing his suit particularly. He was beginning to curse inwardly the artificialities of convention, the forms that bound each man to be a mechanical demonstration of its monotony, extremely aggravated at not having made more sure of the arrangement of his temporary disguise. When they adjourned for coffee he was afraid to rise lest he would disappear and only an evening dress be seen walking about. He held his chair in front of him as he manoeuvred gingerly along.

"And how do you find people take your poetry?" Harris was saying to him. Rudolph sat down. "My poetry? well I find that the poet is to the mass so respected that they consider his creations too sacred even to look at. It would he profanation to open a book of poems. The beggar who carries a menagerie in his rags and the poet are the most respected characters we have. Veneration is carried so far that contact with them is unthought of."

"I have not been so fortunate as you in that respect," replied Harris. "Since I published my poems I have been practically suffocated by the pressure of contact. I am in the throes of a—"

He was interrupted by a crash behind. He turned; the butler had dropped the tray with the coffee and was glaring at Rudolph, and his mouth was open in astonishment.

"What is it?" exclaimed Rudolph amazed. "Surely there is no need to be terrified at so trivial an accident."

"There is," broke in Harris. "It would be an accident if he did not drop it. You are always dropping things, Henry, and—"

"Er–er–I beg pardon, sir," stammered Henry and turning to Rudolph, "I . . . I . . . I . . . you . . . I don't know how to explain myself—" and he pointed to the suit, "you are wearing my clothes," he gasped out.

"Wha . . . what do you mean?" almost whispered Rudolph, oppressed by vague misgivings.

They all stood by, dumbfounded at the strange scene.

The butler pointed to the spots.

"You see these spots, five of 'em, heart shaped. Those very spots were done by my little niece Madge two years ago. That was the very suit I wore when

[A passage is missing here]

the crestfallen Rudolph as by degrees he made himself visible. My extraordinary choice . . . my situation rendered . . . my point of observation was somewhat confusing. I did not notice the ladies." They were all laughing uproariously while Rudolph, having recovered his self-possession, explained the situation.

"You see, Henry," put in Harris, "Mr. Rudolph was under the impression that he was going to a fancy-dress ball; and he borrowed the suit on account of the spots from your lodger."

Rudolph interposed. "I'm sorry, Henry, that your wife has suffered on my account, and I hope you feel more comfortable in your property than I do. And I can't help thinking that if you had paid more attention to your property, and not allowed these spots to find their way on, there would have been no necessity for this disturbance. Besides, your latest additions in coffee stains, although they may be very creditable to your decorative capabilities, do not show a just sense of the relative values of time and place. It positively destroys the harmony. However, Henry, I forgive you."

It was two hours past midnight when he got out into the street and he experienced a wonderful feeling of rejuvenation. The air was tingling and pure, and he walked under the limpid heaven as under a vague, vast tree. The golden lamplights hung in narrowing perspective and shimmered and scintillated on the iridescent bluish pavement. He walked along, the shadowy trees of the park appearing to creep beside him. Some outcasts of the night slept on benches, some looked wistfully: the miserable blasted fruit of this tree of heaven. Praises rang in his ear, fragments of wit, flashes of lyric, and night played vibrations on the chord of emotion. His mind was in a whirl. His past—what a horrible waste of God's faculties—unused. If he had only been taken up and moulded; but life had been cruel to him. Now she showed signs of remorse and atonement. He was young, upon the threshold of life. Life would hold the doors for the golden stairs. Chamber after chamber of the house of delight would be thrown open to him and he would wander in the gardens of pleasure holding the hand of love. The fountains of song would make perpetual music and they would glide down the rivers of twilight in an ecstasy of repose. Glimpses of undulating robes, shimmer of pearl, gleam of dresses, creamy arms and gleaming shoulders—ah! life! was it not time?

And now the dawn broke quietly and rich upon his dream. The vast blue flower of heaven over the dark rim of quaint angular buildings changed dreamily into broken gold and green and rose. The pearly waves of shimmering twilight seemed rising like a tide to meet the dawn, into the light which stole inch by inch the kingdom that was night's.

In October 1911 Rosenberg entered a new social milieu among Slade students. As an East End, working-class Jew with limited awareness of social class expectations, he found life at the Slade to be a difficult shift. He was determined, nevertheless, to make the best of his chance.

A Slade picnic in 1912, with Rosenberg kneeling at left (Isaac Rosenberg Estate)

In order to earn spending money, Rosenberg agreed to teach painting to the son of Mrs. Lily Delissa Joseph. Through Mrs. Joseph, he met Mrs. Herbert Cohen, Mrs. Henriette Löwy, and Mrs. Löwy's artistically inclined daughter, Ruth, who enrolled at the Slade School of Art along with her cousin, Gilbert Solomon. Mrs. Cohen, Mrs. Joseph, and Mrs. Löwy decided to pay Rosenberg's tuition at the Slade School.

Rosenberg's modernist interpretation of art soon conflicted with the more traditional vision held by his patroness, Mrs. Cohen. Following her negative response to Joy, which he painted for the Slade School Competition in summer 1912, he wrote her to defend his aesthetic beliefs and to deny her accusation that he was not working hard.

Rosenberg's letter to Mrs. Herbert Cohen in October 1912 (Ian Parsons, ed., The Collected Works of Isaac Rosenberg, p. 193)

32 Carlingford Rd
Hampstead

Dear Mrs Cohen
    I am very sorry I have disappointed you. If you tell me what was expected of me I shall at least have the satisfaction of knowing by how much I have erred. You

Rosenberg's sketch of Ruth Löwy as the Sleeping Beauty, 1912 (Isaac Rosenberg Estate)

Rosenberg's self-portrait in oil, completed at the Slade in 1912 (Isaac Rosenberg Estate)

were disappointed in my picture for its unfinished state–I have no wish to defend myself–or I might ask what you mean by finish:–and you are convinced I could have done better. I thank you for the compliment but I do not think it deserved–I did my best.

You did ask me whether I had been working hard, and I was so taken back at the question that I couldn't think what to say. If you did not think the work done sufficient evidence, what had I to say? I have no idea what you expected to see. I cannot conceive who gave you the idea that I had such big notions of myself, are you sure the people you enquired of know me, and meant me. You say people I have lately come in contact with. I have hardly seen anyone during the holidays–and I certainly have not been ashamed of my opinions, not about myself, but others–when I have; and if one does say anything in an excited unguarded moment–perhaps an expression of what one would like to be–it is distorted and interpreted as conceit–when in honesty it should be overlooked. I am not very inquisitive naturally, but I think it concerns me to know what you mean by poses and mannerisms–and whose advice do I not take who are in a position to give–and what more healthy style of work do you wish me to adopt?

I feel very grateful for your interest in me–going to the Slade has shown possibilities–has taught me to see more accurately.–but one especial thing it has shown me–Art is not a plaything, it is blood and tears, it must grow up with one; and I believe I have begun too late.

I suppose I go on as I am till Xmas. Till then I will look about. I should like all the money advanced on me considered as a loan–but which you must not expect back for some years as it takes some time settling down in art.

Yours sincerely
I Rosenberg

The Slade pictures will be on view shortly, I will let you know more if you care to see them.

Rosenberg's letter to Laurence Binyon thanking the poet for his encouraging remarks about Rosenberg's poetry (Ian Parsons, ed., The Collected Works of Isaac Rosenberg, *p. 192)*

[1912]

I must thank you very much for your encouraging reply to my poetical efforts.... As you are kind enough to ask about myself, I am sending a sort of autobiography I wrote about a year ago.... You will see from that that my circumstances have not been favourable for artistic production; but generally I am optimistic, I suppose because I am young and do not properly realize the difficulties. I am now attending the Slade, being sent there by some wealthy Jews who are kindly interested in me, and, of course, I spend most of my time drawing. I find writing interferes with drawing a good deal, and is far more exhausting.

After sending his poems to poet Lawrence Binyon for comment in 1912, Rosenberg decided to collect those he had written in the preceding two years and publish them privately in Night and Day. *The longest poem, "Night and Day," marks a farewell to his derivative Romantic poetry and anticipates a response to life based on his actual experiences rather than on literary models.*

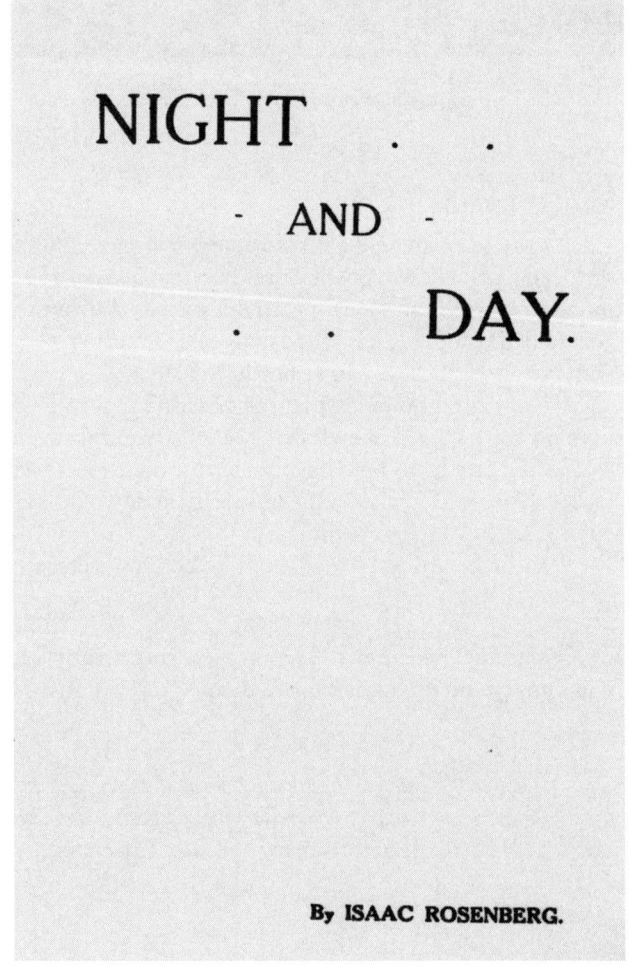

Cover for Rosenberg's privately printed 1912 poetry booklet (Imperial War Museum, London)

Pencil self-portrait of Rosenberg that he drew in 1912 (Isaac Rosenberg Estate)

Description of Rosenberg and Sacred Love *in Edward Marsh's biography (Christopher Hassall,* A Biography of Eddie Marsh, *p. 281)*

Since his last letter abroad Marsh had entertained Rosenberg at breakfast, bought the painting he had come to show, and hung it at the foot of the bed in the spare room over a drawing of Irish peasant women by Currie. The new acquisition, entitled *Sacred Love,* was a small oil-painting of curiously dry texture and pallid tone, like a pastel. In the foreground, a green clearing in a wood, a youth was kneeling by a girl who sat on a rock, and in an attitude of adoration he gathered her hands to his lips. In the background naked figures seemed to be scattering in alarm through the tilted trees. It glowed with a strange, dream-like intensity, reminiscent of Blake—a lovely vision which for the next quarter of a century confronted on their waking all the guests in this little room.

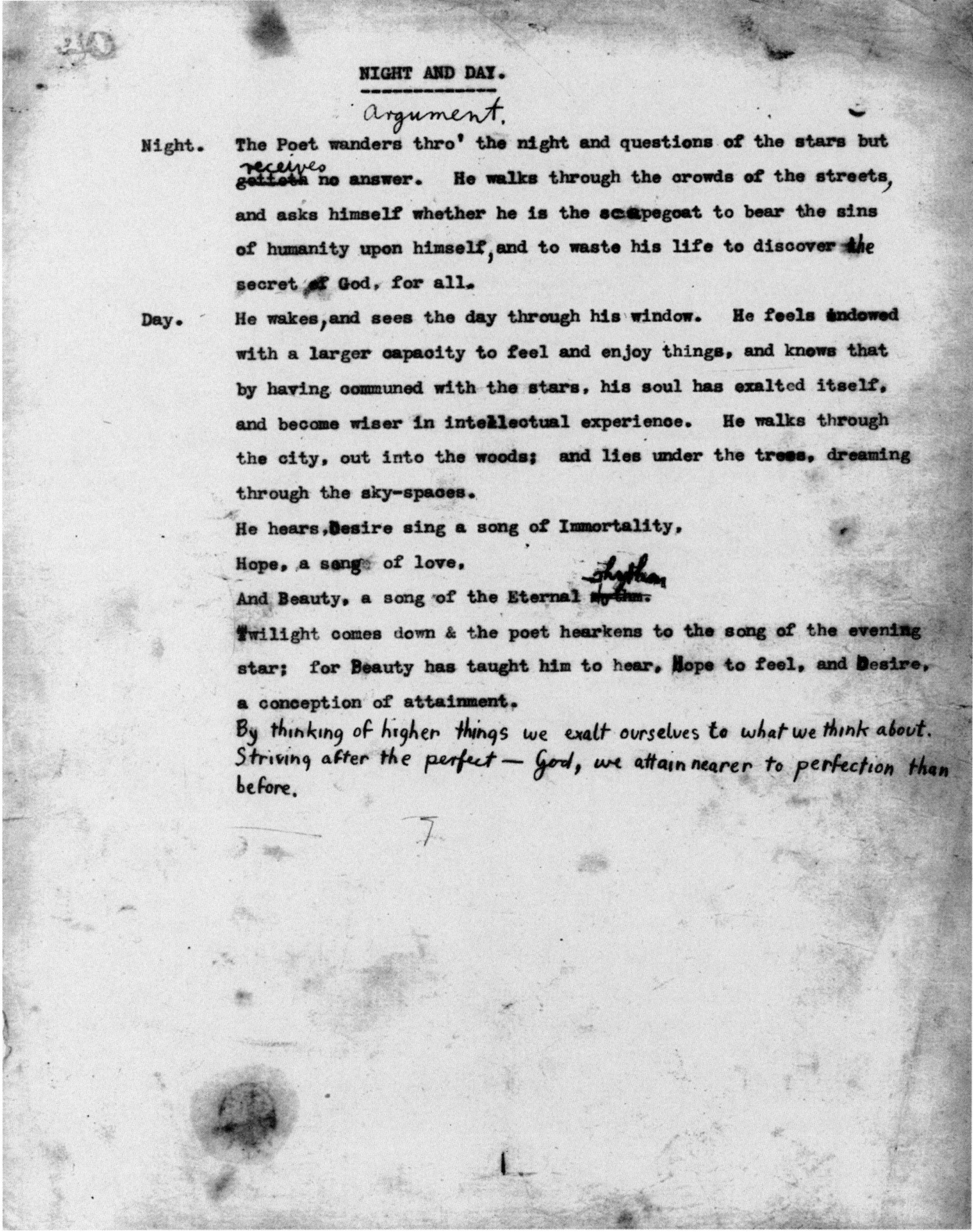

Rosenberg's revised typescript of the "Argument" to his long poem (Imperial War Museum, London)

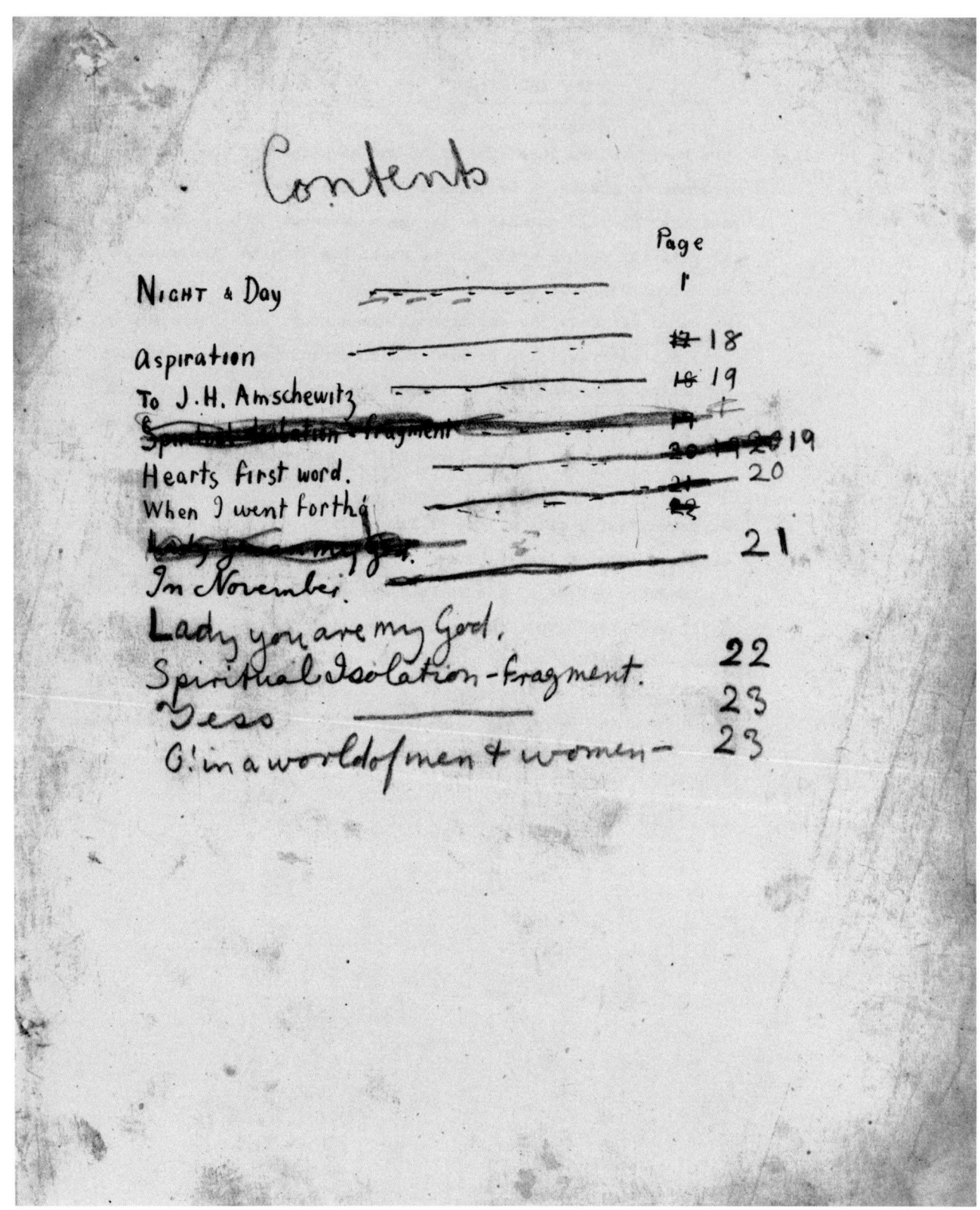

Rosenberg's revised table of contents for Night and Day *(Imperial War Museum, London)*

DAY.

The fiery hoofs of day have trampled the night to dust;
They have broken the censer of darkness and its fumes are lost in light.
Like a smoke blown away by the rushing of the gust
When the doors of the sun flung open, morning leaped and smote the night.

The banners of the day flame from the east.
Its gorgeous hosts assail the heart of dreams.
They brush aside the strange and cowled priest
Who ministers to our pillows with moonbeams
And restful pageantry—or lethe draught.
Sleep——who by day dwells in invisibleness———
Their noising stirs the waking veils of thought.
Ah! I am in the midst of their bright press.

I went to sleep in the night,
In the awed and shadowy night.
Pleading of those birds delight.
Where has the morning borne me to?
What has she done with the night?
And those birds flown whereto?

Surely some God hath breathed upon mine eyes
Between awake and waking, or poured strange wine
Of some large knowledge——for I am grown wise
And big with new life——eager and divine.

Last night I stripped my soul of all alloy
Of earth that did ensphere and fetter it.
I strove to touch the springs of all the night.
My brow felt spray, but hands and eyes were dry.

Rosenberg's working typescript for "Day" (Imperial War Museum, London)

Perhaps Rosenberg's most effective early poem was "Bacchanal," which expressed his strong desire for new opportunities and excitement. He soon got his wish, for he succeeded in showing a drawing and painting at the New English Art Club, where his painter friend Mark Gertler introduced him to Edward Marsh, the influential patron of the arts.

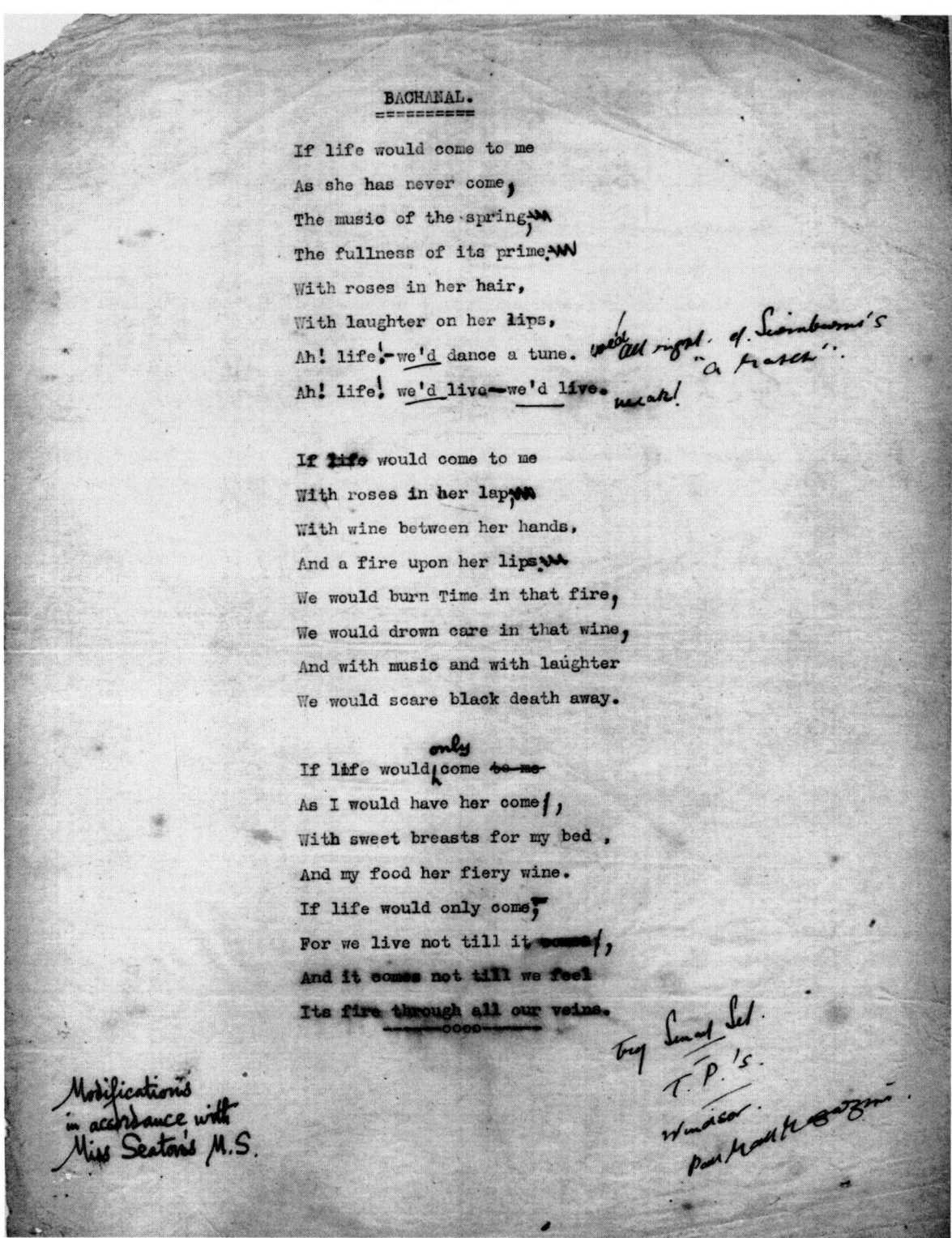

Typescript of "Bacchanal" with notes by Georgian poet Gordon Bottomley (Imperial War Museum, London)

Marsh was impressed with Rosenberg as a painter and a poet. He complimented Rosenberg, encouraged his writing of poetry, and bought two of his artworks: Sacred Love *and the cubist* Hark, Hark, the Lark. *Marsh introduced him to a circle of writers and artists including T. E. Hulme, Ezra Pound, and Jacob Epstein. Spending evenings with these men at the Café Royal helped Rosenberg sharpen his philosophical and artistic views.*

Rosenberg's Sacred Love, *painted in 1912 (Isaac Rosenberg Estate)*

Rosenberg's cubist drawing Hark, Hark, the Lark, *1912 (Isaac Rosenberg Estate)*

By the time Rosenberg completed his course at the Slade School in May 1914, a combination of poor financial prospects and poor health exacerbated by weak lungs forced him to consider career alternatives other than painting.

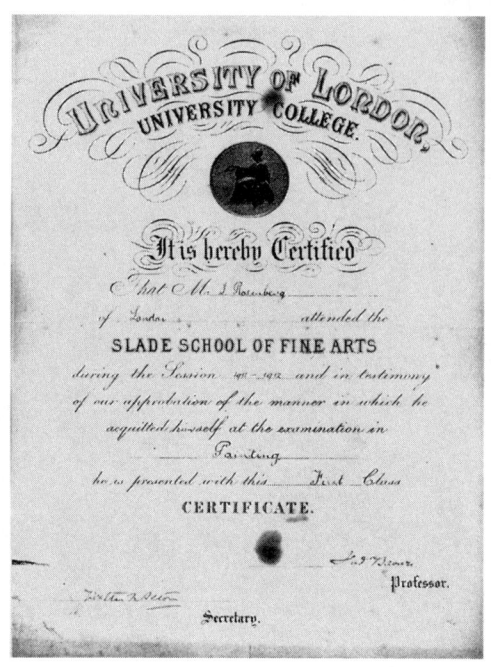

Rosenberg's first-class diploma from the Slade School of Fine Arts (Isaac Rosenberg Estate)

His first thought about alternative employment turned to poetry. He diligently compiled his latest poems (which he eventually published in Youth *[1915]) in a pamphlet and sent them to Marsh for his opinion. Marsh read the collection, saw potential in Rosenberg's work, and wrote favorably to the young poet about the edition. However, Rosenberg could not afford to print the collection at that time. Frustrated by his poverty and hoping for a new challenge, he applied for assistance from the Jewish Educational Aid Society for £12, the boat fare to South Africa, where his sister Minnie was living with her husband, William Horvitch.*

Isaac Rosenberg (standing, far right) at the wedding of his sister Minnie and William Horvitch, August 1913 (Isaac Rosenberg Estate)

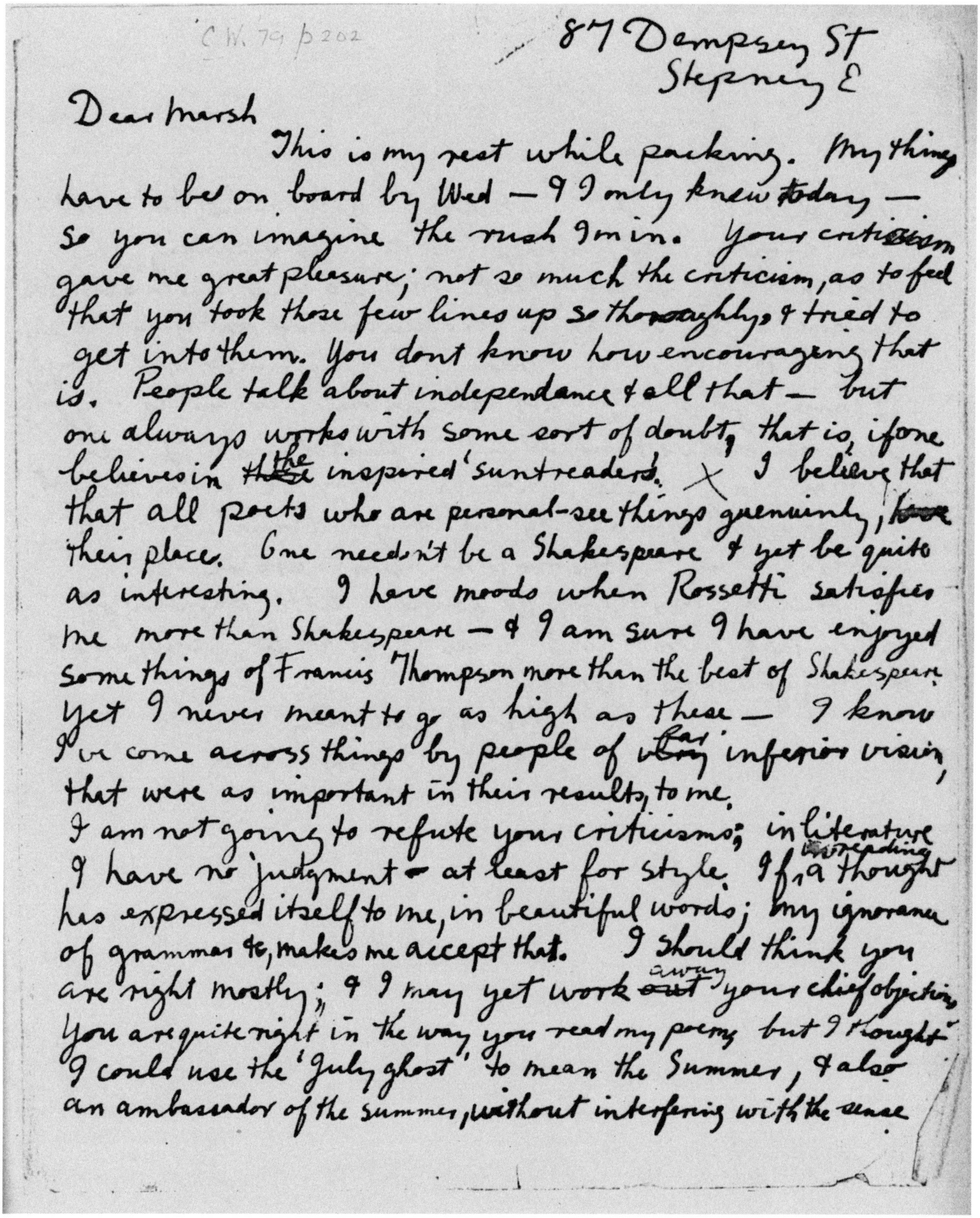

> 87 Dempsey St
> Stepney E
>
> Dear Marsh
>
> This is my rest while packing. My things have to be on board by Wed — & I only knew today — so you can imagine the rush I'm in. Your criticism gave me great pleasure; not so much the criticism, as to feel that you took those few lines up so thoroughly, & tried to get into them. You don't know how encouraging that is. People talk about independance & all that — but one always works with some sort of doubt, that is, if one believes in the inspired 'suntreaders'. × I believe that that all poets who are personal—see things genuinely, have their place. One needn't be a Shakespeare & yet be quite as interesting. I have moods when Rossetti satisfies me more than Shakespeare — & I am sure I have enjoyed some things of Francis Thompson more than the best of Shakespeare. Yet I never meant to go as high as these — I know I've come across things by people of far inferior vision, that were as important in their results, to me.
>
> I am not going to refute your criticisms; in literature I have no judgment — at least for style. If a thought has expressed itself to me, in beautiful words; my ignorance of grammar &c, makes me accept that. I should think you are right mostly; & I may yet work away your chief objection. You are quite right in the way you read my poem; but I thought I could use the 'July ghost' to mean the Summer, & also an ambassador of the summer, without interfering with the sense

Rosenberg's letter to Marsh, thanking the editor for comments on his poetry, just before Rosenberg left for South Africa, May/June 1914 (The Berg Collection, New York Public Library)

The shell of thought is man; you realise the shell has a mouth an opening. Across this opening, the ardours -the sense of heat forms a web — this signifies a sense of summer — the web again becomes another metaphor — a July ghost. — But of course I mean it for summer right through. I think your suggestion of taking out 'woven' is very good. I enclose another thing which is part of this. I told you my idea — The whole thing is to be called the poet. And begins with the way external nature affects him, & goes on to human nature.
In packing my things I found a little painting of a boy that I don't think looks at all bad, I could show it to you if you cared to see it —

Yours sincerely
Isaac Rosenberg

In June 1914 Rosenberg arrived in Cape Town. Within six weeks he wrote Marsh that South Africa was starving for insights about the latest artistic trends and fashions in Europe. Rosenberg felt that he could offer some talks about the European cultural milieu to a grateful audience.

> 43 Devilliers St
> Cape Town
>
> Dear Marsh
>
> I should like you to do me a favour if its not putting you to too much bother. I am in this infernal city by the sea. This city has men in it — and these men have souls in them — or at least have the passages to souls. Though they are millions of years behind time they have yet reached the stage of evolution that knows ears & eyes. But these passages are dreadfully clogged up; gold dust, diamond dust, stocks & shares, & heaven knows what other flinty muck. Well I've made up my mind to clear through all this rubbish. But I want your help. Now I'm going to give a series of lectures on modern art (I'm sending you the first, which I gave in great style. I was asked whether the futurist exhibited at the Royal Academy.) But I want to make the lectures interesting & intelligable by reproductions or slides. Now I wonder whether you have reproductions which you could lend me till I returned or was finished with them. I want to talk about John, Cezanne Vangoch, Innes, the early Piccaso (not the cubistic) Spencer Gertler Lamb. Puvis De Chavannes, Degas. A book of reproductions of the P Impressionist would do & I could get them transfered on slides. I hope this would not put you to any great trouble but if you could manage to do it you don't know how you would help me.

First page of Rosenberg's letter to Marsh discussing his initial impressions of Cape Town and requesting material for his lectures on modern art (The Berg Collection, New York Public Library)

Rosenberg's poetry about the war demonstrates his sense that the destructive power of modern warfare is far beyond comprehension, but his poems also suggest the regenerative power of the conflict. In December 1914 his poems "Our Dead Heroes" and "Beauty" were published in South African Women in Council, a popular South African magazine.

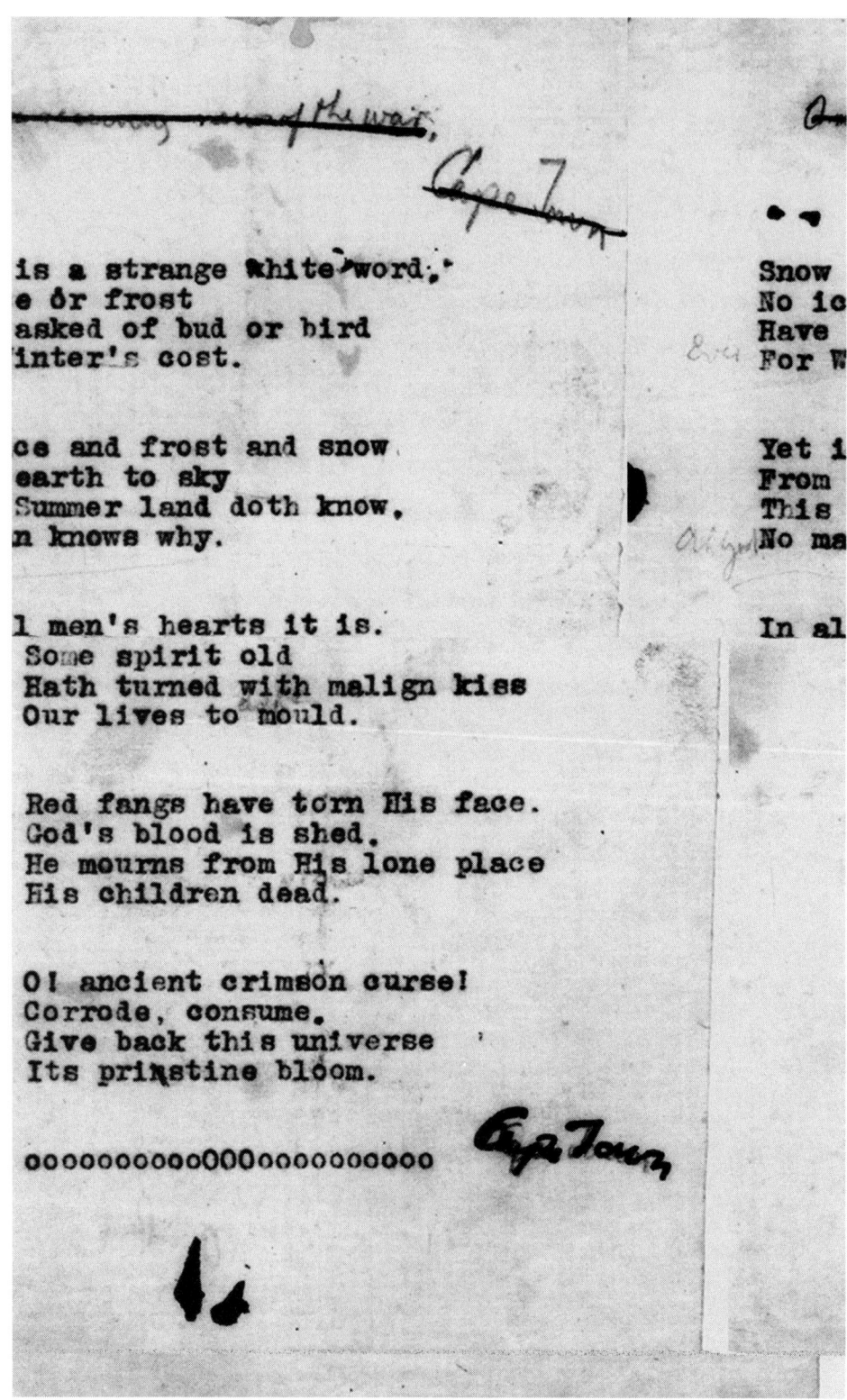

Rosenberg's typescript for "On Receiving News of the War" (Imperial War Museum, London)

Self-portrait that Rosenberg painted in South Africa (Isaac Rosenberg Estate)

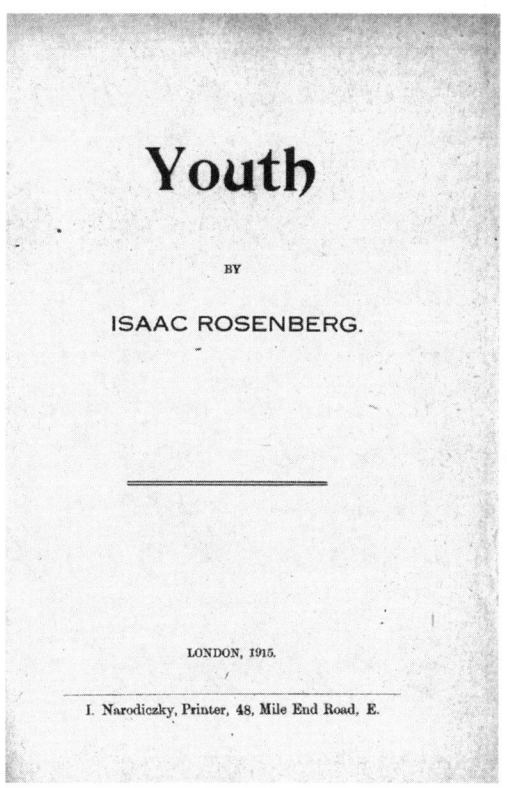

Cover of Youth, *Rosenberg's second poetry booklet, privately printed after he returned from South Africa, May/June 1914 (The Berg Collection, New York Public Library)*

> Dear Mother, Father, & everybody,
>
> I have not read your letters this week as I've been staying out at a pretty suburb with a very pretty name Rondebosch, & with very nice people. It was through my lecture & poems being printed. I went one day to see the lady who is the editor of the paper it was printed in, & there I met a Miss Molteno – who told me how delighted she was with my poems. She asked me to come to Rondebosch where she lives, & there she took me to see some beautiful places, & then asked me whether I'd like to be her guest there for a week or two. She is a sister of the speaker to the House of Parliament here. Her father was a famous author – Sir John Molteno, & she has crowds of relations. Anyway I'm here at Rondebosch having a happy time, you will be glad to hear. I'm anxious to know how you all are & will run down to town about the letters tomorrow; today being Sunday. I'm living like a toff here. Early in the morning coffee is brought to me in bed. My shoes (my only pair) are polished so brightly that the world is pleasantly deceived as to the tragedy that polish covers. I don't know whether there are snakes or wild animals in my room, but in the morning when I get up & look at the soles of my shoes, every morning I see another hole. I shan't make your mouths water by describing my wonderful breakfasts –

Rosenberg's letter to his family discussing South African life, December 1914 (Imperial War Museum, London) the unimaginable lunches – delicious teas, & colossal dinners. You would say all fibs. But I won't tell of the wonderful flowers that look into my window & the magnificent park that surrounds my room. Of the mountain climbing right to the shortest top until the town & the sea & fields were like little picture postcards lying on the pavement to one looking from the top of the monument. In a few months I hope to be back in England – I should like to get there for the warm weather, about March or so.

Isaac

As early as 1915 Rosenberg felt isolated in South Africa from the heady cultural life he had known in London. His poem "The Exile" confirms this isolation and expresses nostalgia for England. Rosenberg was not in sympathy with the aims of the war, but he may have used the war as an excuse to leave South Africa.

THE EXILE.

A northern spray in an all human speech
To this same torrid heart may somewhat reach,
Although its root, its mother tree
Is in the North.
But O! to its cold heart, and fervid eyes,
It sojourns in anothers' paradise,
A loveliness its alien eyes might see,
Could its own roots go forth.

O! dried up waters of deep hungering love!
Far, far, the springs that fed you from above,
And brimmed the wells of happiness
With new delight.
Blinding ourselves to rob another's sun
Only its scorching glory have we won,
And left our own homes in bleak wintryness
Moaning our sunward flight.

Here, where the craggy mountains edge the skies,
Whose profound spaces startle our vain eyes;
Where our thoughts hang, & theirs, who yearn
To know our speech.
O! what winged airs soothe the sharp mountains brow?
From peak to peak with messages they go,
Withering our peering thoughts that crowd to learn
Words from that distant beach.

Typescript of "The Exile," with an additional stanza in Rosenberg's hand, 1914 (Imperial War Museum, London)

By May 1915 Rosenberg was back in England, but under the strain of war there was little interest in the art he was producing. He found little market for his paintings or poetry, and his Youth, at last published privately in June 1915, did little more than bring his work to the attention of Sydney Schiff, the wealthy patron of young Jewish writers and artists living in London.

Chalk drawing of "The First Meeting of Adam and Eve," probably done in 1915 when Rosenberg returned from South Africa
(Isaac Rosenberg Estate)

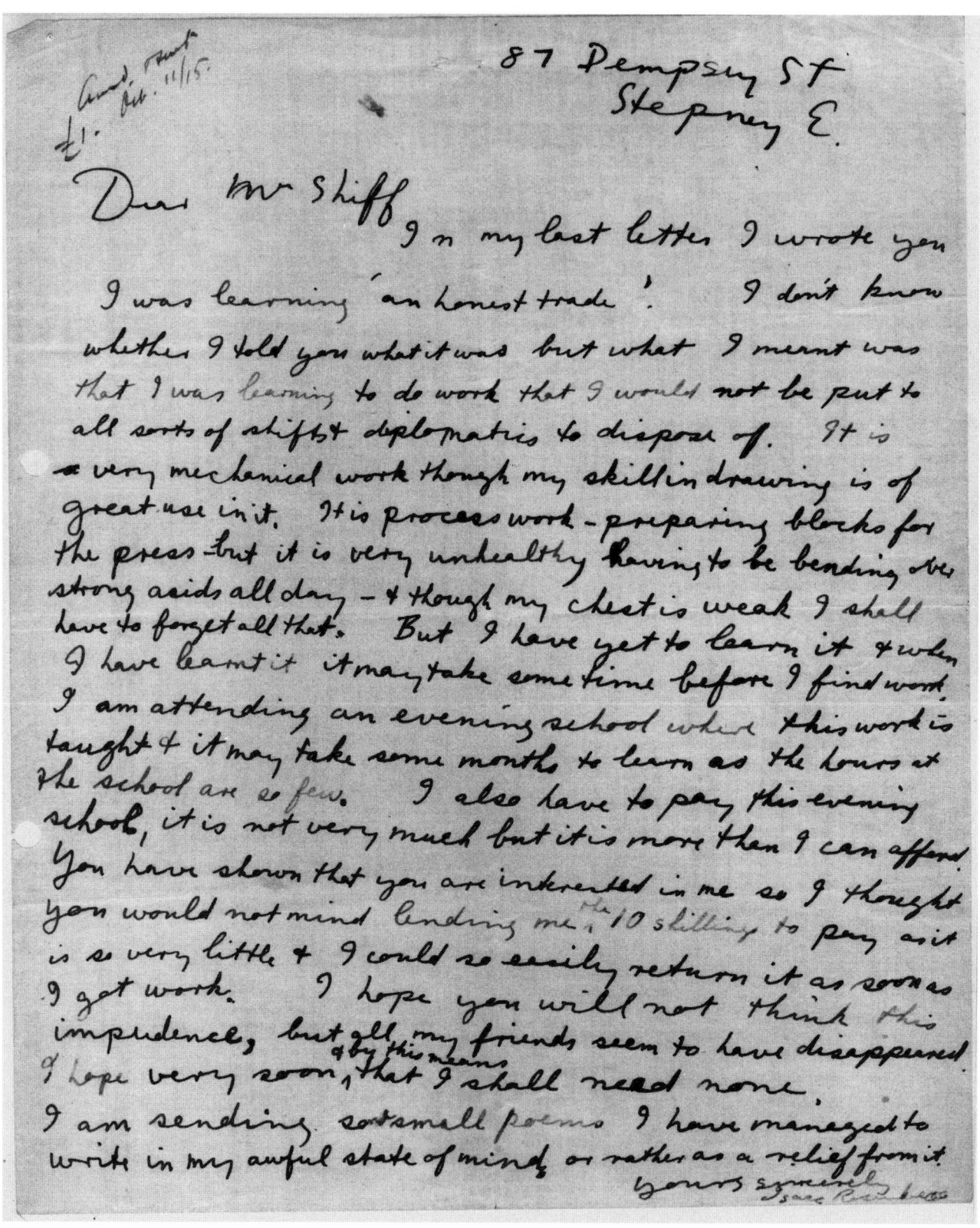

Rosenberg's letter to Sydney Schiff requesting financial aid until he gets resettled in London, October 1915 (Imperial War Museum, London)

Offered a few commissions for painting portraits not long after he arrived, Rosenberg painted portraits of the daughters of Sir Herbert Stanley, a friend of Marsh, for £15. He also began delivering lectures and informal talks at local art clubs. By the time he sent Marsh a copy of his lecture, the Great War had begun.

Rosenberg's letter to Marsh discussing the outbreak of the Great War and his hatred of the conflict, 8 August 1914 (Ian Parsons, ed., The Collected Works of Isaac Rosenberg, *p. 205)*

'Hill House'
43 Deviniers St
Cape Town

Dear Marsh

I enclose the lecture. By the time it reaches you I expect the world will be in convulsions and you'll be in the thick of it. I know my poor innocent essay stands no chance by the side of the bristling legions of war-scented documents on your desk; but know that I despise war and hate war, and hope that the Kaiser William will have his bottom smacked—a naughty aggressive schoolboy who will have *all* the plum pudding. Are we going to have Tennyson's "Battle in the air," and the nations deluging the nations with blood from the air? Now is the time to go on an exploring expedition to the North Pole; to come back and find settled order again.

Yours sincerely
Isaac Rosenberg

Throughout the rest of the year Rosenberg wrote to Schiff with unrealistic fund-raising projects. Once, in order to help his family meet its financial obligations, Rosenberg even resorted to print-block making in a local firm for a short time, but the routine proved impossible for him to stand. Having exhausted his alternatives, his only recourse was to join the army in October 1915. He enlisted largely because of the financial strain that his unemployment had on his family; he was told that on joining the army half of his pay would be go directly to his mother.

Rosenberg in uniform (Isaac Rosenberg Estate)

Because of his short stature and slight build, Rosenberg could join only the Bantam Regiment, which accepted recruits who were physically below standard. However, by early 1916 he was transferred to the Eleventh Battalion of the King's Own Royal Lancasters.

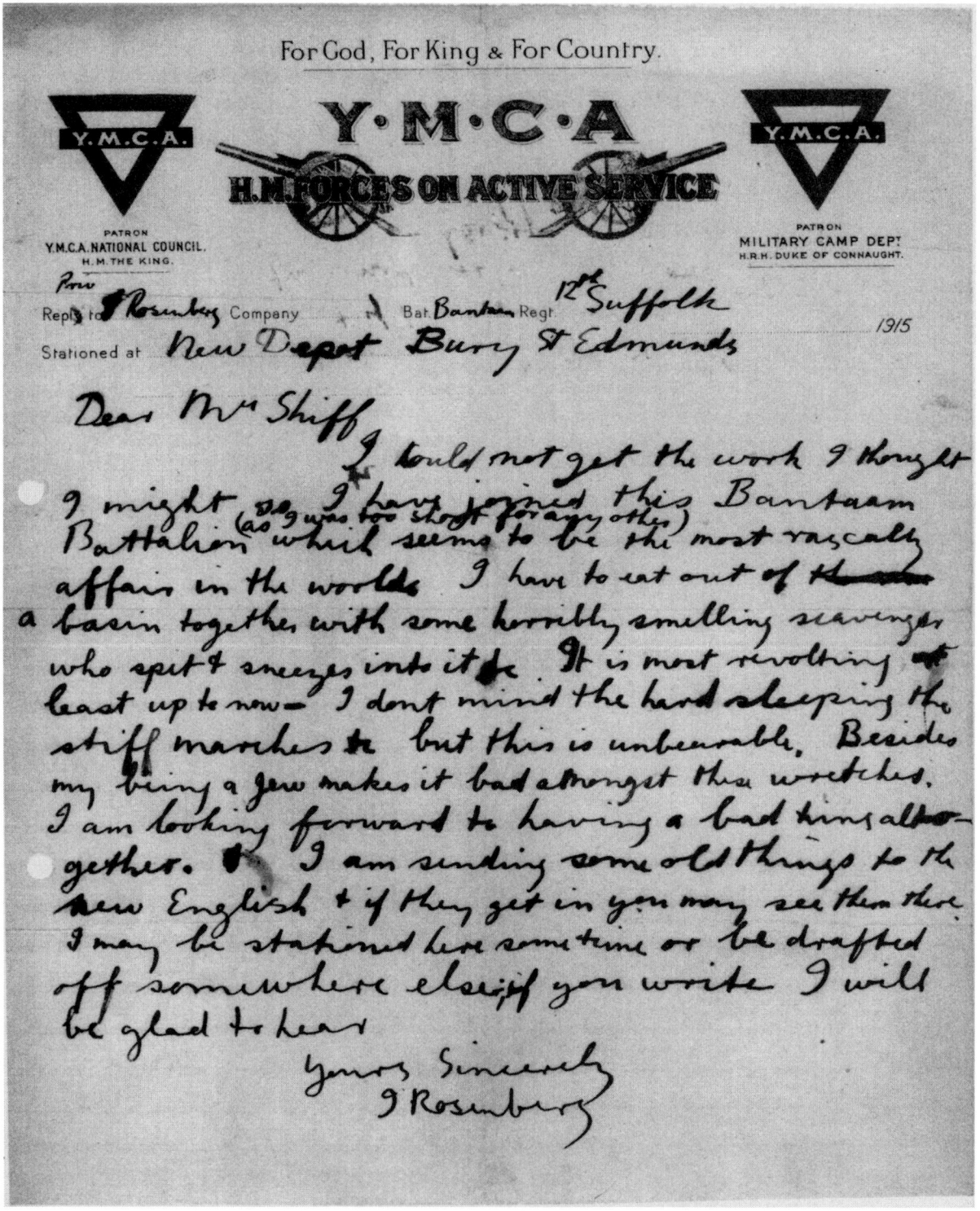

Rosenberg's letter to Sydney Schiff expressing dislike for the Bantam Regiment (Imperial War Museum, London)

Rosenberg's correspondence to Marsh at this time expressed his hatred of war and his despair at the financial bungling of the War Office. He found adjusting to army discipline to be difficult; moreover, he found the officers to be insulting and his fellow enlisted men unkempt. When he experienced anti-Semitic treatment, he wrote a terse poem about it.

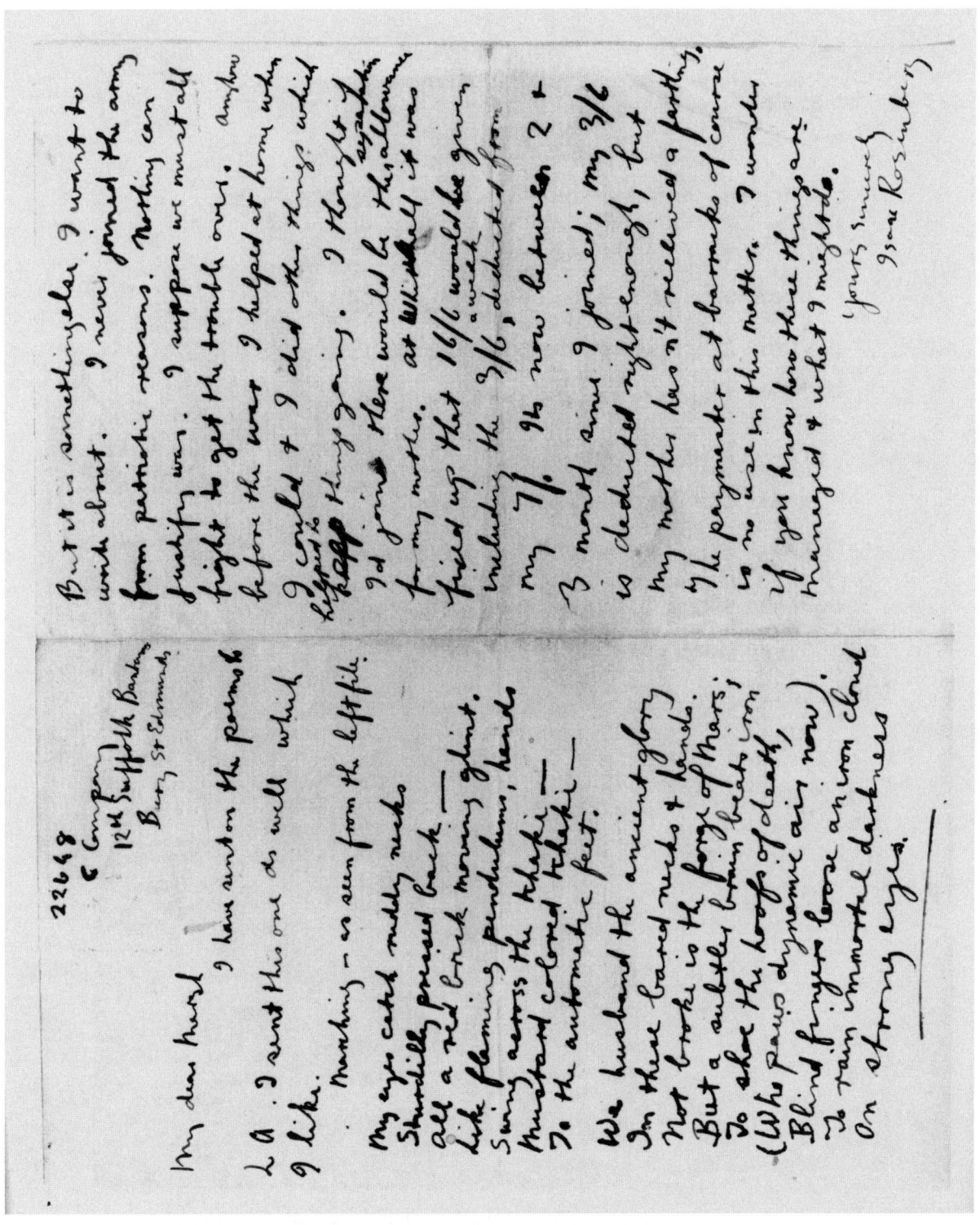

Rosenberg's letter to Marsh complaining about his military pay not being transferred to his mother. The letter includes an early draft of his poem "Marching," December 1915 (The Berg Collection, New York Public Library).

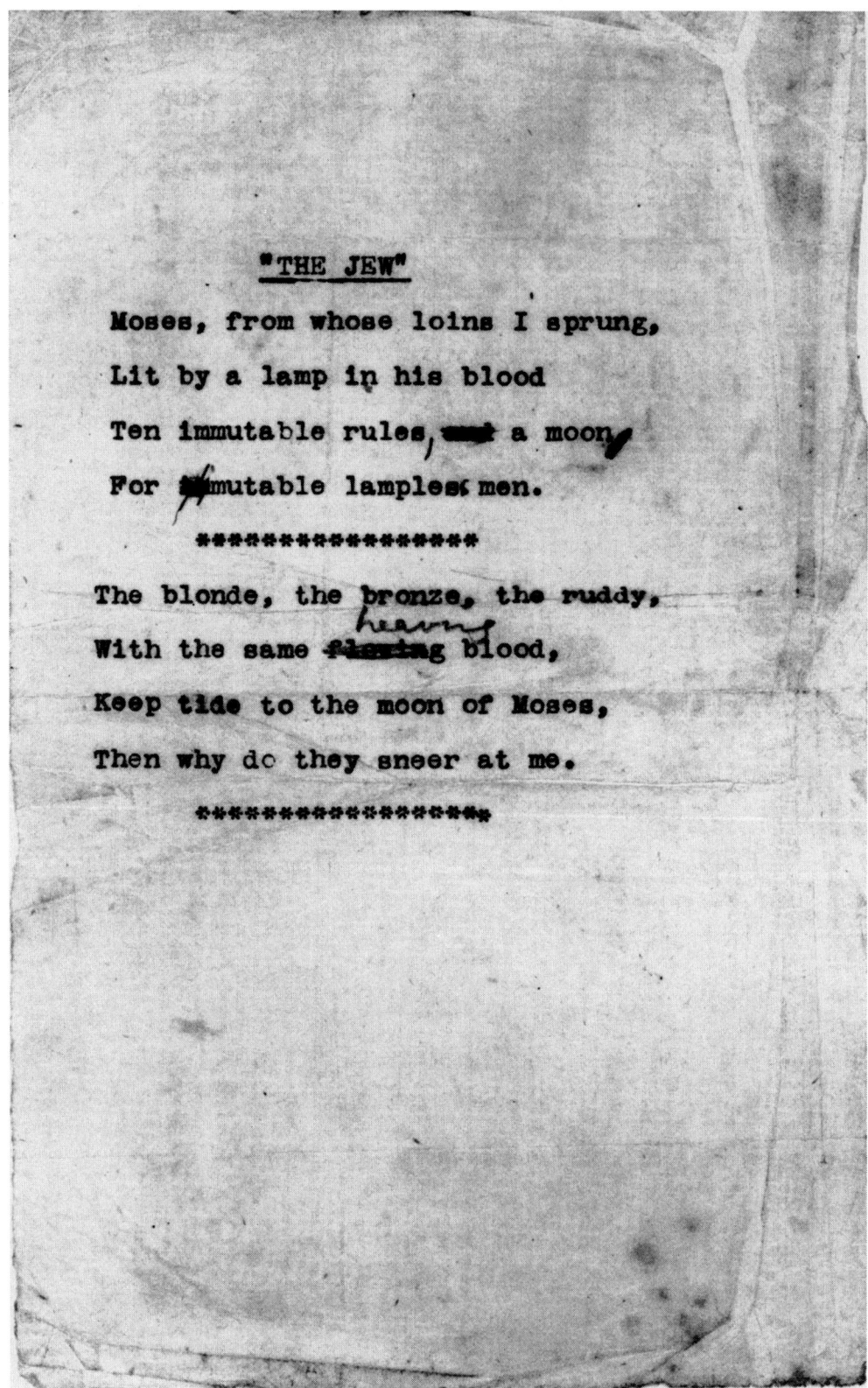

Revised typescript of Rosenberg's poem "The Jew" (Imperial War Museum, London)

Rosenberg found the bullying and overregulation in army life to be unbearable; at first, however, he did grow physically stronger under the tough regimen. Partly to escape the day-to-day drudgery and anti-Semitic harassment during his basic training, Rosenberg concentrated his spare time and energy on Moses (1916). He jotted down bits of this play on scraps of paper in the hope that he could combine all the fragments before he left for France.

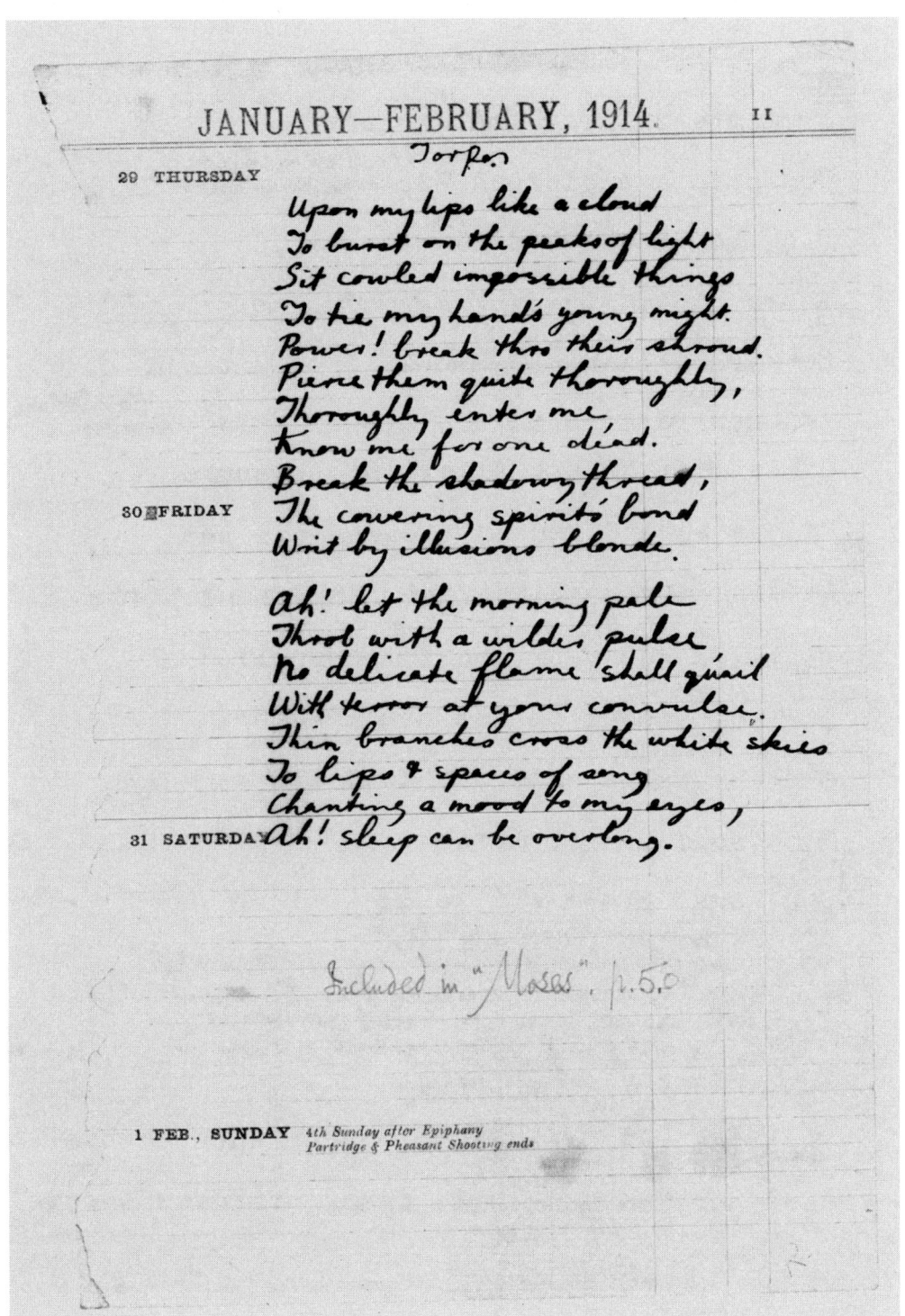

A fragment of Moses that Rosenberg wrote on paper from an old diary during basic training (Imperial War Museum, London)

Hebrew.
    Is not Miriam his sister, Jochabed his mother.

    In the womb he looked round and saw

    From furthermost stretches our wrong.

    From the palaces and schools

    Our pain has pierced ~~hid tunnel ways~~ *dead generations*

    Back to his bloods ~~old~~ *thin* source.

    As we lie chained by Egyptian men

    ~~So has he lain chained by~~ *He lay in nets of* their women,

    And now rejoice, he has broken their ~~chain~~ *meshes*.

    O! his desires are fleets of treasure

    He has squandered in treacherous seas

    Sailing mistrust to find frank ports.

    He fears our fear and tampers mildly

    For our assent to let him save us.

    When he walks amid our toil

    With some master mason

    His tense brows critical

    ~~Of the loose engines~~

    ~~Surposing sore loose machinic laws~~

    Hints famed divines flat ~~imposed~~

    ~~To perfect or builded base to touch~~

    With a scheme scratched on the sand.

    ~~With wisdom bettering it.~~

    Sleek ambush for covert under such council

    Peer muffled meanings, inner mirrored words.

Page from the revised typescript for Moses *(Imperial War Museum, London)*

At the end of May 1916 Rosenberg left the port of Southampton and spent eight hours on a military transport ship to Le Havre. On arriving in France he wrote his first war poem, "The Troop Ship."

Rosenberg's letter to Marsh discussing his embarkation for France, 27 May 1916 (The Berg Collection, New York Public Library)

"The Troop Ship," included in a letter to Rosenberg's friend, R. C. Trevelyan (Imperial War Museum, London)

Rosenberg's first impressions of war-torn France are presented in "From France," a poem that, in its ingenuousness, reflects his literary taste more than the actual military situation at the front.

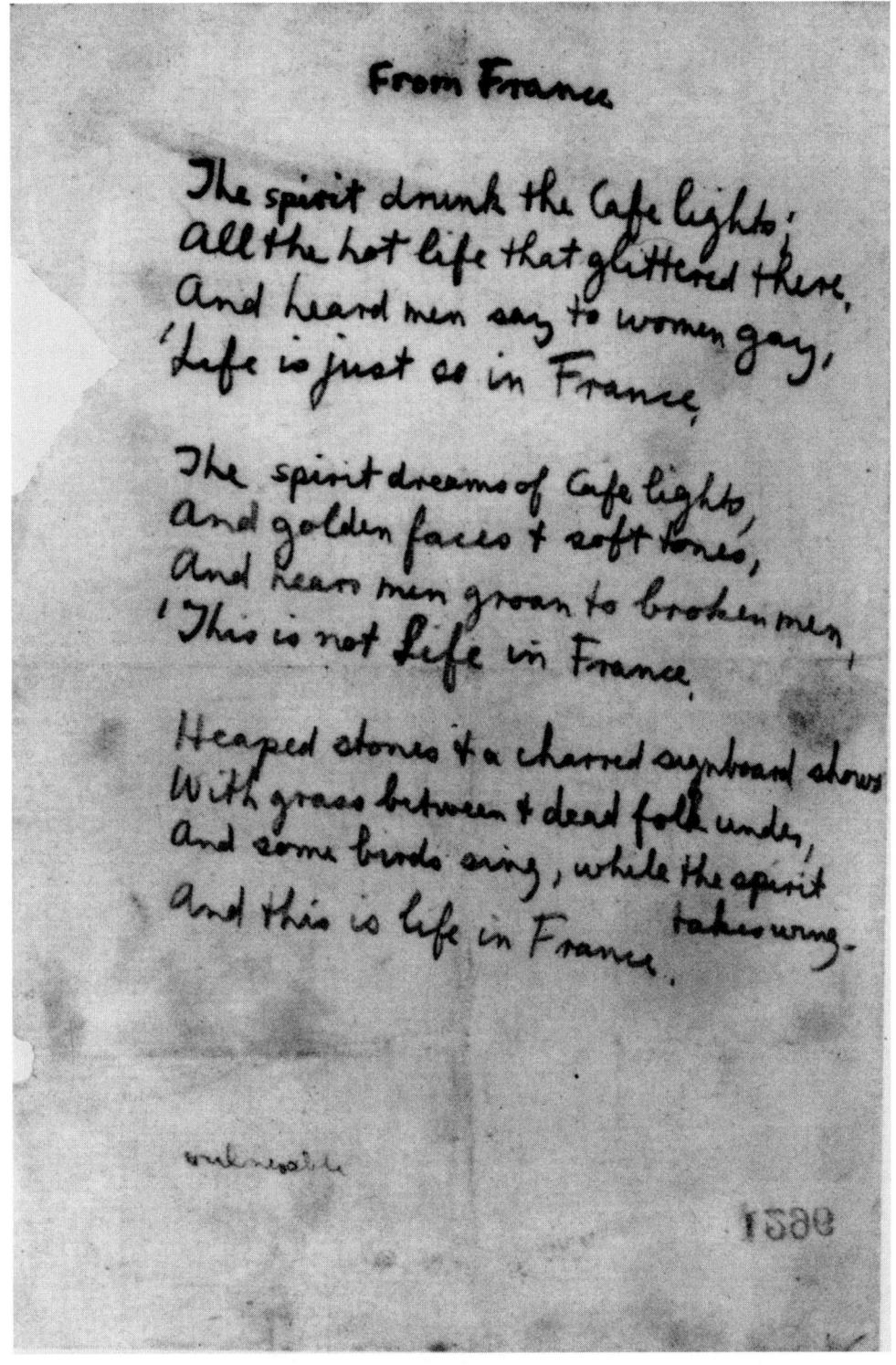

Draft of "From France," 1916 (Ian Parsons, ed., The Collected Works of Isaac Rosenberg)

Throughout June 1916 Rosenberg's Fortieth Division was trained in trench warfare near Bethune in preparation for the anticipated Somme offensive. The unit participated in minor engagements before the actual Battle of the Somme, but once that battle began, the Fortieth Division moved up to the front lines and held trenches in the Loos area. From this position Rosenberg experienced the sodden dugouts, the bombardments, the lice, the cold, the lack of privacy, and the presence of the ubiquitous dead. Many of these experiences were subsequently used in his poetry.

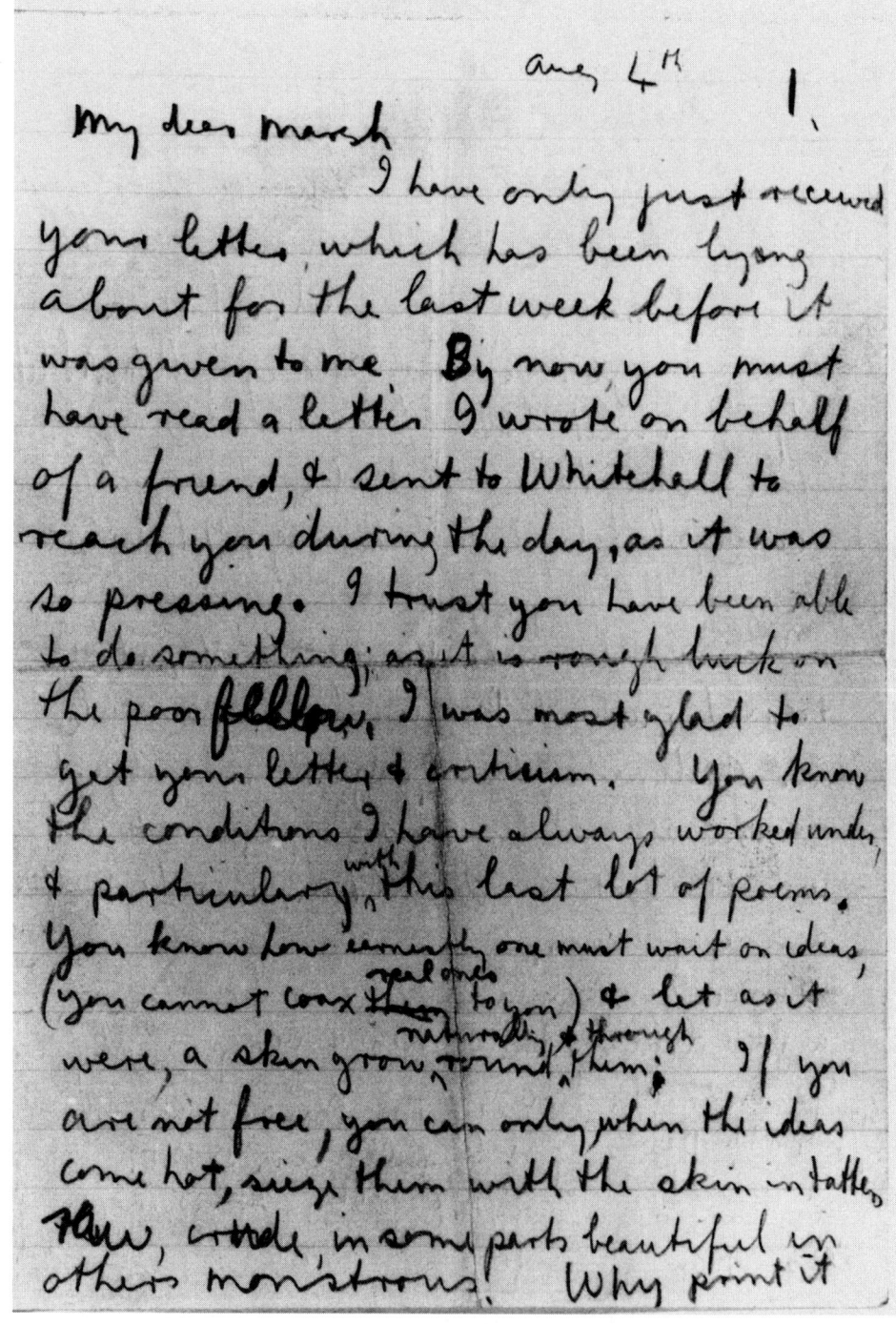

Rosenberg's letter to Marsh accompanying a copy of "Break of Day in the Trenches," one of his well-known war poems, 4 August 1916 (The Berg Collection, New York Public Library)

than? Because the ~~~~ rare parts must not be lost. I work more & more as I write into more depth & lucidity, I am sure. I have a fine idea for a most gorgeous play, Adam & Lilith. If I could get a few months after the war to work & absorb myself completely into the thing, I'd write a great thing.

I am enclosing a poem I wrote in the trenches, which is surely as simple as ordinary talk. You might object to the second line as vague, but that was the best way I could express the sense of dawn.

Since I wrote last I have been given a job behind the lines & very rarely go into the trenches. My address is C/o. 40th Divisional Coy Officer. B.E.F. Pte I Rosenberg 22311. It is more healthy but not absolutely safe from shells as we get those noisy visitors a good many times a day even here. Yours sincerely Isaac Rosenberg

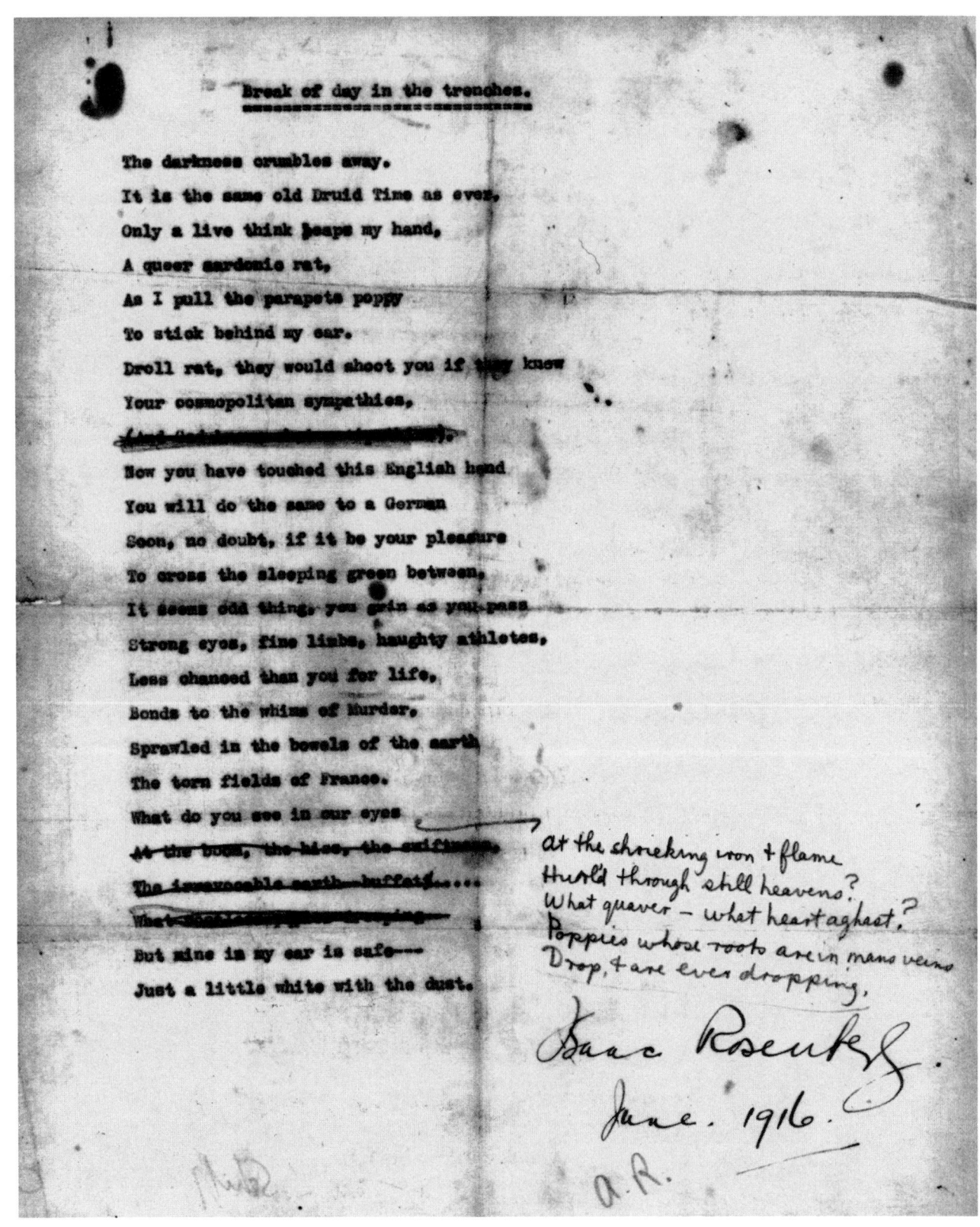

Rosenberg's corrected typescript of "Break of Day in the Trenches," sent to his sister Annie with his emendations (Imperial War Museum, London)

Rosenberg's letter to Marsh informing him of his enlistment and initial responses to military life, October 1915 (Ian Parsons, ed., The Collected Works of Isaac Rosenberg, *pp. 217–218)*

12th Suffolks
Bantam Bat.
New Offices Recruiting Depot
Bury St Edmunds

Dear Marsh

I have just joined the Bantams and am down here amongst a horrible rabble—Falstaff's scarecrows were nothing to these. Three out of every 4 have been scavengers [,] the fourth is a ticket of leave. But that is nothing—though while I'm waiting for my kit I'm roughing it a bit having come down without even a towel. I dry my self with my pocket handkerchief, I don't know whether I will be shifted as soon as I get my rigout—I thought you might like to hear this. I meant to send you some poems I wrote which are better than my usual things but I have left them at home where I am rather afraid to go for a while—I left without saying anything. Abercrombie did not write to me, I hope it is not because he disliked my things. If that is not the reason I should like to send him my new things. Can you tell me anything of Gertler.

Yours sincerely
Isaac Rosenberg

Analysis of "Break of Day in the Trenches" (Desmond Graham, The Truth of War: Owen, Blunden, and Rosenberg, *pp. 149–150)*

The word "they," as in "Break of Day in the Trenches," includes all who are committed to the soulless logic of mechanized destruction for the sake of militant purpose. The soldiers themselves embody this force, but they are a pathetically human and vulnerable component, at the whim of mechanized murder. "Break of Day in the Trenches" continues, addressing the rat:

> It seems you inwardly grin as you pass
> Strong eyes, fine limbs, haughty athletes,
> Less chanced than you for life,
> Bonds to the whims of murder,
> Sprawled in the bowels of the earth,
> The torn fields of France.
> What do you see in our eyes
> At the shrieking iron and flame
> Hurled through still heavens?
> What quaver—what heart aghast?

Rosenberg's pencil self-portrait in France (Imperial War Museum, London)

Conditions for the enlisted man in the trenches did not make writing poetry convenient: few pieces of paper were available; often no light was available in the dugouts; military duties were onerous and time-consuming. Rosenberg frequently gathered his scraps of paper together and mailed them to his sister Annie in England, so she could type them and return them for him to edit. When he finished rewriting the poems, the censors often would not allow him to post them.

The experimental nature of Rosenberg's poetry made it difficult for him to attain critical favor with influential readers. As a result, he was forced to publish his work at his own expense and by using obscure job printers. All these frustrations and the appalling living conditions shaped his poetic responses, which, unlike Siegfried Sassoon's vituperations against those responsible for prolonging the war and Wilfred Owen's appeals to pity, portrayed objectively the catastrophe of the war.

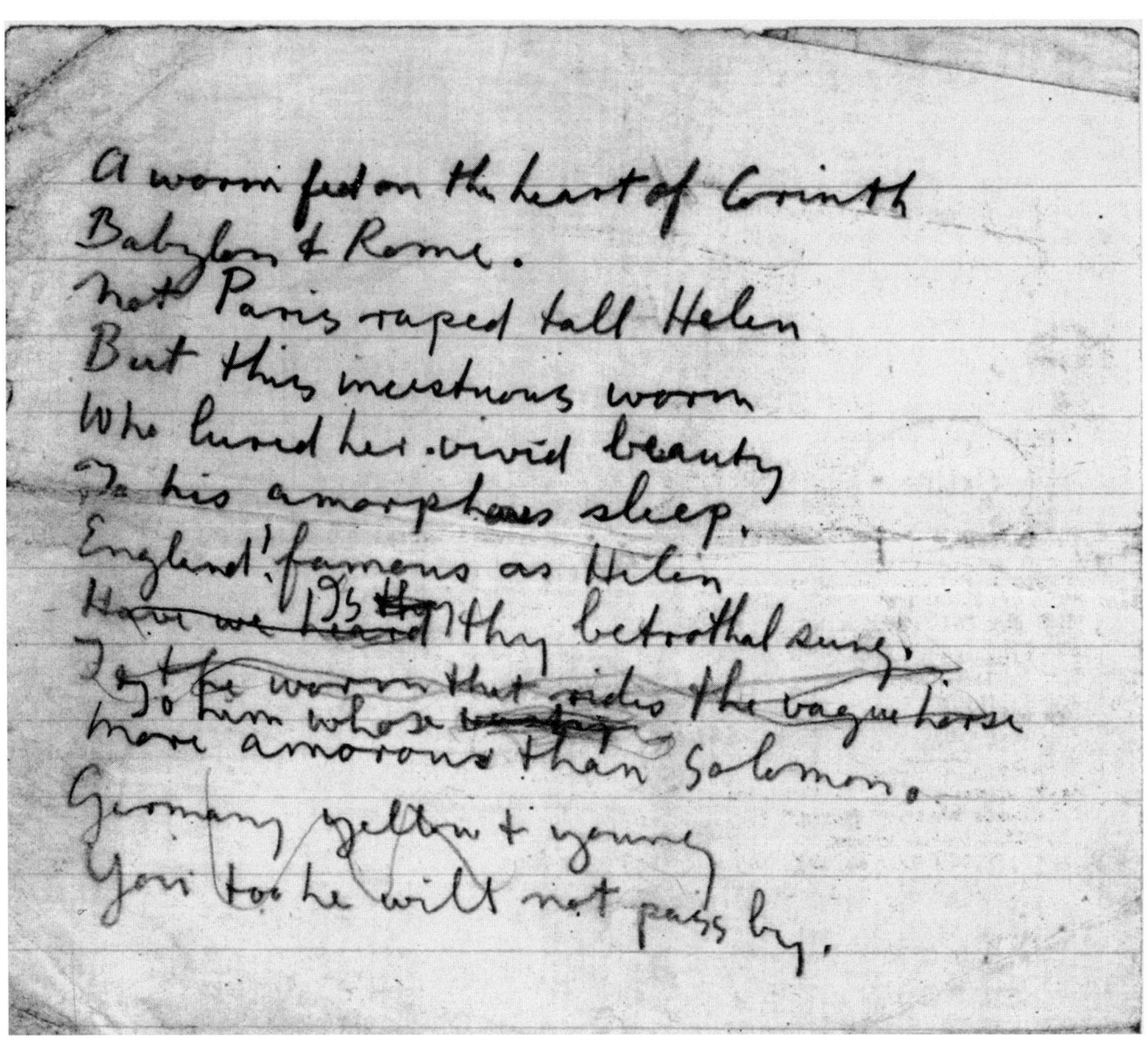

An example of how Rosenberg found scraps of paper on which to write his poems. Using a YMCA mail form, he wrote "A worm fed on the heart of Corinth" on the back (Imperial War Museum, London).

Rosenberg managed to survive the summer and autumn of 1916 in the trenches. The heat and lice-ridden clothes were bothersome, but generally he made light of these discomforts, as in his poem "The Immortals."

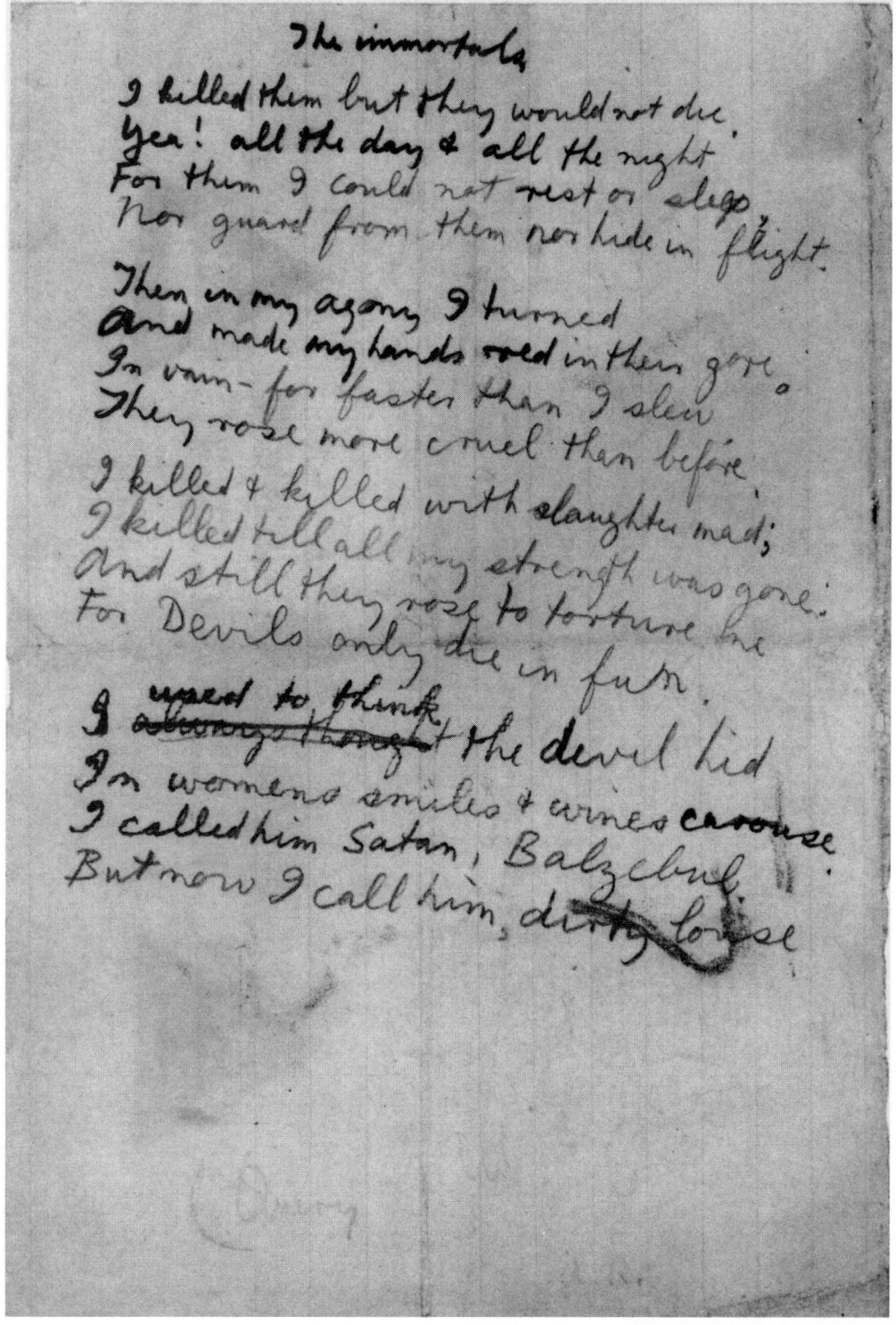

Working manuscript for "The Immortals," 1917 (Imperial War Museum, London)

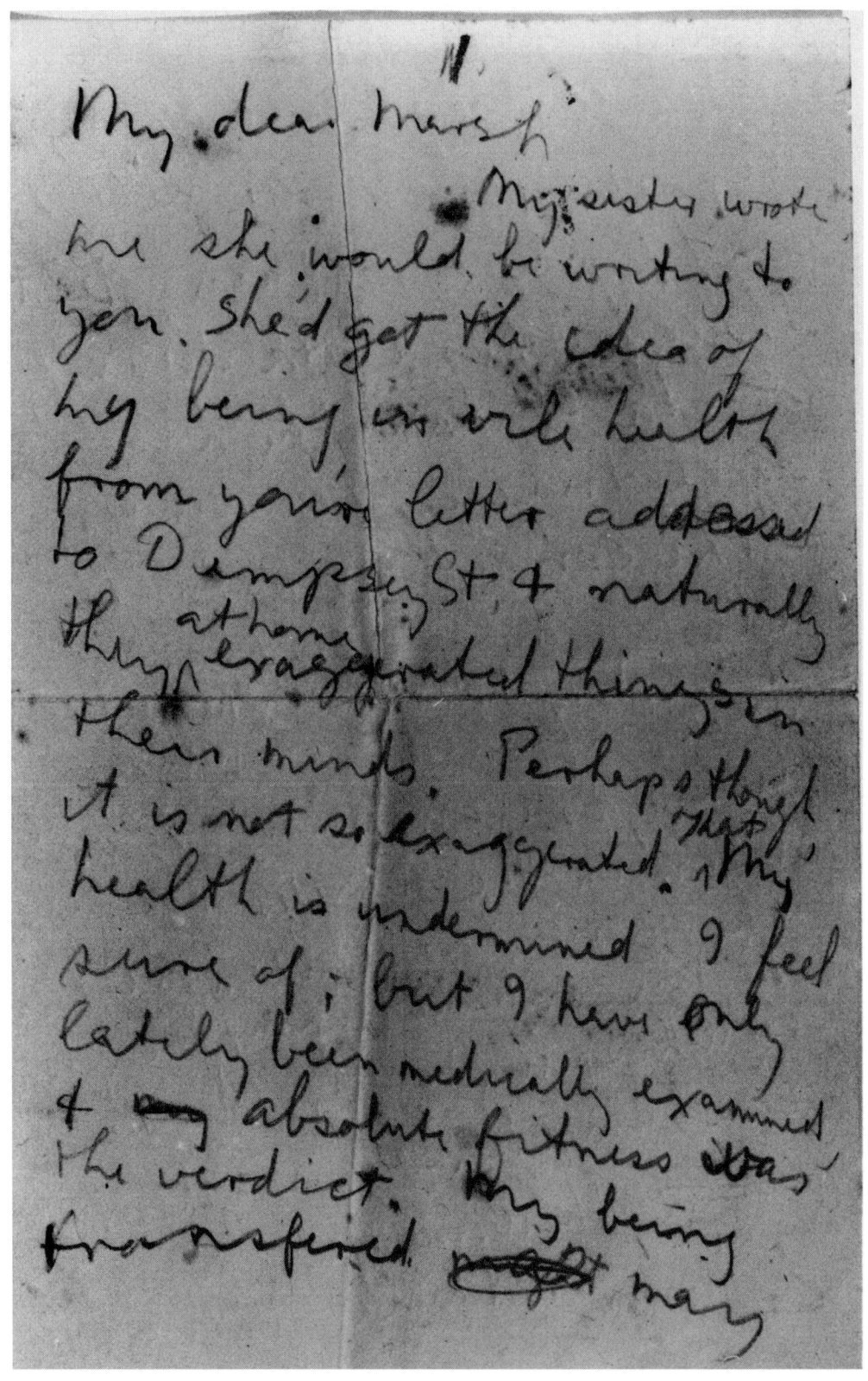

First page from Rosenberg's letter to Marsh suggesting that Marsh might use his influence to have him transferred out of the trenches to a less damp environment, 18 January 1917 (Ian Parsons, ed., The Collected Works of Isaac Rosenberg, pp. 251–252)

The physique of the soldier is no defence against war. Where the rat moves in the open, seems inwardly to grin, the soldiers, living and dead are "Sprawled in the bowels of the earth." What does the rat make of the terror their eyes express, their human anguish amid horror at what they see? The rat is questioned for its interpretation of man's humanity: it keeps its secret. But the "inward grin" which Rosenberg sees in its features tells us of the rat's familiarity with man's destructiveness through experience, its awareness of the fragility of human strength, the power of human destruction.

The joy aroused by the larks' song finally turned to a sombre, pained awareness. The emotion was too intense and too out of place on the battlefield for what it brought to be sustained. But this contemplation, gathering force as it traces over man's destruction and recalls his fear, can draw from an awareness of the rat's resilience a thoughtfulness which finds its own human resilience. Man's pretensions are placed, but consciousness of pervasive destruction has brought with it a sense of brotherhood. A brotherhood which even includes the poppies which grow from the dead and fade. A brotherhood in which he, as his mind's activities prove, is for the moment among the living:

> Poppies whose roots are in man's veins
> Drop, and are ever dropping;
> But mine in my ear is safe—
> Just a little white with the dust.

My dear Marsh

My sister wrote me she would be writing to you. She'd got the idea of my being in vile health from your letter addressed to Dempsey St, and naturally they at home exaggerated things in their minds. Perhaps though it is not so exaggerated. That my health is undermined I feel sure of; but I have only lately been medically examined, and absolute fitness was the verdict. My being transfer[r]ed may be the consequence of my reporting sick, or not; I don't know for certain. But though this work does not entail half the hardships of the trenches, the winter and the conditions naturally tells on me, having once suffered from weak lungs, as you know. I have been in the trenches most of the 8 months I've been here, and the continual damp and exposure is whispering to my old friend consumption, and he may hear the words they say in time. I have nothing outwardly to show yet, but I feel it inwardly. I don't know what you could do in a case like this; perhaps I could be made use of as a

By mid October the Fortieth Division was sent to Abbeville for training and then on to Bapaume in November. Just after Christmas the division entered the Somme valley and found trench conditions and the landscape to be nightmarish. Reports of the icy winter conditions prompted Annie Rosenberg to write Marsh (serving as Winston Churchill's private secretary) about her brother's fragile respiratory condition. Marsh procured a medical examination for Rosenberg, but the poet replied in a subsequent letter that he had received an unexpected verdict of "absolute fitness."

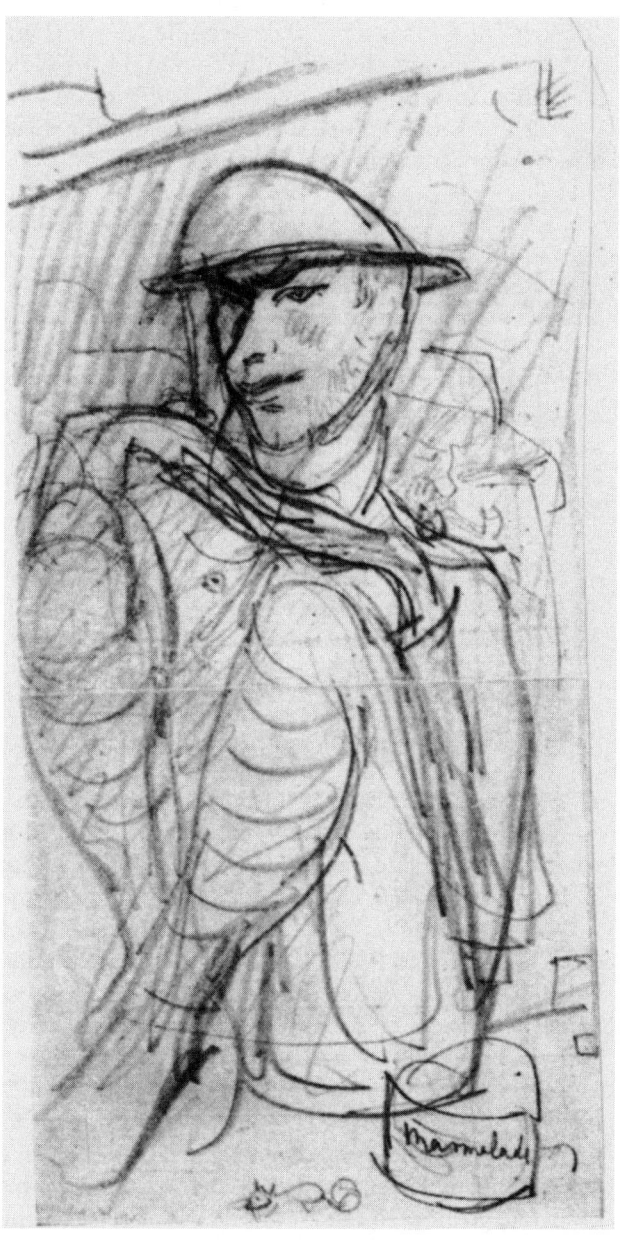

Pencil self-portrait of Rosenberg in the trenches (Isaac Rosenberg Estate)

draughtsman at home; or something else in my own line, or perhaps on munitions. My new address is

>   Pte. I R 22311
>   7 Platoon F. Coy
>   40th Division
>   Works Battalion
>   B.E.F.

I wrote a poem some while ago which Bottomley liked so, and I want you to see it, but I'm writing in most awkward conditions and can't copy it now. "Poetry" of Chicago printed a couple of my things and are paying me. I should think you find the Colonial Office interesting particularly after the war.

I hope however it leaves you leisure for literature; for me its the great thing.

> Yours sincerely
> Isaac Rosenberg

Rosenberg was eventually transferred to a works battalion but ended up as a cook for a trench mortar battalion under the command of a Jewish officer, Captain Frank Waley. In this menial job Rosenberg found time to write, and he showed scraps of his poetry to Waley. Appreciating his improved circumstances, Rosenberg wrote Gordon Bottomley in February that he felt pleased to be out of the trenches, and he enclosed a copy of "Louse Hunting."

Rosenberg's letter to Gordon Bottomley complaining of ill health and enclosing "Louse Hunting," February 1917 (Ian Parsons, ed., The Collected Works of Isaac Rosenberg, *pp. 252–253)*

To Gordon Bottomley

Your letters always give me a strange and large pleasure; and I shall never think I have written poetry in vain, since it has brought your friendliness in my way. Now, feeling as I am, cast away and used up, you don't know what a letter like yours is to me. Ever since November, when we first started on our long marches, I have felt weak; but it seems to be some inscrutable mysterious quality of weakness that defies all doctors. I have been examined most thoroughly several times by our doctor, and there seems to be nothing at all wrong with my lungs. I believe I have strained my abdomen in some way, and I shall know of it later on. We have had desperate weather, but the poor fellows in the trenches where there are no dugouts are the chaps to pity. I am sending a very slight sketch of a lousehunt. It may be a bit vague, as I could not work it out here, but if you can keep it till I get back I can work on it then. I do believe I could make a fine thing of Judas. Judas as a character is more magnanimous than Moses, and I believe I could make it very intense and write a lot from material out here. Thanks very much for your joining in with me to rout the pest out, but I have tried all kinds of stuff; if you can think of any preparation you believe effective I'd be most grateful for it.

A discussion of Rosenberg's "Trench Poems," with particular attention to his developing acceptance of the nature of war (Jack Lindeman, "The 'Trench Poems' of Isaac Rosenberg," The Literary Review, *2 [Summer 1959], pp. 577–585)*

On April 1, 1918, Isaac Rosenberg, at the age of twenty-eight, was killed in action somewhere in France and, like many of his comrades in the British army, buried in an unmarked grave. Though a number of his poems had already appeared in magazines and three pamphlets containing his earlier work had been published at his own expense, his death carried not the same shock of tragedy for those who had their fingers on the pulse beat of English poetry during the war years as did that of either Rupert Brooke or Wilfred Owen. The sense of accomplishment in these latter two soldier-poets was indisputable, and even though both of them had died young, both had written a substantial quantity of poems displaying a definite maturity. The lesser known Rosenberg, on the other hand, was looked upon by even his strongest supporters as a "poet with promise of greatness" rather than a poet who had achieved a certain number of commanding successes. Critics generally held widely divergent opinions as to the quality of his poems. Thus his work never until recently received the attention which it deserves from discriminating poetry lovers.

An English critic, H. Coombes, in a book on Edward Thomas (an English poet and essayist also killed in World War I) refers to the unwarranted indifference shown by the public towards Thomas and states, "No poet of the century, with the exception of Isaac Rosenberg, has been so unjustifiably neglected. It seems clear that Thomas would not have done work of the quality that Rosenberg would unquestionably have done." But Siegfried Sassoon is less qualifying and consequently more willing to put himself out on the limb in behalf of Rosenberg in his "Foreword" to *Collected Poems* (Shocken Books, New York. 1949): "I can only hope that what I say, inadequate though it may be, will help to gain for him the full recognition of his genius which has hitherto been delayed."

Ironically enough, the war which destroyed Rosenberg also provided him with those ideal incidents

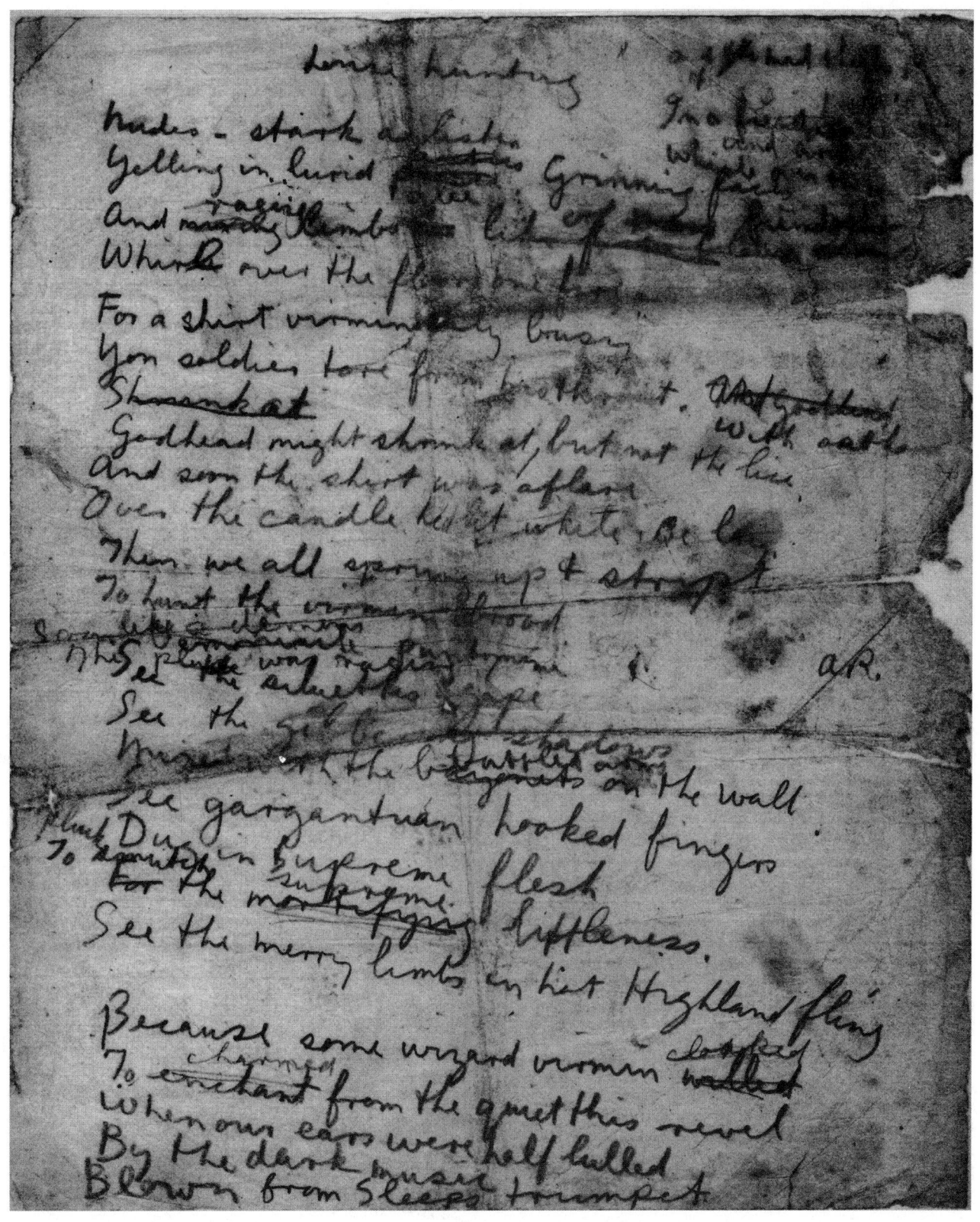

Manuscript for "Louse Hunting" (Imperial War Museum, London)

for which his poetic voice had been vainly searching since the day that it first became aware of its potential power. And though he had no deliberate wish to become a "war poet" it is as a war poet that he did his most effective writing. At the center of *Collected Poems* sits "Trench Poems." They form the vital core of his work; they are the Everest which he finally conquered, and it is around them that any serious discussion of his poetry must invariably begin. . . .

Isaac Rosenberg had three basic loyalties. One, as a member of the human race, was to his fellow man the world over:

> Droll rat, they would shoot you if they knew
> Your cosmopolitan sympathies.

The second was to the England in which he was born and bred and for whom he gave his life:

> Water–water–O water
> For one of England's dying sons.

And the third was to traditional Judaism

> . . . from whose loins I sprung.

In the twenty pieces which go to make up "Trench Poems" we find these three loyalties fused together in perfect harmony. He sees Moses, for example, not as legislator over a small peculiar body of people known as Jews but as one who

> Lit by a lamp in his blood
> Ten immutable rules, a moon
> For mutable lampless men.
>
> The blonde, the bronze, the ruddy,
> With the same heaving blood,
> Keep tide to the moon of Moses.

But then he suddenly asks himself that perennial question which for many centuries the Jews of the Diaspora have never ceased to ask themselves, namely,

> . . . why do they sneer at me?

Moses gave of his wisdom to mankind and mankind accepted it and has attempted to live by it ever since, but because Moses happened to be a Jew–and Mr. Rosenberg is one of his scions,

> Moses, from whose loins I sprung,–

mankind has ungratefully selected his descendant brethren as a target for its spite. Perhaps this spite is in some way connected with its inability to keep abreast of the demands of the "ten immutable rules"?

After a century of virtual peace the guns began to sound once again in Europe. 1914 saw the inheritors of the Sixth Commandment, Thou shalt not kill, do deliberate violence to that commandment. The worm that "fed on the heart of Corinth, / Babylon and Rome" was about to burrow into the heart of his beloved England.

> England! famous as Helen
> Is thy betrothal sung
> To him the shadowless,
> More amorous than Solomon.

The daughters of war "have no softer lure . . . than the savage ways of death." They are Amazons and they drive "the darkness into the flame of day. . . ."

> Over our corroding faces
> That must be broken–broken for evermore
> So the soul can leap out
> Into their huge embraces.

Isaac Rosenberg gladly offered his services to his country:

> I love you, great new Titan!
> Am I not you?
> Napoleon and Caesar
> Out of you grew.

He was well aware of the immemorial fact that "Cruel men were made immortal" by war. Still, England had no other choice, faced as she was with a rapacious enemy bent on giving the entire earth, if necessary, as a gift, to Chaos:

> Chaos! that coincides with this militant purpose.
> Chaos! the heart of this earnest malignancy.

The most impressive and of course the best known of the "Trench Poems" are those which glow with a more personal flame. They are glimpses into the experiences of a common soldier and yet at the same time are aimed high enough so that they surmount the mere temporal ruins of a particular time and trouble. This is not to imply, however, that they lack that touch of intimacy which arouses a feeling of empathy in the reader. Take for example "The Troop Ship":

> We lie all sorts of ways
> And cannot sleep.
> The wet wind is so cold,
> And the lurching men so careless,
> That, should you drop to a doze,
> Winds' fumble or men's feet
> Are on your face.

Anyone who has ever had to endure the careless "lurching men" on a troop ship can vouch for the fidelity of Mr. Rosenberg's observation. But the troop ship is only the beginning of a soldier's adventures. There are more serious and trying ordeals awaiting him in France where only "The spirit" now can dream

> . . . of cafe lights
> And golden faces and soft tones. . . .

He enters that gay, happy land, once the focal point for everything that was advanced in Western culture, and finds

> Heaped stones and a charred signboard show
> With grass between and dead folk under. . . .

The battle is already near at hand. Soon the soldier-poet reaches the front lines and is posted as a sentry in some strategic corner of one of the trenches facing the enemy:

> Somber the night is.
> And though we have our lives, we know
> What sinister threat lurks there.
>
> Dragging these anxious limbs we only know
> This poison-blasted track. . . .
>
> Death could drop from the dark
> As easily as song–

But death does not "drop from the dark," or not yet at least, for there is another dawn to be witnessed:

> the darkness crumbles away–

a dreary awakening in the oozing mud of a trench where everything is quiet for the moment. All's bleak and cheerless in No Man's Land. As the soldier-poet gazes about him nothing seems to be alive but "the parapet's poppy" which he pulls from the earth "to stick behind" his ear, and "a queer sardonic rat" that "leaps my hand–." The rat, universally acknowledged as one of the most despicable creatures on the face of the earth, has a lesson to teach exalted Man. Like the poet, the rat has cosmopolitan sympathies, even in a time of fiercely partisan alliances.

> Now you have touched this English hand
> You will do the same to a German–
> Soon, no doubt, if it be your pleasure
> To cross the sleeping green between.

Certainly the rat with his catholic point of view is more likely to survive the present chaos–the poet believing the rat intuitively senses this, says, "you inwardly grin as you pass"–than the young soldiers with "Strong eyes" and "fine limbs." The "haughty athletes" are doomed simply because they have not learned to touch an English hand and a German one simultaneously. "We must love one another or die" a contemporary poet has warned, and this is exactly what Mr. Rosenberg is telling us.

War has its lighter side too, or if not lighter, its discomforts which are not quite fatal. Lest we forget, our fathers fought without the aid of D.D.T.

> I used to think the Devil hid
> In women's smiles and wine's carouse.
> I called him Satan, Beelzebub.
> But now I call him dirty louse.

It is easy enough for us to laugh over such matters having never been exposed to the torment which this insect is capable of inflicting.

> Nudes–stark and glistening,
> Yelling in lurid glee. Grinning faces
> And raging limbs
> Whirl over the floor one fire.
> For a shirt verminously busy
> Yon soldier tore from his throat, with oaths
> Godhead might shrink at, but not the lice.
> . . . .
> Then we all sprang up and stript
> To hunt the verminous brood.
> Soon like a demons' pantomime
> The place was raging.
> See the silhouettes agape,
> See the gibbering shadows
> Mixed with the battled arms on the wall.
> See gargantuan hooked fingers
> Pluck in supreme flesh
> To smutch supreme littleness.
> See the merry limbs in hot Highland fling. . . .

One reason I have quoted this poem at some length is that it is marvelously photographic and reproduces so authentically the scene of these suffering soldiers that one is almost tempted to reach inside his shirt and begin scratching. Also it illustrates quite effectively some of the hammer-like power which Isaac Rosenberg's poetry possesses to such a high degree: "demons' pantomime," "gibbering shadows," "gargantuan hooked fingers," "supreme littleness." And what could be more lucid than the image of "Nudes–stark and glistening, / Yelling in lurid glee," or "For a shirt verminously busy / Yon soldier tore from his throat, with oaths / Godhead might shrink at . . ." or "Merry limbs in hot Highland fling"?

When the shells begin bursting and the bombs exploding the men quickly forget their lice, some of them, in fact, forget permanently becoming the

Rosenberg in 1917 (Isaac Rosenberg Estate)

"sprawled dead" in "the shattered track" over which the wheels of an ambulance lurch without causing them any pain:

> Their shut mouths made no moan.

Friend and foe born of man and woman are huddled together in an everlasting league of comradeship while the "shells go crying over them / From night till night and now."

> Earth has waited for them
> All the time of their growth
> Fretting for their decay:
> Now she has them at last!
> In the strength of their strength
> Suspended—stopped and held.

William Butler Yeats always insisted that passive suffering was not a proper theme for poetry, and since he felt most of the poems coming out of the First World War fell into this category, he rejected them for The Oxford Book of Modern Verse (1935, edited by W. B. Yeats). In his introduction to that volume he claims that "In all the great tragedies, tragedy is a joy to the man who dies." It seems quite obvious that he was thinking here in terms of the old fashion warrior-hero. What he did not realize was that even by 1914 war had become to a large extent depersonalized. The warrior was no longer heroic in so far as he no longer came into direct contact with his enemy. In modern warfare the soldier seldom if ever sees his opponent before he wounds or kills him. This does not really make him any less heroic than his armored ancestor, for his "passive suffering" is merely a different manifestation of the old heroic tradition for which Mr. Yeats (who was a noncombatant of course) nostalgically yearned. The mode of warfare had changed but Yeats' thinking had not, otherwise he would certainly have recognized not only the poetic quality of such lines as

> Out of those doomed nostrils and the doomed mouth,
> When the swift iron burning bee
> Drained the wild honey of their youth.

Found to be fit after a second medical examination, Rosenberg continued working behind the lines: as a member of the works battalion, he built and repaired roads and trenches as well as buried the dead. But in the winter even a relatively comfortable job behind the lines was exhausting and dangerous.

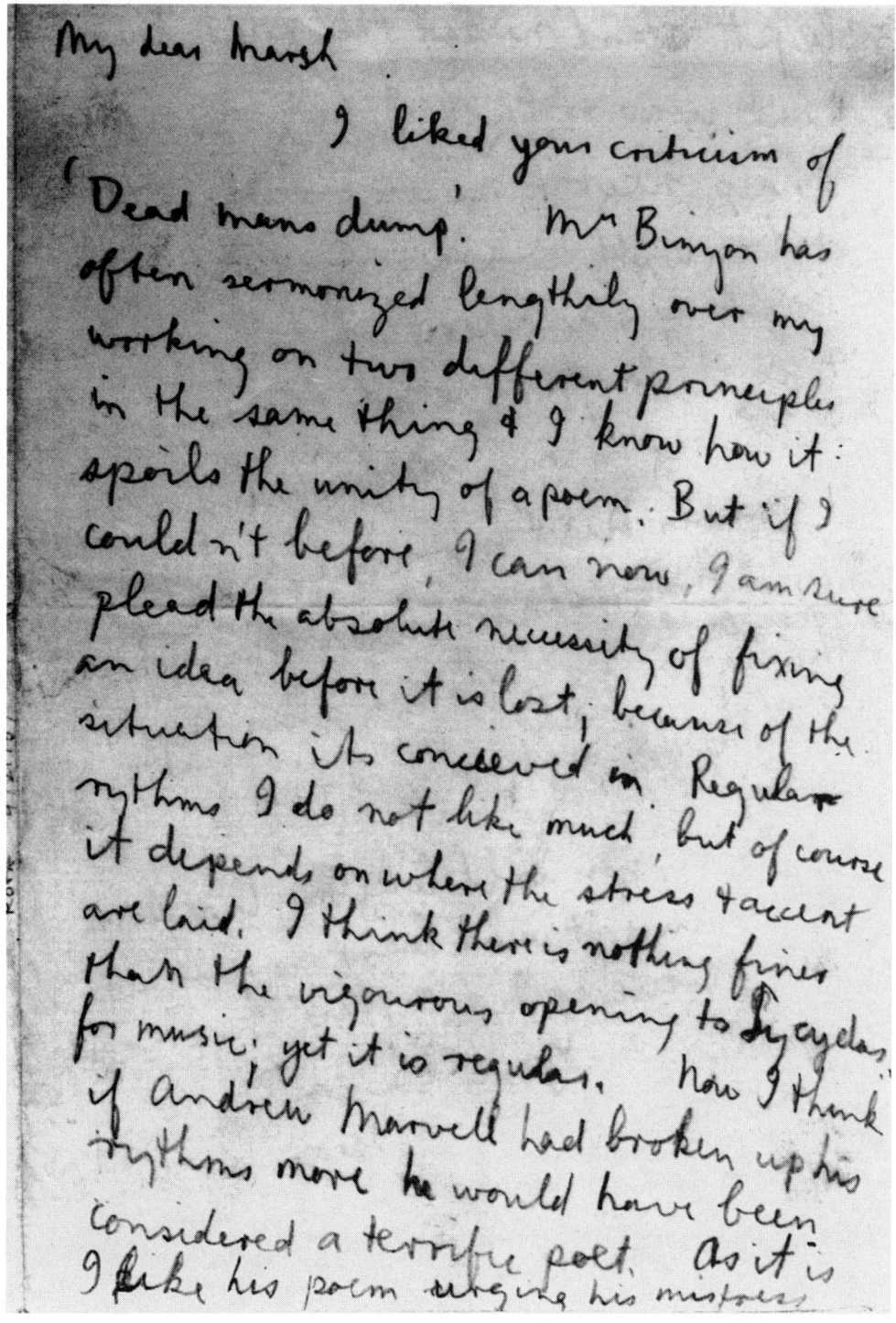

Rosenberg's letter to Marsh discussing poetry amid the horrific conditions on the front, 27 May 1917 (The Berg Collection, New York Public Library)

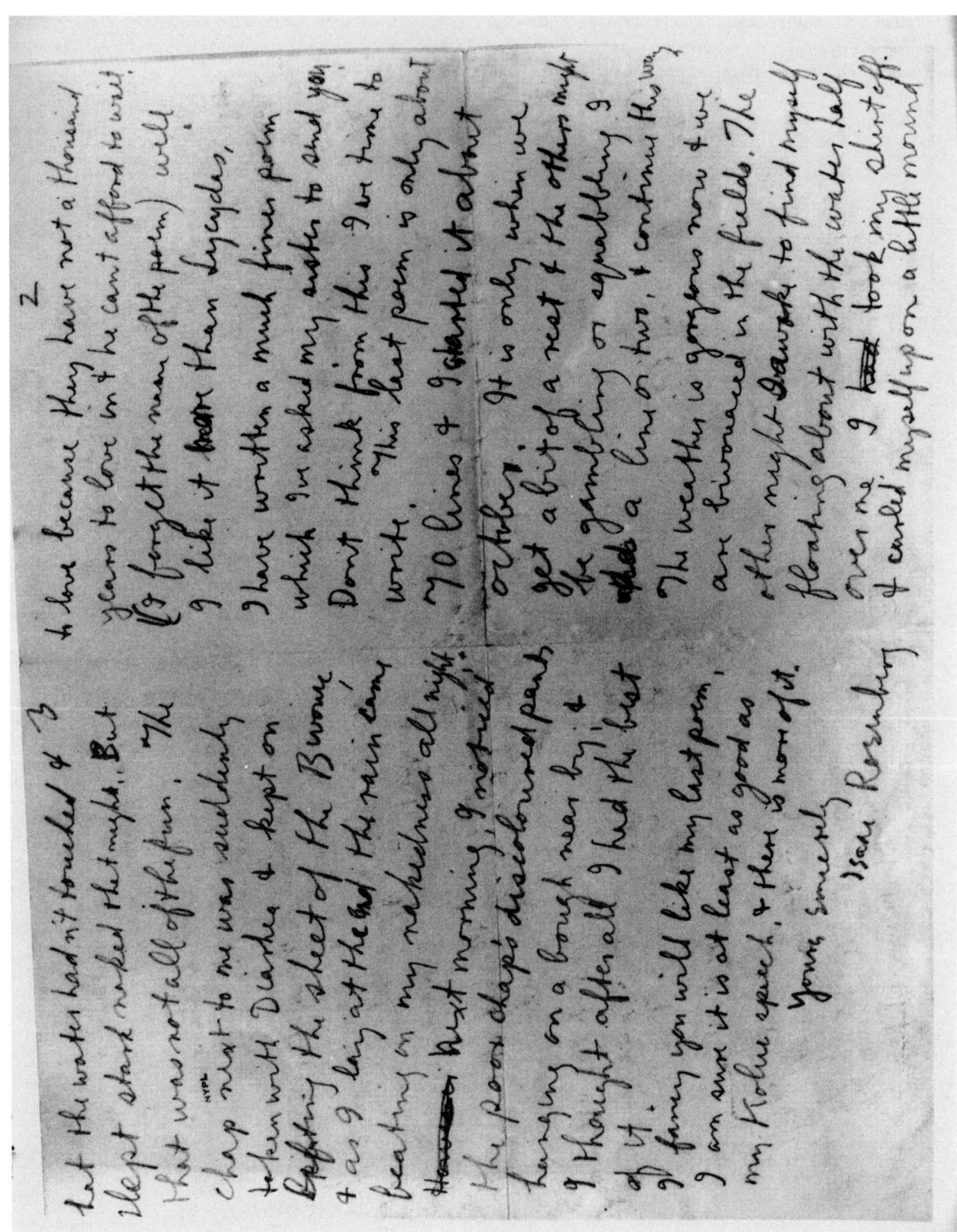

Letter from Rosenberg to Marsh, summer 1917 (from Collected Works, 1937)

but the accuracy with which they reflect the plight of the thousands of young men irredeemably caught in the mouth of that monstrous mechanized fire-breathing serpent of 20th Century warfare. Man is pathetically helpless against the hard explosive metal of the machine when confronting it on its own level. Mr. Rosenberg knew this because he had been to battle:

> What of us who, flung on the shrieking pyre,
> Walk. . . .
> . . . .
> The air is loud with death

against which there is no defense. The poet shouts, "Maniac Earth!" but the roar of the guns drowns his protesting voice. All there is left for him to do is to sympathize with those

> Burnt black by strange decay. . . .

He imagines he hears the "weak scream" of "one not long dead" as the wheels of the truck he is riding in "grazed his dead face." Catching but a glimpse of the "face" he nudges the priest seated next to him and asks if he happened to recognize the dead soldier as someone they knew:

> . . . I heard . . .
> Dimly my brain
> Held words and lost. . . .
> Suddenly my blood ran cold. . . .
> God! God! it could not be.
>
> . . . my brother's name;
> I sank–
> I clutched the priest.
> They did not tell me it was he
> Was killed three days ago.
>
> What are the great sceptered dooms
> To us, caught
> In the wild wave?
> We break ourselves on them,
> My brother, our hearts and years.

A new kind of heroism perhaps, but a heroism that is as genuine as any expressed by those classic examples which Mr. Yeats was referring to and over which we have pored generation after generation with deserving awe.

"*Dead Man's Dump*" (Ian Parsons, ed., *The Collected Works of Isaac Rosenberg, pp. 109–111*)

> The plunging limbers over the shattered track
> Racketed with their rusty freight,
> Stuck out like many crowns of thorns,
> And the rusty stakes like sceptres old
> To stay the flood of brutish men
> Upon our brothers dear.
>
> The wheels lurched over sprawled dead
> But pained them not, though their bones crunched,
> Their shut mouths made no moan,
> They lie there huddled, friend and foeman,
> Man born of man, and born of woman,
> And shells go crying over them
> From night till night and now.
>
> Earth has waited for them
> All the time of their growth
> Fretting for their decay:
> Now she has them at last!
> In the strength of their strength
> Suspended–stopped and held.
>
> What fierce imaginings their dark souls lit
> Earth! have they gone into you?
> Somewhere they must have gone,
> And flung on your hard back
> Is their souls' sack,
> Emptied of God-ancestralled essences.
> Who hurled them out? Who hurled?
>
> None saw their spirits' shadow shake the grass,
> Or stood aside for the half used life to pass
> Out of those doomed nostrils and the doomed mouth,
> When the swift iron burning bee
> Drained the wild honey of their youth.
>
> What of us, who flung on the shrieking pyre,
> Walk, our usual thoughts untouched,
> Our lucky limbs as on ichor fed,
> Immortal seeming ever?
> Perhaps when the flames beat loud on us,
> A fear may choke in our veins
> And the startled blood may stop.
>
> The air is loud with death,
> The dark air spurts with fire
> The explosions ceaseless are.
> Timelessly now, some minutes past,
> These dead strode time with vigorous life,
> Till the shrapnel called "an end!"
> But not to all. In bleeding pangs
> Some borne on stretchers dreamed of home,
> Dear things, war-blotted from their hearts.
>
> A man's brains splattered on
> A stretcher-bearer's face;
> His shook shoulders slipped their load,
> But when they bent to look again
> The drowning soul was sunk too deep
> For human tenderness.
>
> They left this dead with the older dead,
> Stretched at the cross roads.
> Burnt black by strange decay

One of Rosenberg's widely anthologized poems, "Dead Man's Dump," was no doubt inspired by his months laboring with the Works Battalion. The originality of Rosenberg's writings was so startling that many Georgian poets and critics found his poetry too raw for their tastes, and Marsh felt that only the "Ah! Koelue!" section of Moses was worth including in Georgian Poetry, 1916–1917. In the United States, however, Harriet Monroe thought Rosenberg's poetry was inventive enough to be included in her Poetry: A Magazine of Verse in December 1916.

Revised typescript for "Dead Man's Dump," 1917 (Imperial War Museum, London)

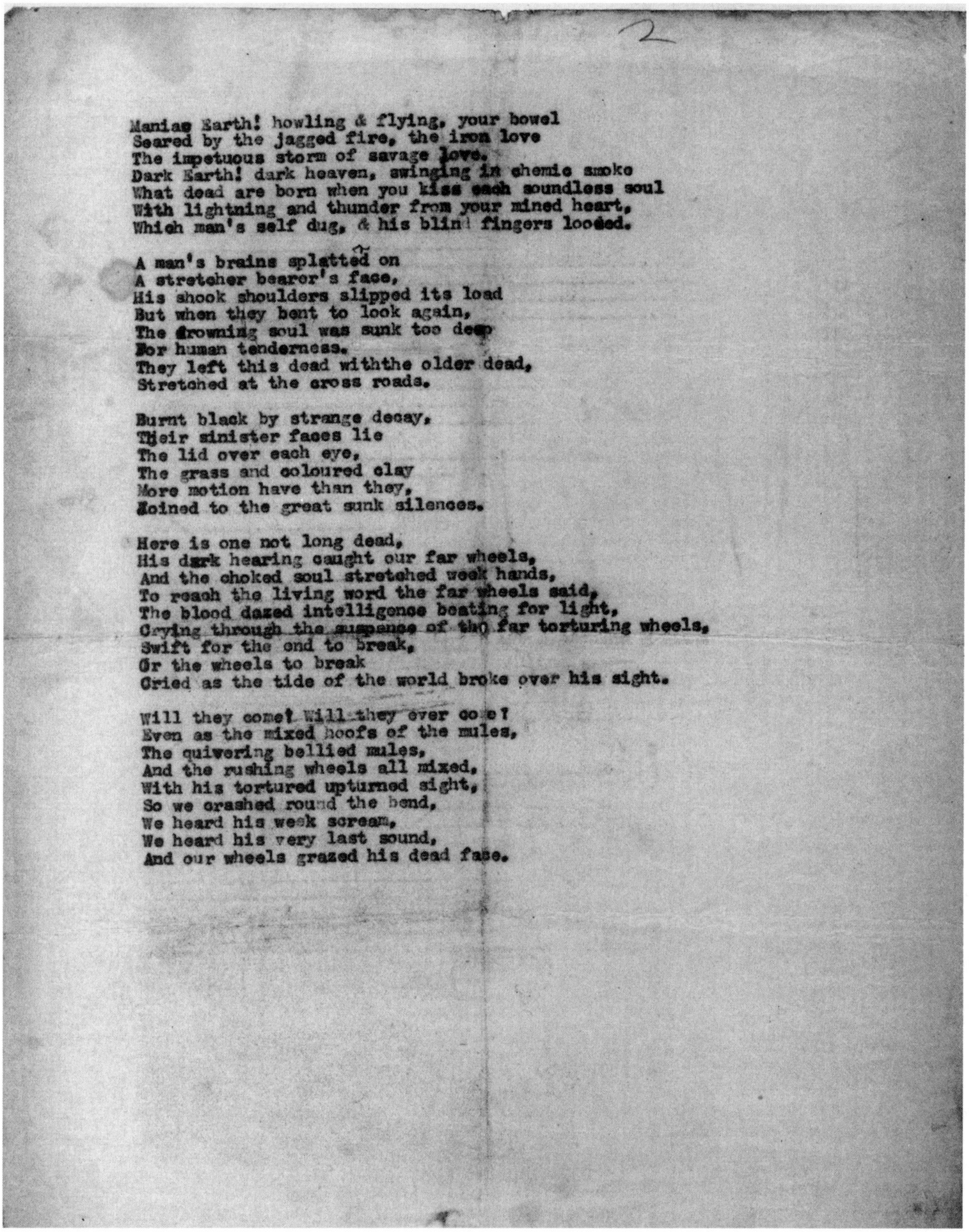

Maniac Earth! howling & flying, your bowel
Seared by the jagged fire, the iron love
The impetuous storm of savage love.
Dark Earth! dark heaven, swinging in chemic smoke
What dead are born when you kiss each soundless soul
With lightning and thunder from your mined heart,
Which man's self dug, & his blind fingers looged.

A man's brains splatted on
A stretcher bearer's face,
His shook shoulders slipped its load
But when they bent to look again,
The drowning soul was sunk too deep
For human tenderness.
They left this dead withthe older dead,
Stretched at the cross roads.

Burnt black by strange decay,
Their sinister faces lie
The lid over each eye,
The grass and coloured clay
More motion have than they,
Joined to the great sunk silences.

Here is one not long dead,
His dark hearing caught our far wheels,
And the choked soul stretched weak hands,
To reach the living word the far wheels said,
The blood dazed intelligence beating for light,
Crying through the suspense of the far torturing wheels,
Swift for the end to break,
Or the wheels to break
Cried as the tide of the world broke over his sight.

Will they come? Will they ever come?
Even as the mixed hoofs of the mules,
The quivering bellied mules,
And the rushing wheels all mixed,
With his tortured upturned sight,
So we crashed round the bend,
We heard his weak scream,
We heard his very last sound,
And our wheels grazed his dead face.

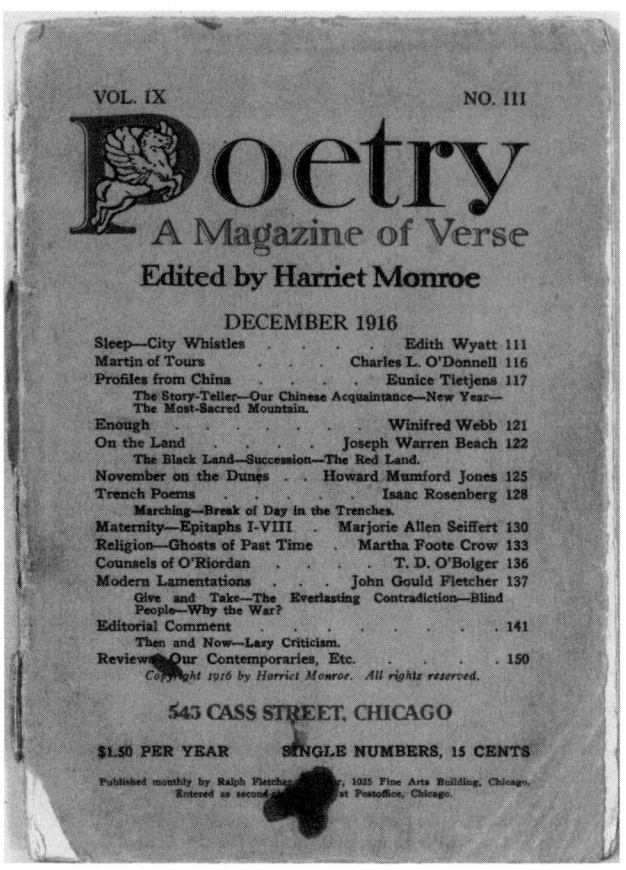

The first publication of Rosenberg's poems in the United States (Imperial War Museum, London)

Their sinister faces lie,
The lid over each eye,
The grass and coloured clay
More motion have than they,
Joined to the great sunk silences.

Here is one not long dead;
His dark hearing caught our far wheels,
And the choked soul stretched weak hands
To reach the living word the far wheels said,
The blood-dazed intelligence beating for light,
Crying through the suspense of the far torturing wheels
Swift for the end to break,
Or the wheels to break,
Cried as the tide of the world broke over his sight.

Will they come? Will they ever come?
Even as the mixed hoofs of the mules,
The quivering-bellied mules,
And the rushing wheels all mixed
With his tortured upturned sight,
So we crashed round the bend,
We heard his weak scream,
We heard his very last sound,
And our wheels grazed his dead face.

Analysis of "Dead Man's Dump" that reads the poem as a symbolic exploration of death as an absolute experience (Bernard Bergonzi, Heroes' Twilight, *pp. 113–115)*

Rosenberg's fullest and most complex crystallization of his experience of war is "Dead Man's Dump." Rosenberg described the genesis of this poem in a letter to Edward Marsh, dated 8 May 1917: "I've written some lines suggested by going out wiring, or rather carrying wire up the line on limbers and running over dead bodies lying about. I don't think what I've written is very good but I think the substance is, and when I work on it I'll make it fine. . . ." Read without reference to the poem itself, this outline might indicate a piece of brutal realism, worked up from personal experience, rather in the manner of Sassoon's frontline sketches. But the finished achievement of "Dead Man's Dump" is very different: realism is transformed into symbolism and, as in his other trench poems, Rosenberg does not dwell on the details of violent death and mutilation. In Harding's words, "he thinks only in terms of death which comes quickly enough to be regarded as a single living experience." "Dead Man's Dump" is indeed an exploration of death as an absolute experience, which at the same time has something of the complexity and gradations of life. From the beginning, Rosenberg's language fuses realism and symbolism:

> The plunging limbers over the shattered track
> Racketed with their rusty freight,
> Stuck out like many crowns of thorns,
> And the rusty stakes like sceptres old
> To stay the flood of brutish men
> Upon our brothers dear.

The bleak phrase from his letter, "carrying wire up the line on limbers," has been thoroughly transformed: the first two lines are direct, realistic observation, but in the third line, the comparison of the coils of barbed wire to "crowns of thorns" is both visually apt and richly associative. In the reference to stakes "like sceptres" which are supposed to stay the enemy flood one is, I think, meant to recall Canute, and no doubt, too, the fact that his attempt to stay the actual flood of the sea was fruitless: so too the wire may fail in its protective function. One sees at this point how Rosenberg has already moved farther away from the particular and the concrete, towards a generalized significance; it is, however, part of his strength that his perceptions are always rooted in the concrete, and he always returns to it:

> The wheels lurched over sprawled dead
> But pained them not, though their bones crunched,
> Their shut mouths made no moan.
> They lie there huddled, friend and foeman,
> Man born of man, and born of woman,
> And shells go crying over them
> From night till night and now.

If one compares this with the huddled corpses in the opening stanza of Sassoon's "Counter-Attack," one can gauge how very different Rosenberg's intentions were. In the third stanza we find a remarkable statement of the idea glanced at in "Break of Day in the Trenches," that there is a relation between man and nature which is brought to fruition when the dead return to the soil:

> Earth has waited for them,
> All the time of their growth
> Fretting for their decay:
> Now she has them at last!
> In the strength of their strength
> Suspended—stopped and held.

In the fifth stanza there is a kind of awe at the absoluteness of the experience of death combined with a sense of loss and pity; the last two lines recall some of the dominant images of "August 1914," here used with greater freedom:

> None saw their spirits' shadow shake the grass,
> Or stood aside for the half used life to pass
> Out of those doomed nostrils and the doomed mouth,
> When the swift iron burning bee
> Drained the wild honey of their youth.

Harding has said of this stanza, "It is noteworthy here that Rosenberg is able and content to present contrasted aspects of the one happening without having to resort to the bitterness or irony which are the easier attitudes to such a contrast." If one believes the best war poetry is essentially a poetry of protest and revolt, Rosenberg's detachment and impersonality may seem disturbing, even a little inhuman. Whilst recognizing this, one must also point out that he moves to a degree of transcendence that takes him far away from his starting point in the realities of frontline activity; in such poetry we have a profound

Self-portrait of Rosenberg in France (Isaac Rosenberg Estate)

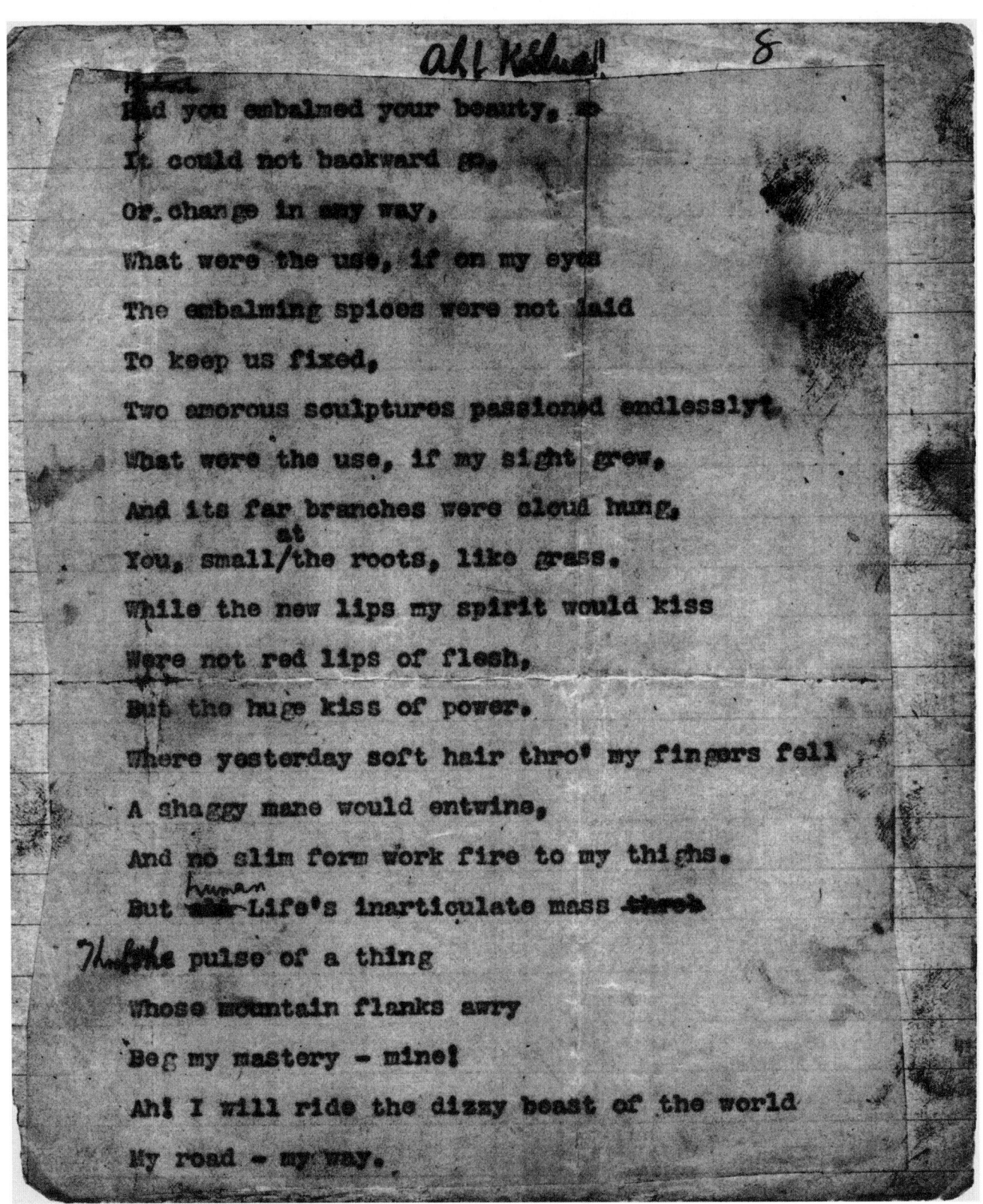

Corrected typescript for "Ah! Koelue!" (Imperial War Museum, London)

The summer of 1917 was relatively quiet; Rosenberg had been transferred to the Royal Engineers, where most days he loaded and unloaded barbed wire, and he was writing some of his more innovative poetry. On 30 July when he wrote Marsh about "Daughters of War," to which he referred as his "Amazon poem," he discussed his evolving philosophy about war and writing. He claimed that he avoided the sensational and depended on a series of poignant images to project his visions of war. "Daughters of War" was written on scraps of paper bound by pieces of string.

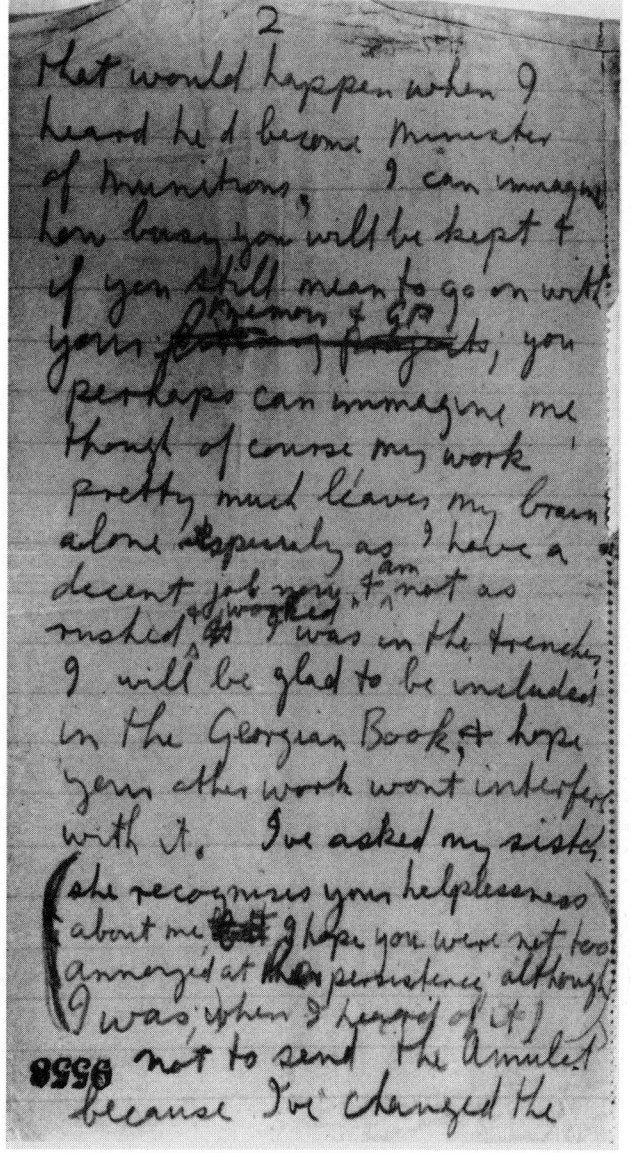

Rosenberg's letter to Marsh written on scraps of paper, 30 July 1917 (The Berg Collection, New York Public Library)

idea plain, as it is to my own mind. 5
I believe my Amazon poem to be my best poem
~~I have~~ ~~to it is~~ If there is any difficulty
it must be in words here & there the change
or elimination of which may make the poem clear
It has taken me about a year to write; for I have
changed & rechanged it & thought hard over that
poem & striven to get that sense of inexorable
the human (or unhuman) side of this war has.
It even penetrates behind human life for
the 'Amazon' who speaks in the second
half of the poem is imagined to be without
her lover yet, while all her sisters have
theirs, the released spirits of the slain
earth men; her love, yet remains to be released.
I hope however, to be home on leave, &
talk it over some time this side of the year.
In my next letter I will try & send
an idea of 'The Unicorn'.
If you are too busy dont
bother about answering;
    Yours sincerely
        Isaac Rosenberg

exploration of the concept of death, startling in its imaginative intensity, which goes beyond simple description, no matter how deeply felt, of the casualties of battle:

> They left this dead with the older dead,
> Stretched at the cross roads.
> Burnt black by strange decay
> Their sinister faces lie,
> The lid over each eye,
> The grass and coloured clay
> More motion have than they,
> Joined to the great sunk silences.
>
> Here is one not long dead;
> His dark hearing caught our far wheels....

In the middle stanza, Rosenberg shows both a painter's eye and an ontological insight; the memorable phrase, "Joined to the great sunk silences," functions like an Arnoldian touchstone. The poem moves towards the sombre paradox of its conclusion when the just dead try to cry out to the living:

> We heard his weak scream,
> We heard his very fast sound,
> And our wheels grazed his dead face.

The last word, in the dialectical development of Rosenberg's poem, rests with the anguish of both the living and the dead.

"Daughters of War" (Ian Parsons, ed., The Collected Works of Isaac Rosenberg, *pp. 112-113)*

> Space beats the ruddy freedom of their limbs—
> Their naked dances with man's spirit naked
> By the root side of the tree of life,
> (The underside of things
> And shut from earth's profoundest eyes).
>
> I saw in prophetic gleams
> These mighty daughters in their dances
> Beckon each soul aghast from its crimson corpse
> To mix in their glittering dances.
> I heard the mighty daughters' giant sighs
> In sleepless passion for the sons of valour,
> And envy of the days of flesh
> Barring their love with mortal boughs across—
> The mortal boughs—the mortal tree of life.
> The old bark burnt with iron wars
> They blow to a live flame
> To char the young green days
> And reach the occult soul; they have no softer lure
> No softer lure than the savage ways of death.
>
> We were satisfied of our lords the moon and the sun
> To take our wage of sleep and bread and warmth—
> These maidens came—these strong ever-living Amazons,
> And in an easy might their wrists
> Of night's sway and noon's sway the sceptres brake,
> Clouding the wild—the soft lustres of our eyes.
> Clouding the wild lustres, the clinging tender lights;
> Driving the darkness into the flame of day,
> With the Amazonian wind of them
> Over our corroding faces
> That must be broken—broken for evermore
> So the soul can leap out
> Into their huge embraces.
> Though there are human faces
> Best sculptures of Deity,
> And sinews lusted after
> By the Archangels tall,
> Even these must leap to the love heat of these maidens
> From the flame of terrene days
> Leaving grey ashes to the wind—to the wind.
>
> One (whose great lifted face,
> Where wisdom's strength and beauty's strength
> And the thewed strength of large beasts
> Moved and merged, gloomed and lit)
> Was speaking, surely, as the earth-men's earth fell away;
> Whose new hearing drunk the sound
> Where pictures, lutes, and mountains mixed
> With the loosed spirit of a thought.
> Essenced to language, thus—
>
> 'My sisters force their males
> From the doomed earth, from the doomed glee
> And hankering of hearts.
> Frail hands gleam up through the human quagmire and lips of ash
> Seem to wail, as in sad faded paintings
> Far sunken and strange.
> My sisters have their males
> Clean of the dust of old days
> That clings about those white hands
> And yearns in those voices sad.
>
> But these shall not see them,
> Or think of them in any days or years,
> They are my sisters' lovers in other days and years.'

Excerpt from Rosenberg's letter to Gordon Bottomley acknowledging his discontent, 21 September 1917 (Ian Parsons, ed., The Collected Works of Isaac Rosenberg, *p. 262)*

To Gordon Bottomley,
    The greatest thing of my leave after seeing my mother was your letter which has just arrived.... I wish I could have seen you, but now I must go on and hope that things will turn out well, and some happy day will give me the chance of meeting you.... I am afraid I can do no writing or reading; I feel so restless here and unanchored. We have lived in

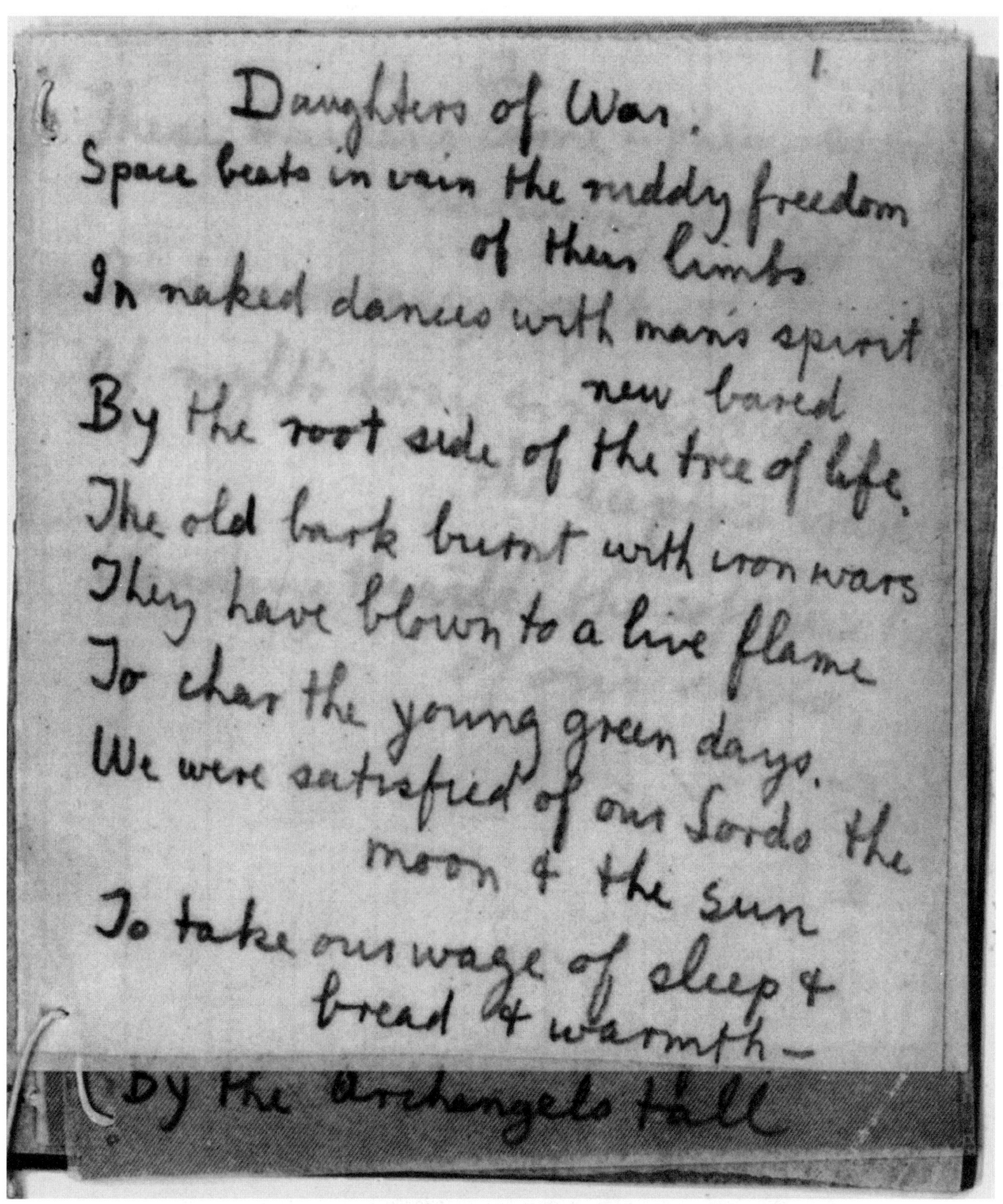

Early draft for Rosenberg's favorite among his poems
(Imperial War Museum, London)

After fourteen consecutive months in combat, Rosenberg was granted home leave in September, but as he confessed to Gordon Bottomley that month, he felt that England had changed significantly during his absence. The contrast between the civilian's heroic suppositions about the nature of war and the combat soldier's awareness of battlefield conditions made communication between the two groups nearly impossible, Rosenberg felt. In "Girl to Soldier on Leave," a satiric poem about the differing perceptions of war held by a soldier and a young woman, he attempted to enlighten civilians about the war.

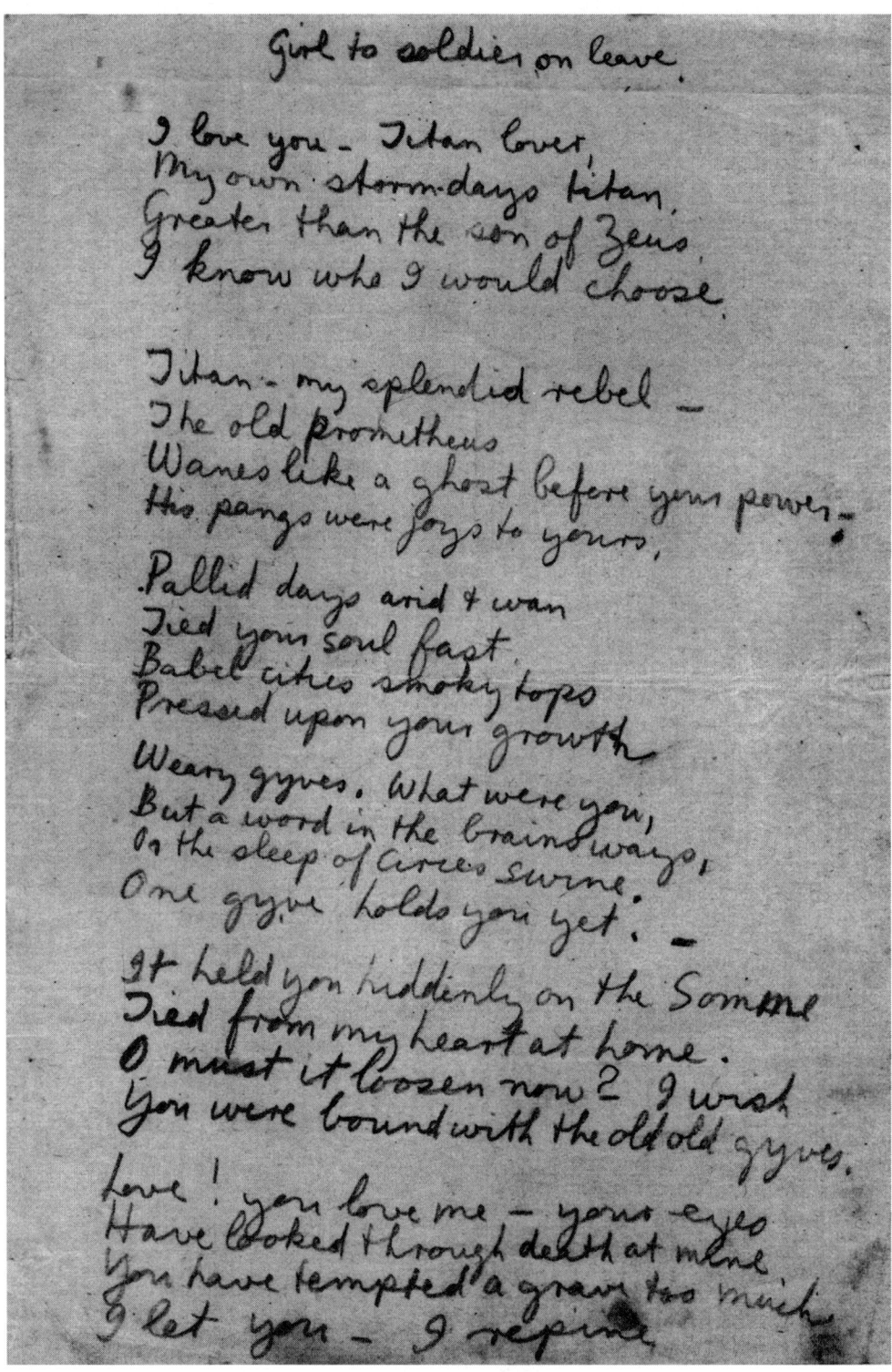

Fair copy of Rosenberg's 1917 poem (Imperial War Museum, London)

When Rosenberg returned to France in October 1917, he was sent to dig communication trenches and lay wire, but by mid October his health broke down, and he was hospitalized for nearly two months. While recovering, he managed to write poetry, but this was his last period of sustained writing. By January he was back in the trenches near Bullecourt, where conditions were abysmal.

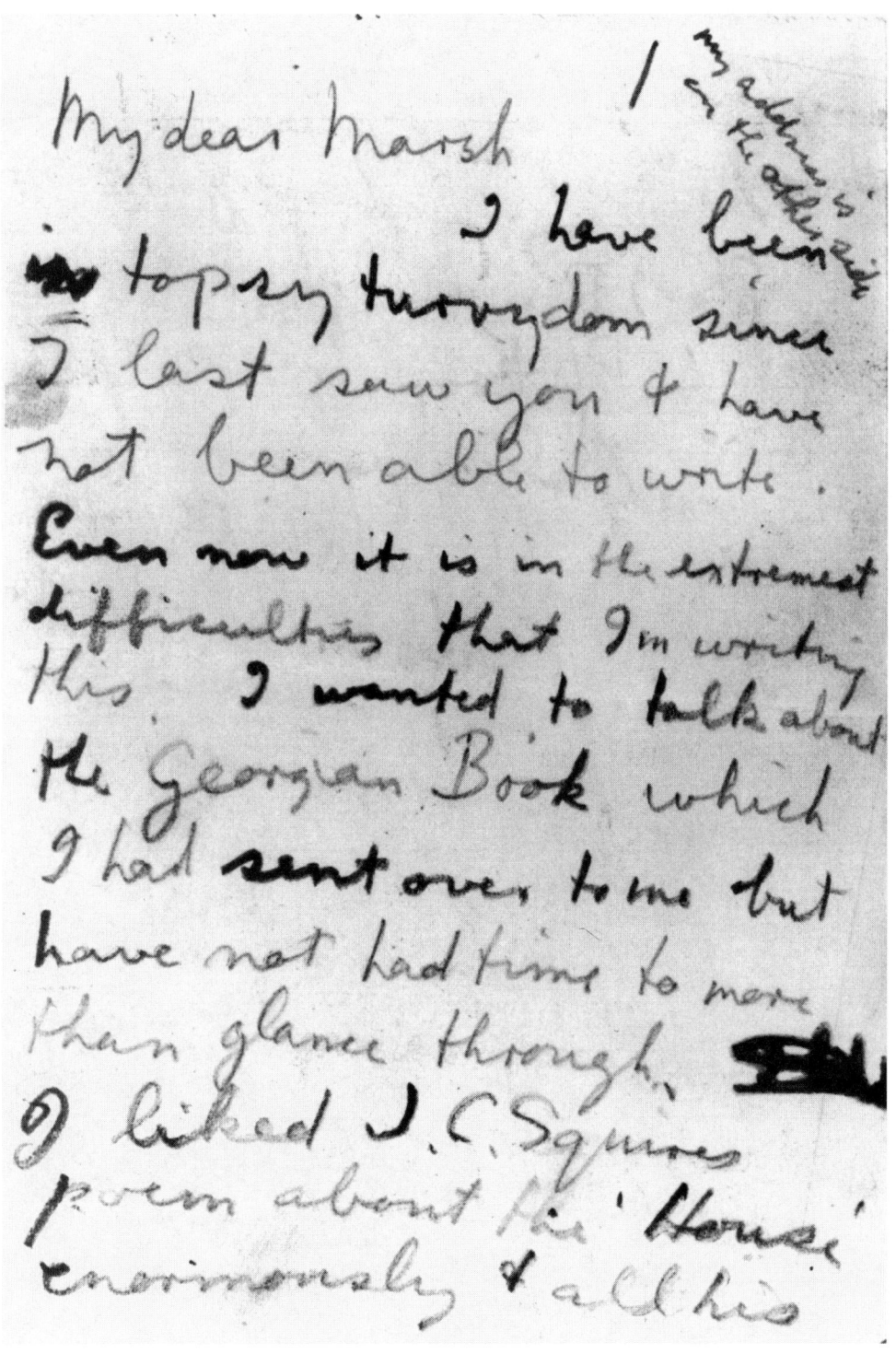

Rosenberg's letter to Edward Marsh commenting on the terrible conditions in the trenches, 26 January 1918
(The Berg Collection, New York Public Library)

other poems. Turners are very beautiful & Sassoon has power. Masefield seemed rather ~~sg~~ commonplace, ~~but~~ please dont take my judgment at anything because I have hardly looked at them. I am back in the trenches which are terrible now. ~~We spend most~~ of our time pulling each other out of the mud. I am not fit at all now & am more in the way than any use.

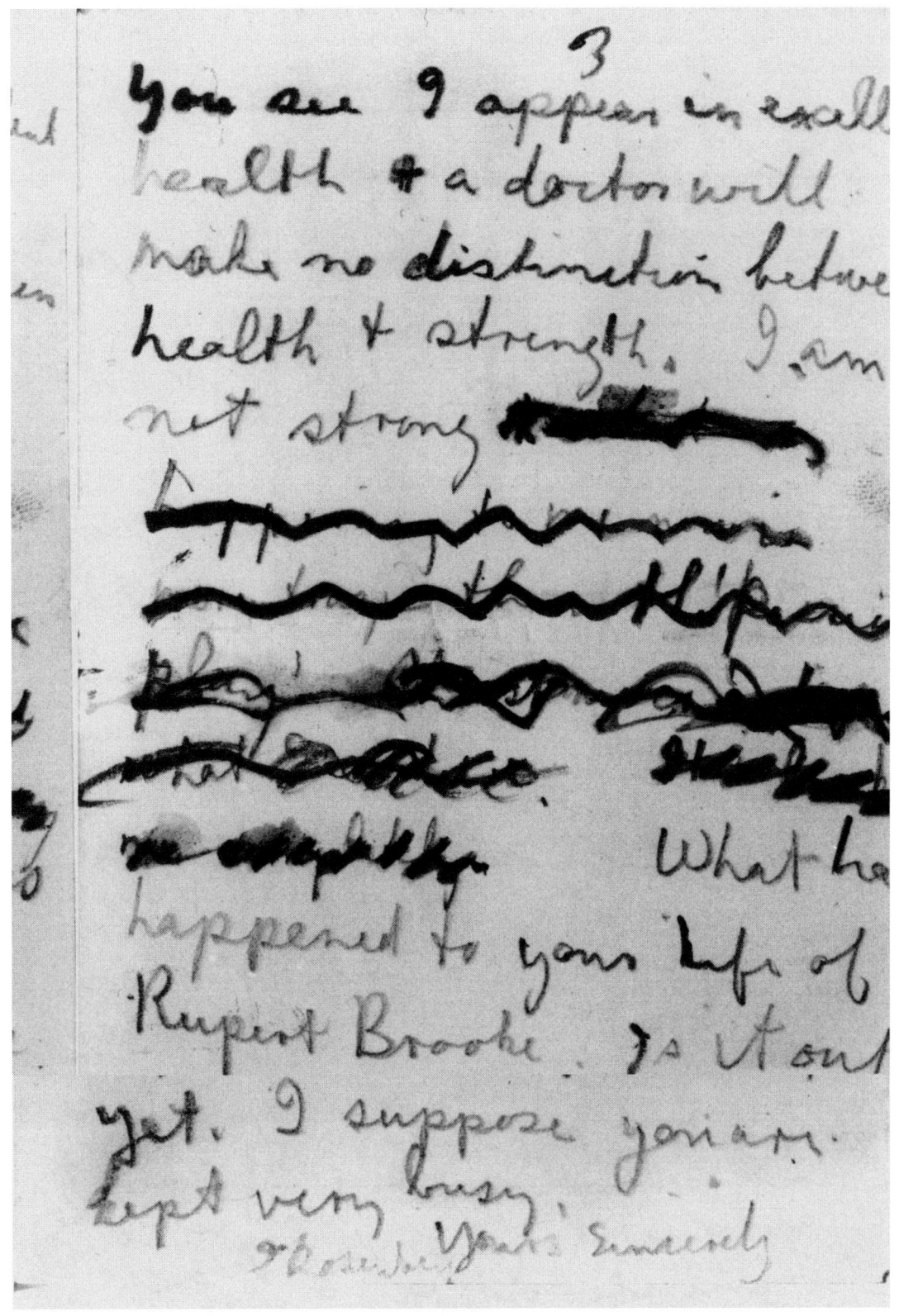

During February, Rosenberg was transferred to the King's Own Rifles as part of the reorganization of the British army, and he wrote his former teacher, Winifreda Seaton, about his annoyance at being retrained again.

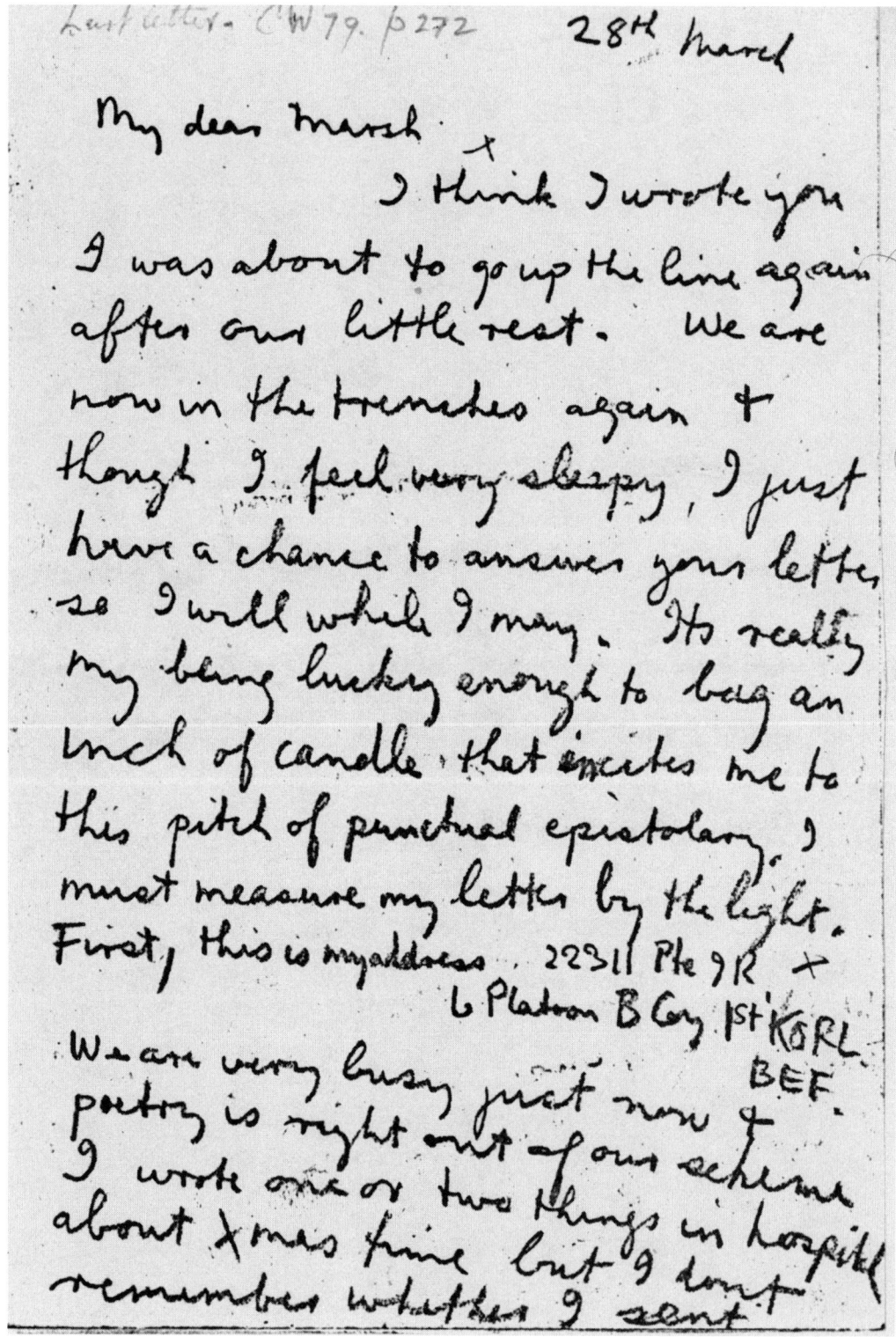

Rosenberg's letter to Winifreda Seaton, 14 February 1918 (Ian Parsons, ed., The Collected Works of Isaac Rosenberg)

them to you or not. I'll
send one, anyhow.

During our little interlude
of rest from the line I managed
to do a bit of sketching — somebody
had colours. & they werent so bad,
I dont think I have forgotten
my art after all. I've heard
nothing further about the G.B.
& of course feel annoyed — more
because no reasons have been
given me. but when we leave
the trenches, I'll enquire further.
I dont remember reading
Freeman. I wanted to write
a battle song for the Judæans
but can think of nothing strong

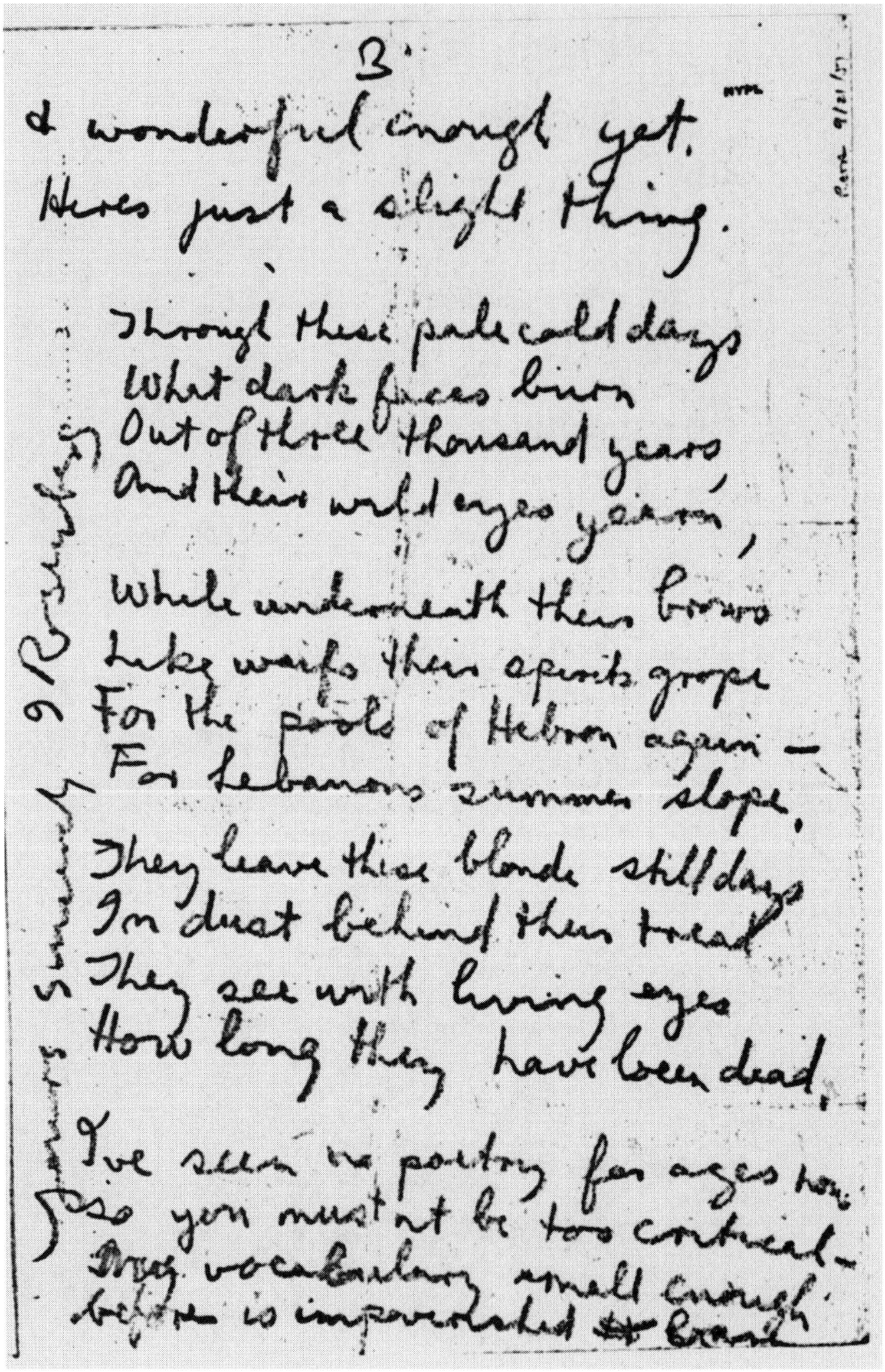

& wonderful enough yet.
Heres just a slight thing.

 Through these pale cold days
 What dark faces burn
 Out of three thousand years,
 And their wild eyes yearn,

 While underneath their brows
 Like waifs their spirits grope
 For the pools of Hebron again —
 For Lebanons summer slope.

 They leave these blonde still days
 In dust behind their tread
 They see with living eyes
 How long they have been dead.

Ive seen no poetry for ages now
so you must'nt be too critical —
My vocabulary small enough
before is impoverished & crass

Rosenberg on leave with his brother Elkon (Isaac Rosenberg Estate)

Rosenberg in England during his last leave (Isaac Rosenberg Estate)

such an elemental way so long, things here don't look quite right to me somehow; or it may be the consciousness of my so limited time here for freedom—so little time to do so many things bewilders me. "The Unicorn," as will be obvious, is just a basis; its final form will be very different, I hope.

Rosenberg's letter to Winifreda Seaton, 14 February 1918 (Ian Parsons, ed., The Collected Works of Isaac Rosenberg, *p. 268)*

We had a rough time in the trenches with the mud, but now we're out for a bit of a rest, and I will try and write longer letters. You must know by now what a rest behind the line means. I can call the evenings—that is, from tea to lights out—my own; but there is no chance whatever for seclusion or any hope of writing poetry now. Sometimes I give way and am appalled at the devastation this life seems to have made in my nature. It seems to have blunted me. I seem to be powerless to compel my will to any direction, and all I do is without energy and interest.

Rosenberg's final poem, 1918 (Ian Parsons, ed., The Collected Works of Isaac Rosenberg, *p. 117)*

"Through These Pale Cold Days"

Through these pale cold days
What dark faces burn
Out of three thousand years,
And their wild eyes yearn,

While underneath their brows
Like waifs their spirits grope
For the pools of Hebron again—
For Lebanon's summer slope.

Military preparations continued during a move to Arras, where in March 1918 Rosenberg wrote his final poems—all with Old Testament themes. He mailed them (including his last poem, "Through These Pale Cold Days") to Edward Marsh on the night the Germans launched a full-scale attack on British lines, which barely held. The next three nights the British were constantly bombarded as Germans hoped to break through the lines, but every night British patrols went out to repair the barbed-wire defenses. On the night of 31 March, Rosenberg left for patrol duty and never returned. His body was never recovered.

Rosenberg's last letter to Edward Marsh, written about art and poetry and including his last poem, 28 March 1918 (The Berg Collection, New York Public Library)

them to you or not. I'll
send one, anyhow.
During our little interlude
of rest from the line I managed
to do a bit of sketching — somebody
had colours & they weren't so bad,
I dont think I have forgotten
my art after all. I've heard
nothing further about the J.B
& of course feel annoyed — more
because no reasons have been
given me — but when we leave
the trenches, I'll enquire farther.
I dont remember reading
Freeman. I wanted to write
a battle song for the Judeans
but can think of nothing strong

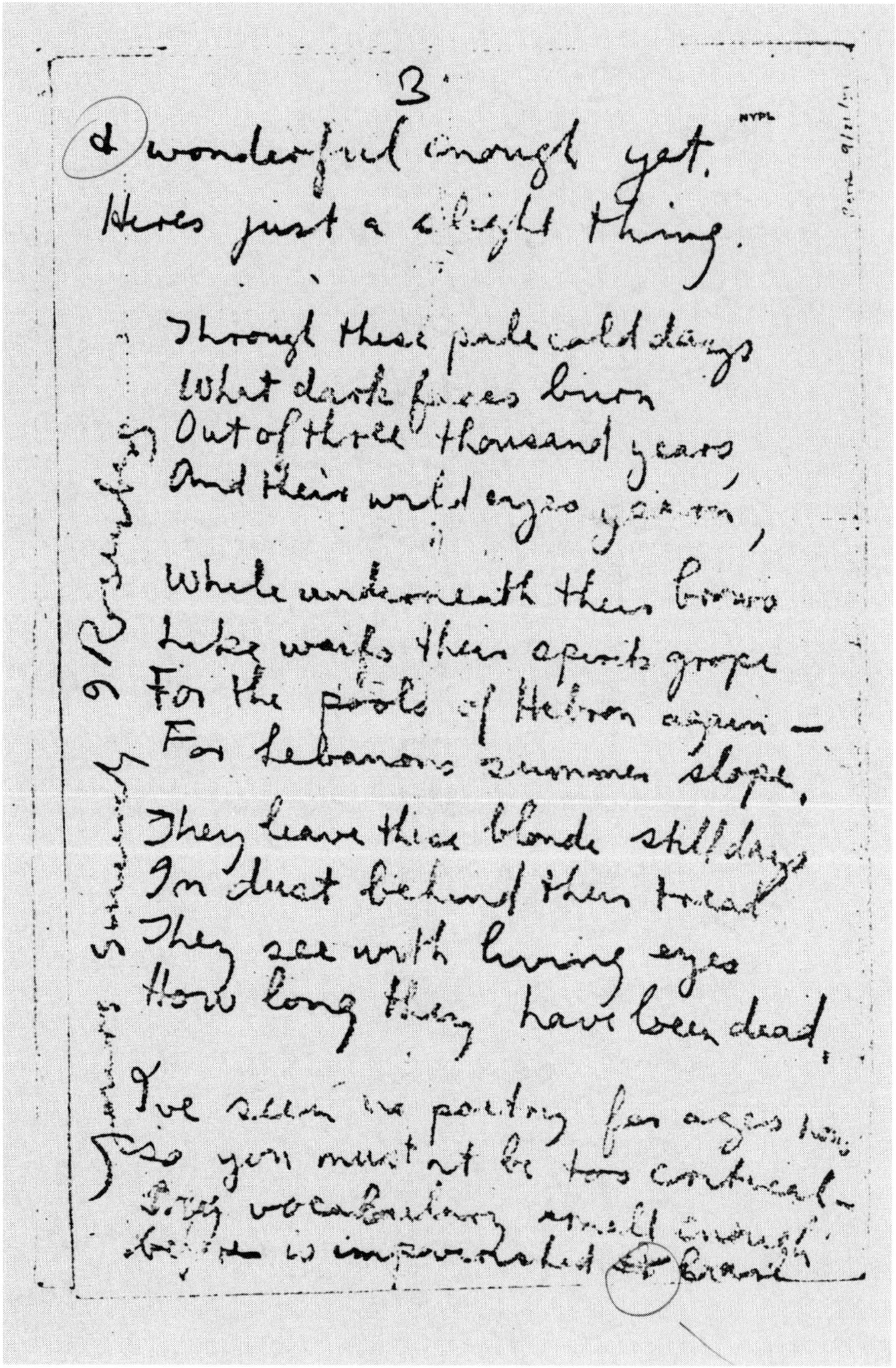

3.

& wonderful enough yet.
Heres just a slight thing.

   Through these pale cold days
   What dark faces burn
   Out of three thousand years,
   And their wild eyes yearn,

   While underneath their brows
   Like waifs their spirits grope
   For the pools of Hebron again —
   For Lebanons summer slope.

   They leave these blonde still days
   In dust behind their tread
   They see with living eyes
   How long they have been dead.

I've seen no poetry for ages now
So you mustnt be too critical —
My vocabulary small enough
before is impoverished & crase

After Rosenberg's death, nearly four years passed before an edition of his works was published. In 1922 Gordon Bottomley edited a selection of Rosenberg's poems and letters, but this collection received little critical attention.

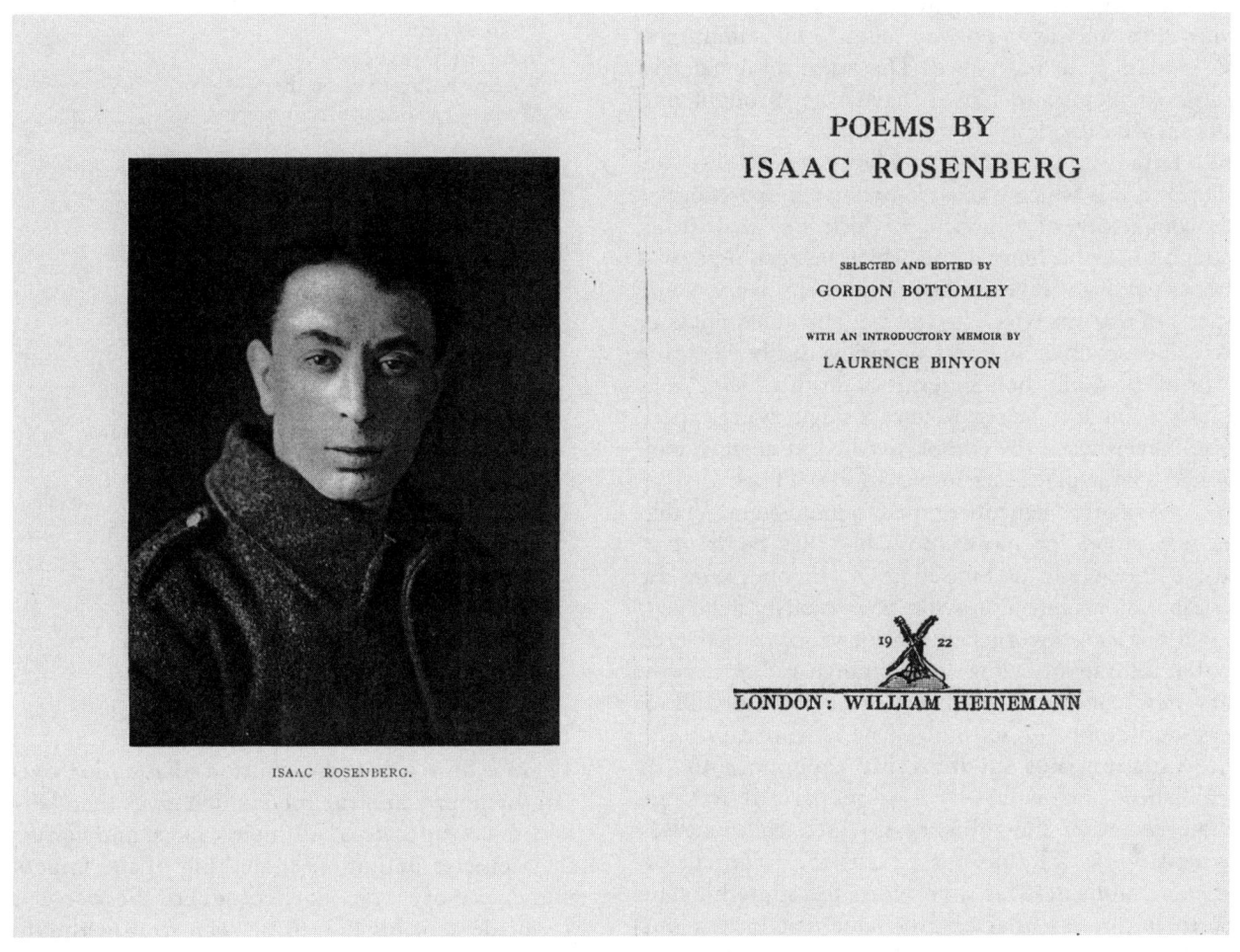

Title page and frontispiece for the first collected edition of Rosenberg's verse

They leave these blond still days
In dust behind their tread
They see with living eyes
Ho long they have been dead.

When D. W. Harding's complimentary article on Rosenberg was published in Scrutiny in 1935, a reassessment of Rosenberg's position in English poetry was deemed necessary, and this revaluation began with the publication of Bottomley and Harding's edition of Rosenberg's Collected Works (1937). Siegfried Sassoon's laudatory foreword to this edition called for a full recognition of Rosenberg's genius, and F. R. Leavis's review of the poems confirmed Sassoon's praise. Rosenberg's place at the forefront of the literature of the Great War is firmly established today, and critics as different as Dennis Silk, Joseph Cohen, and Desmond Graham—who sums up Rosenberg's poetic achievement as "an assertion of the humane spirit against the power of war"—all regard his poetry as an important development in twentieth-century English literature.

Excerpt from D. W. Harding, "Aspects of Poetry of Isaac Rosenberg" (Scrutiny, 3, no. 4 [1935], 91–103)

What most distinguishes Isaac Rosenberg from other English poets who wrote of the last war is the intense significance he saw in the kind of living effort that the war called out, and the way in which his technique enabled him to present both this and the suffering and the waste as inseparable aspects of life in war. Further, there is in his work, without the least touch of coldness, nevertheless a certain impersonality: he tried to feel in the war a significance for life as such, rather than seeing only its convulsion of the human life he knew. . . .

This immortality and the value he glimpses in the living effort of war in no way mitigate his suffering at the human pain and waste. The value of what was destroyed seemed to him to have been brought into sight only by the destruction, and he had to respond to both facts without allowing either to neutralise the other. It is this which is most impressive in Rosenberg—the complexity of experience which he was strong enough to permit himself and which his technique was fine enough to reveal. Naturally there were some aspects of the war which he was not able to compass in his response: maiming and lingering death he never treats of—he thinks only in terms of death which comes quickly enough to be regarded as a single living experience. Nevertheless the complexity he did achieve constituted a large part of his importance as a poet.

To say that Rosenberg tried to understand all that the war stood for means probably that he tried to expose the whole of himself to it. In one letter he describes as an intention what he obviously achieved: "I will not leave a corner of my consciousness covered up, but saturate myself with the strange and extra-ordinary new conditions of this life. . . ." This willingness—and ability—to let himself be newborn into the new situation, not subduing his experience to his established personality, is a large part, if not the whole secret of the robustness which characterises his best work. ("Robustness" is, as the fragment on Emerson indicates, his own word for something he felt to be an essential of great poetry.) It was due largely, no doubt, to his lack of conviction of the adequacy of civilian standards. In "The Troop Ship" and "Louse Hunting" there is no civilian resentment at the conditions he writes of. Here as in all the war poems his suffering and discomfort are unusually direct; there is no secondary distress arising from the sense that these things ought not to be. He was given up to realising fully what was. He has expressed his attitude in "The Unicorn":

> Lilith: I think there is more sorrow in the world
> Than man can bear.
>
> Nubian: None can exceed their limit, lady:
> You either bear or break.

It was Rosenberg's exposure of his whole personality that gave his work its quality of impersonality. Even when he imagines his brother's death he brings it into a poem which is equally concerned with the general destruction and the circumstances of life in war, and which ends with a generalisation of his personal suffering:

> What are the great sceptred dooms
> To us, caught
> In the wild wave?
> We break ourselves on them,
> My brother, our hearts and years.

The same quality is present, most finely, in "Break of Day in the Trenches":

> The darkness crumbles away
> It is the same old druid Time as ever.
> Only a live thing leaps my hand—
> A queer sardonic rat—
> As I pull the parapet's poppy
> To stick behind my ear.
> Droll rat, they would shoot you if they knew
> Your cosmopolitan sympathies
> . . . .
> It seems you inwardly grin as you pass
> Strong eyes, fine limbs, haughty athletes
> Less chanced than you for life,
> . . . .
> Poppies whose roots are in man's veins
> Drop, and are ever dropping;
> But mine in my ear is safe,
> Just a little white with the dust.

There is here a cool distribution of attention over the rat, the poppy and the men which gives them all their due, is considerate of all their values, and conveys in their precise definition something of the impersonal immensity of a war. For Rosenberg the war was not an incident of his life, to be seen from without, but, instead, one kind of life, as unquestionable as any life.

Siegfried Sassoon's foreword to The Collected Works of Isaac Rosenberg

It has been considered appropriate that I should say something about the poems of Isaac Rosenberg. I can only hope that what I say, inadequate though it may be, will help to gain for him the full recognition of his genius which has hitherto been delayed. In reading and re-reading these poems I have been strongly impressed by their depth and integrity. I have found a sensitive and vigorous mind energetically interested in experimenting with language, and I have recognised in Rosenberg a fruitful fusion between English and Hebrew culture. Behind all his poetry there is a racial quality—biblical and prophetic. Scriptural and sculptural are the epithets I would apply to him. His experiments were a strenuous effort for impassioned expression; his imagination had a sinewy and muscular aliveness; often

Dust-jacket front for the 1937 collection edited by George Bottomley and D. W. Harding

he saw things in terms of sculpture, but he did not carve or chisel; he *modelled* words with fierce energy and aspiration, finding ecstasy in form, dreaming in grandeurs of superb light and deep shadow; his poetic visions are mostly in sombre colours and looming sculptural masses, molten and amply wrought. Watching him working with words, I find him a poet of movement; words which express movement are often used by him and are essential to his natural utterance.

Rosenberg was not consciously a "war poet." But the war destroyed him, and his few but impressive "Trench Poems" are a central point in this book. They have the controlled directness of a man finding his true voice and achieving mastery of his material; words and images obey him, instead of leading him into over-elaboration. They are all of them fine poems, but "Break of Day in the Trenches" has for me a poignant and nostalgic quality which eliminates critical analysis. Sensuous front-line existence is there, hateful and repellent, unforgettable and inescapable. And beyond this poem I see the poems he might have written after the war, and the life he might have lived when life began again beyond and behind those trenches which were the limbo of all sane humanity and world-improving imagination. For the spirit of poetry looks beyond life's trench-lines. And Isaac Rosenberg was naturally empowered with something of the divine spirit which touches our human clay to sublimity of expression. . . .

*Excerpt from F. R. Leavis's "The Recognition of Isaac Rosenberg" (*Scrutiny*, 6 [September 1937], pp. 229–234)*

My criticism against this book is that it doesn't contain as introduction the essay that one of its editors, D. W. Harding, contributed to *Scrutiny* for March, 1935. Such an introduction would very much have improved Rosenberg's chances of obtaining, at last, the recognition due to him, and is the more to be desired in that the volume, being exhaustive, includes a bulk of work that isn't in itself strikingly significant. Not that it's a question of vindicating a slender talent; "genius" is the word for Rosenberg, who has all the robustness of genius. But the history of his reputation brings home to one that it is easy to be too optimistic about the chances original genius may expect of getting recognized.

To begin with he had a measure of luck. Circumstanced as he was, how easily he might have escaped all notice, and, dying an insignificant Jewish private with a few pieces of illegible scrawl in his tunic pocket, have disappeared for good (he was killed in 1918), a total loss to English poetry. But he had gained the attention of several representative figures in Georgian letters; patrons who, though the spirit of Rosenberg's work was hardly congenial to what they themselves stood for, kept in benevolent touch with him. And in 1922 the small selection of his verse made by Gordon Bottomley (it was introduced by Laurence Binyon) came out. It is disquieting now to think that that volume did not establish Rosenberg's reputation; did not, although the book was reviewed and Rosenberg became an anthology poet—one of the five hundred, and further distinguished as "one of the war-poets." The history is the more significant in that Mr. T. S. Eliot (it was the occasion of my noting Rosenberg's name as one to remember) mentioned him in a Poetry Bookshop Chapbook as a poet who would have received notice if criticism had been performing its function.

But it is one thing to feel that here is something strange, original and interesting, and another to recognize its nature and significance. I recall the conviction that Mr. Eliot expressed years later regarding Marianne Moore: "that Miss Moore's poems form part of the small body of durable poetry written in our time; of that small body of writings among what passes for poetry, in which an original sensibility and alert intelligence and deep feeling have been engaged in maintaining the life of the English language." I think that something of that kind might have been said, and with far more appropriateness, of Isaac Rosenberg. But, though I knew Gordon Bottomley's selection and was "interested" in Rosenberg, I cannot pretend that it had ever occurred to me to say anything like it. And I confess this with the less confusion since even Mr. Eliot, who stopped to call attention to Rosenberg, appears to have left him with the passing mention.

His early work shows the influence of Rossetti, Swinburne, Francis Thompson, and other poets of the nineteenth century. As for contemporary influences, since he was born in 1890 it will be realized that his debt here, in respect of emancipation and stimulus, cannot have amounted to much: at the time of his adolescence the shocking latest thing in poetry was represented by the little Salvation Army epics of the present Poet Laureate. Yet when, in 1916, Rosenberg writes,

> "Simple Poetry,–that is where an interesting complexity of thought is kept in tone and right value to the dominating idea so that it is understandable and still ungraspable,"

he is describing the spirit of his efforts in poetic technique over the past several years.

He could not, of course, have arrived at this notion of poetry, and at the astonishing technical skill that has been so little appreciated, had he been mainly preoccupied with earning fame as a poet. There are those sentences quoted by Mr. Harding from a letter of 1916:

> "I will not leave a corner of my consciousness covered up but saturate myself with the strange and extraordinary new conditions of this life, and it will all refine itself into poetry later on."

This is the voice of the young man who already before the war was expressing in poetry, not a revolutionary's or social reformer's, but a radical dissatisfaction with civilized life. His interest in life, in fact, is radical and religious in the same sense as D. H. Lawrence's. It has to be added that we must credit him, on the evidence of his best work, with an extraordinarily mature kind of detachment such as is not characteristic of Lawrence–to say this first gives the right force to the observation that of the two Rosenberg was much more an artist.

The spiritual strength manifested in the detachment of his poetry was needed in an almost incredible degree for the writing of it. For it is hardly credible, though it is an indubitable fact, that he wrote his best work while a private (for a while he was a lance-corporal) in the Expeditionary Force–wrote it in pencil on scraps of paper and in improvised notebooks. "I have been forbidden," he tells a correspondent, "to send poems home, as the censor won't be bothered with going through such rubbish. . . ." Actually he managed to send a good deal home, to be typed before it should get lost (and the editors had not only typescript to deal with, but a mass of pencil-scrawl, some of it decipherable, if at all, only by the most unwearying pertinacity). He carried his poetic ideas as they shaped, and his technical problems, about with him in his head, and the kind of concentration that often earned him punishment for absent-mindedness. . . .

It is still, perhaps, not superfluous to insist that the "imperfections" and obscurities of Rosenberg's poetry are not, as some even of his friendly correspondents (one reads between the lines) seem to have thought, of the same order as his faults of grammar, punctuation and spelling, or in any way analogous to them. If he was, like Blake, "uneducated" he was also like Blake in ways in which Blake had the advantage over most educated people; and he appears to have worked more persistently at his problems of poetic technique than Blake did. To criticism of a kind one can imagine, he replies:

> It is much my fault if I am misunderstood, I know; but I also feel a kind of injustice if my idea is not grasped or is ignored, and only petty cavilling at form, which I had known all along was so, is continually knocked into me. I feel quite sure that form is only a question of time.
>
> You will persist in refusing to see my side in our little debate on criticism. Everybody has agreed with you about the faults, and the reason is obvious; the faults are so glaring that nobody can fail to see them. But how many have seen the beauties? And it is here more than any other that the true critic shows himself. And I absolutely disagree that it is blindness or carelessness; it is the brain succumbing to the herculean attempt to enrich the world of ideas.

The "form," it should be plain beyond all question, is achieved, and the world of ideas enriched, at any rate in "Break of Day in the Trenches," "Returning We Hear the Larks," "In War," "Dead Man's Dump" and "Daughters of War," which are great poetry. In *Moses,* "The Amulet" and "The Unicorn" he was extending his technical experience in the creation of myth. To dismiss these draft-fragments, as reviewers have done, with the comment that Rosenberg hadn't got very far in the mastery of dramatic form is not intelligent. They show a richly promising ability to develop into more inclusive organizations the achievement of his verbal technique as exhibited in his best poems.

I was first doubtful about the wisdom of printing the whole bulk of the existing material, but see now the editor's decision was inevitable, given Rosenberg's kind of distinction and his extraordinary history. As they say, it is better that readers should "form their own impression of his developing personality" than "accept an impression conveyed by selective editing." We have also before us some information about Rosenberg's life, the letters and some prose pieces, and the total effect should be, not only the recognized enrichment of the English language by a dozen pages of great poetry, but also the enrichment of tradition by a new legend. And Rosenberg belongs, not with Chatterton, but rather with Keats and Hopkins.

Reminiscences of Isaac Rosenberg written by his sister Minnie, probably in the 1950s (Isaac Rosenberg Estate)

I remember my brother as a sad and discontented child, fervently religious. As a schoolchild he remained the same, but he was continually doing scraps of drawing which we thought of no value at the time.

He would never talk to his family about school life, and after some time I went to the school to discuss him with his teacher. The teacher said he was very capable, but seemed to take little interest in anything but drawing. At playtime even, when all the children were outside, he would sit in the classroom drawing. He did not make friends with the other children, and seemed much too serious for his age.

The teacher, however, thought some of his drawings very good for a child of his age, and took a keen interest. He tried to encourage him, and provided the child with foolscap, pencils and crayons.

At the age of about 10 he drew a picture on cardboard and coloured it, depicting a scene from the history which he had been taught. His teacher thought it so good that he exhibited it at a children's exhibition.

When he was due to leave school we asked him what he would like to do, and he said he wished to become an artist. But of course such an expensive career was impossible because of our poverty, and we decided to approach the Amchewitz's whom we knew well; one of the sons was a prominent artist at the time.

My mother and I visited the Amchewitz's, and discussed the problem with the artist son. My brother had taken some of his drawings which Mr. Amchewitz thought showed promise. He suggested that his brother, who worked for the Board of Guardians, be approached as the Board found apprenticeships for children leaving school. The brother suggested that the nearest approach to art would be engraving or black and white drawing, and Isaac was apprenticed to the firm of Carl Henchel in the City. Isaac was fairly happy there, but still eager to become a "proper" artist. Mr. Amchewitz, the artist, suggested that he go to evening classes at Birbeck College to study art, which he did.

While at Birbeck College he never discussed his progress with the family. We used to ask Mrs. Amchewitz if her son ever mentioned his work at the College, and she told us that he had won a prize—he had never mentioned this to us. He was very modest, and would never show his work to anyone but artists and never boast about it.

He began to read a lot, mostly poetry, and would go to Farringdon Street market and pick up all sorts of books. He once bought a book for ½d and when he showed it to Amchewitz he was told that it was a very valuable first manuscript of Thackeray, which contained a drawing of him. Amchewitz offered to sell it for him and did—for £40!

About this time Isaac started writing little poems. As soon as he thought of something he would jot it down, and he would get the opinion of people well versed in literature. I believe Miss Lowey, who was related to Hubert Cohen, was greatly interested in his poetry and art. He was introduced to prominent people in the literary world, who thought a great deal of his work.

He once did a painting of a young lady which we thought was wonderful, and we were so proud of it that we hung it over the mantelpiece. He was very annoyed, took it down and put it away.

His papers were always scattered on the floor of his room, and nobody dare touch them!

The principal of Birbeck College, Mr. Bentwich, was a very understanding man, and took a great interest in pupils who showed promise. After a while, when my brother was 16, the principal provided him with a card which enabled him to paint in the National Gallery on private viewing days. My brother had started a big canvas of a copy of "The Education of Cupid", and while working on this he was noticed by one of the visitors, Lady Hubert Cohen.

This lady came from a family of artists, amongst them Solomon the portrait painter. She was so impressed by my brother's work that she asked him if he would like to become an artist. When he told her that this was his greatest ambition, she arranged for her secretary to visit my parents. If my parents were willing to allow Isaac to be taken away from home she would send him to the Slade school for five years, and get him a studio in Chelsea. She would pay all the expenses.

Knowing that the boy was interested in nothing but art, the family agreed to this condition.

Once while working under the patronage of Lady Cohen he was asked by her to do a large painting for exhibition at the Royal Academy. The subject chosen was "Joy." She used to send her secretary to inspect the work and report to her. The content of the picture, entitled "Joy", was full of sadness and the secretary criticised it severely. Isaac became so annoyed that he would not finish the canvas and did not exhibit.

In 1913 I married a South African and came to live in Cape Town. About 18 months later my parents wrote saying that Isaac was not well—his lung was affected, and the doctors suggested a warm climate. I asked him to come out to us, which he did.

He brought with him a letter of introduction from Herbert Marshall, Churchill's secretary, to Sir Herbert Stanley of Government. Sir Stanley commissioned him to paint his three daughters, for which he was paid £15.

I introduced him to Advocate Alexander and through him he met many well known artists. A friend of ours belonging to an art club asked my brother to lecture on art, and amongst the audience at the lecture was the editress of a women's magazine—the Womens' Council. I believe her name was Mrs. Cook. His lecture was reported in the magazine, and through this he became acquainted with Miss Molteno.

Miss Molteno was very impressed by his work, and introduced him to many prominent people. She invited him to move to a boarding house in Bishops Court, a very beautiful part of Cape Town, as she thought that district would be better for his health. He visited me frequently.

When the 1914–1918 war broke out he was determined to return to England and join the army. He was not ready to fight, and I and Miss Molteno tried hard to persuade him not to go. She assured him that she could sell all his pictures and he would have no financial difficulties but he refused to be persuaded.

Miss Molteno gave him a letter of introduction to Olive Schreiner, who thought a lot of his work and of him.

Herbert Marshall promised my parents that he would be given a clerical job in the army, but he was sent to the trenches. The letters I received from him written from the trenches were tragic and left me heartbroken. He wrote of the hard discipline enforced by the corporals and officers. He was made to wear boots which hurt his feet so that they bled, and generally he became very embittered by the harshness of army life. For a sensitive and delicate man like my brother, life in the battlefield was unbearable.

An analysis of Rosenberg's three stages of poetic development and his accomplishments as an innovative writer (Dennis Silk, "Isaac Rosenberg (1890–1918)," Judaism, 14 [Fall 1965], pp. 462–474)

Three self-portraits of Isaac Rosenberg, the first painted in London in 1911 or earlier, the second in Cape Town in 1914, the third in France in 1915, conveniently mark the stages of his self-transformation. In his London portrait, intellect is subordinated to sensation, energy and will concealed by an almost ludicrous over-refinement of expression. Exquisiteness survives in the Cape Town portrait, but it is that of a dangerous duelist the prudent would do well to avoid. In his third self-portrait, Rosenberg is a sardonic bombardier, all energy and will, and a squat steel helmet replaces the duelist's hat.

Rosenberg's early work had largely been slack or self-indulgent, although even there a sudden energetic badness, or a poor conceit followed ruthlessly to its conclusion, had disturbed the vacuous Romantic or pre-Raphaelite surface. At its best this early work suggests a powerful experience trapped in the wrong forms, as Rosenberg learned to use, and then to discard, the traditional meters. The poetry of his middle period—of his first experiments with free verse, his first tentative efforts to cope with the visionary experience I believe to underlie his last period—is mannered and obscure. He too often interposes between the reader and himself a thicket of complicated syntax and over-profuse imagery almost impossible to penetrate.

The third, or bombardier's, phase began with his enlistment in late 1915, and ended with his death in action in April 1918. In these two-and-a-half years he pulled tight the knot of his lonely and difficult thought, which underlies and unifies his Trench poems, as well as *Moses* and "The Unicorn," his late dramatic fragments. All his earlier work is finally a laborious preparation for the two-and-a-half years of poetic life with which this essay is primarily concerned.

In 1916, Rosenberg published privately his pamphlet *Moses*. In the dramatic fragment which gives its title to the pamphlet, the extraordinary movement of the verse is based on two opposing principles. In some passages, Rosenberg's verse acquires a stone or monumental quality, though softened by his subtle rhythm. This sense of the ponderable quality of things, of their weight, their resistance, their cutting power, is among contemporary poets to be found only in Robinson Jeffers, but in Jeffers it is too often combined with an obsessive interest in unconscious matter, or matter repudiating consciousness of any kind, any commerce with thought, any volition. With Rosenberg things are moving always to some end; there is a sense of energy, propulsion, destination. The opposing rhythmical principle is one of sharp and emphatic movement. Moses' first soliloquy contains the following verbs: *torn, broken, prick, crack, boil, grip, break, drive, catch*. Rosenberg's prescription for a drawing characterizes this rhythm. "You look at a drawing. Can I read it? Is it clear, concise, definite? It cannot be too harsh for me. The line must cut into my consciousness, the waves of life must be disturbed, sharp and unhesitating. It is nature's consent, her agreement that what we take from her we keep."

The theme of *Moses* is the proper use of the will and imagination, when expressed in action. The fusion of these is Power, Power to break through and down, to create a new life, to destroy the old. Moses had been trapped by an imitation marvel, the pleasures of sensuality. Now he has grown beyond it; he wants instead "the huge kiss of power." His genius will utilize the trapped energies of the Israelite bondmen, "the mauled, sweaty horde" (surely there is a reference here to contemporary Anglo-Jewry, lost either in commercial brutality or pointless over-sensitivity). Rosenberg's Moses is a very free variation on the theme of the hero of *Exodus*–he is sick of priests, of forms, of the miasma of a dying god, yet the Biblical Moses is a great inventor and codifier of priestly forms. He is superb, with nothing of the Biblical Moses' meekness. His power will substitute a new consciousness for the old inertia, but what this consciousness will contemplate is not defined. Only the magnificence of the expectation is there.

Moses speaks a new fierce language. The occasional residual archaicism, oddly embedded there, suggests a pre-Raphaelite caught between swing-doors by a Vorticist, and horribly pummelled. The syntax has been clarified by its relation to the central concept of Power. Rosenberg's earlier obscurity had been caused largely by the fact that more than most poets, even in a period riddled by doctrines of the image as the basic poetic unit, he thought in terms of the image. This cast of thought must have been encouraged by his working habits as a painter. Laurence Binyon describes an early canvas which "was saturated with symbolism and required a good deal of explanation. I liked the mysteriousness of it, and the ideas which inspired the painting had suggested figures and groups and visionary glimpses of landscape which had passages of real beauty, though the whole work had grown impossibly complex with its convolutions of symbolic meaning." Now overmuch imagery, unless held down by a governing impulse, leads to a slush of sensation for its own sake, and to a bombardment of the governing impulse by the accidents of life. This is what occurs in a number of Rosenberg's earlier poems, particularly in the middle period. The governing impulse behind *Moses* is Rosenberg's grasp, at a level beyond the rational or the emotional, of the nature of Power. This governing impulse gave him control of his images, and taught him how to use the normally short-winded Imagist method for longer works. What Rosenberg did is in direct contrast to what happens in Ezra Pound's "Cantos," with their deification of the image at the expense of the intellect, and their consequent passivity in the face of experience.

Rosenberg is nowhere more Jewish, or rather Hebraic, than in the active and dynamic quality of his thinking. In fact, his essentially Hebraic mind is expressed more in how he thought, and the expression it took, than in what he thought. Thorlief Boman, in his comparison of Greek and Hebrew thinking, has several remarks very pertinent to Rosenberg, who habitually, because of his Jewish endowment, sought out possibilities in English that exist more fully in Hebrew. Boman writes: "If Israelite thinking is to be characterized, it is obvious first to call it dynamic, vigorous, passionate, and sometimes explosive in kind: correspondingly, Greek thinking is static, peaceful, moderate and harmonious in kind." Again: "In any case, Hebrew, a language exceptionally unusual in our experience and to our manner of thinking, betrays in many respects the idiosyncrasy of the Israelite psyche. The verbs, especially, whose basic meaning always expresses a movement or an activity, reveal the dynamic activity of the Hebrews' thinking."

The active nature of Rosenberg's poetry makes particularly inept Yeats' decision to omit the war-poets from his Oxford anthology, because of his objection to passive suffering. Rosenberg took pleasure in almost any display of energy, in a wild louse-hunt behind the lines in France, in marching soldiers, in a man straining to lift a cart-wheel deep in mud. Misuse of it might unleash chaos, as in his poem on the destruction of the Lusitania, or it might breed the horrors of trench-warfare. The risk seemed to him worthwhile, when balanced against the chances of new life (although there is in him a poet's hatred of chaos). He constantly protests against the miseries of army life, and maintains that misery drove him to enlist, but he seems at least half-consciously to have chosen military life in order to follow the unleashed energies to their source. In a letter written from Military Hospital before embarkation for France, he writes: "One might succumb, be destroyed–but one might also (and the chances are even greater for it) be renewed, made larger, healthier." And he asks proudly of Wilfred Gibson, "Has your Muse sniffed gunpowder?"

This preoccupation with Power explains why, together with the more immediate poems of trench life, he could write *Moses*, "Daughters Of War," and the "Unicorn" fragments. None of them seems so immediately relevant to the conditions of life in France as the poems of Owen and Sassoon, or some of his own Trench poems. Yet they are engaged, at the deepest level, with war and the energies generating it.

In *Moses*, the man who is the vehicle of Power has to go beyond what Blake calls the "shadowy female." A year later, Rosenberg, with an intensified knowledge of what appears to be a visionary experience never once directly alluded to outside his poetry, thought differently. In his greatest poem, "Dead Man's Dump," and in "The Daughters Of War," his own favorite poem, the energies generating chaos or a new life are traced to their source in a supernatural female will. This will, heroic and demanding, spiritual and voluptuous, destroys to quicken.

In "Dead Man's Dump," a wire-laying party passes with its limber over the bodies of the dead in battle. A grimly physical description alternates with a religious invocation of the supernatural female will.

> Earth has waited for them,
> All the time of their growth
> Fretting for their decay:
> Now she has them at last!
> In the strength of their strength
> Suspended—stopped and held.
>
> What fierce imaginings their dark souls lit?
> Earth! Have they gone into you!
> Somewhere they must have gone,
> And flung on your hard back
> Is their soul's sack
> Emptied of God-ancestralled essences.
> Who hurled them out? Who hurled?
>
> None saw their spirits' shadow shake the grass,
> Or stood aside for the half used life to pass
> Out of those doomed nostrils and the doomed mouth,
> When the swift iron burning bee
> Drained the wild honey of their youth.
> . . . .
>
> Maniac Earth! howling and flying, your bowel
> Seared by the jagged fire, the iron love,
> The impetuous storm of savage love.
> Dark Earth! dark Heavens! swinging in chemic smoke,
> What dead are born when you kiss each soundless soul
> With lightning and thunder from your mined heart,
> Which man's self dug, and his blind fingers loosed?

The casual reader who has not penetrated to the unity underlying Rosenberg's last work may interpret the second stanza as a conventional apostrophization of Mother Earth. This interpretation becomes difficult with the more explicit stanza commencing "Maniac Earth!" which for some reason was excluded from the 1922 Binyon edition but silently inserted in the 1937 Bottomley and Harding edition. When "Dead Man's Dump" is related, as it must be, to the wild "Daughters of War," such an interpretation isn't possible.

This poem is the other side of the legend in *Genesis* of the Sons of God who saw the daughters of men that they were fair. A race of supernatural Amazons need for their fulfillment "the sons of valour," "the earth men" who will be joined to them by death. War then is the instrument for this fusion of mortal and immortal. The Amazons compete with the mortal lovers of these men. At the end an Amazon speaks:

> My sisters force their males
> From the doomed earth, from the doomed glee . . .
> My sisters have their males
> Clean of the dust of old days . . .
> They are my sisters' lovers in other days and years.

One can work out the approximate date for this poem from Rosenberg's letters to Edward Marsh; he was working on "Dead Man's Dump" and "Daughters of War" at roughly the same time. In "Dead Man's Dump" the dark and negative aspect of the Amazonian will is emphasized. The title itself is savage and derisive, the dead are emptied out, diminished, whether they go back into, or sexually enter, the earth, or lie abandoned on its surface. In "Daughters Of War" there is more of creative terror, the sense of a difficult enlargement of men's faculties. Earth, in "Dead Man's Dump," waits morosely for her prisoners: the Amazons wait "in sleepless passion for the sons of valour." Two worlds that need one another, must meet.

Rosenberg writes about "Daughters Of War" in a letter to Edward Marsh: "The end is an attempt to imagine the severance of all human relationship, and the fading away of human life." Such a severance of all human relationship occurs at the end of "Dead Man's Dump," with its great and terrible description of the man who dies at the moment the wiring party reaches him.

It occurs in "Girl to Soldier on Leave." Here the girl addresses her lover, who is a kind of Titan enlarged by his sufferings and released from servitude to an ignoble civilization. The girl is losing in her competition with death, and behind death stand the Amazons. She figures in "Daughters Of War," she is one of the mortal women who lose their earth-men to this fierce supernatural will. Her Titan lover will soon be dead, when the last gyve of heroic life is loosened, and he is fetched home by his Amazonian lover.

Rosenberg's final conception of this female supernatural will follows a series of poems written over a number of years, in which, on the whole, he is kinder to Christ than to Jehovah, but kind finally only to the Daughters of War. Rosenberg's first thought, in thinking of God, usually equated with Jehovah, is how to trick Him. In "Spiritual Isolation," God flees from him as from a leper. In "Invisible Ancient Enemy of Mine," Rosenberg would even amass all of the world's pain, thus cheating God by leaving none for life. In "God Made Blind" we cheat God by keeping Him ignorant of our amorous joy. Then, when our joy has become too evident to conceal, we can cheat Him with it, for what can God do when we have grown to be a part of love, which is itself God? (Here Rosenberg charmingly contradicts himself, for in the earlier part of the poem God is jealous of our love, but to trick Him at the end He has to be made into an embodiment of it.) In "The One Lost," a lover mingles his dust with that of the beloved, so that Jehovah at Judgment Day can't find it. In the only considerable poem of the series, the very beautiful "God," He is just a cowardly bully Whom one must hit back at.

> In his malodorous brain what slugs and mire,
> Lanthorned in his oblique eyes, guttering burned.

His body lodged a rat where men nursed souls.
The world flashed grape-green eyes of a foiled cat
To him. On fragments of an old shrunk power,
On shy and maimed, on women wrung awry,
He lay, a bullying hulk, to crush them more.
But when one, fearless, turned and clawed like bronze,
Cringing was easy to blunt those stern paws,
And he would weigh the heavier on those after.

Finally, in *Moses*, the miasma of a dying god is to be removed, to make way for a new consciousness. The pain inflicted by God is the work of a spiteful bully: inflicted by a Goddess, it becomes necessary suffering.

Just as an earlier series of poems about God culminates in the explosion of *Moses*, in the same way a series of earlier poems preceding and leading directly to "Dead Man's Dump" and "Daughters Of War" are tentative attempts to cope with the visionary experience of the two later poems.

This experience had best be related to what is known of Rosenberg's life, or can be deduced from his poetry. In Maurice de Sausmarez' note on Rosenberg's drawings and paintings, he refers to his "frailty and sensitiveness at this time [circa 1911] . . . the taunting he

Casualties at the Somme (Jay Winter and Blaine Baggett, The Great War and the Shaping of the 20th Century*)*

suffered at the hands of a colleague Guevara until Kramer, who had been learning to box, entered the lists as his champion." De Sausmarez recalls how "his literary ambitions, his continual anxiety about making a living and his natural seriousness set him always somewhat apart." This reinforces the impression made by the poems of a lonely person leading a hard ascetic life. It is difficult to believe that Rosenberg's early love-poems, with their impossibly idealized conception of a woman's nature, were written for a real person. A later cluster of poems, which includes "A Warm Thought Flickers," "First Fruit," "I have lived in the underworld too long," and "Auguries," suggests a relationship entered into, potentially liberating, and turned away from. I believe that Rosenberg's straitened conditions, his ambiguous status, his natural taciturnity, made it difficult for him fully to reveal himself to a woman. The pressure built up by his love-longing probably precipitated the visionary experience at the back of "Auguries," "The Female God," "The Poet (III)," "At Night," "In a concentrated thought a sudden noise startles," and possibly several other poems difficult to pin down because of obscurities of syntax. They lead to the last poems and dramatic fragments, in which the earlier intuitive knowledge is confirmed by later battle experience.

In "At Night," supernatural horsemen, amorous, violent and secretive, sexually assault a sleeper's world. (This poem has obvious connections both with "Daughters Of War" and the "Unicorn" fragments.) In the fragment "In a concentrated thought," the sky itself vibrates with sensuality, "Helpless, obscene and cruel." In "The Poet," at a moment of silence, the street dies to "an essence, a love spirit." In "The Female God," there is an appalled submission to the erotic supernatural will underlying the other poems.

The dividing line between visionary experience of this sort and sexual repression is difficult to draw. It is easy to dismiss as a dishonest deferment of pleasure, or as overreaching symbolism. For me, finally, Rosenberg's experience and his attempt to shape it go beyond personal unhappiness or poetic symbolism.

Rosenberg uncovers in these poems the workings of a supernatural Amazonian will, in need of, and actively seeking out, human lovers transfigured by death in war. In the last year of his life, this will, as represented in his late dramatic fragments, becomes more humanized and in part

After the battle, the Somme (1916)

transformed, so that it is difficult to distinguish in his conception between the superhuman intervening in human life, and human necessity raised to a superhuman pitch.

Between 1917 and his death he wrote three related fragments, "The Amulet," and "The Unicorn" (in two separate versions). They are baffling in their incompleteness, often contradictory, but contain, among a good deal he would certainly have revised, some of his best work. A systematic account of these fragments is impossible, but certain ideas do emerge which are obviously related to the Amazonian cluster, and develop or depart from it. All of them have a vaguely Hebraic or Semitic background, with characters given Hebrew names or roots—Lilith, Saul, Tel, Enoch, Dora—all of them are studies in barrenness.

In "The Amulet," the protagonists are Lilith and a giant Nubian, who goes back ultimately, maybe, to the naked African in *Moses*. They are ambiguous figures. Lilith is at once Eve's predecessor, Lilith Queen of Devils reviled by men, and a desperate wife deprived of her husband Saul's love. I don't believe this ambiguity was intended by Rosenberg. Rather, he attempted to humanize the Amazonian figure of the earlier poems, but with only partial success. The characterization of the Nubian, to whom Lilith bares her heart, is equally ambiguous. He is a kind of miracle-worker, possessing Golden Age wisdom, the gift of happiness, spices to make the brain run wild, bewitching conversation, and a jade amulet to restore lost love. Rosenberg's directions run: "He is an immense man with squat, mule-skinned features, his jet-black curled beard, crisp hair, glistening nude limbs, appear to her like some heathen idol of ancient stories." Yet Lilith wonders whether he is "Law's spirit wandering to us / Through nature's anarchy." Perhaps, even, he had met Moses. And the Nubian is sexually unawoken. Aroused in a shattering way by Lilith, apparently for the first time his glacial coldness is troubled. The law-maker and the coldness are incompatible with the earlier miracle-worker, with his spices, his amulet to restore lost love, his glistening nudeness. I suggest that Rosenberg was wavering between his conception of Moses as a man going beyond sexuality, and his older knowledge, now intensified by battle, of the Daughters of War. The Nubian's soliloquy at the end, when he discovers his passion for Lilith, suggests in its rushing but jagged rhythm a soliloquy of Moses. But Moses turned beyond love, while the Nubian is reaching out for it. A strange reversal.

In the first of the two "Unicorn" fragments, Saul and Lilith appear again, but in a new setting. Saul has been describing to a bookseller his encounter with a unicorn. To the bookseller it seems

Strange as the myth
Of barren men, strange beasts, I lent your wife.

Saul goes on to describe the encounter:

The myth? Ah yes.
Here was the usual road, the usual sky,
The same brown surging flanks, the well thewed legs
Jogging between my thoughts, the queer long ears
That seemed to hear a calling from the town.
Here was Lot's Pool, bare of the shining boys
I looked for, fishing; but it was meal-time then,
As I remembered by a hut I passed,
Then . . . I was nigh jerked from the cart
At the dead stop—like a wind it flew by—
The haughty contours of a swift white horse,
And on its brows a tree, a branching tree.

Whereupon the unicorn rushes by, again terrifying him. It is, at one level of interpretation, the symbol of Saul's barren love for Lilith, of the unused and dammed-up love he had never, because of his taciturn cold ways, sufficiently revealed. Saul declares

This white terror is that virgin will
Of all my unused love.

At another level it carries out Rosenberg's intention, as defined in a letter to Edward Marsh: "Saul and Lilith are ordinary folk into whose ordinary lives the Unicorn bursts. It is to be a play of terror, terror of hidden things and the fear of the supernatural." The unicorn gone, Saul hurries home to Lilith, afraid he may die before revealing his love. The first "Unicorn" fragment ends at this point.

In the second, imperative sexual needs are raised to a superhuman pitch. The protagonists are again Saul, Lilith and the Nubian. Saul is in a woody place in a storm, demoralized, his wagon half-sunk in a quagmire. He has been cowed by his glimpse of a unicorn, a girl bound to its back, and following it a black naked host, the army of a decaying race, enacting a kind of Rape of the Sabines on his people. Almost wiped out for lack of women, they have been forced to breed with animals. Saul is quite lost when Tel—the Nubian—emerges from the storm, helps him lift the wheels from the quagmire, and drives him home to Lilith. On the way, Saul speculates about the nature of Tel, who, unknown to him, is the prince of this race.

Why quails my heart? God riding with
A mortal would absorb him.
He touched my hand, here is my hand the same.
Sure I am whirled in some dark fantasy—
A dizzying cloven wink, the beast, the black,
And I ride now . . . ride, ride, the way I know
That rushing terror . . . I shudder yet.

> The haughty contours of a swift white horse
> And on its brows a tree, a branching tree,
> And on its back a golden girl bound fast . . .
> His monstrous posture, why his neck's turn
> Were our thews' adventure; some Amazon's son doubtless
> From the dark countries.

Tel has already caught a glimpse of Lilith, and turned away, a man who has followed barren ways too long. He enters the house with Saul and there declares his nature, and that of his people, to Lilith.

> Behind impassable places
> Whose air was never warmed by a woman's lips
> Bestial man shapes ride dark impulses
> Through roots in the bleak blood, then hide
> In shuddering light from their self loathing.
> They fade in arid light–
> But unnatured by their craving, for they know
> Obliteration's spectre . . .
> [They] hunt in bleakness for the dread might,
> The incarnate female soul of generation.

The curious thing is that though Tel is directing this Rape of the Sabines, his attitude to Lilith is one of terror; he might be lost in appalled contemplation of the Female God. At the end of this fragment, Tel places the unconscious Lilith on the unicorn and the host ride off "on various animals, the Unicorn leading. A woman is clasped on every one, some are frantic, others white and unconscious, some nestle laughing."

These dramatic fragments, with their study of barrenness, their fear of extinction, can obviously be related to Rosenberg's primary experience as an isolated person dangling between two societies, and to his later war-experiences. But the myth of Tel and his decaying race, with the urgency of their love in the face of extinction, suggests a communal experience transcending one brilliant man's inevitable rootlessness. It may be that, living in a community of men sharing the same hard knowledge of a wasteful isolating war and who, no doubt, after early battle-trials accepted him as one of themselves, Rosenberg came into the power that informs his later work. His invocation of England, as in certain of the Trench poems, has more the feeling of England conceived as a great living entity than is to be found in the work of any other poet of his generation. He spoke for a community.

Rosenberg's position, as a greatly endowed writer with a Jewish background, the son of Tolstoyans and pacifists seeking out battle-trials, resembles that of the amazing Russian-Jewish writer, Isaac Babel, in the Red Cavalry. Babel had to endure the anomaly of being a Jew among Cossacks, to bear the strain of two disciplines, two terribly disparate modes of thought and feeling, to learn how to kill. He made his art out of his burden, but sometimes the joints of his imagination almost crack under the strain. In Rosenberg the particular Jewish background and the more general English and war-experience reinforce one another, and this without self-conscious eclecticism.

The vaguely Hebraic background, already referred to, of the dramatic fragments, is made more explicit in a group of three poems on Jewish themes, written in the trenches, and exploring the same themes of barrenness and extinction. In "The Burning Of The Temple" Rosenberg invokes the wrath of Solomon. This is no exercise in Biblical nostalgia: it is Solomon's wrath that is invoked, not his wisdom, in three curt stanzas.

> Fierce wrath of Solomon
> Where sleepest thou? O see
> The fabric which thou won
> Earth and ocean to give thee–
> O look at the red skies.
>
> Or hath the sun plunged down?
> What is this molten gold–
> These thundering fires blown
> Through heaven–where the smoke rolled?
> Again the great king dies.
>
> His dreams go out in smoke,
> His days he let not pass
> And sculptured here are broke,
> Are charred as the burnt grass,
> Gone as his mouth's last sighs.

Here there is an implicit scorn–identical with that of Moses for Israel in Egypt–of the inertia permitting the Temple's destruction. "The Destruction of Jerusalem By The Babylonian Hordes" is a variation on the same theme, while "Through These Pale Gold Days" resumes, in contemporary terms, the theme of *Moses:* how to touch the rude heart of the mauled, sweaty horde. These Hebrew poems, of the same period as his Trench poems, testify to the noble solidity of Rosenberg's vision. It was possible for him to live at the center of several conflicting faiths, to penetrate to the heart of competing mythologies. First there is creative energy, that Power to remake the world, encountered in *Moses* and traced to its Amazonian source in "Daughters Of War" and "Dead Man's Dump." Against this there is inertia, as in "The Burning of the Temple" or the Israelite bondmen of *Moses,* and Power leading to extinction or chaos when left uncontrolled by a shaping intelligence, as in "The Lusitania" and the "Unicorn" fragments.

Rosenberg performed the heroic double feat of summoning the resources of the Hebrew past and the English present. In his synthesis of almost incompatible elements, he had one advantage denied to later Anglo-

Jewish writers who had to meet the same conflict at their roots.

The Jewish community into which he was born was far more virile, with less of the parvenu, than the same society seventy years on. Whitechapel Jewry around the turn of the century was a poor but energetic community, with many of its members conversant with Hebrew, Yiddish and Russian culture, and possessing a rich folk-background, passionate, voluble and argumentative. At that time it was a sawn-off branch of the Russian-Jewish society which produced Yalag, Peretz, Bialik, Chagall, Isaac Babel, and the powerful body of early Zionist doctrine. The richness of Rosenberg's background must have reinforced his own naturally independent and vigorous nature, empowering him to meet the impact of English culture without demoralization, and to encounter his English contemporaries without selling his birthright.

His achievement is in shocking contrast with that of his generation, who, during the forty years or so since his death, have cheated and impoverished themselves by truckling to the English genius, itself in decline, and, for them, from the very beginning a disease at the roots. When they left the warm if poverty-stricken centers of Jewish life in Whitechapel and elsewhere, they spread out to the suburbs and later to the richer residential centers, became progressively thinned out, vulgarized and diminished, with no roots either in Jewish life or in the contemporary life of post-Christian England. Neither for nor against, and never having dared Rosenberg's synthesis, they possess, in contemporary England, the place

British troops beginning an assault from a trench

of the opportunists in the Inferno of Dante. "Eternally unclassified, they race round and round—pursuing a wavering banner that runs forever before them through the dirty air."

An essay on Rosenberg ought not to end without acknowledging the imperfect nature of most of his work. During his great creative period, from late 1915 to April 1918, he was immersed in the trench warfare which transformed his poetry without allowing him the leisure finally to unify it. Its conflicting characteristics, of fragmentariness and cragginess, repel the lazy-minded. Rosenberg has a capacity to startle and disappoint at once, an awkward combination of delicacy and clumsiness, the relationship to language of a great poet combined with an archaicism of language never fully discarded. Language for him was a form of latent energy, not to be used for the mere passive recording of experience, but rather as an instrument in its exploration and control. Once he peeled off the top layer and penetrated to the deepest level, language became activated energy at the service of the imagination and the will. By a paradox, his penetration to this level has been in part concealed by blunders any smooth amateur could avoid. The residual dead diction is due in the main to Rosenberg's early death; he hadn't the time to organize his discoveries. Another cause is probably his friendship with poets of an older generation, honorable craftsmen who admired his work without understanding his aims.

It would be tragic if these faults permanently concealed Rosenberg's true force. His was a strong nature, with an always active will to dominate experience and extract from it a rigorous discipline. He disliked Turgenev and thought him "immoral" because of the impression he gave of the poverty of life. He must have been a very likeable man, downright in a quiet fashion, keeping his patience with difficult patrons, very taciturn about his own suffering, and saving his visionary thinking for his poems. It is impossible to consider him the victim of his own background or of a war which, though it destroyed him, enlarged his understanding. He had worked on himself, till he reached the point

Title page for the Parsons edition of Rosenberg's writings and art

where English poetry was fit for heroes. He might have given a decadent England standards to judge itself by, and led a generation between two wars. As it is, he emerges as a lonely eminence.

A discussion of the development of Rosenberg's poetry (Joseph Cohen, "Isaac Rosenberg: From Romantic to Classic," Tulane Studies in English, *10 [1960], pp. 129–142)*

In his recent "Writers and Their Work" monograph, entitled "War Poets, 1914–1918," Edmund Blunden, after devoting chapters to Rupert Brooke, Siegfried Sassoon and Wilfred Owen, says only of Isaac Rosenberg that "many still bless the remembrance and feel the passionate idea" of that poet. This superficial treatment of Rosenberg is not accidental. It is representative of much of the writing about him in the past four decades. Beginning with T. S. Eliot in 1920, critics have called attention to Rosenberg and emphasized the significance of his poetry without telling us precisely why we should read it and bless his memory.

The explanation for Rosenberg's neglect is as obvious as that neglect is churlish. Practically every critic who has examined his poetry has assumed that because he died young, leaving only a small quantity of mature verse, most of it on war, that there was no unified development in his poetic thought. They credit him with some achievement but claim that his performance was uneven and static, its limits carefully marked. Within those limits Rosenberg has been classified as an "isolationist" poet, a Georgian poet, a war poet, a "consciously" Jewish poet, an "unconsciously" Jewish poet, and a romantic poet. Readers have had no consistent series of signposts to guide them, and those that have been put up all point in different directions.

Several critics have refused even to erect signposts, maintaining that Rosenberg is unclassifiable, but those who have erected the single ones have seemed dissatisfied with their directions and have hinted that there may be other yet unelucidated routes to the understanding of Rosenberg's work.

. . . Rosenberg was neither more nor less an "isolationist" poet than any other poet who has ever written a line of genuine verse. At the same time, he was not a coterie poet either. To call him a Georgian is simply to recognize that he reached his maturity in the second decade of the twentieth century. To those Georgians who knew him, he was little more than a literary freak. And as for his being a war poet, he made it clear before his death that he did not think of himself as a soldier with a poetic mission, as did both Rupert Brooke and Wilfred Owen.

Certainly Rosenberg was a Jewish poet in that he made both a "conscious" and an "unconscious" use of his religious heritage in his writing. However, he never "aspired to become a representative poet of his own nation" as Laurence Binyon maintained in his well-intentioned but superficial Introduction to Rosenberg's *Poems* published in 1922. On the contrary, there is reason to believe that Rosenberg rejected Judaism's fundamental tenet, the belief in a patriarchal deity, in favor of a pre-Hebraic matriarchal mythology. In any case, he was not orthodox and he could not have been a Jewish poet in any traditionally acceptable theological frame of reference.

We are left with one signpost, romanticism, and the hint of another one, still undisclosed. It takes only the merest glance at the poems to see that romanticism is not only a direction for the reader but is indeed Rosenberg's high road to poetry. But he had a low road too, and it is down that road that the unmarked signpost points. That one should be marked *classicism*. For it was Rosenberg's fate always to be attracted by ambivalent concepts, and any understanding of his work must be based largely on the knowledge that in the last four years of his life when he wrote the poems on which his reputation rests he was unable to choose decisively between romanticism and classicism. Much of the time he used both simultaneously.

The strong romanticism in Rosenberg's poetry developed through his love for the Romantic poets whom he imitated, particularly Shelley, Keats, Tennyson and Browning; his upbringing in an atmosphere where hope eternal fired the imagination of the East European Jews who had settled in Whitechapel; and his rebelling against the socially and religiously restricted ghetto which encompassed him. His classicism, on the other hand, came about through his constant struggle to impose order on his writing; his Hebraic fatalism that manifested itself in a pessimism that grew out of his seeing constantly his hopes thwarted by a cosmic machinery from which he could not escape; his attraction historically to his classical Jewish background, obtained from a study of the Bible; and his response to the impact of the war which made him see clearly the value of contemplating the finite world and using its materials in the conceptualization of poetic images.

Both romanticism and classicism held Rosenberg with such force that he was never able to ignore one or the other. The bulk of his poetry is romantic, but the poems composed after 1915 are essentially though not wholly classical. Since his ambivalent progress coincided with T. E. Hulme's concern with the same subjects, and since there is the possibility that Hulme's ideas were known to Rosenberg, it may prove worthwhile to examine his poetry against the background of

Hulme's "Romanticism and Classicism." However, I do not wish to suggest here either that Hulme's bias against romanticism is justified—clearly he misjudged its role in the twentieth century—or that his classical principles are to be regarded as the norm for classicism. His definitions of classicism simply have a peculiarly direct relevancy to Rosenberg's later development, just as his observations on romanticism relate cogently to Rosenberg's earlier development.

Hulme began his now famous essay (written in 1913 but not published until after his death) with a consideration of the late eighteenth century atmosphere that nurtured romanticism. Out of it came the "religious enthusiasm" that he called "the root of all romanticism," as well as the idea that human progress would be assured once society brought about the destruction of "oppressive order" which interfered with man's drawing upon his "infinite reservoir of possibilities." Though Hulme had the French Revolution in mind, this same religio-political milieu existed in the Whitechapel of Rosenberg's youth, filled as it was with immigrant Russian Jews who had escaped the Czar's "oppressive order" and who now looked optimistically to a bright future for their children where ambition and vision and industry would spell individual success. This attitude, deeply ingrained in Rosenberg's thought when he was a youth, contributed to his seeing the world largely in romantic terms.

Unlike those who planted the seeds of this romanticism within him, Rosenberg did not, however, think of "oppressive order" simply in terms of fierce Russian Cossacks and horses in the synogogue; he saw it symbolized also in the Old Testament figure of God. This stirred his rebellious nature, which had been molded early by constant privation and frustration. It was to be expected that he would rebel, but his rebellion becomes significant when we observe that the method he employed . . . was precisely the method Hulme described as natural for the romantic. Hulme wrote that the romantic will not believe in God, so he begins "to believe that man is a god." This led Hulme to define romanticism as "spilt religion." Since much of Rosenberg's rebellious poetry is poor in quality, Hulme's definition is remarkably appropriate.

"Spilt religion" finds its source in the romantic's view of man as an infinite being, and Hulme wryly observed that the romantic was always talking about the infinite. In his pre-war poetry and prose, Rosenberg talked of little else. Moreover, Hulme argued that the romantic recognizes always a "bitter contrast" between man's estimate of his capabilities and his actual attainments, which results in gloom. Rosenberg's early poetry is filled specifically with this kind of gloom. Hulme argued further that the "whole of the romantic attitude seems to crystallise in verse around metaphors of flight." These metaphors tumble over one another in Rosenberg's verses.

At one time in his youth, Rosenberg's world picture was apparently enveloped in romantic terms. He once composed an informal essay on the symbolism of a door knocker, which begins: "This is essentially an age of romance. We no longer dream but we live the dream. Romance is no more a dim world outside the ordinary world, whose inhabitants are only poets and lovers, but [it is a world] wide, tangible, and universal." At the same time, Rosenberg's theme in a number of poems was the neo-Platonic quest for "the glory of the heavens celestially in glimpses seen." This theme, which Rosenberg took from Shelley and Keats, fitted in well with his view of man as an infinite being seeking celestial perfection. As Hulme observed, the infinite being achieves this perfection by becoming god himself. Rosenberg's "God Made Blind" illustrates fully his use of this concept:

> And then, when Love's power hath increased so
> That we must burst or grow to give it room,
> And we can no more cheat our God with gloom,
> We'll cheat Him with our joy.
> For say! what can God do
> To us, to Love, whom we have grown into?
> Love! the poured rays of God's Eternity!
> We are grown God—and shall His self-hate be?

This idea was sufficiently important to Rosenberg in 1914 that he used it as the basis for the arrangement of *Youth*, a pamphlet of poems published privately in 1915. The idea was outlined in a brief introduction, and "God Made Blind" appeared in the section where the transformation takes place.

The concluding poem in *Youth* Rosenberg called "Expression." It represents the fullest flowering of his romanticism. In a sense it is a manifesto stating vigorously the poet's faith in an imagination freed from "oppressive order":

> Call—call—and bruise the air:
> Shatter dumb space!
> Yea! we will fling this passion everywhere;
> Leaving no place
>
> For the superb and grave
> Magnificent throng,
> The pregnant queens of quietness that brave
> And edge our song
>
> Of wonder at the light.
> (Our life-leased home),

Of greeting to our housemates. And in might
Our song shall roam

Life's heart, a blossoming fire
Blown bright by thought,
While gleams and fades the infinite desire,
Phantasmed nought.

Can this be caught and caged?
Wings can be clipt,
Of eagles, the sun's gaudy measure gauged,
But no sense dipt

In the mystery of sense.
The troubled throng
Of words break out like smother'd fire through dense
And smouldering wrong.

For all its unrestrained enthusiasm, "Expression" is actually Rosenberg's farewell to romanticism as the dominating force in his poetry. He would continue to hold in contempt "oppressive order" in its theological context and, indeed, seek a mythological substitute for it, but by late 1915 he was beginning to differentiate successfully between an all inclusive "oppressive order" and a more limited one which combined unity, simplicity, and clarity in matters of style and expression. He began to see clearly the values in the ancient classical restraints. He was not ready to "leave [a] place" for them, but he did refer to them as a "superb and grave / Magnificent throng." It was not long afterward that Rosenberg crossed over, hesitantly, to his low road of classicism. . . .

Hence it was not unnatural that Rosenberg should become obsessed with order, form, depth, lucidity, unity. By 1916 this obsession was nearly overwhelming. His letters to Gordon Bottomley, Winifred Seaton, Laurence Binyon and Edward Marsh continually allude to his struggles to master his writing. To Gordon Bottomley, he wrote that he wanted to compose simple poetry "where an interesting complexity of thought is kept in tone and right value to the dominating idea so that it is understandable and still ungraspable"; and to Winifred Seaton he said he felt "quite sure that [his achievement of] form is only a question of time"; but in May, 1917, he revealed that he had not escaped his ambivalence when he wrote to Marsh that "Mr. Binyon has often sermonised lengthily over my working on two different principles in the same thing and I know how it spoils the unity of a poem."

In a subsequent letter to Marsh, Rosenberg again took up the subject of poetic composition, relating it directly to one of his poems:

> I think with you that poetry should be definite thought and clear expression, however subtle; I don't think there should be any vagueness at all; but a sense of something hidden and felt to be there. Now when my things fail to be clear I am sure it is because of the luckless choice of a word or the failure to introduce a word that would flash my idea plain as it is to my own mind. I believe my Amazon poem to be my best poem. If there is any difficulty it must be in words here or there the changing or the elimination of which may make the poem clear. It has taken me about a year to write; for I have changed and rechanged it and thought hard over that poem and striven to get that sense of inexorableness the human (or unhuman) side of this war has. It even penetrates behind human life for the "Amazon" who speaks in the second part of the poem is imagined to be without her lover yet, while all her sisters have theirs, the released spirits of the slain earth men; her lover yet remains to be released.

The poem referred to is "Daughters of War." It is an example of Rosenberg's working on two different principles. His material is primarily classical, but his treatment is both classical and romantic. The soldiers who become the Amazons' lovers are first described in a classical context: they were before their deaths "fixed and limited": "We were satisfied of our lords the moon and the sun / To take our wage of sleep and bread and warmth"; but once dead, their spirits romantically transcend the finite to become enamoured of the Amazons: "These maidens came–these strong everliving Amazons . . . Clouding the wild–the soft lustres of our eyes." Subsequent lines revert to the classical and meet Hulme's requirements for classical verse in that they are "all dry and hard," and they have "an actually realised visual object": "My sisters force their males / From the doomed earth, from the doomed glee / And hankering of hearts." But at once the dry, hard quality and the visual object melt away into romantic abstraction: "Frail hands gleam up through the human quagmire and lips of ash / Seem to wail, as in sad faded paintings / Far sunken and strange." But with equal rapidity, Rosenberg moves back to the dry hardness and to the finite through employing classical fatalism to convey to the reader "that sense of inexorableness the human (or unhuman) side of [the] war has":

My sisters have their males
Clean of the dust of old days
That clings about those white hands
And yearns in those voices sad
But these shall not see them
Or think of them in any days or years;
They are my sisters' lovers in other days and years.

"Daughters of War" is one of twenty so-called "trench poems" which, with the privately published play *Moses* and the draft of another short play, "The Unicorn," comprise the bulk of Rosenberg's mature poetry. With the exception of parts of *Moses*, these works are more classical than romantic. Rosenberg no longer reaches totally out of himself, inflating the microcosmic to macrocosmic proportions, seeking through rebellion to escape his destiny. In the trenches he was learning resignation.

Though he became resigned, Rosenberg was not defeated by the severity of military life. In a letter to Binyon in 1916, he wrote: "I am determined that this war, with all its powers for devastation, shall not master my poetry. . . . I will not leave a corner of my consciousness covered, but saturate myself with the strange and extraordinary new conditions of this life, and it will all refine itself into poetry later on."

While the regimentation at the front was odious, the petty tyrannizing of the officers and the harshness of their demands irritating, the weather and the enemy constant killers, Rosenberg and his poetry benefited by his experiences. The war forced on him an orderliness and a continuity his life had lacked. His earlier romantic flights of the imagination gave way to the somber consideration of the finite, his trench poems offering testimony to the changes. There was no sense of rebellion left in him. Unlike the trench poems of Sassoon where rebellious thrusts abound, or the trench poems of Owen where rebellion takes the form of repeated insistence upon the useless sacrifice of human life, Rosenberg's trench poems are simply acknowledgments of man's particularly unfortunate situation on the Western Front. Though Rosenberg never acquiesces, he does not make his verse a poetry of personal appeal. He is classically composed, resolute, disinterested, one of the impersonal many who suffer. There are numerous examples: In "Marching" the "iron cloud" rains "immortal darkness" on *all* "strong eyes"; in "The Troop Ship," Rosenberg sees himself merely as

Irish troops storming German positions at Guillemont, Somme, in the painting by A. Forestier (John Laffin, The Western Front Illustrated 1914–1918 *[Walterboro Falls, N. H.: Sutton, 1991])*

one of the "Grotesque and queerly huddled / Contortionists" seeking sleep; in "Louse Hunting," he is one of the "Nudes—stark and glistening, / Yelling in lurid glee"; in "Returning, We Hear the Larks," he is a member of a patrol coming back to its own lines, "Dragging anguished limbs," knowing, as they all do, that "Death could drop from the dark / As easily as song"; and in "Break of Day in the Trenches," he points to the individuality of the "queer, sardonic rat" in order to emphasize by contrast how man has lost his own identity in combat, returning again to his figure in "Marching" of the vision of death reflected in the eyes of all the soldiers. Taken together, these poems aptly and precisely illustrate Hulme's arguments that in classical verse "man is always man, and never a god," and that "man is an extraordinarily fixed and limited animal whose nature is absolutely constant."

Hulme had emphasized, moreover, that the classical poet "remembers always that [man] is mixed up with the earth." Throughout the trench poems Rosenberg consistently binds his soldiers to the earth but never in the way that Wordsworth would have argued that the common man ought to be close to the soil. "From France" describes the "heaped stones . . . with grass between and dead folks under"; "Break of Day in the Trenches" speaks of the "haughty athletes . . . Sprawled in the bowels of the earth"; "In War" is concerned with grave digging; while "Dead Man's Dump" depicts man's condition in the earth. . . .

Through impersonality, passivity, and the acceptance of man's finiteness, Rosenberg's poetry became a predominantly classical memorial to the war-dead rather than a romantic protest. Man's fundamental dignity and his quiet courage in the face of destruction are simply recorded in the carefully limited images of war Rosenberg presents. This approach, incidentally, was the one taken by the World War II poets. Though they were nurtured on Owen, it was Rosenberg's classical pessimism that they imitated.

This same classical pessimism is found in verses which deal with subjects other than the Western Front. In the months before his death Rosenberg returned occasionally to biblical themes. These poems are marked by their detachment and restraint, and one entitled "The Destruction of Jerusalem by the Babylonian Hordes" illustrates how accomplished Rosenberg was becoming in manipulating classical materials in a thoroughly classical framework:

> They left their Babylon bare
> Of all its tall men,
> Of all its proud horses;
> They made for Lebanon.
>
> And shadowy sowers went
> Before their spears to sow
> The fruit whose taste is ash
> For Judah's soul to know.
>
> They who bowed to the Bull god
> Whose wings roofed Babylon,
> In endless hosts darkened
> The bright-heavened Lebanon.
>
> They washed their grime in pools
> Where laughing girls forgot
> The wiles they used for Solomon.
> Sweet laughter! remembered not.
>
> Sweet laughter charred in the flame
> That clutched the cloud and earth
> While Solomon's towers crashed between,
> The gird of Babylon's mirth.

Accompanying this return to ancient Hebrew materials are numerous allusions from Greek and Roman literature. Where the pre-war poems never went to Greece or Rome for subject-matter, the trench poems allude to Mars, Helen, Paris, the Amazons, Circe, Zeus, and Prometheus. Furthermore, "The Unicorn," Rosenberg's unfinished drama, has for its theme, as he described it, "a kind of 'Rape of the Sabine Woman' idea" . . . . The purpose of "The Unicorn," as Rosenberg wrote to Winifred Seaton, was "to symbolize the war and all the devastating forces let loose by an ambitious and unscrupulous will."

An examination of the draft of "The Unicorn" suggests that, some romantic elements in it notwithstanding, it is Rosenberg's strongest bid for unity along classical lines. Using a Roman myth he superimposes on it Hebraic and Egyptian elements. His chief protagonist, Saul, is Hebrew, his antagonist, Tel, Nubian. His theological system is a combination of Hebraic and Greek fatalism; Saul seeks his security in the conventional Old Testament God, while Tel symbolizes but does not understand the compulsive, irrational force of fate in action. . . . Just before seizing Lilith, Tel comes to understand that he can avoid his fate through procreation with a human female. Addressing Lilith as he sweeps her up, he tells her that the storm has passed into his veins, and that a "Crude vast terrible hunger overpowers" him, motivating his action.

Saul accuses God for the catastrophe of Lilith's rape and abduction and his own imminent death, but nowhere in the play does Rosenberg permit him to contest God's will. Rather he bows to that will, going to his destruction without any reason to believe in infinite purpose, love, or salvation, for he sees clearly that the energy of the universe is invested and regenerated in the forces of terror and violence.

In amalgamating these primarily classical materials, in depicting for us a fixed, limited, and finite Saul, in remaining faithful to the limits he has set for himself, in producing images of terror that lead Saul to self-destruction rather than to rebellion or self-pity, in giving us powerfully created, actually realized visual objects, in following the classical unities of time and space, Rosenberg gives us his most convincing demonstration of the classical approach to the composition of poetry.

Deploring Rosenberg's death in combat, we may observe that it was particularly unfortunate that he was cut off in the midst of putting "The Unicorn" into final shape. What he would have done with the approach it emphasizes had he lived, however, remains one of those uselessly intriguing imponderables that forever surround the poet who dies young and suddenly. But what he did produce along classical lines is sufficient, I believe, for us to resolve the problem of his classification as a poet. By birth and by faith he was a Jew, by chronological and historical reckoning he was a Georgian and a soldier who wrote verse; but most of all, he was a poor romantic whom circumstance was transforming into a remarkably good classically inclined poet at the same time that it was speeding him to his death.

Edward Thomas
(3 March 1878 – 9 April 1917)

See also the Thomas entries in *DLB 19: British Poets, 1880–1914; DLB 98: Modern British Essayists, First Series;* and *DLB 156: British Short-Fiction Writers, 1880–1914: The Romantic Tradition.*

BOOKS:
The Woodland Life (Edinburgh & London: Blackwood, 1897);
Horae Solitariae (London: Duckworth, 1902; New York: Dutton, 1902);
Oxford (London: Black, 1903; revised, 1922);
Rose Acre Papers (London: Brown, Langham, 1904); enlarged, with essays from *Horae Solitariae* (London: Duckworth, 1910);
Beautiful Wales (London: Black, 1905); republished as *Wales* (London: Black, 1924);
The Heart of England (London: Dent / New York: Dutton, 1906);
Richard Jefferies: His Life and Work (London: Hutchinson, 1908; Boston: Little, Brown, 1909);
The South Country (London: Dent, 1909; New York: Dutton, 1909);
Feminine Influence on the Poets (London: Secker, 1910; New York: Lane, 1911);
Rest and Unrest (London: Duckworth, 1910; New York: Dutton, 1910);
Windsor Castle (London: Blackie, 1910; Boston: Estes, 1910);
Celtic Stories (Oxford: Clarendon Press, 1911);
The Isle of Wight (London: Blackie, 1911);
Light and Twilight (London: Duckworth, 1911);
Maurice Maeterlinck (London: Methuen, 1911; New York: Dodd, Mead, 1911);
The Tenth Muse (London: Secker, 1911);
George Borrow: The Man and His Books (London: Chapman & Hall, 1912; New York: Dutton, 1912);
Algernon Charles Swinburne: A Critical Study (London: Secker, 1912; New York: Kennerley, 1912);
Lafcadio Hearn (London: Constable, 1912; Boston & New York: Houghton Mifflin, 1912);
Norse Tales (Oxford: Clarendon Press, 1912);
The Country (London: Batsford, 1913);
The Happy-Go-Lucky Morgans (London: Duckworth, 1913);
The Icknield Way (London: Constable, 1913; New York: Dutton, 1913);
Walter Pater: A Critical Study (London: Secker, 1913; New York: Kennerley, 1913);
Keats (London & Edinburgh: Jack, 1914); republished as *Keats: The Man, His Work and His Friends* (Girard, Kans.: Haldeman-Julius, 1923?); republished as *Keats: His Work and His Character* (Girard, Kans.: Appeal, 193–?);
In Pursuit of Spring (London, Edinburgh, Dublin & New York: Nelson, 1914);
Four-and-Twenty Blackbirds (London: Duckworth, 1915);
The Life of the Duke of Marlborough (London: Chapman & Hall, 1915);
Six Poems, as Edward Eastaway (Flansham: Pear Tree, 1916);
A Literary Pilgrim in England (London: Methuen, 1917; New York: Dodd, Mead, 1917);
Poems, as Eastaway (London: Selwyn & Blount, 1917; New York: Holt, 1917);
Last Poems (London: Selwyn & Blount, 1918);
Collected Poems (London: Selwyn & Blount, 1920; New York: Seltzer, 1921; enlarged edition, London: Ingpen & Grant, 1928);
Cloud Castle, and Other Papers (London: Duckworth, 1922; New York: Dutton, 1922);
Two Poems (London: Ingpen & Grant, 1927);
The Last Sheaf: Essays (London: Cape, 1928);
The Childhood of Edward Thomas: A Fragment of Autobiography, preface by Julian Thomas (London: Faber & Faber, 1938);
The Friend of the Blackbird (Flansham: Pear Tree, 1938);
The Prose of Edward Thomas, edited by Roland Gant (London: Falcon, 1948);
Letters from Edward Thomas to Gordon Bottomley, edited by R. George Thomas (London: Oxford University Press, 1968);
The Diary of Edward Thomas, 1 January – 8 April 1917, foreword by Myfanwy Thomas, introduction by Gant (Andoversford: Whittington, 1977);

The Collected Poems of Edward Thomas, edited by R. George Thomas (Oxford: Clarendon Press, 1978; New York: Oxford University Press, 1978).

BIBLIOGRAPHY:

Robert Paul Eckert, *Edward Thomas: A Biography and a Bibliography* (London: Dent, 1937).

BIOGRAPHICAL STUDIES:

Anthony Berridge, ed., *Letters from Edward Thomas to Jesse Berridge* (London: Enitharmon, 1983);

William Cooke, *Edward Thomas: A Critical Biography, 1878–1917* (London: Faber & Faber, 1970);

Eleanor Farjeon, *Edward Thomas: The Last Four Years* (Oxford: Oxford University Press, 1958);

James Joshua Guthrie, *To the Memory of Edward Thomas* (Flansham: Pear Tree, 1937);

John Cecil Moore, *The Life and Letters of Edward Thomas* (London: Heinemann, 1939);

Vernon Scannell, *Edward Thomas* (London: Longmans, Green, 1963);

Helen Thomas, *As It Was* (London: Heinemann, 1926);

Helen Thomas, *Edward Thomas: A Talk* (Edinburgh: Tragara, 1974);

Helen Thomas, *A Handful of Letters,* edited by R. George Thomas (Edinburgh: Tragara, 1985);

Helen Thomas, *World Without End* (London: Heinemann, 1931);

R. George Thomas, *Edward Thomas* (Cardiff: University of Wales Press, 1972);

R. George Thomas, *Edward Thomas: A Portrait* (Oxford: Oxford University Press, 1985);

R. George Thomas, ed., *Letters to America* (Edinburgh: Tragara, 1989);

R. George Thomas, ed., *Selected Letters* (Oxford & New York: Oxford University Press, 1995).

CRITICAL STUDIES:

Jonathan Barker, ed., *The Art of Edward Thomas* (Mid Glamorgan, Wales: Poetry Wales, 1987);

Henry Coombes, *Edward Thomas: A Critical Study* (London: Chatto & Windus, 1956);

Louis Coxe, *Enabling Acts: Selected Essays in Criticism* (Columbia: University of Missouri Press, 1976);

Piers Gray, *Marginal Men: Edward Thomas, Ivor Gurney, J. R. Ackerley* (London: Macmillan, 1991);

Jeremy Hooker, *Writers in a Landscape* (Cardiff: University of Wales Press, 1996);

Jonathan Kertzer, *Poetic Argument: Studies in Modern Poetry* (Kingston: McGill-Queens University Press, 1988);

Michael Kirkham, *The Imagination of Edward Thomas* (Cambridge: Cambridge University Press, 1986);

Jan Marsh, *Edward Thomas: A Poet for His Country* (London: Elek, 1978);

Andrew Motion, *The Poetry of Edward Thomas* (London: Routledge, 1980);

Robert H. Ross, *The Georgian Revolt: Rise and Fall of a Poetic Ideal, 1910–1922* (Carbondale: Southern Illinois University Press, 1965);

Stan Smith, *Edward Thomas* (London: Faber, 1986).

ARCHIVES:

Edward Thomas materials are held in the C. C. Abbott Collection, University of Durham Library; the Battersea Public Library, London; The Berg Collection, New York Public Library; the Bodleian Library, Oxford; the Lincoln College Library, Oxford; the University of British Columbia Library, Vancouver, Canada; the Dartmouth College Library, Hanover, New Hampshire; the Edward Thomas Collection, Humanities Library, University of Wales, Cardiff; the Harry Ransom Humanities Research Center, University of Texas at Austin; the Lockwood Memorial Library, State University of New York, Buffalo; the National Library of Wales, Aberystwyth; and The British Library, London.

Philip Edward Thomas, the eldest of six sons, was born to Welsh parents in London in 1878. His father, Philip Henry Thomas, was a staff clerk in the Board of Trade whose responsibilities included organizing London's tram traffic. He was by all accounts a stern and demanding parent, and Edward's opinion of him can best be discerned in his poem "P.H.T." In contrast, Mary Elizabeth Townsend, the poet's mother, was a quiet, reserved yet loving traditional Victorian mother who nurtured a strong feeling of intimacy with her son.

Thomas grew up in Battersea, a predominately lower-middle-class suburb of London where the city was gradually encroaching on the open fields and natural surroundings. For Thomas, this loss of open space in his daily surroundings contrasted with the experiences he enjoyed during his summer holidays with relatives in Wales and Wiltshire, where he was free to roam about the local fields and observe the indigenous wildlife and flora. In Wiltshire he was befriended by David Uzzell, a reformed poacher who tutored him to appreciate the countryside. This friendship, which Thomas complemented by reading descriptive sketches of rural life by English nature writer Richard Jefferies, revealed to him the glories of the natural world, a theme that Thomas raised in The Woodland Life *(1897) and* The South Country *(1909).*

Shelgate Road, Battersea, the house on extreme right where Edward Thomas grew up (Jan Marsh, Edward Thomas: A Poet for His Country)

Description of Thomas's experiences in the countryside with Uzzell (R. George Thomas, Edward Thomas: A Portrait, *pp. 14–16)*

We were roach fishing, larking about perhaps more than anything else, and could catch nothing; you see it was a scorching day and the water bright and clear as crystal. Suddenly with a tremendous stroke an old man close by threw a tiny fish up in the air and down it fell. It was Dad.... Then we had a little talk, but it did not end there. Chance acquaintance like this ripened into friendship. We found he had a whole store of out of door knowledge which he was quite ready to impart.

In spite of his clothes—what difference did clothes ever make in a good strong man—he looked a finely made fellow, and we became secretly his admirers. No man at his age ever had a straighter back, that we were sure of, straight and strong, it was as the ground ash stick he always carried. His clear steel blue eyes looked you full in the face without a spark of insolence. It was a kind intelligent eye too, though he could twist a rabbit's neck on occasion with the nonchalance of a professional poacher. Time had left few furrows on that bull strong face, sunburnt like his sinewy neck.... He used to tell us with a sparkle of pride of enormous weights lifted by him in his youth, and of fights where he felled a man like a bullock. Recalling the mad days of youth in fact, a fierceness almost brutal, showed itself, and destroyed the symmetry of his face. In such moments he was not himself, for age had quelled the turbulent spirit, and tamed what must have been a fierce temper indeed....

By pointing out a flower or describing a rarity he could make a walk supremely interesting and was indeed a charming companion on any expedition in the fields. There was not a herb or flowering plant of any sort to be met on our walks that he did not know, and hardly one that was not invaluable as a remedy for some complaint. He certainly had no intention of allowing the old lore concerning herbs to die out. Dried specimens of any sort were always kept by him and roots of many more. Such knowledge as he was full of is fast decaying and it is interesting to come across this old exponent of time-honoured homely skill. He might have made a doctor as well as a poacher....

In modern history as it affected his class he was well informed as ever, and had a memory overflowing with detail. He was bitter against the Church and State though a more truly orthodox man never breathed, and insisted that there was a separate system of law for rich and poor. When bread was a shilling a loaf and men earned less than ten shillings from a long week's work, his father or some other relation was among the most bitterly rebellious

Thomas's fair copy of "P.H.T.," a poem reflecting his strained relationship with his father (Bodleian Library, Oxford)

against a system that could tolerate such things. Every man poached then, and his family with the rest. He remembers hearing it said that each man in one gang at least vowed to kill or disable the keepers if they attempted to thwart their attacks on the game. It was a wild time, and even the old women were poachers, he said, with the aid of a harmless looking dog that barked only when they reached the cottage with a fresh killed rabbit.

Latterly Dad had sobered much when he was no longer able to perform his old feats of strength and daring. To make amends perhaps for the past he had turned tee-totaller and finally Salvationist. It was a strange step from poacher to street corner preacher, but was doubtless sincere. He was loud against "these new religions"; his woodland life and really intense sympathy with Nature could not overcome his adherence to traditional views of religion.

A discussion of how Thomas's appreciation of nature and landscape influence both his critical studies and fiction (Jeremy Hooker, Writers in a Landscape, *pp. 56–64)*

Before the revival of critical interest in Edward Thomas in the late sixties and seventies, it was quite common for critics to dismiss his prose as a whole indiscriminately as hack work. Now, though, we are more in danger of overestimating the continuity of his development, and the consistency of his prose with his poetry. Edward Thomas certainly emerges as an impressive writer from Edna Longley's selection of his prose, *A Language Not to Be Betrayed* (1981). It is, however, an anthology which represents Thomas mainly as a literary critic, and he was the outstanding English critic of his generation. Moreover, he established in his criticism, at least as early as *Richard Jefferies* (1909), and with increasing confidence in his books on Maurice Maeterlinck and Walter Pater, published in 1911 and 1913 respectively, the principles of the poetry that he had still to write. Indeed, he did more than establish the principles; he wrote of language and style with the poet's authority. Yet he continued to write prose that was partially vitiated by the weaknesses characteristic of his earlier work.

In a relatively short writing life, Edward Thomas wrote more than thirty books, edited over a dozen more, and produced a vast number of book reviews. He wrote in a variety of forms—description, diary, itinerary, biography, criticism, fiction, autobiography, prose poetry—and frequently mixed them. His books about nature and the country, in particular, mix description and observation with reverie, imaginative recreation, and lightly disguised spiritual autobiography. The loosely defined "country" book, aimed at a largely urban middle-class readership nostalgic for a pastoral England, was a permissive form; but it is still remarkable how liberally Edward Thomas interpreted his commissions, especially in putting so much of himself into the landscapes. The permissiveness was, at best, a mixed blessing; at worst, it exacerbated the morbid self-consciousness which Thomas himself diagnosed as his greatest ill. The restless, unsatisfactory nature of much of the prose manifests acute formal problems, which Thomas finally overcame only in his poetry. They were not only formal problems, however, but related intimately to problems with the self. Thomas's prose is in part the record of his struggle to achieve an adequate means of self-expression, a struggle which required him to resolve the problem of knowing and believing in the self he desired to express. This in turn meant, in terms that he used in *The Country* (1913), finding something larger than the self "to rest upon." In this sense, Edward Thomas's quest, like that of many Romantic and modern writers who have sought to lose and find themselves in Nature, was essentially religious.

Edward Thomas's first book, *The Woodland Life* (1897), consists of articles and a nature diary which he wrote while still in his teens. As he noted in his maturity, the young writer had "a grandiloquent turn." He had a gift of observation as well, and a microscopic eye, and the ability to arrange his observations. Thus, he perceives a dead leaf:

> On the green mound lies a dead oak-leaf, sober brown and nothing more to the first glance. Through the winter it has lain there, while some of its fellows yet cling wizened and wan about the saplings. Its scalloped edge has kept intact in spite of wind and rain and frost. With the process of the months it has darkened and curled, till now it is a semi-cylinder of the hue of old leather; but underneath the plain brown surface shows a beautiful variety of shades—amber streaks, strange mottlings of chestnut, red and tawny, and, breaking through all, a bloom of faint gold. Each different tinge glows richly as the sunbeams light up the glossy curving surface. It is a last remnant of winter and of the bygone year, pillowed among the tender growths of early spring—sere brown set in the midst of youthful verdure.

In the progressive revelation of what "the first glance" misses, this resembles the descriptive writing of Richard Jefferies, whose great influence on his life and work Edward Thomas acknowledged. Jefferies frequently begins with a small, easily overlooked detail of animate or inanimate nature, and magnifies it until its character, function, and place in the environment are revealed. In "The Pageant of Summer," for example, he begins with rushes:

> Green rushes, long and thick, standing up above the edge of the ditch, told the hour of the year as distinctly as the shadow on the dial the hour of the day. Green and thick and sappy to the touch, they felt like summer, soft and elastic, as if full of life, mere rushes though they were. On the fingers they left a green scent; rushes have a separate scent of green, so, too, have ferns, very different from that of grass or leaves. Rising from brown sheaths, the tall stems enlarged a little in the middle, like classical columns, and heavy with their sap and freshness, leaned against the hawthorn sprays. From the earth they had drawn its moisture, and made the ditch dry; some of the sweetness of the air had entered into their fibres, and the rushes—the common rushes—were full of beautiful summer.

The juxtaposition of the two passages indicates Thomas's debt to Jefferies, but is more revealing of differences. Jefferies is one of the great natural observers of the Victorian age, a period rich in the arts of seeing, in which natural history combined with poetry and painting to produce, in Ruskin and Tennyson and Hardy and Gerard Manley Hopkins, for example, not only minutely detailed perception, but an ocularcentric mode that was both physical and metaphysical. Even among these writers, Jefferies had no equals when it came to natural vision. With him, seeing was both an art and a science, and it had behind it that love of the common and often overlooked thing, like "the common rushes," which we find not only in Gilbert White, but in Wordsworth and Constable and Clare, and in an older tradition with its roots in a religious delight in the natural creation, although in the nineteenth century religious observation of nature was often a substitute for orthodox belief. Jefferies' art, though, is not only visual; it also manifests an acute sensitivity to the life of the thing, both its unique identity and its existence as part of nature. He appeals to the sense of touch and the sense of smell as much as to sight, and he emphasizes the relations of the rushes to their surroundings, their drawing of moisture from the earth and sweetness from the air, and their existence in time, their seasonal life. When he likens them to classical columns the image is not stationary or primarily sculptural, but serves to elevate the common plant to its proper importance. Jefferies knew that civilization depends upon nature; his vision of the ditch shows that it is as interesting and at least as important as any place on earth.

Edward Thomas appears to look at the dead leaf as closely as Jefferies looks at the rushes, but whereas Jefferies reveals the life of the plant, Thomas, in spite of making the dead leaf a symbol of winter among the signs of spring, sees it aesthetically, and makes a picture from its colours and sculptural shape. Jefferies' whole intention, the spirit of his seeing, lies behind the image likening the rushes to classical columns, but "scalloped" and "semi-cylinder" and "curving surface" depict the leaf as an object of aesthetic contemplation. Thomas's method here, in fact, is close to Walter Pater's spectatorial stance, which he would describe later with devastating effect. In *The Woodland Life* the aesthetic mode of perception is dominant, but its tension with natural vision, which sees and depicts the life in things, is largely resolved by the joy of the young writer-cum-naturalist in exercising his gifts. The diary included in the book exhibits an art of naming, with a corresponding delight in the thing named, that is closer to Edward Thomas's poetry. Before he could achieve that, though, he had first to undertake a long struggle to relate aesthetic vision and natural vision, instead of obscuring and even betraying the latter with his word-painting.

Recording his response to the nightingale's song in *The South Country* (1909), Edward Thomas says the notes, with their "inhumanity," convey "the mysterious sense . . . that earth is something more than a human estate." "Here for this hour we are remote from the parochialism of humanity. The bird has admitted a larger air. We breathe deeply of it and are made free citizens of eternity." Thomas, in his writings about nature, often expresses desire for "a larger air" which is at once physical and spiritual. The words echo the close of Jefferies' *The Amateur Poacher,* which for Thomas as a young man were "a gospel, an incantation": "Let us get out of these indoor narrow modern days, whose twelve hours somehow have become shortened, into the sunlight and the pure wind. A something that the ancients called divine can be found and felt there still." Freedom from "the parochialism of humanity" is a great theme, but Thomas is rarely able to pursue it with confidence for long. In *In Pursuit of Spring* (1914), for example, he says Salisbury Plain "makes us feel the age of the earth, the greatness of Time, Space, and Nature; the littleness of man even in an aeroplane, the fact that the earth does not belong to man, but man to the earth." This is a feeling capable of generating awe, and in the writings of Jefferies it frequently does. The same is true of W. H. Hudson, a friend whose prose style Thomas admired. In *The Country* he quotes a passage from *Hampshire Days* in which Hudson, writing of a time by the barrows on Beaulieu Heath in the New Forest, says: "The blue sky, the brown soil beneath, the grass, the trees, the animals, the wind, and rain, and sun, and stars, are never strange to me; for I am in and of and am one with them; and my flesh and the soil are one, and the heat in my blood and in the sunshine are one, and the winds and tempests and my passions are one." Hudson is echoing another writer Thomas admired, Thomas Traherne, whom Hudson has quoted a few pages before: "You never enjoy the earth aright until the sun itself floweth through your veins, till you are clothed with the heavens and crowned with the stars, and perceive yourself to be the sole heir of the whole world." Thomas himself sympathized deeply with the feeling of belonging to the earth, which in Traherne expressed his Christian mysticism and in Hudson was a pagan sentiment, but Thomas's distance from them is marked by his awareness that "cultivation of the instinctive and primitive . . . is the fine flower of a self-conscious civilization, turning in disgust upon itself." And the result, in writing about Salisbury Plain for example, is that he self-consciously turns back upon himself: "And this feeling, or some variety of it, for most men is accompanied by melancholy, or is held to be the same thing. This is perhaps particularly so with townsmen, and above all with writers, because melancholy is the mood most easily given an appearance of profundity, and, therefore, most easily impressive." The loss of emotional impetus, the fragmentation of feeling, and the consequent cynicism or self-dislike, give this and similar passages in Thomas's prose a negative and deadening effect. The problem is that his doctrine of Nature, and his feeling that man belongs to the earth, are at odds with the mode of perception which reflects his self-conscious modernity.

In *Richard Jefferies* Thomas calls self-consciousness "perhaps, the most tragic condition of man's greatness." "If the sea-waves were to be self-conscious," he says, "they would cease to wash the shore; a self-conscious world would fester and stink in a month." He was one who survived "the terror," as he calls it; he even made a virtue of it in his poetry, but time and again in his prose, self-consciousness breaks in, interrupting its rhythmic movement and concentration. It is at the roots of his problems as a prose writer; as he came to realize, it is a psychological dis-ease with social origins.

By the time he wrote his book on Walter Pater, Thomas understood the problem in depth:

> men understand now the impossibility of speaking aloud all that is within them, and if they do not speak it, they cannot write as they speak. The most they can do is to write as they would speak in a less solitary world. A man cannot say all that is in his heart to a woman or another man. The waters are too deep between us. We have not the confidence in what is within us, nor in our voices.

According to Thomas, isolation is the modern condition, which results in inability to communicate, dividing the individual both from others and from his own inner depths, so that he has no confidence either in himself or in his voice. Thomas's understanding of isolation inevitably owed much to his personal history. In *The South Country,* one of the many *alter egos* that wander in and out of his writings, the town-bred clerk escaping to the country, says: "I realize that I belong to the suburbs still." "As for myself," he continues, "I am world-conscious, and hence suffer unutterable loneliness." Such figures at once express Thomas's situation and sentiments, and distance him self-critically from the emotional extravagance.

Born and brought up in the London suburbs, Edward Thomas early identified Wales, his parents' original country, as "my soul's native land." Later, he found in southern England "a kind of home, as I think it is more than any other to those modern people who belong nowhere." Ironically, but not surprisingly, some of his most effective prose, in *The Childhood of Edward Thomas* and *The Happy-Go-Lucky Morgans* (1913), explores the suburbs, while his descriptions of the country are frequently weakened by the escapism arising from his lack of a necessary relation to it. For, as he says in *The Country:* "only a rarefied conscious appreciation is made possible by detachment and the severing of all bonds of necessity." This is by no means the whole truth of his relation to nature and rural England, but the social and psychological forces isolating him were formidable. They were fortified, moreover, by his strongest, and otherwise opposing, literary influences: Richard Jefferies and Walter Pater. Jefferies, in the nature mysticism of *The Story of My Heart,* abstracted himself from the circumstances of his life and from all relationships, and stood "bare-headed before the sun, in the presence of the earth and air, in the presence of the immense forces of the universe." As Jefferies chose to be alone with the elements, Pater elected solipsism, a condition in which experience "is ringed round for each one of us by that thick wall of personality through which no real voice has ever pierced on its way to us, or from us to that which we can only conjecture to be without." For Pater, every impression "is the impression of the individual in his isolation, each mind keeping as a solitary prisoner its own dream of a world." "Dream" is one of the deadly words in Thomas's vocabulary, as it was in the Celtic Twilight and in the English pastoral tradition at large in the quarter-century before the First World War. Solipsism and a vague and isolating nature mysticism were both negative influences upon Edward Thomas's prose. In addition, his contempt for his readership, the "villa residents" that he discusses in *The Country,* exacerbated his lack of confidence and his self-disgust, and increased his uncertainty of tone and focus. Self-consciousness made him his own severest critic, too. "I rarely see much in the country," he confesses in *The Heart of England* (1906); "I always carry out into the fields a vast baggage of prejudices from books and strong characters whom I have met." He then proceeds to condemn in himself "the egoism of an imitative brain." Later, after he had begun to write poetry, he spoke to Eleanor Farjeon of the "rhetoric and formality which left my prose so often with a dead rhythm only." The curiously unmemorable quality of his prose especially at its "finest" is due to its lack of a living rhythm. This in turn is due to its exclusively "written" character, which is a product of the isolated, self-conscious literary mind.

Edward Thomas's strongest description of the imagination occurs in *Richard Jefferies:*

> The clearness of the physical is allied to the penetration of the spiritual vision. For both are nourished to their perfect flowering by the habit of concentration. To see a thing as he saw the sun-painted yellow-hammer in Stewart's Mash is part of the office of the imagination. Imagination is no more than the making of graven images, whether of things on the earth or in the mind. To make them, clear concentrated sight and patient mind are the most necessary things after love, and these two are the children of love.

Thomas is here in process of making a distinction, but has not quite completed it. For clear seeing, which he attributes to Jefferies, is radically different from "graven images," which Pater made from the life of things. In *Walter Pater* Thomas would describe Pater as "a spectator. His aim is to see; if he is to become something it is by seeing." He would describe the style, "free from traces of experience," in which Pater, in words that are "anything but living and social words," turns life into art. What he would diagnose in Pater's "exquisite unnaturalness" is absence of passion, lack of the emotion that commands rhythm and makes an imaginative whole. Pater's "prose embalms choice things, as seen at choice moments, in choice words." Pater's transformation of "animate and inanimate things into words like graven images" is clearly not the kind of seeing or writing that Thomas admires in Jefferies.

Thomas continues his definition of imagination in *Richard Jefferies* by saying that those who have the rare "power of repeating these images by music or language or carved stone" are "aware that human life, nature, and art are every moment continuing and augmenting the Creation—making to-day the first day, and this field Eden, annihilating time." This is a crucial passage for understanding Thomas's own way of seeing: his identification of imagination not with the historical present but with myth, and his vision of Eden. His idea of imagination also contains another meaning, fruitful with possibilities, although it too has a mythical dimension. Thus he mythologizes Jefferies the Wiltshireman, eloquently: "He . . . was the genius, the human expression, of this country, emerging from it, not to be detached from it any more than the curves of some statues from their maternal stone." He sees Jefferies not only as earth-born, however, but as a man with something "to rest upon," a man with a people, who "came to express part of this silence of uncounted generations." Thomas thus sees Jefferies as fulfilling the conditions of poetry, which is "a natural growth," with "roots deep in a substantial past. It springs apparently from an occupation of the land, from long, busy, and quiet tracts of time, wherein a man or a nation may find its own soil. To have a future, it must have had a past." And Thomas sees Jefferies' writing career much as we may now see his own: as a progressive self-revelation. In Thomas's view, Jefferies, by the time he wrote *The Story of My Heart*, was "the poet, the larger man who, though exquisitely sensitive, has no mere delicacy and rejected no part of life in man or nature, country or town." Jefferies had "the clear vision that saw in all forms of life one commonwealth, one law, one beauty." He was, therefore, in spite of his loneliness, the opposite of the "isolated selfconsidering brain," which Thomas felt himself at his worst to be. Jefferies' seeing, then, had nothing in common with that of the spectator, who petrifies life in graven images. Using the bird imagery that would be a crucial element in his poetic vision, Thomas says of Jefferies' style that, "given an entirely suitable subject, he wrote with a natural fineness and richness and a carelessness, too, like the blackbird's singing." It was in Jefferies, then, that Thomas first found his ideal of writing that is the natural speech of the whole man. Jefferies dictated his last essays, and it is significantly of these that Thomas says: "he has found himself; and now it is no longer the sportsman, or the naturalist, or the agriculturalist, or the colourist, or the mystic, that speaks, but a man who has played these parts and been worn and shaped by them, by work and pain." Thomas found, in different degrees, the style that is the speech of "the poet, the larger man" in other writers whom he admired, too—in Cobbett and Hudson, for example, and, at a decisive moment, in the poetry of Robert Frost, whose *North of Boston* "speaks, and it is poetry." The speech of "the larger man" is what poetry finally released in Edward Thomas himself, but his prose almost always withheld.

Thomas was educated at various London schools until he was fourteen years old. Then his ambitious father entered him in a scholarship competition at St. Paul's School, one of the leading British public (that is, private) schools. Although Thomas failed to win the scholarship, his father, anxious to prepare the boy for a civil-service career, reluctantly paid the full fees for his son's admission. As a new boy from the suburbs, Thomas felt not only awed by his socially superior classmates but also isolated from them intellectually.

Early on at St. Paul's he demonstrated his talent in writing, for he had been writing diaries and descriptive notebooks regularly. The local Unitarian minister, a Mr. Tarrant, sensed something special in Thomas's work and introduced him to James Ashcroft Noble, the literary critic for The Spectator, The Academy, *and* The Daily Chronicle. *Noble invited the seventeen-year-old home for tea, grew to like him, and offered to comment on his work. Through this acquaintance Thomas met Noble's three daughters, the second of whom, Helen Berenice, began to demonstrate a romantic interest in the young writer.*

*Thomas's initial response to St. Paul's School (*The Childhood of Edward Thomas: A Fragment of Autobiography, *pp. 142–143)*

The whole school impressed and alarmed me. The head master, a thick old grey-bearded heavy-lidded gruff-voiced man with creased florid face and creased black clothes, impressed and alarmed me. I should have done anything he told me, but he never told me to do anything except, "Speak up. I'm an old man." Once or twice he glanced at my Greek as I sat with a very few other boys in the great hall. I knew nothing; I was humbled but hardly stirred to effort. The hundreds of boys also humbled me. Many of them wore men's clothes, carried their books in bags like clerks', and seemed to me grimly earnest and thinking only of work and success. Many others looked well off, spoke in more refined voices than I was used to. I came alone in the morning, and in the afternoon I went home alone, often in a railway carriage containing three or four schoolfellows, but alone, in a state of discomfort which would I imagined have been multiplied if they had taken any notice of me, which they never once did, in spite of my morbid looking out for signs that they noticed my discomfort. During the middle of the day I was alone: I stood alone watching Rugby football or practice for the sports. For most of the boys in my form went home to lunch; the rest also disappeared. If I had lunch at school I sat alone and was spoken to only once. Opposite me sat several much older boys whose serious faces and eager voices in argument fascinated me, so that I could not but stare, until one day one of them, a pale black-haired youth with strong lean scowling features, asked me why the devil I couldn't mind my own business. Perhaps it was to avoid this school meal that I took to having lunch out, or, rather, buying a few buns to eat in the class room while I read Jefferies. The reasons why I did not play games are that I was never asked to and was shy, and that I was unaccustomed to Rugby football. When I was not reading or watching games I walked along the far side of the river watching the gulls and swans, sometimes in such wretchedness that I wanted to drown myself. My formmaster, seeing me reading when he came in long before afternoon school was to begin, asked me what I did with myself, did I ever skate or take any decent exercise. He was abrupt and looked contemptuous. I muttered something about skating and country walks. My wrists and hands and arms were always decorated with scratches during the bird-nesting season, but of course he knew nothing of that. Nor had he seen the words which I had written, perhaps not quite without ostentation, in the worst possible Latin on the flyleaf of my algebra book: "I love birds more than books."

A discussion of how Thomas's early childhood was revisited when he began writing poetry (Piers Gray, "The Childhood of Edward Thomas," Critical Quarterly, 28 [Autumn 1968], pp. 51–61)

In December of 1914 Edward Thomas wrote this: "When I penetrate backward into my childhood I come perhaps sooner than many people to impassable night. A sweet darkness enfolds with a faint blessing my life up to the age of about four. The task of attempting stubbornly to break up that darkness is one I have never proposed to myself, but I have many times gone up to the edge of it peering, listening, stretching out my hands. . . ." These curious sentences make up the opening of the autobiographical fragment which now bears the title *The Childhood of Edward Thomas*. It was not published until 1938—twenty-one years after Thomas was killed at Arras:

> With regard to his actual death you have probably heard the details. It should be of some comfort to you to know that he died at a moment of victory from a direct hit by a shell, which must have killed him outright without giving him a chance to realise anything,— a gallant death for a very true and gallant gentleman.
>
> We buried him in a little military cemetery a few hundred yards from the battery: the exact spot will be notified to you by the parson. As we stood by the grave the sun came and the guns round seemed to stop firing for a short time. This typified to me what stood out most in your husband's character—the spirit of quiet, sunny, unassuming cheerfulness.

He was—Captain Lushington recalled—"rather older than most of the officers and we all looked up to him as the kind father of our happy family."

But the truth of the matter is that these attempts to make the unbearable bearable lead us away from the recorded reality of the man; for if Edward Thomas did appear to find some kind of contentment in his wartime "family" it must have been a satisfaction quite against the apparent grain: his own father he wrote off thus:

> I may come near loving you
> When you are dead
> And there is nothing to do
> And much to be said.
> . . . .
> But not so long as you live
> Can I love you at all.
> ("P.H.T.")

About his own family he wrote more tortuously; as in the following poem, one of the three bearing the title—most significantly as we shall see—of "Home":

> Fair was the morning, fair our tempers, and
> We had seen nothing fairer than that land,
> Though strange, and the untrodden snow that made
> Wild of the tame, casting out all that was
> Not wild and rustic and old; and we were glad.
>
> Fair too was afternoon, and first to pass
> Were we that league of snow, next the north wind.
>
> There was nothing to return for except need.
>
> And yet we sang nor ever stopped for speed,
> As we did often with the start behind.
> Faster still strode we when we came in sight
> Of the cold roofs where we must spend the night.

Happy we had not been there, nor could be,
Though we had tasted sleep and food and fellowship
Together long.
    "How quick" to someone's lip
The word came, "will the beaten horse run home."

The word "home" raised a smile in us all three,
And one repeated it, smiling just so
That all knew what he meant and none would say.
Between three counties far apart that lay
We were divided and looked strangely each
At the other, and we knew we were not friends
But fellows in a union that ends
With the necessity for it, as it ought.

Never a word was spoken, not a thought
Was thought, of what the look meant with the word
"Home" as we walked and watched the sunset blurred
And then to me the word, only the word,
"Homesick," as it were, playfully occurred:
No more if I should ever more admit
Than the mere word could not endure it
For a day longer: this captivity
Must somehow come to an end, else I should be
Another man, as often now I seem,
Or this life be only an evil dream.

"Homesick": the word becomes the hinge around which the mind swings back into or out away from the space (mental and material) which contains all one is meant to love. The sickness is both of and for the home; appropriately the poem's ending sustains the confusion—the schizophrenic "escape" out of the captivity which keeps Edward Thomas away from home, or the captivity which *is* that very home itself, can only be resolved by creating "another man" to escape from the captivity of the "evil dream" which either is or is not the existence circumscribed by the single word—"home." There are several ways in which one is a captive of—hostage to—one's own creations: the house; the family within that house; the home; the *poem* of the home. For behind—no: within—the writing itself is a highly developed sense of self-hatred which the act of creation only intensifies. For it is the case with Edward Thomas that we have a portrait of the artist as a doomed man; a man for whom the word becomes both the instrument of torture and the tool of escape. It is both the material reality and a sardonic commentary upon that devastating fact. When you are the hack from whose shelter the poet refuses for most of its life to escape, self-criticism will surely seek to state its reservations in the "disease" of "self-contempt"—to use Edward Thomas's own words. And here we have the paradox of Edward Thomas: his life is inseparable from the act of writing; but it is only when in turn the act becomes a protest against such a life that he can contemplate escape: escape, however, takes many different and sometimes unvirtuous forms.

For Edward Thomas material existence had to be supported by hack-work: in 1910 he was working on six books simultaneously; in the autumn of 1911 he published four of them: not surprisingly therefore financial worries and ill-health brought on a severe nervous breakdown. So the act of writing and reviewing, of writing about and reviewing other people and other people's books, is both necessary and futile. There is no escape from this labour: the sacrifice is for a wife and children and with that feeling always present—something of the self being sacrificed—can only come resentment at best or despair at worst. That is why in Edward Thomas's case writing *for* himself—writing selfishly, meanly—becomes a necessary art of negative liberation. He writes poetry to destroy the other writer—the hack: the act of creation is *au fond* an act of violence.

The centre of Edward Thomas's working life is therefore occupied by a chimera—a liberated self which can only grow out of the destruction of the other, the responsible loving father and husband. Ultimately—as we shall see—the condition of absence has to displace the "normal" human emotions and responses. Edward Thomas's life becomes then a preparation for the return to that "sweet darkness" out of which it emerged into painful consciousness. Killing is therefore the ultimate act of liberation for him; killing his self and so his old life—as he obliquely realises in his autobiography—becomes a preparation for that act.

"Homesick"—with the cognates "nostalgic" the word can imply a degree of inadequacy before the facts of adult life; a debilitation in the face of the present and—arguably—a fear of the future. To this extent the emotions suggested by the words seek resolution in flight—escape into the past. On this point I am drawing from D. W. Harding's "Note on Nostalgia" in *Scrutiny* (vol. 1 No. 1) where he observes that the nostalgia which "pervades" Edward Thomas's poetry is subtly bound up with powerful "regressive" tendencies: nostalgia implies a yearning for—ultimately—the conditions of childhood and so flight from the unsympathetic "social group" within which one is trapped. However, adult life becomes horribly complicated if the unsatisfactory "social group" in question is not—say—hostile bourgeois society (*vide* Lawrence) but *one's own created family*. Thus the home may not only fail to provide the support for which the self yearns, it can actually produce an environment in which an unsuccessful provider might feel deeply contemptuous of itself. . . .

Given all this, it seems—none the less—that Harding's account of "nostalgia" is not sufficiently comprehensive to account for our reactions to—say—the poem with which we started, "Home." Part of that inadequacy lies in the fact that Edward Thomas is always ahead of us—as it were; he knows the price to be paid if the word "homesick" becomes more than "the word, only the word." For if that happens then it has to be understood that the group to which he is returning—the family—is the source of his weakness; he is ensnared by it and cannot bear its absence. He feels both inadequate within it and impotent without it.

If we return to the poem's beginning we can now realise how strongly its conclusion is running away from that which Edward Thomas wants to want—namely an aggressive, animalistic freedom which is elemental and utterly hostile to ideas of civilization and home: hence the repetitions of the word "wild." And hence—equally—its laconic opposite, "need" ("There was nothing to return for except need") suggesting excuse rather than explanation. The poem is thus a bitter comment on the need to run away from freedom; to seek home, to become a crippled prisoner of—and here is the twist—an environment from which one ran away in the first place.

"In most of the poems there is no recognition of an underlying social cause for his feeling." Harding's judgement here I take to be with Lawrence—by contrast—in mind. And it certainly would seem to be true in "Home" that the point of dissatisfaction is made without any specific *j'accuse* as its cause; but to limit ourselves to a culpable society—with all its complicated relations—*out there* is to mistake the force of Edward Thomas's writing and—above all—its distressing honesty. For in his work the "social cause" is to be found in the very act of writing itself. In writing the *poem* "Home" he is actually wasting time by working on, making, a thing which is materially useless, unable to sustain the "home."

But even if the poem is a literal rejection of functional writing, it won't do to imagine that the relations between poet and hack are to be balanced around freedom and responsibility; indeed, the poet was the hack's only begetter. For it is the ironic truth of Edward Thomas's life that the very roots of his life's evil dream can be traced back to that moment of his early adult experience when he appeared to have miraculously got it right, the poise between intellectual freedom—writing—and social recognition—more—love. It was through his teenage love affair with Helen Noble that Edward Thomas came to know her father who, as a minor man of London letters, became a patron by helping the precocious young man get a number of essays published in established literary magazines. As the affair became more obviously serious, Helen Noble's mother made the classic parental blunder of forbidding her daughter to have any further dealings with the young "author" and so the business had a Lawrentian aura to it: Edward Thomas became a real-life Paul Morel. At the age of nineteen he went up to Oxford with a published book—*The Woodland Life*—and a mistress. Helen Noble describes the consummation as follows:

> Then I held out my hands to him—for he was standing now, and he raised me to my feet, so that my clothes slid down in a ring. I stepped out of them on to the soft moss and dry leaves, and he kneeling kissed my body from my feet up to my knees, and from my knees up to my hips, and when he had kissed me and let his hand wander all over me he laid me down on the moss, and I lay with my eyes closed, just conscious that he was quickly undressing, and hearing his voice speaking some passionate name. And I knowing he was ready, opened my eyes and saw him standing there naked, said "Come," and drew him to my breast.

Clapham Common became the Garden of Eden—true; but it was mere nature which eventually decided things as Edward Thomas was transformed from the Romantic young writer who actually possessed his own Fanny Brawne into just another undergraduate father-to-be and finally newly-graduated father with little Mervyn and his mother to support. And how else to do that but by the thing at which he was best—writing. The record of that life as recorded by Helen Thomas in *World Without End* is deeply distressing. There is no Romantic passion in their shared misery but a kind of grinding domestic servitude on her part to the love and loyalty of home which could only be reciprocated by her husband's mechanical repetition of materially "meaningful" words. To write out of this *for* this was, in a sense, to be poisoned by the very thing you love. His whole life and hers had become an ironic jest—a tale of romantic fiction mocked by a nightmare of words seeking their reward. But not to be commissioned—not to write—was obviously the worst. Helen Thomas recalls the experience of failure in bitter detail:

> I sat down on the hedge bank, and taking him in my arms mixed my tears with his and bending over him tried to sing his favourite good-night songs to comfort him and stop his sobs. A little bunch of the flowers growing within reach and a feather found on the thorn soon comforted him, and he forgot as I shall never forget that dreadful morning.
>
> I put Philip to bed before going to the study where I found David [i.e. Edward Thomas] sitting as I had left him, not reading, not smoking, with his head in his hands, staring with eyes that saw nothing.
>
> "There are no letters."
>
> "Why tell me what is written on your pale wretched face? I am cursed, and you are cursed because of me. I hate the tears I see you've been crying. Your sympathy and your love are both hateful to me. Hate me, but for God's sake don't stand there, pale and suffering. Leave me, I tell you; get out and leave me."

And Edward Thomas himself reduced some part of it to miserable empty absurdity most terribly in "The long small room":

> The long small room that showed willows in the west
> Narrowed up to the end the fireplace filled,
> Although not wide. I liked it. No one guessed
> What need or accident made them so build.
>
> Only the moon, the mouse and the sparrow peeped
> In from the ivy round the casement thick.
> Of all they saw and heard there they shall keep
> The tale for the old ivy and older brick.
>
> When I look back I am like moon, sparrow and mouse
> That witnessed what they could never understand
> Or alter or prevent in the dark house.
> One thing remains the same—this my right hand
>
> Crawling crab-like over the clean white page,
> Resting awhile each morning on the pillow.
> The once more starting to crawl on towards age.
> The hundred last leaves stream upon the willow.

It seems fair to say that the progress of this poem is—as it were—backwards; that we have a clear example of "nostalgic" writing—until the last stanza, of course. The regressive emotions that lie at the poem's centre are, however, necessary to its *dénouement;* for there is much play with the idea of not being "grown-up" in the main body of the poem. The sense of "childishness" is evoked through the assertion of moods and likes without any justification or explanation: "Although not wide. I liked it. No one guessed / What need or accident made them so build." If we are not yet clear that this is actually the language of escape it becomes obvious in the next two stanzas as the words conjure in the mind's eye a scene from Beatrix Potter. The verb of adult retrospection is displaced by the coyness of "peeped," uniting—as it comfortably does—moon, mouse, sparrow and ivy in a friendly approach, as it were, to the childish bed; a dream of the child's dream. The regression here is much more overt than in "Home" and, if anything, more apparently contemptible. For here there is an insistence upon impotence; the adult excuses his feebleness by assuming the right to childish helplessness:

> When I look back I am like moon, sparrow and mouse
> That witnessed what they could never understand
> Or alter or prevent in the dark house.

Up to this moment the reader has been happily superior to the poem's development within the category of "nostalgic" writing; but even as we condescend to its regression Edward Thomas is preparing to drag us towards adult truths of the most unpleasant kind:

> One thing remains the same—this my right hand
> Crawling crab-like over the clean white page.

Writing: the poem is about the adult Edward Thomas and his condition; the nightmare of the writer. The middle of the poem is, then, part of this cruel irony: the regressive centre is, after all, only possible within *adult* consciousness so that even as Edward Thomas remembers his earlier life in terms of a "nostalgic" language (moon, sparrow, mouse) he is aware that he lived then as he does now—i.e. at the moment of writing the poem: nothing more than (in an ironic recapitulation of the language of diminution) a "right hand." The stanza break offered the illusion of time and space separating past from present even as the words conveyed the opposite message—"one thing remains the same." So that to write "nostalgically" is indeed to emprison oneself—it is after all still to *write*. And to write about that writing to encircle one's own impotence within a hard logic of self-analysis. There is no story then other than the story that there is no story and that one goes on as one can—writing meaninglessly until death. So what's the news? Only this: that the poem is nevertheless—for good or ill—simply that: a poem. It is something other and we are made conscious of this by its last line which seems to let us know what is at stake: "The hundred last leaves stream upon the willow." It is both part of that which preceded it and yet utterly independent; isolated from and yet tied back into the poem through its very first line. It *may* be that the willows were part of the room's likeability—but how can we tell? All we know is that part of the right hand's Lear-like crawl towards death is its act of recording the willow's hundred last leaves *in absentia*. If that is an act of the imagination, it is equally such a deliberately imprecise one that we are left groping towards significance: inferring meaning. The preposition ensures uncertainty: are the leaves attached to the willow or streaming against it? Does the verb suggest the action of life streaming past in a Heraclitean flux or pathetically imply weeping? Are we meant to think across from the leaves to the pages of the right hand's books and so to the right hand itself? Finally are we illuminated by the precise enumeration—"hundred last"? This line is the "real" poem; its freedom of inference plays along the edge of its half-attached Imagist relation to the rest of the verse. It has an anarchic existence which seems to be close to our sense of "modern" poetry. If you want it to "mean" something then you can so make it—nothing is given. In this sense—in the poem's final unaccountability, its mystery, its self-centred irresponsibility—there is both an inescapable moment in the life of a drudge and a privileged secret rejection of all that. It is necessary and irrelevant; its irrelevance we can understand but it is the immaterial necessity (why go on?) which needs explanation and that—it so happens—can be partly found in the document known as *The Childhood of Edward Thomas.*

The passage with which I started—the opening paragraph of *The Childhood of Edward Thomas*—continues as follows:

> . . . and I have heard the voice of one singing as I sat or lay in her arms; and I have become again aware very dimly of being enclosed in rooms that were shadowy, whether by comparison with outer sunlight I know not. The songs, first of my mother, then of her younger sister, I can hear not only afar off behind the veil but on this side of it also. I was, I should think, a very still listener whom the music flowed through and filled to the exclusion of all thought and of all sensation except of blissful easy fullness, so that too early or too sudden ceasing would have meant pangs of expectant emptiness. The one song which, by reason of its repetition or of some aptitude in me, I well remember, was one combining fondness with tranquil if peevish retrospection and regret in a soft heavy twilight. I reach back to it in that effort through a thousand twilights lineally descended from that first one and from the night which gave it birth. If I cried or suffered pain or deprivation in those years nothing remains to star the darkness. Either I asked no question or I had none but sweet answers. I was at peace with life. Indoors, out of the sun, I seem never to have been troubled by heat or cold strong enough to be remembered.

Here is an evocation of warmth before, during and immediately after the emergence of consciousness which certainly suggests a post-Romantic poetic birth—in both senses. The sensitivity to sound ("a very still listener whom the music flowed through") reminds us of Eliot's tribute to De La Mare's early world with its "inexplicable mystery of sound" and "The whispered incantation which allows / Free passage to the phantoms of the mind."

This appeal to the "dark years" and their aural intensity sets up a first emergence into light with an odd negative inclusiveness—"But out of doors, somewhere at the verge of the dark years . . . I lay in the tall grass and buttercups of a narrow field at the edge of London and saw the sky and nothing but the sky"—giving us all and nothing, so disposing us to think again in terms of regressive writing. Here—despite the pleasure of solitude and sky—is the first world, the world of prenatal darkness: that first remembered song combined "fondness with tranquil if peevish retrospection and regret in a soft heavy twilight"—the first of a thousand "twilights lineally descended."

If the fragment were to continue in this manner for long we might soon weary of its sombre grandeur, bored I suspect by its melancholic undertone so much a part of "nostalgic" writing. Not even the connections with the poetry's obsessive desire for the peace of darkness (an absoluteness—in fact—for death) would allow the prose a significant life of its own. But the next paragraph breaks away from these opaque beginnings and sends us mundanely forth into the world of "normal" childhood: "Then I entered the lowest class of a large suburban board school." What then follows is a laconic account of growing up in turn-of-the-century London which develops rapidly into a masterpiece of subversive literature.

The context of its recollections is—perhaps—at first unpromising: Battersea, Wandsworth, Clapham seem solid enough. True there were mean streets south of the river, but Edward Thomas was safely raised in the genteel comfort of the minor Civil Servant's house with domestics and Sunday lunches. No—it was the position of the area on the *margin* of Dickensian London which is important; what mattered were not just the childhood streets and all their dangers but even more the great suburban parks and Commons at Battersea, Wandsworth and Clapham; these were the wild rural woods and untamed downs of the real countryside. Here a boy could find himself:

> The ponds were for paddling in. One of them, a shallow irregular one, weedy and rushy-margined, lying then in some broken ground between the Three Island and the railway, was full of effets and frogs. Bigger boys would torture the frogs, by cutting, skinning or crushing them alive. The sharp penknives sank through the skin and the soft bone into the wood of the seat which was the operating table. This seat and earth under and about it would be strewn with fragments, pale bellies slit up, and complete frogs seeming to be munching their own insides. At that time I could not have done it myself, but my horror lacked pity and turned into a kind of half-shrinking, half-gloating curiosity.

This passage is typical both of the fragment's content and its narrative rhythm: the mind drifts across the landscape until it stops to dwell with detached fascination upon cruelty and suffering, torture and death. The world of children is seen as embedded in brutality: games merge into battles; play is a form of conflict. It is "normal," moreover, to discover oneself in a world characterised by the violence of humans upon animals; in the book's opening chapter—"Infancy"—Edward Thomas's first anecdote concerns a mad dog hiding in a garden; a man takes up a pickaxe: "I do not know that I saw the blow struck, but the idea of heavy sharp steel piercing the shaggy hair, flesh and bone of a living creature has remained horrible and ineffacable ever since." And this is the central theme of this "absurd total" of recollections. At first the violence appears to be indiscriminate, for it is one of the fragment's mysterious qualities to refuse the conventions of any narrative which might suggest a guided development of the self. Incidents happen, events take place, but no purpose is ever suggested; no guidance is ever laid down. Instead a pattern emerges among the different kinds of violence the autobiography records, which sardonically reveals the truth of the man who descends from them.

One extreme of the anecdotal spectrum centres upon those acts of "excusable" violence which human beings explain in terms of survival; there is the moment in the slaughter house when the child finds out how to kill a cow:

> The tall pale butcher came along, shoved her a little sideways to get her perfectly into position, and brought down the pointed knob of the poleaxe smartly upon her forehead. The rope was slackened, she fell heavily. The man thrust a cane into the opening in her forehead, "to stir the brains," said my fellow watcher. The butcher cut her throat and the blood rattled into a bucket, while the man stood, with one foot on the ground clear of her gesticulating legs, and one upon her flank, working it up and down to help the blood out. . . .

The reminiscence closes with the confession that the "only physical pain I could myself inflict with pleasure was upon fish"; and this becomes the opening for a new set of variations upon the techniques of slaughter:

> And there were several ways of destroying a little fish. For example, I could stamp it violently out of existence. Or I could break its head off. Gradually I found myself mildly enjoying the act of driving my thumbnail through the neck or into the back in several places. The body quivered violently; but no sound was made, nor did the eyes express anything. If the root of the tail was squeezed hard between two fingernails the quivering went on for a long time. Several times I forced the bladder out of the body. But these were isolated brief pleasures. I did nothing else of the sort. I never intentionally tortured an animal, though I did protract the drowning of a cat by putting it into a copper that had not been quite filled: as I sat on the lid I sang street tunes very loudly to hide the sounds within and to keep up my courage. I hated having to kill a wounded pigeon. Nevertheless I did it, with a beating heart. When I killed my first snake—it was in reality a blind-worm—I stabbed it so frenziedly that I was lucky not to hurt myself; the frenzy being due partly to suppressed fear, partly to the novelty. As to fish, I very soon began to pride myself on killing what I caught instead of throwing it into the hedge behind, as the factory men usually did, there to die slowly. Pressing the under jaw of the jack against a stone I bent his long body up and over until his neck was broken and his back met his upper jaw. With a smaller fish I inserted the two first fingers into the gills and forced back the head until it was loose. I think that care and pride in doing this neatly and swiftly obliterated any mere pleasure in pain, though it was, I think, accompanied by a slight suffocation and beating of the heart and clouding of the brain.

Although the minor parallels to the anecdote of the slaughterhouse suggest dispassionate reportage, it is the extra-dimension of personal sensations, calmly related, harmonising the experiences of killing, which disturbs us: "I found myself mildly enjoying the act of driving my thumbnail through the neck . . ."; "But these were

Family portrait when Edward was at St. Paul's (Collection of Myfanwy Thomas)

isolated brief pleasures . . ."; "though I did protract the drowning of a cat . . ."; "When I killed my first snake I stabbed it so frenziedly . . ."; "As to fish, I very soon began to pride myself on killing what I caught . . ."; all of which leads up to the conjunction of professional self-regard—"that care and pride in doing this swiftly and neatly"— with personal reaction: "slight suffocation and beating of the heart and clouding of the brain." Act and reaction are there—what we lack is the guidance of an "and therefore," and "I came to realise." It may not even be a moral distancing we seek but simply a narrative control. In the course of reading such recollections we forget the man behind the pen in any other existence than as amanuensis. "These things happened." And then? And then these other things happened.

These anecdotes, as I have suggested, live at one extreme of the spectrum. Their force lies in the fact that they are seen as both "normal" and—as in the parodistic catalogue of the child's own memories of killing—abhorrent. None the less, it is *there* both in adults and children at the centre of life. Equally, another anecdote starts off within that centrality and casually turns itself into a moral fable without judgement. The boy becomes a pigeon-fancier; his particular desire is for a pair of young black-chequers; long-distance homers:

> I was to have them, so I understood, for two-and-six the pair. When I already had them in my hand I learnt they were two-and-six each. This was beyond my means, nor did I want to have one of them at such a price. So he took them back into his hands at the door. Then while I was still lingering he put the head of one bird in his mouth, as I imagined in fun, or to slip a grain into its beak. His teeth closed on the slender neck tighter and tighter, the wings flapped and quivered, and when he opened his jaws the bird was dead. I was speechless, on the edge of tears. He looked down at me with a half-pitying grin, remarking that I was "still softhearted." My tenderness turned to hatred for the man, yet I could not speak. I dared not show my feeling. With only a meek resentfulness I even accepted his gift of the surviving bird. It became the prize of my pigeon house, always distinguished as "the young homer." The man I never did more than nod to again.

In that nod, I take it, lies the point of the story: the gesture remains indecipherable—is it a sign of contempt, gratitude, pride, obeisance?—except as a recognition by the child of the one fact of adult life—compromise. The truth of these "absurd" memories is in their laconic evocation of "normal" experience, of civilisation in all its savage hypocrisy. Violence is necessary even when it is gratuitous—that is the fact of the boy's moral education.

Except that there is a whole other to the autobiography which takes that cruel truth and reworks it so that it is seen *as a truth;* this, in turn, becomes an honesty about life which is at the amoral centre of a genuine anarchic counter-culture; one to which Edward Thomas would—if he could—have truly belonged.

Thomas's school reports while he was at St. Paul's, 1894 (R. George Thomas, Edward Thomas: A Portrait, *p. 20)*

July 1894. *Latin*—Much to learn: starts a long way behind the rest:—works well. *French*—Weak as yet. *Divinity and English Literature*—very fair *Mathematics*—Weak. *Map Drawing*—Very Fair.

General Remarks—Does his work very steadily; backward in languages, but gets on. I wish he seemed to take more interest in life generally.

December 1894. *Classics*—Backward; improves, Greek very little.

French—knows little, improving. *Mathematics*—Fair, making some progress.

Drawing—Good.

General Remarks: I should say quite the ablest in the form considering his age. He has no taste for languages, but his history is very good. I wish he were a more sociable person.

Thomas left St. Paul's to prepare for his civil-service examination in April 1895. Instead, with encouragement from Noble, he concentrated on writing descriptive sketches for magazines such as The Speaker *and* The New Age. *Noble also encouraged the relationship that was developing between his daughter and Thomas, although Mrs. Noble's prejudice against the lower-middle-class Thomas impeded the hopes that the couple had.*

Thomas's letter to James Noble discussing ideas for publications on nature topics, 21 February 1896 (R. George Thomas, ed., Selected Letters, *pp. 2–3)*

> 19 Cambria Place
> New Swindon
> Wilts.
> 21 February 1896

My dear Mr Noble,

I was very sorry indeed to hear of your continued illness, so bad as to keep you in bed. I do hope you have been feeling better and are improving now, that I may have a better account of your health.

I am loth to trouble you with my affairs, but you will be able to judge in a moment whether the paper has a

Title page for the second edition of Thomas's first book

Helen Noble in 1898, at age twenty-one (Collection of Myfanwy Thomas)

chance. I am bewildered in attempting to give a title to it. I think–though I may be wrong–that the Gypsies should be mentioned in the title. "Gypsies and (or in) Wiltshire Meadows"; "Round a Gypsy Camp"; "Meadows and Gypsies"; each of these has something to be said for it though they are very clumsy. It was extremely kind of you to suggest a magazine and I would have tried without troubling you at such a time, but I thought you might see better where to try by looking over the article. After all, it is not very long, but there seems to me *more* information than I can generally give.

My note book would show you that I am not wasting my time–out of doors at least. I have written another paper and hope to be able to write two a week regularly. Father in his letter suggests that I should try the *provincial daily press,* but I know nothing of it, though it seems worth some trouble.

We are having some lovely clear weather now and every day I have been out for long walks. I wish I could hear that yourself had been tempted out by the sun, as you would have been today if better. Though I like the old man's company I really enjoy walks alone best and seem to feel the companionable stillness of the woods, and get more intense calm pleasure thus.

My reading, beyond Civil Service work, is limited to: "Hypatia" and "Selborne" and a snatch at Jefferies rarely as yet.

Besides studying the wild creatures of the fields I have gone so far as to make the acquaintance of a "hedger and ditcher" and a shepherd on the downs. All of them cry out on the farmers who "put no money in the land" and send everything to London; they say that the farmers even forget how to make cheese!

Arthur is in no hurry to write but I suppose he is waiting to let me know the result of his exam.; I hope by this time you will have heard of his *success.*

Again hoping you are already better or well and with kindest regards to all I remain, my dear Mr Noble,

Ever your affectionate
Edwy Thomas

In April 1896 James Noble died suddenly. His widow forbade her daughter to see Thomas, who then was being pressured by his father to take the civil-service examination. When Helen departed for Kent to take up a post as governess, Thomas convinced his father to support his application for a place at Oxford University while the young man finished his first book, The Woodland Life *(1897), a collection of nature essays published by Blackwood. Despite their separation, Edward and Helen continued to write each other regularly, and when she returned to London in the summer of 1896, the two became lovers.*

In autumn 1897 Thomas moved to Oxford to prepare for an entrance scholarship, and the following year he received an award to study history at Lincoln College, where he began undergraduate study in autumn 1898. At Lincoln his social life improved after he was introduced to E. S. P. Haynes, the future writer-solicitor, and Ian MacAlister, the future secretary of the Royal Institute of British Architects. Like many other Oxford students of his day, Thomas pursued a decadent life, with bouts of heavy drinking and opium eating. He continued to visit Helen regularly, and in 1899 during his Easter vacation she became pregnant. As a result of her pregnancy, the two quickly arranged a secret marriage at the Fulham Registry Office on 20 June that year.

Thomas during his first term at Oxford, 1898 (Collection of Myfanwy Thomas)

Comments by Thomas's friend Harry Hooton about the reasons for Thomas's rowdy behavior at Oxford (John Moore, The Life and Letters of Edward Thomas, *p. 41)*

After a summer vacation spent partly at home in London, partly with relations at Pontardulais in South Wales (where he helped with the harvest and made friends with a bard), Edward went back to Oxford in an angry and depressed mood. The reason was an unpleasant row between Helen and her employer, Mrs. Andrews, who had discovered in some way that Edward was Helen's lover. In consequence of this Helen had left the Andrews' and taken a new job, as a sort of general help, with a kind and tolerant and slightly "Bohemian" family who were already her friends and who knew of her relationship with Edward. Here she was happy and at home; and Edward was made welcome too and allowed to come and see her whenever he liked.

But the Andrews affair had upset Edward much more than it had upset Helen. He was ultra-sensitive and secretive about his love (he had not even mentioned Helen to any of his friends at Oxford) and the thought that Mrs. Andrews had read his letters made him both ashamed and furious. He had a queer streak of puritanism in his nature, an inheritance, perhaps, from his Welsh ancestors; he felt that his love was soiled by being pried upon. So he went up for the autumn term in a fit of melancholy. He wrote to Hooton dramatically: "I can only shrink and plan a slinking away out of sight, since I love life too much to die." Probably he only half meant it; but he was experiencing for the first time that mood of bitter brooding and self-torturing introspection which later would trouble him so often, and at such times his despair was so deep that it was like a dark cloud upon his mind.

He sought refuge from his daemon in a kind of life which was quite new to him. He surprised his friends by becoming almost rowdy. He tried all sorts of rather ingenuous experiments with drink and with opium. He "officiated with the scissors at the cutting of an odious lovelock from the brow of a certain freshman." He took up rowing and discovered that he enjoyed it. Altogether he was a changed person. "I can listen to 'Circus Girl' music," he told Hooton with a sort of bravado. "I can topple into bed *off* the verge of drunkenness; swear, use slang creditably; howl the usual foul choruses (for of course it is a fiction that the "Varsity sings 'Who is Sylvia? What is she?'); also I can be heartily sick and well rid of it all."

While Thomas was on holiday in Wales during summer 1899, news of his marriage was revealed to the Thomas family

Thomas after his secret marriage to Helen, October 1899 (Collection of Myfanwy Thomas)

by Harry Hooton, who had been his best man. His parents accepted the marriage with understanding and offered Helen a place in their home until Thomas graduated from Oxford. Thomas's three-week Welsh vacation in Pontardulais was productive, as he was awed by the raw power of the landscape and the harsh beauty of the region. He never lost this affinity for the Welsh countryside.

Thomas's notebook entry concerning the influence of Wales on him, 31 August 1899 (R. George Thomas, Edward Thomas: A Portrait, *p. 80)*

Day by day grows my passion for Wales. It is like a homesickness, but stronger than any homesickness I ever felt–stronger than any passion. Wales indeed, is my soul's native land, if the soul can be said to have a *patria*–or rather, a *matria,* a home with the warm sweetness of a mother's love, and with her influence, too. Today, for example, what yearning thoughts filled my brain as Janet played the tune of *Y Ferch o Landebie* and *Moli merched Cymru lan!* and when I hummed the "Gwlad Gwlad" of the national anthem, my heart broke with thoughts of what I might be and am not, of what I may be–ah! the future in some bookish cottage in the pastoral Towy with Helen!

This feeling is not a new one, born of my visit to the Mumbles in 1896; it really did begin with my visit at five years of age to Caerleon and Swansea–remembered for the Usk and Arthur's Table Island near Aunt Margaret's house, the great red apples from the orchard, and the ivy, the snails and the gloomy well there, and the salmon we ate, the idiot at Caerleon, the porpoise hunt, the churchyard and pigs and snow in May, the house on the hill and the Cinderella (Rachel) in its kitchen, the parrot there and the loaf-like stone I brought to Aunt Mary's house from Langland, where I remember the tall pillars of rock on the near side, and the flying fish pickled in her drawing room, the gulls, too. Hill House, Newport, too, with its great palings–its dogs, its fruit trees, and the sense of mother's girlhood there.

Then came the second visit–to Abertillery, when I was eight or nine. I remember the mountain climbing, the drive to Pontypool, the mountain-ash berries, the shallow Ebbw river where I wanted to fish, being already a fisherman.

Then the reading of Arthurian stories. Then the foolish years between 1890 and 1893.

One always spoke a few Welsh words like "moch" and "achyfi." I was proud of thinking that both Father and Mother came from Wales, and the land was always a Something "beyond these voices."

Then Father's Welsh studies–the Welsh I heard at Swindon which seemed a little Wales,–then Malory in 1895–then Mumbles and Pontardulais, prepared for by my "love of Nature" which was *soi-disant* Celtic.

But now I cherish every shred of a reminder–like the old farm of Mother's grandmother at Tydraw. [Near Margam.]

And how glad I am of such experiences as this. In November last year at Oxford, I met in Trench's rooms in College, two Gypsies (Cornelius aged 25–Buckland aged 70), for about an hour they gave Trench a lesson in the Gypsy tongue. Then, for I had just read *Aylwin,* I asked the elder if he knew Wales. He did. Did he know any Welsh Songs (for I still loved *Y Ferch o Landebie*)? Yes–and he sang right through in that mysterious night

Mae hen wlad fy nhadau yn anwyl i mi
Gwlad beirdd a chantorion enwogion o fri.

In autumn 1899 Thomas returned to Oxford to complete the final year of work for his degree, while Helen reluctantly agreed to live with his parents in London.

Thomas's final year at Oxford was difficult: his child, Philip Merfyn Thomas, was born on 15 January 1900. That summer Thomas graduated with a disappointing second-class

Thomas during his final year at Oxford, 1899 (Collection of Myfanwy Thomas)

degree, and his father began pressuring him, for the sake of a secure position, to enter the civil service. Thomas, however, was determined to make a living as a journalist and sought interviews at various London magazines. He found little work, however, and had almost no income.

Thomas's Oxford notebook records Merfyn's birth, 15 January 1900 (R. George Thomas, Edward Thomas: A Portrait, *p. 83)*

P.M. [Merfyn] appeared at 2 a. m. screaming ferociously. H. took the ordeal as an athlete takes a killing race; and was happy enough at 3 a. m. I sat up all night, fortified (?) by laudanum, writing letters, adding something to my paper on the *Books of my Childhood* and reading Hallam's "Literature," Sir Philip Sidney, and Burton. Thus I reached 7 a. m. when I had the tact to go to Kyrle Road [home of Mrs. Noble] and announce things, so making up the breach that had existed since August. The affair did not have any great effect: sometimes the plasticity of the infant seemed terrible in prospect; sometimes I determined to leave to Providence what Providence has so high-handedly begun. He has blue–ie. "violet" eyes, plenty of dark hair, a pimple of a nose, well-shaped coral lips, a horribly oblong head, long legs, and feet almost too big for his socks, and weighs 9 lbs. at appearance. I saw Haynes at noon; he is anxious to get the family Bible as godfather. The next day I lunched with him at the "Cheshire Cheese". . . . The 15th was a night so clear that the air from height to depth was like one great sapphire: there was a white full moon.

Recollections of interviewing Thomas by Henry Nevinson, editor of the Daily Chronicle *(Henry Nevinson,* Changes and Chances, *pp. 195–196)*

Helen Thomas and Merfyn about the time of Thomas's graduation, 1900 (Collection of Myfanwy Thomas)

One evening after my first return from the Boer War, a person of an unknown name was announced, as many such there were, and, cursing aloud or silently, I awaited his entrance. Can a man stride with a proud and melancholy shyness? If so, he strode in that manner. He was tall, absurdly thin, and a face of attractive distinction and ultra refinement was sicklied over with nervous melancholy and the ill condition of bad food or hunger. Almost too shy to speak, he sat down proudly and asked if I could give him work. I enquired what work he could do, and he said "None." At once recognising my former self in him, I asked whether he would like some reviewing on any subject, and on what. He replied that he knew nothing of any subject, and was quite sure he could not write, but certainly he did want work of some sort. I asked if he would not care to try a short review of a scholarly book I was just throwing away; for if he could not do it, that would make little difference to me or to anyone else. I urged him repeatedly, and at last, with extreme reluctance, he consented, and nervously took his leave, just mentioning that his name was Edward Thomas, lately from Lincoln College, Oxford, and now living in Lavender Hill, Nightingale Lane, Rosemary Cottage, or some such address (for I used afterwards to tell him he chose his wandering homes simply for their pretty names). Of course, at once he became one of my closest friends. Shy and reserved of feeling he always remained; too self-distrustful till nearly the end. Once after visiting him in his home near Petersfield, I told him I was sure he could and did write admirable verse. He answered that he never had and never would. But yet, what fine verse he has written! When last I saw him, only for a moment, during the war, he was in uniform, and had gained incredibly in health and stature and confidence. Very soon afterwards I heard he had been killed at an Observation Post in France. In him also, as in so many of my friends, the war extinguished a nature of singular beauty and power. Early in our friendship, I induced him to write the text for John Fulleylove's pictures of Oxford, and his is the best account of Oxford life ever written. Rather later he dedicated to me his book called "The Heart of England," and I am glad to remember that.

Thomas's father was disturbed by his son's lackadaisical attitude toward caring for a young family. Following a family dispute that resulted from growing tensions between father and son, Thomas and his young family moved to three rooms in the London slums of Earlsfield for three months. They subsequently found more suitable housing in Balham, a London suburb, from February to October 1901, and in order to earn enough to afford this move Thomas wrote many magazine reviews. This hackwork brought a trickle of income, but it provided him neither enough time to concentrate on his creative work nor sufficient finances to justify moving to the countryside, as he and his wife wished to do.

An account of Thomas's depression during his search for employment (Jan Marsh, Edward Thomas: A Poet for His Country, *p. 16)*

He was often disappointed, and thrust into gloom by lack of success. Now for the first time Helen came to know the moods of black despondency that afflicted Edward at times of failure, when he was both depressed and aggressive, taking things out on himself and her. When he came home from seeking work, Helen wrote later,

> with the first glance at his face I knew what the day had been. If it had been a bad one there was no need of words, and none were uttered. I did nothing, for if I said one word which would betray that I knew what he had endured and was enduring, his anger and despair and weariness would break out in angry bitter words which would freeze my heart and afterwards freeze his for having uttered them.

If only Edward could have been happy, Helen would have been radiant in her longed-for role as mother. She took her small son out to the Common as often as possible, letting him lie in the sun and picking flowers for him to hold. She fervently believed that contact with earth and nature were essential to growing things, and that her baby should feel natural beauty around him, even though he was forced to live in a hideous suburb. Perhaps the squalid rented rooms were an added cause of Edward's ill-temper: neither he nor Helen had ever envisaged living anywhere but the country with their child. Not to be able to do so was a negation of all they believed in.

Thomas's letter to Ian MacAlister, his university friend, discussing his frustration as a journalist and providing glimpses of his home life, 29 October 1901 (R. George Thomas, ed., Selected Letters, *pp. 19–20)*

My dear Mac,
Perhaps I am in the promised Land, as you say; but there are still the Canaanites, not to speak of Philistines. That is why I have not written before, in spite of your most welcome letter; I celebrated it, I assure you, like a prodigal's return. I have had troubled times—no work and much expense. I have nevertheless stuck at it in a way that would show bravery in anyone else. Have sent out over 20 articles to journals and magazines. 12

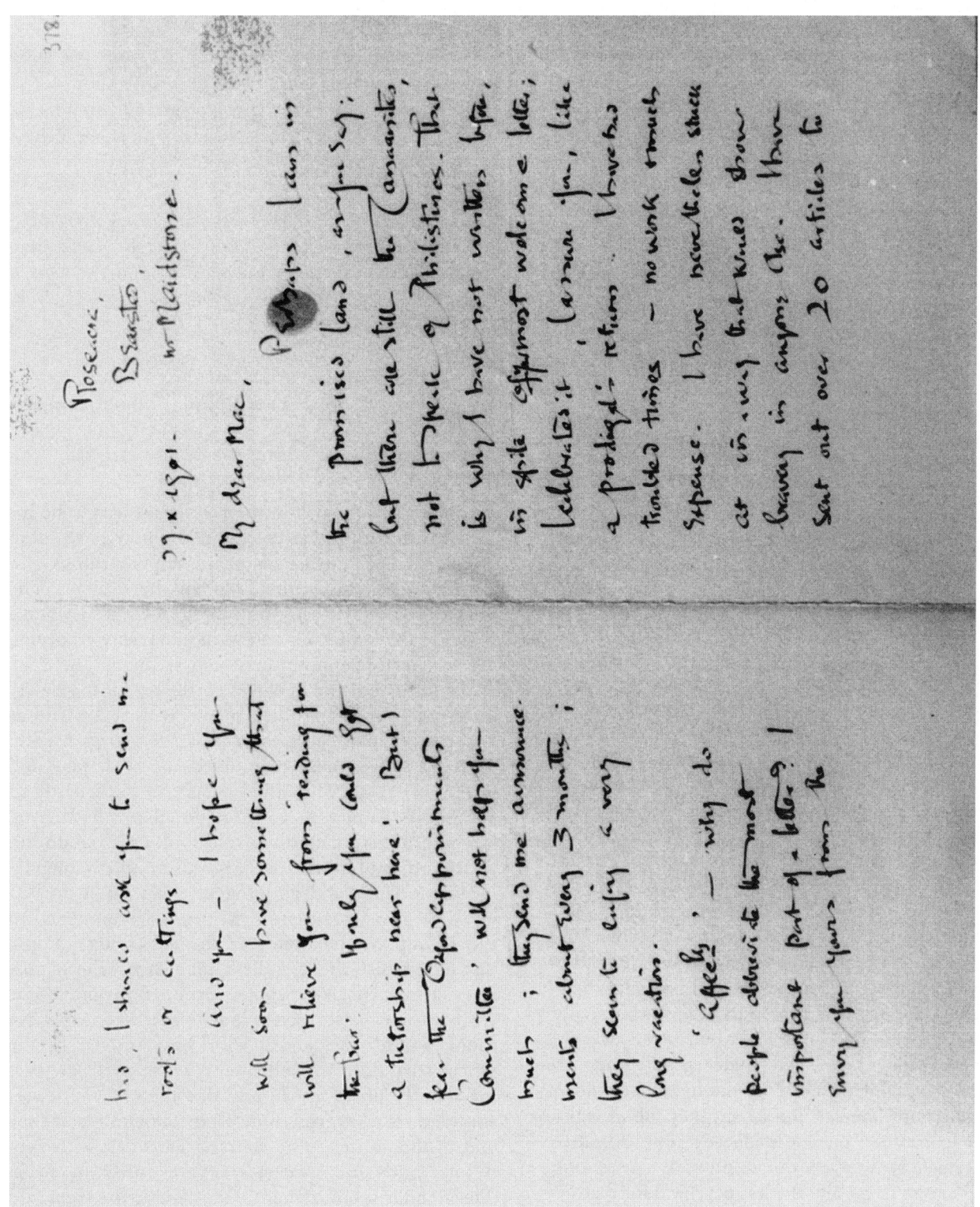

First page of Thomas's letter to Ian MacAlister recounting his frustrations as a journalist and as a family man, 29 October 1901 (Battersea Public Library)

have come back: the other 8 will stay longer because they are with magazines whose decisions take the length of an elephant's pregnancy. I haven't scored one success; yet, showing you how stubborn I have been, the "Globe" and "Pall Mall" between them have rejected 8 articles in a fortnight! And I go on smoking clay pipes and playing with Mervyn who is now going to sleep to the sound of the Bearsted bells. The country is exquisite: yet in a way it soothes me too much and encourages a mild despair which is my favourite vice. Helen and the heir and I have just spent the afternoon out of doors with deep enjoyment, he eating blackberries; I stealing young trees to plant in the garden. As to the garden, now is almost the busiest time. I have turned all the soil up; planted roots, shoots and bulbs; dug a ditch 540 feet long and thrown up a bank the same length; and weeding, etc., illimitable. I suppose you haven't much garden; if you had, I should ask you to send me roots or cuttings.

And you—I hope you will soon have something that will relieve you from "reading for the bar." If only you could get a tutorship near here! But I fear the Oxford Appointments' Committee will not help you much; they send me announcements about every 3 months; they seem to enjoy a very long vacation.

"Affec.ly."—why do people abbreviate the most important part of a letter? I envy you yours from the Malvern boys. The only boys who write to me are grown-up boys at Oxford, and I find the nicest of them all the more foolish because they are old. Still, all Oxford letters are precious to me; and I glance at the post-mark like a philatelist who has got a treasure. You are partly mistaken when you say I valued Oxford more than the people there. It was only because the place acknowledged my love; the people so rarely did. Those that did are far more than the place to me; but a child could count them—1, 2, I can't go on! Now that I am far away, even acquaintances who were unkind or (worse) flippant seem like friends, and now and then I write them letters from my heart; they never reply. Why only lovers understand passion (of any kind) I shall never quite know. And older people—they are never tired of rebuking me. They put melancholy down to crumpets and the like and laugh; they fail to realise the simple fact that "there it is." I know now, of course, that melancholy is largely due to physical causes; only it doesn't seem to me any the less psychical for that.

I shall be very glad if Blackie gives me work, and am most grateful to you for writing to him. I suppose you never meet Crossland of the "Outlook"? If you do, tell him he owes the price of a review done last March, and that he promised me more work. He won't pay and he won't give me work.

It's bad news of Fyfe, but I suppose Garrod was a better man, at any rate by his achievements.

Write again soon especially if you have good news of yourself.

With love from us all,
Yours ever, Edwy.

Financial worries severely depressed Thomas, who boldly—and rather recklessly—decided to move to Rose Acre Cottage near Bearstead, Kent, where the young couple hoped to find solace in the popular "back to the land" environmental philosophy advocated by Edward Carpenter.

Helen Thomas's reflections on moving to the country, from her semi-autobiographical novel World Without End *(pp. 88-90)*

David was busy in the room that was to be his study, and Philip was asleep in the new bare room upstairs, while I washed up the supper things and arranged the cups and plates on the dresser. The kitchen led out directly into the garden, and when I had done my work I stood in the doorway emptying my heart of disappointment and sadness. The dusk was falling, and the dew-wet earth and all the newly born green of spring filled the air with scent, and as I leaned against the door I took in a deep breath. The sweet freshness of it filled me with joy, and again and again I breathed deeply to experience an elation, as from a magic draught, that I had never felt before. I stooped down and took up a handful of earth and crumbling it let it fall through my fingers. Its harsh touch and its pungent clean smell thrilled me with a new awareness. My eyes were opened to the beauty of the night, to the dark ridge of the downs against the cloudless blue sky, where now stars appeared like pebbles dropped from above. Away to the east was a radiance where soon the moon would rise, and a soft wind as of ushering voices stirred on the hill side. A white owl flew past me silently like a ghost, and like the cry of a ghost sounded its quavering note from the elm tree at the end of the garden. The cherry trees thick with pendulous buds breathed—as it were—softly in sleep. The slender moon rising timidly above the trees laid her spell on the earth, and all was silence and darkness and sleep. On me too she laid her spell. I turned to go to David, and met him coming towards me.

"There's a new moon," he said. "You must wish."

Thomas and Merfyn at Rose Acre Cottage, 1902 (Collection of Myfanwy Thomas)

In 1902 Thomas's second collection of essays, Horae Solitariae, was published; few copies were sold, but the book received good reviews. That same year he began corresponding with poet Gordon Bottomley, with whom he began a deliberation about his literary ambitions and writing career that the two men continued throughout Thomas's life. His financial problems were exacerbated when a second child, Bronwen, was born in October, but by the end of the year Thomas learned that he had been chosen to replace Lionel Johnson as the literary reviewer for the prestigious Daily Chronicle. Acquiring this new position meant that Thomas could begin 1903 on a firm financial footing.

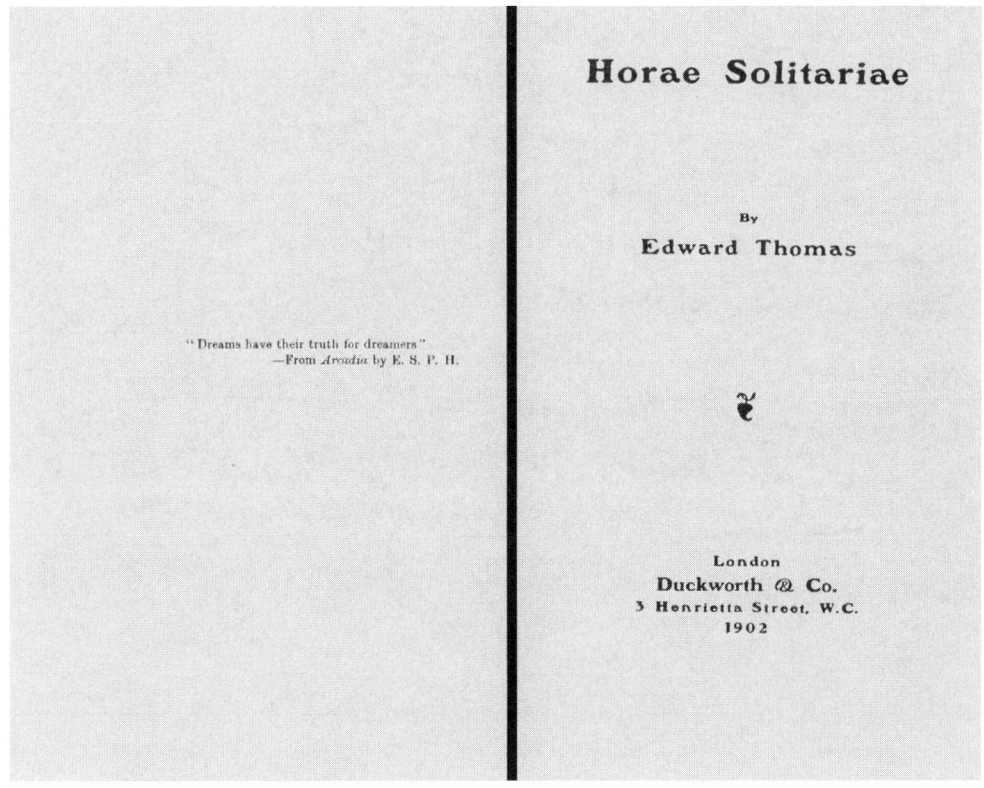

Title page and epigraph for Thomas's collection of fourteen essays comprising his second book

First page of Thomas's letter to MacAlister discussing his financial problems and work, 25 December 1902 (Battersea Public Library)

"There's nothing left to wish for," I said; "we are in the country and it is spring."

We were about a mile from the village of Bearden which lay at the foot of the North Downs. It is a most attractive little place built round a large green. The church with its strangely gargoyled tower is at one corner with the vicarage, and a beautiful manor house encloses the south side. At another corner is the pond where the cows, grazing on the green, drink or stand on hot summer days, ruminating and looking at the ducks who swim about among them. On the north side with their back gardens running down to the railway are the smithy and the wheelwright and the baker all occupying lovely old workshops and houses. There are two inns— "The Black Swan" and "The Lion." "The Black Swan" is the only new building near the green and is ugly and incongruous among a thicket of yews and beeches where often I was to hear the nightingale sing. Near this inn was the station on the main road mounting up to join the important Maidstone and Ashford road. The road up our hill took us past the pond and the grounds of the manor house. The Lion Inn at the other side of the green was an old half-timbered house with uneven roof ridge, and windows in unexpected places, and low, dim, panelled rooms inside, where beer was served in pewter pots, and where in winter the bar parlour, with its brick floor, and great oak settles each side of the fireplace, was bright and cosy with a huge fire of logs. Mr. Tompsett the innkeeper became a friend of ours. He was a splendid gardener as well as host, and helped us with advice and presents of cuttings for our garden.

We made the house as pretty as we could, though I never liked it. David's study, which was also the sitting-room, became homely and comfortable with the books and our most precious possessions, and for the kitchen I had an affection, chiefly because of the view of the downs and the yews which marked the Pilgrims' Way. I spent many hours at the table under the window ironing or sewing or cooking, and Philip sitting in his high chair near me would amuse himself by banging on its deal top with a wooden spoon, or turning over the pages of a linen scrapbook I had made for him, and pointing with his fat finger at the picture for me to name, for he was very late in learning to talk, and his double Dutch became so expressive and I understood it so well that I began to be afraid he would never learn proper speech. He was at this time a splendidly healthy boy, with a mop of loose golden curls, and blue eyes, lively and intelligent and a great joy to us.

Thomas's letter to Ian MacAlister recounting his financial problems and his work, 25 December 1902 (R. George Thomas, ed., Selected Letters, *pp. 22–24)*

Thomas with his parents, son, and paternal grandmother in late 1902 (Edward Thomas: A Portrait)

My dear Mac,

It was very great joy to have even a gloomy letter from you. And on Christmas Day, too. The feast never meant much to me as a child, except from the books and stomach-aches I received. But every year it becomes more and more a remembrancer, and I make up the books of friendship and thought with a sombre pleasure whatever the balance. So you have been with me all day, whether I was playing with Mervyn or drinking hot ale and ginger along with nuts. We had no frost, yet a great fire—and the logs were as idols.

Since I wrote I have had a pretty continuous supply of books, enough to keep me almost continuously employed and to put a stop to original composition; and yet not enough to prevent the quarterly alarm about my rent. I had—but tell it not—Milton's latest book, "*Nova Solyma*," to do for the "Chronicle." And that reminds me that I heard unofficially that I am now to get the review-books which used to go to Lionel Johnson who died last month. I don't know whether to be elated or desperate; for he was a fine scholar and (tho I have only just found it out) a writer of the most beautiful prose.

We are pretty well. Helen is at work now as usual. Rachel Mary Bronwen (for that is her name) grows more agreeable in appearance. Her eyes are changing in the direction of brown, and her hair is to be dark brown, a constrast with Mervyn, who has conspicuous blue eyes and fair yellow hair in long waves. He is a nice boy at times, and by the way he sends you two kisses. He has already quite a store of knowledge—about animals, natural effects and colours, etc., and is a good talker, and most hearty lover of life, with just a tinge of reverie along with a short sharp temper. He runs and climbs and walks often 5 miles a day. He will be 3 next month. I know you would like to see how joyous we can be while he hears me "singing" Welsh airs or "The Old Gray Fox" or "Widdicombe Fair" or "The Lincolnshire Poacher."

Still my progress towards the state of family man is not smooth or invariably pleasant. I often want to go away and walk and walk for a week anywhere so long as it is by an uncertain road. For tho I like to stay in one piece of country I don't like (as I have to, in England) to meet continually some respectable acquaintance with whom I must stop to bore and be bored. I am not a bit of a wanderer, but I like to be thought-free and fancy-free as I can't be in this sweet domestic country. Also my melancholy "grows old along with me."

You don't give me any notion of your work, and so I can only be sick at heart to think of your difficulties. Write to me oftener and talk before your heart gets too full.

Everything you say to encourage me in my work encourages me, partly because I know you used to be unsympathetic. I don't despair because my work is unrecognised. What makes me desperate is the little leisure (from reviewing and much thinking about money) left me to write my best in. In the last three months I have written about 1000 words exclusive of reviews. Yet my head has been so full that I might have done 10,000 much better than I did 1000, and tho' some of that was at the rate of 40 words an hour. Moreover, when for a time I am free from all business, tho my tendency then is to write, I am not always willing to. For I must have some time in which to be non literary, free to think or better still not to think at all, but to let the wind and the sun do my thinking for me, filling my brain. However, that is a trifle and will not be even that when I am part of a great calm under nettles and yews and grass.

Well, I seem to have spent much ink in getting myself on paper. I had better have sent my photograph.

I hope you like "Coldstreamer" [*Horae Solitariae?*] a little. He is now in a 2nd edition, so you can at least make half a crown per head.

We all send our love and good wishes.

Excerpts from Thomas's letter to Gordon Bottomley describing Thomas's personality and ambitions, 17 March 1904 (R. George Thomas, ed., Letters from Edward Thomas to Gordon Bottomley, *pp. 52–54)*

My dear Gordon,

It is not easy for me to think about the future, even about next month. It all seems so improbable, & every day seems to be the last, so tired and unconcentrated am I. . . .

You will find me, I fear, somewhat hard of speech & hearing in the matters you & I really care about. For all my life I have been in the hands of those who care for other & even opposite things; & they have tried to teach me—or by my own imitative nature I have tried to learn—to say much & smartly about things I care nothing for. Perhaps after all they are the only things one can ever sum up & be satisfied with in conversation. And this reminds me of what you say about your own isolated position, away from fellow artists. I know well the desire & the apparent need; for work that depends always & entirely upon a man's own invention & impulse always lets the artist down into deep waters of misery now & then, & at those times I have sought the company of many and various men, & yet I have always been alone & unaided; all I have got from them has been experiences which I never use. I have talked my soul empty to a man who (as I had not the wit to dis-

With the promise of a contract for a book describing the city of Oxford in 1903, Thomas relocated his family to "Ivy Cottage," a more attractive house on Bearstead Green, where he wrote Oxford (1903). The attic room in which he wrote this book became the subject of his later poem, "The Long Small Room." The mental strain that Thomas suffered while working on the book exhausted him, and he lapsed into a depression that was exacerbated by continuing financial difficulties. In addition, the bad drainage and poor insulation at Ivy Cottage caused various illnesses for the family. Both Bronwen and Helen fell seriously ill in the winter, and their doctor advised them to leave the old house for healthier quarters.

Manuscript for "The long small room" (Bodleian Library, Oxford)

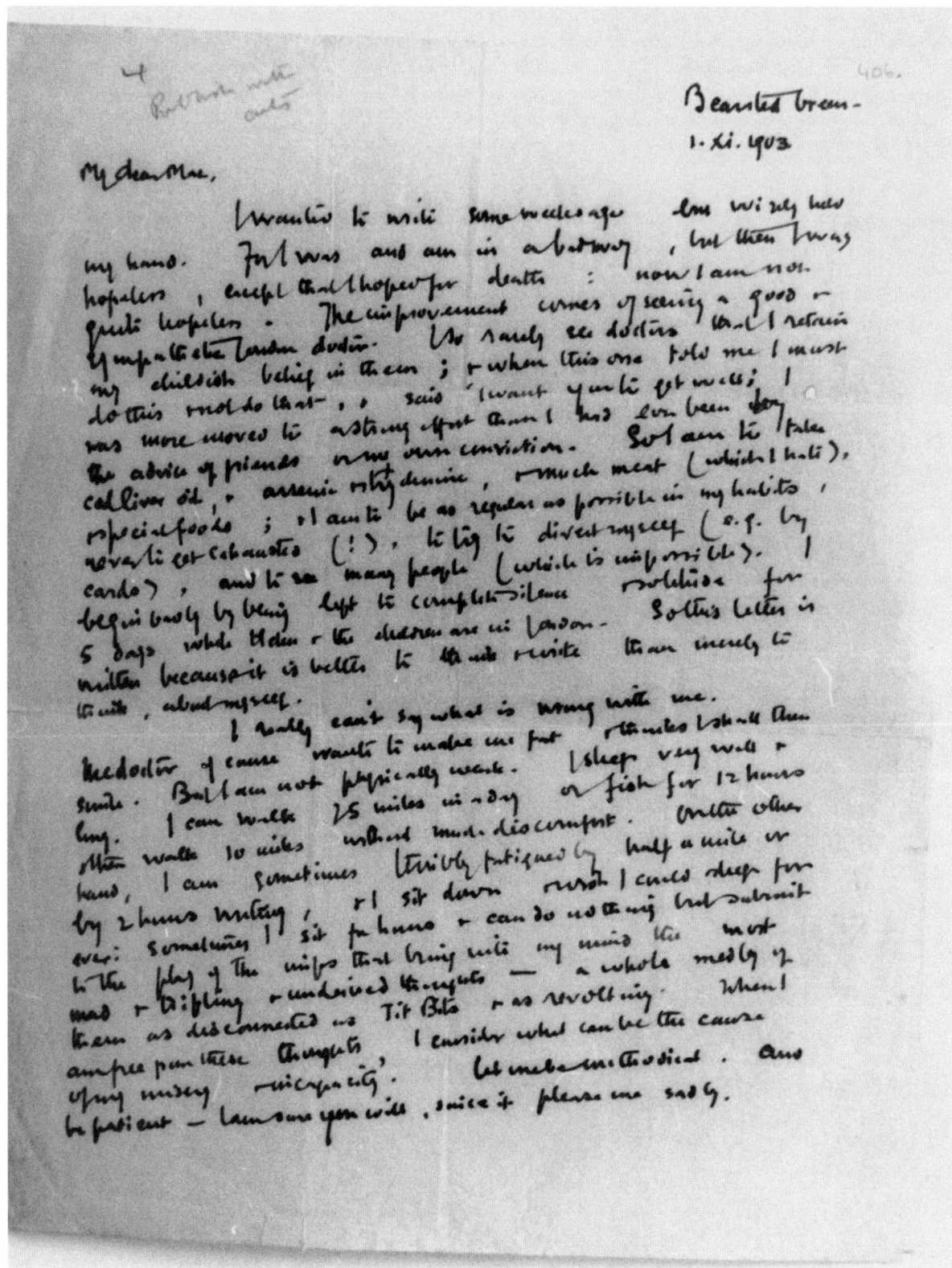

First page of Thomas's letter to Ian MacAlister about his depression, 1 November 1903 (Battersea Public Library)

cover) answered me with his tongue; not one man, but a score: I suppose, as I hinted just now, that my talk was obscure—in "clouds of glory" if you like. Well, are you likely to have better luck? Your work seems to me to be a far lonelier flower than mine, & other artists might change you or swamp you, but couldn't help you to develop.—I think—for the mere health of the brain, a variety of social intercourse should be good: & I wish you were able to try it. But with me, social intercourse is only an intense form of solitude, and as solitude is what I have to avoid, the means are yet to be found. Does this uncomfortable talk comfort you at all? But your poor wrist—that is worse than all my ills—It is a horrible, plain fact that might appal a Berkleian.

I am glad you like "the rapture of the fight." I hardly ever do. I look forward to writing & look back upon it joyfully as if it were an achievement & not an attempt—very often. But while I write, it is a dull blindfold journey through a strange lovely land: I seem to take what I write from the dictation of someone else. Correction is pleasanter. For then I have glimpses of what I was passing through as I wrote. This very morning the sun was shining, wide & pale gold & warm as it has done for two weeks, & the church bells suddenly beginning to ring were at one with it a part of Spring, & they set me writing; for I could not go out, as I have a touch of Helen's illness & am over-weak; but at once, I became dull with the dulness of ecstasy (I suppose)....

Helen is just back & looks quite well. She and I send our love to you all.

Thomas's letter to Ian MacAlister discussing his emotional state, doubts about his writing, and feelings about nature, 1 November 1903 (R. George Thomas, ed., Selected Letters, *pp. 26–28)*

My dear Mac,

I wanted to write some weeks ago but wisely held my hand. For I was and am in a bad way, but then I was hopeless, except that I hoped for death: now I am not quite hopeless. The improvement comes of seeing a good and sympathetic London doctor. I so rarely see doctors that I retain my childish belief in them; and when this one told me I must do this and not do that, and said "I want you to get well," I was more moved to a strong effort than I had ever been by the advice of friends or my own conviction. So I am to take cod liver oil, and arsenic and strychnine, and much meat (which I hate), and special foods; and I am to be as regular as possible in my habits, never to get exhausted (!), to try to divert myself (e.g. by cards), and to see many people (which is impossible). I begin badly by being left to complete silence and solitude for 5 days while Helen and the children are in London. So this letter is written because it is better to think and write than merely to think, about myself.

I really can't say what is wrong with me. The doctor of course wants to make me fat and thinks I shall then smile. But I am not physically weak. I sleep very well and long. I can walk 25 miles in a day or fish for 12 hours and then walk 10 miles without much discomfort. On the other hand, I am sometimes terribly fatigued by half a mile or by 2 hours writing, and I sit down and wish I could sleep for ever: sometimes I sit for hours and can do nothing but submit to the play of the imps that bring into my mind the most mad and trifling and undesired thoughts—a whole medley of them as disconnected as Tit-Bits and as revolting. When I am free from these thoughts, I consider what can be the cause of my misery and incapacity. Let me be methodical. And be patient—I am sure you will, since it pleases me sadly.

First, I wonder if my indiscretions and intemperance in alcohol, opium and tobacco, have at last taken effect. They have been serious, but 2 years ago they became far less so, and in the past 9 months I have lived moderately in every way, unless (which is unlikely) I have worked or walked too much.

Second, has continued journalism at last destroyed my always slender capacity for writing what I like? At first I always tried to leaven my reviews with some thought or fancy which was often irrelevant but often gave me the satisfaction of thinking that I have at least written one or two decent sentences and uttered a part of myself. But those thoughts and fancies had to be very brief: I could not follow them up. So I got, perhaps, into a habit of jerky and unconcluded thinking and imagination. The result *seems* to be that when now I try to write an essay I cannot do more than 2 or 3 sentences: they do not, as they used to do, flow one from the other in a rosary. I hope I am mistaken. Anyhow, the symptom which makes me most wretched is my inability to write an essay. I sit down with my abundant notebooks and find a subject or an apparently suggestive sentence: but nothing moves me.

Third—am I losing my religious attitude towards "Nature"? That is too painful to admit. Yet it may be so. Perhaps my love was not as deep as it seemed. But I seem to notice a change when I sit down to write. One little note used to recall to me much of the glory or joy of former days out of doors. Now it is barren, and that means a great deal, because I cannot bring myself to write about anything else, or at any rate about anything which "Nature" does not unavoidably enter. I argue thus to myself: "I have cared more for Nature than for anything else, therefore if I can write at all, Nature will move me. If, on the other hand, I am unworthy or insincere, if the years of days and nights which I spent in rapture or awe out of doors now mean nothing to me, then I distrust myself wholly and will at least refrain from serving another mistress."

Fourth, shall I ever get used to what I consider the dirtiness and confusion of my house? Practically not an hour of my day passes without some violent irritation caused by this: and either I sit down and curse or I vainly attempt to put things right. In other people's houses I can be contented; never in my own. Some tell me this irritation is an effect of my state of health and mind. Perhaps so: I believe it is the cause and apparently it is ineradicable.

Well there I am writ large. Other things trouble me, lack of company, lack of money (due to small extravagance and great mismanagement). But I have said nearly all—and now I don't feel any better for having told you so much, because I know you will want to help and you can't.

The book is delayed but I hope not for more than a fortnight.

Work is bad, for Nevinson (my greatest patron) has left the "Chronicle" for good and is in Macedonia, and W. J. Fisher, the editor, is not fond of me. So I am advised to look out for something else. But what? Librarianship at a private library would perhaps suit me, but I am unqualified. Who would have me as schoolmaster or secretary? I shall stick to Bearsted as long as possible. Anyway, you will write, I hope: and will you tell, by the way, whom to ask for on the "Outlook"? You remember saying that your father might help me there.

In May 1904 the family moved again—this time to Elses Farm, a country home at Weald, Kent. There, surrounded by agricultural activities, Thomas experienced the rhythms of rural life that inspired his prose and later his poetry. In World Without End *(1931), Helen Thomas's partly fictional account of her life with her husband (called David in the book), she writes of that bucolic life.*

Edward Thomas's praise for the Back-to-the-Land impulse (The South Country, *pp. 147, 133, 135*)

Literature sends us to Nature principally for joy, joy of the senses, of the whole frame, of the contemplative mind, and of the soul, joy which if it is found complete in these several ways might be called religious. Science sends us to Nature for knowledge. Industrialism and the great towns send us to Nature for health, that we may go on manufacturing efficiently, or, if we think right and have the power, that we may escape from it....

I recall many scenes: a church and churchyard and black pigs running down from them towards me in a rocky lane—ladslove and tall, crimson, bitter dahlias in a garden—the sweetness of large, moist yellow apples eaten out of doors—children: ... the moment that I return to them in fancy I am happy....

Some of these scenes, whether repeated or not, come to have a rich, symbolical significance; they return persistently and, as it were, ceremoniously—on festal days—but meaning I know not what. For example, I never see the flowers and scarlet-stained foliage of herb-robert growing out of old stone-heaps by the wayside without a feeling of satisfaction not explained by a long memory of the contrast between the plant and the raw flint; so also with the drenched lilac-bloom leaning out over high walls of unknown gardens; and inland cliffs, covered with beech, jutting out westward into a bottomless valley in the midst of winter twilights, in silence and frost. Something in me belongs to these

Dust jacket for Wales *(1924), Thomas's fifth book, originally published as* Beautiful Wales *(1905)*

To pay the rent for his family's new rural retreat, Thomas undertook a series of commissions to write descriptive travel works such as Beautiful Wales *(1905).*

Elses Farm (Jan Marsh, Edward Thomas: A Poet for His Country*)*

things, but I hardly think that the mere naming of them will mean anything to other people.

A description of rural life as experienced by Helen and David, from Helen Thomas's World Without End, *pp. 107–108*

All this work I loved as I did the housework, the gardening or any work which gave my strong body exercise, and which satisfied my spirit with its human necessity. David too was glad for me to do these things, and I tried my hand at brewing, wine-making, hop-picking and even reaping. Of course hay-making on the lovely slope of Blooming meadow was a festival for us all at the farm, and we learnt how the ricks that rose like a town in the rickyard were shaped so symmetrically, and thatched as carefully as a house. It is this full life of homely doings that I remember chiefly at the farm—the early morning expeditions with David to a large pond about three miles away to fish for perch and roach and even pike; the walks to Penshurst and Leigh and Ightham Moat; the picking and storing of apples; the making of quince jam; the finding of an owl's or a nightingale's nest; the woodpecker which cut the air in scallops as it flew from oak to oak; the white owl which brought its young to the roof ridge to be fed; the beautiful plough-horses with their shining brass ornaments; the cows going into their stalls like people going into their pews in church; the building and thatching of the ricks; the hedging and ditching; the wood-cutting and faggot-binding by men whose fathers had done the same work and whose fathers' fathers too; the work of the farm, leisured as the coming and going of the seasons; the lovely cycle of ploughing, sowing and reaping; the slow experienced labourers, whose knowledge had come to them as the acorns come to the oaks, whose skill had come as the swallow's skill, who are satisfied in their hard life as are the oaks and the swallows in theirs. How I loved it all, and with what joy and strength it filled my being, so that when I needed joy and strength they did not fail me. And often and often I did need them. There were many dark periods while we were here, many days of silence and wretchedness and separation, for sometimes in these moods David would stride away, perhaps for days, wrestling with the devil that tormented his spirit.

In 1905 Thomas met William H. Davies, the Welsh "tramp" poet whose book, The Soul's Destroyer, *Thomas had reviewed with approval in the* Daily Chronicle. *Review-*

Edward Thomas in 1905, about the time he met William H. Davies (Collection of Myfanwy Thomas)

ing works by new poets such as Davies and discovering the originality of their verse encouraged Thomas to pursue a poetic career in the final years of his life. Eventually the two men shared a cottage, largely because Thomas found working at home around his children and his wife to be too distracting. During their period of sharing the cottage, Thomas encouraged Davies to write what became his well-known The Autobiography of a Super-Tramp *(1908), a debt to Thomas that he never forgot.*

A description of Davies in "Men," in Thomas's notebook, 11–12 October 1905 (Edward Thomas: A Portrait, p. 127)

11. x. 05. 11.30 p. m. Farmhouse (Harrow St.), Marshalsea Road, S. E. Called and saw William H. Davies author of "The Soul's Destroyer." A small narrow-headed blackhaired Monmouthshire man, with the childish slightly uncomfortable smile (with the mouth) of Welsh people, and still a Welsh accent. One leg: the

other lost on railway in U.S.A. He is of Maindee near Newport (where Mother lived) and was a picture-frame maker, but had and has eight shillings a week left by his sea-captain grandfather, and left Wales ten years ago, and spent five years in U.S.A. and Canada, doing odd work—fruit farming and railways, and then five years in London.

12. x. 05. He showed me his library—Dick's Wordsworth and Shelley; Enfield's "Speaker," some of Tutin's reprints sent him by Tutin lately; 2 of St. John Adcock's ditto; and (a recent purchase) a book published last year on "How to write verse." I gave him an Oxford Wordsworth in exchange for Dick's—of which the print is cruelly small for a man to read by a coke fire.

He is in Pinker's hands [the literary agent] and apparently neglected—i.e. robbed. He has quite the shy manner of a Welshman who has just come to London, and he looks and speaks as if quite unspoiled by experience or by the glory of a review by Arthur Symons. He talked freely and easily with me about early truancy in Tredegar Park—visits to the Ebbw—England v Wales at Swansea five years ago—working his passage across Atlantic eight or nine times in cattle boats—about "Gambling Fred" who now holds the man who wouldn't lend him sixpence is now in debt for about £50 (because the sixpence was to go on a horse that won and the fifteen shillings thus made would have gone on another and so on.) He paid £19 for printing his book.

*"Killed in Action," W. H. Davies's tribute to Thomas, following Thomas's death in the Great War (*The Complete Poems of W. H. Davies, *pp. 248–249)*

Happy the man whose home is still
    In Nature's green and peaceful ways;
To wake and hear the birds so loud,
    That scream for joy to see the sun
Is shouldering past a sullen cloud.
And we have known those days, when we
    Would wait to hear the cuckoo first;
When you and I, with thoughtful mind,
    Would help a bird to hide her nest,
For fear of other hands less kind.

But thou, my friend, art lying dead:
    War, with its hell-born childishness,
Has claimed thy life, with many more:
    The man that loved this England well,
And never left it once before.

After the Thomases' lease on Elses Cottage ended in October 1906, the family moved to Berryfield Cottage near Steep in Hampshire, in order for their son Merfyn to attend the progressive Bedales

Berryfield Cottage when the Thomas family lived there (R. George Thomas, ed., Letters from Edward Thomas to Gordon Bottomley*)*

School nearby. Their rent for this cottage was more than that for their residence at Kent had been, so Thomas began regular reviewing for the Morning Post *in order to meet the expense that their new accommodations added to the family's already strained budget.*

Description of Berryfield Cottage and the environs (Helen Thomas, World Without End, *pp. 112–114)*

We lived at this farm for three years. Here Elizabeth had learned to walk, and Philip had grown from a baby to a little boy. Here things had gone fairly well with us materially, and here more than anywhere else I had become familiar with farm life. I no longer looked at it eagerly and curiously, but lived it, not unconsciously as the labourers did, but aware all the time of its richness and variety, its crudeness and its beauty, its hardness and its happiness, its cruelty and its innocence, so that when we heard we must leave the farm we could not at first believe that this life had come to an end. The farmer was retiring and had let the farm. As the new man wanted the house, we had to go.

Philip was now six years old and we felt we had better move to a place where there was a school. We remembered the co-educational school in Hampshire I had heard of years ago. So I went to see the school and the country, and, if I liked both, to make inquiries about a house.

I spent a day looking over the school and talking to the headmaster—or rather trying to, but he being very reserved and silent, and I very timid of this austere-looking man, we did not talk nearly as much as I had hoped. However, being prejudiced in favour of the school and liking all I saw, I stayed to see if I could find a house. The country all round was particularly beautiful, being hilly and wooded and untouched by the jerry-builder. I found a house that would suit us perfectly. David approved of the house, but the school he left to me. The country satisfied him completely. So we decided without hesitation to move there and send our children to the famous school.

The house was originally a small farmhouse. It was about a hundred years old and built of flint and brick, with tiny flints let into the pointing. It was a saying that the flint and brick houses were held together by tenpenny nails, because of the likeness of these little round stones to the heads of large nails. It stood on a little rise of a winding lane which ran at the foot of the steep sides of a raised plateau. The irregular sloping edge was in some parts bare like the downs; in other parts covered in a thick growth of trees—beech and yew for the most part—called hang-

Edward Thomas in 1906, just after the move to Berryfield Cottage (Collection of Myfanwy Thomas)

ers. Our cottage lay at the foot of one of the bare slopes—a steep hill dotted here and there with juniper bushes, but crowned with a group of fir trees. To reach this hillside you crossed a rough field sometimes crimson with sainfoin, or orange with dandelions, or silver with dandelion clocks according to the time of the year. A large old-fashioned garden stretched in front of the house running parallel to the lane—and above it, for you entered the garden up half a dozen steps from the lane. Every sort of flower and bush flourished in this garden. Its ancient hedges harboured many kinds of birds, and the yew tree by the gate was the home of a gold-crested wren.

We were very isolated here, for though it was not much more than a mile from the village and the school, we were tucked away among trees and hills, and the winding lane which led to the outer world was the darkest lane I have ever known; so deep and dark it was that the entrance to it on the main road looked like the entrance to a tunnel. On the other side of the house the land sloped down to a stream which flowed through a wild water-meadow full of forget-me-nots, meadow-sweet, mare's tails and loose strife. At night all we could hear was the wind in the hanger, the barking of foxes who lived there, and the hooting of owls. It was a romantic and beautiful spot, and the house belonged to it and we loved it from the first. David of course began exploring the country round, and soon became familiar with the footpaths and byways. We found we were a few miles from Selborne and the place where Cobbett was born, and within a day's walk of Winchester.

In 1907 Thomas was commissioned to write the life of Richard Jefferies, his boyhood hero and literary model. Working arduously on it, he produced an acclaimed biography in 1908, but his home life was deteriorating and his marriage was foundering. His depression eventually compelled him to finish the book in Suffolk, where he became entangled in an embarrassing flirtation with a seventeen-year-old, Hope Webb. Thomas later wrote about the affair in The South Country *and in* Rest and Unrest *(1910).*

Excerpts from Q. D. Leavis's review of Richard Jefferies: His Life and Work *praising Thomas's pioneering work in biography* (Scrutiny, *6 [1938], pp. 436–437)*

Disinterested campaigning for Jefferies would rather ask Messrs. Hutchinson to reprint Edward Thomas's *Richard Jefferies, His Life and Work* (1908) (preferably in the cheap pocket edition); since second-hand booksellers ask a guinea for this Life there must be a long-felt want. This book should be recognized as a classic in critical biography, to stand with Lockhart's Scott and Mrs. Gaskell's Brontë in point of intrinsic interest and containing better literary criticism than many critical works. The well-known fact that Thomas did hack-work for publishers has probably prevented recognition of this book, which he did voluntarily and evidently took much trouble to perfect. Since subsequent writers on Jefferies take all their facts from him as well as his careful bibliography, generally without acknowledgment, and since there is nothing more to be found out about Jefferies (the old inhabitants who knew him having passed away and Thomas anyhow observing "Of the man himself we know, and apparently can know, very little"), to reprint Thomas's work would automatically render further book making unnecessary. His is a model biography. The author is recognized as being present only by the sympathy that informs the narrative and the intelligence that directs the criticism and determines the selections. The selections from Jefferies' works there are so abundant and well-chosen that Thomas's Life of itself will send the reader to their sources.

Excerpts from Thomas's letter to Gordon Bottomley discussing his infatuation with Hope Webb, 7 February 1908 (R.

Bronwen, Helen, and Merfyn Thomas at New Year 1907 (R. George Thomas, Edward Thomas: A Portrait*)*

George Thomas, ed., Letters from Edward Thomas to Gordon Bottomley, *p. 156)*

. . . My health keeps good in this bracing air with few worries & a useful medicine. But I believe my specialist is lazy with me: I am too docile a patient & too schoolboyish & unquestioning with him; as soon as I get into his room I relapse & expect him to discover everything—So I shan't go often again even if I couldn't afford it. Among few disturbances here I got very fond of a girl of 17 with two long plaits of dark brown hair & the richest grey eyes, very wild & shy, to whom I could not say 10 words, nor she to me. She used to milk the 2 cows her father owned, but has now gone away to school. She is a clever child who has begun to write verse. But I liked her for her perfect wild youthfulness & remoteness from myself & now I think of her every day in vain acquiescent dissatisfaction, & shall perhaps never see her again, & shall be sad to hear she ever likes anyone else even tho she will never like me. Which reminds me that Garnett has been praising *The Heart of England*—"The Brook," "A Winter Morning," "First Daffodils," "Fox Hunt" &c. & says I am a poet & says my self-consciousness is akin to my sensitiveness & both due to my *youthfulness*. I suppose I am youthful to like a girl in this way. Yet you have said I am older than the eagle cock that blinks & blinks. Which is right? Both? I used to think him a good & invariably unbiassed critic, but now he praises me I doubt him! . . .

*Thomas's narrative of his affair with Hope Webb (*The South Country, *pp. 84–87)*

It was now that I first accepted the invitation of a relation who lived on the east coast very near the sea. The sea had a sandy shore bounded by a perpendicular sandy cliff, to the edge of which came rough moorland. The sea washed the foot of the cliff at high tide and swept the yellow sand clean twice a day, wiping away all footprints and leaving a fresh arrangement of blue pebbles glistering in the bitter wind. It was impossible to be more alone than on this sand, and I was contented again. The sea brought back the feeling I had when I lay in the buttercup field—the cemetery—and looked into the sky. Walking over the moor the undulations of the land hid and revealed the sea in an always unexpected way, and often as I turned suddenly I seemed to see the blue sky extended so as to reach nearly to my feet and halfway up it went small brown or white clouds like birds—like ships—in fact they were ships sailing on a sea that mingled with the sky. It seemed a beautiful life, where clouds could not help being finely spun or

Thomas in 1907, about the time he became infatuated with Hope Webb (Collection of Myfanwy Thomas)

carved, or pebbles help being delicious to eye and touch. But out of the extremity of my happiness came my worst grief. I fell in love. I fell in love with one of my cousins, a girl of seventeen. She never professed to return my love, but she was a most true friend, and for a time I was intoxicated with the delight; I now envy even the brief moment of pain and misery that I had in those days.

She was clever and understanding so that I was always at my best with her, and yet, too, she was as sweet as a child and strange as an animal. The few moments of pain were when I saw her with the other girls. When they were together, running on the sands or talking or dancing they seemed all to be one, like the wind; and sometimes I thought that like the wind they had no heart amongst them—except mine that raced with the runners and sighed among the laughers. It was lovely to see her with animals! with cows or horses, her implicit motherhood going out to them in an animal kindness, a bluff tenderness without thought. At times I looked carefully and solemnly into her eyes until I was lost in a curious pleasure like that of walking in a shadowy, still, cold place, a cathedral or wintry grove—she had the largest of dark grey eyes; and she did not turn away or smile, but looked fearlessly forward, careless and unashamed like a deep pool in a wood unused to wayfarers. Then she seemed so much a child, and I longed for the days (which I had never really had) when I could have been as careless and bold and free as she was. No, I could never teach those eyes and lips the ways of love: that was for some boy to do. And I thought I will be content to love her and to have her friendliness. I was old for my years, and my life without the influence of women in office and lodgings, I thought, had made me unfit for her delicate ways. I turned away and the sunny ships in the sea were mournful because of my thoughts. But I could not wait. I told her my love. She was not angry or indifferent. She did not reject it. She was afraid. They sent her away to college. She overworked and overplayed, and they have told me she is now a schoolmistress. I see her sad and firm with folded hands. When I knew her she was tall and straight, with long brown hair in two heavy plaits, a shining, rounded brow, dark-lashed, grey eyes, and a smile of inexpressible sweetness in which I once or twice surprised her, pleased with the happiness and beauty of her thoughts and of Nature.

When I had lost her, or thought I had—

> Not comforted to live
> But that there is this jewel in the world
> Which I may see again—

I resolved that I would not be a slave any more. For a few weeks I used to fancy it was only by a chance I had lost her, and every now and then as I mused over it I got heated and my thoughts raced forward as if in the hope of overtaking and averting that very evil chance which had already befallen, and had in fact caused the train of thought.

Excerpt from Thomas's letter to Gordon Bottomley expressing his dislike for London, 6 November 1908 (R.

In July 1908 Thomas began working on another natural history book, The South Country. *Depressed and disillusioned with his literary career, however, he accepted the position of assistant secretary to a Royal Commission studying Welsh monuments the following month. This appointment was brief, for the work was mainly in London, and his dislike of the city and the travel prompted him to resign by Christmas that same year.*

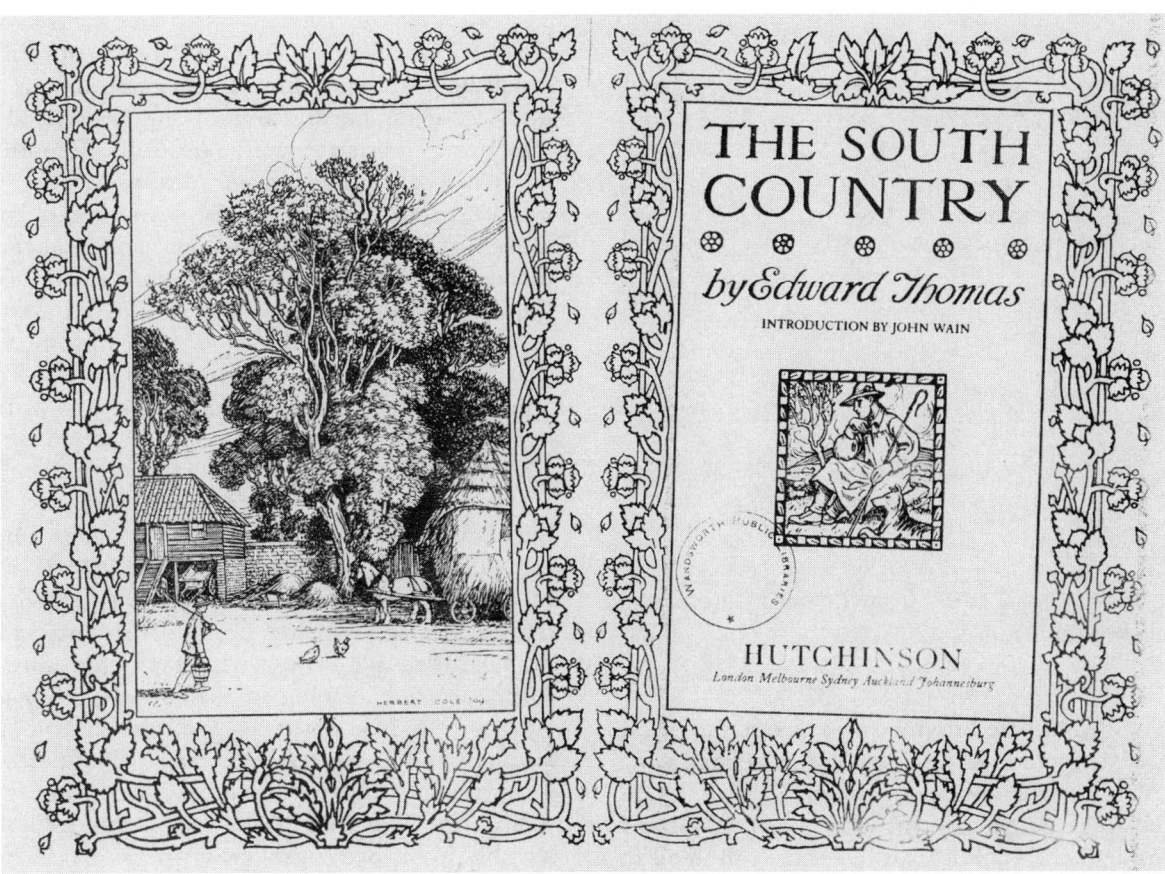

Title page and frontispiece for the book which, in her introduction to the 1932 edition, Helen Thomas describes as "one of the happiest of the prose works of Edward Thomas"

Thomas's earnings from the Royal Commission freed him from financial pressure for a brief period, and he began writing short stories that were later collected in Rest and Unrest *and* Light and Twilight *(1911). During this time he also contributed reviews to the newly founded* The English Review.

Title page for Thomas's prose collection that includes "Winter Music," an essay previously unpublished

George Thomas, ed., Letters from Edward Thomas to Gordon Bottomley, *p. 174)*

... How I hate London; no exercise, no air, & continual bellyache & head ache & discomfort all over. Also I waste time seeing people. It is not good for me to see people as I listen to so much that I don't understand—politics, art & so on—& pretend to take an interest & say (& for the moment think I mean) foolish things. I have a feeling of returning with difficulty to myself after these histrionic bouts. People despise me too—with reservations on account of my superficial amiability & profile. When I saw on a newspaper placard that a Railway Porter had just had £17,000 left him, I was quite seriously thinking how I should like to have that much or a little less so as to be able to stay somewhere alone & not have to work—in fact I hurried back to my lodgings with a sort of flushed expectation of I don't know exactly what, not £17,000 perhaps. I didn't find anything.

How nice it would be to be dead if only we could know we were dead. That is what I hate, the not being able to turn round in the grave & to say It is over. With me I suppose it is vanity: I don't want to do so difficult a thing as dying without any chance of applause after having done it.

Excerpt from Thomas's favorable review of Ezra Pound's Personae (English Review, *2 [June 1909], 627-630)*

To say what this poet has not is not difficult; it will help to define him. He has no obvious grace, no sweetness, hardly any of the superficial good qualities of modern versifiers; not the smooth regularity of the Tennysonian tradition, nor the wavering, uncertain languor of the new, though there is more in his rhythms than is apparent at first through his carelessness of ordinary effects. He has not the current melancholy or resignation or unwillingness to live; nor the kind of feeling for nature that runs to minute description and decorative metaphor. He cannot be usefully compared with any living writers, though he has read Mr. Yeats. Browning and Whitman he respects, and he could easily burlesque Browning if he liked. He knows mediaeval poetry in the popular tongues, and Villon, and Ossian. He is equally fond of strict stanzas of many rhymes, of blank verse with many unfinished lines, of rhymeless or almost rhymeless lyrics, of Pindarics with or without rhyme. But these forms are not striking in themselves, since all are subdued to his spirit; in each he is true in his strength and weakness to himself, full of personality and with such power to express it that from the first to the last lines of most of his poems he holds us steadily in his own pure, grave, passionate world. . . .

In late 1909 the reunited Thomas family moved to new lodgings built in accord with the teachings of utopian architect and designer William Morris. This house at Wick Green, about which Thomas enthusiastically wrote in his poem "Wind and Mist," was a promising domestic setting, but when his wife became pregnant and had to give up her part-time teaching post at Bedales (where the Thomas children were being educated free of charge), Thomas was forced to churn out books as quickly as possible in order to meet the added expenses.

Helen Thomas, about the time of the move to Wick Green in 1909 (Collection of Myfanwy Thomas)

Thomas's poetic reflections on the house at Wick Green (R. George Thomas, ed., The Collected Poems of Edward Thomas, *pp. 153, 155*)

Wind and Mist

They met inside the gateway that gives the view,
A hollow land as vast as heaven. "It is
A pleasant day, sir." "A very pleasant day."
"And what a view here. If you like angled fields
Of grass and grain bounded by oak and thorn,
Here is a league. Had we with Germany
To play upon this board it could not be
More dear than April has made it with a smile.
The fields beyond that league close in together
And merge, even as our days into the past,
Into one wood that has a shining pane
Of water. Then the hills of the horizon—
That is how I should make hills had I to show
One who would never see them what hills were like."
"Yes. Sixty miles of South Downs at one glance.
Sometimes a man feels proud at them, as if
He had just created them with one mighty thought."
"That house, though modern, could not be better planned
For its position. I never liked a new
House better. Could you tell me who lives in it?"
"No one." "Ah—and I was peopling all
Those windows on the south with happy eyes,
The terrace under them with happy feet;
Girls—" "Sir, I know. I know. I have seen that house
Through mist look lovely as a castle in Spain,
And airier. I have thought: 'Twere happy there
To live.' And I have laughed at that
Because I lived there then." "Extraordinary."
"Yes, with my furniture and family
Still in it, I, knowing every nook of it
And loving none, and in fact hating it."
"Dear me! How could that be? But pardon me."
"No offence. Doubtless the house was not to blame,
But the eye watching from those windows saw,
Many a day, day after day, mist—mist
Like chaos surging back—and felt itself
Alone in all the world, marooned alone.
We lived in clouds, on a cliff's edge almost
(You see), and if clouds went, the visible earth
Lay too far off beneath and like a cloud.
I did not know it was the earth I loved
Until I tried to live there in the clouds
And the earth turned to cloud."

"You had a garden
Of flint and clay, too." "True; that was real enough.
The flint was the one crop that never failed.
The clay first broke my heart, and then my back;
And the back heals not. There were other things
Real, too. In that room at the gable a child
Was born while the wind chilled a summer dawn:
Never looked grey mind on a greyer one
Than when the child's cry broke above the groans."
"I hope they were both spared." "They were. Oh yes.
But flint and clay and childbirth were too real
For this cloud castle. I had forgot the wind.
Pray do not let me get on to the wind.
You would not understand about the wind.
It is my subject, and compared with me
Those who have always lived on the firm ground
Are quite unreal in this matter of the wind.
There were whole days and nights when the wind and I
Between us shared the world, and the wind ruled
And I obeyed it and forgot the mist.
My past and the past of the world were in the wind.

Now you will say that though you understand
And feel for me, and so on, you, yourself
Would find it different. You are all like that
If once you stand here free from wind and mist.
I might as well be talking to wind and mist.
You would believe the house-agent's young man
Who gives no heed to anything I say.
Good morning. But one word. I want to admit
That I would try the house once more, if I could;
As I should like to try being young again."

Thomas wrote twelve books to support his family between 1910 and 1912. In September 1911 he suffered an emotional breakdown from this workload, and he hoped to recover by going to Wales to walk and gather material for a new book about George Borrow. In spite of (or perhaps because of) his escape from the family, Thomas continued to feel guilt and depression.

Excerpt from Thomas's letter to Gordon Bottomley about his continuing depression, 5 December 1912 (R. George Thomas, ed., Letters from Edward Thomas to Gordon Bottomley, *p. 226)*

. . . I should have written except that my letters have been getting worse & worse. In fact for 3 months I have been advertising my sorrows & decimating my friends. Briefly this year has been a bad one. I have gone down. I have had less & less work. My habit of introspection & self contempt has at last broken my spirit. Intense irritability made life intolerable in a cottage where I could not suffer without making 4 others suffer with me. So I left home in October & came here as a boarder at [Vivian Locke] Ellis's house for a start, & have worked moderately well & had cloistered days. A couple of days at home were enough to tumble me down again to an abject state from which I am now getting up. Helen & the children come here for Christmas. Tell me when if at all you can see me, supposing you are at the Shiffolds. I am not so bad to meet as to have letters from, as a rule. The thing is to avoid self discussion. In any case forgive what there was to forgive in my last letter & tell me how you & Emily are & believe that such of me as remains is

Biographer's analysis of Thomas's depression (John Moore, The Life and Letters of Edward Thomas, *p. 171)*

He blamed himself overmuch, for at this time he was a very sick man indeed. In the autumn of 1911 his neurasthenia, his "whatever-it-was," reached an acute crisis, and Helen actually feared for his sanity. The doctor had only cured him of doctors; the green pills and the trivial abstentions had done him no good. He had even tried six months of strict vegetarianism, and was no better, was only a bit thinner, as the result of it; and now at Michaelmas, the melancholy was perhaps more profound than it had ever been. His soul was "a blasted heath." "I haven't an ounce of my little courage left, except for endurance," he said. Now he began to fear that he could no longer even endure. "I have got too low," he wrote to Haynes, "and have been down too long to think much about getting up again." The usual money troubles preyed on his mind; he could not work; and he was more savagely self-critical, more bitterly dissatisfied with himself, than ever.

*Helen Thomas's fictional reconstruction of Thomas's state of mind near the time of his breakdown (*World Without End, *pp. 148–149)*

I had merely to give a swift look at his face as he strode in at the gate to see the terrible cloud of melancholy which was hanging low over his spirit, and blotting out like blackest night all light, all joy, all love. Without a word he flung himself in his armchair in the living-room, staring in front of him or at me, while I spoke to him of everyday affairs.

The elder children were at school; the baby playing with a neighbour's child. I prayed they might not come in just yet, but in a moment I saw them coming down the road. I ran out and told them to do an errand for me and then play in the meadow. "Daddy has come home, but he's very tired," I explained, but before they could run off he was there.

"Why are you keeping the children away?" he asked.

"I only thought you were rather tired," I replied, "and, that I'd get you your tea in peace while they played out of doors."

"Why should I be tired when I've just had a fortnight of idleness and not a stroke of work done and none to do—not a book from the *Chronicle*—and my article back from the *New Weekly*. Tired! Tired is not what I am. I'm sick of the whole of life—of myself chiefly, of you and children. You must hate me and despise me, but you can't hate me as much as I hate the whole business, and as I despise myself for not putting an end to it."

After finishing his study of Belgian aesthete Maurice Maeterlinck, Thomas continued to work on his book about Borrow and gathered material for commissions to write about A. C.

Swinburne and Walter Pater. At the same time he received successful medical treatment from Godwin Baynes, a young doctor who was interested in the work of Sigmund Freud and who specialized in nervous conditions. Thomas's writing of The Happy-Go-Lucky Morgans *(1913), his autobiographical novel, also encouraged him to scrutinize his life with some detachment, and with this objectivity he became determined to plod on, despite his personal problems.*

Thomas's studies of Maurice Maeterlinck and Walter Pater compelled him to concentrate on ways language can be used for literary purposes and later affected his own poetry (Stan Smith, "A Language Not To Be Betrayed," Literature and History, *4 [Autumn 1976], pp. 73–80).*

Language's role as the repository and articulation of a culture . . . is a recurrent theme of Thomas's criticism. Folksongs, he says in one review, "imbibed the history of men as abundantly as language itself"; while, in another, he suggests that, for the men who sing them, "England is really old and as full of the past as language is." The antiquity of the language is cognate with the antiquity of the land—both partake of the same mystery. In *Maurice Maeterlinck* he refers to the Belgian's proposition that several words of the Flemish dialect "'still contain images dating from the glacial epochs.'" These "'oldest modes of speech'" express a sensibility all but superseded, "'in which words are really lamps behind ideas, while for us ideas must give light to words.'" He quotes with approval Maeterlinck's description of the transcendent in language:

> "Every language thinks always more than the man, even the man of genius, who employs it, and who is only its heart for the time being. . . . A sincere and honest author is never obscure in the eternal sense of the word, because he always understands himself in a way . . . infinitely beyond anything that he says. It is only artificial ideas which spring up in real darkness and flourish solely in literary epochs and in the insincerity of self-conscious ages, when the thought of the writer is poorer than his expression."

The two studies *Maurice Maeterlinck* (1911) and *Walter Pater* (1913) attempt an extended critique of contemporary aesthetics from the premise afforded by this remark. The pre-eminence of style in Pater, for example, is seen as the inevitable consequence of Pater's supercilious detachment, in which thought, cut off from its sustaining context of action, is necessarily impoverished. The attempt to render language autotelic, as empty of content as music, was the reflex of a situation in which the individual himself had assumed a marginal and self-sufficient character:

The isolation of the individual among the terrible inharmonious multitudes impressed him and made it seem certain to him that art should become "an end in itself, unrelated, unassociated." He himself is one who continually writes of all things as "spectacle."

Uprooting language from its social matrix leads to an inevitable blight:

> Pater was . . . forced, against his judgment, to use words as bricks, as tin soldiers, instead of flesh and blood and genius. Inability to survey the whole history of every word must force the perfectly self-conscious writer into this position. Only when a word has become necessary to him can a man use it safely; if he tries to impress words by force on a sudden occasion, they will either perish of his violence or betray him. No man can decree the value of one word, unless it is his own invention; the value which it will have in his hands has been decreed by his own past, by the past of his race.

"Value" here, as in the poem "What will they do?," is opposed to "price," the intrinsic worth to the externally regulated estimate. Language is not a commodity but a living interchange, in which the individual celebrates an almost sacramental communion with his culture; in his personal appropriation of a common meaning, he both recreates and extends it. Pater's words are dead because he denies their social function as instruments for organizing and articulating a shared subject-world:

> It is clear that they have been carefully chosen as the right and effective words, but they stick out because the labour of composition has become so self-conscious and mechanical that cohesion and perfect consistency are impossible. The words have only an isolated value; they are labels; they are shorthand; they are anything but living and social words.

The congealing of the artist's labour into an alien product seems to be the reflex of a more general alienation of labour-power. The linking of "self-conscious" and "mechanical" is significant. The process by which liberating "creation" (the "ecstasy" of "Words") becomes alienated "labour" produces alienation in the instrument too; the "living and social" becomes "mechanical" and "isolated." The contrast between "significance" and "literal meaning" in the following passage repeats this opposition, as the recurrence of the concept of "mechanical" form suggests:

> Attention to mere physical detail almost seems to be destroying the power to see a thing as one and a whole, and apart from its mechanism and anatomy. . . . He becomes insensible to the significance, apart from the

literal meaning, of some words.... A man so attentive to detail must spoil some at least of that detail by failing to relate it to the whole; and by seeing words singly he must miss their effect on readers who see them in company with others.

"Significance" unites subjective and objective dimensions, when a specious nominalism tries to divorce them. "In the name there's nothing," once that name is detached from the mysterious nexus of experience where it finds its meaning.

The attempt to make words "correspond exactly to any object," Thomas points out in *Feminine Influences on the Poets* (1910), to give them the clinical precision of "scientific terms" requires that "they are first killed." What he calls, in a review, "the absurdity of this sham search for the *mot propre*," and, in *Lafcadio Hearn* (1912), "the ideal of 'one thing, one word,'— one word chosen deliberately as if it were dead and still and powerless to retaliate and live alone," express a fetichized aesthetics appropriate to an age of positivistic science. For Paterian aestheticism is, in reality, an adaptation to literature of the naturalistic fallacy that lies behind contemporary science. "Symbolism," that other *fin-de-siècle* reaction to positivism, succumbed almost as thoroughly to the same delusions. Maeterlinck's assumption that words are products, rather than social processes generated by a commonalty of meaning, is the illusion of a print culture that has dissociated language from speech. "Symbolist" poetry is the ultimate stage of an individualism that privatizes language into a plurality of self-sufficient universes of discourse. Novalis, Thomas notes, had predicted this conclusion:

He foresees poetry such as the Symbolists tried to write when he speaks of

"Poems which are simply sonorous and full of impressive words, but without sense and cohesion, of which at most only penstrokes are comprehensible, like fragments of the most diverse things. This true poetry might have, at most, a general allegoric sense and an indirect action like that of music."

Maeterlinck's Symbolist poetry, he suggests, fails because it substitutes, for the vital commerce of mind and world, a passive cataloguing of sensations and objects in which both mind and world undergo fragmentation. In Maeterlinck's volume *Serres Chaudes,* one poem comes near to acknowledging this:

Here, too, "with their counterparts in my soul," if not a complete explanation is a timid admission of the need for one. But the piece is hardly more than a catalogue of symbols that have no more literary value than words in a dictionary. It ignores the fact that no word . . . has any value beyond its surface value except what it receives from its neighbours and its position among them. Each man makes his own language in the main unconsciously and inexplicably, unless he is still at an age when he is an admiring but purely aesthetic collector of words.

The analogy recurs in a discussion of the "peasant" poet John Clare, who demonstrates that the transcendent quality of language lies in the antiquity of its mediations between men and things and their own past:

He reminds us that words are alive, and not only alive, but still half-wild and imperfectly domesticated. They are quiet and gentle in their ways, but are like cats—to whom night overthrows our civilization and servitude— who seem to love us but will starve in the house which we have left, and thought to have emptied of all worth. . . . The magic of words is due to their living freely among things, and no man knows how they came together in just that order when a beautiful thing is made.... Grown men with dictionaries are as murderous of words as entomologists of butterflies.

The words embody a cultural essence which . . . has the power to survive massive social change (the abandoned house is a frequent image of such change for Thomas). Carnal, vitalistic and evolutionary metaphors are insistent in Thomas's remarks on language: language is a living, "ductile, . . . almost fluid" organism, responsive to every change in sensibility and to the wider social transformations such change expresses.

The shortcoming of Thomas's stylistic reflections is not that he considers form in some unpolitical vacuum but rather that, too often, he assumes an over-simple correspondence between language and social experience. He assumes too readily that language in some straightforward way directly reflects class and culture, so that every countryman speaks with a tangy authenticity that is rooted in the rich humus of English rural culture, while every clerk and intellectual speaks a language which reeks of the lumber-room and the archive.

His critical prose repeatedly finds otherwise, in its shrewdly empirical analysis of a variety of styles; but the core conviction persists. The congruence of language and social identity in fact lies near the centre of Thomas's structure of feeling, a carrying through into critical theory of the populism that led him to admire the folksong, enjoy hard physical labour, and despise privilege, cynicism, and the laws of property. Yet his comments on Pater have some substance. His basic criticism is not that Pater speaks with the intonation of his class but that, because of his self-insulation from any wider discourse in which meanings are made and remade, he fails to speak with the cultural specificity of cadence and inflexion that would, in its fidelity, endow his words with a more universal appeal. Pater has, in a way, imposed a private division of labour upon himself, separating the *littérateur* off from the rest of his personality:

> his words . . . have not been lived with sufficiently. Unless a man write with his whole nature concentrated upon his subject he is unlikely to take hold of another man. For that man will read, not as a scholar, a philologist, a word-fancier, but as a man with all his race, age, class, and personal experience brought to bear on the matter.

. . . The essay "Mothers and Sons" in *Rest and Unrest* (1910) presents an alternative vision. It develops a sustained analogy between language and social identity, opening with a solitary dawn journey over the hills:

> They had been felling much timber, and it lay about on the steep slopes under the moon, more like the crude shapes of chaos out of which trees and men might some day be made.

As a private compensation for this desolate landscape, the fictitious narrator summons up a vision of cosmic harmony which elevates his imagination to an elective superiority over the fragmented world below:

> It was dawn that recalled me to myself. . . . The sky, as quiet as my mind, had brought forth a scene of clouds so harmonious with my unconscious life that at first it seemed some noble dream blessedly given to me than something which all men might see; and I was astonished as perhaps a poet is when he has wrought something lovelier than he knew out of a long silent strife.

This godlike vision cannot for long transcend the world of other men to which it belongs; it is, after all, a common property, even though only one man sees it:

> There I heard the symphony which the stars and the mountains of earth and the hearts of men and the songs of rivers and birds make together in immortal ears.

Hubris rapidly succumbs to disillusion. He feels the need to communicate, but shrinks from doing so in fear of recrimination and mockery, when he awakes to see "black and sinister" chimneys and an earth made "invalid, pathetic, and bereaved" by industrialization. The village he comes to is despoiled, its river polluted, its people, he feels, degraded, by the changeover from an agricultural to an industrial economy. Yet it is the narrator's own sentimentality, with its Wildean flamboyance, which receives the full weight of the prose's indignation:

> As I walked past the shops, neither urban nor rustic, entirely new and as glaring as possible, but awkward, without tradition and without originality, I was full of magnificent regrets. I ought to have had a mantle of tragic hue to swathe myself in mysterious and haughty woe and to flutter ineffable things in the wind, as I trod the streets that were desolate to me.

In contrast with the "raptures of regret about the growth of the village" in which the narrator and the poet he visits "complained together," Thomas sets the speech of the Owens, a working-class family, into whose home he is invited. The "melody" of their speech fulfils, as a social activity, that earlier private vision apparently detached from any imaginable universe of discourse. Language here is simultaneously personal and social, for, though the harmony transcends its individual voices, it enhances their individuality. It represents for Thomas an epitome of the authentic community which redeems the self from unproductive isolation, and sustains it against the encroachments of alienating and divisive economic forces:

> Admirable as they were apart they made an indescribable harmony together. Sometimes all talked at once. . . . Sometimes one told a tale and all attended. Sometimes the talk travelled mysteriously from one to another, and to and fro and crosswise, as if some outside power had descended invisible in their midst and were making a melody out of their lips and eyes, a melody which, I think, never ceased in their hearts.

These are those Welsh "nightingales" of "Words," who "have no wings." Among them, utter frankness is the rule, for deceit would be a decomposition of language, a kind of division of labour in communication. They are "fearless," Thomas's recurrent value-word to describe the spiritual quality of the people:

> The father spoke his thoughts and the boy his, and there was nothing which anyone of them would have said or secretly laughed at with his companions which they would not say before all.

Such candour is capable of taking up and transfiguring the external events which threaten to disrupt the coherence of traditional meanings. It can not only survive but transform the profoundest social revolutions:

> I was disturbed at all the gaiety in the heart of the village darkness, partly because I was unable to see why it should exist, and as foolishly sure that there would never be an end to the darkness unless it eclipsed this gaiety in a revolution of some kind–impious thought and unpardonable if it had not been vain. That gaiety cannot be quenched.

Any renovation of poetic language requires a cultural revolution that would realign the poet with a community of this kind, uncorroded by self-indulgent nostalgia, idealist fantasies, or a disabling cynicism; for all alike express a class attitude, summed up in "Mothers and Sons" as "something between shame and the pride of the convalescent in his tyrant bed." Unlike Wilde, the narrator of the essay can see a cure: convalescence implies a transition to health, a movement which is enacted by the narrative structure of the essay itself.

Only in the recovery of that verbal sincerity and wholeness, that sensuous immediacy of vision and speech which characterized less self-conscious ages, can the poet escape the impasse in which Thomas saw his predecessors transfixed. The successful poet, he argues in an early review, achieves an effect at once "strangely mystical and strangely material," in which fact is transfigured into symbol quite naturally (so that the Hog's Back *is* the Hog's Back). And this "extreme definiteness of imagination," he says, in a passage which connects his literary theory with the social populism that pervades his writings, "is a link between the peasants and the greatest poets, who constantly prove that they have seen what they have imagined."

Thomas's death at Vimy Ridge in 1917 in a way consummated without resolving the contradictions of his life, putting an end to that conflict of populism and isolation, tradition and radicalism, nostalgia and hope which, in the poetry, exists as lived tensions and anxieties, doubts, hesitations and bewilderment. His poetry thus inscribes what Thomas himself once called "a subtler moral" than poetry "in a very obvious way influenced by the spirit of the age," revealing a mind "puzzled to some purpose by the riddles of his own day," able to speak only with the obliquity of "A language not to be betrayed."

Excerpt from Thomas's letter to Gordon Bottomley referring to Dr. Baynes's help in curing his depression, 18 April 1912 (R. George Thomas, ed., Letters from Edward Thomas to Gordon Bottomley, *p. 221)*

Thank you for your book. It has reached me at a Manor House on the Somerset border where I am staying with Clifford Bax and a doctor, a friend of his. This doctor is working magic with my disordered intellects & in a few hours I shall be better able to enjoy *Chambers of Imagery II* than ever before.

Thomas's resolve to continue writing as a livelihood was strengthened by a chance meeting with children's writer Eleanor Farjeon in late 1912. Her role was that of a caring and undemanding platonic lover who did not create sexual tension but offered an understanding, supportive feminine presence from whom Thomas could derive confidence and diversion. Her society emphasized outdoor activities such as walking, camping, and canoeing that offered Thomas an opportunity to relax, to escape the responsibilities of fatherhood and marriage. Helen Thomas accepted the role Farjeon played and was pleased that Thomas had found a female friend who was so compatible.

The foreword to Eleanor Farjeon's Edward Thomas: The Last Four Years *(1958), which recounts her friendship with the poet*

My friendship with Edward Thomas began in the late autumn of 1912. It was a friendship death could not end when, in April 1917, he died.

These years live for me, not only in my heart, but in the many letters Edward wrote to me during them, only a few of which have been published; they will appear in this book with Helen Thomas's loving consent. It is because of them that I have chosen to make Edward's the first book of my memoirs, beginning in midstream before going back to an earlier part of my life. Edward Thomas has his sure place now among our most English poets, and anything connected with him has an importance outside myself. The letters, printed in full without omissions, form a running record of his last four years. Their sequence has much more than a reference value; to lovers of his work it will help to reveal something more of one of the least self-revealing of men: a man whose "central evil" was self-consciousness, "carried as far beyond selfishness as selfishness is beyond self-denial." He could write this of himself in 1913, only two years before the torturing self-consciousness was transformed into the poet's self-expression, and two years later still into the self-denial of the soldier's death in France. He could have been safe, if he had chosen to be.

So, this first book is, in a sense, a double memoir. The continuity of his letters enables me to follow closely the course of those years in my life, with annotations and descriptions of things we did, and friends we had, in common. Many of these friends will reappear in my other books, as they connect themselves with the central object. The object here is Edward.

Helen Thomas on holiday, holding Myfanwy, with Merfyn in Chiswick, about 1912 (Collection of Myfanwy Thomas)

lamentable ignorance of the realities he loved best. I couldn't tell a sycamore from an ash, and was apt to write of trees as temples of Pan. But I could walk and carry a knapsack, and thanks to my father had been brought up on nothing second-rate in poetry. Since 1910 my brother Bertie and I had found our way together into an exciting group of new friends. When among them, I still had to struggle against my childhood's legacy of abnormal shyness, and I was only at ease with those who could dispel it. The reserves peculiar to Edward often made it necessary for his friends to meet him more than half-way; with my want of self-confidence I found this difficult. By some means the difficulty was overcome. He counted on me for friendship; and I loved him with all my heart. He was far too penetrating not to know this, but only by two words, in one of his last letters from France, did he allow himself to show me that he knew. Our four years were undemonstrative, and unfailing.

It is important that this should be made clear, and accepted. Surmise and conjecture may sometimes unravel a truth, but oftener lead away from it. A misconception of the nature of our friendship would make Edward Thomas appear to be what he was not. Helen, my brother Bertie, and one or two close friends, had my confidence; Edward trusted me

When I met him I was thirty-one, and only just merging from a fantasy-life into one of natural human relationships. The strange game of TAR which my brother Harry initiated when I was four years old, and which I have described in the book of our childhood, had continued its powerful influence for far too long. I had indulged myself, night and day, in prolonged states of self-hypnosis of which I did not know the danger, and at twenty-nine was as emotionally immature as a girl of eighteen. My undisciplined delight in writing had developed early through poetry and music, instead of through life, and I had written scarcely anything worth keeping.

I wonder now how the sort of person I was could have become a companion to the sort of person Edward was. No one was quicker than he to distinguish what was genuine from what was sham; and to a quarter-century spent in unreal dreams I added a

"The Ford, Ickleford," a drawing by A. L. Collins for Thomas's The Icknield Way *(1913)*

In July 1913 the Thomases again moved to another house, "Yew Tree Cottage" in Steep, Hampshire. Throughout that year, however, Thomas kept his study room in Wick Green, where he composed his nostalgic study of the pastoral, The Country, *in semi-isolation.*

Thomas just after the move to Steep in 1913 (Collection of Myfanwy Thomas)

never to give it to him. If I had, our friendship must have come to an end.

Helen Thomas's reaction to Eleanor Farjeon (named Margaret), as recorded in World Without End *(pp. 148, 151–152)*

Of all these people David had written to me in his daily letters, but especially of this sister. I knew from him that she was not beautiful, but clever and lively and witty; that she not only equalled the young men in whatever was being discussed, but shone above them all in imagination and humour, and excelled them in the games of mental skill they played. I knew, too, that she had met David very much more than half way in their warm friendship which was necessary to win him from sensitive distrust. I knew also from his letters that among this high-spirited, confident, successful crew, in his heart he was bitter and lonely, and that this girl was the only one with whom he had felt easy. . . .

By the noon post come two letters, one from his chief editor, and one in unknown writing, but I guess whose it is. He is still cold and silent to me. I know the strain of these days shows in my face, and I do things clumsily. Tears are very near my eyes, which before were dry and burning. If only I could be alone to cry and cry. But of course I can't.

The letter, as I guessed, is from Margaret, the new friend.

"Margaret wants to come here for a night. Can we have her? She's walking from Haslemere, and on to Winchester. Shall I say yes or no?"

So this wonder of women is coming, and I am glad.

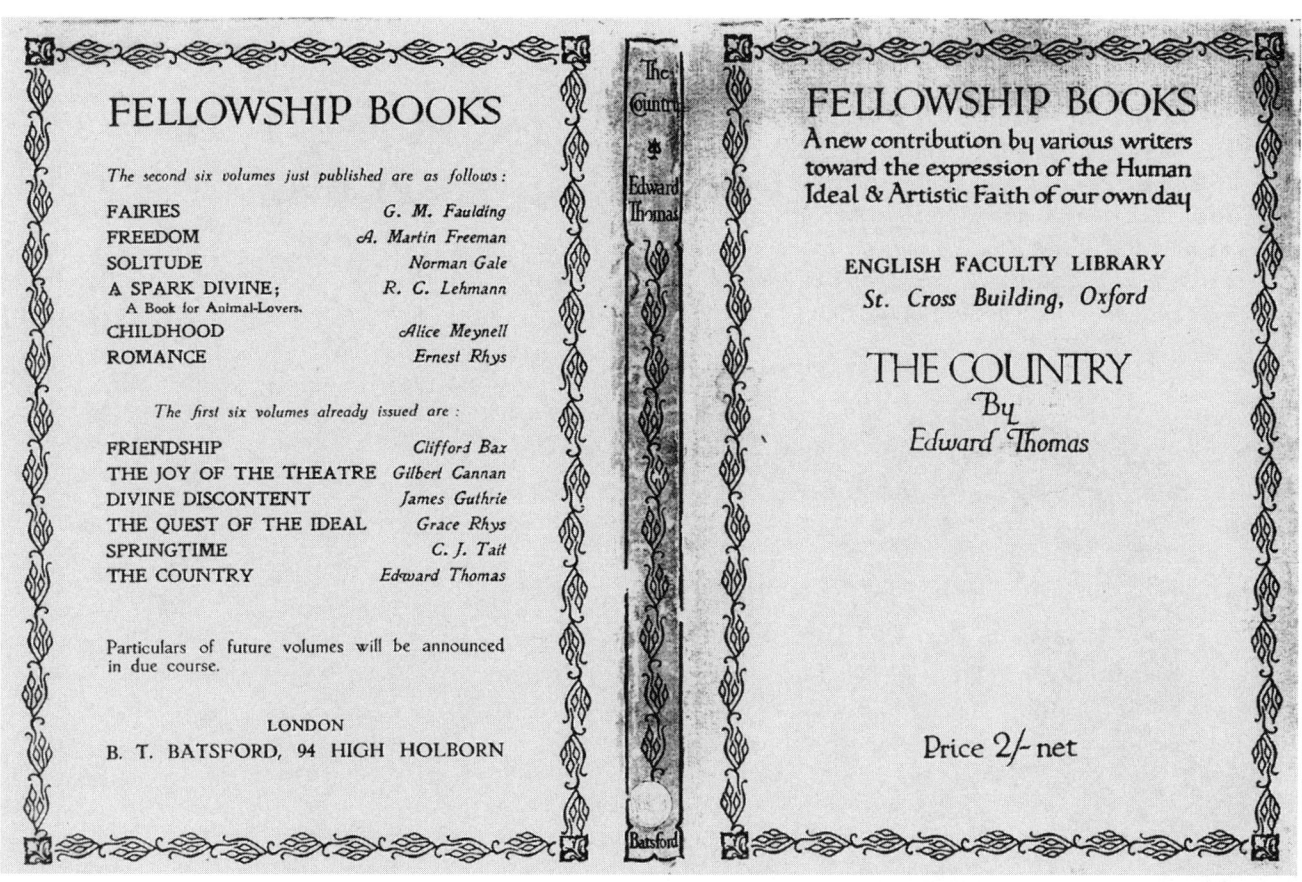

Dust jacket for Thomas's short book in which he expresses his love for rural living: "... it is in the country more often that we become aware, in a sort of majestic quiet, of the destiny which binds us to infinity and eternity."

For somehow, though the thought of meeting strangers, particularly women, fills me with a morbid dread, with her I feel it will be different. But all the same I feel shall not be in any way what she will expect David's wife to be, and this old fear of letting him down to his friend persists. So I write to her, telling her what my fear is, and I dare say revealing to her much more about myself than I had an idea of.

I was busy all the morning making the cottage look its best: scrubbing, polishing, and making cakes. The children and I picked flowers for the rooms—for Margaret's room a shallow bowl of white violets. . . .

David was calm now, but I was still shut out from his love and kindness. He had gone to the study to finish some work, and I was to meet Margaret along the road. I was happily excited, but too conscious of where I fell short of what David's wife should be.

Not far from the village we met.

"You are Margaret!" and "You are Jenny!" was what we said, as we stood for a moment with hands still held. We looked into each other's faces, not inquiringly as if we should say, "Now what are you like, I wonder," but as familiar friends we met; and as friends whose hearts are open to each other we turned together towards the village.

I took her up to her little room of which the window opened to the meadow and the wooded hills beyond.

"You are Margaret!" and "You are Jenny!" we said again, as if Margaret could be no other, and Jenny could be no other and we kissed. While we were unpacking her rucksack, laughing over the way a pretty frock was stuffed in with books and shoes and sponge bag, David's coo-ee came from the wood, and she, leaning out of the window, sent a clear, sweet coo-ee back to him. I hurried her downstairs and showed her the path. "You go to meet him while I butter the potato cakes; the children are there, too."

I thought: "He will be glad to have her. If only I could slip away, so that he would not have the knowledge of my sadness to trouble him; for he punishes himself through me and all is distorted and wrong."

Harold Monro launched his publication of editor Edward Marsh's series of Georgian Poetry *(1912-1922) volumes at the official opening of the Poetry Bookshop in 1913; Thomas subsequently wrote a favorable review of that first 1911-1912 collection. Thomas and Robert Frost met on 6 December of that year, and most literary historians characterize this event as the most important in Thomas's evolution as a poet. Frost gave Thomas the confidence that he needed to write poetry, and the friendship they established became the basis on which Thomas sustained his new artistic endeavors.*

Title page of the book that Robert Frost said included poetry "but in prose form where it did not declare itself"

Robert Frost while living in England, just before he met Edward Thomas (permission of Dartmouth College Library)

Excerpt from Thomas's review of Georgian Poetry 1911-12 *(The Bookman, 43 [March 1913], p. 330)*

"Georgian Poetry" contains "beauteous things." It includes for example long poems by Messrs Abercrombie, Davies, Masefield, Sturge Moore, and James Stephens. It includes the two most impressive of Mr Gordon Bottomley's recent poems, five remarkable pieces by Mr Rupert Brooke, and five representative poems from Mr de la Mare's "Listeners." Altogether it is a brilliant selection from the poetry of 1911 and 1912. But it is less and more than that. It excludes many poems because it aims at showing what young men are typical and promising, what elder men notably reflect the spirit of the moment. Nobody not jaded by excess of poetry or starved for lack of it, will fail to see that there is such a spirit when he meets it thus concentrated. Compare it with a similar book of poetry from 1901 and 1902 and its novelty is apparent. There is, by the way, no anthology of 1901 and 1902, but if it is now too late to make one, it is to be hoped that similar volumes will henceforward be compiled decennially or even quinquennially. If they find editors as generous and impartial as "E.M." they will, like this Georgian anthology, be valuable and delightful.

Thomas's letter to Frost expressing his growing interest in poetry based in the details of daily life, 19 May 1914 (Dartmouth College Library)

Apart from the meeting with Frost, for Thomas the year 1913 proved uneven. Thomas was researching his next book, In Pursuit of Spring *(1914), and he could relieve the constant pressure of work only by relaxing in Norfolk with Farjeon and her circle or by receiving further treatment from Dr. Baynes. As Thomas's meager finances continued to fall short of his expectations, his depression deepened.*

As the friendship between Frost and Thomas grew, the American poet realized that Thomas's emotional state was strained. When Thomas spoke of divorce and expressed concerns about the direction of his writing career, Frost advised him not to divorce Helen and suggested that he consider writing poetry using the subject matter of his prose: Frost clarified this latter recommendation by illustrating what Thomas could do with the prose of In Pursuit of Spring. *Although Thomas did not follow Frost's advice immediately, the suggestion remained with him. He favorably reviewed Frost's* North of Boston *in April 1914, and Thomas celebrated the significance of their friendship in "The Sun Used to Shine."*

Eleanor Farjeon's discussion of the friendship between Thomas and Frost (Edward Thomas: The Last Four Years, *pp. 55–56*)

1914 must be the most important year in Edward's life. In it he discovered his deepest friendship in the American poet Robert Frost, and made in himself the even greater discovery of the English poet Edward Thomas.

When they began to meet in 1913, Frost was a poet unknown in his own country. He had chosen to bring his family to England, where he found a publisher for his first two books of poems. In the second of these, *North of Boston,* Edward made what he knew was the find of his lifetime, and his opinion, more than any other, brought Frost's worth to light in this country. Frost in his eighties is called "the beloved poet" of America; but at forty he had already discovered what he had to say and how he wanted to say it, and what his poetry is now it was in 1914. Over the years he has filled and emptied and refilled his bucket with new water from the same living well. The draught is always fresh, and if Edward had lived to praise the books that followed the first two, he would have praised them no more and no less. He did live to read the third book, *Mountain Interval,* and ten weeks before he died wrote to me from France that the poems were "very good, though never better or different from 'North of Boston.'" He would have said the same of "From Plane to Plane," in one of Frost's latest collections. He would have known that from first to last the poetry was inherent in the man who wrote it.

In the autumn of 1914 Edward's own living stream was undammed. The undamming was Robert's doing when, after reading his friend's prose, he told him he had been a poet all his life, and with plain talk for his tools started the water flowing. From October onwards the poetry came down in a spate, and produced in Edward's being the enharmonic change that made him, not a different man, but the same man in another key. Towards the end of the year the change from minor to major begins to be felt in his letters.

Thomas's letter to Frost expressing his interest in poetry taking the language, people, and events of daily life as its materials—and in the possibilities that Thomas might write such poetry, 19 May 1914 (R. George Thomas, ed., Selected Letters, *pp. 93–94)*

My dear Frost,

I wish I could write a letter. But every day I write a short Welsh sketch and a review and read a bit and weed a bit and every evening type something, not to speak of touching the fiction still sporadically. And then there is the weather to enjoy or (here comes the laugh) to imagine how it should be enjoyed. Today I was out from 12 till sunset bicycling to the pine country by Ascot and back. But it all fleets and one cannot lock up at evening the cake one ate during the day. There must be a world where that is done. I hope you and I will meet in it. I hardly expect it of New Hampshire more than of Old.—I was glad Hudson turned out as I hoped he would. I understand those 3 approaches. If only you were to be in town and he too and he well and not afflicted by his sick wife and age coming on I would take you to see him. He is, if anything, more than his books. Don't get at me about my T.P. article ["How I Began"], which wasn't all that even I could do, but a series of extracts from an essay I shan't do. You could do one now. And you really should start doing a book on speech and literature, or you will find me mistaking your ideas for mine and doing it myself. You can't prevent me from making use of them: I do so daily and want to begin over again with them and wring all the necks of my rhetoric—the geese. However, my *Pater* would show you I had got on to the scent already.

Your second note pleased me. I shall perhaps come soon. My wife and I are to have a week or so very probably early in July. We *have* to get in several calls. If we can we will come to Ledington. I assume there would be room (for 2 whole days).

Did Davies appear? He had left town when I was there last.—I go up next about June 5.

Bronwen is suffering from flat feet and a stoop. She enjoys the new school and the gymnastics. But we miss her. She won't be home till August. Now about August, could we *all* get into the Chandler's for a month and would they have us and at what price? The only difficulty would be a room for me to work in. For work I must. Will you consider? We shall try to let this cottage.

I don't hear when your book is coming. I tried to get T.P. to let me write on it but they won't.

I wonder whether you can imagine me taking to verse. If you can I might get over the feeling that it is impossible—which at once obliges your good nature to say " I can." In any case I must have my "writer's melancholy" though I can quite agree with you that I might spare some of it to the deficient. On the other hand even with registered post, telegraph &c and all modern conveniences I doubt if I could transmit it.

I am pleased with myself for hitting on "Mowing" and "The Tuft of Flowers." For I forgot the names of those you meant me particularly to read, these I suppose being amongst them. You see that conceit consorts with writer's melancholy.

I go on writing something every day. Sometimes brief unstrained impressions of things lately seen, like a drover with 6 newly shorn sheep in a line across a cool woody road on market morning and me looking back to envy him and him looking back at me for some reason which I can't speculate on. Is this North of Bostonism?

Goodbye and I hope you are all well. Mervyn has been writing to Lesley I see. I hope he will go North of Boston before it is too late—North of Boston and West of Me.

Yours ever
Edward Thomas

Thomas's review of Frost's North of Boston *in the* Daily News, *22 July 1914*

This is one of the most revolutionary books of modern times, but one of the quietest and least aggressive. It speaks, and it is poetry. It consists of fifteen poems, from fifty to three hundred lines long, depicting scenes from life, chiefly in the country, in New Hampshire. Two neighbour farmers go along the opposite sides of their boundary wall, mending it and speaking of walls and of boundaries. A husband and wife discuss an old vagabond farm servant who has come home to them, as it falls out, to die. Two travellers sit outside a deserted cottage, talking of those who once lived in it, talking until bees in the wall boards drive them away. A man who has lost his feet in a sawmill talks with a friend, a child, and the lawyer comes from Boston about compensation. The poet himself describes the dreams of his eyes after a long day on a ladder picking apples, and the impression left on him by a neglected woodpile in the snow on an evening walk. All but these last two are dialogue mainly; nearly all are in blank verse.

These poems are revolutionary because they lack the exaggeration of rhetoric, and even at first sight appear to lack the poetic intensity of which rhetoric is an imitation. Their language is free from the poetical words and forms that are the chief material of secondary poets. The metre avoids not only the old-fashioned pomp and sweetness, but the later fashion also of discord and fuss. In fact, the medium is common speech and common decasyllables, and Mr. Frost is at no pains to exclude blank verse lines resembling those employed, I think, by Andrew Lang in a leading article printed as prose. Yet almost all these poems are beautiful. They depend not at all on objects commonly admitted to be beautiful; neither have they merely a homely beauty, but are often grand, sometimes magical. Many, if not most of the separate lines and separate sentences are plain and, in themselves, nothing. But they are bound together and made elements of beauty by a calm eagerness of emotion.

What the poet might have done, could he have permitted himself egoistic rhetoric, we have a glimpse of once or twice where one of his characters tastes a fanciful mood to the full: as where one of the men by the deserted cottage, who has been describing an old-style inhabitant, says:

> "As I sit here, and often times I wish
> I could be monarch of a desert land
> I could devote and dedicate for ever
> To the truths we keep coming back and back to.
> So desert it would have to be, so walled
> By mountain ranges half in summer snow,
> No one would covet it or think it worth
> The pains of conquering to force change on.
> Scattered oases where men dwelt, but mostly
> Sand dunes held loosely in tamarisk
> Blown over and over themselves in idleness.
> Sand grains should sugar in the natal dew
> The babe born to the desert, the sand storm
> Retard mid-waste my cowering caravans—
>
> There are bees in this wall." He struck the clapboards,
> Fierce heads looked out; small bodies pivoted.
> We rose to go. Sunset blazed on the windows.

This passage stands alone. But it is a solitary emotion also that gives him another which I feel obligated to quote in order to hint at the poetry elsewhere spread evenly over the whole poems. It is the end of "The Wood Pile":

> I thought that only
> Someone who lived in turning to fresh tasks
> Could so forget his handiwork on which
> He spent himself, the labor of his axe,
> And leave it there far from a useful fireplace
> To warm the frozen swamp as best it could
> With the slow smokeless burning of decay.

The more dramatic pieces have the same beauty in solution, the beauty of life seen by one in whom mystery and tenderness together just outstrip humour and curiosity. This beauty grows like grass over the whole, and blossoms with simple flowers which the reader gradually sets a greater and greater value on, in lines such as these about the dying labourer:

> She put out her hand
> Among the harp-like morning-glory strings
> Taut with the dew from garden bed to eaves,
> As if she played unheard the tenderness
> That wrought on him beside her in the night.
> "Warren," she said, "he has come home to die:
> You needn't be afraid he'll leave you this time."
> "Home," he mocked gently.
> "Yes, what else but home?
> It all depends on what you mean by home.
> Of course, he's nothing to us, any more
> Than was the hound that came a stranger to us
> Out of the woods, worn out upon the trail."
> "Home is the place where, when you have to go there,
> They have to take you in."
> "I should have called it
> Something you somehow haven't to deserve."

The book is not without failures. Mystery falls into obscurity. In some lines I cannot hit upon the required accents. But his successes, like "The Death of the Hired Man," put Mr Frost above all other writers of verse in America. He will be accused of keeping monotonously at a low level, because his characters are quiet people, and he has chosen the unresisting medium of blank verse. I will only remark that he would lose far less than most modern writers by being printed as prose. If his work were so printed, it would have little in common with the kind of prose that runs to blank verse: in fact, it would turn out to be closer knit and more intimate than the finest prose is except in its finest passages. It is poetry because it is better than prose.

Thomas's memories of his friendship with Frost, as expressed in "The Sun Used to Shine," finished in 1916 (R. George Thomas, ed., The Collected Poems of Edward Thomas, *pp. 319, 321)*

Rumors about the possibility of war at this time did not seem to affect Thomas. He was interested in visiting Frost and the poets who lived nearby in Gloucestershire, writers such as Lascelles Abercrombie and John Drinkwater who, along with Rupert Brooke, were preparing New Numbers, *a poetry anthology. Thomas's discussions with Frost, especially about "the sense of sound," stirred his developing poetic imagination.*

Thomas at Steep, summer 1914, between visits to Robert Frost (Collection of Myfanwy Thomas)

> The sun used to shine while we two walked
> Slowly together, paused and started
> Again, and sometimes mused, sometimes talked
> As either pleased, and cheerfully parted
>
> Each night. We never disagreed
> Which gate to rest on. The to be
> And the late past we gave small heed.
> We turned from men or poetry
>
> To rumours of the war remote
> Only till both stood disinclined
> For aught but the yellow flavorous coat
> Of an apple wasps had undermined;
>
> Or a sentry of dark betonies,
> The stateliest of small flowers on earth,
> At the forest verge; or crocuses
> Pale purple as if they had their birth

Helen Thomas at Steep, summer 1914 (R. George Thomas, Edward Thomas: A Portrait)

My dear Eleanor,

Thank you for your two letters and a postscript. At anyrate the p.s. was deserved. But talk is worse for letters than writing is. It is bad for writing too. At least its *immediate* effect is bad on *mine*. And talk and strolling and odd games of cricket fill most days; or I might have written—you know if I should. Things are quietly disturbing away here where there are few papers, those late. Mr Chandler is a soldier of 44 who saw 21 years' service and has this morning been sent for to Hereford. It may be that Frost and I will do some of the work he will leave behind. But if not, other things have postponed our Welsh trip. We can't go now in any case till after Baba's birthday. And Abercrombie is to join us. It might be Tuesday. That would perhaps mean not returning till the 22nd. Would you like to know definitely, or would you come in any case on the 20th.? We are doing rather moderately here. The boys are bored. Peter [Mrosowsky] is here—he helps to raise the standard of what boys may do, I suppose. Bronwen is alright. Baby is, too, tho she had a very bad fall from a swing a few days ago and I thought she was going to lose a birthday. Helen is not up to very much, and I don't help. One thing and another leaves me very irritable indeed. The quarters are too close. I want to get away to Wales and should like a full week, but travel-

Edward Thomas at Steep near the outbreak of the Great War (Collection of Myfanwy Thomas)

In sunless Hades fields. The war
Came back to mind with the moonrise
Which soldiers in the east afar
Beheld then. Nevertheless, our eyes

Could as well imagine the Crusades
Or Caesar's battles. Everything
To faintness like those rumours fades—
Like the brook's water glittering

Under the moonlight—like those walks
Now—like us two that took them, and
The fallen apples, all the talks
And silences—like memory's sand

When the tide covers it late or soon,
And other men through other flowers
In those fields under the same moon
Go talking and have easy hours.

Thomas's letter to Eleanor Farjeon on the brink of World War I reveals little awareness of the ramifications of the impending conflict, 14 August 1914 (R. George Thomas, ed., Selected Letters, pp. 96–97).

After war was declared, Frost decided to return to his native New England. He invited Thomas and his family to join him there, but Thomas's feelings of patriotism were already evident in his letters to Frost and in a series of essays he wrote early in the war.

First page of Thomas's letter to Frost expressing his growing interest in writing poetry, October 1914 (Dartmouth College Library)

Lascelles Abercrombie at Grange-Over-Sands, Lancashire (Robert H. Ross, The Georgian Revolt: Rise and Fall of a Poetic Ideal, 1910–1922)

ling has new inconveniences and things cost more than ever here, so I don't know what they'll be at inns. I haven't thought of serving my country, or of putting one leg round my neck and singing those songs that Clifford and Olga [Bax] and Bertie and Joan [Farjeon] like so much, but don't say so. I did think of turning plain reporter and giving unvarnished reports of country conversations about the war. But Frost discourages. In any case varnish is the thing. Do you read Harold Begbie for example? But this sounds as if I imagined myself a James Thomson or Richard Middleton who was going to die unrecognised and got some consolation from the imagining.

The one advantage of waiting a week to write to you is that Joan appears to have escaped the water bailiff. Of course if I could have done anything I would. But witty replies to water bailiffs are not my long suit.

Baby is grizzling upstairs. The Frosts are all over the house seeing Mr Chandler off. Peter's chair creaks as he reads the Baroness Orczy and Mervyn sounds completely satisfied with the old Strand Magazines. But it is a very fine hot day. God is in *His* heaven all right, obviously and ostentatiously. Mr Chandler will be in *his* in Hereford. Goodbye. I am sorry this letter turns out so. Please remember me to Clifford or is he serving our country?

Part of Thomas's "On Poets and Poetry in War Time," discussing the nature of patriotic poetry (Poetry and Drama, *2 [December 1914], pp. 51–58)*

If they also serve who only sit and write, poets are doing their work well. Several of them, it seems to me, with names known and unknown, have been turned into poets by the war, printing verse now for the first time. Whatever other virtues they show, courage at least is not lacking—the courage to write for oblivion. . . .

It is a fact that in the past but a small number of poems destined to endure are directly or entirely concerned with the public triumphs, calamities, or trepidations that helped to beget them. The public, crammed with mighty facts and ideas it will never digest, must look coldly on poetry where already those mighty things have sunk away far into "The still sad music of humanity." For his insults to their feelings, the newspapers, history, they might call the poet a pro-Boer. They want something raw and solid, or vague and lofty or sentimental. They must have Mr Begbie to express their thoughts, or "Tipperary" to drown them.

A patriotic poem pure and simple hardly exists, as a man who was a patriot pure and simple could not live outside a madhouse. Very seldom are poems written for occasions, great or small, more seldom for great than for small. But verses are, and they may be excellent. Virtually all hymns are occasional verses. They are written for certain people or a certain class. The writer of hymns or patriotic verses appears to be a man who feels himself always or at the time at one with the class, perhaps the whole nation, or he is a smart fellow who can simulate or exaggerate this sympathy. Experience, reality, truth, unless suffused or submerged by popular sentiment, are out of place. What we like is Mr. J. A. Nicklin's city clerk (*And They Went to the War,* Sidgwick & Jackson, 6d net) singing:

> When the air with hurtling shrapnel's all aquiver
>   And the smoke of battle through the valley swirls,
> It's better than our Sundays up the river,
>   And the rifle's hug is closer than a girl's.

Mr Arthur K. Sabin's sonnet called "Harvest Moon at Midnight," and dated September 8th (*War Harvest, 1914,* Temple, Sheen Press, 6d), is equally the thing, though nearer truth—it ends:

Thomas, his daughter Myfanwy, and Tommy Dodd, a neighborhood friend, in December 1914 (Collection of Myfanwy Thomas)

Ah, underneath this Moon, in fields of France,
How many of our old companionship
Snatch hurried rest, with hearts that burn and glow,
Longing to hear the bugles sound *Advance!*
To seize their weapons with unfaltering grip,
And for old England strike another blow.

. . . But this is not great poetry, nor is it what is wanted. It is the hour of the writer who picks up popular views or phrases, or coins them, and has the power to turn them into downright stanzas. Most newspapers have one or more of these gentlemen. They could take the easy words of a statesman, such as "No price is too high when honour and freedom are at stake," and dish them up so that the world next morning, ready to be thrilled by anything lofty and noble-looking, is thrilled. These poems are not to be attacked any more than hymns. Like hymns, they play with common ideas, with words and names which most people have in their heads at the time. Most seem to me bombastic, hypocritical, or senseless; but either they go straight to the heart of the great public which does not read poetry, or editors expect them to, and accordingly supply the articles.

There is a smaller class of better or more honest work which can hardly last longer. I mean the work of true poets which has been occasioned by the war. A few men are in an exceptional position: Messrs Newbolt and Kipling belong to a professional class apart, and may be supposed to suffer less drastic modifications from the war. It was their hour, and they have not been silent. They have written as well as in times of peace. The one silence which can be felt is Mr Charles M. Doughty's. But it might easily have been forecast. He has lived through this time long ago, and *The Cliffs* (reissue: Duckworth, 3/6 net.) and *The Clouds* show that modern warfare and German politics had no surprises for him. Other men who stood on old foundations of character and tradition were not suddenly transported out of themselves. Mr Bridges, Mr de la Mare, Mr Binyon, among others, remained themselves. Years before this they had proved themselves English poets. They have not done more now. Their private and social emotion does them credit, but with few exceptions, such as Messrs Binyon, Chesterton, and John Freeman, they have fallen various distances below their natural level. Nor am I surprised. I should have expected the shock to silence them, had it not been counterbalanced by a powerful social sense genuinely aroused. I have not liked any of these poems, but fancy tells me that they do for persons with more social sense than I, what the noisy stuff does for the man who normally lives without poetry. They are suddenly made old-fashioned: Mr Chesterton's "Hymn of War," for example (*Lord God of Battles: A War Anthology,* compiled by A. E. Manning Foster, Cope & Fenwick, 1/ net), is archaic and Hebraic, after this fashion:

> O God of earth and altar,
>   Bow down and hear our cry,
> Our earthly rulers falter,
>   Our people drift and die;
>
> The walls of gold entomb us,
>   The swords of scorn divide,
> Take not the thunder from us,
>   But take away our pride.

They revert, and they may be right, though I cannot follow them if I would.

Thomas began writing poetry about this time, and from 3 December through 7 December 1914 he wrote "Up in the Wind," "November," "March," "Old Man," and "The Sign-post." With hopes of having these poems published, he sent copies of them to Harold Monro, but Monro rejected them.

"Old Man," written at Steep, 6 December 1914 (R. George Thomas, ed., *The Collected Poems of Edward Thomas, pp. 19, 21*)

> Old Man, or Lad's-love,–in the name there's nothing
> To one that knows not Lad's-love, or Old Man,
> The hoar-green feathery herb, almost a tree,
> Growing with rosemary and lavender.
> Even to one that knows it well, the names
> Half decorate, half perplex, the thing it is:
> At least, what that is clings not to the names
> In spite of time. And yet I like the names.
>
> The herb itself I like not, but for certain
> I love it, as some day the child will love it
> Who plucks a feather from the door-side bush
> Whenever she goes in or out of the house.
> Often she waits there, snipping the tips and shrivelling
> The shreds at last on to the path, perhaps
> Thinking, perhaps of nothing, till she sniffs
> Her fingers and runs off. The bush is still
> But half as tall as she, though it is as old;
> So well she clips it. Not a word she says;
> And I can only wonder how much hereafter
> She will remember, with that bitter scent,
> Of garden rows, and ancient damson-trees
> Topping a hedge, a bent path to a door,
> A low thick bush beside the door, and me
> Forbidding her to pick.
>
>   As for myself,
> Where first I met the bitter scent is lost.
> I, too, often shrivel the grey, shreds,
> Sniff them and think and sniff again and try
> Once more to think what it is I am remembering,
> Always in vain. I cannot like the scent,
> Yet I would rather give up others more sweet,
> With no meaning, than this bitter one.
>
> I have mislaid the key. I sniff the spray
> And think of nothing; I see and I hear nothing;
> Yet seem, too, to be listening, lying in wait
> For what I should, yet never can, remember:
> No garden appears, no path, no hoar-green bush
> Of Lad's-love, or Old Man, no child beside,
> Neither father nor mother, nor any playmate;
> Only an avenue, dark, nameless, without end.

Analysis of "Old Man" (Andrew Motion, The Poetry of Edward Thomas, *pp. 164–169)*

The first prose draft was written on 17 November 1914, nearly three weeks before the poem was finished, but that draft was itself based on childhood and adult memories. Thomas's autobiography contains what is probably the earliest source, in its description of a London friend's back garden where "I first saw dark crimson dahlias and smelt bitter crushed stalks in plucking them. As I stood with my back to the house among the tall blossoming bushes I had no sense of any end to the garden between its brown fences. There remains in my mind a greenness, at once lowly and endless." Several years later, another friend, Bottomley, inadvertently started the sequence of events which was to produce the poem when he sent Thomas a cutting of the herb called "old man." In time Thomas was to tell him, "The Old Man or Lad's-Love you gave me is now a beautiful great bush at my study door." Helen Thomas confirms this precise context. In her account of Yewtree Cottage (where they moved in 1913), she noted "By the only door into the house we planted the herbs which [Edward] so loved. Rosemary, thyme, lavender, bergamot and old man were there, all direct descendants of our first country garden, which we had propagated from cuttings each time we moved." A further step towards the poem–the connection between smelling the "bitter crushed stalks" of the dahlias as a child and the later act of plucking the "bitter" herb as an aid to memory—was taken in *The South Country*. Describing "many scenes" from his childhood, Thomas recalls "a church and churchyard and black pigs running down from them towards me in a rocky lane–lad's-love and tall, crimson, bitter dahlias in a garden–the sweetness of large, moist yellow apples eaten out of doors–children." One of the children he sees in this passage is walking "down a long grassy path in an old garden," and is "content only to brush the tips of the flowers with her outstretched hands." For her, Thomas imagines, "there was no end to the path," and he watches her "gravely walk" on into the shadow and into Eternity, dimly foreknowing her life's days. This acknowledgment that the pursuit of childhood memories is a pursuit of happiness, and that the child's absorption in the present gives her a sense of stability, provided the basis for "Old Man." Moreover, the prose also contains a submerged paradox which was to be crucially developed later. The girl's experience is both limited and defined by the shadows which surround her, and by the fact that her goal recedes as she advances towards it. As was to be the case with Thomas himself, her "content" is the result of exploration rather than attainment.

The poem's paradoxical foundation is established in the opening lines. This hiatus between the herb's names and "the thing it is" reaffirms Thomas's belief that language cannot adequately re-create the object that it describes. The "thisness" of the herb, and the memories to which it is a means of access, hover so close to the edge of consciousness that any attempt to articulate them risks destroying their elusive nature. But this loss is offset by Thomas's gain in realizing that the plant's principal characteristics are paradoxical. The proper names–their age and youth–initiate a series of reconciled opposites that define the one context in which harmony becomes possible. The same balance is evident in its appearance: the "hoar-green" colouring blends faded antiquity with youthful health, and its being "almost a tree"–with its suggestion of transition–reconciles the states of maturity and immaturity. Like the names, these qualities "Half decorate, half perplex" Thomas by enlarging the herb's significance: as he stands watching, in middle age, he remembers his own past while looking forward to the child's future. His hopes of recalling "something out of [his] youth" are increased by the fact that the old man is placed between rosemary and lavender. The former's connotations of remembrance, and the latter's of preservation, combine to shelter the old man's potential harmony.

In this first stanza Thomas erects a platform upon which to build the main burden of the poem. The contradictory names of the herb have become, in Marie Quinn's words, "an image of the speaker's goal, because to retrieve past time is also to conquer the discreteness of time, to live in the past and present simultaneously." But in addition to this, the names have established him in a catalogue of distinct age groups ranging from the old man of the title to the child on whom he now concentrates his attention. Here too a paradox is implicit. While the gradations of age emphasise the remorseless passage of time, they also suggest a regenerative, cyclical movement. Child, adult and "old man" discover that their patterns of experience are repeated when they look back.

Thomas's original examination of the hiatus between "thing" and name is here subtly enlarged to accommodate the discrepancy between his attitude to the herb itself and the consoling memories that it inspires. Their value has so far only been conveyed by "hints and whispers," and his emphatic escalation of "like" to "love" is made while realising that he cannot entirely repossess the harmony they embody. Only the child has a pure and simple sense of integration with her surroundings.

So complete is her absorption and sympathy with the herb that she undertakes a literally physical process of identification with it. She shares its age, and trims it regularly as if to keep it a child like herself. And this outward harmony is complemented by evidence of an internal, invisible sympathy. By "perhaps / Thinking, perhaps of nothing," and by saying "not a word," the child exemplifies the same rapt, wordless communion described by Thomas in "Digging." "It is enough" for her to sniff the shreds, just as it was "enough" for him "To smell, to crumble the dark earth": both states make the need for verbal expression redundant, and deny the possibility that language will betray them.

The child has in fact "run off" by now, and Thomas's memory is free to ponder her future. But he does so knowing that he cannot imitate her silent communion; although he shares her intuitive knowledge that "the ultimate language is that of the thing," he is unable to use it. His "Forbidding her to pick" is a stern proof of this: it replaces "hints and whispers" with forthright disapproval. Where the child was content with "perhaps / Thinking, perhaps of nothing," Thomas wrestles with the fugitive "meaning" of the scent. As he pulls the leaves from the herb, the repetitiveness of his actions conveys a sense of frustrated bafflement. But this does not prevent him from introducing a few more hopeful signs. The present tense of "am remembering" suggests that the mere operation of memory produces some–albeit unspecified–results. This promise is strengthened by the admission that "I would rather give up others more sweet, / With no meaning, than this bitter one." The confession indicates clear knowledge of his own shortcomings, and emphasises his reluctance to settle for less elusive—and less rewarding—goals.

In the poem's final stanza, however, these potential pleasures are overshadowed. The original location of the herb's scent has already been described as "lost," but its disappearance is here translated into incontrovertible, concrete terms, By saying he has "mislaid the key," Thomas recalls the fact that the bush itself is "door-side," and that one of the things the child might remember is "a bent path to a door." It is as if the bush—which was touched by the child "Whenever she [went] in or out of the house"—actually facilitated her passage from one state (indoors/outdoors) to another (outdoors/indoors). All the apartments of experience, and all the divisions of time, were available to her, whereas for Thomas there is no free access. The past, in terms of his image, is locked to him, and so is the harmony he once enjoyed there. When he repeats the mnemonic of his former happiness by sniffing the spray, it is not the absorbed and receptive "nothing" of the child that he sees, but merely a shadowy telescopic view of emptiness. His failure is exacerbated by the very insistence of his longing for success. Not only is he looking and listening, but even "lying in wait"— as if to ambush "what I should, yet never can, remember." His anxious self-consciousness is aggravated by his knowledge of what to expect, were it possible to realise his ambition.

Because Thomas is trying to reproduce, rather than originate, a sense of integration, his closing account of natural and social isolation is a tormenting mixture of visible and invisible qualities. This is most obviously apparent in the superb closing line: customary expectations that an avenue should lead towards a specific place are rebuffed by a vacant darkness. It is, however, an avenue "without end." While this suggests that his search for harmony will repeatedly be compromised, it also contains at least the potential for fulfilment. As Edna Longley says, "despite the poem's overt statements, it has itself explored and illuminated as much of the avenue as is humanly and imaginatively possible."

Thomas's letter to Harold Monro after the publisher rejected his poems, 15 December 1914 (R. George Thomas, ed., Selected Letters, *p. 104)*

Many thanks for saying it. I am sorry because I feel utterly sure they are me. I expect obstacles and I get them. It was chiefly to save myself what I think unnecessary pain that I asked for no explanations. One blow was better. I assume the verses expressed nothing clearly that you cared about, as that is the only ground for not liking written work. But don't let us talk about it. I have to be at the Museum next week, far too busy for my liking. If I have time I will suggest an evening.

Early in 1915 Thomas sprained his ankle seriously and was incapacitated for almost three months. While recuperating, he continued to write poetry at a rapid rate and also to edit This England *(1915), a collection of reflections about wartime England. Under the pseudonym of Edward Eastaway, he included two of his own poems in this volume. About this time Frost and his family left for the United States, but the two writers continued to correspond regularly until Thomas's death.*

Letter to Robert Frost discussing Thomas's evolving poetic vision and the impact of Rupert Brooke's death, 3 May 1915 (R. George Thomas, ed., Selected Letters, *pp. 109–110)*

My dear Robert,

I got a letter from you on Friday, the one I have been gladdest to yet, and not only because you said you liked "Lob." I was glad to hear of you going off to Stowe "tomorrow." You are enjoying this period, but it is silly of me to tell you so. If you weren't you ought to be, because you are not writing about Marlborough. But we have one piece of luck. Two pairs of nightingales have come to us. One sings in our back hedge nearly all day and night. My only regret when I first heard it was that you hadn't stayed another Spring and heard it too. I hope the Gods don't think I'm the sort of poet who will be content with a nightingale, though. You don't think they could have made that mistake do you? What does it mean?–I get quite annoyed with people complaining of the weather as soon as it greys a little. Am I really ripe for being all sound content, or what? 2nd piece of luck (still embryonic) is that Scott-James has some connection with an American literary journal called *The Bellman* and is recommending them things by me, beginning with a remark on Rupert Brooke. You heard perhaps that he died on April 23rd of sunstroke on the way to the Dardanelles? All the papers are full of his "beauty" and an eloquent last sonnet beginning "If I should die." He was eloquent. Men never spoke ill of him.

After recovering from his injury, Thomas began a patriotic study of John Churchill, first Duke of Marlborough, which he completed in less than a month, and then began regularly sending his poems to literary acquaintances. Their responses were hardly reassuring; indeed, his only poems that he ever saw in print were published in James Guthrie's quarterlies and in Six Poems *(1916), a small collection that Thomas published under his pseudonym, Edward Eastaway.*

Title page of the first collection of Thomas's poetry, published in an edition of one hundred copies

But you have some poems by you fit to send out, haven't you? These editors mustn't go sour with waiting.

I find I can't write. Re-reading Rupert Brooke and putting a few things together about him have rather messed me up and there's Marlborough behind and Marlborough before. I shall have to go up to London for the last time next week—for the last bout at the Museum, I mean. Bronwen is now at school again. I shall take Baba up and leave Helen to contrive some spring cleaning. I tell you—I should like another April week in Gloucestershire with you like that one last year. You are the only person I can be idle with. That's natural history, not eloquence. If you were there I might even break away from the Duke for 3 days, but it would be hard.

Are the children at school now? Or are you still "neglecting" them? God bless them all. By the way, there was a beautiful return of sun yesterday after a misty moisty morning, and everything smelt wet and warm and cuckoos called, and I found myself with nothing to say but "God bless it." I laughed a little as I came over the field, thinking about the "it" in "God bless it."

Yours and Elinor's ever
Edward Thomas

In late spring 1915 Frost almost succeeded in convincing Thomas to leave England for the United States, but Thomas worried that no foreseeable work awaited him there. His uncertainty about finding employment in the United States, coupled with a sense of patriotic guilt about abandoning his country in time of war, finally persuaded him to enlist in the armed forces. On 11 July 1915 Thomas wrote to Frost that he planned to volunteer, and two days later he enlisted in the Artists' Rifles.

Thomas's letter to Frost discussing the war, prospects for finding a livelihood in the United States, and Frost's poetry, 13 June 1915 (R. George Thomas, ed., Selected Letters, *pp. 111–114)*

Steep, Petersfield

My dear Robert,

Your two letters came together Friday night. When I saw the Franconia postmark on the smaller I guessed it was the second and that you were there. I hope very much you still are and will be almost as long as you would like to be. My next hope is that I shall see you there. But this is a funny world, as I think you said before I did. "Rum job, painting," Turner used to say when Ruskin had poured out a can of words. I wish I hadn't to say more about poetry. I wished it on Friday night particularly as I had to spoil the effect of your letter by writing 1000 words about Rupert Brooke's posthumous book—not daring to say that those sonnets about him enlisting (?) are probably not very personal but a nervous attempt to connect with himself the very widespread idea that self sacrifice is the highest self indulgence. You know. And I don't dispute it. Only I doubt if he knew it or would he have troubled to drag in the fact that enlisting cleared him of

All the little emptiness of love?

. . . Still, I am thinking about America as my only chance (apart from Paradise). Tell me when would be the best time to begin. Are people back in town in September? I suppose I ought to take what introductions I can get. You will tell me if there is any way of living cheaply and yet not being in the wilderness. But what will your distance be from Boston and what the fare? . . .

I read "The road not taken" to Helen just now and she liked it entirely and agreed with me how naturally symbolical it was. You won't go and exaggerate what I say about that one phrase.

This moment a letter from Haines telling me I am free to drop in on him next week as I hope to do. The weather keeps so fine though that each day it seems must be the last—just like last year.

People are getting pretty black about the war, realising they have not got the Germans beaten yet. It is said however that we are really through the Dardanelles and the price of wheat is falling. It is said to be kept back to prevent rowdyism in the rejoicing.

Good luck to you at Franconia and all our loves to you six.

          Yours ever
          E. Thomas

Thomas's letter to his parents announcing his enlistment, 9 July 1915 (R. George Thomas, ed., Selected Letters, *pp. 115–116)*

          Steep

Dear Father and Mother,

I have got on a step in the half decision I came to while I was with you of enlisting. I saw a sergeant of the Artists Rifles at their H.Q. to-day. They are virtually an Officers Training Corps now. If I joined I should be for a week or two in London, and able (I believe) to stay with you. Then I should spend a month or two in Richmond Park in camp and then a similar period of training at H.Q. in France. If I were then considered fit for a commission I should be at liberty to apply for one. But if I got one it would not (on account of my age) be for service, at first at any rate, if at all, in the trenches, but for training men in England. I have practically come to the decision to go up next week and offer myself to the doctor. The alternative is the Sportsman's Battalion of the Royal Fusiliers, but there (I am told) I might find a rowdy set, no better company than the ordinary crowd of privates, whereas the Artists would be largely professional men. Of course there are still some things to consider, but Helen is willing, and I believe my savings and pay would if necessary cover her expenses during as long an absence as two years. She does not want to go to the Ellises and for the present she and the two girls would stay on here. If I am accepted next week I can have several days for putting my things in order.

I hope this will not seem to you very unreasonable. The conditions being as I say you will have little cause for anxiety unless some unforeseeable changes take place. . . .

Duckworths offer me £10 in advance for the *Proverbs*. It is something but I have not accepted it yet.

I am inquiring how if at all my insurance policies will be affected.

The *English Review* rejects my poem. Perhaps if I am in khaki they will be more genial. I am not troubled. I never felt easier in my mind except for a fear that the doctor will not pass me.

         Every your loving son
         Edwy

Helen's reaction to Thomas's enlistment (World Without End, *pp. 152–157*)

But now indeed things were bad for us, and after our friends sailed back to America taking Philip with them for a year, David became torn in his mind as to what he ought to do. There was hardly any literary work to be had, and we were hard put to it to keep going. He got one or two commissions for special articles having an indirect war interest, but naturally the papers did not want his reflective and critical essays, and reviewing had almost ceased. Besides the anxiety of providing for us all there was the deep conviction that he ought to enlist. He hated the newspaper patriotism. He saw through the lies and deception of the press as he had always seen through untruths. He was not even carried away by the abnormal condition of the national emotion. Indeed his attitude to the war was inexplicable to his father who was roused to fury by what he thought was his son's disloyalty when David suggested that the Germans were as brave as the English, and that "cold steel" would bring fear to the hearts of any man be he German or English. The old antagonism broke out again and was never healed.

One day when he was in London ostensibly looking for work, he sent me a telegram telling me he had enlisted in the Artists' Rifles. I had known that the struggle going on in his spirit would end like this, and I had tried to prepare myself for it. But when that telegram came I felt suddenly faint and despairing. "No, no, no," was all I could say; "not that." But I knew it had to be and that it was right. He was—so the telegram said—to come home in a few days a soldier.

During our life there had been many bitter partings and many joyous home-comings. The bitterness of the partings has faded from my consciousness; I know it was so, but I forget how and why. But the memory of the joy and hope and happiness

Thomas (second row, second from left) at Hare Hill Camp, December 1915 (Collection of Myfanwy Thomas)

of the reunions has stayed with me, and for ever, so it seems to me, part of me will stand at the gate and listen for his step, watch for his long stride; feel the strong embrace of his arms, and his kiss. . . .

David got out [at the Steep train station] just where I stood. I noticed with a shock that his hair was cut very short, and that the thinness of his face was accentuated, but that he looked trim and soldierly in his uniform.

As he stooped to kiss me I smelt for the first time that queer sour smell of khaki, so different from David's usual smell of peaty Harris tweed and tobacco. What a difference the clothes made! The stiffness and tightness too were so strange after his easy loose things. I could not now walk with my hand in his pocket and his hand over mine.

I looked up at his face as we walked along, and in a flash I saw the sensitiveness, the suffering, the strength and the sincerity which had determined for him the rightness of this step. I was proud of him, and my heart silently responded to the cheers with which the crowd welcomed their hero. I passed again the woman who had spoken to me. "You be luckier than us," she said, "with a V.C. all of your own." David saluted her, and I nodded in acknowledgement of the truth of what she said.

The children were excited and eager to hear all about soldiers, and after tea, as we sat round the table polishing his buttons and badges and buckles, he told us about enlisting, and how he was now a soldier for the duration of the war. He had already learned some soldiers' songs which had good choruses in which we all joined.

The three days he had before joining his regiment were busy with gardening and putting papers and books in order in the hill-top study, and making preparations for a long absence from home. We had one glorious walk together. On that day he discarded his khaki, and but for his shorn hair, which I could not get used to, was his old self. We talked of ways and means, of the children and the garden, of the men mostly painters and writers like himself who were to be his companions and to learn with him the uncongenial business of warfare. Sometimes, walking through familiar country which we loved, we talked of that, and sometimes in the old way we walked silently. I remember thinking, "Oh if only we could walk on like this for ever, and for ever it be summer, and for ever we be happy!" And then I remembered that after all the war itself was the reason of this very walk, and had its part in the depth of our deep content with the English country

Thomas's fair copy of "This is no case of petty right or wrong," his poem about the realities of war (Bodleian Library, Oxford)

Thomas's emotional preparation for the horrors of battle did little to palliate his melancholy, but perhaps his military service soothed some feelings of guilt about having abandoned his family. His army training not only improved his physical condition but also gave him a greater confidence than he had achieved previously in his literary accomplishments. Life in the military permitted spare time in which to write, and he wrote twenty-eight poems in the first five months of 1916. Before he went to France, Thomas wrote "Home," a poem in which he ponders the loss of liberty he feels from having the military discipline imposed on his life. This is the only poem he wrote that reflects his response to army routine.

Thomas's fair copy of the first page of "Home" (Bodleian Library, Oxford)

In 1916 Thomas succeeded in obtaining a place as an officer cadet at the Royal Artillery School in London, where in November he passed his exams and was commissioned as a second lieutenant with the Royal Artillery, initially stationed in Kent.

Part of Thomas's letter to Frost about enlisting in the artillery, 28 July 1916 (Dartmouth College Library)

Part of Thomas's letter to Frost explaining why he wants to go to France to fight, 24 November 1916 (Dartmouth College Library) and with each other. Because of the war our souls were now drawn into the circle that was our love, and we understood and loved each other completely.

Thomas spent his first two months of army training in London. Despite the mundane routines of drills, latrine duty, and restrictions imposed on him by the military life, he willingly accepted the spirit of military discipline. By November 1915 he had been promoted to lance corporal and moved to Hare Hill Camp in Essex, where he pursued the outdoor life of a map-reading instructor. Thomas's patriotism and sense of duty were undoubtedly sincere; however, he was not blind to the harsh realities of war, and his poetry of the period reflects this awareness.

Analysis of "Home" (Andrew Motion, The Poetry of Edward Thomas, *pp. 116–118)*

Thomas and Bottomley during Thomas's last visit home, November 1916 (William Cooke, Edward Thomas: A Critical Biography, 1878–1917)

The poem opens with a panorama of content which prefigures his experience of army comradeship—morning, tempers and land are all "fair." And this fusion of mental and natural landscapes is given physical expression by the unifying and "untrodden snow that made / Wild of the tame." The snow momentarily restores a "wild and rustic and old" appearance to the place, and thereby makes it resemble "quintessential England." Moreover, the fact that "first to pass / Were we that league of snow, next the north wind" suggests that the walkers are the original, uncompromised possessors of the landscape. Their ownership of it is confirmed by the wind blurring their tracks behind them. It is an action which literally seals them in an exalted, refined state. Thomas acknowledges that practical needs will ensure their return, but this does not impede present enjoyment, which manifests itself in their singing and hurrying "As we did often with the start behind." The significance of this phrase emerges when it is recalled that because they must start walking from, and in the end return to, "the cold roofs" of the camp, their journey will inevitably be circular. Like racehorses (an image developed from the reference to "the start" in line 10, to "the beaten horse" in line 16), their appearance of free movement conceals a reality of predetermined constraint. Thomas and his companions are invisibly chained to the beginning of the course of which they walk the extent, by their obligation to fulfil military duties.

The disadvantages of camp life, though real enough, are minimised by the congestion of the line which mentions them: "Happy we had not been there, nor could be." This suppression of unhappiness is confirmed by Thomas's attention to benefits inherent in the same context. "Sleep and food and fellowship" are not simply enumerated, they are intensified and relished by the verb "tasted." It is a miniature ascending scale of pleasures which aptly introduce and justify his protracted discussion of "home." Of the three walkers, it is Thomas's two companions who first toss the word between them, savouring the irony of its being applied to an army camp. Yet there is a sense in which it is appropriate. In the poem, Thomas is reconciled to his patriotic duty, whatever its inconveniences; and until the demands that war makes on him are ended, the camp and his companions define an appreciation of national identity. Between the comforts of domestic homes and the ideal homes of imagination, they constitute a third, which is inadequate in many respects, but admitted to be necessary.

It is, in addition, one which resolves individual differences, however briefly, and forms a unique, practical friendship in which Thomas scrupulously identifies the shortcomings, as well as the virtues. The nervous balance of their relationship is as fine as their interpretation of the word "home." In his letters, he expanded on the reasons for this, employing the same terminology as he did in the poem. The day before it was written he had said to Frost: "here I have to like people because they are more my sort than the others, although I realise at certain times they are not my sort at all and will vanish away after the war. What almost completes the illusion is that I can't help talking to them as if they were friends." But by the time he embarked for France he had made it clear that it was not simply the quality of his comrades' characters which made friendship difficult. It was rather that he was reluctant to form ties which would almost certainly be broken painfully: "I don't want *friends* here," he told Bottomley, "I should be too introspective or too happy to meet the circumstances."

The tacit suggestion of a perfect state of friendship, from which these fall short, emphasises the similarly missed ideal of home. But Thomas—only now speaking for the first time—refuses to visualise this clearly.

In December, Thomas volunteered for service in France and began making the rounds of his friends to say farewell before being sent to the front, but he was able to enjoy a short Christmas leave at home with his wife and family before he left to begin active service in France. In 1917 he began keeping a private diary that detailed his assigned movements and described the cold western front.

Gordon Bottomley's recollection of Thomas's visit in November 1916 (R. George Thomas, Edward Thomas: A Portrait, *p. 277)*

I have no written record of that time, but the memory . . . is still vivid and new. There was talk and music, and he sang (he always sang when he came to us): beside his folk-songs he had acquired a riotous collection of army-songs, which he sang with a mischievous quietness that made the rowdy ones much funnier even than they were meant to be. He went one or two long walks with my wife; at other times he sat with me in my open garden-house. [Bottomley was still an invalid.] One afternoon we spent a long time indoors watching a marvellous storm gather about Ill Bell and High Street and come sweeping down Kentmere and the estuary: the cross-lights among the dark veils were unearthly: he said reflectively "You are lucky." I replied "What, with my health?" He was silent for an appreciable time, then said still more quietly "Yes". . . . While he was here I asked him why he had chosen to ask for a commission in the artillery, when that might be thought to be the professional soldier's particular province, with its special training and special risks. He replied "To get a larger pension for Helen!"

Thomas arrived at Le Havre on 30 January and requested an immediate transfer to the front lines. By 11 February 1917 he was near Arras, where he was to spend all but a fortnight of the rest of his life. Just after his thirty-ninth birthday he learned from Frost that three of his poems had been included in Harriet Monroe's Poetry. *At the same time, news reached him from Bottomley that* An Annual of New Poetry *had been published with his poems included, and people were inquiring about the identity of Edward Eastaway. Thomas's poetic reputa-tion was just beginning to flourish as the Allies' preparations for the spring assault on the German lines began.*

Second Lieutenant Thomas a few days before he left for France, January 1917 (Collection of Myfanwy Thomas)

Helen Thomas's letter to Jane Hooton recounting her final farewell to Edward, 29 January 1920 (William Cooke, Edward Thomas: A Critical Biography, 1878-1917, *pp. 48-49)*

Three years ago today Edward went away from me. The snow was deep on the ground and he soon disappeared in a thick fog, and we cooied to each other until we could not hear any more. I was left alone knowing I would never see him, never hear him, never hold him in my arms again. Tonight I think of all our life together, and I think of my life during these three years. Our life together was a restless sea, tide in, tide out, calm and glorious despair and ecstasy; never still, never easy, but always vivid and moving, wave upon wave, a wild deep glorious sea. Our life was terrible and glorious but always life. And I think of my life these three years. And again it has been like a sea, calm and cruel, happy and despairing, just the same as always but without a harbour, without an anchorage, and I have been tired to death of its tossing to and fro on to this beach and that, on to this rock and that. For life to me cannot be otherwise until that new life comes to me and I am gathered into my anchorage and him and get a calm.

Thomas's letter to Frost detailing the dangers of an artillery officer at the front, 6 March 1917 (R. George Thomas, ed., Selected Letters, pp. 145–146)

Arras

My dear Robert,

I still don't hear from you, but I had better write when I can. One never knows. I have now been living 2 weeks in a city that is only 2400 yds from the enemy, is shelled every day and night and is likely to be heavily bombarded some day. Of course the number of shells that fall is larger than the number of casualties although the place is crowded and falling masonry helps the shells, but this does not really appeal to anything but the brains that may be knocked out by them. Nor is it consoling to know that the enemy has put shells into the orchard where the battery is and all round it without injuring anybody. However it may console those who are not out here.

For these 2 weeks I have been detached from my battery to work at headquarters, which has meant getting to know something of how battle is conducted, and also going about with maps and visiting observation posts, some of which give a view of No Man's Land like a broad river very clear and close. We went out yesterday morning to see the Gordons cross to raid the enemy but it was snowing and we only saw snow and something moving and countless shell bursts beyond. Our artillery made a roof over our heads of shells singing and shuffling along in shoals.–I return to the battery, a mile away, very soon now.

We are having many fine days, bright and warm even at times, and we begin to see larks as well as aeroplanes. I wish we did not see so many of the enemy's. Every clear day we are continually hearing the whistle blowing the alarm. It incenses the artillery very much as the planes spot us and then tell their batteries how to hit us.

I have not a great deal to do as a rule. Long hours of waiting, nothing that has to be done and yet not free to do what I want, in fact not consciously wanting anything except, I suppose, the end. Wisdom perhaps trickles in, perhaps not. There is nobody I like much, that is the worst of it. I don't want friends. I don't think I should like to have friends out here. I am sure I shouldn't. But I want companions and I hardly expect to find them. This may not be final. There are plenty of likeable people. There is also one very intelligent man here, the Signalling Officer, an architect before the war, a hard clever pungent fellow who knows the *New Age*, *Georgian Poetry* (and doesn't like it) &c. He didn't seem to know "Mountain Interval" or the author.

A letter from de la Mare came yesterday. So he has seen you. He says you don't look as well as you ought to. Whatever he said would be little or nothing, so I needn't complain that he said nothing. He said he wished we could have a talk. Fancy being polite to me out here. Well, there is nothing I want to forget so far. Is that right?

I have time to spare but I can't talk. You don't answer, and I am inhibiting introspection except when I wake up and hear the shelling and wonder whether I ought to move my bed away from the window to the inner side where there is more masonry—more to resist and more to fall on me. But it is no use thinking like this. I am half awake when I do. Besides I have hardly learnt yet to distinguish between shells going out and shells coming in—my worst alarm was really shells going out. So far it excites but doesn't disturb, or at any rate doesn't upset and unfit.

I hear my book is coming out soon. Did the duplicate verses ever reach you? You have never said so. But don't think I mind. I should like to be a poet, just as I should like to live, but I know as much about my chances in either case, and I don't really trouble about either. Only I want to come back more or less complete. Goodbye. My dearest love to you all.

Yours ever
Edward Thomas

Thomas's diary entries from 4 March through 7 March 1917 (University College Library, Cardiff)

4. Cold but bright clear and breezy. Nothing to do all morning but trace a map and its contours. Colonel and I went down to 244 before lunch to see the shell holes of last night and this morning. Hun planes over. More shells came in the afternoon. The fire is warm but the room cold. Tea with Lushington and Thorburn. Shelling at 5.30 I don't like it. I wonder where I shall be hit as in bed I wonder if it is better to be on the window or outer side of room or on the chimney or inner side, whether better to be upstairs where you may fall or on the ground floor where you may be worse crushed. Birthday parcels from home.

5. Out early to see a raid by VI Corps, but snow hid most but singing of Field shells and snuffling of 6 ins. Ronville's desolate streets. TO 244's orchard which has had numerous 4.2 shells over, meant for the road. Wrote to Helen, Mervyn and Bronwen. Afternoon indoors paying etc. After tea to 244 to dine, not very happy with Lushington, Horton and Smith. They have the wind up because of the shells (which may have been meant for the road behind). Letters from de la Mare, Helen, Bronwen and de la Mare. A beautiful clear

moonlit night after a beautiful high blue day combed white clouds.

6. Bright and clear early and all day and warm at 1. Walked over to 244's position with Colonel and then up to 234 beyond Dainville station, and listened to larks and watched aeroplane fights. 2 planes down, one in flames, a Hun. Sometimes 10 of our planes together very high. Shells into Arras in afternoon.

7. A cold raw dull day with nothing to do except walk round to 244 to get a pair of socks. The wind made a noise in the house and trees and a dozen black crumpled sycamore leaves dance round and round on terrace. Wrote to Pearce and Irene. Rather cold and depressed and solitary.

Review in The New Statesman *(31 March 1917, p. 617) of poems by Edward Eastaway (Thomas) included in* An Annual of New Poetry

The one poet whose contributions make this book really worth having is Mr Edward Eastaway. This name is a pseudonym; I happen to be aware that it conceals the identity of a man who has written large numbers of prose works; but as it appears to be his wish to remain pseudonymous, I leave it for someone else to strip off the disguise. One's knowledge did not prepossess one in favour of his poetry; one did not think that a real gift for verse could remain so long unexploited without becoming atrophied. But the unlikely has happened; and his poems are better than his prose, good though some of this has been. There are not enough of them here to give an exact notion of his power and his limitations. But "The Wood," "Aspens," "The Brook," "Wind and Mist," and "For These" would, by themselves, be enough to show that he is worth fifty Frosts. His verse does not sing, and it never shouts; yet the absence of music in the words is compensated for by a sort of music of the mind. He seizes a moment's mood, and gives it with all the circumstances that lead to it and the ripples it leaves behind it; and if you find his moods monotonous he gives his answer in the last stanza of "Aspens":

> All day and night, save winter, every weather,
> Above the inn, the smithy and the shop,
> The aspens at the crossroads talk together
> Of rain, until their last leaves fall from the top.
>
> Out of the blacksmith's cavern comes the ringing
> Of hammer, shoe and anvil; out of the inn

> The clink, the hum, the roar, the random singing,
> The sounds that for these fifty years have been.
>
> Whatever wind blows, while they and I have leaves
> We cannot other than an aspen be
> That ceaselessly, unreasonably grieves,
> Or so men think who like a different tree.

One of the best of his poems is "Wind and Mist," in which a man describes a house that he used to occupy on the edge of the downs, and on winter days it was like being on a cliff's edge above a gulf of mist. I hear that the author (who is now in the army in France) intends shortly to issue a volume of his own. If they are as interesting as those given here they will give him his place among contemporary poets at once.

On 1 April 1917 the British began bombarding German lines along fourteen miles of the Arras front. Five days later the army began a rolling barrage to cover the advance of the infantry. On 6 April, Thomas wrote about the impending attack in a letter to Helen. Easter Sunday fell two days later, and as Thomas made his way to the battery that day, he was knocked over by the impact of a dud shell that fell within yards of him. He was not wounded, but the incident was the subject of much good-natured humor among the men under his command, who commented on his good luck. On the morning of 9 April 1917 Thomas was killed by a German shell at his battery.

Letter from John Thorburn, fellow officer, to Helen relating the death of Edward Thomas, 9 April 1917 (R. George Thomas, Edward Thomas: A Portrait, *pp. 293-294)*

Dear Mrs. Thomas,

It is a great trial to me to write to inform you that your husband was killed this morning. As I have been very closely associated with him since we first met at Trowbridge, I thought it would be well to take upon myself the duty of letting you know of his death. It happened this morning, by shell fire, in the observation post.

I think, before anything else, I have to express to you the great debt of gratitude I owe to your husband. He has been so much my support through this difficult—and to me, uncongenial,—work; and has been so wise and kind in the help he has given me. His friendship has meant a great deal to me. I don't know whether you would want me to say this,— but it seems to me he has got on splendidly,—magnificently,—in the army; as well as much younger, men who have just the knack. And I am sure that his other gifts, and the depth and strength of his character, have been gratefully valued by all of us who were at work with him.

I claim, at least, his friendship; and just now I am terribly lonely out here without him. I hope I may not have given you needless pain by anything I have said. But will you accept my most sincere and earnest sympathy in your sorrow.

I shall be very glad to look after your husband's personal effects.

A tribute to Edward Thomas's life and work with critical comment by John Freeman (The Bookman, 53 *[December 1917], pp. 93-94)*

Until he became an artilleryman, Edward Thomas had written all his poetry in prose. There was a delicate play of fancy and imagination and a lapidary cunning in the verbal artistry of his essays and criticisms which make it less surprising that he should at last have found a medium of expression in verse than that he did not find it earlier; but none even of his intimates can have foreseen that with his gentle manners, his diffident self-distrust and bookish preoccupations, he had in him the makings of a soldier. Certainly, he was no lover of war; he took up arms solely because he felt that to be his duty; then, with his usual thoroughness, he was not satisfied to make a pretence of doing what he had set out to do. He devoted himself as keenly, as conscientiously to his military work as he had done to the work that was more properly his. It was this impulse, since he was a soldier, to be the real thing, that took him to his death in the British advance of last April. "For," says Mr. John Freeman, "in France he was detached from his battery for staff duties, and was dissatisfied until he had succeeded in returning to his old post of danger. Just the same scrupulous spirit had moved him years before when he gave up a permanent appointment sans duties because there was no way in which he could earn or was expected to earn his pay. There were things he could not endure; no one who knew him could be surprised."

But though all his poems were written in the atmosphere of war, except for a rousing call in "The Trumpet"

"To the old wars,
Arise. Arise!"

the "In Memoriam" quatrain for Easter, 1915, and a stray line or so glooming in some picture of country life like a cloud that drifts momentarily across the sun, there is little of the touch of war in them—as little as there is in the songs of Ledwidge. The war stirred both profoundly and absorbed all their energies for the time, but when they had leisure to withdraw into themselves, for them as for others of their temper old sources of inspiration reopened, old habits of thought closed round them again, and in such hours of respite the war dwindled to a beating of rain on the window, a wind that roared in the darkness and rattled at the door which had shut it out.

An overview of Thomas's poetry and his poetic achievement, which are linked with those of John Keats (Hugh Underhill, "The 'Poetic Character' of Edward Thomas," Essays in Criticism, *23 [1973], pp. 236-253)*

One of the distinctive features of Edward Thomas's poetry is its concern with the "feel" of an experience, with what the mind does to an experience. Moreover, the recording of experiential phenomena of this order comes together with an ontological concern with the perception of essences. It might be said that a great deal of poetry attempts to convey the exact nature or essence of a thing or an experience, but Thomas delves into the mental processes attendant upon this in a peculiarly obsessive way. This is apparent in the poem called "Parting":

The Past is a strange land, most strange.
Wind blows not there, nor does rain fall:
If they do, they cannot hurt at all.
Men of all kinds as equals range

The soundless fields and streets of it.
Pleasure and pain there have no sting,
The perished self not suffering
That lacks all blood and nerve and wit,

And is in shadow-land a shade.
Remembered joy and misery
Bring joy to the joyous equally;
Both sadden the sad. So memory made

Parting today a double pain:
First because it was parting; next
Because the ill it ended vexed
And mocked me from the Past again,

Not as what had been remedied
Had I gone on,–not that, oh no!
But as itself no longer woe;
Sighs, angry word and look and deed

Being faded: rather a kind of bliss,
For there spiritualized it lay
In the perpetual yesterday
That naught can stir and strain like this.

(Captain Bruce Fairfeather, Fragments from France, *1917)*

This is not a simple piece of nostalgia or lament at parting, nor is it just saying that the past always appears less painful than the present. The poem's fluctuations of thought and feeling and the corrugations of the verse realise for us the acute discomfort of a state of consciousness, a psychological disposition, in which more or less normal experience becomes an almost intolerable burden, to be mentally heaved and strained at in an effort to get it into some sort of manageable form. "Parting today" is "a double pain," while the present—many Thomas poems debate the relative value or reality of past and present—is a state of being in which, almost by definition for Thomas, the pressure is never taken off; the movement of the verse itself "stirs" and "strains" to convey this state. What sort of a mental condition is this and what sort of a "poetical character"—the appropriateness of Keats's phrase will, I hope, become evident—makes poetry out of it? "Parting" has perhaps a certain affinity of character with the Metaphysicals: the lively speech-movement, the tendency towards involved and paradoxical thought, and something of an explorative habit accompanying a record of "the thought at the moment it arose in the mind." Thomas's verse in general displays an oblique, angular play of mind involving the repetition of words and syntactical arrangements with progressive shifts of meaning, and a terse conjoining of perceptions or ideas which is almost wit were it not for the reticence. All of this embodies a particular self-conscious and analytic attitude towards experience, and to note that Thomas shares this with the Metaphysicals goes some way towards answering my question. But we can also talk about affinities in Thomas with very different writers, Hardy and Robert Frost, for example, or Keats.

The association of Thomas with Keats was made by John Burrow in *Essays in Criticism* in 1957 (Vol. VII, No. 4, pp. 404–15). Mr. Burrow's starting-point is the "rotten little book on Keats" which Thomas told Eleanor Farjeon he had undertaken in the autumn of 1913: "Between the writing of this book and its publication in 1916, Thomas produced nearly all the poems by which he is now known." Mr. Burrow proceeded to argue that "the particular strength of these poems testifies as much to an intelligent reading of Keats as to the acknowledged friendship and advice of Robert Frost." Replying to this article in *E. in C.,* Vol. VIII, No. 2, H. Coombes complained that "Many writers helped to form the man who is the Edward Thomas of the poems," but that nothing in Keats "'became' anything in Thomas's poetry in the simple way Mr. Burrow suggests." This is true; the presence of those "many writers" has been well demonstrated, notably by Mr. Coombes himself and by William Cooke in their books on Thomas. Even so, Mr. Burrow was justified in his perception that "the intimate relation of [Thomas's] critical judgements to his habits as a poet" reveals particular affiliations between his own poetry and Keats's.

I should like, first, to add to Mr. Burrow's evidence a few examples. Observations of natural phenomena such as this in "To Autumn":

> While barred clouds bloom the soft-dying day,
> And touch the stubble-plains with rosy hue

are remarkably similar in the two poets—compare Thomas's

> The pack of scarlet clouds running across
> The harvest evening that seemed endless then.
>   ("Over the Hills")

Though Keats refers here to the dawn, Thomas may be remembering in his *pack* of clouds the "dismal *rack* of clouds Upon the boundaries of day and night," where the sorrowing Hyperion "stretch'd himself" (Book 1, ll. 302–5). In any case the comparison serves to illustrate the strongly metaphorical and concrete habit of expression which the two poets have in common. We will find, too, the same play in both poets with oppositions of cold and warmth, darkness and brightness. Thomas amply qualifies as a possessor of that "poetical Character" which in Keats's definition "enjoys light and shade." When in his book he quotes from the closing stanza of "Ode to Psyche" one senses him savouring the complex of contrasts in "bright torch," the darkness and coolness of night, "warm Love," and (an especially positive sympathy here) "dark-cluster'd trees." Of the quality and character of Keats's Englishness, Thomas says:

> English literature, English poetry, the Muse of his native land . . . was a main part of what England meant for Keats. Nature and poetry joined influences. . . . "I like, I love England–I like its living men. . . ."

This is something very like his own deep-rooted Englishness, and for Thomas, too, English poetry and nature join influences. In his book, Thomas brings out excellently the interdependence for Keats of books—his reading–and nature; to Keats, he says, "The beauty of Nature immediately suggested the beauty of poetry and the translation of one into the other." This is the case for both poets, and not only does Thomas record with obvious satisfaction various aspects of Keats's observation and appreciation of nature, but their particular ways of perceiving and experiencing are similar. One of these is suggested by Thomas, for example, when he admires in Keats's letters the "direct presentation of the moment's phases of mind and moods of temperament," or when he notes "Keats's fidelity to the observation or feeling of the hour."

Thomas's critical study (the finished book was not so "rotten" after all) is, then, the expression of a self-implicating sympathy, a kinship of sensibility and of "poetical character." Thomas recognises in Keats the kind of passive extinction of self in the experience of the moment, the same kind of giving of himself to the weather and other natural manifestations, that is present in his own poems:

> So he could lie awake listening to the night rain "with a sense of being drowned and rotted like a grain of

Snavernake Forest, a part of rural England memorialized by naturalist Richard Jefferies, whom Thomas admired (Edward Thomas, A Literary Pilgrim in England, *1917*)

wheat"; if a sparrow came before his window he could "take part in its existence and pick about the gravel. . . ."

Thomas's "Rain" begins with a similar surrender to the night rain, and draws to a close:

> Like me who have no love which this wild rain
> Has not dissolved except the love of death. . . .

Here Thomas allows the surrender to find its ultimate form in a Keatsian embracing of death. Something like Keats's "taking part in" the life of the sparrow extends in Thomas to virtually all natural objects, to the weather and the seasons. "Digging" ("To-day I think Only with scents. . . .") is a compact expression of the Keatsian abdication to sense-impressions, to the moment's experience. In another poem Thomas loses himself in the life of a butterfly:

> And down upon the dome
> Of the stone the cart-horse kicks against so oft
> A butterfly alighted. From aloft
> He took the heat of the sun, and from below.
> On the hot stone he perched contented so,
> As if never a cart would pass again
> That way; as if I were the last of men
> And he the first of insects to have earth
> And sun together and to know their worth.
> ("The Brook")

In "Sleep and Poetry," we may recall, a butterfly was one of those "peaceful images" which helped to bring Keats release from "Despondence! miserable bane!" (l. 281, ll. 339–45), and we may note in passing, bearing in mind such Thomas poems as "Lights Out" where he speaks of "sleep that is sweeter Than tasks most noble," its alliance with release in sleep. But in Thomas's lines as in Keats's, even the butterfly appears to be losing itself, dissolving its being, in a moment of intense sensuous experience ("As if never a cart would pass again. . . ."), echoing the poet's abdication to such a moment; the identification of man and creature is in "to have earth And sun together. . . ." These points of rest and self-extinction are always bounded by a sense of the continuing reality from which they are an escape: "as if" registers in the reader's mind that a cart will pass again that way, so that much of the poem's effect and meaning emerges from this playing-off of the moment against the continuing reality. Dr. Cooke speaks (though in relation to Frost rather than Keats) of Thomas's "psychological theme of attempted escape and necessary return." And the poem does end with a partial breaking of the spell, a breaking of a kind even more notable in, for example, "The Lane."

Many of Thomas's poems enact in their perplexity both a reconciliation with, and an alienation from, the actual. Keats sometimes effects a reconciliation with life through his escape, by means of a gathering-up of sense-impressions into a concentrated flight of the imagination. There is invariably a rueful return to reality (the ending of "Ode to a Nightingale" is the obvious example), but it is the escape which makes life meaningful and tolerable. "All that I could lose / I lost" says Thomas in "The Brook," indicating by this very statement that the losing is never total. And Thomas is quick to find in Keats his own anti-mystical bent and mode of experiencing through fully physical phenomena:

> . . . though a lover of the moon, a most sublunary poet, earthly, substantial, and precise, a man, but for his intensity, singularly like his fellow-men. . . .

The emphasis could not be more exactly correct for Thomas himself; even his metaphysics are rooted in physical reality; as Mr. Coombes has written, "The grasp of the actual makes us firmly discard 'mystical.'"

This problem of escape from life yet reconciliation with it is again engaged by Thomas when he draws attention to the closing stanza of "Ode to Psyche," with its placing of "a sanctuary" among dark-clustered trees. Keats's wish to build a fane to Psyche "In some untrodden region of my mind" is echoed in, among other poems, Thomas's "Over the Hills":

> Often and often it came back again
> To mind, the day I passed the horizon ridge
> To a new country, the path I had to find
> By half-gaps that were stiles once in the hedge.

Despite the physicality and particularity of detail, it becomes evident as the poem progresses—one notices, for example, the poised effect of "horizon ridge" with the enjambment suggesting some climactic passing from the known into the unknown—that this "new country" does indeed only have its existence in the poet's mind. The phenomenon is symbolised elsewhere as in the song of "The Unknown Bird." The poet told "the naturalists" about the bird, but they were at a loss to identify it. The moment of escape which the symbolism represents, furthermore, cannot be reclaimed. The bird "never came again." "I did not know my loss Till one day twelve months later" says the poet in "Over the Hills," and continues:

> Recall
> Was vain: no more could the restless brook
> Ever turn back and climb the waterfall
> To the lake that rests and stirs not in its nook
> As in the hollow of the collar-bone
> Under the mountain's head of rush and stone.

"Loss" suggests the losing, or extinction, of self in the moment of release, as well the failure to rediscover the moment. And the final lines, with their remarkable representation of a psychological phenomenon in terms of physical phenomena, form a secondary image of the poet's restless and impossible quest, ramifying the poem in a characteristic Thomas manner. The symbolic features in the poem—the horizon, the path, an inn, some "strangers"—are consistent with their use in other poems; they intimate the fulfilment which constantly eludes Thomas. Now, different as this is from the escape into the imagination which is Keats's "untrodden region of my mind," it is like in its representation of an inward quest for fulfilment or self-extinction, for "sanctuary" or rest, and it is like in the imaging of this quest in terms of physical scenery (the dark-clustered trees and mountain ridges of Keats's poem). Neither poet makes mystical claims for his moment of release; it remains a slightly bewildering psychological oddity:

> Surely I dreamt today, or did I see
> The winged Psyche with awaken'd eyes?

or as Thomas puts it: "As if the bird or I were in a dream." But Keats's *cri de coeur* to Reynolds, "lord! a man should have the fine point of his soul taken off to become fit for this world," is what both poets felt acutely, and for both this paradoxical means of reconciliation with life through escape is a mode of rendering experience manageable for the ultra-sensitive man.

The centre of his sympathy for Keats is found by Thomas early in his book:

> In spite of his energy, courage, and independence, he enjoyed and suffered from what he himself called his morbidity of temperament. . . . His morbidity of temperament was inseparably kin to the sensitive passive qualities without which his poetry would have been nothing. I do not mean that his poetry sprang from his morbidity simply, but that both had to do with this brooding intensity of his receptiveness, that they inhabited the same enchanted treasure-caves. Eagerness and joy went with it also.

It must, I think, be admitted that an element of morbidity is there in both poets, and it is this "brooding intensity of receptiveness" which is so alike. Two aspects of this are closely linked: one, a certain imaginative medium, represented by the phrase "enchanted treasure caves" and the other by the terms in which Thomas writes of the Odes and "The Eve of St. Agnes":

> Love for vanished, inaccessible, inhuman things, almost for death itself—regret—and the consolation

Dove Cottage at Grasmere, William Wordsworth's home, which Thomas discusses in his A Literary Pilgrim in England *(1917)*

offered by the intensity which makes pleasure and pain so much alike—are the principal moods of these poems.

Though Thomas is far from the Gothic Revivalism of "The Eve of St. Agnes," he is sometimes able to integrate expressively a touch of fancy into a poem, as with the "castle in Spain" in "Wind and Mist." In "The Path" he refers to:

> the path that looks
> As if it led on to some legendary
> Or fancied place where men have wished to go
> And stay....

This "place" might be compared with Keats's "sanctuary" built in the mind, with its "gardener Fancy." R. P. Eckert writes of Thomas's childhood: "He had always a lively fancy; he used to wander alone about the country near his home with an imaginary companion, 'a spiritual self,' and the country became an almost mythic land." So the "legendary or fancied place" and the curious *alter ego* that figures in several of his poems have their origin in childhood imaginings. The interdependence of books and nature is again apparent in an unobtrusive but repeated tapping in Thomas's poetry of a reservoir of reading in folklore, legend and fairy-tale; the allusions are made discretely to play off a touch of mystery, of the unknown, against his solid natural physicalities. And the allusions stand, fairly obviously, for those regions of the mind in which Thomas and Keats quest for their intangible and elusive fulfilment, the "place where men have wished to go and stay." That this is partly looking back to a legendary past, partly nostalgia for childhood dreams, indicates its close connection with the pervading retrospection, the "groundwork of regret," the "love for vanished" inaccessible, inhuman things, almost for death itself which his poetry shares with Keats's.

This very similar psychological patterning in the work of the two poets brings me to the question of melancholy and its association with "sensitive passive qualities." In writing of Keats, Thomas dwells almost obsessively on passivity and stillness. The "Ode to Melancholy," he writes,

> is one of the central poems of this period, admitting, as it does so fully, and celebrating, the relationship between melancholy and certain still pleasures. Nowhere is the connoisseurship of the quiet, withdrawn spectator so extremely and remorselessly put...

I have already touched upon "The Brook"—there are many such poems—where Thomas himself appears as something of a "quiet, withdrawn spectator," absorbing mood and sense-impressions, passively opening himself up to the perceptions and experience of the moment. He also presents a connoisseur's delicate handling of that experience. Of his own passive temper he wrote to Gordon Bottomley in 1907:

> Why have I no energies like other men? I long for some hatred or indignation or even sharp despair, since love is impossible, to send me out on the road that leads over the hills & among the stars sometimes. I was told the other day that I seemed a calm dispassionate observer with no opinions. I hope I am more. I have no opinions, I know. But cannot the passive temperament do something a little? For I have impressions of men places & books. They often overawe me as a tree or a crowd does the sensitized paper; & is that nothing or as good as nothing?

In a sense, neither poet was without energies, but both seemed susceptible to this lassitude. "I have this morning such a Lethargy that I cannot write," wrote Keats on one occasion, "I am in that temper that if I were under water I would scarcely kick to come to the top." And this incapacity for strong active drives not only sets the poet somewhat apart from "other men," but is also, it seems to me, a constituent of the famous "negative capability." The photographic analogy (I take Thomas to mean this) is apt: the Keatsian or Thomasian temperament is able to give itself up totally to "impressions" or images of an "overawing" kind, to receive their imprint with minute fidelity, in the process undergoing an extinction of self, a "taking part in." It will be remembered that the "poetical Character" which "enjoys light and shade" is usually linked by Keats's commentators with the separate reference in the letters to "negative capability."

Thomas, too, repeatedly admits and celebrates "the relationship between melancholy and certain still pleasures," and records "the consolations offered by the intensity which makes pleasure and pain so much alike." He seems to be pointing to this intensity in himself when he writes again to Bottomley:

> But seriously I wonder whether for a person like myself whose most intense moments were those of depression a cure that destroys the depression may not destroy the intensity....

The "Ode on Melancholy," writes Thomas,

> taken literally, seems to say that the bitter with the sweet is worth while—is the necessary woof of life....

It is an essentially romantic idea, and many of his own poems turn on something very like it. The coupling of "Pleasure and pain" that we notice in "Parting" recurs in many poems. His own "Melancholy"

British troops on the way to the Somme, June 1916 (Jay Winter and Blaine Baggett, The Great War and the Shaping of the 20th Century, *1996)*

employs throughout a Keatsian-romantic notation; the misting over, the retreating into vagueness at the end, is also deeply romantic:

> Yet naught did my despair
> But sweeten the strange sweetness, while through the wild air
> All day long I heard a distant cuckoo calling
> And, soft as dulcimers, sounds of near water falling,
> And, softer, and remote as if in history,
> Rumours of what had touched my friends, my foes, or me.

In part, the poem is a posing of the Keatsian question, "Do I wake or sleep?" The poem pivots, however, on the line and a half preceding those quoted–"What I desired I knew not, but whate'er my choice / Vain it must be" denotes Thomas's central dilemma, the crippling incapacity to define the fulfilment which is always sought; yet growing directly out of this–inextricably bound to it–is the melancholy which is so savoured, the strangely sweet despair (not a "sharp despair"). The dilemma is voiced in "The Glory" with a typical simplicity of paradox: "In hope to find whatever it is I seek," while a more convoluted statement of the paradox occurs in the fourth stanza of "The Other." The desire is active enough, one might say, but the passivity lies in the recalcitrance towards that "choice"; the longing is, in its strange sweetness, its "pleasant pain," almost self-sufficient. Keats's version of the same psychological phenomenon is famous:

> Ay, in the very temple of Delight
> Veil'd Melancholy has her sovran shrine,
> Though seen of none save him whose strenuous tongue
> Can burst joy's grape against his palate fine.

Keats and Thomas share the fine palate. Referring to this passage in his *Romantic Image,* Professor Kermode says it is necessary for the romantic artist in the modern world to "be cut off from life and action, in one way or another. . . . a man who experiences it [the power of joy] will also suffer exceptionally. . . ." Such an artist's isolation is strongly suggested in "Melancholy"; the poet is drawn towards and intensely conscious of the "dear" human world, and at the same time jealous of his own difference. He wishes to lose contact with human voices, and yet regrets doing so—joy and suffering come together: the vacillation and ambiguity of feeling are wholly typical of the kind of temper to which "negative capability" is natural. There is no pressure towards a resolution of dilemmas and ambiguities; it would seem to be the case that in such poetry a cure for the depression would be a destruction of the intensity.

"Melancholy" certainly betrays traces of that temper which when under water would "scarcely kick to come to the top"; elsewhere in the poetry there are references to a certain "Poison" at work, recalling Keats's dreamer who because he cannot keep pain and pleasure apart "venoms all his days" (*The Fall of Hyperion,* Canto 1, 1. 175). There is also in "Melancholy" something of what Thomas finds in relation to Keats's sonnet "Bright Star":

> a man troubled by the principal unrest of life cries out for that same calm, for the oblivion of "melting out his essence fine into the winds," for "soothest sleep that saves from curious conscience"....

Thomas is also attracted in "Bright Star" to "would I were steadfast as thou art" and "steadfast, still unchangeable"; he is like Keats in his apprehension of mortality and transience. The continually changing effects of light and weather and of the seasons on the English countryside seem to image for him "sublunary" alteration; but these changing effects are valued. Detail is unnecessary here; Thomas's critics have shown how, in poems such as "Health," Thomas is at once infinitely troubled by the burden of human consciousness, and yet celebrates its uniqueness. Some poems may exhibit a Keatsian embracing of death, but at the other pole there is the statement in "The Other": "And yet Life stayed on within my soul." He himself makes a point of Keats's love of life: "But he loved life too well to turn his back on anything by which men were moved." The poetry of both is finally affirmative, but the affirmations are interpenetrated with indulged attitudes in the treatment of transience, melancholy, the past, death itself.

A romantic intensity thus characterised, then, is intrinsic to the psychological condition which disposes the poet towards a handling of experience like that in "Parting." But I must elucidate the point more exactly. Thomas's well-known "Wind and Mist" dramatises the "psychological theme of attempted escape (to the house on the hill) and necessary return (to the earth below)." In doing so, it records the ceaseless flux of Thomas's consciousness, in which what is "in the mind" can become actual, the "firm ground" can turn to cloud ("the visible earth . . . like a cloud"), in which reality and "fancy" co-exist and interchange. The "one word" with which the poet leaves us confirms the vacillation between earth and cloud-castle, the impossibility of "choice"—

> "I want to admit
> That I would try the house once more, if I could;
> As I should like to try being young again."

—other than that imposed by irresistible external circumstances. The subject of "Wind and Mist" was the house at Steep in Hampshire in which Thomas and his family lived from 1909 to 1913. Dr. Cooke puts it succinctly: "The house was magnificent, but they never felt at home there." Thomas's wavering about Frost's invitation to return with him to New Hampshire in 1914 shows itself as part of an inveterate indecision, and of a deep sense of his own incapacity to "feel at home" any more in New Hampshire, as he put it to Frost, than in old. In his book *The South Country* he spoke of "those modern people who belong nowhere," and no less than three poems have the title "Home." One of these takes stock of the poet's past life, and adopts a posture for whatever the future may bring:

> Not the end: but there's nothing more.
> Sweet Summer and Winter rude
> I have loved, and friendship and love,
> The crowd and solitude;
>
> But I know them: I weary not;
> But all that they mean I know.
> I would go back again home
> Now. Yet how should I go?
>
> This is my grief. That land,
> My home, I have never seen;
> No traveller tells of it,
> However far he has been.
>
> And could I discover it,
> I fear my happiness there,
> Or my pain, might be dreams of return
> Here, to these things that were.
>
> Remembering ills, though slight
> Yet irremediable,
> Brings a worse, an impurer pang
> Than remembering what was well.
>
> No: I cannot go back,
> And would not if I could.
> Until blindness come, I must wait
> And blink at what is not good.

This and "Parting" (both written, as Dr. Cooke shows, in February 1915 under the pressure of Thomas's impending enlistment) not only have similar movement and verse-form, but are obviously contiguous in terms of material. "Remembering ills" here, for example, immediately connects with "Remembered joy and misery" in the other poem. But here the mood modulates, clearly enough, into an acceptance barely suggested in "Parting." The first two stanzas, despite "I weary not," express the Thomasian longing for release from the burden of consciousness, but then comes the definitive self-diagnosis—"This is my grief": it provides a fixed point of reference for much of the rest of his poetry. Not only is "my home" almost certainly a delusion, like the cloud-castle in "Wind and Mist," but the poet knows that he can never escape the curse of dissatisfaction. He can never be finally certain that it is "there" he wants more than "here," just as there can be no final abandonment of the present—"I cannot go back"—for the refuge of that "strange land," the past. The dilemma is complicated by the fact that he *does* value the here and now, and such a poem as "The Sign-Post" indicates a possible preference for this over the unknown. So, in the final quatrain of "Home" both aspects of the romantic solution to the dilemma—refuge in nostalgia and retrospection, or release into "countries of the mind," "enchanted treasure-caves," death or "whatever it is I seek"—are rejected.

A poem which satisfactorily objectifies this dilemma, by reflecting the dialectic of romantic and counter-romantic tendencies in Thomas's consciousness, is "The Chalk-Pit." Like "Wind and Mist" the poem is a dramatic dialogue between two voices, here more clearly than ever the two sides of Thomas's mind. The two speakers have followed a road which leads to an abandoned chalk-pit and one thinks that he has visited "the place"—these are familiar Thomas symbols—before, looking like an "amphitheatre," with a few trees for actors; but these have now been cut down. There is a certain Hamlet-like note in the poem, a straining to peer into the unknown:

> its emptiness and silence
> And stillness haunt me, as if just before
> It was not empty, silent, still, but full
> Of life of some kind, perhaps tragical . . .
> . . . better leave it like the end of a play
> Actors and audience and lights all gone;
> For so it looks now. In my memory
> Again and again I see it, strangely dark,
> And vacant of a life but just withdrawn.
> We have not seen the woodman with the axe.
> Some ghost has left it now. . . .

That "In my memory . . . strangely dark" recalls again "Parting"; there is something of that Keatsian hovering between stillness and action which is so often for Thomas an effect of the way memory operates. This, indeed, is again what Thomas seems to be examining, while at the same time battling with the way the mind colours reality—the shape, the feel which consciousness gives to an experience. In fact, the whole of the old conundrum about appearance and reality is under debate here:

> For another place
> Real or painted, may have combined with it.

The poem shares with "Parting" and "Home" a sense of the past being just beyond reach and yet impinging crucially on the present; there is, too, something of the same curious distancing of the experiencing mind from the subject of its ruminations, together with a similar "feel" and intensity of that mind's operations realised in the structure and movement of the verse.

Each speaker in "The Chalk-Pit" attempts to come at some suspected inner "core" of significance ("I cannot bite the day to the core," says Thomas in "The Glory") from a different direction. But this never totally yields itself to the mind's grasp, as the last of the two to speak virtually admits. At the same time, he again rejects the "romantic" solution; he will have nothing to do with what his companion calls "fancies":

> "You please yourself. I should prefer the truth
> Or nothing. Here, in fact, is nothing at all
> Except a silent place that once rang loud,
> And trees and us—imperfect friends, we men
> And trees since time began; and nevertheless
> Between us still we breed a mystery."

Yet still there is no positive resolution of romantic and counter-romantic, or of the dilemma of which is more real—here and now, or "there," the past, the "legendary or fancied place." The potency of the romantic experience is still felt: the speaker cannot deny that "mystery" existing in the relation of man to nature, and the implication seems to be that any "truth" which does not take account of it will be insufficient. The emphasis of these final lines, though, confirms our sense of the poem's metaphysics again having primarily to do with psychological rather than mystical phenomena. But Thomas is, more fully than most, a poet who can never come to the point of "final truth"; this is absolutely characteristic of the sort of temper, something very close to "negative capability," we have seen Thomas to possess in common with Keats. His chronic restlessness and acute self-consciousness—he repeatedly complained of both in his letters—combine to eliminate from his poetry the possibility of experience being precipitated towards some definite end. Hence we are left with the experience itself, which is pored over incessantly; valued, and despaired in, for its own sake alone.

No doubt we can diagnose a certain maladjustment in the ambivalent attitude towards reality and in the endemic dissatisfaction and irresolution. At the same time, this is a "poetical character" which, in giving concrete verse form to the process of the acutely conscious, sensitive individual attempting to manage experience, imparts an astonishing freshness to some

Flanders fields (Jay Winter and Blaine Baggett, The Great War and the Shaping of the 20th Century, *1996)*

permanent enigmas. The Keatsian "intensity," the passive, melancholic mental state in which desire and fulfilment are held in almost willing solution, helps to make the poetical character what it is. It is in large part what allows Thomas to make poetry from his peculiar troubled "connoisseurship" of certain kinds of experiential phenomena.

Critical study claiming that Thomas's pastoral poetry can be regarded as a call for ecological balance in the overindustrialized modern world (Edna Longley, "The Business of Earth: Edward Thomas and Ecocentrism," High and Low Moderns: Literature and Culture, 1889–1939, *edited by Maria Di Battista and Lucy McDiarmid [New York: Oxford University Press, 1996], pp. 106–129)*

Modernism and Marxism fetishize the city, but in different ways. The one neglects "nature poetry" as having refused a cognitive and aesthetic revolution; the other criticizes "pastoral" as repressing the exploitation not only of urban workers in the present but of rural workers in the past. For example, the unreal city of American poetic modernism—cosmopolitan London or Paris refracted through "the simultaneity of the ambient"—does not meet the political demands that Raymond Williams (in *The Country and the City*) sees cities as making on the literary imagination. To Williams, T. S. Eliot's urban impressions appear "as relentless and as conventional as pastoral . . . neo-urban imagery, of the same literary kind as the isolated neo-pastoral . . . [mediating] a general despair in the isolated observer." Ultimately he diagnoses a continuing, and perhaps necessary, conflict between modernist urban myth making (best represented by the related but disconnected consciousness streams of *Ulysses*) and the collectivist "social ideas and movements" also produced by the modern city. This dialectical model, with its 1930s aura, still excludes most twentieth-century rural writing in the British Isles. Although Williams finds among the texts of that tradition occasional resistance to an "elegiac, neo-pastoral mode," nonetheless "[t]he underlying pattern is . . . clear. A critique of a whole dimension of modern life, and with it many necessary general questions, was expressed but also reduced to a convention, which took the form of a detailed version of a part-imagined, part-observed rural England . . . [a] strange formation in which observation, myth, record and half-history are . . . deeply entwined."

These remarks follow an analysis of Edward Thomas's poetry in which Williams discerns a few unpastoral sparks, but which he accuses of falling back on "inexpressible alienation." Thomas has often been squeezed by a pincer movement of modernist and Marxist preconceptions—not that this has put off his many "common readers." I want to change the perceptual ground by looking at his "alienation" in the light of contemporary environmental theory, an approach that also reinserts him into the Edwardian period. Formerly I have suggested that various factors prevented Thomas (1878-1917) from becoming a poet of 1900, that he became inevitably a poet of 1914. But the late twentieth century may both reopen some of Thomas's Edwardian contexts and link his "critique of a whole dimension of modern life" (Williams) with issues now on the global political agenda. Perhaps Edward Thomas is, in fact, a poet of the year 2000. Perhaps his symbolic "warning" looks much farther ahead than Wilfred Owen's, just as it had a deeper hinterland. His sonnet "February Afternoon," which thrice repeats the phrase "a thousand years" suggests how readily Thomas himself could think in terms of millennia—although the cumulative effect is hardly millenarian:

> Men heard this roar of parleying starlings, saw,
> A thousand years ago, even as now,
> Black rooks with white gulls following the plough
> So that the first are last until a caw
> Commands that last are first again,—a law
> That was of old when one, like me, dreamed how
> A thousand years might dust lie on his brow
> Yet thus would birds do between hedge and shaw.
>
> Time swims before me, making as a day
> A thousand years, while the broad ploughland oak
> Roars mill-like and men strike and bear the stroke
> Of war as ever, audacious or resigned,
> And God still sits aloft in the array
> That we have wrought him, stone-deaf and stone-blind.

Williams finds here "a tension between [a] sense of timelessness and the sense of war in which, in a different sense 'Time swims before me.'" But "February Afternoon" (to be discussed later) may, in fact, introduce a third perspective whereby human actors and constructs share in a larger earthly drama. This perspective defines Thomas's ecocentric sense of history.

In her book *Environmentalism and Political Theory* (1992) Robyn Eckersley sums up ecocentrism as follows: "Ecocentrism is based on a . . . philosophy of *internal relatedness*, according to which all organisms are not simply interrelated with their environment but also *constituted* by those very environmental interrelationships." Ecocentrism perceives the world as "an intrinsically dynamic interconnected web . . . in which there are no absolutely discrete entities and no absolute dividing lines between . . . the animate and the inanimate, or the human and the nonhuman." Or, as Edward Thomas put it more monosyllabically and musically in 1915:

> There's nothing like the sun as the year dies,
> Kind as it can be, this world being made so,
> To stones and men and beasts and birds and flies,
> To all things that it touches except snow,
> Whether on mountain side or street of town. . . .

The irony that touches the leveling third line, with its regular iambics, denies humanity a primary or Promethean role in "this world" and its making. I argue, first, that Edward Thomas is a prophet of ecocentrism (cognate terms are biocentrism and geocentrism) not only conceptually but also in terms of poetic structure; and second, that to read his poetry (and prose) in this light is to vindicate its Green politics/poetics against criticism from precisely those theoretical quarters that, for Eckersley, fall short of an ecocentric vision. Thus she finds that the "orthodox eco-Marxist approach turned out to be the most active kind of discrimination against the nonhuman world." This is because of its anthropocentric "focus on the relations of production at the expense of the forces of production, and its uncritical acceptance of industrial technology and instrumental reason." Eckersley also analyzes revisionist forms of eco-Marxism as modified by humanism and eco-socialism. Although she discovers more common ground here with the ecocentric perspective, her conclusion is that anthropocentrism keeps sneaking back in, whether as a benign domestication of nature or as the recruitment of Green politics for an anticapitalist agenda. Ultimately, the need for a paradigm shift that would reorient humanity's relation to the rest of nature is not accepted even by the most heretical Marxist thinkers.

Some of Eckersley's arguments have a literary-critical counterpart in Jonathan Bate's innovative *Romantic Ecology* (1991) and a geographic counterpart in Anne Buttimer's *Geography and the Human Spirit* (1993). Bate says in his introduction:

> The 1960s gave us an idealist reading of romanticism which was implicitly bourgeois in its privileging of the individual imagination; the 1980s gave us a post-Althusserian Marxist critique of Romanticism. The first of these readings assumed that the human mind is superior to nature; the second assumed that the economy of human society is more important than . . . the economy of nature. It is precisely these assumptions that are now being questioned by green politics.

In arguing that "there is not an opposition but a continuity between [Wordsworth's] 'love of nature' and his revolutionary politics," Bate several times relies on the insights of Edward Thomas. But he limits Thomas's ecocentric radicalism, his metaphysical and political leaps beyond Wordsworth, by highlighting only his "localism" and concern with place names. These emphases should be construed as strands of a larger web which amounts to more than "connecting the self to the environment." Also, no writer more profoundly tested the romantic poets' legacy to modernity than did Thomas in his criticism and poetry—even testing it to destruction. One problem with Bate's tentatively proposed "ecocriticism" might be the soft streak in English readings of the English "nature" tradition. Here a merely personal subjectivity is the anthropocentrism that keeps sneaking back in. Nor should *every* nature or country poem be identified with the Green revolution—or all versified Green propaganda with poetry. Such traps were latent and occasionally articulated in a "Green" issue of *Poetry Review* (London) that appeared in 1990. Yet something more is required than the editor's reassurance that poets "have remained animists ... [exploring] the mini-Gaia of our daily life" or a reviewer's dismissal of "telling one another how much we care in the worn-out words of greenspeak and sociobabble." The absent element might be historical and critical feeling for where (and how) poetry has pioneered Green themes. Otherwise it will lack the means to carry these themes further.

In her introduction to *Geography and the Human Spirit*, Anne Buttimer calls for freedom from academic and ideological "Faustian frames ... which are no longer appropriate for the challenge of understanding humanity and earth!" She also states (her findings stem from the International Dialogue Project, 1978–88): "Proclamations about the meaning of humanness ... make little sense geographically until they are orchestrated with the more basic nature of dwelling.... Neither humanism nor geography can be regarded as an autonomous field of enquiry.... The common concern is terrestrial dwelling; *humanus* literally means 'earth dweller.'" Earth, man, and home are crucial and interactive terms in the poetry Edward Thomas wrote from his particular "temporal, geographic and cultural setting" (Buttimer's phrase). By persistently asking what it is to be an "inhabitant of earth" ("The Other"), he anticipates the ecohumanism for which various theorists are arguing today. In "The New Year" he takes a fresh look at the sphinx's riddle, at man the earth dweller:

> Fifty yards off, I could not tell how much
> Of the strange tripod was a man. His body,
> Bowed horizontal, was supported equally
> By legs at one end, by a rake at the other:
> Thus he rested, far less like a man than
> His wheel-barrow in profile was like a pig.

Thomas's historical position and cultural coordinates place him at a nodal point in relation to current ecological issues and their intellectual repercussions. "Mainly Welsh" but brought up in London, he moved physically and imaginatively from city to country, from metropolis to region, border and rural parish, from built to natural environments. He walked all over the south of England at a time when its suburbanization, behind which lay agricultural depression, marked a new frontier, and perhaps limit, of the industrial revolution. The rapid erosion of rural England had no counterpart in any other European country. Thomas saw himself as a product of the London suburbs which had mushroomed without being conceptualized or imagined. One of his personae speaks of "belonging to no class or race and having no traditions" and calls people of the suburbs "a muddy, confused, hesitating mass." This is not just alienation that might have been voiced at any time since industrialization or since the always-lost "golden age." It belongs specifically and oppositionally to Edwardian England. Jose Harris, in *Private Lives, Public Spirit: Britain, 1870–1914* (1993) emphasizes how

"Old Somersby Rectory," from the drawing of Alfred Tennyson's birthplace by W. E. F. Britten (Edward Thomas, *A Literary Pilgrim in England, 1917*)

between 1871 and 1881 "the population of the most heavily urbanised counties increased by 75 per cent—the fastest decade of urban growth for the whole of the nineteenth century." Consequently, the "prolonged building boom of the 1870s and 1880s encircled all towns and cities with the middle- and working-class red or yellow brick suburbs, which remain the most enduring physical monument of the late Victorian age." Thomas's irritation with the title of Edward Marsh's "Georgian" anthologies ("Not a few of these [poets] had attained their qualities under Victoria and Edward") might have extended to his own posthumous periodization in such terms.

Edward Thomas's career as a writer, including its poetic apotheosis from December 1914 until his death, coincides with the trajectory traced by Samuel Hynes in *The Edwardian Turn of Mind*: "[T]o think of Edwardian England as a peaceful, opulent world before the flood is to misread the age and to misunderstand the changes that were dramatised by the First World War." At the same time, Hynes exhibits a certain (possibly American, metropolitan, and postmodernist) impatience toward those who failed to swim with tidal waves of social transformation. For example, he criticizes C. F. G. Masterman's literary rural nostalgia—such as his regard for W. H. Davies's *Autobiography of a Super-Tramp* (also promoted by Thomas)—and Masterman's "problem of accepting the idea of a twentieth-century, urban, industrial England." This was not necessarily an idea, a cultural or imaginative accommodation, that could be made overnight. The "shock of the new," as an aesthetic thrill, may bypass culture shocks which literature needs time to absorb. The 1930s, when English society had supposedly got used to the city, saw a back-to-nature movement as striking as that of the 1900s—Louis MacNeice's "hiking cockney lovers." The scenario detailed by *Private Lives, Public Spirit* makes more room for Masterman's hankerings and for Thomas's disquiet with the suburbs. Throughout her study Harris stresses not a Victorian national solidarity beginning to crumble after near-defeat in the Boer War, but a more volcanic and more variegated historical, temporal, and spatial picture. She concludes by underlining "the varying pace of time, the idiosyncrasy of local habits and the frequent conjunction of quite dissimilar or contradictory social structures," and continues:

> Yet my overall point—that the true watershed came at the beginning [1870] rather than the end of the period . . . can be supported on many levels. The shift to a "modern" demographic structure began in the 1870s, and in the eyes of many contemporaries was already alarmingly advanced by 1914. The structural and qualitative transformation of cities did not come with the Industrial Revolution but with the arrival of public utilities and municipal socialism after 1867. . . . It was not the early nineteenth-century factory system, but the onset of mass-production and the retailing and financial revolutions of the 1880s that created the distinctive class, status, and consumer groups that were to characterise British society for much of the twentieth century.

As a reviewer for the *Daily Chronicle* (from 1901) and the *Morning Post*—this was also the period when mass newspapers proliferated—and in his other literary criticism, Thomas was explicit about contemporary instabilities and the challenges they posed to poetry in particular. In 1905, reviewing a book by the feminist Frances Power Cobbe, he describes the present as "an age of doubt and balancing and testing—of distrusting the old and not very confidently expecting the new." In the same year, reviewing new verse, he rebukes both literary arcadianism and arcadian literariness:

> [A] country life is neither more easy nor more simple than a city life. If it were, the world would now be ruled by the brewers, bankers, and journalists who are now taking the place of hops in Kent. And just as, in thinking about life, we cry out for a return to Nature and her beneficent simplicity, so we are apt to cry out for a return to simplicity in literature. . . . A critic has lately spoken of *Tom Jones* and *Pendennis* as unrolling "the infinite variety of human nature before us," and has compared Mr Meredith most unfavourably with them. They are simpler, and they do not disturb. Nothing could be more false than this attitude. If it were also strong, it might endanger much that is most characteristic of our age. . . . Here, before us, are many views which would seem to have been inspired by a cunning search for simplicity. These men are trying to write as if there were no such thing as a Tube, Grape Nuts, love of Nature, a Fabian Society, A Bill for the reform of the Marriage Laws; nor do they show that they are in possession of any grace or virtue which can be set up against those wonders of our age.

Evidently, however, this is no straightforward hurrah for modernity. Thomas's allusions to economic and demographic change and to "wonders of our age" are as ironic as "cunning search for simplicity." As for the political reformism also glanced at, it featured in his disagreements with his father, and his reaction to the Bedales intelligentsia again suggests dissidence from its ethos, if not its aims. Bedales was the progressive school in Hampshire near which Thomas and his family lived from December 1906. Although Helen Thomas, who taught in the kindergarten, was inspired by the school's staff, she records, "[Edward] frankly did not like them, and to them he was an enigma—a solitary wandering creature . . . who had no political beliefs or social theories, and who was not impressed by the school or its ideals.... [T]hey could not like him or rope him in at all."

Helen Thomas may take her husband's lack of politics too literally; but there might be good warrant for a writer's not being impressed by any school and its ideals: Samuel Hynes quotes Beatrice Webb's admission "without apparent regret, that she was 'poetry-blind.'" Yet Thomas then faced the task of developing a literary mode, and perhaps an alternative politics, which would at once interpret what was happening to Kent, remember that Grape Nuts could not be uninvented, and go beyond the false simplicities of the poets under review. It has to be said that it took him nearly ten more years, in the course of which his own "love of Nature" (there is self-irony in the review, too) still perpetrated cunning simplicities: "But at morning twilight I see the moon low in the west like a broken and dinted shield of silver hanging long forgotten outside the tent of a great knight in a wood...." Thomas himself mocked "my soarings & flutterings" over *The South Country* (1909), from which that sentence comes. Yet some parts of the book organize his perceptions in a way that would eventually help to recharge the "nature poem," while other chapters contain literary-critical, sociological, and ecological thinking that tends in the same direction. The literary-critical dimension matters: the Green movement does not always acknowledge its literary origins. Thomas returned to origins (early English and Welsh transactions with nature); read not only all nature poetry up to its romantic apotheosis, but the entire tradition of "country books" culminating in Richard Jefferies and W. H. Hudson: and asked questions about the meaning of this literature in irretrievably complex times. His study *Richard Jefferies* (1909) charts Jefferies's discontent "to some purpose . . . with modernity" and hard-won holistic awareness of "the diverse life of the world, in man, in beast, in tree, in earth and sky, and sea, and stars." Thomas looked for contemporary works "which really show, in verse or prose, the inseparableness of Nature and Man" and approved a modern "diminution of man's importance in the landscape." At the same time, he savaged the "chattering" nature-trash he received for review, and (prefiguring *Romantic Ecology*) regretted the scientific and literary specialization that seemed to "make impossible a grand concerted advance like that which accompanied the French Revolution."

On the sociological front, Thomas's prose abounds in semidocumentary portraits of obsolescent, displaced, or potentially displaced country people. These figures flesh out Jose Harris's representation of "a society in which rootlessness was endemic and in which people felt themselves to be living in many different layers of historic time." What Harris terms "a lurking grief at the memory of a lost domain" (also a feature of Irish cultural nationalism) is, of course, partly Thomas's own grief coloring the canvas. But he does not merely foist his feelings on to real casualties of "the 1880s when, alone among European countries, Britain chose not to protect home producers against American wheat, with a consequent collapse of archaic rural communities, an explosion of migration to great cities...." His father's more upwardly mobile migration from Wales enabled Thomas to connect an autobiographical deracination with the wider forces whereby the countryman was "sinking before the *Daily Mail* like a savage before pox or whisky." Childhood holidays in Wales and Wiltshire had indelibly, if precariously, reconstituted the lost domain. A central trope in *The South Country,* as in Thomas's other prose, is a passage from country to city; then, usually by a second generation, from city to country in an attempted retrieval of loss. This reflexive narrative occupies Chapter 6, "A Return to Nature," which concludes with a last glimpse of "the man from Caermarthenshire," back once more in London "ill-dressed" and "thin" amid a pathetic march of the unemployed: "Comfortable clerks and others of the servile realised that here were the unemployed about whom the newspapers had said this and that . . . and they repeated the word 'Socialism' and smiled at the bare legs of the son of man and the yellow boots of the orator."

In *Edward Thomas* (1986) Stan Smith stresses "A Return to Nature" in his interesting analysis of Thomas's situation as "a superfluous man," a term that Thomas himself borrowed from Turgenev. But while Smith highlights the depopulation of the countryside, arguing that some of the natural beauties of Thomas's England depended on dereliction and that Thomas was responsibly aware of this, he may point his sense of superfluousness too much toward class, too little toward the lost domain with its cultural as well as aesthetic pull. For example, he identifies "the crisis of a generation," which Thomas's writings enact, as "the dilemma of a middle-class liberal individualism under strain, faced with the prospect of its own redundancy in the changed world of a new era, and struggling, with remarkable intensity and integrity, to understand the flux in which it is to go down." First, it is not clear that the Edwardian period was such a bad time for middle-class liberalism. Second, even if there never has been a golden age but only "an *imaginary* plenitude, a utopian land of lost content which is precisely nowhere," Harris's study suggests that Thomas internalized a "crisis" which can be seen as major historical watershed–and not only in the context of England. What Smith perceives as Thomas's symptomatic political paralysis, his deadlock between resignation and revolution, may be a

Pro patria

search for other parameters in addition to class politics. His ultimate discovery of those parameters coincided with his discovery of distinctive poetic forms, and with the impact of the war on his existing sense of crisis.

Thomas's prose is undeniably romantic about "children of earth," about men "five generations thick," about the innocence or earth-motherhood of rural women. Yet his empathy with the London unemployed, which includes their pre-London history, questions whether socialism is the only answer, and whether even rural poverty might not have harbored valuable communal and local meanings now dispersed. (This is not the same as claiming "organicism" for any community: the clearances in the Soviet Union were to prove as socially disastrous as those in the Scottish Highlands.) Similarly, he says of Gypsies: "They belong to the little roads that are dying out." One aspect of Thomas's thought, his inner western rather than southern landscape, understands depopulation, change, obsolescence, dereliction, though not with a consoling nuance: Cornwall's "deserted mines are frozen cries of despair, as if they had perished in conflict with the waste." On a longer time scale the mines consort with "cromlech, camp, circle, hut and tumulus of the unwritten years . . . a silent bedlam of history, a senseless cemetery or museum, amidst which we walk as animals must do when they see those valleys full of skeletons where their kind are said to go punctually to die." Yet the very intensity of this reaction suggests that Thomas sees the current transformations as uniquely ominous for man. The peril is exemplified by the situation of an old man, living in a London suburb where once his father farmed, and mourning the final loss of elm trees which "had come unconsciously to be part of the real religion of men in that neighbourhood . . . and helped to build and keep firm that sanctuary of beauty to which we must be able to retire if we are to be more than eaters and drinkers and newspaper readers." Today's deep ecologists would endorse that interconnectedness, rephrased in "The Chalk Pit": "imperfect friends, we men / And trees since time began; and nevertheless / Between us still we breed a mystery."

Thomas's prose writings criticize "the parochialism of humanity" with respect to larger evolutionary processes. This critique, which chimes with the Green stress on the short-termism of our species, comes to a head in *The South Country,* where he exclaims: "How little do we know of the business of the earth, not to speak of the universe; of time, not to speak of eternity." Or, as Edward O. Wilson puts it in *The Diversity of Life* (1992): "The biosphere . . . remains obscure." "Earth" in Thomas's poetry is not only a spatial but also a temporal domain. Although (or because) he was a historian himself by academic training, *The South Country* attacks the tunnel vision of orthodox historians, comparing them to "a child planting flowers severed from their stalks and roots, expecting them to grow." This covers not only "the unwritten years" but also the excluded species and ignorance of how our own has survived. Similarly, Wilson observes: "Humanity is part of nature. . . . Only in the last moment of human history has the delusion arisen that people can flourish apart from the rest of the living world." Thomas understands this delusion when he says, "We are not merely twentieth-century Londoners or Kentish men or Welshmen," or appeals for a holistic approach to human and natural history. This would show us "in animals, in plants . . . what life is, how our own is related to theirs . . . in fact, our position, responsibilities and debts among the other inhabitants of the earth." "Digging" is both an eco-historical poem (like "February Afternoon") and a symbolic model for eco-historical research:

> What matter makes my spade for tears or mirth,
> Letting down two lay pipes into the earth?
> The one I smoked, the other a soldier
> Of Blenheim, Ramillies, and Malplaquet
> Perhaps. The dead man's immortality
> Lies represented lightly with my own,
> A yard or two nearer the living air
> Than bones of ancients who, amazed to see

Almighty God erect the mastodon,
Once laughed, or wept, in this same light of day.

Thomas's eco-history provides a tough and agnostic basis for his ecocentric philosophy. He anticipated (by eighty years) Andrew Dobson's précis: "The science of ecology teaches us that we are part of a system that stretches back into an unfathomable past and reaches forward into an incalculable future...." Thomas writes in the chapter of *The South Country* called "History and the Parish": "In some places history has wrought like an earthquake, in others like an ant or mole; everywhere, permanently; so that if we but knew or cared, every swelling of the grass, every wavering line of hedge or path or road were an inscription, brief as an epitaph, in many languages and characters. But most of us know only a few of these unspoken languages of the past...." The text of the earth remains to be read, and not all its inscriptions are human. In "November" the speaker exclaims:

the prettiest thing on ground are the paths
With morning and evening hobnails dinted,
With foot and wing-tip overprinted
Or separately charactered,
Of little beast and little bird.

It is often claimed that any such long-term view is merely a device for discouraging protest. Here I want to bring together Thomas's historical situation and his ecocentrism, at their wartime crisis point, as a preliminary to exploring some of their structural and epistemological consequences in his poetry. Just as Raymond Williams sees "February Afternoon" as simply opposing a sense of timelessness to a sense of war, so Robert Wells has criticized Thomas for being philosophically "unable to protest; not against the destruction of [English rural] culture nor against the mass slaughter of the men who embodied the culture." It all depends on what you mean by "protest." In "In Memoriam (Easter, 1915)" Thomas does not minimize a catastrophe when, rather than comparing the dead to flowers, or ridiculing that comparison, he points to a socio-ecological alteration:

The flowers left thick at nightfall in the wood
This eastertide call into mind the men,
Now far from home, who, with their sweethearts, should,
Have gathered them and will do never again.

Similarly, "February Afternoon" and "Digging" are not really saying it will be or was "all the same in a thousand years" or several thousand years. Both poems are partly framed as ironical questions to human powers-that-be—political and religious—in the context of an ecosystem to which they belong and from which they might learn. Anger works through perspectives such as "The dead man's immortality / Lies represented lightly with my own," with the ambiguity of "immortality" (as in "Haymaking," quoted later) and the oxymoronic pun on "represented lightly." Here, you might say, war recruits achieve solidarity beyond the parochialism of the contemporary. Also, "living air" and "light of day" seem ecological accusations. They contrast with the (self-sponsored) reduction of the human element to dead "matter" and the doubt as to whom it matters in another sense. Indeed, "the living air," the biosphere, questions the binary opposition of "tears or mirth." One sign of such questioning is that "Digging" (the first poem Thomas wrote after his enlistment) is a revision of an earlier poem of the same title. Initially he picks up on its final rhyme, given more emphasis and some irony by a rhyming couplet. Thus the rhyme sequence from poem to poem runs as follows: earth, mirth, mirth, earth. "Earth," the key word in common and enclosing term of the chiasmus, shifts in meaning from soil, humus, to more global suggestions. The disturbing archaeology of "Digging" [II] upsets a harmony, above ground, in "Digging" [I], whereby "It is enough / To smell, to crumble the dark earth, / While the robin sings over again / Sad songs of Autumn mirth." Here the robin's song is said to integrate what the later poem perceives as a split in (or owing to) human consciousness: we laugh or weep. "February Afternoon" also inquires into the oppositional habits that produce wars in which "men" can be only "audacious or resigned." The sonnet incorporates a political bird fable in its use of a starlings' parliament, perhaps in democratic contrast to imagery of gulls led by rooks. But if the natural world is competitive, too, it seems better regulated. Men who plow (or dig) contribute to the system. Men at war become unable to see or hear what the animal or vegetable creation might be suggesting. This blindness and deafness is totalized in a patriarchal Judaeo-Christian God "aloft," transcendental, out of touch with the earth: "And God still sits aloft in the array / That we have wrought him...." "Array" hits at religious forms lacking the substance that a genuine "humanus" might have put there. ("Almighty God" in "Digging" is a similar construct on the part of our inability to read an evolutionary environment in which we have survived the mastodon.) When "the broad plough land oak / Roars mill-like" with starlings, like the mastodon it is both an emblem of earth at war and a reminder of older "laws." Thomas's historical sense in the poem functions in the same microcosmic way as his spatial sense. If he uses millennia to get into focus one day in 1916, one day in 1916 also focuses millennia.

A war fought in mud (Jay Winter and Blaine Baggett, The Great War and the Shaping of the 20th Century, *1996)*

Thomas's eco-history is equal to interpreting briefer timespans and individual lifespans. "Man and Dog" and "A Private" complement each other as concentrations of Thomas's earlier rural biographies, which themselves culminated in several articles about rural and urban England preparing or unprepared for war: "I shall write down, as nearly as possible, what I saw and heard, hoping not to offend too much those who had ready-made notions as to how an Imperial people should or would behave in time of war, of such a war. . . ." Robert Wells cites "Man and Dog" when he faults Thomas for merely elegizing a culture, thereby assenting in its "general will to die." This political and critical naivete suggests that Wells, rather than Thomas, has succumbed to fatalism and "shows little sense of the common tragedy in which Europe was caught by the war." England was a window for Thomas, not an insular limit, and "elegy" is a wide-ranging genre, not an invariably passive lament.

"'Twill take some getting." "Sir, I think 'twill so."
The old man stared up at the mistletoe
That hung too high in the poplar's nest for plunder
Of any climber, though not for kissing under:
Then he went on against the northeast wind—
Straight but lame, leaning on a staff new-skinned,
Carrying a brolly, flag-basket, and old coat,—
Towards Alton, ten miles off. And he had not
Done less from Chilgrove where he pulled up docks. . . .

At certain historical junctures the artist's most useful action may be to point the camera. But there is analysis and criticism in this subtly blended elegy. As the speaker attends to oral history stemming from the last third of the nineteenth century, we learn in a seemingly incidental phrase that the man's "sons, three sons, were fighting." This information takes its place in a shifting history of hard work, hardship, and environmental change. Industrial casual labor has encroached on farm laboring, itself grown casual, and the old man, too, has been a soldier:

His mind was running on the work he had done
Since he left Christchurch in the New Forest, one
Spring in the 'seventies,–navvying on dock and line
From Southampton to Newcastle-on-Tyne.
In 'seventy-four a year of soldiering
With the Berkshires,–hoeing and harvesting
In half the shires where corn and couch will grow.

If the close of the poem moves with an autumnal rhythm, it simultaneously condemns the exploitative ethic that has led to the war and the man's obsolescence:

> "Many a man sleeps worse tonight
> Than I shall." "In the trenches." "Yes, that's right.
> But they'll be out of that–I hope they be–
> This weather, marching after the enemy."
> "And so I hope. Good luck." And there I nodded
> "Good night. You keep straight on." Stiffly he plodded;
> And at his heels the crisp leaves scurried fast,
> And the leaf-coloured robin watched. They passed,
> The robin till next day, the man for good,
> Together in the twilight of the wood.

This counterpoints the histories of man, robin, and trees. All the life in the poem belongs in different but interconnected ways to what is "passing," to the business of the earth. There is, however, an implied question about the accelerating human impact on natural systems and cycles. The old man's relationship to the earth, on balance–and in balance–positive, is becoming a thing of the past. And yet, within the politics of this scenario, the nonhuman creation is shown to resist subjugation: mistletoe plays hard to get; couch grass grows with corn; the man can skin a staff but has been lamed by a fall from a tree; the robin appears noncommittal; the leaves "scurry" as if speeding a departure. Meanwhile, humanity's self-destructive tendencies are accelerating too: "shires" have become regiments. Thus the poem's valedictory vista disturbingly implicates all its readers ("the man for good"). According to eco-history, human endings matter but are not all that matter. As the conclusion of another poem, "The Mountain Chapel," reminds us: "When gods were young / This wind was old."

The old man's passing, individually if not culturally, might be seen as a fitting evolutionary return to the earth (compare the death of Lok in William Golding's novel *The Inheritors*). But this does not apply to the swifter recycling implied by "Digging" or grimly encapsulated in Thomas's lines "when the war began / To turn young men to dung" ("Gone, Gone Again"). The death of "A Private" covers the intolerable plight of the old man's sons:

> This ploughman dead in battle slept out of doors
> Many a frozen night, and merrily
> Answered staid drinkers, good bedmen, and all bores:
> "At Mrs Greenland's Hawthorn Bush," said he,
> "I slept." None knew which bush. Above the town,
> Beyond "The Drover," a hundred spot the down
> In Wiltshire. And where now at last he sleeps
> More sound in France–that, too, he secret keeps.

The war has prematurely violated the ploughman/private's bonds with "Mrs Greenland"– a joke that anticipates Gaia. And his riddle about where he sleeps, together with the poem's own ironic, riddling play on "privacy" and secrecy, further accuses human agencies of usurping earth-mysteries. When Thomas himself got to the front (in January 1917), it is not incongruous that his "War Diary" should have intermingled nature notes and battle log, thus conveying a whole environment under bombardment. The second-to-last entry (April 7) reads: "A cold bright day of continuous shelling. . . . Larks, partridges, hedgesparrows, magpies by O[bservation] P[ost]. A great burst in red brick building in N. Vitasse stood up like a birch tree or fountain. Back at 7.30 in peace. Then at 8.30 a continuous roar of artillery."

. . . Ecology, like economy, derives from the Greek *oikos,* home. "Home" is a key word in Thomas's meditation on England (as is "England" in his meditation on home), a much-canvassed topic, to which David Gervais has made a contribution. Gervais stresses the "partial, private," and provisional nature of Thomas's England, criticizes any attempt to recruit his poetry for a pure elixir of Englishness, and says: "We rarely find [Hardy's] shared meaning in the rural life Thomas writes about. . . . Thomas did not come to his England from a position sufficiently inside and of it to think of it as more than special and local. He was reticent when it came to investing it with any significance beyond itself (as later readers have been tempted to do)." Hardy's kind of "shared meaning" may still be accessible in "the inn, the smithy, and the shop" but the aspen-poet listens to other winds. If Thomas sought and found Englishness most persuasively in particulars, localities, and momentary epiphanies, this in itself deconstructs the totalizing, centralizing propensities that "Great Britain" was beginning to assume in the Edwardian era, and which were eventually to culminate in the Thatcherite project. Commentators such as John Lucas in *England and Englishness* (1990), who maintain that "rootedness is always something wished on others," unwittingly testify to the success of that century-long hegemonic trend. Thomas's local emphases, including his interest in dialect and folk song, can also be seen as intelligently conservationist. Jose Harris writes: "[An] intense and variegated local and provincial culture was still a major strand in British social life between 1870 and 1914 . . . [although] the late Victorian period saw a subterranean shift in the balance of social life away from the locality to the metropolis and the nation. The elements in this shift were complex and only partly visible to contemporaries...." Evidently they were visible to Edward Thomas, and he looked for countervailing elements in communities farther from the metropolis. Hence his alertness to the literature of "intimate reality" inspired by Ireland as contrasted with Britannia—"a frigid personification." *Beautiful Wales* (1905) devotes half a page of its first chapter to reciting the names of places visited, and attributes extreme and holistic local loyalties to some of the people met. Of course, as *Beautiful Wales* indicates, the suburbs had reached Wales, too, though change was slower there. Thomas's Anglo-Welshness may or may not have involved "contradictions." It certainly gave him insights that dramatized the conflict, throughout the British Isles, between modernization and traditional kinds of communal self-understanding, a conflict that is not quite over yet. I have already argued that, for Thomas, "shared meaning" requires participation in a wider web than the social nexus Gervais finds lacking in his work.

Thomas wrote three poems called "Home," and two of them are unhappy. The first (February 1915) begins "Not the end: but there's nothing more," and turns on an unresolved tension between utopian or arcadian possibility ("That land, / My home, I have never seen") and the "fear [that] my happiness there, / Or my pain, might be dreams of return / Here, to the things that were." On its social level, this parable sticks with the present while registering the lost domain. The third in the series, written in March 1916, after his enlistment, has a more exclusively cultural focus. The title is given in quotation marks, and the poem concerns a walk taken by three soldiers over "untrodden snow" in the "strange" countryside around their training camp:

> The word "home" raised a smile in us all three,
> And one repeated it, smiling just so
> That all knew what he meant and none would say.
> Between three counties far apart that lay
> We were divided and looked strangely each
> At the other, and we knew we were not friends
> But fellows in a union that ends
> With the necessity for it, as it ought. . . .

In this poem of division and estrangement, "shared meaning" is precluded because the meaning shared is that "home" means different things, different places, different perceptions. The men have been constrained into a military, and perhaps national, "union" that overrides local particularisms. Thomas's poetry is shaped by the antinomies: familiar/strange; known/unknown or unknowable; solitude/society. These antinomies raise overlapping questions about psychic, cultural, and eco-

Memorial window dedicated to Edward Thomas and etched by Laurence Whistler at Eastbury Church (Collection of Myfanwy Thomas)

logical belonging which are most affirmatively answered in the second "Home" poem (April 1915). Here, to quote Robyn Eckersley, the various "organisms" are harmoniously "constituted by environmental interrelationships," while psychology and culture also achieve equilibrium:

> Often I had gone this way before:
> But now it seemed I never could be
> And never had been anywhere else;
> Twas home; one nationality
> We had, I and the birds that sang,
> One memory.
>
> They welcomed me. I had come back
> That eve somehow from somewhere far:
> The April mist, the chill, the calm,
> Meant the same thing familiar
> And pleasant to us, and strange too,
> Yet with no bar.

The extension of "nationality," historical "memory," and shared meaning to birds is a subversive stroke in 1915. It sharpens the similar transferrals in Thomas's prose, of sociopolitical vocabulary to "this commonwealth of things that live in the sun, the air, the earth, the sea, now and through all time." That phrase occurs in his meditation on "the business of the earth" and on the reality that the "rumour of much toil and scheming and triumph may never reach the stars. . . . We know not by what we survive." The poem ends by including in its local ecosystem a laborer who "went along, his tread / Slow, half with weariness, half with ease," and the "sound of [his] sawing" is given the last word. This construction of "Home" partly endorses, partly qualifies, Thomas's wartime redefinition of "England" as "a system of vast circumferences circling round the minute neighbouring points of home." Its ecosystem is not necessarily a national microcosm but cognitively self-sufficient. Thus the centrifugal implications converge on those of "Home" in quotation marks. "England," as well as "Great Britain," has to be broken down. Thomas's originality in reimagining the "knowable community," however, is to fuse ecology and sociality, to unite environmental and local/regional priorities against the metropolis. Yet, as a poet concerned about the condition of England, Thomas sometimes insinuates that its "system of vast circumferences" becomes the interconnected web of his own poems, which might have various local meanings. In the camp, talking to fellow recruits about England, he was pleased to find "There isn't a man I don't share some part with."

Thomas's poetry destabilizes authority, perception, and time in a spirit often regarded as peculiar to modernist aesthetics. It does so with precise reference to environmental and epistemological issues latent in his immediate historical context. And it exhibits a kind of historical imagination usually precluded by the premises of American and Irish modernism. His antinomial landscape is also compounded of presence and absence: a matter not of theoretical protocols but of lost domains, senseless cemeteries, and human departures—the "flowers left thick at nightfall," "two clay pipes," "a ghostly room." Stan Smith has demonstrated that the "ghost is one of the commonest tropes in Thomas's poetry." But absence in Thomas not only laments or prophesies loss but also marks what ought to be there. The poet returns from the margin, "comes back . . . from somewhere far," with meanings for community.

Thomas is as occupied with meaning and language as modernist writing is supposed to be, and often more disturbingly. "I read the sign. Which way shall I go?" says "The Signpost," one of his first poems, and the poetry that follows reads many ambiguous natural and cultural signs that are missed by contemporary theorists (Robyn Eckersley attacks "The Failed Promise of Critical Theory" from an ecocentric viewpoint). Indeed, Thomas's interest in language pivots on relations between nature and culture: not just the anthropocentric question whether culture seeks to "naturalize" itself for suspect political reasons, but the ecocentric question whether human languages remain in touch with their environmental origins. "The Combe" begins, "The Combe was ever dark, ancient and dark. / Its mouth is stopped with bramble, thorn, and briar." If this suggests the impenetrability of some earth languages, the poem goes on to find the Combe's stopped mouth less dismaying than an ecological violence that bears on England at war, not only with Germany but with itself:

> But far more ancient and dark
> The Combe looks since they killed the badger there,
> Dug him out and gave him to the hounds,
> That most ancient Briton of English beasts.

Thomas's humanizing language for the badger (which invokes Celtic rather than imperial Britain) tries to heal a split in home and in natural man. In "Words" Thomas celebrates the English language for being "as dear / As the earth which you prove / That we love." Language, too, has a long ecohistory, being "[a]s our hills are, old." Similarly, the elusive "Lob" represents one language's evolutionary fitness in speech and writing: "Calling the wild cherry tree the merry tree." In this positive linguistic scenario, it is not that "word" exactly or referentially reproduces "thing," but that the associations of words, in an ecological sense, testify to the development of language (and literature) as a function of bodily, sensory, local, and earthly existence. The likeness/difference of bird language is not just a sentimentality on Thomas's part. Humanity kept itself in the text through language. And our ability to ensure that language is "Worn new / Again and again" ("Words") depends on recognizing the "lost homes" it harbors.

But the dark alternative is that man's textual inscriptions may wear thin or lose touch. Two of Thomas's first poems, "March" and "Old Man, "written on consecutive days, stand in an antinomial symbolic relation to each other. In "March" Thomas identifies his own artistic release with thrushes imposing their song after bad weather has "kept them quiet as the primroses" and postponed spring: "So they could keep off silence / And night, they cared not what they sang or screamed." At the end of "March" there is a sense that the linked vocal efforts of poet and birds have been productive. "Old Man" begins by holding the human and nonhuman creation in a precarious balance:

> Old Man, or Lad's-love,–in the name there's nothing
> To one that knows not Lad's-love, or Old Man,
> The hoar-green feathery herb, almost a tree,
> Growing with rosemary and lavender.
> Even to one that knows it well, the names
> Half decorate, half perplex, the thing it is:
> At least, what that is clings not to the names
> In spite of time. And yet I like the names.

Certainly this does not subscribe to a correspondence theory of language, or suggest contradictory names that any single verbal formula can get at "the thing it is."

The contradictory names of the plant, and the speaker's liking for them, however, belong to a history of proximate if not shared meanings. In contrast, the end of "Old Man" unravels the interconnected web ("I have mislaid the key. I sniff the spray / And think of nothing; I see and I hear nothing") to open up a vista devoid of human presence, history, memory, meaning, and language: "Only an avenue, dark, nameless, without end." Nonhuman creatures can cope with nameless things, or speak "thingless names," but not mankind. This ultimate or original absence is not the silence and night that Thomas sometimes welcomes as an earthly requiescat. It forebodes the premature encroachment of "nothingness" if we "mislay the key" to the domain, if we cease desiring to be "not a transitory member of a parochial species, but a citizen of the Earth."

Appendix:
Other British Poets Who Fell in the Great War

Brian Brooke
Captain, Second Battalion, Gordon Highlanders
Wounded 1 July 1916, died 25 July

Poems, foreword by M. P. Willcocks (London: John Lane, Bodley Head, 1917).

Leslie Coulson
Sergeant, Twelfth London Battalion, Royal Fusiliers
Died of wounds 7 October 1916 near Lesboeufs in the Somme valley

From an Outpost and Other Poems, introduction by F. Raymond Coulson (London: Macdonald, 1917).

Richard Molesworth Dennys
Captain, Loyal North Lancashire Regiment
Wounded in the Somme advance 12 July 1916, died 24 July

There Is No Death: Poems, foreword by Captain Desmond Coke (London: John Lane, Bodley Head, 1917).

Hugh Reginald "Rex" Freston
Second Lieutenant, Third Royal Berkshire Regiment
Killed in action in France 24 January 1916

The Quest of Beauty, and Other Poems (Oxford: Blackwell, 1915);
The Quest of Truth, and Other Poems (Oxford: Blackwell, 1916);
Collected Poems (Oxford: Blackwell, 1916).

Hon. Julian Grenfell, D.S.O.
Captain, Royal Dragoons
Wounded 12 May 1915 near the Ypres-Menen road, died 26 May

Into Battle, as J. G. (London: Privately printed by the Medici Society, 1915).

William Noel Hodgson, M.C.
(Edward Melbourne)
Lieutenant, Ninth Devon Regiment
Killed in the Somme advance 1 July 1916

Verse and Prose in Peace and War (London: Smith, Elder, 1916).

Thomas Michael Kettle
Lieutenant, Ninth Dublin Fusiliers
Killed in the First Battle of the Somme 8 September 1916

Poems and Parodies, preface by William Dawson (London: Duckworth, 1916).

Francis Ledwidge
*Lance-Corporal, Fifth Battalion, Royal Inniskilling Fusiliers
Killed in Flanders 31 July 1917*

Songs of Peace, introduction by Lord Dunsany (London: Jenkins, 1917);
Last Songs, introduction by Lord Dunsany (London: Jenkins, 1918);
The Complete Poems of Francis Ledwidge, introduction by Lord Dunsany (London: Jenkins, 1919; New York: Brentano's, 1919).

Ewart Alan Mackintosh, M.C.
Lieutenant, Seaforth Highlanders
Killed at Cambrai 21 November 1917

A Highland Regiment (London: John Lane / New York: John Lane, 1917);
War, the Liberator, and Other Pieces: With a Memoir (London: Bodley Head / New York: John Lane, 1918).

Charles John Beech Masefield, M.C.
Acting Captain, Fifth North Staffordshire Regiment
Wounded in action 1 July 1917, died in prisoner of war camp 2 July

Gilbert Hermer: The Memory of a Man, His Ways and His Words. Written by the Friend of His Age (Edinburgh & London: Blackwood, 1908);
Staffordshire (London: Methuen, 1910);
The Seasons' Difference, and Other Poems (London: Fifield, 1911);
Dislikes: Some Modern Satires (London: Fifield, 1914);
Poems, introduction by A. St. John Adcock (Oxford: Blackwell, 1919).

Francis St. Vincent Morris
Second Lieutenant, Third Battalion, Sherwood Foresters
Died of wounds 29 April 1917

The Poems of F. St. V. Morris, with a Memoir by L. A. G. S. (Oxford: Blackwell, 1917).

Hon. Colwyn Erasmus Arnold Philipps
Captain, Royal Horse Guards
Killed near Ypres 13 May 1915

Colwyn Erasmus Arnold Philipps, Captain, Royal Horse Guards . . . Verses—Prose Fragments—Extracts from Letters from the Front . . . November 1914 to April 1915 (London: Smith, Elder, 1915).

Alexander Robertson
Corporal, Twelfth York and Lancaster Regiment
Killed in action 1 July 1916

Comrades (London: Elkin Mathews, 1916);
Last Poems, preface by P. Hume Brown (London: Elkin Mathews, 1918).

Charles Hamilton Sorley
Captain, Suffolk Regiment
Killed at Loos 13 October 1915

Marlborough, and Other Poems, preface by W. R. Sorley (Cambridge: Cambridge University Press, 1916);
Letters from Germany and from the Army, edited by W. R. Sorley (Cambridge: Privately printed, 1916);
The Letters of Charles Sorley: With a Chapter of Biography (Cambridge: Cambridge University Press, 1919);
Charles Hamilton Sorley: Selected Poems (London: Benn, 1931).

John William Streets
Sergeant, Twelfth York and Lancaster Regiment
Mortally wounded in the Somme advance 1 July 1916

Truth! An Allegory; The Temple of Youth, and the Spirit of Melancholy: Poems (London: Arthur H. Stockwell, 1912); *The Undying Splendour* (London: Macdonald, 1917).

Hon. Edward Wyndham Tennant
Lieutenant, Fourth Battalion, Grenadier Guards
Killed in the First Battle of the Somme 22 September 1916

Worple Flit, and Other Poems (Oxford: Blackwell, 1916).

Robert Ernest Vernède
Lieutenant, Third Rifle Brigade, Ninth Royal Fusiliers
Killed at Havrincourt Wood 9 April 1917

Meriel of the Moors: A Romance. From the MSS. of T. T. Redd, Esq. (London: Alston Rivers, 1906);
The Judgement of Illingborough (London: Hodder & Stoughton, 1908);
The Fair Dominion: A Record of Canadian Impressions (London: Kegan Paul, Trench, Trübner, 1911);
An Ignorant in India (Edinburgh & London: Blackwood, 1911);
The June Lady (London: Constable, 1912);
The Pursuit of Mr. Faviel (London: Nelson, 1913);
Letters to His Wife, edited by C. H. Vernède (London: Collins, 1917);
War Poems, and Other Verses, introduction by Edmund Gosse (London: Heinemann, 1917);
The Quietness of Dick (London: Collins, 1918);
The Port Allington Stories and Others (London: Heinemann, 1921).

Eric Fitzwater Wilkinson, M.C.
Captain, Leeds Rifles, West Yorkshire Regiment
Killed in the attack on Passchendaele Ridge 9 October 1917

Sunrise Dreams, and Other Poems (London: Macdonald, 1916).

Cumulative Index

Dictionary of Literary Biography, Volumes 1-216
Dictionary of Literary Biography Yearbook, 1980-1998
Dictionary of Literary Biography Documentary Series, Volumes 1-19

Cumulative Index

DLB before number: *Dictionary of Literary Biography,* Volumes 1-216
Y before number: *Dictionary of Literary Biography Yearbook,* 1980-1998
DS before number: *Dictionary of Literary Biography Documentary Series,* Volumes 1-19

A

Aakjær, Jeppe 1866-1930 .... DLB-214
Abbey, Edwin Austin 1852-1911 .... DLB-188
Abbey, Maj. J. R. 1894-1969 .... DLB-201
Abbey Press DLB-49
The Abbey Theatre and Irish Drama,
  1900-1945 .... DLB-10
Abbot, Willis J. 1863-1934 .... DLB-29
Abbott, Jacob 1803-1879 .... DLB-1
Abbott, Lee K. 1947- DLB-130
Abbott, Lyman 1835-1922 .... DLB-79
Abbott, Robert S. 1868-1940 .... DLB-29, 91
Abe Kōbō 1924-1993 .... DLB-182
Abelard, Peter circa 1079-1142? DLB-115, 208
Abelard-Schuman DLB-46
Abell, Arunah S. 1806-1888 .... DLB-43
Abell, Kjeld 1901-1961 .... DLB-214
Abercrombie, Lascelles 1881-1938 .... DLB-19
Aberdeen University Press Limited DLB-106
Abish, Walter 1931- DLB-130
Ablesimov, Aleksandr Onisimovich
  1742-1783 .... DLB-150
Abraham à Sancta Clara 1644-1709 ...... DLB-168
Abrahams, Peter 1919- DLB-117
Abrams, M. H. 1912- DLB-67
Abrogans circa 790-800 .... DLB-148
Abschatz, Hans Aßmann von
  1646-1699 .... DLB-168
Abse, Dannie 1923- DLB-27
Abutsu-ni 1221-1283 .... DLB-203
Academy Chicago Publishers DLB-46
Accius circa 170 B.C.-circa 80 B.C. DLB-211
Accrocca, Elio Filippo 1923- DLB-128
Ace Books DLB-46
Achebe, Chinua 1930- DLB-117
Achtenberg, Herbert 1938- DLB-124
Ackerman, Diane 1948- DLB-120
Ackroyd, Peter 1949- DLB-155
Acorn, Milton 1923-1986 .... DLB-53
Acosta, Oscar Zeta 1935?- DLB-82
Acosta Torres, José 1925- DLB-209
Actors Theatre of Louisville DLB-7
Adair, Gilbert 1944- DLB-194
Adair, James 1709?-1783? DLB-30
Adam, Graeme Mercer 1839-1912 .... DLB-99
Adam, Robert Borthwick II 1863-1940 ... DLB-187
Adame, Leonard 1947- DLB-82
Adamic, Louis 1898-1951 .... DLB-9
Adams, Abigail 1744-1818 .... DLB-200
Adams, Alice 1926- Y-86
Adams, Brooks 1848-1927 .... DLB-47
Adams, Charles Francis, Jr. 1835-1915 ... DLB-47
Adams, Douglas 1952- Y-83
Adams, Franklin P. 1881-1960 .... DLB-29
Adams, Hannah 1755-1832 .... DLB-200
Adams, Henry 1838-1918 .... DLB-12, 47, 189
Adams, Herbert Baxter 1850-1901 ...... DLB-47
Adams, J. S. and C. [publishing house] ... DLB-49
Adams, James Truslow
  1878-1949 .... DLB-17; DS-17
Adams, John 1735-1826 .... DLB-31, 183
Adams, John 1735-1826 and
  Adams, Abigail 1744-1818 .... DLB-183
Adams, John Quincy 1767-1848 .... DLB-37
Adams, Léonie 1899-1988 .... DLB-48
Adams, Levi 1802-1832 .... DLB-99
Adams, Samuel 1722-1803 .... DLB-31, 43
Adams, Sarah Fuller Flower
  1805-1848 .... DLB-199
Adams, Thomas 1582 or 1583-1652 .... DLB-151
Adams, William Taylor 1822-1897 .... DLB-42
Adamson, Sir John 1867-1950 .... DLB-98
Adcock, Arthur St. John 1864-1930 ..... DLB-135
Adcock, Betty 1938- DLB-105
Adcock, Fleur 1934- DLB-40
Addison, Joseph 1672-1719 .... DLB-101
Ade, George 1866-1944 .... DLB-11, 25
Adeler, Max (see Clark, Charles Heber)
Adonias Filho 1915-1990 .... DLB-145
Advance Publishing Company DLB-49
Ady, Endre 1877-1919 .... DLB-215
AE 1867-1935 .... DLB-19
Ælfric circa 955-circa 1010 .... DLB-146
Aeschines circa 390 B.C.-circa 320 B.C.
  .... DLB-176
Aeschylus
  525-524 B.C.-456-455 B.C. DLB-176
Aesthetic Poetry (1873), by Walter Pater ... DLB-35
After Dinner Opera Company Y-92
Afro-American Literary Critics:
  An Introduction DLB-33
Agassiz, Elizabeth Cary 1822-1907 ...... DLB-189
Agassiz, Jean Louis Rodolphe
  1807-1873 .... DLB-1
Agee, James 1909-1955 .... DLB-2, 26, 152
The Agee Legacy: A Conference at the University
  of Tennessee at Knoxville Y-89
Aguilera Malta, Demetrio 1909-1981 .... DLB-145
Ai 1947- DLB-120
Aichinger, Ilse 1921- DLB-85
Aidoo, Ama Ata 1942- DLB-117
Aiken, Conrad 1889-1973 .... DLB-9, 45, 102
Aiken, Joan 1924- DLB-161
Aikin, Lucy 1781-1864 .... DLB-144, 163
Ainsworth, William Harrison 1805-1882 .. DLB-21
Aitken, George A. 1860-1917 .... DLB-149
Aitken, Robert [publishing house] DLB-49
Akenside, Mark 1721-1770 .... DLB-109
Akins, Zoë 1886-1958 .... DLB-26
Aksahov, Sergei Timofeevich
  1791-1859 .... DLB-198
Akutagawa, Ryūnosuke 1892-1927 ...... DLB-180
Alabaster, William 1568-1640 .... DLB-132
Alain de Lille circa 1116-1202/1203 ..... DLB-208
Alain-Fournier 1886-1914 .... DLB-65
Alanus de Insulis (see Alain de Lille)
Alarcón, Francisco X. 1954- DLB-122
Alarcón, Justo S. 1930- DLB-209
Alba, Nanina 1915-1968 .... DLB-41
Albee, Edward 1928- DLB-7
Albert the Great circa 1200-1280 .... DLB-115
Alberti, Rafael 1902- DLB-108
Albertinus, Aegidius circa 1560-1620 .... DLB-164
Alcaeus born circa 620 B.C. DLB-176
Alcott, Amos Bronson 1799-1888 .... DLB-1
Alcott, Louisa May
  1832-1888 .... DLB-1, 42, 79; DS-14
Alcott, William Andrus 1798-1859 .... DLB-1
Alcuin circa 732-804 .... DLB-148
Alden, Henry Mills 1836-1919 .... DLB-79
Alden, Isabella 1841-1930 .... DLB-42
Alden, John B. [publishing house] DLB-49
Alden, Beardsley and Company DLB-49

321

Aldington, Richard 1892-1962 . . . . DLB-20, 36, 100, 149

Aldis, Dorothy 1896-1966 . . . . DLB-22

Aldis, H. G. 1863-1919 . . . . DLB-184

Aldiss, Brian W. 1925- DLB-14

Aldrich, Thomas Bailey 1836-1907 . . . . DLB-42, 71, 74, 79

Alegría, Ciro 1909-1967 . . . . DLB-113

Alegría, Claribel 1924- DLB-145

Aleixandre, Vicente 1898-1984 . . . . DLB-108

Aleksandrov, Aleksandr Andreevich (see Durova, Nadezhda Andreevna)

Aleramo, Sibilla 1876-1960 . . . . DLB-114

Alexander, Cecil Frances 1818-1895 . . . . . DLB-199

Alexander, Charles 1868-1923 . . . . DLB-91

Alexander, Charles Wesley [publishing house] DLB-49

Alexander, James 1691-1756 . . . . DLB-24

Alexander, Lloyd 1924- DLB-52

Alexander, Sir William, Earl of Stirling 1577?-1640 . . . . DLB-121

Alexie, Sherman 1966- DLB-175, 206

Alexis, Willibald 1798-1871 . . . . DLB-133

Alfred, King 849-899 . . . . DLB-146

Alger, Horatio, Jr. 1832-1899 . . . . DLB-42

Algonquin Books of Chapel Hill DLB-46

Algren, Nelson 1909-1981 . . . . . DLB-9; Y-81, Y-82

Allan, Andrew 1907-1974 . . . . DLB-88

Allan, Ted 1916- DLB-68

Allbeury, Ted 1917- DLB-87

Alldritt, Keith 1935- DLB-14

Allen, Ethan 1738-1789 . . . . DLB-31

Allen, Frederick Lewis 1890-1954 . . . . DLB-137

Allen, Gay Wilson 1903-1995 . . . . . DLB-103; Y-95

Allen, George 1808-1876 . . . . DLB-59

Allen, George [publishing house] DLB-106

Allen, George, and Unwin Limited DLB-112

Allen, Grant 1848-1899 . . . . DLB-70, 92, 178

Allen, Henry W. 1912- Y-85

Allen, Hervey 1889-1949 . . . . DLB-9, 45

Allen, James 1739-1808 . . . . DLB-31

Allen, James Lane 1849-1925 . . . . DLB-71

Allen, Jay Presson 1922- DLB-26

Allen, John, and Company DLB-49

Allen, Paula Gunn 1939- DLB-175

Allen, Samuel W. 1917- DLB-41

Allen, Woody 1935- DLB-44

Allende, Isabel 1942- DLB-145

Alline, Henry 1748-1784 . . . . DLB-99

Allingham, Margery 1904-1966 . . . . DLB-77

Allingham, William 1824-1889 . . . . DLB-35

Allison, W. L. [publishing house] DLB-49

The *Alliterative Morte Arthure and the Stanzaic Morte Arthur* circa 1350-1400 . . . . DLB-146

Allott, Kenneth 1912-1973 . . . . DLB-20

Allston, Washington 1779-1843 . . . . DLB-1

Almon, John [publishing house] DLB-154

Alonzo, Dámaso 1898-1990 . . . . DLB-108

Alsop, George 1636-post 1673 . . . . DLB-24

Alsop, Richard 1761-1815 . . . . DLB-37

Altemus, Henry, and Company DLB-49

Altenberg, Peter 1885-1919 . . . . DLB-81

Altolaguirre, Manuel 1905-1959 . . . . DLB-108

Aluko, T. M. 1918- DLB-117

Alurista 1947- DLB-82

Alvarez, A. 1929- DLB-14, 40

Amadi, Elechi 1934- DLB-117

Amado, Jorge 1912- DLB-113

Ambler, Eric 1909- DLB-77

America: or, a Poem on the Settlement of the British Colonies (1780?), by Timothy Dwight DLB-37

American Conservatory Theatre DLB-7

American Fiction and the 1930s DLB-9

American Humor: A Historical Survey
East and Northeast
South and Southwest
Midwest
West DLB-11

The American Library in Paris Y-93

American News Company DLB-49

The American Poets' Corner: The First Three Years (1983-1986) Y-86

American Proletarian Culture: The 1930s . . . DS-11

American Publishing Company DLB-49

American Stationers' Company DLB-49

American Sunday-School Union DLB-49

American Temperance Union DLB-49

American Tract Society DLB-49

The American Trust for the British Library Y-96

The American Writers Congress (9-12 October 1981) Y-81

The American Writers Congress: A Report on Continuing Business Y-81

Ames, Fisher 1758-1808 . . . . DLB-37

Ames, Mary Clemmer 1831-1884 . . . . DLB-23

Amini, Johari M. 1935- DLB-41

Amis, Kingsley 1922-1995 . . . . DLB-15, 27, 100, 139, Y-96

Amis, Martin 1949- DLB-194

Ammianus Marcellinus circa A.D. 330-A.D. 395 . . . . DLB-211

Ammons, A. R. 1926- DLB-5, 165

Amory, Thomas 1691?-1788 . . . . DLB-39

Anania, Michael 1939- DLB-193

Anaya, Rudolfo A. 1937- DLB-82, 206

Ancrene Riwle circa 1200-1225 . . . . DLB-146

Andersch, Alfred 1914-1980 . . . . DLB-69

Andersen, Benny 1929- DLB-214

Anderson, Alexander 1775-1870 . . . . DLB-188

Anderson, Frederick Irving 1877-1947 . . . DLB-202

Anderson, Margaret 1886-1973 . . . . . . DLB-4, 91

Anderson, Maxwell 1888-1959 . . . . DLB-7

Anderson, Patrick 1915-1979 . . . . DLB-68

Anderson, Paul Y. 1893-1938 . . . . DLB-29

Anderson, Poul 1926- DLB-8

Anderson, Robert 1750-1830 . . . . DLB-142

Anderson, Robert 1917- DLB-7

Anderson, Sherwood 1876-1941 . . . . DLB-4, 9, 86; DS-1

Andreae, Johann Valentin 1586-1654 . . . . DLB-164

Andreas Capellanus flourished circa 1185 . . . . DLB-208

Andreas-Salomé, Lou 1861-1937 . . . . DLB-66

Andres, Stefan 1906-1970 . . . . DLB-69

Andreu, Blanca 1959- DLB-134

Andrewes, Lancelot 1555-1626 . . . . . DLB-151, 172

Andrews, Charles M. 1863-1943 . . . . DLB-17

Andrews, Miles Peter ?-1814 . . . . DLB-89

Andrian, Leopold von 1875-1951 . . . . DLB-81

Andrić, Ivo 1892-1975 . . . . DLB-147

Andrieux, Louis (see Aragon, Louis)

Andrus, Silas, and Son DLB-49

Andrzejewski, Jerzy 1909-1983 . . . . DLB-215

Angell, James Burrill 1829-1916 . . . . DLB-64

Angell, Roger 1920- DLB-171, 185

Angelou, Maya 1928- DLB-38

Anger, Jane flourished 1589 . . . . DLB-136

Angers, Félicité (see Conan, Laure)

Anglo-Norman Literature in the Development of Middle English Literature DLB-146

The Anglo-Saxon Chronicle circa 890-1154 . . . . DLB-146

The "Angry Young Men" DLB-15

Angus and Robertson (UK) Limited DLB-112

Anhalt, Edward 1914- DLB-26

Anners, Henry F. [publishing house] DLB-49

Annolied between 1077 and 1081 . . . . DLB-148

Annual Awards for *Dictionary of Literary Biography* Editors and Contributors Y-98

Anselm of Canterbury 1033-1109 . . . . . . DLB-115

Anstey, F. 1856-1934 . . . . DLB-141, 178

Anthony, Michael 1932- DLB-125

Anthony, Piers 1934- DLB-8

Anthony, Susanna 1726-1791 . . . . DLB-200

The Anthony Burgess Archive at the Harry Ransom Humanities Research Center Y-98

Anthony Burgess's 99 Novels: An Opinion Poll Y-84

Antin, David 1932- DLB-169

Antin, Mary 1881-1949 . . . . Y-84

Anton Ulrich, Duke of Brunswick-Lüneburg 1633-1714 . . . . DLB-168

Antschel, Paul (see Celan, Paul)

Anyidoho, Kofi 1947- DLB-157

Anzaldúa, Gloria 1942- DLB-122

Anzengruber, Ludwig 1839-1889 . . . . DLB-129

Apess, William 1798-1839 . . . . DLB-175

Apodaca, Rudy S. 1939- DLB-82

Apollonius Rhodius third century B.C. DLB-176

Apple, Max 1941- DLB-130	Arnold, Edwin 1832-1904.............DLB-35	Augier, Emile 1820-1889.............DLB-192
Appleton, D., and Company DLB-49	Arnold, Edwin L. 1857-1935 .... DLB-178	Augustine 354-430...................DLB-115
Appleton-Century-Crofts..............DLB-46	Arnold, Matthew 1822-1888 .... DLB-32, 57	Aulus Cellius
Applewhite, James 1935- DLB-105	Arnold, Thomas 1795-1842............DLB-55	circa A.D. 125-circa A.D. 180?......DLB-211
Applewood Books DLB-46	Arnold, Edward [publishing house]......DLB-112	Austen, Jane 1775-1817 ....DLB-116
Apuleius circa A.D. 125-post A.D. 164 ...DLB-211	Arnow, Harriette Simpson 1908-1986......DLB-6	Austin, Alfred 1835-1913.............DLB-35
Aquin, Hubert 1929-1977 ....DLB-53	Arp, Bill (see Smith, Charles Henry)	Austin, Jane Goodwin 1831-1894 ......DLB-202
Aquinas, Thomas 1224 or	Arpino, Giovanni 1927-1987 ....DLB-177	Austin, Mary 1868-1934 .... DLB-9, 78, 206
1225-1274 ....DLB-115	Arreola, Juan José 1918- DLB-113	Austin, William 1778-1841.............DLB-74
Aragon, Louis 1897-1982..............DLB-72	Arrian circa 89-circa 155 ....DLB-176	Author-Printers, 1476–1599............DLB-167
Aralica, Ivan 1930- DLB-181	Arrowsmith, J. W. [publishing house] ...DLB-106	Author Websites Y-97
Aratus of Soli circa 315 B.C.-circa 239 B.C.	The Art and Mystery of Publishing:	The Author's Apology for His Book
...........................DLB-176	Interviews Y-97	(1684), by John Bunyan DLB-39
Arbasino, Alberto 1930- DLB-196	Arthur, Timothy Shay	An Author's Response, by Ronald Sukenick.. Y-82
Arbor House Publishing Company DLB-46	1809-1885 .... DLB-3, 42, 79; DS-13	Authors and Newspapers Association DLB-46
Arbuthnot, John 1667-1735 ....DLB-101	The Arthurian Tradition and Its European	Authors' Publishing Company DLB-49
Arcadia House DLB-46	Context.....................DLB-138	Avalon Books.........................DLB-46
Arce, Julio G. (see Ulica, Jorge)	Artmann, H. C. 1921- DLB-85	Avancini, Nicolaus 1611-1686..........DLB-164
Archer, William 1856-1924............DLB-10	Arvin, Newton 1900-1963.............DLB-103	Avendaño, Fausto 1941- DLB-82
Archilochhus mid seventh century B.C.E.	As I See It, by Carolyn Cassady DLB-16	Averroëö 1126-1198..................DLB-115
...........................DLB-176	Asch, Nathan 1902-1964 ....DLB-4, 28	Avery, Gillian 1926- DLB-161
The Archpoet circa 1130?-?...........DLB-148	Ash, John 1948- DLB-40	Avicenna 980-1037....................DLB-115
Archpriest Avvakum (Petrovich)	Ashbery, John 1927- DLB-5, 165; Y-81	Avison, Margaret 1918- DLB-53
1620?-1682 ....DLB-150	Ashbridge, Elizabeth 1713-1755 ....DLB-200	Avon Books.........................DLB-46
Arden, John 1930- DLB-13	Ashburnham, Bertram Lord	Awdry, Wilbert Vere 1911- DLB-160
Arden of Faversham.....................DLB-62	1797-1878 ....DLB-184	Awoonor, Kofi 1935- DLB-117
Ardis Publishers....................... Y-89	Ashendene Press DLB-112	Ayckbourn, Alan 1939- DLB-13
Ardizzone, Edward 1900-1979..........DLB-160	Asher, Sandy 1942- Y-83	Aymé, Marcel 1902-1967...............DLB-72
Arellano, Juan Estevan 1947- DLB-122	Ashton, Winifred (see Dane, Clemence)	Aytoun, Sir Robert 1570-1638 ....DLB-121
The Arena Publishing Company DLB-49	Asimov, Isaac 1920-1992.......... DLB-8; Y-92	Aytoun, William Edmondstoune
Arena Stage DLB-7	Askew, Anne circa 1521-1546 ....DLB-136	1813-1865 .... DLB-32, 159
Arenas, Reinaldo 1943-1990 ....DLB-145	Asselin, Olivar 1874-1937 ....DLB-92	
Arensberg, Ann 1937- Y-82	Asturias, Miguel Angel 1899-1974 ......DLB-113	**B**
Arguedas, José María 1911-1969 ....DLB-113	Atheneum Publishers.................DLB-46	B. V. (see Thomson, James)
Argueta, Manilio 1936- DLB-145	Atherton, Gertrude 1857-1948..... DLB-9, 78, 186	Babbitt, Irving 1865-1933 ....DLB-63
Arias, Ron 1941- DLB-82	Athlone Press........................DLB-112	Babbitt, Natalie 1932- DLB-52
Arishima, Takeo 1878-1923...........DLB-180	Atkins, Josiah circa 1755-1781 ....DLB-31	Babcock, John [publishing house] DLB-49
Aristophanes	Atkins, Russell 1926- DLB-41	Babits, Mihály 1883-1941 ....DLB-215
circa 446 B.C.-circa 386 B.C. DLB-176	The Atlantic Monthly Press............DLB-46	Babrius circa 150-200..................DLB-176
Aristotle 384 B.C.-322 B.C..............DLB-176	Attaway, William 1911-1986............DLB-76	Baca, Jimmy Santiago 1952- DLB-122
Ariyoshi Sawako 1931-1984 ....DLB-182	Atwood, Margaret 1939- DLB-53	Bache, Benjamin Franklin 1769-1798......DLB-43
Arland, Marcel 1899-1986..............DLB-72	Aubert, Alvin 1930- DLB-41	Bacheller, Irving 1859-1950............DLB-202
Arlen, Michael 1895-1956 .... DLB-36, 77, 162	Aubert de Gaspé, Phillipe-Ignace-François	Bachmann, Ingeborg 1926-1973 ....DLB-85
Armah, Ayi Kwei 1939- DLB-117	1814-1841 ....DLB-99	Bacon, Delia 1811-1859................DLB-1
Armantrout, Rae 1947- DLB-193	Aubert de Gaspé, Phillipe-Joseph	Bacon, Francis 1561-1626.............DLB-151
Der arme Hartmann ?-after 1150........DLB-148	1786-1871 ....DLB-99	Bacon, Roger circa 1214/1220-1292 .....DLB-115
Armed Services Editions DLB-46	Aubin, Napoléon 1812-1890 ....DLB-99	Bacon, Sir Nicholas circa 1510-1579 .....DLB-132
Armstrong, Martin Donisthorpe	Aubin, Penelope 1685-circa 1731 ....DLB-39	Bacon, Thomas circa 1700-1768..........DLB-31
1882-1974 ....DLB-197	Aubrey-Fletcher, Henry Lancelot (see Wade, Henry)	Badger, Richard G., and Company........DLB-49
Armstrong, Richard 1903- DLB-160	Auchincloss, Louis 1917- DLB-2; Y-80	Bage, Robert 1728-1801................DLB-39
Arndt, Ernst Moritz 1769-1860 ....DLB-90	Auden, W. H. 1907-1973...........DLB-10, 20	Bagehot, Walter 1826-1877.............DLB-55
Arnim, Achim von 1781-1831 ....DLB-90	Audio Art in America: A Personal Memoir... Y-85	Bagley, Desmond 1923-1983............DLB-87
Arnim, Bettina von 1785-1859 ....DLB-90	Audubon, John Woodhouse	Bagnold, Enid 1889-1981 ...... DLB-13, 160, 191
Arnim, Elizabeth von (Countess Mary Annette	1812-1862 ....DLB-183	Bagryana, Elisaveta 1893-1991 ....DLB-147
Beauchamp Russell) 1866-1941......DLB-197	Auerbach, Berthold 1812-1882 ....DLB-133	Bahr, Hermann 1863-1934 .... DLB-81, 118
Arno Press..........................DLB-46	Auernheimer, Raoul 1876-1948..........DLB-81	

Bailey, Abigail Abbot 1746-1815........ DLB-200
Bailey, Alfred Goldsworthy 1905- DLB-68
Bailey, Francis [publishing house]........ DLB-49
Bailey, H. C. 1878-1961................ DLB-77
Bailey, Jacob 1731-1808 .... DLB-99
Bailey, Paul 1937- DLB-14
Bailey, Philip James 1816-1902......... DLB-32
Baillargeon, Pierre 1916-1967.......... DLB-88
Baillie, Hugh 1890-1966............... DLB-29
Baillie, Joanna 1762-1851 .... DLB-93
Bailyn, Bernard 1922- DLB-17
Bainbridge, Beryl 1933- DLB-14
Baird, Irene 1901-1981............... DLB-68
Baker, Augustine 1575-1641 .... DLB-151
Baker, Carlos 1909-1987 .... DLB-103
Baker, David 1954- DLB-120
Baker, Herschel C. 1914-1990 .... DLB-111
Baker, Houston A., Jr. 1943- DLB-67
Baker, Samuel White 1821-1893 .... DLB-166
Baker, Thomas 1656-1740 .... DLB-213
Baker, Walter H., Company
  ("Baker's Plays") DLB-49
The Baker and Taylor Company........ DLB-49
Balaban, John 1943- DLB-120
Bald, Wambly 1902- DLB-4
Balde, Jacob 1604-1668................ DLB-164
Balderston, John 1889-1954 .... DLB-26
Baldwin, James 1924-1987 ..... DLB-2, 7, 33; Y-87
Baldwin, Joseph Glover 1815-1864..... DLB-3, 11
Baldwin, Richard and Anne
  [publishing house] DLB-170
Baldwin, William circa 1515-1563 ...... DLB-132
Bale, John 1495-1563 .... DLB-132
Balestrini, Nanni 1935- DLB-128, 196
Balfour, Sir Andrew 1630-1694 .... DLB-213
Balfour, Arthur James 1848-1930...... DLB-190
Balfour, Sir James 1600-1657 .... DLB-213
Ballantine Books................... DLB-46
Ballantyne, R. M. 1825-1894 .... DLB-163
Ballard, J. G. 1930- DLB-14, 207
Ballard, Martha Moore 1735-1812 ...... DLB-200
Ballerini, Luigi 1940- DLB-128
Ballou, Maturin Murray
  1820-1895 .... DLB-79, 189
Ballou, Robert O. [publishing house] DLB-46
Balzac, Honoré de 1799-1855 .... DLB-119
Bambara, Toni Cade 1939- DLB-38
Bamford, Samuel 1788-1872 .... DLB-190
Bancroft, A. L., and Company DLB-49
Bancroft, George 1800-1891 ...... DLB-1, 30, 59
Bancroft, Hubert Howe 1832-1918 ...DLB-47, 140
Bandelier, Adolph F. 1840-1914 .... DLB-186
Bangs, John Kendrick 1862-1922 ... DLB-11, 79
Banim, John 1798-1842.........DLB-116, 158, 159
Banim, Michael 1796-1874 .... DLB-158, 159

Banks, Iain 1954- DLB-194
Banks, John circa 1653-1706........... DLB-80
Banks, Russell 1940- DLB-130
Bannerman, Helen 1862-1946 .... DLB-141
Bantam Books DLB-46
Banti, Anna 1895-1985................DLB-177
Banville, John 1945- DLB-14
Baraka, Amiri 1934- DLB-5, 7, 16, 38; DS-8
Baratynsky, Evgenii Abramovich
  1800-1844 .... DLB-205
Barbauld, Anna Laetitia
  1743-1825........... DLB-107, 109, 142, 158
Barbeau, Marius 1883-1969 .... DLB-92
Barber, John Warner 1798-1885......... DLB-30
Bàrberi Squarotti, Giorgio 1929- DLB-128
Barbey d'Aurevilly, Jules-Amédée
  1808-1889 .... DLB-119
Barbour, John circa 1316-1395......... DLB-146
Barbour, Ralph Henry 1870-1944 ...... DLB-22
Barbusse, Henri 1873-1935............ DLB-65
Barclay, Alexander circa 1475-1552 ..... DLB-132
Barclay, E. E., and Company.......... DLB-49
Bardeen, C. W. [publishing house]....... DLB-49
Barham, Richard Harris 1788-1845 ..... DLB-159
Barich, Bill 1943- DLB-185
Baring, Maurice 1874-1945............ DLB-34
Baring-Gould, Sabine
  1834-1924 .... DLB-156, 190
Barker, A. L. 1918- DLB-14, 139
Barker, George 1913-1991 .... DLB-20
Barker, Harley Granville 1877-1946...... DLB-10
Barker, Howard 1946- DLB-13
Barker, James Nelson 1784-1858 .... DLB-37
Barker, Jane 1652-1727............ DLB-39, 131
Barker, Lady Mary Anne 1831-1911 .... DLB-166
Barker, William
  circa 1520-after 1576 .... DLB-132
Barker, Arthur, Limited DLB-112
Barkov, Ivan Semenovich
  1732-1768 .... DLB-150
Barks, Coleman 1937- DLB-5
Barlach, Ernst 1870-1938 .... DLB-56, 118
Barlow, Joel 1754-1812................. DLB-37
Barnard, John 1681-1770 .... DLB-24
Barne, Kitty (Mary Catherine Barne)
  1883-1957 .... DLB-160
Barnes, Barnabe 1571-1609 .... DLB-132
Barnes, Djuna 1892-1982.......... DLB-4, 9, 45
Barnes, Jim 1933- DLB-175
Barnes, Julian 1946- DLB-194; Y-93
Barnes, Margaret Ayer 1886-1967 .... DLB-9
Barnes, Peter 1931- DLB-13
Barnes, William 1801-1886 .... DLB-32
Barnes, A. S., and Company DLB-49
Barnes and Noble Books DLB-46
Barnet, Miguel 1940- DLB-145

Barney, Natalie 1876-1972 .... DLB-4
Barnfield, Richard 1574-1627 ....DLB-172
Baron, Richard W.,
  Publishing Company DLB-46
Barr, Amelia Edith Huddleston
  1831-1919 .... DLB-202
Barr, Robert 1850-1912 .... .DLB-70, 92
Barral, Carlos 1928-1989 .... DLB-134
Barrax, Gerald William 1933- DLB-41, 120
Barrès, Maurice 1862-1923............. DLB-123
Barrett, Eaton Stannard 1786-1820...... DLB-116
Barrie, J. M. 1860-1937.........DLB-10, 141, 156
Barrie and Jenkins DLB-112
Barrio, Raymond 1921- DLB-82
Barrios, Gregg 1945- DLB-122
Barry, Philip 1896-1949 .... DLB-7
Barry, Robertine (see Françoise)
Barse and Hopkins.................. DLB-46
Barstow, Stan 1928- DLB-14, 139
Barth, John 1930- DLB-2
Barthelme, Donald
  1931-1989 ....DLB-2; Y-80, Y-89
Barthelme, Frederick 1943- Y-85
Bartholomew, Frank 1898-1985........DLB-127
Bartlett, John 1820-1905................ DLB-1
Bartol, Cyrus Augustus 1813-1900....... DLB-1
Barton, Bernard 1784-1849............. DLB-96
Barton, Thomas Pennant 1803-1869 .... DLB-140
Bartram, John 1699-1777 .... DLB-31
Bartram, William 1739-1823 .... DLB-37
Basic Books DLB-46
Basille, Theodore (see Becon, Thomas)
Bass, Rick 1958- DLB-212
Bass, T. J. 1932- Y-81
Bassani, Giorgio 1916- DLB-128, 177
Basse, William circa 1583-1653 .... DLB-121
Bassett, John Spencer 1867-1928..........DLB-17
Bassler, Thomas Joseph (see Bass, T.J.)
Bate, Walter Jackson 1918- DLB-67, 103
Bateman, Christopher
  [publishing house] DLB-170
Bateman, Stephen circa 1510-1584...... DLB-136
Bates, H. E. 1905-1974 .... DLB-162, 191
Bates, Katharine Lee 1859-1929......... DLB-71
Batiushkov, Konstantin Nikolaevich
  1787-1855 .... DLB-205
Batsford, B. T. [publishing house] DLB-106
Battiscombe, Georgina 1905- DLB-155
The Battle of Maldon circa 1000........ DLB-146
Bauer, Bruno 1809-1882 .... DLB-133
Bauer, Wolfgang 1941- DLB-124
Baum, L. Frank 1856-1919 .... DLB-22
Baum, Vicki 1888-1960 .... DLB-85
Baumbach, Jonathan 1933- Y-80
Bausch, Richard 1945- DLB-130
Bawden, Nina 1925- DLB-14, 161, 207

Bax, Clifford 1886-1962 . . . . DLB-10, 100	Belasco, David 1853-1931 . . . . DLB-7	Benni, Stefano 1947- DLB-196
Baxter, Charles 1947- DLB-130	Belford, Clarke and Company. DLB-49	Benoit, Jacques 1941- DLB-60
Bayer, Eleanor (see Perry, Eleanor)	Belinksy, Vissarion Grigor'evich 1811-1848 . . . . DLB-198	Benson, A. C. 1862-1925. . . . . DLB-98
Bayer, Konrad 1932-1964 . . . . DLB-85	Belitt, Ben 1911- DLB-5	Benson, E. F. 1867-1940. . . . . DLB-135, 153
Baynes, Pauline 1922- DLB-160	Belknap, Jeremy 1744-1798 . . . . DLB-30, 37	Benson, Jackson J. 1930- DLB-111
Bazin, Hervé 1911- DLB-83	Bell, Adrian 1901-1980 . . . . DLB-191	Benson, Robert Hugh 1871-1914. . . . . . . DLB-153
Beach, Sylvia 1887-1962. . . . . DLB-4; DS-15	Bell, Clive 1881-1964. . . . . DS-10	Benson, Stella 1892-1933. . . . . DLB-36, 162
Beacon Press DLB-49	Bell, Gertrude Margaret Lowthian 1868-1926 . . . . DLB-174	Bent, James Theodore 1852-1897 . . . . DLB-174
Beadle and Adams DLB-49	Bell, James Madison 1826-1902. . . . . DLB-50	Bent, Mabel Virginia Anna ?-? DLB-174
Beagle, Peter S. 1939- Y-80	Bell, Marvin 1937- DLB-5	Bentham, Jeremy 1748-1832 . . . . DLB-107, 158
Beal, M. F. 1937- Y-81	Bell, Millicent 1919- DLB-111	Bentley, E. C. 1875-1956 . . . . DLB-70
Beale, Howard K. 1899-1959. . . . . DLB-17	Bell, Quentin 1910- DLB-155	Bentley, Phyllis 1894-1977. . . . . DLB-191
Beard, Charles A. 1874-1948 . . . . DLB-17	Bell, Vanessa 1879-1961 . . . . DS-10	Bentley, Richard [publishing house] DLB-106
A Beat Chronology: The First Twenty-five Years, 1944-1969. . . . . DLB-16	Bell, George, and Sons. DLB-106	Benton, Robert 1932- and Newman, David 1937- DLB-44
Beattie, Ann 1947- Y-82	Bell, Robert [publishing house] DLB-49	Benziger Brothers DLB-49
Beattie, James 1735-1803 . . . . DLB-109	Bellamy, Edward 1850-1898 . . . . DLB-12	*Beowulf* circa 900-1000 or 790-825 . . . . DLB-146
Beatty, Chester 1875-1968 . . . . DLB-201	Bellamy, John [publishing house]. DLB-170	Berent, Wacław 1873-1940 . . . . DLB-215
Beauchemin, Nérée 1850-1931 . . . . DLB-92	Bellamy, Joseph 1719-1790 . . . . DLB-31	Beresford, Anne 1929- DLB-40
Beauchemin, Yves 1941- DLB-60	Bellezza, Dario 1944- DLB-128	Beresford, John Davys 1873-1947 . . . . DLB-162, 178, 197
Beaugrand, Honoré 1848-1906 . . . . DLB-99	*La Belle Assemblée* 1806-1837 . . . . DLB-110	Beresford-Howe, Constance 1922- DLB-88
Beaulieu, Victor-Lévy 1945- DLB-53	Belloc, Hilaire 1870-1953 . . . . DLB-19, 100, 141, 174	Berford, R. G., Company DLB-49
Beaumont, Francis circa 1584-1616 and Fletcher, John 1579-1625 . . . . . . DLB-58	Bellonci, Maria 1902-1986. . . . . DLB-196	Berg, Stephen 1934- DLB-5
Beaumont, Sir John 1583?-1627. . . . . DLB-121	Bellow, Saul 1915- DLB-2, 28; Y-82; DS-3	Bergengruen, Werner 1892-1964 . . . . DLB-56
Beaumont, Joseph 1616-1699. . . . . DLB-126	Belmont Productions DLB-46	Berger, John 1926- DLB-14, 207
Beauvoir, Simone de 1908-1986 . . . . DLB-72; Y-86	Bemelmans, Ludwig 1898-1962. . . . . DLB-22	Berger, Meyer 1898-1959 . . . . DLB-29
Becher, Ulrich 1910- DLB-69	Bemis, Samuel Flagg 1891-1973 . . . . DLB-17	Berger, Thomas 1924- DLB-2; Y-80
Becker, Carl 1873-1945 . . . . DLB-17	Bemrose, William [publishing house] DLB-106	Berkeley, Anthony 1893-1971 . . . . DLB-77
Becker, Jurek 1937- DLB-75	Ben no Naishi 1228?-1271? DLB-203	Berkeley, George 1685-1753 . . . . DLB-31, 101
Becker, Jurgen 1932- DLB-75	Benchley, Robert 1889-1945 . . . . DLB-11	The Berkley Publishing Corporation. DLB-46
Beckett, Samuel 1906-1989 . . . . . DLB-13, 15; Y-90	Bencúr, Matej (see Kukučín, Martin)	Berlin, Lucia 1936- DLB-130
Beckford, William 1760-1844. . . . . DLB-39	Benedetti, Mario 1920- DLB-113	Bernal, Vicente J. 1888-1915 . . . . DLB-82
Beckham, Barry 1944- DLB-33	Benedictus, David 1938- DLB-14	Bernanos, Georges 1888-1948. . . . . DLB-72
Becon, Thomas circa 1512-1567 . . . . DLB-136	Benedikt, Michael 1935- DLB-5	Bernard, Harry 1898-1979 . . . . DLB-92
Becque, Henry 1837-1899 . . . . DLB-192	Benediktov, Vladimir Grigor'evich 1807-1873. . . . . DLB-205	Bernard, John 1756-1828 . . . . DLB-37
Beùkoviù, Matija 1939- DLB-181	Benét, Stephen Vincent 1898-1943 . . . . DLB-4, 48, 102	Bernard of Chartres circa 1060-1124? DLB-115
Beddoes, Thomas 1760-1808 . . . . DLB-158	Benét, William Rose 1886-1950 . . . . DLB-45	Bernard of Clairvaux 1090-1153 . . . . DLB-208
Beddoes, Thomas Lovell 1803-1849 . . . . . DLB-96	Benford, Gregory 1941- Y-82	Bernard Silvestris flourished circa 1130-1160 . . . . DLB-208
Bede circa 673-735 . . . . DLB-146	Benjamin, Park 1809-1864. . . . . DLB-3, 59, 73	Bernari, Carlo 1909-1992 . . . . DLB-177
Beecher, Catharine Esther 1800-1878 . . . . . DLB-1	Benjamin, S. G. W. 1837-1914. . . . . DLB-189	Bernhard, Thomas 1931-1989. . . . . . . DLB-85, 124
Beecher, Henry Ward 1813-1887 . . . . . . DLB-3, 43	Benlowes, Edward 1602-1676 . . . . DLB-126	Bernstein, Charles 1950- DLB-169
Beer, George L. 1872-1920 . . . . DLB-47	Benn, Gottfried 1886-1956 . . . . DLB-56	Berriault, Gina 1926- DLB-130
Beer, Johann 1655-1700 . . . . DLB-168	Benn Brothers Limited. DLB-106	Berrigan, Daniel 1921- DLB-5
Beer, Patricia 1919- DLB-40	Bennett, Arnold 1867-1931 . . . DLB-10, 34, 98, 135	Berrigan, Ted 1934-1983. . . . . DLB-5, 169
Beerbohm, Max 1872-1956 . . . . DLB-34, 100	Bennett, Charles 1899- DLB-44	Berry, Wendell 1934- DLB-5, 6
Beer-Hofmann, Richard 1866-1945. . . . . . DLB-81	Bennett, Emerson 1822-1905. . . . . DLB-202	Berryman, John 1914-1972 . . . . DLB-48
Beers, Henry A. 1847-1926 . . . . DLB-71	Bennett, Gwendolyn 1902- DLB-51	Bersianik, Louky 1930- DLB-60
Beeton, S. O. [publishing house] DLB-106	Bennett, Hal 1930- DLB-33	Berthelet, Thomas [publishing house] DLB-170
Bégon, Elisabeth 1696-1755 . . . . DLB-99	Bennett, James Gordon 1795-1872. . . . . . . DLB-43	Berto, Giuseppe 1914-1978 . . . . DLB-177
Behan, Brendan 1923-1964 . . . . DLB-13	Bennett, James Gordon, Jr. 1841-1918. . . . DLB-23	Bertolucci, Attilio 1911- DLB-128
Behn, Aphra 1640?-1689 . . . . DLB-39, 80, 131	Bennett, John 1865-1956 . . . . DLB-42	Berton, Pierre 1920- DLB-68
Behn, Harry 1898-1973 . . . . DLB-61	Bennett, Louise 1919- DLB-117	Besant, Sir Walter 1836-1901 . . . . DLB-135, 190
Behrman, S. N. 1893-1973. . . . . DLB-7, 44		Bessette, Gerard 1920- DLB-53
Belaney, Archibald Stansfeld (see Grey Owl)		

Cumulative Index

Bessie, Alvah 1904-1985................ DLB-26

Bester, Alfred 1913-1987................ DLB-8

Besterman, Theodore 1904-1976....... DLB-201

The Bestseller Lists: An Assessment........ Y-84

Bestuzhev, Aleksandr Aleksandrovich (Marlinsky) 1797-1837..................... DLB-198

Bestuzhev, Nikolai Aleksandrovich 1791-1855..................... DLB-198

Betham-Edwards, Matilda Barbara (see Edwards, Matilda Barbara Betham-)

Betjeman, John 1906-1984......... DLB-20; Y-84

Betocchi, Carlo 1899-1986............. DLB-128

Bettarini, Mariella 1942-............. DLB-128

Betts, Doris 1932-..................... Y-82

Beveridge, Albert J. 1862-1927........... DLB-17

Beverley, Robert circa 1673-1722..... DLB-24, 30

Bevilacqua, Alberto 1934-............. DLB-196

Bevington, Louisa Sarah 1845-1895..... DLB-199

Beyle, Marie-Henri (see Stendhal)

Bianco, Margery Williams 1881-1944... DLB-160

Bibaud, Adèle 1854-1941............... DLB-92

Bibaud, Michel 1782-1857................ DLB-99

Bibliographical and Textual Scholarship Since World War II.................. Y-89

The Bicentennial of James Fenimore Cooper: An International Celebration........... Y-89

Bichsel, Peter 1935-................... DLB-75

Bickerstaff, Isaac John 1733-circa 1808.... DLB-89

Biddle, Drexel [publishing house]........ DLB-49

Bidermann, Jacob 1577 or 1578-1639............... DLB-164

Bidwell, Walter Hilliard 1798-1881....... DLB-79

Bienek, Horst 1930-................... DLB-75

Bierbaum, Otto Julius 1865-1910....... DLB-66

Bierce, Ambrose 1842-1914?...... DLB-11, 12, 23, 71, 74, 186

Bigelow, William F. 1879-1966........... DLB-91

Biggle, Lloyd, Jr. 1923-................. DLB-8

Bigiaretti, Libero 1905-1993............. DLB-177

Bigland, Eileen 1898-1970............. DLB-195

Biglow, Hosea (see Lowell, James Russell)

Bigongiari, Piero 1914-................ DLB-128

Billinger, Richard 1890-1965........... DLB-124

Billings, Hammatt 1818-1874........... DLB-188

Billings, John Shaw 1898-1975......... DLB-137

Billings, Josh (see Shaw, Henry Wheeler)

Binding, Rudolf G. 1867-1938........... DLB-66

Bingham, Caleb 1757-1817............. DLB-42

Bingham, George Barry 1906-1988..... DLB-127

Bingley, William [publishing house]..... DLB-154

Binyon, Laurence 1869-1943........... DLB-19

Biographia Brittanica................. DLB-142

Biographical Documents I............. Y-84

Biographical Documents II............ Y-85

Bioren, John [publishing house]........ DLB-49

Bioy Casares, Adolfo 1914-............. DLB-113

Bird, Isabella Lucy 1831-1904......... DLB-166

Bird, Robert Montgomery 1806-1854... DLB-202

Bird, William 1888-1963........ DLB-4; DS-15

Birken, Sigmund von 1626-1681....... DLB-164

Birney, Earle 1904-................... DLB-88

Birrell, Augustine 1850-1933........... DLB-98

Bisher, Furman 1918-................. DLB-171

Bishop, Elizabeth 1911-1979........ DLB-5, 169

Bishop, John Peale 1892-1944...... DLB-4, 9, 45

Bismarck, Otto von 1815-1898......... DLB-129

Bisset, Robert 1759-1805............. DLB-142

Bissett, Bill 1939-.................... DLB-53

Bitzius, Albert (see Gotthelf, Jeremias)

Björnvig, Thorkild 1918-............. DLB-214

Black, David (D. M.) 1941-........... DLB-40

Black, Winifred 1863-1936........... DLB-25

Black, Walter J. [publishing house]..... DLB-46

The Black Aesthetic: Background......... DS-8

The Black Arts Movement, by Larry Neal..................... DLB-38

Black Theaters and Theater Organizations in America, 1961-1982: A Research List............... DLB-38

Black Theatre: A Forum [excerpts]....... DLB-38

Blackamore, Arthur 1679-?........ DLB-24, 39

Blackburn, Alexander L. 1929-........... Y-85

Blackburn, Paul 1926-1971........ DLB-16; Y-81

Blackburn, Thomas 1916-1977......... DLB-27

Blackmore, R. D. 1825-1900............ DLB-18

Blackmore, Sir Richard 1654-1729...... DLB-131

Blackmur, R. P. 1904-1965............. DLB-63

Blackwell, Basil, Publisher............. DLB-106

Blackwood, Algernon Henry 1869-1951.............. DLB-153, 156, 178

Blackwood, Caroline 1931-........ DLB-14, 207

Blackwood, William, and Sons, Ltd..... DLB-154

Blackwood's Edinburgh Magazine 1817-1980..................... DLB-110

Blades, William 1824-1890............ DLB-184

Blagden, Isabella 1817?-1873........... DLB-199

Blair, Eric Arthur (see Orwell, George)

Blair, Francis Preston 1791-1876......... DLB-43

Blair, James circa 1655-1743........... DLB-24

Blair, John Durburrow 1759-1823....... DLB-37

Blais, Marie-Claire 1939-.............. DLB-53

Blaise, Clark 1940-................... DLB-53

Blake, George 1893-1961............. DLB-191

Blake, Lillie Devereux 1833-1913....... DLB-202

Blake, Nicholas 1904-1972............. DLB-77 (see Day Lewis, C.)

Blake, William 1757-1827....... DLB-93, 154, 163

The Blakiston Company............... DLB-49

Blanchot, Maurice 1907-............. DLB-72

Blanckenburg, Christian Friedrich von 1744-1796..................... DLB-94

Blaser, Robin 1925-.................. DLB-165

Bledsoe, Albert Taylor 1809-1877...... DLB-3, 79

Bleecker, Ann Eliza 1752-1783......... DLB-200

Blelock and Company................ DLB-49

Blennerhassett, Margaret Agnew 1773-1842..................... DLB-99

Bles, Geoffrey [publishing house]...... DLB-112

Blessington, Marguerite, Countess of 1789-1849..................... DLB-166

The Blickling Homilies circa 971....... DLB-146

Blind, Mathilde 1841-1896............ DLB-199

Blish, James 1921-1975................ DLB-8

Bliss, E., and E. White [publishing house]................ DLB-49

Bliven, Bruce 1889-1977.............. DLB-137

Blixen, Karen 1885-1962............. DLB-214

Bloch, Robert 1917-1994.............. DLB-44

Block, Rudolph (see Lessing, Bruno)

Blondal, Patricia 1926-1959............ DLB-88

Bloom, Harold 1930-................. DLB-67

Bloomer, Amelia 1818-1894............ DLB-79

Bloomfield, Robert 1766-1823......... DLB-93

Bloomsbury Group.................. DS-10

Blotner, Joseph 1923-................ DLB-111

Bloy, Léon 1846-1917................ DLB-123

Blume, Judy 1938-................... DLB-52

Blunck, Hans Friedrich 1888-1961...... DLB-66

Blunden, Edmund 1896-1974.... DLB-20, 100, 155

Blunt, Lady Anne Isabella Noel 1837-1917..................... DLB-174

Blunt, Wilfrid Scawen 1840-1922..... DLB-19, 174

Bly, Nellie (see Cochrane, Elizabeth)

Bly, Robert 1926-..................... DLB-5

Blyton, Enid 1897-1968.............. DLB-160

Boaden, James 1762-1839............. DLB-89

Boas, Frederick S. 1862-1957........... DLB-149

The Bobbs-Merrill Archive at the Lilly Library, Indiana University........ Y-90

The Bobbs-Merrill Company............ DLB-46

Bobrov, Semen Sergeevich 1763?-1810..................... DLB-150

Bobrowski, Johannes 1917-1965......... DLB-75

Bodenheim, Maxwell 1892-1954...... DLB-9, 45

Bodenstedt, Friedrich von 1819-1892.... DLB-129

Bodini, Vittorio 1914-1970............ DLB-128

Bodkin, M. McDonnell 1850-1933....... DLB-70

Bodley, Sir Thomas 1545-1613........ DLB-213

Bodley Head....................... DLB-112

Bodmer, Johann Jakob 1698-1783....... DLB-97

Bodmershof, Imma von 1895-1982...... DLB-85

Bodsworth, Fred 1918-............... DLB-68

Boehm, Sydney 1908-................ DLB-44

Boer, Charles 1939-................... DLB-5

Boethius circa 480-circa 524........... DLB-115

Boethius of Dacia circa 1240-?......... DLB-115

Bogan, Louise 1897-1970......... DLB-45, 169

Bogarde, Dirk 1921-................. DLB-14

Bogdanovich, Ippolit Fedorovich
  circa 1743-1803 ....DLB-150
Bogue, David [publishing house] DLB-106
Böhme, Jakob 1575-1624 ....DLB-164
Bohn, H. G. [publishing house] DLB-106
Bohse, August 1661-1742 ....DLB-168
Boie, Heinrich Christian 1744-1806 ......DLB-94
Bok, Edward W. 1863-1930 ......DLB-91; DS-16
Boland, Eavan 1944- DLB-40
Bolingbroke, Henry St. John, Viscount
  1678-1751 ....DLB-101
Böll, Heinrich 1917-1985 ....DLB-69; Y-85
Bolling, Robert 1738-1775 ....DLB-31
Bolotov, Andrei Timofeevich
  1738-1833 ....DLB-150
Bolt, Carol 1941- DLB-60
Bolt, Robert 1924- DLB-13
Bolton, Herbert E. 1870-1953 ....DLB-17
Bonaventura DLB-90
Bonaventure circa 1217-1274 ....DLB-115
Bonaviri, Giuseppe 1924- DLB-177
Bond, Edward 1934- DLB-13
Bond, Michael 1926- DLB-161
Boni, Albert and Charles
  [publishing house] DLB-46
Boni and Liveright DLB-46
Bonner, Paul Hyde 1893-1968. . . . . DS-17
Bonner, Sherwood 1849-1883 ....DLB-202
Robert Bonner's Sons DLB-49
Bonnin, Gertrude Simmons (see Zitkala-Ša)
Bonsanti, Alessandro 1904-1984 ....DLB-177
Bontemps, Arna 1902-1973 ....DLB-48, 51
The Book Arts Press at the University
  of Virginia Y-96
The Book League of America DLB-46
Book Publishing Accounting: Some Basic
  Concepts Y-98
Book Reviewing in America: I. Y-87
Book Reviewing in America: II Y-88
Book Reviewing in America: III Y-89
Book Reviewing in America: IV Y-90
Book Reviewing in America: V Y-91
Book Reviewing in America: VI Y-92
Book Reviewing in America: VII Y-93
Book Reviewing in America: VIII Y-94
Book Reviewing in America and the
  Literary Scene Y-95
Book Reviewing and the
  Literary Scene Y-96, Y-97
Book Supply Company DLB-49
The Book Trade History Group Y-93
The Booker Prize......................Y-96
The Booker Prize
  Address by Anthony Thwaite,
  Chairman of the Booker Prize Judges
  Comments from Former Booker
  Prize Winners Y-86
Boorde, Andrew circa 1490-1549 ....DLB-136

Boorstin, Daniel J. 1914- DLB-17
Booth, Mary L. 1831-1889 ....DLB-79
Booth, Franklin 1874-1948 ....DLB-188
Booth, Philip 1925- Y-82
Booth, Wayne C. 1921- DLB-67
Booth, William 1829-1912 ....DLB-190
Borchardt, Rudolf 1877-1945 ....DLB-66
Borchert, Wolfgang 1921-1947 .....DLB-69, 124
Borel, Pétrus 1809-1859 ....DLB-119
Borges, Jorge Luis 1899-1986 .....DLB-113; Y-86
Börne, Ludwig 1786-1837 ....DLB-90
Bornstein, Miriam 1950- DLB-209
Borowski, Tadeusz 1922-1951 ....DLB-215
Borrow, George 1803-1881 ......DLB-21, 55, 166
Bosch, Juan 1909- DLB-145
Bosco, Henri 1888-1976 ....DLB-72
Bosco, Monique 1927- DLB-53
Boston, Lucy M. 1892-1990 ....DLB-161
Boswell, James 1740-1795 ....DLB-104, 142
Botev, Khristo 1847-1876 ....DLB-147
Bote, Hermann
  circa 1460-circa 1520 ....DLB-179
Botta, Anne C. Lynch 1815-1891 ....DLB-3
Botto, Ján (see Krasko, Ivan)
Bottome, Phyllis 1882-1963 ....DLB-197
Bottomley, Gordon 1874-1948 ....DLB-10
Bottoms, David 1949- DLB-120; Y-83
Bottrall, Ronald 1906- DLB-20
Bouchardy, Joseph 1810-1870 ....DLB-192
Boucher, Anthony 1911-1968 ....DLB-8
Boucher, Jonathan 1738-1804 ....DLB-31
Boucher de Boucherville, George
  1814-1894 ....DLB-99
Boudreau, Daniel (see Coste, Donat)
Bourassa, Napoléon 1827-1916 ....DLB-99
Bourget, Paul 1852-1935 ....DLB-123
Bourinot, John George 1837-1902 ....DLB-99
Bourjaily, Vance 1922- DLB-2, 143
Bourne, Edward Gaylord
  1860-1908 ....DLB-47
Bourne, Randolph 1886-1918 ....DLB-63
Bousoño, Carlos 1923- DLB-108
Bousquet, Joë 1897-1950 ....DLB-72
Bova, Ben 1932- Y-81
Bovard, Oliver K. 1872-1945 ....DLB-25
Bove, Emmanuel 1898-1945 ....DLB-72
Bowen, Elizabeth 1899-1973 ....DLB-15, 162
Bowen, Francis 1811-1890 ....DLB-1, 59
Bowen, John 1924- DLB-13
Bowen, Marjorie 1886-1952 ....DLB-153
Bowen-Merrill Company DLB-49
Bowering, George 1935- DLB-53
Bowers, Bathsheba 1671-1718 ....DLB-200
Bowers, Claude G. 1878-1958 ....DLB-17
Bowers, Edgar 1924- DLB-5

Bowers, Fredson Thayer
  1905-1991 ....DLB-140; Y-91
Bowles, Paul 1910- DLB-5, 6
Bowles, Samuel III 1826-1878 ....DLB-43
Bowles, William Lisles 1762-1850 ....DLB-93
Bowman, Louise Morey 1882-1944 ....DLB-68
Boyd, James 1888-1944 ....DLB-9; DS-16
Boyd, John 1919- DLB-8
Boyd, Thomas 1898-1935 ....DLB-9; DS-16
Boyesen, Hjalmar Hjorth
  1848-1895 ....DLB-12, 71; DS-13
Boyle, Kay
  1902-1992 ....DLB-4, 9, 48, 86; Y-93
Boyle, Roger, Earl of Orrery
  1621-1679 ....DLB-80
Boyle, T. Coraghessan 1948- Y-86
Božić, Mirko 1919- DLB-181
Brackenbury, Alison 1953- DLB-40
Brackenridge, Hugh Henry
  1748-1816 ....DLB-11, 37
Brackett, Charles 1892-1969 ....DLB-26
Brackett, Leigh 1915-1978 ....DLB-8, 26
Bradburn, John [publishing house] DLB-49
Bradbury, Malcolm 1932- DLB-14, 207
Bradbury, Ray 1920- DLB-2, 8
Bradbury and Evans DLB-106
Braddon, Mary Elizabeth
  1835-1915 ....DLB-18, 70, 156
Bradford, Andrew 1686-1742 ....DLB-43, 73
Bradford, Gamaliel 1863-1932 ....DLB-17
Bradford, John 1749-1830 ....DLB-43
Bradford, Roark 1896-1948 ....DLB-86
Bradford, William 1590-1657 ....DLB-24, 30
Bradford, William III 1719-1791 ......DLB-43, 73
Bradlaugh, Charles 1833-1891 ....DLB-57
Bradley, David 1950- DLB-33
Bradley, Marion Zimmer 1930- DLB-8
Bradley, William Aspenwall
  1878-1939 ....DLB-4
Bradley, Ira, and Company DLB-49
Bradley, J. W., and Company DLB-49
Bradshaw, Henry 1831-1886 ....DLB-184
Bradstreet, Anne
  1612 or 1613-1672 ....DLB-24
Bradwardine, Thomas circa
  1295-1349 ....DLB-115
Brady, Frank 1924-1986 ....DLB-111
Brady, Frederic A. [publishing house] DLB-49
Bragg, Melvyn 1939- DLB-14
Brainard, Charles H. [publishing house] ...DLB-49
Braine, John 1922-1986 ....DLB-15; Y-86
Braithwait, Richard 1588-1673 ....DLB-151
Braithwaite, William Stanley
  1878-1962 ....DLB-50, 54
Braker, Ulrich 1735-1798 ....DLB-94
Bramah, Ernest 1868-1942 ....DLB-70
Branagan, Thomas 1774-1843 ....DLB-37

Branch, William Blackwell 1927- DLB-76	*The British Critic* 1793-1843 .... DLB-110	Broster, Dorothy Kathleen 1877-1950 .... DLB-160
Branden Press DLB-46	The British Library and the Regular Readers' Group Y-91	Brother Antoninus (see Everson, William)
Branner, H.C. 1903-1966 .... DLB-214	British Literary Prizes Y-98	Brotherton, Lord 1856-1930 .... DLB-184
Brant, Sebastian 1457-1521 .... DLB-179	*The British Review and London Critical Journal* 1811-1825 .... DLB-110	Brougham and Vaux, Henry Peter Brougham, Baron 1778-1868 .... DLB-110, 158
Brassey, Lady Annie (Allnutt) 1839-1887 .... DLB-166	British Travel Writing, 1940-1997 ...... DLB-204	Brougham, John 1810-1880 .... DLB-11
Brathwaite, Edward Kamau 1930- DLB-125	Brito, Aristeo 1942- DLB-122	Broughton, James 1913- DLB-5
Brault, Jacques 1933- DLB-53	Brittain, Vera 1893-1970 .... DLB-191	Broughton, Rhoda 1840-1920 .... DLB-18
Braun, Matt 1932- DLB-212	Broadway Publishing Company DLB-46	Broun, Heywood 1888-1939 .... DLB-29, 171
Braun, Volker 1939- DLB-75	Broch, Hermann 1886-1951 .... DLB-85, 124	Brown, Alice 1856-1948 .... DLB-78
Brautigan, Richard 1935-1984 .... DLB-2, 5, 206; Y-80, Y-84	Brochu, André 1942- DLB-53	Brown, Bob 1886-1959 .... DLB-4, 45
Braxton, Joanne M. 1950- DLB-41	Brock, Edwin 1927- DLB-40	Brown, Cecil 1943- DLB-33
Bray, Anne Eliza 1790-1883 .... DLB-116	Brockes, Barthold Heinrich 1680-1747 .... DLB-168	Brown, Charles Brockden 1771-1810 .... DLB-37, 59, 73
Bray, Thomas 1656-1730 .... DLB-24	Brod, Max 1884-1968 .... DLB-81	Brown, Christy 1932-1981 .... DLB-14
Braziller, George [publishing house] DLB-46	Brodber, Erna 1940- DLB-157	Brown, Dee 1908- Y-80
The Bread Loaf Writers' Conference 1983 .... Y-84	Brodhead, John R. 1814-1873 .... DLB-30	Brown, Frank London 1927-1962 ..... DLB-76
The Break-Up of the Novel (1922), by John Middleton Murry DLB-36	Brodkey, Harold 1930- DLB-130	Brown, Fredric 1906-1972 .... DLB-8
Breasted, James Henry 1865-1935 ...... DLB-47	Brodsky, Joseph 1940-1996 .... Y-87	Brown, George Mackay 1921- DLB-14, 27, 139
Brecht, Bertolt 1898-1956 .... DLB-56, 124	Broeg, Bob 1918- DLB-171	Brown, Harry 1917-1986 .... DLB-26
Bredel, Willi 1901-1964 .... DLB-56	Brøgger, Suzanne 1944- DLB-214	Brown, Marcia 1918- DLB-61
Bregendahl, Marie 1867-1940 .... DLB-214	Brome, Richard circa 1590-1652 ...... DLB-58	Brown, Margaret Wise 1910-1952 .... DLB-22
Breitinger, Johann Jakob 1701-1776 ...... DLB-97	Brome, Vincent 1910- DLB-155	Brown, Morna Doris (see Ferrars, Elizabeth)
Bremser, Bonnie 1939- DLB-16	Bromfield, Louis 1896-1956 .... DLB-4, 9, 86	Brown, Oliver Madox 1855-1874 .... DLB-21
Bremser, Ray 1934- DLB-16	Bromige, David 1933- DLB-193	Brown, Sterling 1901-1989 .... DLB-48, 51, 63
Brentano, Bernard von 1901-1964 ...... DLB-56	Broner, E. M. 1930- DLB-28	Brown, T. E. 1830-1897 .... DLB-35
Brentano, Clemens 1778-1842 .... DLB-90	Bronk, William 1918- DLB-165	Brown, William Hill 1765-1793 .... DLB-37
Brentano's DLB-49	Bronnen, Arnolt 1895-1959 .... DLB-124	Brown, William Wells 1814-1884 .... DLB-3, 50, 183
Brenton, Howard 1942- DLB-13	Brontë, Anne 1820-1849 .... DLB-21, 199	Browne, Charles Farrar 1834-1867 .... DLB-11
Breslin, Jimmy 1929- DLB-185	Brontë, Charlotte 1816-1855 ... DLB-21, 159, 199	Browne, Frances 1816-1879 .... DLB-199
Breton, André 1896-1966 .... DLB-65	Brontë, Emily 1818-1848 .... DLB-21, 32, 199	Browne, Francis Fisher 1843-1913 ...... DLB-79
Breton, Nicholas circa 1555-circa 1626 .... DLB-136	Brook, Stephen 1947- DLB-204	Browne, J. Ross 1821-1875 .... DLB-202
The Breton Lays 1300-early fifteenth century DLB-146	Brooke, Frances 1724-1789 .... DLB-39, 99	Browne, Michael Dennis 1940- DLB-40
Brewer, Luther A. 1858-1933 .... DLB-187	Brooke, Henry 1703?-1783 .... DLB-39	Browne, Sir Thomas 1605-1682 .... DLB-151
Brewer, Warren and Putnam DLB-46	Brooke, L. Leslie 1862-1940 .... DLB-141	Browne, William, of Tavistock 1590-1645 .... DLB-121
Brewster, Elizabeth 1922- DLB-60	Brooke, Margaret, Ranee of Sarawak 1849-1936 .... DLB-174	Browne, Wynyard 1911-1964 .... DLB-13
Bridge, Ann (Lady Mary Dolling Sanders O'Malley) 1889-1974 .... DLB-191	Brooke, Rupert 1887-1915 .... DLB-19, 216	Browne and Nolan DLB-106
Bridge, Horatio 1806-1893 .... DLB-183	Brooker, Bertram 1888-1955 .... DLB-88	Brownell, W. C. 1851-1928 .... DLB-71
Bridgers, Sue Ellen 1942- DLB-52	Brooke-Rose, Christine 1926- DLB-14	Browning, Elizabeth Barrett 1806-1861 .... DLB-32, 199
Bridges, Robert 1844-1930 .... DLB-19, 98	Brookner, Anita 1928- DLB-194; Y-87	Browning, Robert 1812-1889 .... DLB-32, 163
The Bridgewater Library DLB-213	Brooks, Charles Timothy 1813-1883 ...... DLB-1	Brownjohn, Allan 1931- DLB-40
Bridie, James 1888-1951 .... DLB-10	Brooks, Cleanth 1906-1994 .... DLB-63; Y-94	Brownson, Orestes Augustus 1803-1876 .... DLB-1, 59, 73
Brieux, Eugene 1858-1932 .... DLB-192	Brooks, Gwendolyn 1917- DLB-5, 76, 165	Bruccoli, Matthew J. 1931- DLB-103
Bright, Mary Chavelita Dunne (see Egerton, George)	Brooks, Jeremy 1926- DLB-14	Bruce, Charles 1906-1971 .... DLB-68
Brimmer, B. J., Company DLB-46	Brooks, Mel 1926- DLB-26	Bruce, Leo 1903-1979 .... DLB-77
Brines, Francisco 1932- DLB-134	Brooks, Noah 1830-1903 .... DLB-42; DS-13	Bruce, Philip Alexander 1856-1933 ...... DLB-47
Brinley, George, Jr. 1817-1875 .... DLB-140	Brooks, Richard 1912-1992 .... DLB-44	Bruce Humphries [publishing house] DLB-46
Brinnin, John Malcolm 1916- DLB-48	Brooks, Van Wyck 1886-1963 .... DLB-45, 63, 103	Bruce-Novoa, Juan 1944- DLB-82
Brisbane, Albert 1809-1890 .... DLB-3	Brophy, Brigid 1929- DLB-14	Bruckman, Clyde 1894-1955 .... DLB-26
Brisbane, Arthur 1864-1936 .... DLB-25	Brophy, John 1899-1965 .... DLB-191	Bruckner, Ferdinand 1891-1958 .... DLB-118
British Academy DLB-112	Brossard, Chandler 1922-1993 .... DLB-16	Brundage, John Herbert (see Herbert, John)
	Brossard, Nicole 1943- DLB-53	

Brutus, Dennis 1924- DLB-117
Bryan, C. D. B. 1936- DLB-185
Bryant, Arthur 1899-1985 ....DLB-149
Bryant, William Cullen
  1794-1878................DLB-3, 43, 59, 189
Bryce Echenique, Alfredo 1939- DLB-145
Bryce, James 1838-1922............DLB-166, 190
Brydges, Sir Samuel Egerton
  1762-1837 ....DLB-107
Bryskett, Lodowick 1546?-1612.........DLB-167
Buchan, John 1875-1940 ....DLB-34, 70, 156
Buchanan, George 1506-1582 ....DLB-132
Buchanan, Robert 1841-1901 ....DLB-18, 35
Buchman, Sidney 1902-1975 ....DLB-26
Buchner, Augustus 1591-1661 ....DLB-164
Büchner, Georg 1813-1837 ....DLB-133
Bucholtz, Andreas Heinrich
  1607-1671.......................DLB-168
Buck, Pearl S. 1892-1973 ....DLB-9, 102
Bucke, Charles 1781-1846 ....DLB-110
Bucke, Richard Maurice
  1837-1902 ....DLB-99
Buckingham, Joseph Tinker 1779-1861 and
  Buckingham, Edwin 1810-1833 ....DLB-73
Buckler, Ernest 1908-1984..............DLB-68
Buckley, William F., Jr. 1925- DLB-137; Y-80
Buckminster, Joseph Stevens 1784-1812 ...DLB-37
Buckner, Robert 1906- DLB-26
Budd, Thomas ?-1698...................DLB-24
Budrys, A. J. 1931- DLB-8
Buechner, Frederick 1926- Y-80
Buell, John 1927- DLB-53
Bufalino, Gesualdo 1920-1996..........DLB-196
Buffum, Job [publishing house] DLB-49
Bugnet, Georges 1879-1981 ....DLB-92
Buies, Arthur 1840-1901 ....DLB-99
Building the New British Library
  at St Pancras Y-94
Bukowski, Charles 1920-1994....DLB-5, 130, 169
Bulatović, Miodrag 1930-1991..........DLB-181
Bulgarin, Faddei Venediktovich
  1789-1859 ....DLB-198
Bulger, Bozeman 1877-1932.............DLB-171
Bullein, William
  between 1520 and 1530-1576 ....DLB-167
Bullins, Ed 1935- DLB-7, 38
Bulwer-Lytton, Edward (also Edward Bulwer)
  1803-1873 ....DLB-21
Bumpus, Jerry 1937- Y-81
Bunce and Brother....................DLB-49
Bunner, H. C. 1855-1896 ....DLB-78, 79
Bunting, Basil 1900-1985..............DLB-20
Buntline, Ned (Edward Zane Carroll Judson)
  1821-1886 ....DLB-186
Bunyan, John 1628-1688 ....DLB-39
Burch, Robert 1925- DLB-52
Burciaga, José Antonio 1940- DLB-82

Bürger, Gottfried August 1747-1794.......DLB-94
Burgess, Anthony 1917-1993 ....DLB-14, 194
Burgess, Gelett 1866-1951 ....DLB-11
Burgess, John W. 1844-1931 ....DLB-47
Burgess, Thornton W. 1874-1965 ....DLB-22
Burgess, Stringer and Company DLB-49
Burick, Si 1909-1986 ....DLB-171
Burk, John Daly circa 1772-1808 ....DLB-37
Burk, Ronnie 1955- DLB-209
Burke, Edmund 1729?-1797 ....DLB-104
Burke, Kenneth 1897-1993..........DLB-45, 63
Burke, Thomas 1886-1945 ....DLB-197
Burlingame, Edward Livermore
  1848-1922 ....DLB-79
Burnet, Gilbert 1643-1715 ....DLB-101
Burnett, Frances Hodgson
  1849-1924 ....DLB-42, 141; DS-13, 14
Burnett, W. R. 1899-1982................DLB-9
Burnett, Whit 1899-1973 and
  Martha Foley 1897-1977 ....DLB-137
Burney, Fanny 1752-1840 ....DLB-39
Burns, Alan 1929- DLB-14, 194
Burns, John Horne 1916-1953............Y-85
Burns, Robert 1759-1796 ....DLB-109
Burns and Oates DLB-106
Burnshaw, Stanley 1906- DLB-48
Burr, C. Chauncey 1815?-1883 ....DLB-79
Burr, Esther Edwards 1732-1758 ....DLB-200
Burroughs, Edgar Rice 1875-1950 ....DLB-8
Burroughs, John 1837-1921 ....DLB-64
Burroughs, Margaret T. G. 1917- DLB-41
Burroughs, William S., Jr. 1947-1981 ....DLB-16
Burroughs, William Seward
  1914-.........DLB-2, 8, 16, 152; Y-81, Y-97
Burroway, Janet 1936- DLB-6
Burt, Maxwell Struthers
  1882-1954 ....DLB-86; DS-16
Burt, A. L., and Company..............DLB-49
Burton, Hester 1913- DLB-161
Burton, Isabel Arundell 1831-1896 .....DLB-166
Burton, Miles (see Rhode, John)
Burton, Richard Francis
  1821-1890 ....DLB-55, 166, 184
Burton, Robert 1577-1640 ....DLB-151
Burton, Virginia Lee 1909-1968 ....DLB-22
Burton, William Evans 1804-1860.......DLB-73
Burwell, Adam Hood 1790-1849 ....DLB-99
Bury, Lady Charlotte 1775-1861 ....DLB-116
Busch, Frederick 1941- DLB-6
Busch, Niven 1903-1991 ....DLB-44
Bushnell, Horace 1802-1876 ....DS-13
Bussieres, Arthur de 1877-1913 ....DLB-92
Butler, Josephine Elizabeth 1828-1906....DLB-190
Butler, Juan 1942-1981 ....DLB-53
Butler, Octavia E. 1947- DLB-33

Butler, Pierce 1884-1953 ....DLB-187
Butler, Robert Olen 1945- DLB-173
Butler, Samuel 1613-1680 ....DLB-101, 126
Butler, Samuel 1835-1902 ....DLB-18, 57, 174
Butler, William Francis 1838-1910 .....DLB-166
Butler, E. H., and Company DLB-49
Butor, Michel 1926- DLB-83
Butter, Nathaniel [publishing house] DLB-170
Butterworth, Hezekiah 1839-1905.......DLB-42
Buttitta, Ignazio 1899- DLB-114
Buzzati, Dino 1906-1972 ....DLB-177
Byars, Betsy 1928- DLB-52
Byatt, A. S. 1936- DLB-14, 194
Byles, Mather 1707-1788................DLB-24
Bynneman, Henry [publishing house] DLB-170
Bynner, Witter 1881-1968 ....DLB-54
Byrd, William circa 1543-1623 ....DLB-172
Byrd, William II 1674-1744 ....DLB-24, 140
Byrne, John Keyes (see Leonard, Hugh)
Byron, George Gordon, Lord
  1788-1824 ....DLB-96, 110
Byron, Robert 1905-1941 ....DLB-195

C

Caballero Bonald, José Manuel
  1926- DLB-108
Cabañero, Eladio 1930- DLB-134
Cabell, James Branch 1879-1958 ....DLB-9, 78
Cabeza de Baca, Manuel 1853-1915 .....DLB-122
Cabeza de Baca Gilbert, Fabiola
  1898- DLB-122
Cable, George Washington
  1844-1925 ....DLB-12, 74; DS-13
Cable, Mildred 1878-1952 ....DLB-195
Cabrera, Lydia 1900-1991..............DLB-145
Cabrera Infante, Guillermo 1929- DLB-113
Cadell [publishing house]..............DLB-154
Cady, Edwin H. 1917- DLB-103
Caedmon flourished 658-680 ....DLB-146
Caedmon School circa 660-899 ....DLB-146
Cafés, Brasseries, and Bistros DS-15
Cage, John 1912-1992 ....DLB-193
Cahan, Abraham 1860-1951 ....DLB-9, 25, 28
Cain, George 1943- DLB-33
Caird, Mona 1854-1932 ....DLB-197
Caldecott, Randolph 1846-1886 ....DLB-163
Calder, John (Publishers), Limited DLB-112
Calderón de la Barca, Fanny
  1804-1882 ....DLB-183
Caldwell, Ben 1937- DLB-38
Caldwell, Erskine 1903-1987..........DLB-9, 86
Caldwell, H. M., Company DLB-49
Caldwell, Taylor 1900-1985 ....DS-17
Calhoun, John C. 1782-1850 ....DLB-3
Calisher, Hortense 1911- DLB-2

A Call to Letters and an Invitation
   to the Electric Chair,
   by Siegfried Mandel DLB-75

Callaghan, Mary Rose 1944- DLB-207

Callaghan, Morley 1903-1990 .... DLB-68

Callahan, S. Alice 1868-1894 .... DLB-175

Callaloo Y-87

Callimachus circa 305 B.C.-240 B.C.
   .... DLB-176

Calmer, Edgar 1907- DLB-4

Calverley, C. S. 1831-1884 .... DLB-35

Calvert, George Henry 1803-1889 ..... DLB-1, 64

Calvino, Italo 1923-1985 .... DLB-196

Cambridge Press DLB-49

Cambridge Songs (Carmina Cantabrigensia)
   circa 1050 .... DLB-148

Cambridge University Press DLB-170

Camden, William 1551-1623 .... DLB-172

Camden House: An Interview with
   James Hardin Y-92

Cameron, Eleanor 1912- DLB-52

Cameron, George Frederick
   1854-1885 .... DLB-99

Cameron, Lucy Lyttelton 1781-1858 ... DLB-163

Cameron, William Bleasdell
   1862-1951 .... DLB-99

Camm, John 1718-1778 .... DLB-31

Camon, Ferdinando 1935- DLB-196

Campana, Dino 1885-1932 .... DLB-114

Campbell, Gabrielle Margaret Vere
   (see Shearing, Joseph, and Bowen, Marjorie)

Campbell, James Dykes 1838-1895 ..... DLB-144

Campbell, James Edwin 1867-1896 ..... DLB-50

Campbell, John 1653-1728 .... DLB-43

Campbell, John W., Jr. 1910-1971 .... DLB-8

Campbell, Roy 1901-1957 .... DLB-20

Campbell, Thomas
   1777-1844 .... DLB-93, 144

Campbell, William Wilfred
   1858-1918 .... DLB-92

Campion, Edmund 1539-1581 .... DLB-167

Campion, Thomas
   1567-1620 .... DLB-58, 172

Camus, Albert 1913-1960 .... DLB-72

The Canadian Publishers' Records
   Database Y-96

Canby, Henry Seidel 1878-1961 .... DLB-91

Candelaria, Cordelia 1943- DLB-82

Candelaria, Nash 1928- DLB-82

Candour in English Fiction (1890),
   by Thomas Hardy DLB-18

Canetti, Elias 1905-1994 .... DLB-85, 124

Canham, Erwin Dain 1904-1982 .... DLB-127

Canitz, Friedrich Rudolph Ludwig von
   1654-1699 .... DLB-168

Cankar, Ivan 1876-1918 .... DLB-147

Cannan, Gilbert 1884-1955 .... DLB-10, 197

Cannan, Joanna 1896-1961 .... DLB-191

Cannell, Kathleen 1891-1974 .... DLB-4

Cannell, Skipwith 1887-1957 .... DLB-45

Canning, George 1770-1827 .... DLB-158

Cannon, Jimmy 1910-1973 .... DLB-171

Cano, Daniel 1947- DLB-209

Cantú, Norma Elia 1947- DLB-209

Cantwell, Robert 1908-1978 .... DLB-9

Cape, Jonathan, and Harrison Smith
   [publishing house] DLB-46

Cape, Jonathan, Limited DLB-112

Čapek, Karel 1890-1938 .... DLB-215

Capen, Joseph 1658-1725 .... DLB-24

Capes, Bernard 1854-1918 .... DLB-156

Capote, Truman
   1924-1984 .... DLB-2, 185; Y-80, Y-84

Caproni, Giorgio 1912-1990 .... DLB-128

Cardarelli, Vincenzo 1887-1959 ...... DLB-114

Cárdenas, Reyes 1948- DLB-122

Cardinal, Marie 1929- DLB-83

Carew, Jan 1920- DLB-157

Carew, Thomas 1594 or 1595-1640 .... DLB-126

Carey, Henry
   circa 1687-1689-1743 .... DLB-84

Carey, Mathew 1760-1839 .... DLB-37, 73

Carey and Hart DLB-49

Carey, M., and Company DLB-49

Carlell, Lodowick 1602-1675 .... DLB-58

Carleton, William 1794-1869 .... DLB-159

Carleton, G. W. [publishing house] . DLB-49

Carlile, Richard 1790-1843 ...... DLB-110, 158

Carlyle, Jane Welsh 1801-1866 ...... DLB-55

Carlyle, Thomas 1795-1881 .... DLB-55, 144

Carman, Bliss 1861-1929 .... DLB-92

Carmina Burana circa 1230 .... DLB-138

Carnero, Guillermo 1947- DLB-108

Carossa, Hans 1878-1956 .... DLB-66

Carpenter, Humphrey 1946- DLB-155

Carpenter, Stephen Cullen ?-1820? .. DLB-73

Carpentier, Alejo 1904-1980 .... DLB-113

Carrier, Roch 1937- DLB-53

Carrillo, Adolfo 1855-1926 .... DLB-122

Carroll, Gladys Hasty 1904- DLB-9

Carroll, John 1735-1815 .... DLB-37

Carroll, John 1809-1884 .... DLB-99

Carroll, Lewis 1832-1898 ...... DLB-18, 163, 178

Carroll, Paul 1927- DLB-16

Carroll, Paul Vincent 1900-1968 .... DLB-10

Carroll and Graf Publishers DLB-46

Carruth, Hayden 1921- DLB-5, 165

Carryl, Charles E. 1841-1920 .... DLB-42

Carson, Anne 1950- DLB-193

Carswell, Catherine 1879-1946 ...... DLB-36

Carter, Angela 1940-1992 .... DLB-14, 207

Carter, Elizabeth 1717-1806 .... DLB-109

Carter, Henry (see Leslie, Frank)

Carter, Hodding, Jr. 1907-1972 ..... DLB-127

Carter, John 1905-1975 .... DLB-201

Carter, Landon 1710-1778 .... DLB-31

Carter, Lin 1930- Y-81

Carter, Martin 1927- DLB-117

Carter and Hendee DLB-49

Carter, Robert, and Brothers DLB-49

Cartwright, John 1740-1824 .... DLB-158

Cartwright, William circa 1611-1643 .. DLB-126

Caruthers, William Alexander
   1802-1846 .... DLB-3

Carver, Jonathan 1710-1780 .... DLB-31

Carver, Raymond
   1938-1988 .... DLB-130; Y-84, Y-88

Cary, Alice 1820-1871 .... DLB-202

Cary, Joyce 1888-1957 .... DLB-15, 100

Cary, Patrick 1623?-1657 .... DLB-131

Casey, Juanita 1925- DLB-14

Casey, Michael 1947- DLB-5

Cassady, Carolyn 1923- DLB-16

Cassady, Neal 1926-1968 .... DLB-16

Cassell and Company DLB-106

Cassell Publishing Company DLB-49

Cassill, R. V. 1919- DLB-6

Cassity, Turner 1929- DLB-105

Cassius Dio circa 155/164-post 229
   .... DLB-176

Cassola, Carlo 1917-1987 .... DLB-177

The Castle of Perserverance
   circa 1400-1425 .... DLB-146

Castellano, Olivia 1944- DLB-122

Castellanos, Rosario 1925-1974 ..... DLB-113

Castillo, Ana 1953- DLB-122

Castillo, Rafael C. 1950- DLB-209

Castlemon, Harry (see Fosdick, Charles Austin)

Čašule, Kole 1921- DLB-181

Caswall, Edward 1814-1878 .... DLB-32

Catacalos, Rosemary 1944- DLB-122

Cather, Willa 1873-1947 ...... DLB-9, 54, 78; DS-1

Catherine II (Ekaterina Alekseevna), "TheGreat,"
   Empress of Russia 1729-1796 ...... DLB-150

Catherwood, Mary Hartwell
   1847-1902 .... DLB-78

Catledge, Turner 1901-1983 .... DLB-127

Catlin, George 1796-1872 .... DLB-186, 189

Cato the Elder 234 B.C.-149 B.C. DLB-211

Cattafi, Bartolo 1922-1979 .... DLB-128

Catton, Bruce 1899-1978 .... DLB-17

Catullus circa 84 B.C.-54 B.C. DLB-211

Causley, Charles 1917- DLB-27

Caute, David 1936- DLB-14

Cavendish, Duchess of Newcastle,
   Margaret Lucas 1623-1673 .... DLB-131

Cawein, Madison 1865-1914 .... DLB-54

The Caxton Printers, Limited DLB-46

Caxton, William [publishing house] .. DLB-170

Cayrol, Jean 1911- DLB-83

Cecil, Lord David 1902-1986 . . . . .DLB-155
Cela, Camilo José 1916- Y-89
Celan, Paul 1920-1970. . . . . .DLB-69
Celati, Gianni 1937- DLB-196
Celaya, Gabriel 1911-1991 . . . . .DLB-108
A Celebration of Literary Biography Y-98
Céline, Louis-Ferdinand 1894-1961. . . . . . .DLB-72
The Celtic Background to Medieval English
 Literature. DLB-146
Celtis, Conrad 1459-1508 . . . . .DLB-179
Center for Bibliographical Studies and
 Research at the University of
 California, Riverside Y-91
The Center for the Book in the Library
 of Congress. Y-93
Center for the Book Research Y-84
Centlivre, Susanna 1669?-1723 . . . . .DLB-84
The Century Company. DLB-49
Cernuda, Luis 1902-1963 . . . . .DLB-134
"Certain Gifts," by Betty Adcock. DLB-105
Cervantes, Lorna Dee 1954- DLB-82
Chaadaev, Petr Iakovlevich
 1794-1856 .DLB-198
Chacel, Rosa 1898- DLB-134
Chacón, Eusebio 1869-1948 . . . . .DLB-82
Chacón, Felipe Maximiliano 1873-?. DLB-82
Chadwyck-Healey's Full-Text Literary Data-bases:
 Editing Commercial Databases of
 Primary Literary Texts Y-95
Challans, Eileen Mary (see Renault, Mary)
Chalmers, George 1742-1825. . . . . .DLB-30
Chaloner, Sir Thomas 1520-1565 . . . . . . .DLB-167
Chamberlain, Samuel S. 1851-1916. . . . . . .DLB-25
Chamberland, Paul 1939- DLB-60
Chamberlin, William Henry
 1897-1969 . . . . .DLB-29
Chambers, Charles Haddon
 1860-1921 . . . . .DLB-10
Chambers, María Cristina (see Mena, María Cristina)
Chambers, Robert W. 1865-1933 . . . . . . .DLB-202
Chambers, W. and R.
 [publishing house] DLB-106
Chamisso, Albert von 1781-1838. . . . . .DLB-90
Champfleury 1821-1889 . . . . .DLB-119
Chandler, Harry 1864-1944 . . . . .DLB-29
Chandler, Norman 1899-1973 . . . . .DLB-127
Chandler, Otis 1927- DLB-127
Chandler, Raymond 1888-1959 . . . . DS-6
Channing, Edward 1856-1931. . . . . .DLB-17
Channing, Edward Tyrrell 1790-1856. . .DLB-1, 59
Channing, William Ellery 1780-1842. . . .DLB-1, 59
Channing, William Ellery, II
 1817-1901 . . . . .DLB-1
Channing, William Henry
 1810-1884 . . . . .DLB-1, 59
Chaplin, Charlie 1889-1977 . . . . .DLB-44
Chapman, George
 1559 or 1560 - 1634 . . . . .DLB-62, 121

Chapman, John .DLB-106
Chapman, Olive Murray 1892-1977 . . . . .DLB-195
Chapman, R. W. 1881-1960 . . . . .DLB-201
Chapman, William 1850-1917 . . . . .DLB-99
Chapman and Hall DLB-106
Chappell, Fred 1936- DLB-6, 105
Charbonneau, Jean 1875-1960 . . . . .DLB-92
Charbonneau, Robert 1911-1967 . . . . .DLB-68
Charles d'Orléans 1394-1465 . . . . .DLB-208
Charles, Gerda 1914- DLB-14
Charles, William [publishing house] DLB-49
The Charles Wood Affair:
 A Playwright Revived Y-83
Charley (see Mann, Charles)
Charlotte Forten: Pages from her Diary . . .DLB-50
Charteris, Leslie 1907-1993 . . . . .DLB-77
Chartier, Alain circa 1385-1430. . . . . .DLB-208
Charyn, Jerome 1937- Y-83
Chase, Borden 1900-1971 . . . . .DLB-26
Chase, Edna Woolman 1877-1957. . . . . . . .DLB-91
Chase-Riboud, Barbara 1936- DLB-33
Chateaubriand, François-René de
 1768-1848 .DLB-119
Chatterton, Thomas 1752-1770 . . . . .DLB-109
Chatto and Windus. DLB-106
Chatwin, Bruce 1940-1989 . . . . .DLB-194, 204
Chaucer, Geoffrey 1340?-1400 . . . . .DLB-146
Chauncy, Charles 1705-1787 . . . . .DLB-24
Chauveau, Pierre-Joseph-Olivier
 1820-1890 . . . . .DLB-99
Chávez, Denise 1948- DLB-122
Chávez, Fray Angélico 1910- DLB-82
Chayefsky, Paddy 1923-1981 . . . . DLB-7, 44; Y-81
Cheesman, Evelyn 1881-1969 . . . . .DLB-195
Cheever, Ezekiel 1615-1708 . . . . .DLB-24
Cheever, George Barrell 1807-1890 . . . . . . .DLB-59
Cheever, John
 1912-1982 . . . . DLB-2, 102; Y-80, Y-82
Cheever, Susan 1943- Y-82
Cheke, Sir John 1514-1557 . . . . .DLB-132
Chelsea House. .DLB-46
Cheney, Ednah Dow (Littlehale)
 1824-1904 . . . . .DLB-1
Cheney, Harriet Vaughn 1796-1889 . . . . . .DLB-99
Chénier, Marie-Joseph 1764-1811 . . . . . . .DLB-192
Cherry, Kelly 1940 . . . . Y-83
Cherryh, C. J. 1942- Y-80
Chesebro', Caroline 1825-1873 . . . . .DLB-202
Chesnutt, Charles Waddell
 1858-1932 . . . . DLB-12, 50, 78
Chesney, Sir George Tomkyns
 1830-1895 . . . . .DLB-190
Chester, Alfred 1928-1971 . . . . .DLB-130
Chester, George Randolph 1869-1924 . . . .DLB-78
The Chester Plays circa 1505-1532;
 revisions until 1575 . . . . .DLB-146

Chesterfield, Philip Dormer Stanhope,
 Fourth Earl of 1694-1773. . . . . .DLB-104
Chesterton, G. K. 1874-1936
 . . . . .DLB-10, 19, 34, 70, 98, 149, 178
Chettle, Henry
 circa 1560-circa 1607. . . . . .DLB-136
Chew, Ada Nield 1870-1945 . . . . .DLB-135
Cheyney, Edward P. 1861-1947 . . . . .DLB-47
Chiara, Piero 1913-1986 . . . . .DLB-177
Chicano History DLB-82
Chicano Language. DLB-82
Child, Francis James 1825-1896. . . . . . .DLB-1, 64
Child, Lydia Maria 1802-1880 . . . . .DLB-1, 74
Child, Philip 1898-1978 . . . . .DLB-68
Childers, Erskine 1870-1922 . . . . .DLB-70
Children's Book Awards and Prizes DLB-61
Children's Illustrators, 1800-1880 . . . . . . .DLB-163
Childress, Alice 1920-1994 . . . . .DLB-7, 38
Childs, George W. 1829-1894. . . . . .DLB-23
Chilton Book Company DLB-46
Chin, Frank 1940- DLB-206
Chinweizu 1943- DLB-157
Chitham, Edward 1932- DLB-155
Chittenden, Hiram Martin 1858-1917. . . . .DLB-47
Chivers, Thomas Holley 1809-1858 . . . . . . .DLB-3
Cholmondeley, Mary 1859-1925 . . . . .DLB-197
Chopin, Kate 1850-1904 . . . . .DLB-12, 78
Chopin, Rene 1885-1953. . . . . .DLB-92
Choquette, Adrienne 1915-1973 . . . . .DLB-68
Choquette, Robert 1905- DLB-68
Chrétien de Troyes
 circa 1140-circa 1190. . . . . .DLB-208
Christensen, Inger 1935- DLB-214
The Christian Publishing Company DLB-49
Christie, Agatha 1890-1976 . . . . .DLB-13, 77
Christine de Pizan
 circa 1365-circa 1431. . . . . .DLB-208
Christus und die Samariterin circa 950 . . . . . .DLB-148
Christy, Howard Chandler
 1873-1952 .DLB-188
Chulkov, Mikhail Dmitrievich
 1743?-1792. . . . . .DLB-150
Church, Benjamin 1734-1778. . . . . .DLB-31
Church, Francis Pharcellus 1839-1906 . . . .DLB-79
Church, Peggy Pond 1903-1986 . . . . .DLB-212
Church, Richard 1893-1972. . . . . .DLB-191
Church, William Conant 1836-1917 . . . . . .DLB-79
Churchill, Caryl 1938- DLB-13
Churchill, Charles 1731-1764. . . . . .DLB-109
Churchill, Winston 1871-1947. . . . . .DLB-202
Churchill, Sir Winston
 1874-1965 . . . . .DLB-100; DS-16
Churchyard, Thomas 1520?-1604. . . . . . .DLB-132
Churton, E., and Company. DLB-106
Chute, Marchette 1909-1994 . . . . .DLB-103
Ciardi, John 1916-1986 . . . . .DLB-5; Y-86
Cibber, Colley 1671-1757. . . . . .DLB-84

Cicero 106 B.C.-43 B.C. ... DLB-211
Cima, Annalisa 1941- ... DLB-128
Čingo, Živko 1935-1987 ... DLB-181
Cirese, Eugenio 1884-1955 ... DLB-114
Cisneros, Sandra 1954- ... DLB-122, 152
City Lights Books ... DLB-46
Cixous, Hélène 1937- ... DLB-83
Clampitt, Amy 1920-1994 ... DLB-105
Clapper, Raymond 1892-1944 ... DLB-29
Clare, John 1793-1864 ... DLB-55, 96
Clarendon, Edward Hyde, Earl of 1609-1674 ... DLB-101
Clark, Alfred Alexander Gordon (see Hare, Cyril)
Clark, Ann Nolan 1896- ... DLB-52
Clark, C. E. Frazer Jr. 1925- ... DLB-187
Clark, C. M., Publishing Company ... DLB-46
Clark, Catherine Anthony 1892-1977 ... DLB-68
Clark, Charles Heber 1841-1915 ... DLB-11
Clark, Davis Wasgatt 1812-1871 ... DLB-79
Clark, Eleanor 1913- ... DLB-6
Clark, J. P. 1935- ... DLB-117
Clark, Lewis Gaylord 1808-1873 ... DLB-3, 64, 73
Clark, Walter Van Tilburg 1909-1971 ... DLB-9, 206
Clark, William (see Lewis, Meriwether)
Clark, William Andrews Jr. 1877-1934 ... DLB-187
Clarke, Austin 1896-1974 ... DLB-10, 20
Clarke, Austin C. 1934- ... DLB-53, 125
Clarke, Gillian 1937- ... DLB-40
Clarke, James Freeman 1810-1888 ... DLB-1, 59
Clarke, Pauline 1921- ... DLB-161
Clarke, Rebecca Sophia 1833-1906 ... DLB-42
Clarke, Robert, and Company ... DLB-49
Clarkson, Thomas 1760-1846 ... DLB-158
Claudel, Paul 1868-1955 ... DLB-192
Claudius, Matthias 1740-1815 ... DLB-97
Clausen, Andy 1943- ... DLB-16
Clawson, John L. 1865-1933 ... DLB-187
Claxton, Remsen and Haffelfinger ... DLB-49
Clay, Cassius Marcellus 1810-1903 ... DLB-43
Cleary, Beverly 1916- ... DLB-52
Cleaver, Vera 1919- and Cleaver, Bill 1920-1981 ... DLB-52
Cleland, John 1710-1789 ... DLB-39
Clemens, Samuel Langhorne (Mark Twain) 1835-1910 ... DLB-11, 12, 23, 64, 74, 186, 189
Clement, Hal 1922- ... DLB-8
Clemo, Jack 1916- ... DLB-27
Clephane, Elizabeth Cecilia 1830-1869 ... DLB-199
Cleveland, John 1613-1658 ... DLB-126
Cliff, Michelle 1946- ... DLB-157
Clifford, Lady Anne 1590-1676 ... DLB-151
Clifford, James L. 1901-1978 ... DLB-103
Clifford, Lucy 1853?-1929 ... DLB-135, 141, 197

Clifton, Lucille 1936- ... DLB-5, 41
Clines, Francis X. 1938- ... DLB-185
Clive, Caroline (V) 1801-1873 ... DLB-199
Clode, Edward J. [publishing house] ... DLB-46
Clough, Arthur Hugh 1819-1861 ... DLB-32
Cloutier, Cécile 1930- ... DLB-60
Clutton-Brock, Arthur 1868-1924 ... DLB-98
Coates, Robert M. 1897-1973 ... DLB-4, 9, 102
Coatsworth, Elizabeth 1893- ... DLB-22
Cobb, Charles E., Jr. 1943- ... DLB-41
Cobb, Frank I. 1869-1923 ... DLB-25
Cobb, Irvin S. 1876-1944 ... DLB-11, 25, 86
Cobbe, Frances Power 1822-1904 ... DLB-190
Cobbett, William 1763-1835 ... DLB-43, 107
Cobbledick, Gordon 1898-1969 ... DLB-171
Cochran, Thomas C. 1902- ... DLB-17
Cochrane, Elizabeth 1867-1922 ... DLB-25, 189
Cockerell, Sir Sydney 1867-1962 ... DLB-201
Cockerill, John A. 1845-1896 ... DLB-23
Cocteau, Jean 1889-1963 ... DLB-65
Coderre, Emile (see Jean Narrache)
Coffee, Lenore J. 1900?-1984 ... DLB-44
Coffin, Robert P. Tristram 1892-1955 ... DLB-45
Cogswell, Fred 1917- ... DLB-60
Cogswell, Mason Fitch 1761-1830 ... DLB-37
Cohen, Arthur A. 1928-1986 ... DLB-28
Cohen, Leonard 1934- ... DLB-53
Cohen, Matt 1942- ... DLB-53
Colbeck, Norman 1903-1987 ... DLB-201
Colden, Cadwallader 1688-1776 ... DLB-24, 30
Colden, Jane 1724-1766 ... DLB-200
Cole, Barry 1936- ... DLB-14
Cole, George Watson 1850-1939 ... DLB-140
Colegate, Isabel 1931- ... DLB-14
Coleman, Emily Holmes 1899-1974 ... DLB-4
Coleman, Wanda 1946- ... DLB-130
Coleridge, Hartley 1796-1849 ... DLB-96
Coleridge, Mary 1861-1907 ... DLB-19, 98
Coleridge, Samuel Taylor 1772-1834 ... DLB-93, 107
Coleridge, Sara 1802-1852 ... DLB-199
Colet, John 1467-1519 ... DLB-132
Colette 1873-1954 ... DLB-65
Colette, Sidonie Gabrielle (see Colette)
Colinas, Antonio 1946- ... DLB-134
Coll, Joseph Clement 1881-1921 ... DLB-188
Collier, John 1901-1980 ... DLB-77
Collier, John Payne 1789-1883 ... DLB-184
Collier, Mary 1690-1762 ... DLB-95
Collier, Robert J. 1876-1918 ... DLB-91
Collier, P. F. [publishing house] ... DLB-49
Collin and Small ... DLB-49
Collingwood, W. G. 1854-1932 ... DLB-149
Collins, An floruit circa 1653 ... DLB-131

Collins, Merle 1950- ... DLB-157
Collins, Mortimer 1827-1876 ... DLB-21, 35
Collins, Wilkie 1824-1889 ... DLB-18, 70, 159
Collins, William 1721-1759 ... DLB-109
Collins, William, Sons and Company ... DLB-154
Collins, Isaac [publishing house] ... DLB-49
Collis, Maurice 1889-1973 ... DLB-195
Collyer, Mary 1716?-1763? ... DLB-39
Colman, Benjamin 1673-1747 ... DLB-24
Colman, George, the Elder 1732-1794 ... DLB-89
Colman, George, the Younger 1762-1836 ... DLB-89
Colman, S. [publishing house] ... DLB-49
Colombo, John Robert 1936- ... DLB-53
Colquhoun, Patrick 1745-1820 ... DLB-158
Colter, Cyrus 1910- ... DLB-33
Colum, Padraic 1881-1972 ... DLB-19
Columella fl. first century A.D. ... DLB-211
Colvin, Sir Sidney 1845-1927 ... DLB-149
Colwin, Laurie 1944-1992 ... Y-80
Comden, Betty 1919- and Green, Adolph 1918- ... DLB-44
Comi, Girolamo 1890-1968 ... DLB-114
The Comic Tradition Continued [in the British Novel] ... DLB-15
Commager, Henry Steele 1902- ... DLB-17
The Commercialization of the Image of Revolt, by Kenneth Rexroth ... DLB-16
Community and Commentators: Black Theatre and Its Critics ... DLB-38
Commynes, Philippe de circa 1447-1511 ... DLB-208
Compton-Burnett, Ivy 1884?-1969 ... DLB-36
Conan, Laure 1845-1924 ... DLB-99
Conde, Carmen 1901- ... DLB-108
Conference on Modern Biography ... Y-85
Congreve, William 1670-1729 ... DLB-39, 84
Conkey, W. B., Company ... DLB-49
Connell, Evan S., Jr. 1924- ... DLB-2; Y-81
Connelly, Marc 1890-1980 ... DLB-7; Y-80
Connolly, Cyril 1903-1974 ... DLB-98
Connolly, James B. 1868-1957 ... DLB-78
Connor, Ralph 1860-1937 ... DLB-92
Connor, Tony 1930- ... DLB-40
Conquest, Robert 1917- ... DLB-27
Conrad, Joseph 1857-1924 ... DLB-10, 34, 98, 156
Conrad, John, and Company ... DLB-49
Conroy, Jack 1899-1990 ... Y-81
Conroy, Pat 1945- ... DLB-6
The Consolidation of Opinion: Critical Responses to the Modernists ... DLB-36
Consolo, Vincenzo 1933- ... DLB-196
Constable, Henry 1562-1613 ... DLB-136
Constable and Company Limited ... DLB-112
Constable, Archibald, and Company ... DLB-154
Constant, Benjamin 1767-1830 ... DLB-119

Constant de Rebecque, Henri-benjamin de (see Constant, Benjamin)

Constantine, David 1944- DLB-40

Constantin-Weyer, Maurice 1881-1964 ....DLB-92

Contempo Caravan: Kites in a Windstorm Y-85

A Contemporary Flourescence of Chicano Literature Y-84

"Contemporary Verse Story-telling," by Jonathan Holden DLB-105

The Continental Publishing Company DLB-49

A Conversation with Chaim Potok Y-84

Conversations with Editors Y-95

Conversations with Publishers I: An Interview with Patrick O'Connor Y-84

Conversations with Publishers II: An Interview with Charles Scribner III Y-94

Conversations with Publishers III: An Interview with Donald Lamm.................Y-95

Conversations with Publishers IV: An Interview with James Laughlin Y-96

Conversations with Rare Book Dealers I: An Interview with Glenn Horowitz Y-90

Conversations with Rare Book Dealers II: An Interview with Ralph Sipper Y-94

Conversations with Rare Book Dealers (Publishers) III: An Interview with Otto Penzler Y-96

The Conversion of an Unpolitical Man, by W. H. Bruford DLB-66

Conway, Moncure Daniel 1832-1907......DLB-1

Cook, Ebenezer circa 1667-circa 1732 ....DLB-24

Cook, Edward Tyas 1857-1919 ....DLB-149

Cook, Eliza 1818-1889................DLB-199

Cook, Michael 1933- DLB-53

Cook, David C., Publishing Company DLB-49

Cooke, George Willis 1848-1923.........DLB-71

Cooke, Increase, and Company.........DLB-49

Cooke, John Esten 1830-1886 ....DLB-3

Cooke, Philip Pendleton 1816-1850.....DLB-3, 59

Cooke, Rose Terry 1827-1892.........DLB-12, 74

Cook-Lynn, Elizabeth 1930- DLB-175

Coolbrith, Ina 1841-1928..............DLB-54, 186

Cooley, Peter 1940- DLB-105

Coolidge, Clark 1939- DLB-193

Coolidge, Susan (see Woolsey, Sarah Chauncy)

Coolidge, George [publishing house]......DLB-49

Cooper, Giles 1918-1966 ....DLB-13

Cooper, J. California 19??- DLB-212

Cooper, James Fenimore 1789-1851....DLB-3, 183

Cooper, Kent 1880-1965 ....DLB-29

Cooper, Susan 1935- DLB-161

Cooper, William [publishing house] DLB-170

Coote, J. [publishing house] DLB-154

Coover, Robert 1932- DLB-2; Y-81

Copeland and Day....................DLB-49

Ćopić, Branko 1915-1984 ....DLB-181

Copland, Robert 1470?-1548 ....DLB-136

Coppard, A. E. 1878-1957 ....DLB-162

Coppel, Alfred 1921- Y-83

Coppola, Francis Ford 1939- DLB-44

Copway, George (Kah-ge-ga-gah-bowh) 1818-1869 ....DLB-175, 183

Corazzini, Sergio 1886-1907 ....DLB-114

Corbett, Richard 1582-1635 ....DLB-121

Corcoran, Barbara 1911- DLB-52

Cordelli, Franco 1943- DLB-196

Corelli, Marie 1855-1924...........DLB-34, 156

Corle, Edwin 1906-1956 ....Y-85

Corman, Cid 1924- DLB-5, 193

Cormier, Robert 1925- DLB-52

Corn, Alfred 1943- DLB-120; Y-80

Cornish, Sam 1935- DLB-41

Cornish, William circa 1465-circa 1524................DLB-132

Cornwall, Barry (see Procter, Bryan Waller)

Cornwallis, Sir William, the Younger circa 1579-1614 ....DLB-151

Cornwell, David John Moore (see le Carré, John)

Corpi, Lucha 1945- DLB-82

Corrington, John William 1932- DLB-6

Corrothers, James D. 1869-1917 ....DLB-50

Corso, Gregory 1930- DLB-5, 16

Cortázar, Julio 1914-1984 ....DLB-113

Cortéz, Carlos 1923- DLB-209

Cortez, Jayne 1936- DLB-41

Corvinus, Gottlieb Siegmund 1677-1746 ..DLB-168

Corvo, Baron (see Rolfe, Frederick William)

Cory, Annie Sophie (see Cross, Victoria)

Cory, William Johnson 1823-1892 ....DLB-35

Coryate, Thomas 1577?-1617 ......DLB-151, 172

Ćosić, Dobrica 1921- DLB-181

Cosin, John 1595-1672............DLB-151, 213

Cosmopolitan Book Corporation DLB-46

Costain, Thomas B. 1885-1965 ....DLB-9

Coste, Donat 1912-1957 ....DLB-88

Costello, Louisa Stuart 1799-1870........DLB-166

Cota-Cárdenas, Margarita 1941- DLB-122

Cotten, Bruce 1873-1954...............DLB-187

Cotter, Joseph Seamon, Sr. 1861-1949....DLB-50

Cotter, Joseph Seamon, Jr. 1895-1919....DLB-50

Cottle, Joseph [publishing house].......DLB-154

Cotton, Charles 1630-1687 ....DLB-131

Cotton, John 1584-1652................DLB-24

Cotton, Sir Robert Bruce 1571-1631 .....DLB-213

Coulter, John 1888-1980 ....DLB-68

Cournos, John 1881-1966 ....DLB-54

Courteline, Georges 1858-1929 ....DLB-192

Cousins, Margaret 1905- DLB-137

Cousins, Norman 1915-1990...........DLB-137

Coventry, Francis 1725-1754 ....DLB-39

Coverdale, Miles 1487 or 1488-1569.....DLB-167

Coverly, N. [publishing house] DLB-49

Covici-Friede DLB-46

Coward, Noel 1899-1973...............DLB-10

Coward, McCann and Geoghegan DLB-46

Cowles, Gardner 1861-1946 ....DLB-29

Cowles, Gardner ("Mike"), Jr. 1903-1985 ....DLB-127, 137

Cowley, Abraham 1618-1667 ......DLB-131, 151

Cowley, Hannah 1743-1809 ....DLB-89

Cowley, Malcolm 1898-1989...........DLB-4, 48; Y-81, Y-89

Cowper, William 1731-1800 ....DLB-104, 109

Cox, A. B. (see Berkeley, Anthony)

Cox, James McMahon 1903-1974 ....DLB-127

Cox, James Middleton 1870-1957 ....DLB-127

Cox, Palmer 1840-1924.................DLB-42

Coxe, Louis 1918-1993 ....DLB-5

Coxe, Tench 1755-1824.................DLB-37

Cozzens, Frederick S. 1818-1869........DLB-202

Cozzens, James Gould 1903-1978 ....DLB-9; Y-84; DS-2

Cozzens's Michael Scarlett Y-97

Crabbe, George 1754-1832 ....DLB-93

Crackanthorpe, Hubert 1870-1896 ......DLB-135

Craddock, Charles Egbert (see Murfree, Mary N.)

Cradock, Thomas 1718-1770 ....DLB-31

Craig, Daniel H. 1811-1895.............DLB-43

Craik, Dinah Maria 1826-1887 ......DLB-35, 136

Cramer, Richard Ben 1950- DLB-185

Cranch, Christopher Pearse 1813-1892..DLB-1, 42

Crane, Hart 1899-1932 ....DLB-4, 48

Crane, R. S. 1886-1967 ....DLB-63

Crane, Stephen 1871-1900........DLB-12, 54, 78

Crane, Walter 1845-1915 ....DLB-163

Cranmer, Thomas 1489-1556 .....DLB-132, 213

Crapsey, Adelaide 1878-1914...........DLB-54

Crashaw, Richard 1612 or 1613-1649 ....DLB-126

Craven, Avery 1885-1980 ....DLB-17

Crawford, Charles 1752-circa 1815 ....DLB-31

Crawford, F. Marion 1854-1909 ....DLB-71

Crawford, Isabel Valancy 1850-1887 .....DLB-92

Crawley, Alan 1887-1975...............DLB-68

Crayon, Geoffrey (see Irving, Washington)

Creamer, Robert W. 1922- DLB-171

Creasey, John 1908-1973 ....DLB-77

Creative Age Press....................DLB-46

Creech, William [publishing house]......DLB-154

Creede, Thomas [publishing house] DLB-170

Creel, George 1876-1953 ....DLB-25

Creeley, Robert 1926- DLB-5, 16, 169; DS-17

Creelman, James 1859-1915 ....DLB-23

Cregan, David 1931- DLB-13

Creighton, Donald Grant 1902-1979......DLB-88

Cremazie, Octave 1827-1879 ....DLB-99

Crémer, Victoriano 1909?- DLB-108

Crescas, Hasdai circa 1340-1412?	DLB-115
Crespo, Angel 1926-	DLB-134
Cresset Press	DLB-112
Cresswell, Helen 1934-	DLB-161
Crèvecoeur, Michel Guillaume Jean de 1735-1813	DLB-37
Crewe, Candida 1964-	DLB-207
Crews, Harry 1935-	DLB-6, 143, 185
Crichton, Michael 1942-	Y-81
A Crisis of Culture: The Changing Role of Religion in the New Republic	DLB-37
Crispin, Edmund 1921-1978	DLB-87
Cristofer, Michael 1946-	DLB-7
"The Critic as Artist" (1891), by Oscar Wilde	DLB-57
"Criticism In Relation To Novels" (1863), by G. H. Lewes	DLB-21
Crnjanski, Miloš 1893-1977	DLB-147
Crocker, Hannah Mather 1752-1829	DLB-200
Crockett, David (Davy) 1786-1836	DLB-3, 11, 183
Croft-Cooke, Rupert (see Bruce, Leo)	
Crofts, Freeman Wills 1879-1957	DLB-77
Croker, John Wilson 1780-1857	DLB-110
Croly, George 1780-1860	DLB-159
Croly, Herbert 1869-1930	DLB-91
Croly, Jane Cunningham 1829-1901	DLB-23
Crompton, Richmal 1890-1969	DLB-160
Cronin, A. J. 1896-1981	DLB-191
Crosby, Caresse 1892-1970	DLB-48
Crosby, Caresse 1892-1970 and Crosby, Harry 1898-1929	DLB-4; DS-15
Crosby, Harry 1898-1929	DLB-48
Cross, Gillian 1945-	DLB-161
Cross, Victoria 1868-1952	DLB-135, 197
Crossley-Holland, Kevin 1941-	DLB-40, 161
Crothers, Rachel 1878-1958	DLB-7
Crowell, Thomas Y., Company	DLB-49
Crowley, John 1942-	Y-82
Crowley, Mart 1935-	DLB-7
Crown Publishers	DLB-46
Crowne, John 1641-1712	DLB-80
Crowninshield, Edward Augustus 1817-1859	DLB-140
Crowninshield, Frank 1872-1947	DLB-91
Croy, Homer 1883-1965	DLB-4
Crumley, James 1939-	Y-84
Cruz, Victor Hernández 1949-	DLB-41
Csokor, Franz Theodor 1885-1969	DLB-81
Cuala Press	DLB-112
Cullen, Countee 1903-1946	DLB-4, 48, 51
Culler, Jonathan D. 1944-	DLB-67
The Cult of Biography Excerpts from the Second Folio Debate: "Biographies are generally a disease of English Literature" – Germaine Greer, Victoria Glendinning, Auberon Waugh, and Richard Holmes	Y-86
Cumberland, Richard 1732-1811	DLB-89
Cummings, Constance Gordon 1837-1924	DLB-174
Cummings, E. E. 1894-1962	DLB-4, 48
Cummings, Ray 1887-1957	DLB-8
Cummings and Hilliard	DLB-49
Cummins, Maria Susanna 1827-1866	DLB-42
Cumpián, Carlos 1953-	DLB-209
Cundall, Joseph [publishing house]	DLB-106
Cuney, Waring 1906-1976	DLB-51
Cuney-Hare, Maude 1874-1936	DLB-52
Cunningham, Allan 1784-1842	DLB-116, 144
Cunningham, J. V. 1911-	DLB-5
Cunningham, Peter F. [publishing house]	DLB-49
Cunquiero, Alvaro 1911-1981	DLB-134
Cuomo, George 1929-	Y-80
Cupples and Leon	DLB-46
Cupples, Upham and Company	DLB-49
Cuppy, Will 1884-1949	DLB-11
Curiel, Barbara Brinson 1956-	DLB-209
Curll, Edmund [publishing house]	DLB-154
Currie, James 1756-1805	DLB-142
Currie, Mary Montgomerie Lamb Singleton, Lady Currie (see Fane, Violet)	
Cursor Mundi circa 1300	DLB-146
Curti, Merle E. 1897-	DLB-17
Curtis, Anthony 1926-	DLB-155
Curtis, Cyrus H. K. 1850-1933	DLB-91
Curtis, George William 1824-1892	DLB-1, 43
Quintus Curtius Rufus fl. A.D. 35	DLB-211
Curzon, Robert 1810-1873	DLB-166
Curzon, Sarah Anne 1833-1898	DLB-99
Cushing, Harvey 1869-1939	DLB-187
Cynewulf circa 770-840	DLB-146
Czepko, Daniel 1605-1660	DLB-164

D

D. M. Thomas: The Plagiarism Controversy	Y-82
Dabit, Eugène 1898-1936	DLB-65
Daborne, Robert circa 1580-1628	DLB-58
Dacey, Philip 1939-	DLB-105
Dach, Simon 1605-1659	DLB-164
Daggett, Rollin M. 1831-1901	DLB-79
D'Aguiar, Fred 1960-	DLB-157
Dahl, Roald 1916-1990	DLB-139
Dahlberg, Edward 1900-1977	DLB-48
Dahn, Felix 1834-1912	DLB-129
Dal', Vladimir Ivanovich (Kazak Vladimir Lugansky) 1801-1872	DLB-198
Dale, Peter 1938-	DLB-40
Daley, Arthur 1904-1974	DLB-171
Dall, Caroline Wells (Healey) 1822-1912	DLB-1
Dallas, E. S. 1828-1879	DLB-55
The Dallas Theater Center	DLB-7
D'Alton, Louis 1900-1951	DLB-10
Daly, T. A. 1871-1948	DLB-11
Damon, S. Foster 1893-1971	DLB-45
Damrell, William S. [publishing house]	DLB-49
Dana, Charles A. 1819-1897	DLB-3, 23
Dana, Richard Henry, Jr. 1815-1882	DLB-1, 183
Dandridge, Ray Garfield	DLB-51
Dane, Clemence 1887-1965	DLB-10, 197
Danforth, John 1660-1730	DLB-24
Danforth, Samuel, I 1626-1674	DLB-24
Danforth, Samuel, II 1666-1727	DLB-24
Dangerous Years: London Theater, 1939-1945	DLB-10
Daniel, John M. 1825-1865	DLB-43
Daniel, Samuel 1562 or 1563-1619	DLB-62
Daniel Press	DLB-106
Daniells, Roy 1902-1979	DLB-68
Daniels, Jim 1956-	DLB-120
Daniels, Jonathan 1902-1981	DLB-127
Daniels, Josephus 1862-1948	DLB-29
Danis Rose and the Rendering of *Ulysses*	Y-97
Dannay, Frederic 1905-1982 and Manfred B. Lee 1905-1971	DLB-137
Danner, Margaret Esse 1915-	DLB-41
Danter, John [publishing house]	DLB-170
Dantin, Louis 1865-1945	DLB-92
Danzig, Allison 1898-1987	DLB-171
D'Arcy, Ella circa 1857-1937	DLB-135
Darley, Felix Octavious Carr 1822-1888	DLB-188
Darley, George 1795-1846	DLB-96
Darwin, Charles 1809-1882	DLB-57, 166
Darwin, Erasmus 1731-1802	DLB-93
Daryush, Elizabeth 1887-1977	DLB-20
Dashkova, Ekaterina Romanovna (née Vorontsova) 1743-1810	DLB-150
Dashwood, Edmée Elizabeth Monica de la Pasture (see Delafield, E. M.)	
Daudet, Alphonse 1840-1897	DLB-123
d'Aulaire, Edgar Parin 1898- and d'Aulaire, Ingri 1904-	DLB-22
Davenant, Sir William 1606-1668	DLB-58, 126
Davenport, Guy 1927-	DLB-130
Davenport, Marcia 1903-1996	DS-17
Davenport, Robert ?-?	DLB-58
Daves, Delmer 1904-1977	DLB-26
Davey, Frank 1940-	DLB-53
Davidson, Avram 1923-1993	DLB-8
Davidson, Donald 1893-1968	DLB-45
Davidson, John 1857-1909	DLB-19
Davidson, Lionel 1922-	DLB-14
Davidson, Robyn 1950-	DLB-204
Davidson, Sara 1943-	DLB-185

Davie, Donald 1922- ... DLB-27	De Bow, James Dunwoody Brownson 1820-1867 ... DLB-3, 79	Deloney, Thomas died 1600 ... DLB-167
Davie, Elspeth 1919- ... DLB-139	de Bruyn, Günter 1926- ... DLB-75	Deloria, Ella C. 1889-1971 ... DLB-175
Davies, Sir John 1569-1626 ... DLB-172	de Camp, L. Sprague 1907- ... DLB-8	Deloria, Vine, Jr. 1933- ... DLB-175
Davies, John, of Hereford 1565?-1618 ... DLB-121	De Carlo, Andrea 1952- ... DLB-196	del Rey, Lester 1915-1993 ... DLB-8
Davies, Rhys 1901-1978 ... DLB-139, 191	De Casas, Celso A. 1944- ... DLB-209	Del Vecchio, John M. 1947- ... DS-9
Davies, Robertson 1913- ... DLB-68	The Decay of Lying (1889), by Oscar Wilde [excerpt] ... DLB-18	Del'vig, Anton Antonovich 1798-1831 ... DLB-205
Davies, Samuel 1723-1761 ... DLB-31	Dechert, Robert 1895-1975 ... DLB-187	de Man, Paul 1919-1983 ... DLB-67
Davies, Thomas 1712?-1785 ... DLB-142, 154	Dedication, *Ferdinand Count Fathom* (1753), by Tobias Smollett ... DLB-39	Demby, William 1922- ... DLB-33
Davies, W. H. 1871-1940 ... DLB-19, 174		Deming, Philander 1829-1915 ... DLB-74
Davies, Peter, Limited ... DLB-112	Dedication, *The History of Pompey the Little* (1751), by Francis Coventry ... DLB-39	Deml, Jakub 1878-1961 ... DLB-215
Daviot, Gordon 1896?-1952 ... DLB-10 (see also Tey, Josephine)	Dedication, *Lasselia* (1723), by Eliza Haywood [excerpt] ... DLB-39	Demorest, William Jennings 1822-1895 ... DLB-79
Davis, Charles A. 1795-1867 ... DLB-11		De Morgan, William 1839-1917 ... DLB-153
Davis, Clyde Brion 1894-1962 ... DLB-9	Dedication, *The Wanderer* (1814), by Fanny Burney ... DLB-39	Demosthenes 384 B.C.-322 B.C. ... DLB-176
Davis, Dick 1945- ... DLB-40	Dee, John 1527-1608 or 1609 ... DLB-136, 213	Denham, Henry [publishing house] ... DLB-170
Davis, Frank Marshall 1905-? ... DLB-51	Deeping, George Warwick 1877-1950 ... DLB 153	Denham, Sir John 1615-1669 ... DLB-58, 126
Davis, H. L. 1894-1960 ... DLB-9, 206	Defense of *Amelia* (1752), by Henry Fielding ... DLB-39	Denison, Merrill 1893-1975 ... DLB-92
Davis, John 1774-1854 ... DLB-37		Denison, T. S., and Company ... DLB-49
Davis, Lydia 1947- ... DLB-130	Defoe, Daniel 1660-1731 ... DLB-39, 95, 101	Dennery, Adolphe Philippe 1811-1899 ... DLB-192
Davis, Margaret Thomson 1926- ... DLB-14	de Fontaine, Felix Gregory 1834-1896 ... DLB-43	
Davis, Ossie 1917- ... DLB-7, 38	De Forest, John William 1826-1906 ... DLB-12, 189	Dennie, Joseph 1768-1812 ... DLB-37, 43, 59, 73
Davis, Paxton 1925-1994 ... Y-94		Dennis, John 1658-1734 ... DLB-101
Davis, Rebecca Harding 1831-1910 ... DLB-74	DeFrees, Madeline 1919- ... DLB-105	Dennis, Nigel 1912-1989 ... DLB-13, 15
Davis, Richard Harding 1864-1916 ... DLB-12, 23, 78, 79, 189; DS-13	DeGolyer, Everette Lee 1886-1956 ... DLB-187	Denslow, W. W. 1856-1915 ... DLB-188
	de Graff, Robert 1895-1981 ... Y-81	Dent, Tom 1932- ... DLB-38
Davis, Samuel Cole 1764-1809 ... DLB-37	de Graft, Joe 1924-1978 ... DLB-117	Dent, J. M., and Sons ... DLB-112
Davis, Samuel Post 1850-1918 ... DLB-202	*De Heinrico* circa 980? ... DLB-148	Denton, Daniel circa 1626-1703 ... DLB-24
Davison, Peter 1928- ... DLB-5	Deighton, Len 1929- ... DLB-87	dePaola, Tomie 1934- ... DLB-61
Davydov, Denis Vasil'evich 1784-1839 ... DLB-205	DeJong, Meindert 1906-1991 ... DLB-52	Department of Library, Archives, and Institutional Research, American Bible Society ... Y-97
Davys, Mary 1674-1732 ... DLB-39	Dekker, Thomas circa 1572-1632 ... DLB-62, 172	
DAW Books ... DLB-46	Delacorte, Jr., George T. 1894-1991 ... DLB-91	De Quille, Dan 1829-1898 ... DLB-186
Dawn Powell, Where Have You Been All Our lives? ... Y-97	Delafield, E. M. 1890-1943 ... DLB-34	De Quincey, Thomas 1785-1859 ... DLB-110, 144
	Delahaye, Guy 1888-1969 ... DLB-92	Derby, George Horatio 1823-1861 ... DLB-11
Dawson, Ernest 1882-1947 ... DLB-140	de la Mare, Walter 1873-1956 ... DLB-19, 153, 162	Derby, J. C., and Company ... DLB-49
Dawson, Fielding 1930- ... DLB-130		Derby and Miller ... DLB-49
Dawson, William 1704-1752 ... DLB-31	Deland, Margaret 1857-1945 ... DLB-78	De Ricci, Seymour 1881-1942 ... DLB-201
Day, Angel flourished 1586 ... DLB-167	Delaney, Shelagh 1939- ... DLB-13	Derleth, August 1909-1971 ... DLB-9; DS-17
Day, Benjamin Henry 1810-1889 ... DLB-43	Delano, Amasa 1763-1823 ... DLB-183	The Derrydale Press ... DLB-46
Day, Clarence 1874-1935 ... DLB-11	Delany, Martin Robinson 1812-1885 ... DLB-50	Derzhavin, Gavriil Romanovich 1743-1816 ... DLB-150
Day, Dorothy 1897-1980 ... DLB-29	Delany, Samuel R. 1942- ... DLB-8, 33	
Day, Frank Parker 1881-1950 ... DLB-92	de la Roche, Mazo 1879-1961 ... DLB-68	Desaulniers, Gonsalve 1863-1934 ... DLB-92
Day, John circa 1574-circa 1640 ... DLB-62	Delavigne, Jean François Casimir 1793-1843 ... DLB-192	Deschamps, Eustache 1340?-1404 ... DLB-208
Day, John [publishing house] ... DLB-170		Desbiens, Jean-Paul 1927- ... DLB-53
Day Lewis, C. 1904-1972 ... DLB-15, 20 (see also Blake, Nicholas)	Delbanco, Nicholas 1942- ... DLB-6	des Forêts, Louis-Rene 1918- ... DLB-83
	Del Castillo, Ramón 1949- ... DLB-209	Desiato, Luca 1941- ... DLB-196
Day, Thomas 1748-1789 ... DLB-39	De León, Nephtal 1945- ... DLB-82	Desnica, Vladan 1905-1967 ... DLB-181
Day, The John, Company ... DLB-46	Delgado, Abelardo Barrientos 1931- ... DLB-82	DesRochers, Alfred 1901-1978 ... DLB-68
Day, Mahlon [publishing house] ... DLB-49	Del Giudice, Daniele 1949- ... DLB-196	Desrosiers, Léo-Paul 1896-1967 ... DLB-68
Dazai Osamu 1909-1948 ... DLB-182	De Libero, Libero 1906-1981 ... DLB-114	Dessì, Giuseppe 1909-1977 ... DLB-177
Dąbrowska, Maria 1889-1965 ... DLB-215	DeLillo, Don 1936- ... DLB-6, 173	Destouches, Louis-Ferdinand (see Céline, Louis-Ferdinand)
Deacon, William Arthur 1890-1977 ... DLB-68	de Lisser H. G. 1878-1944 ... DLB-117	
Deal, Borden 1922-1985 ... DLB-6	Dell, Floyd 1887-1969 ... DLB-9	De Tabley, Lord 1835-1895 ... DLB-35
de Angeli, Marguerite 1889-1987 ... DLB-22	Dell Publishing Company ... DLB-46	"A Detail in a Poem," by Fred Chappell ... DLB-105
De Angelis, Milo 1951- ... DLB-128	delle Grazie, Marie Eugene 1864-1931 ... DLB-81	Deutsch, Babette 1895-1982 ... DLB-45

Deutsch, Niklaus Manuel (see Manuel, Niklaus)
Deutsch, André, Limited DLB-112
Deveaux, Alexis 1948- DLB-38
The Development of the Author's Copyright
   in Britain DLB-154
The Development of Lighting in the Staging
   of Drama, 1900-1945 .... DLB-10
The Development of Meiji Japan DLB-180
De Vere, Aubrey 1814-1902............ DLB-35
Devereux, second Earl of Essex, Robert
   1565-1601 .... DLB-136
The Devin-Adair Company DLB-46
De Vinne, Theodore Low 1828-1914.... DLB-187
De Voto, Bernard 1897-1955 .... DLB-9
De Vries, Peter 1910-1993 .... DLB-6; Y-82
Dewdney, Christopher 1951- DLB-60
Dewdney, Selwyn 1909-1979 .... DLB-68
DeWitt, Robert M., Publisher DLB-49
DeWolfe, Fiske and Company DLB-49
Dexter, Colin 1930- DLB-87
de Young, M. H. 1849-1925............ DLB-25
Dhlomo, H. I. E. 1903-1956........... DLB-157
Dhuoda circa 803-after 843 .... DLB-148
The Dial Press DLB-46
Diamond, I. A. L. 1920-1988 .... DLB-26
Dibble, L. Grace 1902-1998 .... DLB-204
Dibdin, Thomas Frognall
   1776-1847 .... DLB-184
Di Cicco, Pier Giorgio 1949- DLB-60
Dick, Philip K. 1928-1982 .... DLB-8
Dick and Fitzgerald................... DLB-49
Dickens, Charles
   1812-1870........DLB-21, 55, 70, 159, 166
Dickinson, Peter 1927- DLB-161
Dickey, James 1923-1997
   ....DLB-5, 193; Y-82, Y-93, Y-96; DS-7, DS-19
Dickey, William 1928-1994 .... DLB-5
Dickinson, Emily 1830-1886 .... DLB-1
Dickinson, John 1732-1808............ DLB-31
Dickinson, Jonathan 1688-1747......... DLB-24
Dickinson, Patric 1914- DLB-27
Dickinson, Peter 1927- DLB-87
Dicks, John [publishing house] DLB-106
Dickson, Gordon R. 1923- DLB-8
*Dictionary of Literary Biography
   Yearbook* Awards....... Y-92, Y-93, Y-97, Y-98
The Dictionary of National Biography
   .... DLB-144
Didion, Joan 1934-
   .... DLB-2, 173, 185; Y-81, Y-86
Di Donato, Pietro 1911- DLB-9
Die Fürstliche Bibliothek Corvey Y-96
Diego, Gerardo 1896-1987 .... DLB-134
Digges, Thomas circa 1546-1595 ...... DLB-136
The Digital Millennium Copyright Act:
   Expanding Copyright Protection in
   Cyberspace and Beyond Y-98
Dillard, Annie 1945- Y-80

Dillard, R. H. W. 1937- DLB-5
Dillingham, Charles T., Company....... DLB-49
The Dillingham, G. W., Company DLB-49
Dilly, Edward and Charles
   [publishing house] DLB-154
Dilthey, Wilhelm 1833-1911 .... DLB-129
Dimitrova, Blaga 1922- DLB-181
Dimov, Dimitr 1909-1966 .... DLB-181
Dimsdale, Thomas J. 1831?-1866....... DLB-186
Dinesen, Isak (see Blixen, Karen)
Dingelstedt, Franz von 1814-1881 ...... DLB-133
Dintenfass, Mark 1941- Y-84
Diogenes, Jr. (see Brougham, John)
Diogenes Laertius circa 200 ....DLB-176
DiPrima, Diane 1934- DLB-5, 16
Disch, Thomas M. 1940- DLB-8
Disney, Walt 1901-1966............... DLB-22
Disraeli, Benjamin 1804-1881........ DLB-21, 55
D'Israeli, Isaac 1766-1848 ....DLB-107
Ditlevsen, Tove 1917-1976 .... DLB-214
Ditzen, Rudolf (see Fallada, Hans)
Dix, Dorothea Lynde 1802-1887 .... DLB-1
Dix, Dorothy (see Gilmer, Elizabeth Meriwether)
Dix, Edwards and Company DLB-49
Dix, Gertrude circa 1874-? DLB-197
Dixie, Florence Douglas 1857-1905 .....DLB-174
Dixon, Ella Hepworth 1855 or
   1857-1932...................... DLB-197
Dixon, Paige (see Corcoran, Barbara)
Dixon, Richard Watson 1833-1900 ...... DLB-19
Dixon, Stephen 1936- DLB-130
Dmitriev, Ivan Ivanovich 1760-1837..... DLB-150
Dobell, Bertram 1842-1914 .... DLB-184
Dobell, Sydney 1824-1874 .... DLB-32
Dobie, J. Frank 1888-1964 .... DLB-212
Döblin, Alfred 1878-1957 .... DLB-66
Dobson, Austin 1840-1921 .... DLB-35, 144
Doctorow, E. L. 1931- DLB-2, 28, 173; Y-80
Documents on Sixteenth-Century
   Literature DLB-167, 172
Dodd, William E. 1869-1940 .... DLB-17
Dodd, Anne [publishing house] DLB-154
Dodd, Mead and Company DLB-49
Doderer, Heimito von 1896-1968........ DLB-85
Dodge, Mary Mapes
   1831?-1905.............DLB-42, 79; DS-13
Dodge, B. W., and Company........... DLB-46
Dodge Publishing Company DLB-49
Dodgson, Charles Lutwidge (see Carroll, Lewis)
Dodsley, Robert 1703-1764............ DLB-95
Dodsley, R. [publishing house]........ DLB-154
Dodson, Owen 1914-1983 .... DLB-76
Dodwell, Christina 1951- DLB-204
Doesticks, Q. K. Philander, P. B. (see Thomson,
   Mortimer)
Doheny, Carrie Estelle 1875-1958 ...... DLB-140

Doherty, John 1798?-1854 .... DLB-190
Doig, Ivan 1939- DLB-206
Domínguez, Sylvia Maida 1935- DLB-122
Donahoe, Patrick [publishing house] DLB-49
Donald, David H. 1920- DLB-17
Donaldson, Scott 1928- DLB-111
Doni, Rodolfo 1919- DLB-177
Donleavy, J. P. 1926- DLB-6, 173
Donnadieu, Marguerite (see Duras, Marguerite)
Donne, John 1572-1631 .... DLB-121, 151
Donnelley, R. R., and Sons Company DLB-49
Donnelly, Ignatius 1831-1901........... DLB-12
Donohue and Henneberry DLB-49
Donoso, José 1924- DLB-113
Doolady, M. [publishing house] DLB-49
Dooley, Ebon (see Ebon)
Doolittle, Hilda 1886-1961........... DLB-4, 45
Doplicher, Fabio 1938- DLB-128
Dor, Milo 1923- DLB-85
Doran, George H., Company.......... DLB-46
Dorgelès, Roland 1886-1973........... DLB-65
Dorn, Edward 1929- DLB-5
Dorr, Rheta Childe 1866-1948........ DLB-25
Dorris, Michael 1945-1997 ....DLB-175
Dorset and Middlesex, Charles Sackville,
   Lord Buckhurst, Earl of 1643-1706 ... DLB-131
Dorst, Tankred 1925- DLB-75, 124
Dos Passos, John
   1896-1970............DLB-4, 9; DS-1, DS-15
John Dos Passos: A Centennial
   Commemoration Y-96
Doubleday and Company DLB-49
Dougall, Lily 1858-1923............... DLB-92
Doughty, Charles M.
   1843-1926 .... DLB-19, 57, 174
Douglas, Gavin 1476-1522 .... DLB-132
Douglas, Keith 1920-1944 .... DLB-27
Douglas, Norman 1868-1952 .... DLB-34, 195
Douglass, Frederick 1817?-1895. .DLB-1, 43, 50, 79
Douglass, William circa 1691-1752....... DLB-24
Dourado, Autran 1926- DLB-145
Dove, Arthur G. 1880-1946 .... DLB-188
Dove, Rita 1952- DLB-120
Dover Publications DLB-46
Doves Press DLB-112
Dowden, Edward 1843-1913 .... DLB-35, 149
Dowell, Coleman 1925-1985 .... DLB-130
Dowland, John 1563-1626 ....DLB-172
Downes, Gwladys 1915- DLB-88
Downing, J., Major (see Davis, Charles A.)
Downing, Major Jack (see Smith, Seba)
Dowriche, Anne
   before 1560-after 1613 ....DLB-172
Dowson, Ernest 1867-1900......... DLB-19, 135
Doxey, William [publishing house] DLB-49

Doyle, Sir Arthur Conan 1859-1930 .... DLB-18, 70, 156, 178
Doyle, Kirby 1932- DLB-16
Doyle, Roddy 1958- DLB-194
Drabble, Margaret 1939- DLB-14, 155
Drach, Albert 1902- DLB-85
Dragojević, Danijel 1934- DLB-181
Drake, Samuel Gardner 1798-1875 ...... DLB-187
The Dramatic Publishing Company DLB-49
Dramatists Play Service DLB-46
Drant, Thomas early 1540s?-1578 .... DLB-167
Draper, John W. 1811-1882 .... DLB-30
Draper, Lyman C. 1815-1891 .... DLB-30
Drayton, Michael 1563-1631 .... DLB-121
Dreiser, Theodore 1871-1945 .... DLB-9, 12, 102, 137; DS-1
Drewitz, Ingeborg 1923-1986 .... DLB-75
Drieu La Rochelle, Pierre 1893-1945 ...... DLB-72
Drinker, Elizabeth 1735-1807 .... DLB-200
Drinkwater, John 1882-1937 .... DLB-10, 19, 149
Droste-Hülshoff, Annette von 1797-1848 .... DLB-133
The Drue Heinz Literature Prize Excerpt from "Excerpts from a Report of the Commission," in David Bosworth's *The Death of Descartes* An Interview with David Bosworth. . Y-82
Drummond, William Henry 1854-1907 .... DLB-92
Drummond, William, of Hawthornden 1585-1649 .... DLB-121, 213
Dryden, Charles 1860?-1931 .... DLB-171
Dryden, John 1631-1700 ...... DLB-80, 101, 131
Držić, Marin circa 1508-1567 .... DLB-147
Duane, William 1760-1835 .... DLB-43
Dubé, Marcel 1930- DLB-53
Dubé, Rodolphe (see Hertel, François)
Dubie, Norman 1945- DLB-120
Du Bois, W. E. B. 1868-1963 .... DLB-47, 50, 91
Du Bois, William Pène 1916- DLB-61
Dubus, Andre 1936- DLB-130
Ducange, Victor 1783-1833 .... DLB-192
Du Chaillu, Paul Belloni 1831?-1903 ..... DLB-189
Ducharme, Réjean 1941- DLB-60
Dučić, Jovan 1871-1943 .... DLB-147
Duck, Stephen 1705?-1756 .... DLB-95
Duckworth, Gerald, and Company Limited DLB-112
Dudek, Louis 1918- DLB-88
Duell, Sloan and Pearce DLB-46
Duerer, Albrecht 1471-1528 .... DLB-179
Dufief, Nicholas Gouin 1776-1834 .... DLB-187
Duff Gordon, Lucie 1821-1869 .... DLB-166
Dufferin, Helen Lady, Countess of Gifford 1807-1867 .... DLB-199
Duffield and Green DLB-46
Duffy, Maureen 1933- DLB-14

Dugan, Alan 1923- DLB-5
Dugard, William [publishing house] DLB-170
Dugas, Marcel 1883-1947 .... DLB-92
Dugdale, William [publishing house] DLB-106
Duhamel, Georges 1884-1966 .... DLB-65
Dujardin, Edouard 1861-1949 .... DLB-123
Dukes, Ashley 1885-1959 .... DLB-10
du Maurier, Daphne 1907-1989 .... DLB-191
Du Maurier, George 1834-1896 .... DLB-153, 178
Dumas, Alexandre *fils* 1824-1895 .... DLB-192
Dumas, Alexandre *père* 1802-1870 ..... DLB-119, 192
Dumas, Henry 1934-1968 .... DLB-41
Dunbar, Paul Laurence 1872-1906 .... DLB-50, 54, 78
Dunbar, William circa 1460-circa 1522 DLB-132, 146
Duncan, Norman 1871-1916 .... DLB-92
Duncan, Quince 1940- DLB-145
Duncan, Robert 1919-1988 .... DLB-5, 16, 193
Duncan, Ronald 1914-1982 .... DLB-13
Duncan, Sara Jeannette 1861-1922 .... DLB-92
Dunigan, Edward, and Brother DLB-49
Dunlap, John 1747-1812 .... DLB-43
Dunlap, William 1766-1839 .... DLB-30, 37, 59
Dunn, Douglas 1942- DLB-40
Dunn, Harvey Thomas 1884-1952 ...... DLB-188
Dunn, Stephen 1939- DLB-105
Dunne, Finley Peter 1867-1936 .... DLB-11, 23
Dunne, John Gregory 1932- Y-80
Dunne, Philip 1908-1992 .... DLB-26
Dunning, Ralph Cheever 1878-1930 ...... DLB-4
Dunning, William A. 1857-1922 .... DLB-17
Duns Scotus, John circa 1266-1308 ...... DLB-115
Dunsany, Lord (Edward John Moreton Drax Plunkett, Baron Dunsany) 1878-1957 .... DLB-10, 77, 153, 156
Dunton, John [publishing house] DLB-170
Dunton, W. Herbert 1878-1936 .... DLB-188
Dupin, Amantine-Aurore-Lucile (see Sand, George)
Durand, Lucile (see Bersianik, Louky)
Duranti, Francesca 1935- DLB-196
Duranty, Walter 1884-1957 .... DLB-29
Duras, Marguerite 1914- DLB-83
Durfey, Thomas 1653-1723 .... DLB-80
Durova, Nadezhda Andreevna (Aleksandr Andreevich Aleksandrov) 1783-1866 . DLB-198
Durrell, Lawrence 1912-1990 DLB-15, 27, 204; Y-90
Durrell, William [publishing house] DLB-49
Dürrenmatt, Friedrich 1921-1990 .... DLB-69, 124
Duston, Hannah 1657-1737 .... DLB-200
Dutton, E. P., and Company DLB-49
Duvoisin, Roger 1904-1980 .... DLB-61
Duyckinck, Evert Augustus 1816-1878 .... DLB-3, 64
Duyckinck, George L. 1823-1863 .... DLB-3
Duyckinck and Company DLB-49
Dwight, John Sullivan 1813-1893 .... DLB-1

Dwight, Timothy 1752-1817 .... DLB-37
Dybek, Stuart 1942- DLB-130
Dyer, Charles 1928- DLB-13
Dyer, George 1755-1841 .... DLB-93
Dyer, John 1699-1757 .... DLB-95
Dyer, Sir Edward 1543-1607 .... DLB-136
Dyk, Viktor 1877-1931 .... DLB-215
Dylan, Bob 1941- DLB-16

E

Eager, Edward 1911-1964 .... DLB-22
Eames, Wilberforce 1855-1937 .... DLB-140
Earle, James H., and Company DLB-49
Earle, John 1600 or 1601-1665 .... DLB-151
Early American Book Illustration, by Sinclair Hamilton DLB-49
Eastlake, William 1917-1997 .... DLB-6, 206
Eastman, Carol ?- DLB-44
Eastman, Charles A. (Ohiyesa) 1858-1939 .... DLB-175
Eastman, Max 1883-1969 .... DLB-91
Eaton, Daniel Isaac 1753-1814 .... DLB-158
Eberhart, Richard 1904- DLB-48
Ebner, Jeannie 1918- DLB-85
Ebner-Eschenbach, Marie von 1830-1916 .... DLB-81
Ebon 1942- DLB-41
E-Books Turn the Corner Y-98
Ecbasis Captivi circa 1045 .... DLB-148
Ecco Press DLB-46
Eckhart, Meister circa 1260-circa 1328 .... DLB-115
The Eclectic Review 1805-1868 .... DLB-110
Eco, Umberto 1932- DLB-196
Edel, Leon 1907- DLB-103
Edes, Benjamin 1732-1803 .... DLB-43
Edgar, David 1948- DLB-13
Edgeworth, Maria 1768-1849 .... DLB-116, 159, 163
The Edinburgh Review 1802-1929 .... DLB-110
Edinburgh University Press DLB-112
The Editor Publishing Company DLB-49
Editorial Statements DLB-137
Edmonds, Randolph 1900- DLB-51
Edmonds, Walter D. 1903- DLB-9
Edschmid, Kasimir 1890-1966 .... DLB-56
Edwards, Amelia Anne Blandford 1831-1892 .... DLB-174
Edwards, Edward 1812-1886 .... DLB-184
Edwards, James [publishing house] DLB-154
Edwards, Jonathan 1703-1758 .... DLB-24
Edwards, Jonathan, Jr. 1745-1801 .... DLB-37
Edwards, Junius 1929- DLB-33
Edwards, Matilda Barbara Betham- 1836-1919 .... DLB-174
Edwards, Richard 1524-1566 .... DLB-62

Edwards, Sarah Pierpont 1710-1758 ..... DLB-200

Effinger, George Alec 1947- DLB-8

Egerton, George 1859-1945 .... DLB-135

Eggleston, Edward 1837-1902.......... DLB-12

Eggleston, Wilfred 1901-1986 .... DLB-92

Ehrenstein, Albert 1886-1950........... DLB-81

Ehrhart, W. D. 1948- DS-9

Ehrlich, Gretel 1946- DLB-212

Eich, Günter 1907-1972............ DLB-69, 124

Eichendorff, Joseph Freiherr von
  1788-1857 .... DLB-90

Eifukumon'in 1271-1342............. DLB-203

1873 Publishers' Catalogues DLB-49

Eighteenth-Century Aesthetic Theories ... DLB-31

Eighteenth-Century Philosophical
  Background DLB-31

Eigner, Larry 1926-1996........... DLB-5, 193

Eikon Basilike 1649................... DLB-151

Eilhart von Oberge
  circa 1140-circa 1195 .... DLB-148

Einhard circa 770-840................. DLB-148

Eiseley, Loren 1907-1977 ....DS-17

Eisenreich, Herbert 1925-1986.......... DLB-85

Eisner, Kurt 1867-1919................ DLB-66

Eklund, Gordon 1945- Y-83

Ekwensi, Cyprian 1921- DLB-117

Eld, George [publishing house].........DLB-170

Elder, Lonne III 1931- DLB-7, 38, 44

Elder, Paul, and Company DLB-49

The Electronic Text Center and the Electronic
  Archive of Early American Fiction at the University of Virginia Library Y-98

Elements of Rhetoric (1828; revised, 1846),
  by Richard Whately [excerpt] DLB-57

Elie, Robert 1915-1973 .... DLB-88

Elin Pelin 1877-1949 .... DLB-147

Eliot, George 1819-1880......... DLB-21, 35, 55

Eliot, John 1604-1690.................. DLB-24

Eliot, T. S. 1888-1965.......DLB-7, 10, 45, 63

Eliot's Court Press DLB-170

Elizabeth I 1533-1603................. DLB-136

Elizabeth of Nassau-Saarbrücken
  after 1393-1456 ....DLB-179

Elizondo, Salvador 1932- DLB-145

Elizondo, Sergio 1930- DLB-82

Elkin, Stanley 1930- DLB-2, 28; Y-80

Elles, Dora Amy (see Wentworth, Patricia)

Ellet, Elizabeth F. 1818?-1877 .... DLB-30

Elliot, Ebenezer 1781-1849 .... DLB-96, 190

Elliot, Frances Minto (Dickinson)
  1820-1898 .... DLB-166

Elliott, Charlotte 1789-1871 .... DLB-199

Elliott, George 1923- DLB-68

Elliott, Janice 1931- DLB-14

Elliott, William 1788-1863 .... DLB-3

Elliott, Thomes and Talbot DLB-49

Ellis, Alice Thomas (Anna Margaret Haycraft)
  1932- DLB-194

Ellis, Edward S. 1840-1916............. DLB-42

Ellis, Frederick Staridge
  [publishing house] DLB-106

The George H. Ellis Company.......... DLB-49

Ellis, Havelock 1859-1939 .... DLB-190

Ellison, Harlan 1934- DLB-8

Ellison, Ralph Waldo
  1914-1994 ....DLB-2, 76; Y-94

Ellmann, Richard 1918-1987 ......DLB-103; Y-87

The Elmer Holmes Bobst Awards in Arts
  and Letters Y-87

Elyot, Thomas 1490?-1546............. DLB-136

Emanuel, James Andrew 1921- DLB-41

Emecheta, Buchi 1944- DLB-117

The Emergence of Black Women Writers DS-8

Emerson, Ralph Waldo
  1803-1882 ....DLB-1, 59, 73, 183

Emerson, William 1769-1811 .... DLB-37

Emerson, William 1923-1997 .... Y-97

Emin, Fedor Aleksandrovich
  circa 1735-1770................... DLB-150

Empedocles fifth century B.C. DLB-176

Empson, William 1906-1984 .... DLB-20

Enchi Fumiko 1905-1986 .... DLB-182

Encounter with the West DLB-180

The End of English Stage Censorship,
  1945-1968 .... DLB-13

Ende, Michael 1929- DLB-75

Endō Shūsaku 1923-1996............. DLB-182

Engel, Marian 1933-1985 .... DLB-53

Engels, Friedrich 1820-1895 .... DLB-129

Engle, Paul 1908- DLB-48

English, Thomas Dunn 1819-1902...... DLB-202

English Composition and Rhetoric (1866),
  by Alexander Bain [excerpt]......... DLB-57

The English Language: 410 to 1500..... DLB-146

The English Renaissance of Art (1908),
  by Oscar Wilde DLB-35

Ennius 239 B.C.-169 B.C. DLB-211

Enright, D. J. 1920- DLB-27

Enright, Elizabeth 1909-1968 .... DLB-22

L'Envoi (1882), by Oscar Wilde DLB-35

Epic and Beast Epic DLB-208

Epictetus circa 55-circa 125-130 ....DLB-176

Epicurus 342/341 B.C.-271/270 B.C.
  ....DLB-176

Epps, Bernard 1936- DLB-53

Epstein, Julius 1909- and
  Epstein, Philip 1909-1952 .... DLB-26

Equiano, Olaudah circa 1745-1797 .....DLB-37, 50

Eragny Press.................... DLB-112

Erasmus, Desiderius 1467-1536 .... DLB-136

Erba, Luciano 1922- DLB-128

Erdrich, Louise 1954- DLB-152, 175, 206

Erichsen-Brown, Gwethalyn Graham
  (see Graham, Gwethalyn)

Eriugena, John Scottus circa 810-877 .... DLB-115

Ernest Hemingway's Reaction to James Gould
  Cozzens Y-98

Ernest Hemingway's Toronto Journalism
  Revisited: With Three Previously
  Unrecorded Stories Y-92

Ernst, Paul 1866-1933 .... DLB-66, 118

Ershov, Petr Pavlovich 1815-1869...... DLB-205

Erskine, Albert 1911-1993 .... Y-93

Erskine, John 1879-1951............. DLB-9, 102

Erskine, Mrs. Steuart ?-1948 .... DLB-195

Ervine, St. John Greer 1883-1971........ DLB-10

Eschenburg, Johann Joachim
  1743-1820...................... DLB-97

Escoto, Julio 1944- DLB-145

Esdaile, Arundell 1880-1956........... DLB-201

Eshleman, Clayton 1935- DLB-5

Espriu, Salvador 1913-1985 .... DLB-134

Ess Ess Publishing Company DLB-49

Essay on Chatterton (1842), by
  Robert Browning................. DLB-32

Essex House Press DLB-112

Estes, Eleanor 1906-1988 .... DLB-22

Eszterhas, Joe 1944- DLB-185

Estes and Lauriat DLB-49

Etherege, George 1636-circa 1692 .... DLB-80

Ethridge, Mark, Sr. 1896-1981..........DLB-127

Ets, Marie Hall 1893- DLB-22

Etter, David 1928- DLB-105

Ettner, Johann Christoph 1654-1724 .... DLB-168

Eudora Welty: Eye of the Storyteller Y-87

Eugene O'Neill Memorial Theater
  Center DLB-7

Eugene O'Neill's Letters: A Review......... Y-88

Eupolemius flourished circa 1095....... DLB-148

Euripides circa 484 B.C.-407/406 B.C.
  ....DLB-176

Evans, Caradoc 1878-1945............ DLB-162

Evans, Charles 1850-1935 ....DLB-187

Evans, Donald 1884-1921 .... DLB-54

Evans, George Henry 1805-1856........ DLB-43

Evans, Hubert 1892-1986............. DLB-92

Evans, Mari 1923- DLB-41

Evans, Mary Ann (see Eliot, George)

Evans, Nathaniel 1742-1767 .... DLB-31

Evans, Sebastian 1830-1909 .... DLB-35

Evans, M., and Company............. DLB-46

Everett, Alexander Hill 1790-1847 .... DLB-59

Everett, Edward 1794-1865 .... DLB-1, 59

Everson, R. G. 1903- DLB-88

Everson, William 1912-1994 ......DLB-5, 16, 212

Every Man His Own Poet; or, The
  Inspired Singer's Recipe Book (1877),
  by W. H. Mallock DLB-35

Ewart, Gavin 1916- DLB-40

Ewing, Juliana Horatia 1841-1885 ... DLB-21, 163

The Examiner 1808-1881............. DLB-110

Exley, Frederick 1929-1992 . . . . DLB-143; Y-81

Experiment in the Novel (1929),
by John D. Beresford DLB-36

von Eyb, Albrecht 1420-1475 . . . . DLB-179

"Eyes Across Centuries: Contemporary
Poetry and 'That Vision Thing,'"
by Philip Dacey DLB-105

Eyre and Spottiswoode DLB-106

Ezzo ?-after 1065 . . . . DLB-148

F

"F. Scott Fitzgerald: St. Paul's Native Son
and Distinguished American Writer":
University of Minnesota Conference,
29-31 October 1982. . . . . Y-82

Faber, Frederick William 1814-1863 . . . . . . DLB-32

Faber and Faber Limited DLB-112

Faccio, Rena (see Aleramo, Sibilla)

Fagundo, Ana María 1938- DLB-134

Fair, Ronald L. 1932- DLB-33

Fairfax, Beatrice (see Manning, Marie)

Fairlie, Gerard 1899-1983 . . . . DLB-77

Fallada, Hans 1893-1947 . . . . DLB-56

Falsifying Hemingway Y-96

Fancher, Betsy 1928- Y-83

Fane, Violet 1843-1905 . . . . DLB-35

Fanfrolico Press DLB-112

Fanning, Katherine 1927 . . . . DLB-127

Fanshawe, Sir Richard 1608-1666 . . . . DLB-126

Fantasy Press Publishers DLB-46

Fante, John 1909-1983 . . . . DLB-130; Y-83

Al-Farabi circa 870-950 . . . . DLB-115

Farah, Nuruddin 1945- DLB-125

Farber, Norma 1909-1984 . . . . DLB-61

Farigoule, Louis (see Romains, Jules)

Farjeon, Eleanor 1881-1965 . . . . DLB-160

Farley, Walter 1920-1989 . . . . DLB-22

Farmborough, Florence 1887-1978 . . . . . . DLB-204

Farmer, Penelope 1939- DLB-161

Farmer, Philip José 1918- DLB-8

Farquhar, George circa 1677-1707 . . . . DLB-84

Farquharson, Martha (see Finley, Martha)

Farrar, Frederic William 1831-1903 . . . . . . DLB-163

Farrar and Rinehart DLB-46

Farrar, Straus and Giroux DLB-46

Farrell, James T. 1904-1979 . . . . DLB-4, 9, 86; DS-2

Farrell, J. G. 1935-1979 . . . . DLB-14

Fast, Howard 1914- DLB-9

Faulks, Sebastian 1953- DLB-207

Faulkner and Yoknapatawpha Conference,
Oxford, Mississippi Y-97

"Faulkner 100–Celebrating the Work," University of
South Carolina, Columbia Y-97

Faulkner, William 1897-1962
. . . . DLB-9, 11, 44, 102; DS-2; Y-86

Faulkner, George [publishing house] DLB-154

Fauset, Jessie Redmon 1882-1961 . . . . DLB-51

Faust, Irvin 1924- DLB-2, 28; Y-80

Fawcett, Edgar 1847-1904 . . . . DLB-202

Fawcett, Millicent Garrett 1847-1929 . . . . . DLB-190

Fawcett Books DLB-46

Fay, Theodore Sedgwick 1807-1898 . . . . . DLB-202

Fearing, Kenneth 1902-1961 . . . . DLB-9

Federal Writers' Project DLB-46

Federman, Raymond 1928- Y-80

Feiffer, Jules 1929- DLB-7, 44

Feinberg, Charles E. 1899-1988 . . . . DLB-187; Y-88

Feind, Barthold 1678-1721 . . . . DLB-168

Feinstein, Elaine 1930- DLB-14, 40

Feiss, Paul Louis 1875-1952 . . . . DLB-187

Feldman, Irving 1928- DLB-169

Felipe, Léon 1884-1968 . . . . DLB-108

Fell, Frederick, Publishers DLB-46

Fellowship of Southern Writers Y-98

Felltham, Owen 1602?-1668 . . . . DLB-126, 151

Fels, Ludwig 1946- DLB-75

Felton, Cornelius Conway 1807-1862 . . . . . . DLB-1

Fenn, Harry 1837-1911 . . . . DLB-188

Fennario, David 1947- DLB-60

Fenno, Jenny 1765?-1803 . . . . DLB-200

Fenno, John 1751-1798 . . . . DLB-43

Fenno, R. F., and Company DLB-49

Fenoglio, Beppe 1922-1963 . . . . DLB-177

Fenton, Geoffrey 1539?-1608. . . . . DLB-136

Fenton, James 1949- DLB-40

Ferber, Edna 1885-1968 . . . . DLB-9, 28, 86

Ferdinand, Vallery III (see Salaam, Kalamu ya)

Ferguson, Sir Samuel 1810-1886 . . . . DLB-32

Ferguson, William Scott 1875-1954 . . . . . . DLB-47

Fergusson, Robert 1750-1774 . . . . DLB-109

Ferland, Albert 1872-1943 . . . . DLB-92

Ferlinghetti, Lawrence 1919- DLB-5, 16

Fermor, Patrick Leigh 1915- DLB-204

Fern, Fanny (see Parton, Sara Payson Willis)

Ferrars, Elizabeth 1907- DLB-87

Ferré, Rosario 1942- DLB-145

Ferret, E., and Company DLB-49

Ferrier, Susan 1782-1854 . . . . DLB-116

Ferril, Thomas Hornsby 1896-1988 . . . . . DLB-206

Ferrini, Vincent 1913- DLB-48

Ferron, Jacques 1921-1985 . . . . DLB-60

Ferron, Madeleine 1922- DLB-53

Ferrucci, Franco 1936- DLB-196

Fetridge and Company DLB-49

Feuchtersleben, Ernst Freiherr von
1806-1849 . . . . DLB-133

Feuchtwanger, Lion 1884-1958 . . . . DLB-66

Feuerbach, Ludwig 1804-1872 . . . . DLB-133

Feuillet, Octave 1821-1890 . . . . DLB-192

Feydeau, Georges 1862-1921 . . . . DLB-192

Fichte, Johann Gottlieb 1762-1814 . . . . DLB-90

Ficke, Arthur Davison 1883-1945 . . . . DLB-54

Fiction Best-Sellers, 1910-1945 . . . . DLB-9

Fiction into Film, 1928-1975: A List of Movies
Based on the Works of Authors in
British Novelists, 1930-1959 . . . . DLB-15

Fiedler, Leslie A. 1917- DLB-28, 67

Field, Edward 1924- DLB-105

Field, Eugene
1850-1895 . . . . DLB-23, 42, 140; DS-13

Field, John 1545?-1588 . . . . DLB-167

Field, Marshall, III 1893-1956 . . . . DLB-127

Field, Marshall, IV 1916-1965 . . . . DLB-127

Field, Marshall, V 1941- DLB-127

Field, Nathan 1587-1619 or 1620 . . . . DLB-58

Field, Rachel 1894-1942 . . . . DLB-9, 22

A Field Guide to Recent Schools of American
Poetry Y-86

Fielding, Henry 1707-1754 . . . . DLB-39, 84, 101

Fielding, Sarah 1710-1768 . . . . DLB-39

Fields, James Thomas 1817-1881 . . . . DLB-1

Fields, Julia 1938- DLB-41

Fields, W. C. 1880-1946 . . . . DLB-44

Fields, Osgood and Company DLB-49

Fifty Penguin Years Y-85

Figes, Eva 1932- DLB-14

Figuera, Angela 1902-1984 . . . . DLB-108

Filmer, Sir Robert 1586-1653 . . . . DLB-151

Filson, John circa 1753-1788 . . . . DLB-37

Finch, Anne, Countess of Winchilsea
1661-1720 . . . . DLB-95

Finch, Robert 1900- DLB-88

"Finding, Losing, Reclaiming: A Note on My
Poems," by Robert Phillips DLB-105

Findley, Timothy 1930- DLB-53

Finlay, Ian Hamilton 1925- DLB-40

Finley, Martha 1828-1909 . . . . DLB-42

Finn, Elizabeth Anne (McCaul)
1825-1921 . . . . DLB-166

Finney, Jack 1911- DLB-8

Finney, Walter Braden (see Finney, Jack)

Firbank, Ronald 1886-1926 . . . . DLB-36

Fire at Thomas Wolfe Memorial Y-98

Firmin, Giles 1615-1697 . . . . DLB-24

Fischart, Johann
1546 or 1547-1590 or 1591 . . . . DLB-179

First Edition Library/Collectors'
Reprints, Inc. Y-91

First International F. Scott Fitzgerald
Conference Y-92

First Strauss "Livings" Awarded to Cynthia
Ozick and Raymond Carver
An Interview with Cynthia Ozick
An Interview with Raymond
Carver Y-83

Fischer, Karoline Auguste Fernandine
1764-1842 . . . . DLB-94

Fish, Stanley 1938- DLB-67

Fishacre, Richard 1205-1248 . . . . DLB-115

Fisher, Clay (see Allen, Henry W.)

Cumulative Index

Fisher, Dorothy Canfield 1879-1958................ DLB-9, 102

Fisher, Leonard Everett 1924-......... DLB-61

Fisher, Roy 1930-................. DLB-40

Fisher, Rudolph 1897-1934......... DLB-51, 102

Fisher, Sydney George 1856-1927....... DLB-47

Fisher, Vardis 1895-1968........... DLB-9, 206

Fiske, John 1608-1677............... DLB-24

Fiske, John 1842-1901............. DLB-47, 64

Fitch, Thomas circa 1700-1774......... DLB-31

Fitch, William Clyde 1865-1909......... DLB-7

FitzGerald, Edward 1809-1883......... DLB-32

Fitzgerald, F. Scott 1896-1940
........DLB-4, 9, 86; Y-81; DS-1, 15, 16

F. Scott Fitzgerald Centenary Celebrations.... Y-96

Fitzgerald, Penelope 1916-....... DLB-14, 194

Fitzgerald, Robert 1910-1985............. Y-80

Fitzgerald, Thomas 1819-1891......... DLB-23

Fitzgerald, Zelda Sayre 1900-1948......... Y-84

Fitzhugh, Louise 1928-1974........... DLB-52

Fitzhugh, William circa 1651-1701....... DLB-24

Flagg, James Montgomery 1877-1960.... DLB-188

Flanagan, Thomas 1923-................. Y-80

Flanner, Hildegarde 1899-1987......... DLB-48

Flanner, Janet 1892-1978................. DLB-4

Flaubert, Gustave 1821-1880.......... DLB-119

Flavin, Martin 1883-1967................ DLB-9

Fleck, Konrad (flourished circa 1220)
.... DLB-138

Flecker, James Elroy 1884-1915....... DLB-10, 19

Fleeson, Doris 1901-1970............. DLB-29

Fleißer, Marieluise 1901-1974....... DLB-56, 124

Fleming, Ian 1908-1964............. DLB-87, 201

Fleming, Paul 1609-1640............. DLB-164

Fleming, Peter 1907-1971............. DLB-195

The Fleshly School of Poetry and Other Phenomena of the Day (1872), by Robert Buchanan....................... DLB-35

The Fleshly School of Poetry: Mr. D. G. Rossetti (1871), by Thomas Maitland (Robert Buchanan)................. DLB-35

Fletcher, Giles, the Elder 1546-1611..... DLB-136

Fletcher, Giles, the Younger 1585 or 1586-1623................. DLB-121

Fletcher, J. S. 1863-1935............... DLB-70

Fletcher, John (see Beaumont, Francis)

Fletcher, John Gould 1886-1950....... DLB-4, 45

Fletcher, Phineas 1582-1650.......... DLB-121

Flieg, Helmut (see Heym, Stefan)

Flint, F. S. 1885-1960................. DLB-19

Flint, Timothy 1780-1840........... DLB-73, 186

Flores-Williams, Jason 1969-......... DLB-209

Florio, John 1553?-1625............. DLB-172

Fo, Dario 1926-......................... Y-97

Foix, J. V. 1893-1987................ DLB-134

Foley, Martha (see Burnett, Whit, and Martha Foley)

Folger, Henry Clay 1857-1930......... DLB-140

Folio Society....................... DLB-112

Follen, Eliza Lee (Cabot) 1787-1860....... DLB-1

Follett, Ken 1949-............... DLB-87; Y-81

Follett Publishing Company........... DLB-46

Folsom, John West [publishing house].... DLB-49

Folz, Hans between 1435 and 1440-1513........DLB-179

Fontane, Theodor 1819-1898......... DLB-129

Fontes, Montserrat 1940-........... DLB-209

Fonvisin, Denis Ivanovich 1744 or 1745-1792............... DLB-150

Foote, Horton 1916-.................. DLB-26

Foote, Mary Hallock 1847-1938............. DLB-186, 188, 202

Foote, Samuel 1721-1777............. DLB-89

Foote, Shelby 1916-.................DLB-2, 17

Forbes, Calvin 1945-................ DLB-41

Forbes, Ester 1891-1967.............. DLB-22

Forbes, Rosita 1893?-1967........... DLB-195

Forbes and Company................ DLB-49

Force, Peter 1790-1868............... DLB-30

Forché, Carolyn 1950-........... DLB-5, 193

Ford, Charles Henri 1913-......... DLB-4, 48

Ford, Corey 1902-1969................ DLB-11

Ford, Ford Madox 1873-1939.... DLB-34, 98, 162

Ford, Jesse Hill 1928-................. DLB-6

Ford, John 1586-?..................... DLB-58

Ford, R. A. D. 1915-................. DLB-88

Ford, Worthington C. 1858-1941........ DLB-47

Ford, J. B., and Company............. DLB-49

Fords, Howard, and Hulbert........... DLB-49

Foreman, Carl 1914-1984.............. DLB-26

Forester, C. S. 1899-1966............ DLB-191

Forester, Frank (see Herbert, Henry William)

"Foreword to *Ludwig of Baviria*," by Robert Peters................... DLB-105

Forman, Harry Buxton 1842-1917...... DLB-184

Fornés, María Irene 1930-............. DLB-7

Forrest, Leon 1937-................. DLB-33

Forster, E. M. 1879-1970
.... DLB-34, 98, 162, 178, 195; DS-10

Forster, Georg 1754-1794............. DLB-94

Forster, John 1812-1876............. DLB-144

Forster, Margaret 1938-............ DLB-155

Forsyth, Frederick 1938-............. DLB-87

Forten, Charlotte L. 1837-1914......... DLB-50

Fortini, Franco 1917-................ DLB-128

Fortune, T. Thomas 1856-1928......... DLB-23

Fosdick, Charles Austin 1842-1915...... DLB-42

Foster, Genevieve 1893-1979........... DLB-61

Foster, Hannah Webster 1758-1840....................DLB-37, 200

Foster, John 1648-1681............... DLB-24

Foster, Michael 1904-1956............. DLB-9

Foster, Myles Birket 1825-1899....... DLB-184

Foulis, Robert and Andrew / R. and A. [publishing house]............... DLB-154

Fouqué, Caroline de la Motte 1774-1831..................... DLB-90

Fouqué, Friedrich de la Motte 1777-1843..................... DLB-90

Four Essays on the Beat Generation, by John Clellon Holmes............ DLB-16

Four Seas Company................ DLB-46

Four Winds Press................... DLB-46

Fournier, Henri Alban (see Alain-Fournier)

Fowler and Wells Company........... DLB-49

Fowles, John 1926-..........DLB-14, 139, 207

Fox, John, Jr. 1862 or 1863-1919... DLB-9; DS-13

Fox, Paula 1923-.................... DLB-52

Fox, Richard Kyle 1846-1922........... DLB-79

Fox, William Price 1926-........DLB-2; Y-81

Fox, Richard K. [publishing house]...... DLB-49

Foxe, John 1517-1587................ DLB-132

Fraenkel, Michael 1896-1957............ DLB-4

France, Anatole 1844-1924........... DLB-123

France, Richard 1938-................. DLB-7

Francis, Convers 1795-1863............ DLB-1

Francis, Dick 1920-................. DLB-87

Francis, Sir Frank 1901-1988......... DLB-201

Francis, Jeffrey, Lord 1773-1850........DLB-107

Francis, C. S. [publishing house]........ DLB-49

François 1863-1910................. DLB-92

François, Louise von 1817-1893........ DLB-129

Franck, Sebastian 1499-1542..........DLB-179

Francke, Kuno 1855-1930............. DLB-71

Frank, Bruno 1887-1945.............. DLB-118

Frank, Leonhard 1882-1961........ DLB-56, 118

Frank, Melvin (see Panama, Norman)

Frank, Waldo 1889-1967............ DLB-9, 63

Franken, Rose 1895?-1988.............. Y-84

Franklin, Benjamin 1706-1790..............DLB-24, 43, 73, 183

Franklin, James 1697-1735............. DLB-43

Franklin Library.................... DLB-46

Frantz, Ralph Jules 1902-1979........... DLB-4

Franzos, Karl Emil 1848-1904......... DLB-129

Fraser, G. S. 1915-1980............... DLB-27

Fraser, Kathleen 1935-............. DLB-169

Frattini, Alberto 1922-............. DLB-128

Frau Ava ?-1127.................... DLB-148

Frayn, Michael 1933-........DLB-13, 14, 194

Frederic, Harold 1856-1898............. DLB-12, 23; DS-13

Freeling, Nicolas 1927-............... DLB-87

Freeman, Douglas Southall 1886-1953..................DLB-17; DS-17

Freeman, Legh Richmond 1842-1915.... DLB-23

Freeman, Mary E. Wilkins 1852-1930....................DLB-12, 78

Freeman, R. Austin 1862-1943......... DLB-70

Freidank circa 1170-circa 1233......... DLB-138

Freiligrath, Ferdinand 1810-1876 . . . . .DLB-133

Frémont, John Charles 1813-1890 . . . . . . .DLB-186

Frémont, John Charles 1813-1890 and Frémont, Jessie Benton 1834-1902 . . .DLB-183

French, Alice 1850-1934 . . . . .DLB-74; DS-13

French Arthurian Literature. DLB-208

French, David 1939- DLB-53

French, Evangeline 1869-1960. . . . . .DLB-195

French, Francesca 1871-1960 . . . . .DLB-195

French, James [publishing house] DLB-49

French, Samuel [publishing house]. DLB-49

Samuel French, Limited DLB-106

Freneau, Philip 1752-1832 . . . . DLB-37, 43

Freni, Melo 1934- DLB-128

Freshfield, Douglas W. 1845-1934. . . . . . .DLB-174

Freytag, Gustav 1816-1895 . . . . .DLB-129

Fried, Erich 1921-1988. . . . . .DLB-85

Friedman, Bruce Jay 1930- DLB-2, 28

Friedrich von Hausen circa 1171-1190. . . .DLB-138

Friel, Brian 1929- DLB-13

Friend, Krebs 1895?-1967? DLB-4

Fries, Fritz Rudolf 1935- DLB-75

Fringe and Alternative Theater in Great Britain DLB-13

Frisch, Max 1911-1991 . . . . .DLB-69, 124

Frischlin, Nicodemus 1547-1590 . . . . .DLB-179

Frischmuth, Barbara 1941- DLB-85

Fritz, Jean 1915- .DLB-52

Froissart, Jean circa 1337-circa 1404. . . . . .DLB-208

Fromentin, Eugene 1820-1876 . . . . .DLB-123

From *The Gay Science*, by E. S. Dallas DLB-21

Frontinus circa A.D. 35-A.D. 103/104 . . . .DLB-211

Frost, A. B. 1851-1928. . . . . .DLB-188; DS-13

Frost, Robert 1874-1963. . . . . .DLB-54; DS-7

Frothingham, Octavius Brooks 1822-1895 . . . . .DLB-1

Froude, James Anthony 1818-1894 . . . . DLB-18, 57, 144

Fry, Christopher 1907- DLB-13

Fry, Roger 1866-1934 . . . . .DS-10

Fry, Stephen 1957- DLB-207

Frye, Northrop 1912-1991 . . . . .DLB-67, 68

Fuchs, Daniel 1909-1993 . . . . .DLB-9, 26, 28; Y-93

Fuentes, Carlos 1928- DLB-113

Fuertes, Gloria 1918- DLB-108

The Fugitives and the Agrarians: The First Exhibition Y-85

Fujiwara no Shunzei 1114-1204 . . . . .DLB-203

Fujiwara no Tameaki 1230s?-1290s? DLB-203

Fujiwara no Tameie 1198-1275 . . . . .DLB-203

Fujiwara no Teika 1162-1241 . . . . .DLB-203

Fulbecke, William 1560-1603?. DLB-172

Fuller, Charles H., Jr. 1939- DLB-38

Fuller, Henry Blake 1857-1929. . . . . .DLB-12

Fuller, John 1937- DLB-40

Fuller, Margaret (see Fuller, Sarah Margaret, Marchesa D'Ossoli)

Fuller, Roy 1912-1991 . . . . .DLB-15, 20

Fuller, Samuel 1912- DLB-26

Fuller, Sarah Margaret, Marchesa D'Ossoli 1810-1850. . . . . . . DLB-1, 59, 73, 183

Fuller, Thomas 1608-1661 . . . . .DLB-151

Fullerton, Hugh 1873-1945 . . . . .DLB-171

Fulton, Alice 1952- DLB-193

Fulton, Len 1934- Y-86

Fulton, Robin 1937- DLB-40

Furbank, P. N. 1920- DLB-155

Furman, Laura 1945- Y-86

Furness, Horace Howard 1833-1912. . . . . .DLB-64

Furness, William Henry 1802-1896. . . . . . . .DLB-1

Furnivall, Frederick James 1825-1910 . . . .DLB-184

Furthman, Jules 1888-1966 . . . . .DLB-26

Furui Yoshikichi 1937- DLB-182

Fushimi, Emperor 1265-1317 . . . . .DLB-203

Futabatei, Shimei (Hasegawa Tatsunosuke) 1864-1909 . . . . .DLB-180

The Future of the Novel (1899), by Henry James .DLB-18

Fyleman, Rose 1877-1957. . . . . .DLB-160

G

The G. Ross Roy Scottish Poetry Collection at the University of South Carolina Y-89

Gadda, Carlo Emilio 1893-1973 . . . . .DLB-177

Gaddis, William 1922- DLB-2

Gág, Wanda 1893-1946. . . . . .DLB-22

Gagarin, Ivan Sergeevich 1814-1882 . . . . .DLB-198

Gagnon, Madeleine 1938- DLB-60

Gaine, Hugh 1726-1807 . . . . .DLB-43

Gaine, Hugh [publishing house] DLB-49

Gaines, Ernest J. 1933- DLB-2, 33, 152; Y-80

Gaiser, Gerd 1908-1976 . . . . .DLB-69

Galarza, Ernesto 1905-1984. . . . . .DLB-122

Galaxy Science Fiction Novels DLB-46

Gale, Zona 1874-1938 . . . . .DLB-9, 78

Galen of Pergamon 129-after 210 . . . . . . .DLB-176

Gales, Winifred Marshall 1761-1839 . . . . .DLB-200

Gall, Louise von 1815-1855 . . . . .DLB-133

Gallagher, Tess 1943- DLB-120, 212

Gallagher, Wes 1911- DLB-127

Gallagher, William Davis 1808-1894. . . . . .DLB-73

Gallant, Mavis 1922- DLB-53

Gallegos, María Magdalena 1935- DLB-209

Gallico, Paul 1897-1976 . . . . DLB-9, 171

Galloway, Grace Growden 1727-1782 . . . .DLB-200

Gallup, Donald 1913- DLB-187

Galsworthy, John 1867-1933 . . . . . . .DLB-10, 34, 98, 162; DS-16

Galt, John 1779-1839 . . . . .DLB-99, 116

Galton, Sir Francis 1822-1911 . . . . .DLB-166

Galvin, Brendan 1938- DLB-5

Gambit. DLB-46

Gamboa, Reymundo 1948- DLB-122

Gammer Gurton's Needle DLB-62

Gan, Elena Andreevna (Zeneida R-va) 1814-1842 . . . . .DLB-198

Gannett, Frank E. 1876-1957 . . . . .DLB-29

Gaos, Vicente 1919-1980. . . . . .DLB-134

García, Andrew 1854?-1943 . . . . .DLB-209

García, Lionel G. 1935- DLB-82

García, Richard 1941- DLB-209

García-Camarillo, Cecilio 1943- DLB-209

García Lorca, Federico 1898-1936. . . . . . .DLB-108

García Márquez, Gabriel 1928- . . .DLB-113; Y-82

Gardam, Jane 1928- DLB-14, 161

Garden, Alexander circa 1685-1756. . . . . . .DLB-31

Gardiner, Margaret Power Farmer (see Blessington, Marguerite, Countess of)

Gardner, John 1933-1982 . . . . .DLB-2; Y-82

Garfield, Leon 1921- DLB-161

Garis, Howard R. 1873-1962 . . . . .DLB-22

Garland, Hamlin 1860-1940 . . . . DLB-12, 71, 78, 186

Garneau, Francis-Xavier 1809-1866 . . . . . .DLB-99

Garneau, Hector de Saint-Denys 1912-1943 . . . . .DLB-88

Garneau, Michel 1939- DLB-53

Garner, Alan 1934- DLB-161

Garner, Hugh 1913-1979 . . . . .DLB-68

Garnett, David 1892-1981 . . . . .DLB-34

Garnett, Eve 1900-1991 . . . . .DLB-160

Garnett, Richard 1835-1906 . . . . .DLB-184

Garrard, Lewis H. 1829-1887 . . . . .DLB-186

Garraty, John A. 1920- DLB-17

Garrett, George 1929- DLB-2, 5, 130, 152; Y-83

Garrett, John Work 1872-1942 . . . . .DLB-187

Garrick, David 1717-1779. . . . . .DLB-84, 213

Garrison, William Lloyd 1805-1879 . . . .DLB-1, 43

Garro, Elena 1920- DLB-145

Garth, Samuel 1661-1719. . . . . .DLB-95

Garve, Andrew 1908- . . . . .DLB 87

Gary, Romain 1914-1980 . . . . .DLB-83

Gascoigne, George 1539?-1577 . . . . .DLB-136

Gascoyne, David 1916- DLB-20

Gaskell, Elizabeth Cleghorn 1810-1865 . . . . .DLB-21, 144, 159

Gaspey, Thomas 1788-1871 . . . . .DLB-116

Gass, William Howard 1924- DLB-2

Gates, Doris 1901- DLB-22

Gates, Henry Louis, Jr. 1950- DLB-67

Gates, Lewis E. 1860-1924 . . . . .DLB-71

Gatto, Alfonso 1909-1976 . . . . .DLB-114

Gaunt, Mary 1861-1942 . . . . .DLB-174

Gautier, Théophile 1811-1872 . . . . .DLB-119

Gauvreau, Claude 1925-1971 . . . . .DLB-88

Cumulative Index

The *Gawain*-Poet
    flourished circa 1350-1400 .... DLB-146

Gay, Ebenezer 1696-1787 .... DLB-24

Gay, John 1685-1732 .... DLB-84, 95

The Gay Science (1866), by E. S. Dallas
    [excerpt] DLB-21

Gayarré, Charles E. A. 1805-1895 .... DLB-30

Gaylord, Edward King 1873-1974 ...... DLB-127

Gaylord, Edward Lewis 1919- DLB-127

Gaylord, Charles [publishing house] DLB-49

Geddes, Gary 1940- DLB-60

Geddes, Virgil 1897- DLB-4

Gedeon (Georgii Andreevich Krinovsky)
    circa 1730-1763 .... DLB-150

Gee, Maggie 1948- DLB-207

Geibel, Emanuel 1815-1884 .... DLB-129

Geiogamah, Hanay 1945- DLB-175

Geis, Bernard, Associates DLB-46

Geisel, Theodor Seuss 1904-1991... DLB-61; Y-91

Gelb, Arthur 1924- DLB-103

Gelb, Barbara 1926- DLB-103

Gelber, Jack 1932- DLB-7

Gelinas, Gratien 1909- DLB-88

Gellert, Christian Füerchtegott
    1715-1769 .... DLB-97

Gellhorn, Martha 1908-1998 .... Y-82, Y-98

Gems, Pam 1925- DLB-13

A General Idea of the College of Mirania (1753),
    by William Smith [excerpts] DLB-31

Genet, Jean 1910-1986 .... DLB-72; Y-86

Genevoix, Maurice 1890-1980 .... DLB-65

Genovese, Eugene D. 1930- DLB-17

Gent, Peter 1942- Y-82

Geoffrey of Monmouth
    circa 1100-1155 .... DLB-146

George, Henry 1839-1897 .... DLB-23

George, Jean Craighead 1919- DLB-52

George, W. L. 1882-1926............. DLB-197

George III, King of Great Britain and Ireland
    1738-1820....................... DLB-213

Georgslied 896? DLB-148

Gerhardie, William 1895-1977 .... DLB-36

Gerhardt, Paul 1607-1676 .... DLB-164

Gérin, Winifred 1901-1981 .... DLB-155

Gérin-Lajoie, Antoine 1824-1882 .... DLB-99

German Drama 800-1280 .... DLB-138

German Drama from Naturalism
    to Fascism: 1889-1933 .... DLB-118

German Literature and Culture from
    Charlemagne to the Early Courtly
    Period......................... DLB-148

German Radio Play, The DLB-124

German Transformation from the Baroque
    to the Enlightenment, The DLB-97

The Germanic Epic and Old English Heroic
    Poetry: *Widseth, Waldere,* and *The
    Fight at Finnsburg* DLB-146

Germanophilism, by Hans Kohn DLB-66

Gernsback, Hugo 1884-1967 .... DLB-8, 137

Gerould, Katharine Fullerton
    1879-1944....................... DLB-78

Gerrish, Samuel [publishing house] DLB-49

Gerrold, David 1944- DLB-8

The Ira Gershwin Centenary Y-96

Gerson, Jean 1363-1429 .... DLB-208

Gersonides 1288-1344 .... DLB-115

Gerstäcker, Friedrich 1816-1872 .... DLB-129

Gerstenberg, Heinrich Wilhelm von
    1737-1823....................... DLB-97

Gervinus, Georg Gottfried
    1805-1871....................... DLB-133

Geßner, Salomon 1730-1788........... DLB-97

Geston, Mark S. 1946- DLB-8

"Getting Started: Accepting the Regions You Own—
    or Which Own You," by
    Walter McDonald DLB-105

Al-Ghazali 1058-1111 .... DLB-115

Gibbings, Robert 1889-1958........... DLB-195

Gibbon, Edward 1737-1794........... DLB-104

Gibbon, John Murray 1875-1952 .... DLB-92

Gibbon, Lewis Grassic (see Mitchell, James Leslie)

Gibbons, Floyd 1887-1939 .... DLB-25

Gibbons, Reginald 1947- DLB-120

Gibbons, William ?-? DLB-73

Gibson, Charles Dana 1867-1944 .... DS-13

Gibson, Charles Dana
    1867-1944................ DLB-188; DS-13

Gibson, Graeme 1934- DLB-53

Gibson, Margaret 1944- DLB-120

Gibson, Margaret Dunlop 1843-1920.....DLB-174

Gibson, Wilfrid 1878-1962 .... DLB-19

Gibson, William 1914- DLB-7

Gide, André 1869-1951 .... DLB-65

Giguère, Diane 1937- DLB-53

Giguère, Roland 1929- DLB-60

Gil de Biedma, Jaime 1929-1990 .... DLB-108

Gil-Albert, Juan 1906- DLB-134

Gilbert, Anthony 1899-1973........... DLB-77

Gilbert, Michael 1912- DLB-87

Gilbert, Sandra M. 1936- DLB-120

Gilbert, Sir Humphrey 1537-1583....... DLB-136

Gilchrist, Alexander 1828-1861 .... DLB-144

Gilchrist, Ellen 1935- DLB-130

Gilder, Jeannette L. 1849-1916......... DLB-79

Gilder, Richard Watson 1844-1909 ... DLB-64, 79

Gildersleeve, Basil 1831-1924 .... DLB-71

Giles, Henry 1809-1882 .... DLB-64

Giles of Rome circa 1243-1316 .... DLB-115

Gilfillan, George 1813-1878 .... DLB-144

Gill, Eric 1882-1940 .... DLB-98

Gill, Sarah Prince 1728-1771 .... DLB-200

Gill, William F., Company DLB-49

Gillespie, A. Lincoln, Jr. 1895-1950 ...... DLB-4

Gilliam, Florence ?-? DLB-4

Gilliatt, Penelope 1932-1993............ DLB-14

Gillott, Jacky 1939-1980 .... DLB-14

Gilman, Caroline H. 1794-1888 .... DLB-3, 73

Gilman, W. and J. [publishing house]..... DLB-49

Gilmer, Elizabeth Meriwether
    1861-1951 .... DLB-29

Gilmer, Francis Walker 1790-1826....... DLB-37

Gilroy, Frank D. 1925- DLB-7

Gimferrer, Pere (Pedro) 1945- DLB-134

Gingrich, Arnold 1903-1976............DLB-137

Ginsberg, Allen 1926- DLB-5, 16, 169

Ginzburg, Natalia 1916-1991 ....DLB-177

Ginzkey, Franz Karl 1871-1963 .... DLB-81

Gioia, Dana 1950- DLB-120

Giono, Jean 1895-1970 .... DLB-72

Giotti, Virgilio 1885-1957............. DLB-114

Giovanni, Nikki 1943- DLB-5, 41

Gipson, Lawrence Henry 1880-1971 ......DLB-17

Girard, Rodolphe 1879-1956 .... DLB-92

Giraudoux, Jean 1882-1944 .... DLB-65

Gissing, George 1857-1903 ...... DLB-18, 135, 184

Giudici, Giovanni 1924- DLB-128

Giuliani, Alfredo 1924- DLB-128

Glackens, William J. 1870-1938 .... DLB-188

Gladstone, William Ewart
    1809-1898 ....DLB-57, 184

Glaeser, Ernst 1902-1963 .... DLB-69

Glancy, Diane 1941- DLB-175

Glanville, Brian 1931- DLB-15, 139

Glapthorne, Henry 1610-1643? DLB-58

Glasgow, Ellen 1873-1945 .... DLB-9, 12

Glasier, Katharine Bruce 1867-1950..... DLB-190

Glaspell, Susan 1876-1948 ....DLB-7, 9, 78

Glass, Montague 1877-1934 .... DLB-11

The Glass Key and Other Dashiell Hammett
    Mysteries Y-96

Glassco, John 1909-1981 .... DLB-68

Glauser, Friedrich 1896-1938........... DLB-56

F. Gleason's Publishing Hall............ DLB-49

Gleim, Johann Wilhelm Ludwig
    1719-1803....................... DLB-97

Glendinning, Victoria 1937- DLB-155

Glinka, Fedor Nikolaevich
    1786-1880....................... DLB-205

Glover, Richard 1712-1785............. DLB-95

Glück, Louise 1943- DLB-5

Glyn, Elinor 1864-1943 .... DLB-153

Gnedich, Nikolai Ivanovich
    1784-1833....................... DLB-205

Go-Toba 1180-1239 .... DLB-203

Gobineau, Joseph-Arthur de
    1816-1882 .... DLB-123

Godbout, Jacques 1933- DLB-53

Goddard, Morrill 1865-1937 .... DLB-25

Goddard, William 1740-1817 .... DLB-43

Godden, Rumer 1907- DLB-161

Godey, Louis A. 1804-1878 . . . . DLB-73	"The Good, The Not So Good," by Stephen Dunn DLB-105	Graham, Jorie 1951- DLB-120
Godey and McMichael DLB-49		Graham, Katharine 1917- DLB-127
Godfrey, Dave 1938- DLB-60	Goodbye, Gutenberg? A Lecture at the New York Public Library, 18 April 1995 . . . . Y-95	Graham, Lorenz 1902-1989 . . . . DLB-76
Godfrey, Thomas 1736-1763 . . . . DLB-31		Graham, Philip 1915-1963 . . . . DLB-127
Godine, David R., Publisher DLB-46	Goodison, Lorna 1947- DLB-157	Graham, R. B. Cunninghame 1852-1936 . . . . DLB-98, 135, 174
Godkin, E. L. 1831-1902 . . . . DLB-79	Goodman, Paul 1911-1972 . . . . DLB-130	
Godolphin, Sidney 1610-1643 . . . . DLB-126	The Goodman Theatre DLB-7	Graham, Shirley 1896-1977 . . . . DLB-76
Godwin, Gail 1937- DLB-6	Goodrich, Frances 1891-1984 and Hackett, Albert 1900- DLB-26	Graham, Stephen 1884-1975 . . . . DLB-195
Godwin, Mary Jane Clairmont 1766-1841 . . . . DLB-163	Goodrich, Samuel Griswold 1793-1860 . . . . DLB-1, 42, 73	Graham, W. S. 1918- DLB-20
		Graham, William H. [publishing house] . . . DLB-49
Godwin, Parke 1816-1904 . . . . DLB-3, 64	Goodrich, S. G. [publishing house] DLB-49	Graham, Winston 1910- DLB-77
Godwin, William 1756-1836 . . . . DLB-39, 104, 142, 158, 163	Goodspeed, C. E., and Company DLB-49	Grahame, Kenneth 1859-1932 . . . . DLB-34, 141, 178
Godwin, M. J., and Company DLB-154	Goodwin, Stephen 1943- Y-82	
Goering, Reinhard 1887-1936 . . . . DLB-118	Googe, Barnabe 1540-1594 . . . . DLB-132	Grainger, Martin Allerdale 1874-1941 . . . . . DLB-92
Goes, Albrecht 1908- DLB-69	Gookin, Daniel 1612-1687 . . . . DLB-24	Gramatky, Hardie 1907-1979 . . . . DLB-22
Goethe, Johann Wolfgang von 1749-1832 . . . . DLB-94	Gordimer, Nadine 1923- Y-91	Grand, Sarah 1854-1943 . . . . DLB-135, 197
	Gordon, Caroline 1895-1981 . . . . DLB-4, 9, 102; DS-17; Y-81	Grandbois, Alain 1900-1975 . . . . DLB-92
Goetz, Curt 1888-1960 . . . . DLB-124		Grandson, Oton de circa 1345-1397 . . . . . DLB-208
Goffe, Thomas circa 1592-1629 . . . . DLB-58	Gordon, Giles 1940- DLB-14, 139, 207	Grange, John circa 1556-? DLB-136
Goffstein, M. B. 1940- DLB-61	Gordon, Helen Cameron, Lady Russell 1867-1949 . . . . DLB-195	Granich, Irwin (see Gold, Michael)
Gogarty, Oliver St. John 1878-1957 . . . . DLB-15, 19		Granovsky, Timofei Nikolaevich 1813-1855 . . . . DLB-198
Gogol, Nikolai Vasil'evich 1809-1852 . . . . DLB-198	Gordon, Lyndall 1941- DLB-155	
Goines, Donald 1937-1974 . . . . DLB-33	Gordon, Mary 1949- DLB-6; Y-81	Grant, Anne MacVicar 1755-1838 . . . . DLB-200
Gold, Herbert 1924- DLB-2; Y-81	Gordone, Charles 1925- DLB-7	Grant, Duncan 1885-1978 . . . . DS-10
Gold, Michael 1893-1967 . . . . DLB-9, 28	Gore, Catherine 1800-1861 . . . . DLB-116	Grant, George 1918-1988 . . . . DLB-88
Goldbarth, Albert 1948- DLB-120	Gorey, Edward 1925- DLB-61	Grant, George Monro 1835-1902 . . . . DLB-99
Goldberg, Dick 1947- DLB-7	Gorgias of Leontini circa 485 B.C.-376 B.C. DLB-176	Grant, Harry J. 1881-1963 . . . . DLB-29
Golden Cockerel Press DLB-112		Grant, James Edward 1905-1966 . . . . DLB-26
Golding, Arthur 1536-1606 . . . . DLB-136	Görres, Joseph 1776-1848 . . . . DLB-90	Grass, Günter 1927- DLB-75, 124
Golding, Louis 1895-1958 . . . . DLB-195	Gosse, Edmund 1849-1928 . . . . . DLB-57, 144, 184	Grasty, Charles H. 1863-1924 . . . . DLB-25
Golding, William 1911-1993 . . . DLB-15, 100; Y-83	Gosson, Stephen 1554-1624 . . . . DLB-172	Grau, Shirley Ann 1929- DLB-2
Goldman, William 1931- DLB-44	Gotlieb, Phyllis 1926- DLB-88	Graves, John 1920- Y-83
Goldring, Douglas 1887-1960 . . . . DLB-197	Gottfried von Straßburg died before 1230 . . . . DLB-138	Graves, Richard 1715-1804 . . . . DLB-39
Goldsmith, Oliver 1730?-1774 . . . . DLB-39, 89, 104, 109, 142		Graves, Robert 1895-1985 . . . . DLB-20, 100, 191; DS-18; Y-85
	Gotthelf, Jeremias 1797-1854 . . . . DLB-133	
Goldsmith, Oliver 1794-1861 . . . . DLB-99	Gottschalk circa 804/808-869 . . . . DLB-148	Gray, Alasdair 1934- DLB-194
Goldsmith Publishing Company DLB-46	Gottsched, Johann Christoph 1700-1766 . . . . DLB-97	Gray, Asa 1810-1888 . . . . DLB-1
Goldstein, Richard 1944- DLB-185		Gray, David 1838-1861 . . . . DLB-32
Gollancz, Sir Israel 1864-1930 . . . . DLB-201	Götz, Johann Nikolaus 1721-1781 . . . . DLB-97	Gray, Simon 1936- DLB-13
Gollancz, Victor, Limited DLB-112	Goudge, Elizabeth 1900-1984 . . . . DLB-191	Gray, Thomas 1716-1771 . . . . DLB-109
Gombrowicz, Witold 1904-1969 . . . . DLB-215	Gould, Wallace 1882-1940 . . . . DLB-54	Grayson, William J. 1788-1863 . . . . DLB-3, 64
Gómez-Quiñones, Juan 1942- DLB-122	Govoni, Corrado 1884-1965 . . . . DLB-114	The Great Bibliographers Series Y-93
Gomme, Laurence James [publishing house] DLB-46	Gower, John circa 1330-1408 . . . . DLB-146	The Great Modern Library Scam Y-98
	Goyen, William 1915-1983 . . . . DLB-2; Y-83	The Great War and the Theater, 1914-1918 [Great Britain] DLB-10
Goncourt, Edmond de 1822-1896 . . . . DLB-123	Goytisolo, José Augustín 1928- DLB-134	
Goncourt, Jules de 1830-1870 . . . . DLB-123	Gozzano, Guido 1883-1916 . . . . DLB-114	The Great War Exhibition and Symposium at the University of South Carolina Y-97
Gonzales, Rodolfo "Corky" 1928- DLB-122	Grabbe, Christian Dietrich 1801-1836 . . . . DLB-133	
Gonzales-Berry, Erlinda 1942- DLB-209		Grech, Nikolai Ivanovich 1787-1867 . . . . . DLB-198
González, Angel 1925- DLB-108	Gracq, Julien 1910- DLB-83	Greeley, Horace 1811-1872 . . . . DLB-3, 43, 189
Gonzalez, Genaro 1949- DLB-122	Grady, Henry W. 1850-1889 . . . . DLB-23	Green, Adolph (see Comden, Betty)
Gonzalez, Ray 1952- DLB-122	Graf, Oskar Maria 1894-1967 . . . . DLB-56	Green, Anna Katharine 1846-1935 . . . . . . DLB-202
González de Mireles, Jovita 1899-1983 . . . . DLB-122	Graf Rudolf between circa 1170 and circa 1185 . . . . DLB-148	Green, Duff 1791-1875 . . . . DLB-43
		Green, Elizabeth Shippen 1871-1954 . . . . . DLB-188
	Grafton, Richard [publishing house] DLB-170	Green, Gerald 1922- DLB-28
González-T., César A. 1931- DLB-82	Graham, George Rex 1813-1894 . . . . DLB-73	Green, Henry 1905-1973 . . . . DLB-15
	Graham, Gwethalyn 1913-1965 . . . . DLB-88	Green, Jonas 1712-1767 . . . . DLB-31

Green, Joseph 1706-1780 .... DLB-31
Green, Julien 1900- DLB-4, 72
Green, Paul 1894-1981 .... DLB-7, 9; Y-81
Green, T. and S. [publishing house] DLB-49
Green, Thomas Hill 1836-1882 .... DLB-190
Green, Timothy [publishing house] DLB-49
Greenaway, Kate 1846-1901 .... DLB-141
Greenberg: Publisher DLB-46
Green Tiger Press DLB-46
Greene, Asa 1789-1838 .... DLB-11
Greene, Belle da Costa 1883-1950 ...... DLB-187
Greene, Benjamin H.
  [publishing house] DLB-49
Greene, Graham 1904-1991 ....
  DLB-13, 15, 77, 100, 162, 201, 204; Y-85, Y-91
Greene, Robert 1558-1592 .... DLB-62, 167
Greene Jr., Robert Bernard (Bob)
  1947- DLB-185
Greenhow, Robert 1800-1854 .... DLB-30
Greenlee, William B. 1872-1953 .... DLB-187
Greenough, Horatio 1805-1852 .... DLB-1
Greenwell, Dora 1821-1882 .... DLB-35, 199
Greenwillow Books DLB-46
Greenwood, Grace (see Lippincott, Sara Jane Clarke)
Greenwood, Walter 1903-1974 ...... DLB-10, 191
Greer, Ben 1948- DLB-6
Greflinger, Georg 1620?-1677 .... DLB-164
Greg, W. R. 1809-1881 .... DLB-55
Greg, W. W. 1875-1959 .... DLB-201
Gregg, Josiah 1806-1850 .... DLB-183, 186
Gregg Press DLB-46
Gregory, Isabella Augusta
  Persse, Lady 1852-1932 .... DLB-10
Gregory, Horace 1898-1982 .... DLB-48
Gregory of Rimini circa 1300-1358 ..... DLB-115
Gregynog Press DLB-112
Greiffenberg, Catharina Regina von
  1633-1694 .... DLB-168
Grenfell, Wilfred Thomason
  1865-1940 .... DLB-92
Gress, Elsa 1919-1988 .... DLB-214
Greve, Felix Paul (see Grove, Frederick Philip)
Greville, Fulke, First Lord Brooke
  1554-1628 .... DLB-62, 172
Grey, Sir George, K.C.B. 1812-1898 .... DLB-184
Grey, Lady Jane 1537-1554 .... DLB-132
Grey Owl 1888-1938 .... DLB-92; DS-17
Grey, Zane 1872-1939 .... DLB-9, 212
Grey Walls Press DLB-112
Griboedov, Aleksandr Sergeevich
  1795?-1829 .... DLB-205
Grier, Eldon 1917- DLB-88
Grieve, C. M. (see MacDiarmid, Hugh)
Griffin, Bartholomew flourished 1596 .... DLB-172
Griffin, Gerald 1803-1840 .... DLB-159
Griffith, Elizabeth 1727?-1793 .... DLB-39, 89
Griffith, George 1857-1906 .... DLB-178

Griffiths, Trevor 1935- DLB-13
Griffiths, Ralph [publishing house] DLB-154
Griggs, S. C., and Company DLB-49
Griggs, Sutton Elbert 1872-1930 .... DLB-50
Grignon, Claude-Henri 1894-1976 .... DLB-68
Grigson, Geoffrey 1905- DLB-27
Grillparzer, Franz 1791-1872 .... DLB-133
Grimald, Nicholas
  circa 1519-circa 1562 .... DLB-136
Grimké, Angelina Weld
  1880-1958 .... DLB-50, 54
Grimm, Hans 1875-1959 .... DLB-66
Grimm, Jacob 1785-1863 .... DLB-90
Grimm, Wilhelm 1786-1859 .... DLB-90
Grimmelshausen, Johann Jacob Christoffel von
  1621 or 1622-1676 .... DLB-168
Grimshaw, Beatrice Ethel 1871-1953 ..... DLB-174
Grindal, Edmund 1519 or 1520-1583 .... DLB-132
Griswold, Rufus Wilmot 1815-1857 .... DLB-3, 59
Grosart, Alexander Balloch 1827-1899 ... DLB-184
Gross, Milt 1895-1953 .... DLB-11
Grosset and Dunlap DLB-49
Grossman, Allen 1932- DLB-193
Grossman Publishers DLB-46
Grosseteste, Robert circa 1160-1253 .... DLB-115
Grosvenor, Gilbert H. 1875-1966 .... DLB-91
Groth, Klaus 1819-1899 .... DLB-129
Groulx, Lionel 1878-1967 .... DLB-68
Grove, Frederick Philip 1879-1949 .... DLB-92
Grove Press DLB-46
Grubb, Davis 1919-1980 .... DLB-6
Gruelle, Johnny 1880-1938 .... DLB-22
von Grumbach, Argula
  1492-after 1563? DLB-179
Grymeston, Elizabeth
  before 1563-before 1604 .... DLB-136
Gryphius, Andreas 1616-1664 .... DLB-164
Gryphius, Christian 1649-1706 .... DLB-168
Guare, John 1938- DLB-7
Guerra, Tonino 1920- DLB-128
Guest, Barbara 1920- DLB-5, 193
Guèvremont, Germaine 1893-1968 ..... DLB-68
Guidacci, Margherita 1921-1992 ..... DLB-128
Guide to the Archives of Publishers, Journals,
  and Literary Agents in North American
  Libraries Y-93
Guillén, Jorge 1893-1984 .... DLB-108
Guilloux, Louis 1899-1980 .... DLB-72
Guilpin, Everard
  circa 1572-after 1608? DLB-136
Guiney, Louise Imogen 1861-1920 ..... DLB-54
Guiterman, Arthur 1871-1943 .... DLB-11
Günderrode, Caroline von 1780-1806 ... DLB-90
Gundulić, Ivan 1589-1638 .... DLB-147
Gunn, Bill 1934-1989 .... DLB-38
Gunn, James E. 1923- DLB-8
Gunn, Neil M. 1891-1973 .... DLB-15

Gunn, Thom 1929- DLB-27
Gunnars, Kristjana 1948- DLB-60
Günther, Johann Christian 1695-1723 ... DLB-168
Gurik, Robert 1932- DLB-60
Gustafson, Ralph 1909- DLB-88
Gütersloh, Albert Paris 1887-1973 .... DLB-81
Guthrie, A. B., Jr. 1901-1991 .... DLB-6, 212
Guthrie, Ramon 1896-1973 .... DLB-4
The Guthrie Theater DLB-7
Guthrie, Thomas Anstey (see Anstey, FC)
Gutzkow, Karl 1811-1878 .... DLB-133
Guy, Ray 1939- DLB-60
Guy, Rosa 1925- DLB-33
Guyot, Arnold 1807-1884 .... DS-13
Gwynne, Erskine 1898-1948 .... DLB-4
Gyles, John 1680-1755 .... DLB-99
Gysin, Brion 1916- DLB-16

H

H. D. (see Doolittle, Hilda)
Habington, William 1605-1654 .... DLB-126
Hacker, Marilyn 1942- DLB-120
Hackett, Albert (see Goodrich, Frances)
Hacks, Peter 1928- DLB-124
Hadas, Rachel 1948- DLB-120
Hadden, Briton 1898-1929 .... DLB-91
Hagedorn, Friedrich von 1708-1754 ..... DLB-168
Hagelstange, Rudolf 1912-1984 .... DLB-69
Haggard, H. Rider
  1856-1925 .... DLB-70, 156, 174, 178
Haggard, William 1907-1993 .... Y-93
Hahn-Hahn, Ida Gräfin von
  1805-1880 .... DLB-133
Haig-Brown, Roderick 1908-1976 ...... DLB-88
Haight, Gordon S. 1901-1985 .... DLB-103
Hailey, Arthur 1920- DLB-88; Y-82
Haines, John 1924- DLB-5, 212
Hake, Edward flourished 1566-1604 .... DLB-136
Hake, Thomas Gordon 1809-1895 ...... DLB-32
Hakluyt, Richard 1552?-1616 .... DLB-136
Halas, František 1901-1949 .... DLB-215
Halbe, Max 1865-1944 .... DLB-118
Haldone, Charlotte 1894-1969 .... DLB-191
Haldane, J. B. S. 1892-1964 .... DLB-160
Haldeman, Joe 1943- DLB-8
Haldeman-Julius Company DLB-46
Hale, E. J., and Son DLB-49
Hale, Edward Everett 1822-1909 ... DLB-1, 42, 74
Hale, Janet Campbell 1946- DLB-175
Hale, Kathleen 1898- DLB-160
Hale, Leo Thomas (see Ebon)
Hale, Lucretia Peabody 1820-1900 ...... DLB-42
Hale, Nancy
  1908-1988 .... DLB-86; DS-17; Y-80, Y-88

Hale, Sarah Josepha (Buell)
1788-1879....................DLB-1, 42, 73

Hales, John 1584-1656................DLB-151

Halévy, Ludovic 1834-1908............DLB-192

Haley, Alex 1921-1992.................DLB-38

Haliburton, Thomas Chandler
1796-1865.....................DLB-11, 99

Hall, Anna Maria 1800-1881..........DLB-159

Hall, Donald 1928- DLB-5

Hall, Edward 1497-1547................DLB-132

Hall, James 1793-1868..............DLB-73, 74

Hall, Joseph 1574-1656...........DLB-121, 151

Hall, Radclyffe 1880-1943............DLB-191

Hall, Sarah Ewing 1761-1830..........DLB-200

Hall, Samuel [publishing house]........DLB-49

Hallam, Arthur Henry 1811-1833........DLB-32

Halleck, Fitz-Greene 1790-1867..........DLB-3

Haller, Albrecht von 1708-1777........DLB-168

Halliwell-Phillipps, James Orchard
1820-1889.....................DLB-184

Hallmann, Johann Christian
1640-1704 or 1716?..............DLB-168

Hallmark Editions DLB-46

Halper, Albert 1904-1984 ....DLB-9

Halperin, John William 1941- DLB-111

Halstead, Murat 1829-1908.............DLB-23

Hamann, Johann Georg 1730-1788.......DLB-97

Hamburger, Michael 1924- DLB-27

Hamilton, Alexander 1712-1756.........DLB-31

Hamilton, Alexander 1755?-1804........DLB-37

Hamilton, Cicely 1872-1952......DLB-10, 197

Hamilton, Edmond 1904-1977............DLB-8

Hamilton, Elizabeth 1758-1816.....DLB-116, 158

Hamilton, Gail (see Corcoran, Barbara)

Hamilton, Ian 1938- DLB-40, 155

Hamilton, Janet 1795-1873............DLB-199

Hamilton, Mary Agnes 1884-1962......DLB-197

Hamilton, Patrick 1904-1962.......DLB-10, 191

Hamilton, Virginia 1936- DLB-33, 52

Hamilton, Hamish, Limited............DLB-112

Hammett, Dashiell 1894-1961.............DS-6

Dashiell Hammett: An Appeal in *TAC* Y-91

Hammon, Jupiter 1711-died between
1790 and 1806.................DLB-31, 50

Hammond, John ?-1663..................DLB-24

Hamner, Earl 1923- DLB-6

Hampson, John 1901-1955.............DLB-191

Hampton, Christopher 1946- DLB-13

Handel-Mazzetti, Enrica von 1871-1955...DLB-81

Handke, Peter 1942- DLB-85, 124

Handlin, Oscar 1915- DLB-17

Hankin, St. John 1869-1909............DLB-10

Hanley, Clifford 1922- DLB-14

Hanley, James 1901-1985..............DLB-191

Hannah, Barry 1942- DLB-6

Hannay, James 1827-1873...............DLB-21

Hansberry, Lorraine 1930-1965........DLB-7, 38

Hansen, Martin A. 1909-1955..........DLB-214

Hansen, Thorkild 1927-1989...........DLB-214

Hanson, Elizabeth 1684-1737..........DLB-200

Hapgood, Norman 1868-1937............DLB-91

Happel, Eberhard Werner 1647-1690....DLB-168

Harcourt Brace Jovanovich.............DLB-46

Hardenberg, Friedrich von (see Novalis)

Harding, Walter 1917- DLB-111

Hardwick, Elizabeth 1916- DLB-6

Hardy, Thomas 1840-1928......DLB-18, 19, 135

Hare, Cyril 1900-1958.................DLB-77

Hare, David 1947- DLB-13

Hargrove, Marion 1919- DLB-11

Häring, Georg Wilhelm Heinrich (see Alexis, Willibald)

Harington, Donald 1935- DLB-152

Harington, Sir John 1560-1612........DLB-136

Harjo, Joy 1951- DLB-120, 175

Harkness, Margaret (John Law)
1854-1923.....................DLB-197

Harley, Edward, second Earl of Oxford
1689-1741.....................DLB-213

Harley, Robert, first Earl of Oxford
1661-1724.....................DLB-213

Harlow, Robert 1923- DLB-60

Harman, Thomas
flourished 1566-1573..............DLB-136

Harness, Charles L. 1915- DLB-8

Harnett, Cynthia 1893-1981............DLB-161

Harper, Fletcher 1806-1877.............DLB-79

Harper, Frances Ellen Watkins
1825-1911......................DLB-50

Harper, Michael S. 1938- DLB-41

Harper and Brothers DLB-49

Harraden, Beatrice 1864-1943.........DLB-153

Harrap, George G., and Company
Limited........................DLB-112

Harriot, Thomas 1560-1621............DLB-136

Harris, Benjamin ?-circa 1720......DLB-42, 43

Harris, Christie 1907- DLB-88

Harris, Frank 1856-1931..........DLB-156, 197

Harris, George Washington
1814-1869......................DLB-3, 11

Harris, Joel Chandler
1848-1908..........DLB-11, 23, 42, 78, 91

Harris, Mark 1922- DLB-2; Y-80

Harris, Wilson 1921- DLB-117

Harrison, Charles Yale 1898-1954.......DLB-68

Harrison, Frederic 1831-1923.....DLB-57, 190

Harrison, Harry 1925- DLB-8

Harrison, Jim 1937- Y-82

Harrison, Mary St. Leger Kingsley
(see Malet, Lucas)

Harrison, Paul Carter 1936- DLB-38

Harrison, Susan Frances 1859-1935......DLB-99

Harrison, Tony 1937- DLB-40

Harrison, William 1535-1593..........DLB-136

Harrison, James P., Company...........DLB-49

Harrisse, Henry 1829-1910.............DLB-47

Harryman, Carla 1952- DLB-193

Harsdörffer, Georg Philipp 1607-1658....DLB-164

Harsent, David 1942- DLB-40

Hart, Albert Bushnell 1854-1943.......DLB-17

Hart, Anne 1768-1834.................DLB-200

Hart, Elizabeth 1771-1833............DLB-200

Hart, Julia Catherine 1796-1867........DLB-99

The Lorenz Hart Centenary Y-95

Hart, Moss 1904-1961....................DLB-7

Hart, Oliver 1723-1795.................DLB-31

Hart-Davis, Rupert, Limited...........DLB-112

Harte, Bret 1836-1902....DLB-12, 64, 74, 79, 186

Harte, Edward Holmead 1922- DLB-127

Harte, Houston Harriman 1927- DLB-127

Hartlaub, Felix 1913-1945..............DLB-56

Hartleben, Otto Erich 1864-1905.......DLB-118

Hartley, L. P. 1895-1972...........DLB-15, 139

Hartley, Marsden 1877-1943............DLB-54

Hartling, Peter 1933- DLB-75

Hartman, Geoffrey H. 1929- DLB-67

Hartmann, Sadakichi 1867-1944.........DLB-54

Hartmann von Aue
circa 1160-circa 1205............DLB-138

Harvey, Gabriel 1550?-1631......DLB-167, 213

Harvey, Jean-Charles 1891-1967........DLB-88

Harvill Press Limited.................DLB-112

Harwood, Lee 1939- DLB-40

Harwood, Ronald 1934- DLB-13

Hašek, Jaroslav 1883-1923............DLB-215

Haskins, Charles Homer 1870-1937......DLB-47

Haslam, Gerald 1937- DLB-212

Hass, Robert 1941- DLB-105, 206

Határ, Győző 1914- DLB-215

The Hatch-Billops Collection DLB-76

Hathaway, William 1944- DLB-120

Hauff, Wilhelm 1802-1827..............DLB-90

A Haughty and Proud Generation (1922),
by Ford Madox Hueffer DLB-36

Haugwitz, August Adolph von
1647-1706......................DLB-168

Hauptmann, Carl 1858-1921........DLB-66, 118

Hauptmann, Gerhart 1862-1946.....DLB-66, 118

Hauser, Marianne 1910- Y-83

Havergal, Frances Ridley 1836-1879....DLB-199

Hawes, Stephen 1475?-before 1529......DLB-132

Hawker, Robert Stephen 1803-1875.......DLB-32

Hawkes, John 1925-1998....DLB-2, 7; Y-80, Y-98

Hawkesworth, John 1720-1773..........DLB-142

Hawkins, Sir Anthony Hope (see Hope, Anthony)

Hawkins, Sir John 1719-1789......DLB-104, 142

Hawkins, Walter Everette 1883-?.......DLB-50

345

Cumulative Index DLB 216

Hawthorne, Nathaniel
    1804-1864 ....DLB-1, 74, 183

Hawthorne, Nathaniel 1804-1864 and
    Hawthorne, Sophia Peabody
    1809-1871...................... DLB-183

Hay, John 1835-1905 ....DLB-12, 47, 189

Hayashi, Fumiko 1903-1951........... DLB-180

Haycox, Ernest 1899-1950 .... DLB-206

Haycraft, Anna Margaret (see Ellis, Alice Thomas)

Hayden, Robert 1913-1980 .... DLB-5, 76

Haydon, Benjamin Robert
    1786-1846...................... DLB-110

Hayes, John Michael 1919- DLB-26

Hayley, William 1745-1820 .... DLB-93, 142

Haym, Rudolf 1821-1901............ DLB-129

Hayman, Robert 1575-1629 .... DLB-99

Hayman, Ronald 1932- DLB-155

Hayne, Paul Hamilton 1830-1886 .. DLB-3, 64, 79

Hays, Mary 1760-1843............ DLB-142, 158

Hayward, John 1905-1965 .... DLB-201

Haywood, Eliza 1693?-1756 .... DLB-39

Hazard, Willis P. [publishing house]...... DLB-49

Hazlitt, William 1778-1830 .... DLB-110, 158

Hazzard, Shirley 1931- Y-82

Head, Bessie 1937-1986 .... DLB-117

Headley, Joel T. 1813-1897 .. DLB-30, 183; DS-13

Heaney, Seamus 1939- DLB-40; Y-95

Heard, Nathan C. 1936- DLB-33

Hearn, Lafcadio 1850-1904 ......DLB-12, 78, 189

Hearne, John 1926- DLB-117

Hearne, Samuel 1745-1792 .... DLB-99

Hearne, Thomas 1678?-1735 .... DLB-213

Hearst, William Randolph 1863-1951 .... DLB-25

Hearst, William Randolph, Jr.
    1908-1993 .... DLB-127

Heartman, Charles Frederick
    1883-1953 .... DLB-187

Heath, Catherine 1924- DLB-14

Heath, Roy A. K. 1926- DLB-117

Heath-Stubbs, John 1918- DLB-27

Heavysege, Charles 1816-1876.......... DLB-99

Hebbel, Friedrich 1813-1863 .... DLB-129

Hebel, Johann Peter 1760-1826........ DLB-90

Heber, Richard 1774-1833 .... DLB-184

Hébert, Anne 1916- DLB-68

Hébert, Jacques 1923- DLB-53

Hecht, Anthony 1923- DLB-5, 169

Hecht, Ben 1894-1964
    ....DLB-7, 9, 25, 26, 28, 86

Hecker, Isaac Thomas 1819-1888 .... DLB-1

Hedge, Frederic Henry 1805-1890 ..... DLB-1, 59

Hefner, Hugh M. 1926- DLB-137

Hegel, Georg Wilhelm Friedrich
    1770-1831...................... DLB-90

Heidish, Marcy 1947- Y-82

Heißenbüttel 1921- DLB-75

Heike monogatari.................. DLB-203

Hein, Christoph 1944- DLB-124

Hein, Piet 1905-1996 .... DLB-214

Heine, Heinrich 1797-1856 .... DLB-90

Heinemann, Larry 1944- DS-9

Heinemann, William, Limited DLB-112

Heinesen, William 1900-1991 .... DLB-214

Heinlein, Robert A. 1907-1988 .... DLB-8

Heinrich Julius of Brunswick
    1564-1613 .... DLB-164

Heinrich von dem Türlîn
    flourished circa 1230 .... DLB-138

Heinrich von Melk
    flourished after 1160 .... DLB-148

Heinrich von Veldeke
    circa 1145-circa 1190 .... DLB-138

Heinrich, Willi 1920- DLB-75

Heiskell, John 1872-1972............ DLB-127

Heinse, Wilhelm 1746-1803 .... DLB-94

Heinz, W. C. 1915- DLB-171

Hejinian, Lyn 1941- DLB-165

Heliand circa 850................. DLB-148

Heller, Joseph 1923- DLB-2, 28; Y-80

Heller, Michael 1937- DLB-165

Hellman, Lillian 1906-1984 ....DLB-7; Y-84

Hellwig, Johann 1609-1674........... DLB-164

Helprin, Mark 1947- Y-85

Helwig, David 1938- DLB-60

Hemans, Felicia 1793-1835 .... DLB-96

Hemingway, Ernest
    1899-1961 .... DLB-4, 9, 102, 210;
    Y-81, Y-87; DS-1, DS-15, DS-16

Hemingway: Twenty-Five Years Later....... Y-85

Hémon, Louis 1880-1913 .... DLB-92

Hemphill, Paul 1936- Y-87

Hénault, Gilles 1920- DLB-88

Henchman, Daniel 1689-1761 .... DLB-24

Henderson, Alice Corbin 1881-1949 ..... DLB-54

Henderson, Archibald 1877-1963 .... DLB-103

Henderson, David 1942- DLB-41

Henderson, George Wylie 1904- DLB-51

Henderson, Zenna 1917-1983........... DLB-8

Henisch, Peter 1943- DLB-85

Henley, Beth 1952- Y-86

Henley, William Ernest 1849-1903 ...... DLB-19

Henningsen, Agnes 1868-1962 .... DLB-214

Henniker, Florence 1855-1923 .... DLB-135

Henry, Alexander 1739-1824 .... DLB-99

Henry, Buck 1930- DLB-26

Henry VIII of England 1491-1547...... DLB-132

Henry, Marguerite 1902- DLB-22

Henry, O. (see Porter, William Sydney)

Henry of Ghent
    circa 1217-1229 - 1293 .... DLB-115

Henry, Robert Selph 1889-1970 .... DLB-17

Henry, Will (see Allen, Henry W.)

Henryson, Robert
    1420s or 1430s-circa 1505 .... DLB-146

Henschke, Alfred (see Klabund)

Hensley, Sophie Almon 1866-1946 ...... DLB-99

Henson, Lance 1944- DLB-175

Henty, G. A. 1832?-1902 .... DLB-18, 141

Hentz, Caroline Lee 1800-1856 .... DLB-3

Heraclitus flourished circa 500 B.C.
    ....DLB-176

Herbert, Agnes circa 1880-1960.........DLB-174

Herbert, Alan Patrick 1890-1971 .....DLB-10, 191

Herbert, Edward, Lord, of Cherbury
    1582-1648 .... DLB-121, 151

Herbert, Frank 1920-1986 .... DLB-8

Herbert, George 1593-1633 .... DLB-126

Herbert, Henry William 1807-1858 .... DLB-3, 73

Herbert, John 1926- DLB-53

Herbert, Mary Sidney, Countess of Pembroke
    (see Sidney, Mary)

Herbst, Josephine 1892-1969 .... DLB-9

Herburger, Gunter 1932- DLB-75, 124

Hercules, Frank E. M. 1917- DLB-33

Herder, Johann Gottfried 1744-1803 ..... DLB-97

Herder, B., Book Company DLB-49

Herford, Charles Harold 1853-1931 .... DLB-149

Hergesheimer, Joseph 1880-1954..... DLB-9, 102

Heritage Press................... DLB-46

Hermann the Lame 1013-1054 .... DLB-148

Hermes, Johann Timotheus
    1738-1821...................... DLB-97

Hermlin, Stephan 1915-1997 .... DLB-69

Hernández, Alfonso C. 1938- DLB-122

Hernández, Inés 1947- DLB-122

Hernández, Miguel 1910-1942 .... DLB-134

Hernton, Calvin C. 1932- DLB-38

"The Hero as Man of Letters: Johnson,
    Rousseau, Burns" (1841), by Thomas
    Carlyle [excerpt]................ DLB-57

The Hero as Poet. Dante; Shakspeare (1841),
    by Thomas Carlyle DLB-32

Herodotus circa 484 B.C.-circa 420 B.C.
    ....DLB-176

Heron, Robert 1764-1807............. DLB-142

Herr, Michael 1940- DLB-185

Herrera, Juan Felipe 1948- DLB-122

Herrick, Robert 1591-1674 .... DLB-126

Herrick, Robert 1868-1938.........DLB-9, 12, 78

Herrick, William 1915- Y-83

Herrick, E. R., and Company DLB-49

Herrmann, John 1900-1959 .... DLB-4

Hersey, John 1914-1993............ DLB-6, 185

Hertel, François 1905-1985............ DLB-68

Hervé-Bazin, Jean Pierre Marie (see Bazin, Hervé)

Hervey, John, Lord 1696-1743 .... DLB-101

Herwig, Georg 1817-1875............. DLB-133

Herzog, Emile Salomon Wilhelm (see
    Maurois, André)

Hesiod eighth century B.C. DLB-176

Hesse, Hermann 1877-1962 .... DLB-66

Hessus, Helius Eobanus 1488-1540......DLB-179	Hingley, Ronald 1920-................DLB-155	Hohl, Ludwig 1904-1980...............DLB-56
Hewat, Alexander circa 1743-circa 1824 ...DLB-30	Hinojosa-Smith, Rolando 1929-........DLB-82	Holbrook, David 1923-...........DLB-14, 40
Hewitt, John 1907-....................DLB-27	Hippel, Theodor Gottlieb von 1741-1796....................DLB-97	Holcroft, Thomas 1745-1809.....DLB-39, 89, 158
Hewlett, Maurice 1861-1923........DLB-34, 156	Hippocrates of Cos flourished circa 425 B.C. DLB-176	Holden, Jonathan 1941-..............DLB-105
Heyen, William 1940-.................DLB-5	Hirabayashi, Taiko 1905-1972.........DLB-180	Holden, Molly 1927-1981..............DLB-40
Heyer, Georgette 1902-1974........DLB-77, 191	Hirsch, E. D., Jr. 1928-...............DLB-67	Hölderlin, Friedrich 1770-1843.........DLB-90
Heym, Stefan 1913-..................DLB-69	Hirsch, Edward 1950-...............DLB-120	Holiday House.......................DLB-46
Heyse, Paul 1830-1914...............DLB-129	*The History of the Adventures of Joseph Andrews* (1742), by Henry Fielding [excerpt]....DLB-39	Holinshed, Raphael died 1580.........DLB-167
Heytesbury, William circa 1310-1372 or 1373............DLB-115	Hoagland, Edward 1932-................DLB-6	Holland, J. G. 1819-1881................DS-13
Heyward, Dorothy 1890-1961...........DLB-7	Hoagland, Everett H., III 1942-........DLB-41	Holland, Norman N. 1927-............DLB-67
Heyward, DuBose 1885-1940.......DLB-7, 9, 45	Hoban, Russell 1925-.................DLB-52	Hollander, John 1929-.................DLB-5
Heywood, John 1497?-1580?.........DLB-136	Hobbes, Thomas 1588-1679...........DLB-151	Holley, Marietta 1836-1926.............DLB-11
Heywood, Thomas 1573 or 1574-1641..................DLB-62	Hobby, Oveta 1905-.................DLB-127	Hollinghurst, Alan 1954-..............DLB-207
Hibbs, Ben 1901-1975................DLB-137	Hobby, William 1878-1964............DLB-127	Hollingsworth, Margaret 1940-.........DLB-60
Hichens, Robert S. 1864-1950..........DLB-153	Hobsbaum, Philip 1932-...............DLB-40	Hollo, Anselm 1934-..................DLB-40
Hickey, Emily 1845-1924..............DLB-199	Hobson, Laura Z. 1900-...............DLB-28	Holloway, Emory 1885-1977...........DLB-103
Hickman, William Albert 1877-1957......DLB-92	Hobson, Sarah 1947-................DLB-204	Holloway, John 1920-.................DLB-27
Hidalgo, José Luis 1919-1947..........DLB-108	Hoby, Thomas 1530-1566.............DLB-132	Holloway House Publishing Company....DLB-46
Hiebert, Paul 1892-1987...............DLB-68	Hoccleve, Thomas circa 1368-circa 1437..............DLB-146	Holme, Constance 1880-1955...........DLB-34
Hieng, Andrej 1925-.................DLB-181	Hochhuth, Rolf 1931-................DLB-124	Holmes, Abraham S. 1821?-1908.........DLB-99
Hierro, José 1922-..................DLB-108	Hochman, Sandra 1936-................DLB-5	Holmes, John Clellon 1926-1988.........DLB-16
Higgins, Aidan 1927-.................DLB-14	Hocken, Thomas Morland 1836-1910....................DLB-184	Holmes, Mary Jane 1825-1907.........DLB-202
Higgins, Colin 1941-1988..............DLB-26	Hodder and Stoughton, Limited........DLB-106	Holmes, Oliver Wendell 1809-1894...DLB-1, 189
Higgins, George V. 1939-....DLB-2; Y-81, Y-98	Hodgins, Jack 1938-..................DLB-60	Holmes, Richard 1945-...............DLB-155
Higginson, Thomas Wentworth 1823-1911....................DLB-1, 64	Hodgman, Helen 1945-...............DLB-14	Holmes, Thomas James 1874-1959......DLB-187
Highwater, Jamake 1942?-.......DLB-52; Y-85	Hodgskin, Thomas 1787-1869..........DLB-158	Holroyd, Michael 1935-...............DLB-155
Hijuelos, Oscar 1951-................DLB-145	Hodgson, Ralph 1871-1962............DLB-19	Holst, Hermann E. von 1841-1904.......DLB-47
Hildegard von Bingen 1098-1179........DLB-148	Hodgson, William Hope 1877-1918.........DLB-70, 153, 156, 178	Holt, John 1721-1784..................DLB-43
Das Hildesbrandslied circa 820...........DLB-148	Hoe, Robert III 1839-1909.............DLB-187	Holt, Henry, and Company.............DLB-49
Hildesheimer, Wolfgang 1916-1991...................DLB-69, 124	Hoeg, Peter 1957-...................DLB-214	Holt, Rinehart and Winston............DLB-46
Hildreth, Richard 1807-1865.......DLB-1, 30, 59	Højholt, Per 1928-..................DLB-214	Holtby, Winifred 1898-1935............DLB-191
Hill, Aaron 1685-1750.................DLB-84	Hoffenstein, Samuel 1890-1947..........DLB-11	Holthusen, Hans Egon 1913-...........DLB-69
Hill, Geoffrey 1932-...................DLB-40	Hoffman, Charles Fenno 1806-1884......DLB-3	Hölty, Ludwig Christoph Heinrich 1748-1776.......................DLB-94
Hill, "Sir" John 1714?-1775..............DLB-39	Hoffman, Daniel 1923-.................DLB-5	Holz, Arno 1863-1929................DLB-118
Hill, Leslie 1880-1960..................DLB-51	Hoffmann, E. T. A. 1776-1822..........DLB-90	Home, Henry, Lord Kames (see Kames, Henry Home, Lord)
Hill, Susan 1942-.................DLB-14, 139	Hoffman, Frank B. 1888-1958..........DLB-188	Home, John 1722-1808................DLB-84
Hill, Walter 1942-....................DLB-44	Hoffmanswaldau, Christian Hoffman von 1616-1679.....................DLB-168	Home, William Douglas 1912-..........DLB-13
Hill and Wang........................DLB-46	Hofmann, Michael 1957-..............DLB-40	Home Publishing Company.............DLB-49
Hill, George M., Company..............DLB-49	Hofmannsthal, Hugo von 1874-1929....................DLB-81, 118	Homer circa eighth-seventh centuries B.C. DLB-176
Hill, Lawrence, and Company, Publishers........................DLB-46	Hofstadter, Richard 1916-1970..........DLB-17	Homer, Winslow 1836-1910...........DLB-188
Hillberry, Conrad 1928-...............DLB-120	Hogan, Desmond 1950-...............DLB-14	Homes, Geoffrey (see Mainwaring, Daniel)
Hillerman, Tony 1925-................DLB-206	Hogan, Linda 1947-.................DLB-175	Honan, Park 1928-..................DLB-111
Hilliard, Gray and Company............DLB-49	Hogan and Thompson..................DLB-49	Hone, William 1780-1842........DLB-110, 158
Hills, Lee 1906-....................DLB-127	Hogarth Press.......................DLB-112	Hongo, Garrett Kaoru 1951-...........DLB-120
Hillyer, Robert 1895-1961..............DLB-54	Hogg, James 1770-1835........DLB-93, 116, 159	Honig, Edwin 1919-...................DLB-5
Hilton, James 1900-1954............DLB-34, 77	Hohberg, Wolfgang Helmhard Freiherr von 1612-1688.....................DLB-168	Hood, Hugh 1928-...................DLB-53
Hilton, Walter died 1396..............DLB-146	von Hohenheim, Philippus Aureolus Theophrastus Bombastus (see Paracelsus)	Hood, Thomas 1799-1845.............DLB-96
Hilton and Company..................DLB-49		Hook, Theodore 1788-1841...........DLB-116
Himes, Chester 1909-1984........DLB-2, 76, 143		Hooker, Jeremy 1941-.................DLB-40
Hindmarsh, Joseph [publishing house]....DLB-170		Hooker, Richard 1554-1600............DLB-132
Hine, Daryl 1936-....................DLB-60		Hooker, Thomas 1586-1647............DLB-24
		Hooper, Johnson Jones 1815-1862......DLB-3, 11

Hope, Anthony 1863-1933 . . . . DLB-153, 156
Hopkins, Ellice 1836-1904 . . . . DLB-190
Hopkins, Gerard Manley
   1844-1889 . . . . DLB-35, 57
Hopkins, John (see Sternhold, Thomas)
Hopkins, Lemuel 1750-1801 . . . . DLB-37
Hopkins, Pauline Elizabeth 1859-1930 . . . . DLB-50
Hopkins, Samuel 1721-1803 . . . . DLB-31
Hopkins, John H., and Son DLB-46
Hopkinson, Francis 1737-1791 . . . . DLB-31
Hoppin, Augustus 1828-1896 . . . . DLB-188
Hora, Josef 1891-1945 . . . . DLB-215
Horace 65 B.C.-8 B.C. DLB-211
Horgan, Paul 1903-1995 . . . . . DLB-102, 212; Y-85
Horizon Press DLB-46
Hornby, C. H. St. John 1867-1946 . . . . . . DLB-201
Hornby, Nick 1957- DLB-207
Horne, Frank 1899-1974 . . . . DLB-51
Horne, Richard Henry (Hengist)
   1802 or 1803-1884 . . . . DLB-32
Hornung, E. W. 1866-1921 . . . . DLB-70
Horovitz, Israel 1939- DLB-7
Horton, George Moses 1797?-1883? DLB-50
Horváth, Ödön von 1901-1938 . . . . . DLB-85, 124
Horwood, Harold 1923- DLB-60
Hosford, E. and E. [publishing house] DLB-49
Hoskens, Jane Fenn 1693-1770? DLB-200
Hoskyns, John 1566-1638 . . . . DLB-121
Hosokawa Yūsai 1535-1610 . . . . DLB-203
Hostovský, Egon 1908-1973 . . . . DLB-215
Hotchkiss and Company DLB-49
Hough, Emerson 1857-1923 . . . . DLB-9, 212
Houghton Mifflin Company DLB-49
Houghton, Stanley 1881-1913 . . . . DLB-10
Household, Geoffrey 1900-1988 . . . . DLB-87
Housman, A. E. 1859-1936 . . . . DLB-19
Housman, Laurence 1865-1959 . . . . DLB-10
Houwald, Ernst von 1778-1845 . . . . DLB-90
Hovey, Richard 1864-1900 . . . . DLB-54
Howard, Donald R. 1927-1987 . . . . DLB-111
Howard, Maureen 1930- Y-83
Howard, Richard 1929- DLB-5
Howard, Roy W. 1883-1964 . . . . DLB-29
Howard, Sidney 1891-1939 . . . . DLB-7, 26
Howard, Thomas, second Earl of Arundel
   1585-1646 . . . . DLB-213
Howe, E. W. 1853-1937 . . . . DLB-12, 25
Howe, Henry 1816-1893 . . . . DLB-30
Howe, Irving 1920-1993 . . . . DLB-67
Howe, Joseph 1804-1873 . . . . DLB-99
Howe, Julia Ward 1819-1910 . . . . DLB-1, 189
Howe, Percival Presland 1886-1944 . . . . . DLB-149
Howe, Susan 1937- DLB-120
Howell, Clark, Sr. 1863-1936 . . . . DLB-25
Howell, Evan P. 1839-1905 . . . . DLB-23

Howell, James 1594?-1666 . . . . DLB-151
Howell, Warren Richardson
   1912-1984 . . . . DLB-140
Howell, Soskin and Company DLB-46
Howells, William Dean
   1837-1920 . . . . DLB-12, 64, 74, 79, 189
Howitt, Mary 1799-1888 . . . . DLB-110, 199
Howitt, William 1792-1879 and
   Howitt, Mary 1799-1888 . . . . DLB-110
Hoyem, Andrew 1935- DLB-5
Hoyers, Anna Ovena 1584-1655 . . . . DLB-164
Hoyos, Angela de 1940- DLB-82
Hoyt, Palmer 1897-1979 . . . . DLB-127
Hoyt, Henry [publishing house] DLB-49
Hrabanus Maurus 776?-856 . . . . DLB-148
Hronský, Josef Cíger 1896-1960 . . . . DLB-215
Hrotsvit of Gandersheim
   circa 935-circa 1000 . . . . DLB-148
Hubbard, Elbert 1856-1915 . . . . DLB-91
Hubbard, Kin 1868-1930 . . . . DLB-11
Hubbard, William circa 1621-1704 . . . . . . DLB-24
Huber, Therese 1764-1829 . . . . DLB-90
Huch, Friedrich 1873-1913 . . . . DLB-66
Huch, Ricarda 1864-1947 . . . . DLB-66
Huck at 100: How Old Is
   Huckleberry Finn? Y-85
Huddle, David 1942- DLB-130
Hudgins, Andrew 1951- DLB-120
Hudson, Henry Norman 1814-1886 . . . . . DLB-64
Hudson, Stephen 1868?-1944 . . . . DLB-197
Hudson, W. H. 1841-1922 . . . . . DLB-98, 153, 174
Hudson and Goodwin DLB-49
Huebsch, B. W. [publishing house] DLB-46
Hueffer, Oliver Madox 1876-1931 . . . . . . DLB-197
Hugh of St. Victor circa 1096-1141 . . . . . DLB-208
Hughes, David 1930- DLB-14
Hughes, John 1677-1720 . . . . DLB-84
Hughes, Langston
   1902-1967 . . . . DLB-4, 7, 48, 51, 86
Hughes, Richard 1900-1976 . . . . DLB-15, 161
Hughes, Ted 1930- DLB-40, 161
Hughes, Thomas 1822-1896 . . . . DLB-18, 163
Hugo, Richard 1923-1982 . . . . DLB-5, 206
Hugo, Victor 1802-1885 . . . . DLB-119, 192
Hugo Awards and Nebula Awards DLB-8
Hull, Richard 1896-1973 . . . . DLB-77
Hulme, T. E. 1883-1917 . . . . DLB-19
Hulton, Anne ?-1779? DLB-200
Humboldt, Alexander von 1769-1859 . . . . DLB-90
Humboldt, Wilhelm von 1767-1835 . . . . . DLB-90
Hume, David 1711-1776 . . . . DLB-104
Hume, Fergus 1859-1932 . . . . DLB-70
Hume, Sophia 1702-1774 . . . . DLB-200
Hummer, T. R. 1950- DLB-120
Humorous Book Illustration DLB-11

Humphrey, Duke of Gloucester
   1391-1447 . . . . DLB-213
Humphrey, William 1924-1997 . . . . . DLB-6, 212
Humphreys, David 1752-1818 . . . . DLB-37
Humphreys, Emyr 1919- DLB-15
Huncke, Herbert 1915- DLB-16
Huneker, James Gibbons 1857-1921 . . . . . DLB-71
Hunold, Christian Friedrich
   1681-1721 . . . . DLB-168
Hunt, Irene 1907- DLB-52
Hunt, Leigh 1784-1859 . . . . DLB-96, 110, 144
Hunt, Violet 1862-1942 . . . . DLB-162, 197
Hunt, William Gibbes 1791-1833 . . . . DLB-73
Hunter, Evan 1926- Y-82
Hunter, Jim 1939- DLB-14
Hunter, Kristin 1931- DLB-33
Hunter, Mollie 1922- DLB-161
Hunter, N. C. 1908-1971 . . . . DLB-10
Hunter-Duvar, John 1821-1899 . . . . DLB-99
Huntington, Henry E. 1850-1927 . . . . . . DLB-140
Huntington, Susan Mansfield
   1791-1823 . . . . DLB-200
Hurd and Houghton DLB-49
Hurst, Fannie 1889-1968 . . . . DLB-86
Hurst and Blackett DLB-106
Hurst and Company DLB-49
Hurston, Zora Neale 1901?-1960 . . . . . DLB-51, 86
Husson, Jules-François-Félix (see Champfleury)
Huston, John 1906-1987 . . . . DLB-26
Hutcheson, Francis 1694-1746 . . . . DLB-31
Hutchinson, R. C. 1907-1975 . . . . DLB-191
Hutchinson, Thomas 1711-1780 . . . . . DLB-30, 31
Hutchinson and Company
   (Publishers) Limited DLB-112
von Hutton, Ulrich 1488-1523 . . . . DLB-179
Hutton, Richard Holt 1826-1897 . . . . DLB-57
Huxley, Aldous
   1894-1963 . . . . DLB-36, 100, 162, 195
Huxley, Elspeth Josceline
   1907-1997 . . . . DLB-77, 204
Huxley, T. H. 1825-1895 . . . . DLB-57
Huyghue, Douglas Smith 1816-1891 . . . . . DLB-99
Huysmans, Joris-Karl 1848-1907 . . . . DLB-123
Hwang, David Henry 1957- DLB-212
Hyde, Donald 1909-1966 and
   Hyde, Mary 1912- DLB-187
Hyman, Trina Schart 1939- DLB-61

I

Iavorsky, Stefan 1658-1722 . . . . DLB-150
Iazykov, Nikolai Mikhailovich
   1803-1846 . . . . DLB-205
Ibáñez, Armando P. 1949- DLB-209
Ibn Bajja circa 1077-1138 . . . . DLB-115
Ibn Gabirol, Solomon
   circa 1021-circa 1058 . . . . DLB-115
Ibuse, Masuji 1898-1993 . . . . DLB-180

Ichijō Kanera (see Ichijō Kaneyoshi)

Ichijō Kaneyoshi (Ichijō Kanera)
 1402-1481 ....DLB-203

The Iconography of Science-Fiction Art DLB-8

Iffland, August Wilhelm 1759-1814 ....DLB-94

Ignatow, David 1914- DLB-5

Ike, Chukwuemeka 1931- DLB-157

Ikkyū Sōjun 1394-1481 ....DLB-203

Iles, Francis (see Berkeley, Anthony)

The Illustration of Early German
 Literary Manuscripts,
 circa 1150-circa 1300 ....DLB-148

Illyés, Gyula 1902-1983 ....DLB-215

"Images and 'Images,'" by
 Charles Simic DLB-105

Imbs, Bravig 1904-1946 ....DLB-4

Imbuga, Francis D. 1947- DLB-157

Immermann, Karl 1796-1840 ....DLB-133

Impressions of William Faulkner Y-97

Inchbald, Elizabeth 1753-1821 ....DLB-39, 89

Inge, William 1913-1973 ....DLB-7

Ingelow, Jean 1820-1897 ....DLB-35, 163

Ingersoll, Ralph 1900-1985 ....DLB-127

The Ingersoll Prizes Y-84

Ingoldsby, Thomas (see Barham, Richard Harris)

Ingraham, Joseph Holt 1809-1860 ....DLB-3

Inman, John 1805-1850 ....DLB-73

Innerhofer, Franz 1944- DLB-85

Innis, Harold Adams 1894-1952 ....DLB-88

Innis, Mary Quayle 1899-1972 ....DLB-88

Inō Sōgi 1421-1502 ....DLB-203

Inoue Yasushi 1907-1991 ....DLB-181

International Publishers Company DLB-46

Interview with Benjamin Anastas Y-98

An Interview with David Rabe Y-91

An Interview with George Greenfield,
 Literary Agent......................Y-91

Interview with George V. Higgins Y-98

An Interview with James Ellroy Y-91

Interview with Melissa Bank Y-98

Interview with Norman Mailer Y-97

An Interview with Peter S. Prescott Y-86

An Interview with Russell Hoban Y-90

Interview with Stanley Burnshaw Y-97

Interview with Thomas McCormack Y-98

An Interview with Tom Jenks Y-86

"Into the Mirror," by Peter Cooley DLB-105

Introduction to Paul Laurence Dunbar,
 Lyrics of Lowly Life (1896),
 by William Dean Howells DLB-50

Introductory Essay: Letters of Percy Bysshe
 Shelley (1852), by Robert Browning....DLB-32

Introductory Letters from the Second Edition
 of Pamela (1741), by Samuel
 Richardson DLB-39

Irving, John 1942- DLB-6; Y-82

Irving, Washington 1783-1859
 .... DLB-3, 11, 30, 59, 73, 74, 183, 186

Irwin, Grace 1907- DLB-68

Irwin, Will 1873-1948 ....DLB-25

Isherwood, Christopher
 1904-1986 .... DLB-15, 195; Y-86

Ishiguro, Kazuo 1954- DLB-194

Ishikawa Jun 1899-1987 ....DLB-182

The Island Trees Case: A Symposium on
 School Library Censorship
 An Interview with Judith Krug
 An Interview with Phyllis Schlafly
 An Interview with Edward B. Jenkinson
 An Interview with Lamarr Mooneyham
 An Interview with Harriet Bernstein Y-82

Islas, Arturo 1938-1991 ....DLB-122

Ivanišević, Drago 1907-1981 ....DLB-181

Ivers, M. J., and Company..............DLB-49

Iwaniuk, Wacław 1915- DLB-215

Iwano, Hōmei 1873-1920 ....DLB-180

Iwaszkiewicz, Jarosław 1894-1980 ......DLB-215

Iyayi, Festus 1947- DLB-157

Izumi, Kyōka 1873-1939 ....DLB-180

J

Jackmon, Marvin E. (see Marvin X)

Jacks, L. P. 1860-1955 ....DLB-135

Jackson, Angela 1951- DLB-41

Jackson, Helen Hunt
 1830-1885 .... DLB-42, 47, 186, 189

Jackson, Holbrook 1874-1948 ....DLB-98

Jackson, Laura Riding 1901-1991 ....DLB-48

Jackson, Shirley 1919-1965 ....DLB-6

Jacob, Naomi 1884?-1964 ....DLB-191

Jacob, Piers Anthony Dillingham
 (see Anthony, Piers)

Jacobi, Friedrich Heinrich 1743-1819 .....DLB-94

Jacobi, Johann Georg 1740-1841 ....DLB-97

Jacobs, Joseph 1854-1916................DLB-141

Jacobs, W. W. 1863-1943 ....DLB-135

Jacobs, George W., and Company DLB-49

Jacobsen, Jørgen-Frantz 1900-1938 ......DLB-214

Jacobson, Dan 1929- DLB-14, 207

Jacobson, Howard 1942- DLB-207

Jacques de Vitry
 circa 1160/1170-1240................DLB-208

Jæger, Frank 1926-1977 ....DLB-214

Jaggard, William [publishing house] DLB-170

Jahier, Piero 1884-1966 ....DLB-114

Jahnn, Hans Henny 1894-1959 .....DLB-56, 124

Jakes, John 1932- Y-83

James, C. L. R. 1901-1989 ....DLB-125

James Dickey Tributes...................Y-97

James, George P. R. 1801-1860 ....DLB-116

James Gould Cozzens—A View from Afar....Y-97

James Gould Cozzens Case Re-opened Y-97

James Gould Cozzens: How to Read Him....Y-97

James, Henry
 1843-1916 .... DLB-12, 71, 74, 189; DS-13

James, John circa 1633-1729..............DLB-24

James Jones Papers in the Handy Writers' Colony
 Collection at the University of Illinois at
 Springfield.........................Y-98

The James Jones Society Y-92

James Laughlin Tributes Y-97

James, M. R. 1862-1936...........DLB-156, 201

James, Naomi 1949- DLB-204

James, P. D. 1920- DLB-87; DS-17

James, Thomas 1572?-1629...........DLB-213

James, Will 1892-1942................. DS-16

James Joyce Centenary: Dublin, 1982.......Y-82

James Joyce Conference..................Y-85

James VI of Scotland, I of England
 1566-1625 ....DLB-151, 172

James, U. P. [publishing house] DLB-49

Jameson, Anna 1794-1860 ....DLB-99, 166

Jameson, Fredric 1934- DLB-67

Jameson, J. Franklin 1859-1937 ....DLB-17

Jameson, Storm 1891-1986 ....DLB-36

Jančar, Drago 1948- DLB-181

Janés, Clara 1940- DLB-134

Janevski, Slavko 1920- DLB-181

Janvier, Thomas 1849-1913............DLB-202

Jaramillo, Cleofas M. 1878-1956 ....DLB-122

Jarman, Mark 1952- DLB-120

Jarrell, Randall 1914-1965............DLB-48, 52

Jarrold and Sons DLB-106

Jarry, Alfred 1873-1907 ....DLB-192

Jarves, James Jackson 1818-1888........DLB-189

Jasmin, Claude 1930- DLB-60

Jay, John 1745-1829....................DLB-31

Jean de Garlande (see John of Garland)

Jefferies, Richard 1848-1887 ....DLB-98, 141

Jeffers, Lance 1919-1985 ....DLB-41

Jeffers, Robinson 1887-1962..........DLB-45, 212

Jefferson, Thomas 1743-1826.........DLB-31, 183

Jégé 1866-1940......................DLB-215

Jelinek, Elfriede 1946- DLB-85

Jellicoe, Ann 1927- DLB-13

Jenkins, Elizabeth 1905- DLB-155

Jenkins, Robin 1912- DLB-14

Jenkins, William Fitzgerald (see Leinster, Murray)

Jenkins, Herbert, Limited DLB-112

Jennings, Elizabeth 1926- DLB-27

Jens, Walter 1923- DLB-69

Jensen, Johannes V. 1873-1950 ....DLB-214

Jensen, Merrill 1905-1980 ....DLB-17

Jensen, Thit 1876-1957 ....DLB-214

Jephson, Robert 1736-1803 ....DLB-89

Jerome, Jerome K. 1859-1927 ....DLB-10, 34, 135

Jerome, Judson 1927-1991 ....DLB-105

Jerrold, Douglas 1803-1857 ....DLB-158, 159

Jesse, F. Tennyson 1888-1958 ....DLB-77

Jewett, Sarah Orne 1849-1909........DLB-12, 74

Jewett, John P., and Company..........DLB-49

Cumulative Index

The Jewish Publication Society.......... DLB-49
Jewitt, John Rodgers 1783-1821 .... DLB-99
Jewsbury, Geraldine 1812-1880 .... DLB-21
Jewsbury, Maria Jane 1800-1833 .... DLB-199
Jhabvala, Ruth Prawer 1927- DLB-139, 194
Jiménez, Juan Ramón 1881-1958 ...... DLB-134
Joans, Ted 1928- DLB-16, 41
Jōha 1525-1602..................... DLB-203
Johannis de Garlandia (see John of Garland)
John, Eugenie (see Marlitt, E.)
John of Dumbleton circa 1310-circa 1349 .... DLB-115
John of Garland (Jean de Garlande, Johannis de Garlandia) circa 1195-circa 1272 .... DLB-208
John Edward Bruce: Three Documents ... DLB-50
John Hawkes: A Tribute Y-98
John O'Hara's Pottsville Journalism........ Y-88
John Steinbeck Research Center............ Y-85
John Updike on the Internet............... Y-97
John Webster: The Melbourne Manuscript....................... Y-86
Johns, Captain W. E. 1893-1968 .... DLB-160
Johnson, B. S. 1933-1973 .... DLB-14, 40
Johnson, Charles 1679-1748 .... DLB-84
Johnson, Charles R. 1948- DLB-33
Johnson, Charles S. 1893-1956...... DLB-51, 91
Johnson, Denis 1949- DLB-120
Johnson, Diane 1934- Y-80
Johnson, Dorothy M. 1905–1984....... DLB-206
Johnson, Edgar 1901- DLB-103
Johnson, Edward 1598-1672 .... DLB-24
Johnson E. Pauline (Tekahionwake) 1861-1913......................DLB-175
Johnson, Fenton 1888-1958 .... DLB-45, 50
Johnson, Georgia Douglas 1886-1966 .... DLB-51
Johnson, Gerald W. 1890-1980 .... DLB-29
Johnson, Helene 1907- DLB-51
Johnson, James Weldon 1871-1938 ...... DLB-51
Johnson, John H. 1918- DLB-137
Johnson, Linton Kwesi 1952- DLB-157
Johnson, Lionel 1867-1902 .... DLB-19
Johnson, Nunnally 1897-1977 .... DLB-26
Johnson, Owen 1878-1952 .... Y-87
Johnson, Pamela Hansford 1912- DLB-15
Johnson, Pauline 1861-1913 .... DLB-92
Johnson, Ronald 1935- DLB-169
Johnson, Samuel 1696-1772 .... DLB-24
Johnson, Samuel 1709-1784 ....DLB-39, 95, 104, 142, 213
Johnson, Samuel 1822-1882 .... DLB-1
Johnson, Susanna 1730-1810........... DLB-200
Johnson, Uwe 1934-1984 .... DLB-75
Johnson, Benjamin [publishing house] DLB-49
Johnson, Benjamin, Jacob, and Robert [publishing house] DLB-49
Johnson, Jacob, and Company DLB-49

Johnson, Joseph [publishing house] DLB-154
Johnston, Annie Fellows 1863-1931 ...... DLB-42
Johnston, David Claypole 1798?-1865 ... DLB-188
Johnston, Basil H. 1929- DLB-60
Johnston, Denis 1901-1984............. DLB-10
Johnston, Ellen 1835-1873 .... DLB-199
Johnston, George 1913- DLB-88
Johnston, Sir Harry 1858-1927.........DLB-174
Johnston, Jennifer 1930- DLB-14
Johnston, Mary 1870-1936 .... DLB-9
Johnston, Richard Malcolm 1822-1898 ... DLB-74
Johnstone, Charles 1719?-1800?.......... DLB-39
Johst, Hanns 1890-1978 .... DLB-124
Jolas, Eugene 1894-1952............. DLB-4, 45
Jones, Alice C. 1853-1933 .... DLB-92
Jones, Charles C., Jr. 1831-1893......... DLB-30
Jones, D. G. 1929- DLB-53
Jones, David 1895-1974 .... DLB-20, 100
Jones, Diana Wynne 1934- DLB-161
Jones, Ebenezer 1820-1860............. DLB-32
Jones, Ernest 1819-1868 .... DLB-32
Jones, Gayl 1949- DLB-33
Jones, George 1800-1870 .... DLB-183
Jones, Glyn 1905- DLB-15
Jones, Gwyn 1907- DLB-15, 139
Jones, Henry Arthur 1851-1929 .... DLB-10
Jones, Hugh circa 1692-1760 .... DLB-24
Jones, James 1921-1977........DLB-2, 143; DS-17
Jones, Jenkin Lloyd 1911- DLB-127
Jones, John Beauchamp 1810-1866...... DLB-202
Jones, LeRoi (see Baraka, Amiri)
Jones, Lewis 1897-1939................ DLB-15
Jones, Madison 1925- DLB-152
Jones, Major Joseph (see Thompson, William Tappan)
Jones, Preston 1936-1979 .... DLB-7
Jones, Rodney 1950- DLB-120
Jones, Sir William 1746-1794 .... DLB-109
Jones, William Alfred 1817-1900......... DLB-59
Jones's Publishing House DLB-49
Jong, Erica 1942- DLB-2, 5, 28, 152
Jonke, Gert F. 1946- DLB-85
Jonson, Ben 1572?-1637 .... DLB-62, 121
Jordan, June 1936- DLB-38
Joseph, Jenny 1932- DLB-40
Joseph, Michael, Limited DLB-112
Josephson, Matthew 1899-1978 .... DLB-4
Josephus, Flavius 37-100 ....DLB-176
Josiah Allen's Wife (see Holley, Marietta)
Josipovici, Gabriel 1940- DLB-14
Josselyn, John ?-1675 .... DLB-24
Joudry, Patricia 1921- DLB-88
Jovine, Giuseppe 1922- DLB-128
Joyaux, Philippe (see Sollers, Philippe)

Joyce, Adrien (see Eastman, Carol)
A Joyce (Con)Text: Danis Rose and the Remaking of Ulysses.................... Y-97
Joyce, James 1882-1941 ......DLB-10, 19, 36, 162
Jozsef, Attila 1905-1937................. DLB-215
Judd, Sylvester 1813-1853 .... DLB-1
Judd, Orange, Publishing Company...... DLB-49
Judith circa 930..................... DLB-146
Julian of Norwich 1342-circa 1420 ..... DLB-1146
Julian Symons at Eighty Y-92
Julius Caesar 100 B.C.-44 B.C......... DLB-211
June, Jennie (see Croly, Jane Cunningham)
Jung, Franz 1888-1963 .... DLB-118
Jünger, Ernst 1895- DLB-56
Der jüngere Titurel circa 1275 .... DLB-138
Jung-Stilling, Johann Heinrich 1740-1817..................... DLB-94
Justice, Donald 1925- Y-83
Juvenal circa A.D. 60-circa A.D. 130 .... DLB-211
The Juvenile Library (see Godwin, M. J., and Company)

K

Kacew, Romain (see Gary, Romain)
Kafka, Franz 1883-1924 .... DLB-81
Kahn, Roger 1927- DLB-171
Kaikō Takeshi 1939-1989................ DLB-182
Kaiser, Georg 1878-1945 .... DLB-124
Kaiserchronik circca 1147.............. DLB-148
Kaleb, Vjekoslav 1905- DLB-181
Kalechofsky, Roberta 1931- DLB-28
Kaler, James Otis 1848-1912 .... DLB-12
Kames, Henry Home, Lord 1696-1782.................... DLB-31, 104
Kamo no Chōmei (Kamo no Nagaakira) 1153 or 1155-1216................ DLB-203
Kamo no Nagaakira (see Kamo no Chōmei)
Kampmann, Christian 1939-1988 .... DLB-214
Kandel, Lenore 1932- DLB-16
Kanin, Garson 1912- DLB-7
Kant, Hermann 1926- DLB-75
Kant, Immanuel 1724-1804 .... DLB-94
Kantemir, Antiokh Dmitrievich 1708-1744..................... DLB-150
Kantor, MacKinlay 1904-1977 .... DLB-9, 102
Kanze Kōjirō Nobumitsu 1435-1516 .... DLB-203
Kanze Motokiyo (see Zeimi)
Kaplan, Fred 1937- DLB-111
Kaplan, Johanna 1942- DLB-28
Kaplan, Justin 1925- DLB-111
Kapnist, Vasilii Vasilevich 1758?-1823 ... DLB-150
Karadžić, Vuk Stefanović 1787-1864 .....DLB-147
Karamzin, Nikolai Mikhailovich 1766-1826.................... DLB-150
Karinthy, Frigyes 1887-1938........... DLB-215
Karsch, Anna Louisa 1722-1791 .... DLB-97

Kasack, Hermann 1896-1966............DLB-69
Kasai, Zenzō 1887-1927..............DLB-180
Kaschnitz, Marie Luise 1901-1974........DLB-69
Kassák, Lajos 1887-1967.............DLB-215
Kaštelan, Jure 1919-1990.............DLB-147
Kästner, Erich 1899-1974..............DLB-56
Katenin, Pavel Aleksandrovich
   1792-1853.....................DLB-205
Kattan, Naim 1928-...................DLB-53
Katz, Steve 1935-.......................Y-83
Kauffman, Janet 1945-..................Y-86
Kauffmann, Samuel 1898-1971.........DLB-127
Kaufman, Bob 1925-..............DLB-16, 41
Kaufman, George S. 1889-1961..........DLB-7
Kavanagh, P. J. 1931-.................DLB-40
Kavanagh, Patrick 1904-1967......DLB-15, 20
Kawabata, Yasunari 1899-1972.........DLB-180
Kaye-Smith, Sheila 1887-1956..........DLB-36
Kazin, Alfred 1915-....................DLB-67
Keane, John B. 1928-..................DLB-13
Keary, Annie 1825-1879...............DLB-163
Keating, H. R. F. 1926-................DLB-87
Keats, Ezra Jack 1916-1983............DLB-61
Keats, John 1795-1821..........DLB-96, 110
Keble, John 1792-1866.............DLB-32, 55
Keeble, John 1944-.....................Y-83
Keeffe, Barrie 1945-...................DLB-13
Keeley, James 1867-1934...............DLB-25
W. B. Keen, Cooke and Company.......DLB-49
Keillor, Garrison 1942-..................Y-87
Keith, Marian 1874?-1961..............DLB-92
Keller, Gary D. 1943-..................DLB-82
Keller, Gottfried 1819-1890............DLB-129
Kelley, Edith Summers 1884-1956........DLB-9
Kelley, William Melvin 1937-...........DLB-33
Kellogg, Ansel Nash 1832-1886.........DLB-23
Kellogg, Steven 1941-..................DLB-61
Kelly, George 1887-1974................DLB-7
Kelly, Hugh 1739-1777.................DLB-89
Kelly, Robert 1935-...........DLB-5, 130, 165
Kelly, Piet and Company...............DLB-49
Kelman, James 1946-.................DLB-194
Kelmscott Press......................DLB-112
Kemble, E. W. 1861-1933..............DLB-188
Kemble, Fanny 1809-1893..............DLB-32
Kemelman, Harry 1908-...............DLB-28
Kempe, Margery circa 1373-1438.......DLB-146
Kempner, Friederike 1836-1904........DLB-129
Kempowski, Walter 1929-..............DLB-75
Kendall, Claude [publishing company]....DLB-46
Kendell, George 1809-1867.............DLB-43
Kenedy, P. J., and Sons................DLB-49
Kenkō circa 1283-circa 1352..........DLB-203
Kennan, George 1845-1924............DLB-189

Kennedy, Adrienne 1931-..............DLB-38
Kennedy, John Pendleton 1795-1870......DLB-3
Kennedy, Leo 1907-....................DLB-88
Kennedy, Margaret 1896-1967..........DLB-36
Kennedy, Patrick 1801-1873...........DLB-159
Kennedy, Richard S. 1920-............DLB-111
Kennedy, William 1928-........DLB-143; Y-85
Kennedy, X. J. 1929-...................DLB-5
Kennelly, Brendan 1936-...............DLB-40
Kenner, Hugh 1923-...................DLB-67
Kennerley, Mitchell [publishing house]...DLB-46
Kenneth Dale McCormick Tributes........Y-97
Kenny, Maurice 1929-................DLB-175
Kent, Frank R. 1877-1958..............DLB-29
Kenyon, Jane 1947-..................DLB-120
Keough, Hugh Edmund 1864-1912.....DLB-171
Keppler and Schwartzmann............DLB-49
Ker, John, third Duke of Roxburghe
   1740-1804.....................DLB-213
Ker, N. R. 1908-1982.................DLB-201
Kerlan, Irvin 1912-1963...............DLB-187
Kern, Jerome 1885-1945..............DLB-187
Kerner, Justinus 1776-1862............DLB-90
Kerouac, Jack 1922-1969.......DLB-2, 16; DS-3
The Jack Kerouac Revival................Y-95
Kerouac, Jan 1952-....................DLB-16
Kerr, Orpheus C. (see Newell, Robert Henry)
Kerr, Charles H., and Company.........DLB-49
Kesey, Ken 1935-.............DLB-2, 16, 206
Kessel, Joseph 1898-1979..............DLB-72
Kessel, Martin 1901-..................DLB-56
Kesten, Hermann 1900-...............DLB-56
Keun, Irmgard 1905-1982..............DLB-69
Key and Biddle.......................DLB-49
Keynes, Sir Geoffrey 1887-1982........DLB-201
Keynes, John Maynard 1883-1946.......DS-10
Keyserling, Eduard von 1855-1918......DLB-66
Khan, Ismith 1925-..................DLB-125
Khaytov, Nikolay 1919-...............DLB-181
Khemnitser, Ivan Ivanovich
   1745-1784.....................DLB-150
Kheraskov, Mikhail Matveevich
   1733-1807.....................DLB-150
Khomiakov, Aleksei Stepanovich
   1804-1860.....................DLB-205
Khristov, Boris 1945-.................DLB-181
Khvostov, Dmitrii Ivanovich
   1757-1835.....................DLB-150
Kidd, Adam 1802?-1831................DLB-99
Kidd, William [publishing house].......DLB-106
Kidder, Tracy 1945-..................DLB-185
Kiely, Benedict 1919-.................DLB-15
Kieran, John 1892-1981...............DLB-171
Kiggins and Kellogg...................DLB-49
Kiley, Jed 1889-1962....................DLB-4
Kilgore, Bernard 1908-1967...........DLB-127

Killens, John Oliver 1916-.............DLB-33
Killigrew, Anne 1660-1685............DLB-131
Killigrew, Thomas 1612-1683...........DLB-58
Kilmer, Joyce 1886-1918...............DLB-45
Kilwardby, Robert circa 1215-1279....DLB-115
Kimball, Richard Burleigh 1816-1892....DLB-202
Kincaid, Jamaica 1949-...............DLB-157
King, Charles 1844-1933..............DLB-186
King, Clarence 1842-1901..............DLB-12
King, Florence 1936.....................Y-85
King, Francis 1923-...............DLB-15, 139
King, Grace 1852-1932.............DLB-12, 78
King, Harriet Hamilton 1840-1920.....DLB-199
King, Henry 1592-1669...............DLB-126
King, Stephen 1947-.............DLB-143; Y-80
King, Thomas 1943-..................DLB-175
King, Woodie, Jr. 1937-...............DLB-38
King, Solomon [publishing house].......DLB-49
Kinglake, Alexander William
   1809-1891..................DLB-55, 166
Kingsley, Charles
   1819-1875........DLB-21, 32, 163, 178, 190
Kingsley, Mary Henrietta 1862-1900....DLB-174
Kingsley, Henry 1830-1876............DLB-21
Kingsley, Sidney 1906-.................DLB-7
Kingsmill, Hugh 1889-1949...........DLB-149
Kingsolver, Barbara 1955-............DLB-206
Kingston, Maxine Hong
   1940-...............DLB-173, 212; Y-80
Kingston, William Henry Giles
   1814-1880.....................DLB-163
Kinnan, Mary Lewis 1763-1848.........DLB-200
Kinnell, Galway 1927-...........DLB-5; Y-87
Kinsella, Thomas 1928-................DLB-27
Kipling, Rudyard
   1865-1936..........DLB-19, 34, 141, 156
Kipphardt, Heinar 1922-1982.........DLB-124
Kirby, William 1817-1906..............DLB-99
Kircher, Athanasius 1602-1680........DLB-164
Kireevsky, Ivan Vasil'evich
   1806-1856.....................DLB-198
Kireevsky, Petr Vasil'evich
   1808-1856.....................DLB-205
Kirk, Hans 1898-1962................DLB-214
Kirk, John Foster 1824-1904............DLB-79
Kirkconnell, Watson 1895-1977........DLB-68
Kirkland, Caroline M.
   1801-1864...........DLB-3, 73, 74; DS-13
Kirkland, Joseph 1830-1893............DLB-12
Kirkman, Francis [publishing house]....DLB-170
Kirkpatrick, Clayton 1915-............DLB-127
Kirkup, James 1918-...................DLB-27
Kirouac, Conrad (see Marie-Victorin, Frère)
Kirsch, Sarah 1935-...................DLB-75
Kirst, Hans Hellmut 1914-1989.........DLB-69
Kiš, Danilo 1935-1989................DLB-181
Kita Morio 1927-....................DLB-182

Kitcat, Mabel Greenhow 1859-1922 ..... DLB-135
Kitchin, C. H. B. 1895-1967 .... DLB-77
Kittredge, William 1932- DLB-212
Kiukhel'beker, Vil'gel'm Karlovich 1797-1846 .... DLB-205
Kizer, Carolyn 1925- DLB-5, 169
Klabund 1890-1928 .... DLB-66
Klaj, Johann 1616-1656 .... DLB-164
Klappert, Peter 1942- DLB-5
Klass, Philip (see Tenn, William)
Klein, A. M. 1909-1972................ DLB-68
Kleist, Ewald von 1715-1759 .... DLB-97
Kleist, Heinrich von 1777-1811 .... DLB-90
Klinger, Friedrich Maximilian 1752-1831 .... DLB-94
Klopstock, Friedrich Gottlieb 1724-1803 .... DLB-97
Klopstock, Meta 1728-1758 .... DLB-97
Kluge, Alexander 1932- DLB-75
Knapp, Joseph Palmer 1864-1951 .... DLB-91
Knapp, Samuel Lorenzo 1783-1838 ...... DLB-59
Knapton, J. J. and P. [publishing house] DLB-154
Kniazhnin, Iakov Borisovich 1740-1791 .... DLB-150
Knickerbocker, Diedrich (see Irving, Washington)
Knigge, Adolph Franz Friedrich Ludwig, Freiherr von 1752-1796 .... DLB-94
Knight, Damon 1922- DLB-8
Knight, Etheridge 1931-1992 .... DLB-41
Knight, John S. 1894-1981 .... DLB-29
Knight, Sarah Kemble 1666-1727 .... DLB-24, 200
Knight, Charles, and Company DLB-106
Knight-Bruce, G. W. H. 1852-1896 ......DLB-174
Knister, Raymond 1899-1932........... DLB-68
Knoblock, Edward 1874-1945 .... DLB-10
Knopf, Alfred A. 1892-1984 .... Y-84
Knopf, Alfred A. [publishing house]...... DLB-46
Knorr von Rosenroth, Christian 1636-1689 .... DLB-168
"Knots into Webs: Some Autobiographical Sources," by Dabney Stuart DLB-105
Knowles, John 1926- DLB-6
Knox, Frank 1874-1944 .... DLB-29
Knox, John circa 1514-1572 .... DLB-132
Knox, John Armoy 1850-1906 .... DLB-23
Knox, Ronald Arbuthnott 1888-1957 ..... DLB-77
Knox, Thomas Wallace 1835-1896 ...... DLB-189
Kobayashi, Takiji 1903-1933 .... DLB-180
Kober, Arthur 1900-1975 .... DLB-11
Kocbek, Edvard 1904-1981 .... DLB-147
Koch, Howard 1902- DLB-26
Koch, Kenneth 1925- DLB-5
Kōda, Rohan 1867-1947 .... DLB-180
Koenigsberg, Moses 1879-1945.......... DLB-25
Koeppen, Wolfgang 1906-1996 .... DLB-69
Koertge, Ronald 1940- DLB-105

Koestler, Arthur 1905-1983 .... Y-83
Kohn, John S. Van E. 1906-1976 and Papantonio, Michael 1907-1978 ..... DLB-187
Kokoschka, Oskar 1886-1980 .... DLB-124
Kolb, Annette 1870-1967 .... DLB-66
Kolbenheyer, Erwin Guido 1878-1962................ DLB-66, 124
Kolleritsch, Alfred 1931- DLB-85
Kolodny, Annette 1941- DLB-67
Kol'tsov, Aleksei Vasil'evich 1809-1842 .... DLB-205
Komarov, Matvei circa 1730-1812 ..... DLB-150
Komroff, Manuel 1890-1974............ DLB-4
Komunyakaa, Yusef 1947- DLB-120
Koneski, Blaže 1921-1993............ DLB-181
Konigsburg, E. L. 1930- DLB-52
Konparu Zenchiku 1405-1468? DLB-203
Konrad von Würzburg circa 1230-1287 .... DLB-138
Konstantinov, Aleko 1863-1897 .... DLB-147
Kooser, Ted 1939- DLB-105
Kopit, Arthur 1937- DLB-7
Kops, Bernard 1926?- DLB-13
Kornbluth, C. M. 1923-1958 .... DLB-8
Körner, Theodor 1791-1813............ DLB-90
Kornfeld, Paul 1889-1942............. DLB-118
Kosinski, Jerzy 1933-1991 ....DLB-2; Y-82
Kosmač, Ciril 1910-1980 .... DLB-181
Kosovel, Srečko 1904-1926 .... DLB-147
Kostrov, Ermil Ivanovich 1755-1796..... DLB-150
Kotzebue, August von 1761-1819 .... DLB-94
Kotzwinkle, William 1938- DLB-173
Kovačić, Ante 1854-1889 .... DLB-147
Kovič, Kajetan 1931- DLB-181
Kozlov, Ivan Ivanovich 1779-1840 ..... DLB-205
Kraf, Elaine 1946- Y-81
Kramer, Jane 1938- DLB-185
Kramer, Mark 1944- DLB-185
Kranjčević, Silvije Strahimir 1865-1908 .... DLB-147
Krasko, Ivan 1876-1958 .... DLB-215
Krasna, Norman 1909-1984............ DLB-26
Kraus, Hans Peter 1907-1988 .... DLB-187
Kraus, Karl 1874-1936 .... DLB-118
Krauss, Ruth 1911-1993.............. DLB-52
Kreisel, Henry 1922- DLB-88
Kreuder, Ernst 1903-1972............. DLB-69
Kreymborg, Alfred 1883-1966 .... DLB-4, 54
Krieger, Murray 1923- DLB-67
Krim, Seymour 1922-1989 .... DLB-16
Kristensen, Tom 1893-1974 .... DLB-214
Krleža, Miroslav 1893-1981 .... DLB-147
Krock, Arthur 1886-1974 .... DLB-29
Kroetsch, Robert 1927- DLB-53
Krúdy, Gyula 1878-1933 .... DLB-215
Krutch, Joseph Wood 1893-1970 .... DLB-63, 206

Krylov, Ivan Andreevich 1769-1844..... DLB-150
Kubin, Alfred 1877-1959............... DLB-81
Kubrick, Stanley 1928-1999 .... DLB-26
Kudrun circa 1230-1240............... DLB-138
Kuffstein, Hans Ludwig von 1582-1656 .... DLB-164
Kuhlmann, Quirinus 1651-1689........ DLB-168
Kuhnau, Johann 1660-1722 .... DLB-168
Kukol'nik, Nestor Vasil'evich 1809-1868 .... DLB-205
Kukučín, Martin 1860-1928 .... DLB-215
Kumin, Maxine 1925- DLB-5
Kuncewicz, Maria 1895-1989 .... DLB-215
Kunene, Mazisi 1930- DLB-117
Kunikida, Doppo 1869-1908 .... DLB-180
Kunitz, Stanley 1905- DLB-48
Kunjufu, Johari M. (see Amini, Johari M.)
Kunnert, Gunter 1929- DLB-75
Kunze, Reiner 1933- DLB-75
Kupferberg, Tuli 1923- DLB-16
Kurahashi Yumiko 1935- DLB-182
Kureishi, Hanif 1954- DLB-194
Kürnberger, Ferdinand 1821-1879 ..... DLB-129
Kurz, Isolde 1853-1944................ DLB-66
Kusenberg, Kurt 1904-1983 .... DLB-69
Kuttner, Henry 1915-1958 .... DLB-8
Kyd, Thomas 1558-1594 .... DLB-62
Kyffin, Maurice circa 1560?-1598.. DLB-136
Kyger, Joanne 1934- DLB-16
Kyne, Peter B. 1880-1957.............. DLB-78
Kyōgoku Tamekane 1254-1332 .... DLB-203

L

L. E. L. (see Landon, Letitia Elizabeth)
Laberge, Albert 1871-1960 .... DLB-68
Laberge, Marie 1950- DLB-60
Labiche, Eugène 1815-1888 .... DLB-192
La Capria, Raffaele 1922- DLB-196
Lacombe, Patrice (see Trullier-Lacombe, Joseph Patrice)
Lacretelle, Jacques de 1888-1985 .... DLB-65
Lacy, Sam 1903- DLB-171
Ladd, Joseph Brown 1764-1786 .... DLB-37
La Farge, Oliver 1901-1963 .... DLB-9
Lafferty, R. A. 1914- DLB-8
La Flesche, Francis 1857-1932..........DLB-175
Lagorio, Gina 1922- DLB-196
La Guma, Alex 1925-1985 ....DLB-117
Lahaise, Guillaume (see Delahaye, Guy)
Lahontan, Louis-Armand de Lom d'Arce, Baron de 1666-1715? DLB-99
Laing, Kojo 1946- DLB-157
Laird, Carobeth 1895- Y-82
Laird and Lee.................... DLB-49
Lalić, Ivan V. 1931-1996 .... DLB-181

Lalić, Mihailo 1914-1992..............DLB-181
Lalonde, Michèle 1937- DLB-60
Lamantia, Philip 1927- DLB-16
Lamb, Charles 1775-1834 ...... DLB-93, 107, 163
Lamb, Lady Caroline 1785-1828.........DLB-116
Lamb, Mary 1764-1874 ....DLB-163
Lambert, Betty 1933-1983 ....DLB-60
Lamming, George 1927- DLB-125
L'Amour, Louis 1908-1988 .... DLB-206; Y-80
Lampman, Archibald 1861-1899 ....DLB-92
Lamson, Wolffe and Company DLB-49
Lancer Books.........................DLB-46
Landesman, Jay 1919- and
  Landesman, Fran 1927- DLB-16
Landolfi, Tommaso 1908-1979 ....DLB-177
Landon, Letitia Elizabeth 1802-1838......DLB-96
Landor, Walter Savage 1775-1864.... DLB-93, 107
Landry, Napoléon-P. 1884-1956..........DLB-92
Lane, Charles 1800-1870 ....DLB-1
Lane, Laurence W. 1890-1967............DLB-91
Lane, M. Travis 1934- DLB-60
Lane, Patrick 1939- DLB-53
Lane, Pinkie Gordon 1923- DLB-41
Lane, John, Company DLB-49
Laney, Al 1896-1988 ....DLB-4, 171
Lang, Andrew 1844-1912 ...... DLB-98, 141, 184
Langevin, André 1927- DLB-60
Langgässer, Elisabeth 1899-1950.........DLB-69
Langhorne, John 1735-1779 ....DLB-109
Langland, William
  circa 1330-circa 1400.................DLB-146
Langton, Anna 1804-1893 ....DLB-99
Lanham, Edwin 1904-1979 ....DLB-4
Lanier, Sidney 1842-1881 ....DLB-64; DS-13
Lanyer, Aemilia 1569-1645 ....DLB-121
Lapointe, Gatien 1931-1983..............DLB-88
Lapointe, Paul-Marie 1929- DLB-88
Lardner, John 1912-1960................DLB-171
Lardner, Ring
  1885-1933 .... DLB-11, 25, 86, 171; DS-16
Lardner, Ring, Jr. 1915- DLB-26
Lardner 100: Ring Lardner
  Centennial Symposium...............Y-85
Larkin, Philip 1922-1985 ....DLB-27
La Roche, Sophie von 1730-1807.........DLB-94
La Rocque, Gilbert 1943-1984............DLB-60
Laroque de Roquebrune, Robert (see Roquebrune,
  Robert de)
Larrick, Nancy 1910- DLB-61
Larsen, Nella 1893-1964 ....DLB-51
La Sale, Antoine de
  circa 1386-1460/1467 ....DLB-208
Lasker-Schüler, Else 1869-1945......DLB-66, 124
Lasnier, Rina 1915- DLB-88
Lassalle, Ferdinand 1825-1864..........DLB-129
Latham, Robert 1912-1995 ....DLB-201

Lathrop, Dorothy P. 1891-1980 ....DLB-22
Lathrop, George Parsons 1851-1898......DLB-71
Lathrop, John, Jr. 1772-1820 ....DLB-37
Latimer, Hugh 1492?-1555 ....DLB-136
Latimore, Jewel Christine McLawler (see Amini,
  Johari M.)
Latymer, William 1498-1583............DLB-132
Laube, Heinrich 1806-1884 ....DLB-133
Laud, William 1573-1645 ....DLB-213
Laughlin, James 1914- DLB-48
Laumer, Keith 1925- DLB-8
Lauremberg, Johann 1590-1658 ....DLB-164
Laurence, Margaret 1926-1987 ....DLB-53
Laurentius von Schnüffis 1633-1702 .....DLB-168
Laurents, Arthur 1918- DLB-26
Laurie, Annie (see Black, Winifred)
Laut, Agnes Christiana 1871-1936........DLB-92
Lauterbach, Ann 1942- DLB-193
Lavater, Johann Kaspar 1741-1801 ......DLB-97
Lavin, Mary 1912- DLB-15
Law, John (see Harkness, Margaret)
Lawes, Henry 1596-1662................DLB-126
Lawless, Anthony (see MacDonald, Philip)
Lawrence, D. H.
  1885-1930 ...... DLB-10, 19, 36, 98, 162, 195
Lawrence, David 1888-1973 ....DLB-29
Lawrence, Seymour 1926-1994 ....Y-94
Lawrence, T. E. 1888-1935 ....DLB-195
Lawson, George 1598-1678 ....DLB-213
Lawson, John ?-1711 ....DLB-24
Lawson, Robert 1892-1957 ....DLB-22
Lawson, Victor F. 1850-1925 ....DLB-25
Layard, Sir Austen Henry
  1817-1894 ....DLB-166
Layton, Irving 1912- DLB-88
LaZamon flourished circa 1200..........DLB-146
Lazarević, Laza K. 1851-1890 ....DLB-147
Lazarus, George 1904-1997 ....DLB-201
Lazhechnikov, Ivan Ivanovich
  1792-1869 ....DLB-198
Lea, Henry Charles 1825-1909 ....DLB-47
Lea, Sydney 1942- DLB-120
Lea, Tom 1907- DLB-6
Leacock, John 1729-1802................DLB-31
Leacock, Stephen 1869-1944 ....DLB-92
Lead, Jane Ward 1623-1704............DLB-131
Leadenhall Press DLB-106
Leapor, Mary 1722-1746 ....DLB-109
Lear, Edward 1812-1888........ DLB-32, 163, 166
Leary, Timothy 1920-1996 ....DLB-16
Leary, W. A., and Company............DLB-49
Léautaud, Paul 1872-1956 ....DLB-65
Leavitt, David 1961- DLB-130
Leavitt and Allen DLB-49
Le Blond, Mrs. Aubrey 1861-1934 ......DLB-174

le Carré, John 1931- DLB-87
Lécavelé, Roland (see Dorgeles, Roland)
Lechlitner, Ruth 1901- DLB-48
Leclerc, Félix 1914- DLB-60
Le Clézio, J. M. G. 1940- DLB-83
Lectures on Rhetoric and Belles Lettres (1783),
  by Hugh Blair [excerpts]............DLB-31
Leder, Rudolf (see Hermlin, Stephan)
Lederer, Charles 1910-1976..............DLB-26
Ledwidge, Francis 1887-1917 ....DLB-20
Lee, Dennis 1939- DLB-53
Lee, Don L. (see Madhubuti, Haki R.)
Lee, George W. 1894-1976 ....DLB-51
Lee, Harper 1926- DLB-6
Lee, Harriet (1757-1851) and
  Lee, Sophia (1750-1824) DLB-39
Lee, Laurie 1914- DLB-27
Lee, Li-Young 1957- DLB-165
Lee, Manfred B. (see Dannay, Frederic, and
  Manfred B. Lee)
Lee, Nathaniel circa 1645 - 1692 ....DLB-80
Lee, Sir Sidney 1859-1926......... DLB-149, 184
Lee, Sir Sidney, "Principles of Biography," in
  Elizabethan and Other Essays DLB-149
Lee, Vernon
  1856-1935 .... DLB-57, 153, 156, 174, 178
Lee and Shepard DLB-49
Le Fanu, Joseph Sheridan
  1814-1873 .... DLB-21, 70, 159, 178
Leffland, Ella 1931- Y-84
le Fort, Gertrud von 1876-1971 ....DLB-66
Le Gallienne, Richard 1866-1947 ....DLB-4
Legaré, Hugh Swinton 1797-1843 ... DLB-3, 59, 73
Legaré, James M. 1823-1859 ....DLB-3
The Legends of the Saints and a Medieval
  Christian Worldview DLB-148
Léger, Antoine-J. 1880-1950 ....DLB-88
Le Guin, Ursula K. 1929- DLB-8, 52
Lehman, Ernest 1920- DLB-44
Lehmann, John 1907- DLB-27, 100
Lehmann, Rosamond 1901-1990.........DLB-15
Lehmann, Wilhelm 1882-1968 ....DLB-56
Lehmann, John, Limited DLB-112
Leiber, Fritz 1910-1992 ....DLB-8
Leibniz, Gottfried Wilhelm 1646-1716....DLB-168
Leicester University Press DLB-112
Leigh, W. R. 1866-1955................DLB-188
Leinster, Murray 1896-1975 ....DLB-8
Leisewitz, Johann Anton 1752-1806......DLB-94
Leitch, Maurice 1933- DLB-14
Leithauser, Brad 1943- DLB-120
Leland, Charles G. 1824-1903..........DLB-11
Leland, John 1503?-1552..............DLB-136
Lemay, Pamphile 1837-1918 ....DLB-99
Lemelin, Roger 1919- DLB-88
Lemercier, Louis-Jean-Népomucène
  1771-1840 ....DLB-192

Lemon, Mark 1809-1870 .... DLB-163

Le Moine, James MacPherson 1825-1912. .... DLB-99

Le Moyne, Jean 1913- DLB-88

Lemperly, Paul 1858-1939 .... DLB-187

L'Engle, Madeleine 1918- DLB-52

Lennart, Isobel 1915-1971. .... DLB-44

Lennox, Charlotte 1729 or 1730-1804 .... DLB-39

Lenox, James 1800-1880. .... DLB-140

Lenski, Lois 1893-1974. .... DLB-22

Lenz, Hermann 1913- DLB-69

Lenz, J. M. R. 1751-1792. .... DLB-94

Lenz, Siegfried 1926- DLB-75

Leonard, Elmore 1925- DLB-173

Leonard, Hugh 1926- DLB-13

Leonard, William Ellery 1876-1944 ..... DLB-54

Leonowens, Anna 1834-1914 .... DLB-99, 166

LePan, Douglas 1914- DLB-88

Leprohon, Rosanna Eleanor 1829-1879 ... DLB-99

Le Queux, William 1864-1927 .... DLB-70

Lermontov, Mikhail Iur'evich 1814-1841. .... DLB-205

Lerner, Max 1902-1992 .... DLB-29

Lernet-Holenia, Alexander 1897-1976 ..... DLB-85

Le Rossignol, James 1866-1969 .... DLB-92

Lescarbot, Marc circa 1570-1642 .... DLB-99

LeSeur, William Dawson 1840-1917 ..... DLB-92

LeSieg, Theo. (see Geisel, Theodor Seuss)

Leslie, Doris before 1902-1982 .... DLB-191

Leslie, Eliza 1787-1858 .... DLB-202

Leslie, Frank 1821-1880 .... DLB-43, 79

Leslie, Frank, Publishing House DLB-49

Leśmian, Bolesław 1878-1937 .... DLB-215

Lesperance, John 1835?-1891 .... DLB-99

Lessing, Bruno 1870-1940. .... DLB-28

Lessing, Doris 1919- DLB-15, 139; Y-85

Lessing, Gotthold Ephraim 1729-1781 .... DLB-97

Lettau, Reinhard 1929- DLB-75

Letter from Japan Y-94, Y-98

Letter from London Y-96

Letter to [Samuel] Richardson on *Clarissa* (1748), by Henry Fielding DLB-39

A Letter to the Editor of *The Irish Times* Y-97

Lever, Charles 1806-1872. .... DLB-21

Leverson, Ada 1862-1933. .... DLB-153

Levertov, Denise 1923- DLB-5, 165

Levi, Peter 1931- DLB-40

Levi, Primo 1919-1987 .... DLB-177

Levien, Sonya 1888-1960 .... DLB-44

Levin, Meyer 1905-1981 .... DLB-9, 28; Y-81

Levine, Norman 1923- DLB-88

Levine, Philip 1928- DLB-5

Levis, Larry 1946- DLB-120

Levy, Amy 1861-1889 .... DLB-156

Levy, Benn Wolfe 1900-1973 .... DLB-13; Y-81

Lewald, Fanny 1811-1889 .... DLB-129

Lewes, George Henry 1817-1878 .... DLB-55, 144

Lewis, Agnes Smith 1843-1926. .... DLB-174

Lewis, Alfred H. 1857-1914 .... DLB-25, 186

Lewis, Alun 1915-1944. .... DLB-20, 162

The Lewis Carroll Centenary Y-98

Lewis, C. Day (see Day Lewis, C.)

Lewis, C. S. 1898-1963 .... DLB-15, 100, 160

Lewis, Charles B. 1842-1924 .... DLB-11

Lewis, Henry Clay 1825-1850 .... DLB-3

Lewis, Janet 1899- Y-87

Lewis, Matthew Gregory 1775-1818 .... DLB-39, 158, 178

Lewis, Meriwether 1774-1809 and Clark, William 1770-1838 ..... DLB-183, 186

Lewis, Norman 1908- DLB-204

Lewis, R. W. B. 1917- DLB-111

Lewis, Richard circa 1700-1734. .... DLB-24

Lewis, Sinclair 1885-1951 ...... DLB-9, 102; DS-1

Lewis, Wilmarth Sheldon 1895-1979 ..... DLB-140

Lewis, Wyndham 1882-1957 .... DLB-15

Lewisohn, Ludwig 1882-1955 ... DLB-4, 9, 28, 102

Leyendecker, J. C. 1874-1951 .... DLB-188

Lezama Lima, José 1910-1976 .... DLB-113

The Library of America DLB-46

The Licensing Act of 1737 .... DLB-84

Lichfield, Leonard I [publishing house] ...DLB-170

Lichtenberg, Georg Christoph 1742-1799 .... DLB-94

The Liddle Collection. Y-97

Lieb, Fred 1888-1980 .... DLB-171

Liebling, A. J. 1904-1963 .... DLB-4, 171

Lieutenant Murray (see Ballou, Maturin Murray)

The Life of James Dickey: A Lecture to the Friends of the Emory Libraries, by Henry Hart ... Y-98

Lighthall, William Douw 1857-1954 ...... DLB-92

Lilar, Françoise (see Mallet-Joris, Françoise)

Lillo, George 1691-1739 .... DLB-84

Lilly, J. K., Jr. 1893-1966 .... DLB-140

Lilly, Wait and Company DLB-49

Lily, William circa 1468-1522 .... DLB-132

Limited Editions Club DLB-46

Limón, Graciela 1938- DLB-209

Lincoln and Edmands. DLB-49

Lindesay, Ethel Forence (see Richardson, Henry Handel)

Lindsay, Alexander William, Twenty-fifth Earl of Crawford 1812-1880 .... DLB-184

Lindsay, Sir David circa 1485-1555 .... DLB-132

Lindsay, Jack 1900- Y-84

Lindsay, Lady (Caroline Blanche Elizabeth Fitzroy Lindsay) 1844-1912 .... DLB-199

Lindsay, Vachel 1879-1931. .... DLB-54

Linebarger, Paul Myron Anthony (see Smith, Cordwainer)

Link, Arthur S. 1920- DLB-17

Linn, John Blair 1777-1804 .... DLB-37

Lins, Osman 1¹24-1978. .... DLB-145

Linton, Eliza Lynn 1822-1898 .... DLB-18

Linton, William James 1812-1897 ...... DLB-32

Lintot, Barnaby Bernard [publishing house] DLB-170

Lion Books DLB-46

Lionni, Leo 1910- DLB-61

Lippard, George 1822-1854 .... DLB-202

Lippincott, Sara Jane Clarke 1823-1904 .... DLB-43

Lippincott, J. B., Company DLB-49

Lippmann, Walter 1889-1974. .... DLB-29

Lipton, Lawrence 1898-1975 .... DLB-16

Liscow, Christian Ludwig 1701-1760 ..... DLB-97

Lish, Gordon 1934- DLB-130

Lispector, Clarice 1925-1977 .... DLB-113

The Literary Chronicle and Weekly Review 1819-1828 .... DLB-110

Literary Documents: William Faulkner and the People-to-People Program Y-86

Literary Documents II: *Library Journal* Statements and Questionnaires from First Novelists Y-87

Literary Effects of World War II [British novel]. DLB-15

Literary Prizes [British] DLB-15

Literary Research Archives: The Humanities Research Center, University of Texas Y-82

Literary Research Archives II: Berg Collection of English and American Literature of the New York Public Library. Y-83

Literary Research Archives III: The Lilly Library. Y-84

Literary Research Archives IV: The John Carter Brown Library Y-85

Literary Research Archives V: Kent State Special Collections Y-86

Literary Research Archives VI: The Modern Literary Manuscripts Collection in the Special Collections of the Washington University Libraries. Y-87

Literary Research Archives VII: The University of Virginia Libraries. Y-91

Literary Research Archives VIII: The Henry E. Huntington Library. Y-92

Literary Societies Y-98

"Literary Style" (1857), by William Forsyth [excerpt] DLB-57

Literatura Chicanesca: The View From Without DLB-82

Literature at Nurse, or Circulating Morals (1885), by George Moore. DLB-18

Littell, Eliakim 1797-1870 .... DLB-79

Littell, Robert S. 1831-1896 .... DLB-79

Little, Brown and Company. DLB-49

Little Magazines and Newspapers DS-15

The Little Review 1914-1929 . . . . DS-15
Littlewood, Joan 1914- DLB-13
Lively, Penelope 1933- DLB-14, 161, 207
Liverpool University Press DLB-112
The Lives of the Poets. DLB-142
Livesay, Dorothy 1909- DLB-68
Livesay, Florence Randal 1874-1953 . . . . . . DLB-92
"Living in Ruin," by Gerald Stern DLB-105
Livings, Henry 1929- DLB-13
Livingston, Anne Howe 1763-1841 . . . DLB-37, 200
Livingston, Myra Cohn 1926- DLB-61
Livingston, William 1723-1790 . . . . DLB-31
Livingstone, David 1813-1873 . . . . DLB-166
Livy 59 B.C.-A.D. 17 . . . . DLB-211
Liyong, Taban lo (see Taban lo Liyong)
Lizárraga, Sylvia S. 1925- DLB-82
Llewellyn, Richard 1906-1983 . . . . DLB-15
Lloyd, Edward [publishing house] DLB-106
Lobel, Arnold 1933- DLB-61
Lochridge, Betsy Hopkins (see Fancher, Betsy)
Locke, David Ross 1833-1888 . . . . DLB-11, 23
Locke, John 1632-1704 . . . . DLB-31, 101, 213
Locke, Richard Adams 1800-1871 . . . . DLB-43
Locker-Lampson, Frederick
  1821-1895 . . . . DLB-35, 184
Lockhart, John Gibson
  1794-1854 . . . . DLB-110, 116 144
Lockridge, Ross, Jr. 1914-1948 . . . . DLB-143; Y-80
Locrine and Selimus DLB-62
Lodge, David 1935- DLB-14, 194
Lodge, George Cabot 1873-1909 . . . . DLB-54
Lodge, Henry Cabot 1850-1924 . . . . DLB-47
Lodge, Thomas 1558-1625 . . . . DLB-172
Loeb, Harold 1891-1974 . . . . DLB-4
Loeb, William 1905-1981 . . . . DLB-127
Lofting, Hugh 1886-1947 . . . . DLB-160
Logan, Deborah Norris 1761-1839 . . . . . . DLB-200
Logan, James 1674-1751 . . . . DLB-24, 140
Logan, John 1923- DLB-5
Logan, Martha Daniell 1704?-1779 . . . . . . DLB-200
Logan, William 1950- DLB-120
Logau, Friedrich von 1605-1655 . . . . DLB-164
Logue, Christopher 1926- DLB-27
Lohenstein, Daniel Casper von
  1635-1683 . . . . DLB-168
Lomonosov, Mikhail Vasil'evich
  1711-1765 . . . . DLB-150
London, Jack 1876-1916 . . . . . . DLB-8, 12, 78, 212
The London Magazine 1820-1829 . . . . DLB-110
Long, Haniel 1888-1956 . . . . DLB-45
Long, Ray 1878-1935 . . . . DLB-137
Long, H., and Brother DLB-49
Longfellow, Henry Wadsworth
  1807-1882 . . . . DLB-1, 59
Longfellow, Samuel 1819-1892 . . . . DLB-1
Longford, Elizabeth 1906- DLB-155

Longinus circa first century DLB-176
Longley, Michael 1939- DLB-40
Longman, T. [publishing house] DLB-154
Longmans, Green and Company DLB-49
Longmore, George 1793?-1867 . . . . DLB-99
Longstreet, Augustus Baldwin
  1790-1870 . . . . DLB-3, 11, 74
Longworth, D. [publishing house] DLB-49
Lonsdale, Frederick 1881-1954 . . . . DLB-10
A Look at the Contemporary Black Theatre
  Movement DLB-38
Loos, Anita 1893-1981 . . . . DLB-11, 26; Y-81
Lopate, Phillip 1943- Y-80
López, Diana (see Isabella, Ríos)
López, Josefina 1969- DLB-209
Loranger, Jean-Aubert 1896-1942 . . . . DLB-92
Lorca, Federico García 1898-1936 . . . . DLB-108
Lord, John Keast 1818-1872 . . . . DLB-99
The Lord Chamberlain's Office and Stage
  Censorship in England DLB-10
Lorde, Audre 1934-1992 . . . . DLB-41
Lorimer, George Horace 1867-1939 . . . . . . DLB-91
Loring, A. K. [publishing house] DLB-49
Loring and Mussey DLB-46
Lorris, Guillaume de (see Roman de la Rose)
Lossing, Benson J. 1813-1891 . . . . DLB-30
Lothar, Ernst 1890-1974 . . . . DLB-81
Lothrop, Harriet M. 1844-1924 . . . . DLB-42
Lothrop, D., and Company DLB-49
Loti, Pierre 1850-1923 . . . . DLB-123
Lotichius Secundus, Petrus 1528-1560 . . . DLB-179
Lott, Emeline ?-? DLB-166
The Lounger, no. 20 (1785), by Henry
  Mackenzie DLB-39
Louisiana State University Press Y-97
Lounsbury, Thomas R. 1838-1915 . . . . DLB-71
Louÿs, Pierre 1870-1925 . . . . DLB-123
Lovelace, Earl 1935- DLB-125
Lovelace, Richard 1618-1657 . . . . DLB-131
Lovell, Coryell and Company DLB-49
Lovell, John W., Company DLB-49
Lover, Samuel 1797-1868 . . . . DLB-159, 190
Lovesey, Peter 1936- DLB-87
Lovingood, Sut (see Harris, George Washington)
Low, Samuel 1765-? DLB-37
Lowell, Amy 1874-1925 . . . . DLB-54, 140
Lowell, James Russell
  1819-1891 . . . . DLB-1, 11, 64, 79, 189
Lowell, Robert 1917-1977 . . . . DLB-5, 169
Lowenfels, Walter 1897-1976 . . . . DLB-4
Lowndes, Marie Belloc 1868-1947 . . . . DLB-70
Lowndes, William Thomas 1798-1843 . . . DLB-184
Lownes, Humphrey [publishing house] . . . DLB-170
Lowry, Lois 1937- DLB-52
Lowry, Malcolm 1909-1957 . . . . DLB-15
Lowther, Pat 1935-1975 . . . . DLB-53

Loy, Mina 1882-1966 . . . . DLB-4, 54
Lozeau, Albert 1878-1924 . . . . DLB-92
Lubbock, Percy 1879-1965 . . . . DLB-149
Lucan A.D. 39-A.D. 65 . . . . DLB-211
Lucas, E. V. 1868-1938 . . . . DLB-98, 149, 153
Lucas, Fielding, Jr. [publishing house] DLB-49
Luce, Henry R. 1898-1967 . . . . DLB-91
Luce, John W., and Company DLB-46
Lucian circa 120-180 . . . . DLB-176
Lucie-Smith, Edward 1933- DLB-40
Lucilius circa 180 B.C.-102/101 B.C. DLB-211
Lucini, Gian Pietro 1867-1914 . . . . DLB-114
Lucretius circa 94 B.C.-circa 49 B.C. DLB-211
Luder, Peter circa 1415-1472 . . . . DLB-179
Ludlum, Robert 1927- Y-82
Ludus de Antichristo circa 1160 . . . . DLB-148
Ludvigson, Susan 1942- DLB-120
Ludwig, Jack 1922- DLB-60
Ludwig, Otto 1813-1865 . . . . DLB-129
Ludwigslied 881 or 882 . . . . DLB-148
Luera, Yolanda 1953- DLB-122
Luft, Lya 1938- DLB-145
Lugansky, Kazak Vladimir (see
  Dal', Vladimir Ivanovich)
Lukács, György 1885-1971 . . . . DLB-215
Luke, Peter 1919- DLB-13
Lummis, Charles F. 1859-1928 . . . . DLB-186
Lupton, F. M., Company DLB-49
Lupus of Ferrières circa 805-circa 862 . . . . DLB-148
Lurie, Alison 1926- DLB-2
Luther, Martin 1483-1546 . . . . DLB-179
Luzi, Mario 1914- DLB-128
L'vov, Nikolai Aleksandrovich
  1751-1803 . . . . DLB-150
Lyall, Gavin 1932- DLB-87
Lydgate, John circa 1370-1450 . . . . DLB-146
Lyly, John circa 1554-1606 . . . . DLB-62, 167
Lynch, Patricia 1898-1972 . . . . DLB-160
Lynch, Richard flourished 1596-1601 . . . . DLB-172
Lynd, Robert 1879-1949 . . . . DLB-98
Lyon, Matthew 1749-1822 . . . . DLB-43
Lysias circa 459 B.C.-circa 380 B.C. DLB-176
Lytle, Andrew 1902-1995 . . . . DLB-6; Y-95
Lytton, Edward (see Bulwer-Lytton, Edward)
Lytton, Edward Robert Bulwer
  1831-1891 . . . . DLB-32

M

Maass, Joachim 1901-1972 . . . . DLB-69
Mabie, Hamilton Wright 1845-1916 . . . . . . DLB-71
Mac A'Ghobhainn, Iain (see Smith, Iain Crichton)
MacArthur, Charles 1895-1956 . . . . . DLB-7, 25, 44
Macaulay, Catherine 1731-1791 . . . . DLB-104
Macaulay, David 1945- DLB-61
Macaulay, Rose 1881-1958 . . . . DLB-36

Macaulay, Thomas Babington 1800-1859 . . . . DLB-32, 55	Macmillan's English Men of Letters, First Series (1878-1892) DLB-144	Malerba, Luigi 1927- DLB-196
Macaulay Company DLB-46	MacNamara, Brinsley 1890-1963 . . . . DLB-10	Malet, Lucas 1852-1931 . . . . DLB-153
MacBeth, George 1932- DLB-40	MacNeice, Louis 1907-1963 . . . . DLB-10, 20	Malleson, Lucy Beatrice (see Gilbert, Anthony)
Macbeth, Madge 1880-1965 . . . . DLB-92	MacPhail, Andrew 1864-1938 . . . . DLB-92	Mallet-Joris, Françoise 1930- DLB-83
MacCaig, Norman 1910- DLB-27	Macpherson, James 1736-1796 . . . . DLB-109	Mallock, W. H. 1849-1923 . . . . DLB-18, 57
MacDiarmid, Hugh 1892-1978 . . . . DLB-20	Macpherson, Jay 1931- DLB-53	Malone, Dumas 1892-1986 . . . . DLB-17
MacDonald, Cynthia 1928- DLB-105	Macpherson, Jeanie 1884-1946 . . . . DLB-44	Malone, Edmond 1741-1812 . . . . DLB-142
MacDonald, George 1824-1905 . . . . DLB-18, 163, 178	Macrae Smith Company DLB-46	Malory, Sir Thomas circa 1400-1410 - 1471 . . . . DLB-146
MacDonald, John D. 1916-1986 . . . . DLB-8; Y-86	Macrone, John [publishing house] DLB-106	Malraux, André 1901-1976 . . . . DLB-72
MacDonald, Philip 1899?-1980 . . . . DLB-77	MacShane, Frank 1927- DLB-111	Malthus, Thomas Robert 1766-1834 . . . . DLB-107, 158
Macdonald, Ross (see Millar, Kenneth)	Macy-Masius DLB-46	Maltz, Albert 1908-1985 . . . . DLB-102
MacDonald, Wilson 1880-1967 . . . . DLB-92	Madden, David 1933- DLB-6	Malzberg, Barry N. 1939- DLB-8
Macdonald and Company (Publishers) . . DLB-112	Madden, Sir Frederic 1801-1873 . . . . DLB-184	Mamet, David 1947- DLB-7
MacEwen, Gwendolyn 1941- DLB-53	Maddow, Ben 1909-1992 . . . . DLB-44	Manaka, Matsemela 1956- DLB-157
Macfadden, Bernarr 1868-1955 . . . . . . DLB-25, 91	Maddux, Rachel 1912-1983 . . . . Y-93	Manchester University Press DLB-112
MacGregor, John 1825-1892 . . . . DLB-166	Madgett, Naomi Long 1923- DLB-76	Mandel, Eli 1922- DLB-53
MacGregor, Mary Esther (see Keith, Marian)	Madhubuti, Haki R. 1942- DLB-5, 41; DS-8	Mandeville, Bernard 1670-1733 . . . . DLB-101
Machado, Antonio 1875-1939 . . . . DLB-108	Madison, James 1751-1836 . . . . DLB-37	Mandeville, Sir John mid fourteenth century DLB-146
Machado, Manuel 1874-1947 . . . . DLB-108	Madsen, Svend Åge 1939- DLB-214	Mandiargues, André Pieyre de 1909- . . . DLB-83
Machar, Agnes Maule 1837-1927 . . . . DLB-92	Maeterlinck, Maurice 1862-1949 . . . . DLB-192	Manfred, Frederick 1912-1994 . . . . . DLB-6, 212
Machaut, Guillaume de circa 1300-1377 . . . . DLB-208	Magee, David 1905-1977 . . . . DLB-187	Manfredi, Gianfranco 1948- DLB-196
Machen, Arthur Llewelyn Jones 1863-1947 . . . . DLB-36, 156, 178	Maginn, William 1794-1842 . . . . DLB-110, 159	Mangan, Sherry 1904-1961 . . . . DLB-4
MacInnes, Colin 1914-1976 . . . . DLB-14	Mahan, Alfred Thayer 1840-1914 . . . . DLB-47	Manganelli, Giorgio 1922-1990 . . . . DLB-196
MacInnes, Helen 1907-1985 . . . . DLB-87	Maheux-Forcier, Louise 1929- DLB-60	Manilius fl. first century A.D DLB-211
Mack, Maynard 1909- DLB-111	Mafūz, Najīb 1911- Y-88	Mankiewicz, Herman 1897-1953 . . . . DLB-26
Mackall, Leonard L. 1879-1937 . . . . DLB-140	Mahin, John Lee 1902-1984 . . . . DLB-44	Mankiewicz, Joseph L. 1909-1993 . . . . DLB-44
MacKaye, Percy 1875-1956 . . . . DLB-54	Mahon, Derek 1941- DLB-40	Mankowitz, Wolf 1924- DLB-15
Macken, Walter 1915-1967 . . . . DLB-13	Maikov, Vasilii Ivanovich 1728-1778 . . . . DLB-150	Manley, Delarivière 1672?-1724 . . . . . . DLB-39, 80
Mackenzie, Alexander 1763-1820 . . . . DLB-99	Mailer, Norman 1923- DLB-2, 16, 28, 185; Y-80, Y-83; DS-3	Mann, Abby 1927- DLB-44
Mackenzie, Alexander Slidell 1803-1848 . . . . DLB-183	Maillart, Ella 1903-1997 . . . . DLB-195	Mann, Charles 1929-1998 . . . . Y-98
Mackenzie, Compton 1883-1972 . . . . DLB-34, 100	Maillet, Adrienne 1885-1963 . . . . DLB-68	Mann, Heinrich 1871-1950 . . . . DLB-66, 118
Mackenzie, Henry 1745-1831 . . . . DLB-39	Maimonides, Moses 1138-1204 . . . . DLB-115	Mann, Horace 1796-1859 . . . . DLB-1
Mackenzie, William 1758-1828 . . . . DLB-187	Maillet, Antonine 1929- DLB-60	Mann, Klaus 1906-1949 . . . . DLB-56
Mackey, Nathaniel 1947- DLB-169	Maillu, David G. 1939- DLB-157	Mann, Thomas 1875-1955 . . . . DLB-66
Mackey, William Wellington 1937- DLB-38	Main Selections of the Book-of-the-Month Club, 1926-1945 . . . . DLB-9	Mann, William D'Alton 1839-1920 . . . . . . DLB-137
Mackintosh, Elizabeth (see Tey, Josephine)	Main Trends in Twentieth-Century Book Clubs DLB-46	Mannin, Ethel 1900-1984 . . . . DLB-191, 195
Mackintosh, Sir James 1765-1832 . . . . . . DLB-158	Mainwaring, Daniel 1902-1977 . . . . DLB-44	Manning, Marie 1873?-1945 . . . . DLB-29
Maclaren, Ian (see Watson, John)	Mair, Charles 1838-1927 . . . . DLB-99	Manning and Loring DLB-49
Macklin, Charles 1699-1797 . . . . DLB-89	Mais, Roger 1905-1955 . . . . DLB-125	Mannyng, Robert flourished 1303-1338 . . . . DLB-146
MacLean, Katherine Anne 1925- DLB-8	Major, Andre 1942- DLB-60	Mano, D. Keith 1942- DLB-6
Maclean, Norman 1902-1990 . . . . DLB-206	Major, Charles 1856-1913 . . . . DLB-202	Manor Books DLB-46
MacLeish, Archibald 1892-1982 . . . . DLB-4, 7, 45; Y-82	Major, Clarence 1936- DLB-33	Mansfield, Katherine 1888-1923 . . . . DLB-162
MacLennan, Hugh 1907-1990 . . . . DLB-68	Major, Kevin 1949- DLB-60	Manuel, Niklaus circa 1484-1530 . . . . DLB-179
Macleod, Fiona (see Sharp, William)	Major Books DLB-46	Manzini, Gianna 1896-1974 . . . . DLB-177
MacLeod, Alistair 1936- DLB-60	Makemie, Francis circa 1658-1708 . . . . . . DLB-24	Mapanje, Jack 1944- DLB-157
Macleod, Norman 1906-1985 . . . . DLB-4	The Making of Americans Contract Y-98	Maraini, Dacia 1936- DLB-196
Mac Low, Jackson 1922- DLB-193	The Making of a People, by J. M. Ritchie DLB-66	March, William 1893-1954 . . . . DLB-9, 86
Macmillan and Company DLB-106	Maksimović, Desanka 1898-1993 . . . . DLB-147	Marchand, Leslie A. 1900- DLB-103
The Macmillan Company DLB-49	Malamud, Bernard 1914-1986 . . . . . . DLB-2, 28, 152; Y-80, Y-86	Marchant, Bessie 1862-1941 . . . . DLB-160
		Marchessault, Jovette 1938- DLB-60
		Marcus, Frank 1928- DLB-13

Marden, Orison Swett 1850-1924 . . . . DLB-137	Martin, Jay 1935- DLB-111	Maugham, W. Somerset 1874-1965 . . . . . . DLB-10, 36, 77, 100, 162, 195
Marechera, Dambudzo 1952-1987. . . . . . . DLB-157	Martin, Johann (see Laurentius von Schnüffis)	Maupassant, Guy de 1850-1893 . . . . DLB-123
Marek, Richard, Books DLB-46	Martin, Thomas 1696-1771 . . . . DLB-213	Mauriac, Claude 1914- DLB-83
Mares, E. A. 1938- DLB-122	Martin, Violet Florence (see Ross, Martin)	Mauriac, François 1885-1970 . . . . DLB-65
Mariani, Paul 1940- DLB-111	Martin du Gard, Roger 1881-1958 . . . . DLB-65	Maurice, Frederick Denison 1805-1872 . . . . DLB-55
Marie de France flourished 1160-1178. . . . DLB-208	Martineau, Harriet 1802-1876 . . . . DLB-21, 55, 159, 163, 166, 190	
Marie-Victorin, Frère 1885-1944 . . . . DLB-92	Martínez, Demetria 1960- DLB-209	Maurois, André 1885-1967 . . . . DLB-65
Marin, Biagio 1891-1985 . . . . DLB-128	Martínez, Eliud 1935- DLB-122	Maury, James 1718-1769 . . . . DLB-31
Marincovič, Ranko 1913- DLB-147	Martínez, Max 1943- DLB-82	Mavor, Elizabeth 1927- DLB-14
Marinetti, Filippo Tommaso 1876-1944 . . . . DLB-114	Martínez, Rubén 1962- DLB-209	Mavor, Osborne Henry (see Bridie, James)
	Martyn, Edward 1859-1923. . . . . DLB-10	Maxwell, Gavin 1914-1969 . . . . DLB-204
Marion, Frances 1886-1973 . . . . DLB-44	Marvell, Andrew 1621-1678 . . . . DLB-131	Maxwell, William 1908- Y-80
Marius, Richard C. 1933- Y-85	Marvin X 1944- DLB-38	Maxwell, H. [publishing house]. DLB-49
The Mark Taper Forum DLB-7	Marx, Karl 1818-1883 . . . . DLB-129	Maxwell, John [publishing house] DLB-106
Mark Twain on Perpetual Copyright Y-92	Marzials, Theo 1850-1920 . . . . DLB-35	May, Elaine 1932- DLB-44
Markfield, Wallace 1926- DLB-2, 28	Masefield, John 1878-1967 . . . . DLB-10, 19, 153, 160	May, Karl 1842-1912. . . . . DLB-129
Markham, Edwin 1852-1940 . . . . DLB-54, 186		May, Thomas 1595 or 1596-1650 . . . . DLB-58
Markle, Fletcher 1921-1991 . . . . DLB-68; Y-91	Mason, A. E. W. 1865-1948 . . . . DLB-70	Mayer, Bernadette 1945- DLB-165
Marlatt, Daphne 1942- DLB-60	Mason, Bobbie Ann 1940- DLB-173; Y-87	Mayer, Mercer 1943- DLB-61
Marlitt, E. 1825-1887. . . . . DLB-129	Mason, William 1725-1797. . . . . DLB-142	Mayer, O. B. 1818-1891 . . . . DLB-3
Marlowe, Christopher 1564-1593 . . . . DLB-62	Mason Brothers DLB-49	Mayes, Herbert R. 1900-1987 . . . . DLB-137
Marlyn, John 1912- DLB-88	Massey, Gerald 1828-1907. . . . . DLB-32	Mayes, Wendell 1919-1992. . . . . DLB-26
Marmion, Shakerley 1603-1639. . . . . DLB-58	Massey, Linton R. 1900-1974 . . . . DLB-187	Mayfield, Julian 1928-1984 . . . . DLB-33; Y-84
Der Marner before 1230-circa 1287 . . . . . . DLB-138	Massinger, Philip 1583-1640 . . . . DLB-58	Mayhew, Henry 1812-1887 . . . . . . DLB-18, 55, 190
Marnham, Patrick 1943- DLB-204	Masson, David 1822-1907 . . . . DLB-144	Mayhew, Jonathan 1720-1766 . . . . DLB-31
The *Marprelate Tracts* 1588-1589 . . . . DLB-132	Masters, Edgar Lee 1868-1950 . . . . DLB-54	Mayne, Ethel Colburn 1865-1941 . . . . DLB-197
Marquand, John P. 1893-1960 . . . . DLB-9, 102	Mastronardi, Lucio 1930-1979 . . . . DLB-177	Mayne, Jasper 1604-1672 . . . . DLB-126
Marqués, René 1919-1979 . . . . DLB-113	Matevski, Mateja 1929- DLB-181	Mayne, Seymour 1944- DLB-60
Marquis, Don 1878-1937 . . . . DLB-11, 25	Mather, Cotton 1663-1728. . . . . . . DLB-24, 30, 140	Mayor, Flora Macdonald 1872-1932 . . . . . . DLB-36
Marriott, Anne 1913- DLB-68	Mather, Increase 1639-1723 . . . . DLB-24	Mayrocker, Friederike 1924- DLB-85
Marryat, Frederick 1792-1848 . . . . DLB-21, 163	Mather, Richard 1596-1669 . . . . DLB-24	Mazrui, Ali A. 1933- DLB-125
Marsh, George Perkins 1801-1882 . . . . . DLB-1, 64	Matheson, Richard 1926- DLB-8, 44	Mažuranić, Ivan 1814-1890 . . . . DLB-147
Marsh, James 1794-1842 . . . . DLB-1, 59	Matheus, John F. 1887- DLB-51	Mazursky, Paul 1930- DLB-44
Marsh, Capen, Lyon and Webb DLB-49	Matthew of Vendôme circa 1130-circa 1200 . . . . DLB-208	McAlmon, Robert 1896-1956 . . . . DLB-4, 45; DS-15
Marsh, Narcissus 1638-1713 . . . . DLB-213		
Marsh, Ngaio 1899-1982 . . . . DLB-77	Mathews, Cornelius 1817?-1889 . . . . DLB-3, 64	McArthur, Peter 1866-1924 . . . . DLB-92
Marshall, Edison 1894-1967 . . . . DLB-102	Mathews, John Joseph 1894-1979 . . . . . . DLB-175	McBride, Robert M., and Company DLB-46
Marshall, Edward 1932- DLB-16	Mathews, Elkin [publishing house] DLB-112	McCabe, Patrick 1955- DLB-194
Marshall, Emma 1828-1899 . . . . DLB-163	Mathias, Roland 1915- DLB-27	McCaffrey, Anne 1926- DLB-8
Marshall, James 1942-1992 . . . . DLB-61	Mathis, June 1892-1927 . . . . DLB-44	McCarthy, Cormac 1933- DLB-6, 143
Marshall, Joyce 1913- DLB-88	Mathis, Sharon Bell 1937- DLB-33	McCarthy, Mary 1912-1989 . . . . DLB-2; Y-81
Marshall, Paule 1929- DLB-33, 157	Matković, Marijan 1915-1985 . . . . DLB-181	McCay, Winsor 1871-1934 . . . . DLB-22
Marshall, Tom 1938- DLB-60	Matoš, Antun Gustav 1873-1914 . . . . DLB-147	McClane, Albert Jules 1922-1991 . . . . DLB-171
Marsilius of Padua circa 1275-circa 1342 . . . . DLB-115	Matsumoto Seichō 1909-1992 . . . . DLB-182	McClatchy, C. K. 1858-1936. . . . . DLB-25
	The Matter of England 1240-1400 . . . . . . DLB-146	McClellan, George Marion 1860-1934 . . . . DLB-50
Mars-Jones, Adam 1954- DLB-207	The Matter of Rome early twelfth to late fifteenth century DLB-146	McCloskey, Robert 1914- DLB-22
Marson, Una 1905-1965 . . . . DLB-157		McClung, Nellie Letitia 1873-1951 . . . . . . DLB-92
Marston, John 1576-1634 . . . . DLB-58, 172	Matthews, Brander 1852-1929 . . . . DLB-71, 78; DS-13	McClure, Joanna 1930- DLB-16
Marston, Philip Bourke 1850-1887 . . . . DLB-35		McClure, Michael 1932- DLB-16
Martens, Kurt 1870-1945 . . . . DLB-66	Matthews, Jack 1925- DLB-6	McClure, Phillips and Company DLB-46
Martial circa A.D. 40-circa A.D. 103 . . . . . DLB-211	Matthews, William 1942- DLB-5	McClure, S. S. 1857-1949 . . . . DLB-91
Martien, William S. [publishing house] DLB-49	Matthiessen, F. O. 1902-1950 . . . . DLB-63	McClurg, A. C., and Company DLB-49
Martin, Abe (see Hubbard, Kin)	Maturin, Charles Robert 1780-1824 . . . . . DLB-178	McCluskey, John A., Jr. 1944- DLB-33
Martin, Charles 1942- DLB-120	Matthiessen, Peter 1927- DLB-6, 173	McCollum, Michael A. 1946 . . . . Y-87
Martin, Claire 1914- DLB-60		

McConnell, William C. 1917- DLB-88	McLuhan, Marshall 1911-1980 .... DLB-88	Meredith, George 1828-1909 .... DLB-18, 35, 57, 159
McCord, David 1897- DLB-61	McMaster, John Bach 1852-1932 .... DLB-47	Meredith, Louisa Anne 1812-1895...... DLB-166
McCorkle, Jill 1958- Y-87	McMurtry, Larry 1936- DLB-2, 143; Y-80, Y-87	Meredith, Owen (see Lytton, Edward Robert Bulwer)
McCorkle, Samuel Eusebius 1746-1811....................... DLB-37	McNally, Terrence 1939- DLB-7	Meredith, William 1919- DLB-5
McCormick, Anne O'Hare 1880-1954.... DLB-29	McNeil, Florence 1937- DLB-60	Mergerle, Johann Ulrich (see Abraham à Sancta Clara)
McCormick, Robert R. 1880-1955....... DLB-29	McNeile, Herman Cyril 1888-1937 ...... DLB-77	
McCourt, Edward 1907-1972 .... DLB-88	McNickle, D'Arcy 1904-1977 .... DLB-175, 212	Mérimée, Prosper 1803-1870 .... DLB-119, 192
McCoy, Horace 1897-1955................ DLB-9	McPhee, John 1931- DLB-185	Merivale, John Herman 1779-1844....... DLB-96
McCrae, John 1872-1918 .... DLB-92	McPherson, James Alan 1943- DLB-38	Meriwether, Louise 1923- DLB-33
McCullagh, Joseph B. 1842-1896 .... DLB-23	McPherson, Sandra 1943- Y-86	Merlin Press DLB-112
McCullers, Carson 1917-1967....... DLB-2, 7, 173	McWhirter, George 1939- DLB-60	Merriam, Eve 1916-1992 .... DLB-61
McCulloch, Thomas 1776-1843 .... DLB-99	McWilliams, Carey 1905-1980......... DLB-137	The Merriam Company............. DLB-49
McDonald, Forrest 1927- DLB-17	Mead, L. T. 1844-1914................. DLB-141	Merrill, James 1926-1995 ....DLB-5, 165; Y-85
McDonald, Walter 1934- DLB-105, DS-9	Mead, Matthew 1924- DLB-40	Merrill and Baker................. DLB-49
McDougall, Colin 1917-1984 .... DLB-68	Mead, Taylor ?- DLB-16	The Mershon Company.............. DLB-49
McDowell, Obolensky DLB-46	Meany, Tom 1903-1964................DLB-171	Merton, Thomas 1915-1968........DLB-48; Y-81
McEwan, Ian 1948- DLB-14, 194	Mechthild von Magdeburg circa 1207-circa 1282 .... DLB-138	Merwin, W. S. 1927- DLB-5, 169
McFadden, David 1940- DLB-60		Messner, Julian [publishing house]....... DLB-46
McFall, Frances Elizabeth Clarke (see Grand, Sarah)	Medieval French Drama............. DLB-208	Metcalf, J. [publishing house] DLB-49
	Medieval Travel Diaries.............. DLB-203	Metcalf, John 1938- DLB-60
McFarlane, Leslie 1902-1977............ DLB-88	Medill, Joseph 1823-1899 .... DLB-43	The Methodist Book Concern DLB-49
McFee, William 1881-1966............ DLB-153	Medoff, Mark 1940- DLB-7	Methuen and Company DLB-112
McGahern, John 1934- DLB-14	Meek, Alexander Beaufort 1814-1865 ..... DLB-3	Meun, Jean de (see Roman de la Rose)
McGee, Thomas D'Arcy 1825-1868...... DLB-99	Meeke, Mary ?-1816?................ DLB-116	Mew, Charlotte 1869-1928......... DLB-19, 135
McGeehan, W. O. 1879-1933...........DLB-25, 171	Meinke, Peter 1932- DLB-5	Mewshaw, Michael 1943- Y-80
McGill, Ralph 1898-1969 .... DLB-29	Mejia Vallejo, Manuel 1923- DLB-113	Meyer, Conrad Ferdinand 1825-1898 ... DLB-129
McGinley, Phyllis 1905-1978 .... DLB-11, 48	Melanchthon, Philipp 1497-1560 ....DLB-179	Meyer, E. Y. 1946- DLB-75
McGinniss, Joe 1942- DLB-185	Melançon, Robert 1947- DLB-60	Meyer, Eugene 1875-1959 .... DLB-29
McGirt, James E. 1874-1930 .... DLB-50	Mell, Max 1882-1971 .... DLB-81, 124	Meyer, Michael 1921- DLB-155
McGlashan and Gill DLB-106	Mellow, James R. 1926- DLB-111	Meyers, Jeffrey 1939- DLB-111
McGough, Roger 1937- DLB-40	Meltzer, David 1937- DLB-16	Meynell, Alice 1847-1922 .... DLB-19, 98
McGraw-Hill..................... DLB-46	Meltzer, Milton 1915- DLB-61	Meynell, Viola 1885-1956 .... DLB-153
McGuane, Thomas 1939- DLB-2, 212; Y-80	Melville, Elizabeth, Lady Culross circa 1585-1640 ....DLB-172	Meyrink, Gustav 1868-1932............. DLB-81
McGuckian, Medbh 1950- DLB-40		Mézières, Philipe de circa 1327-1405 .... DLB-208
McGuffey, William Holmes 1800-1873 ... DLB-42	Melville, Herman 1819-1891 .... DLB-3, 74	Michael, Ib 1945- DLB-214
McHenry, James 1785-1845 .... DLB-202	Memoirs of Life and Literature (1920), by W. H. Mallock [excerpt]......... DLB-57	Michael M. Rea and the Rea Award for the Short Story................... Y-97
McIlvanney, William 1936- DLB-14, 207		
McIlwraith, Jean Newton 1859-1938 ..... DLB-92	Mena, María Cristina (María Cristina Chambers) 1893-1965 .... DLB-209	Michaëlis, Karen 1872-1950 .... DLB-214
McIntyre, James 1827-1906............ DLB-99		Michaels, Leonard 1933- DLB-130
McIntyre, O. O. 1884-1938 .... DLB-25	Menander 342-341 B.C.-circa 292-291 B.C. DLB-176	Micheaux, Oscar 1884-1951............. DLB-50
McKay, Claude 1889-1948.....DLB-4, 45, 51, 117		Michel of Northgate, Dan circa 1265-circa 1340 .... DLB-146
The David McKay Company........... DLB-49	Menantes (see Hunold, Christian Friedrich)	
McKean, William V. 1820-1903......... DLB-23	Mencke, Johann Burckhard 1674-1732...................... DLB-168	Micheline, Jack 1929- DLB-16
McKenna, Stephen 1888-1967 .... DLB-197		Michener, James A. 1907?- DLB-6
The McKenzie Trust Y-96	Mencken, H. L. 1880-1956 ....DLB-11, 29, 63, 137	Micklejohn, George circa 1717-1818.................. DLB-31
McKerrow, R. B. 1872-1940 .... DLB-201		
McKinley, Robin 1952- DLB-52	Mencken and Nietzsche: An Unpublished Excerpt from H. L. Mencken's My Life as Author and Editor Y-93	Middle English Literature: An Introduction................. DLB-146
McLachlan, Alexander 1818-1896 .... DLB-99		The Middle English Lyric DLB-146
McLaren, Floris Clark 1904-1978........ DLB-68	Mendelssohn, Moses 1729-1786 .... DLB-97	Middle Hill Press DLB-106
McLaverty, Michael 1907- DLB-15	Méndez M., Miguel 1930- DLB-82	Middleton, Christopher 1926- DLB-40
McLean, John R. 1848-1916............ DLB-23	Mens Rea (or Something)................. Y-97	Middleton, Richard 1882-1911 .... DLB-156
McLean, William L. 1852-1931 .... DLB-25	The Mercantile Library of New York Y-96	Middleton, Stanley 1919- DLB-14
McLennan, William 1856-1904 .... DLB-92	Mercer, Cecil William (see Yates, Dornford)	Middleton, Thomas 1580-1627 .... DLB-58
McLoughlin Brothers................ DLB-49	Mercer, David 1928-1980................ DLB-13	
	Mercer, John 1704-1768 .... DLB-31	

Miegel, Agnes 1879-1964 . . . . DLB-56
Mihailović, Dragoslav 1930- DLB-181
Mihalić, Slavko 1928- DLB-181
Miles, Josephine 1911-1985 . . . . DLB-48
Miliković, Branko 1934-1961 . . . . DLB-181
Milius, John 1944- DLB-44
Mill, James 1773-1836 . . . . DLB-107, 158
Mill, John Stuart 1806-1873 . . . . DLB-55, 190
Millar, Kenneth 1915-1983 . . . . DLB-2; Y-83; DS-6
Millar, Andrew [publishing house] DLB-154
Millay, Edna St. Vincent 1892-1950 . . . . . . DLB-45
Miller, Arthur 1915- DLB-7
Miller, Caroline 1903-1992 . . . . DLB-9
Miller, Eugene Ethelbert 1950- DLB-41
Miller, Heather Ross 1939- DLB-120
Miller, Henry 1891-1980 . . . . DLB-4, 9; Y-80
Miller, Hugh 1802-1856 . . . . DLB-190
Miller, J. Hillis 1928- DLB-67
Miller, James [publishing house] DLB-49
Miller, Jason 1939- DLB-7
Miller, Joaquin 1839-1913 . . . . DLB-186
Miller, May 1899- DLB-41
Miller, Paul 1906-1991 . . . . DLB-127
Miller, Perry 1905-1963 . . . . DLB-17, 63
Miller, Sue 1943- DLB-143
Miller, Vassar 1924- DLB-105
Miller, Walter M., Jr. 1923- DLB-8
Miller, Webb 1892-1940 . . . . DLB-29
Millhauser, Steven 1943- DLB-2
Millican, Arthenia J. Bates 1920- DLB-38
Mills and Boon DLB-112
Milman, Henry Hart 1796-1868 . . . . DLB-96
Milne, A. A. 1882-1956 . . . . . DLB-10, 77, 100, 160
Milner, Ron 1938- DLB-38
Milner, William [publishing house] DLB-106
Milnes, Richard Monckton (Lord Houghton) 1809-1885 . . . . DLB-32, 184
Milton, John 1608-1674 . . . . DLB-131, 151
Miłosz, Czesław 1911- DLB-215
Minakami Tsutomu 1919- DLB-182
Minamoto no Sanetomo 1192-1219 . . . . . DLB-203
The Minerva Press DLB-154
Minnesang circa 1150-1280 . . . . DLB-138
Minns, Susan 1839-1938 . . . . DLB-140
Minor Illustrators, 1880-1914 . . . . DLB-141
Minor Poets of the Earlier Seventeenth Century DLB-121
Minton, Balch and Company DLB-46
Mirbeau, Octave 1848-1917 . . . . DLB-123, 192
Mirk, John died after 1414? DLB-146
Miron, Gaston 1928- DLB-60
A Mirror for Magistrates DLB-167
Mishima Yukio 1925-1970 . . . . DLB-182
Mitchel, Jonathan 1624-1668 . . . . DLB-24
Mitchell, Adrian 1932- DLB-40

Mitchell, Donald Grant 1822-1908 . . . . DLB-1; DS-13
Mitchell, Gladys 1901-1983 . . . . DLB-77
Mitchell, James Leslie 1901-1935 . . . . DLB-15
Mitchell, John (see Slater, Patrick)
Mitchell, John Ames 1845-1918 . . . . DLB-79
Mitchell, Joseph 1908-1996 . . . . DLB-185; Y-96
Mitchell, Julian 1935- DLB-14
Mitchell, Ken 1940- DLB-60
Mitchell, Langdon 1862-1935 . . . . DLB-7
Mitchell, Loften 1919- DLB-38
Mitchell, Margaret 1900-1949 . . . . DLB-9
Mitchell, S. Weir 1829-1914 . . . . DLB-202
Mitchell, W. O. 1914- DLB-88
Mitchison, Naomi Margaret (Haldane) 1897- DLB-160, 191
Mitford, Mary Russell 1787-1855 . . . . DLB-110, 116
Mitford, Nancy 1904-1973 . . . . DLB-191
Mittelholzer, Edgar 1909-1965 . . . . DLB-117
Mitterer, Erika 1906- DLB-85
Mitterer, Felix 1948- DLB-124
Mitternacht, Johann Sebastian 1613-1679 . . . . DLB-168
Miyamoto, Yuriko 1899-1951 . . . . DLB-180
Mizener, Arthur 1907-1988 . . . . DLB-103
Mo, Timothy 1950- DLB-194
Modern Age Books DLB-46
"Modern English Prose" (1876), by George Saintsbury DLB-57
The Modern Language Association of America Celebrates Its Centennial Y-84
The Modern Library DLB-46
"Modern Novelists – Great and Small" (1855), by Margaret Oliphant DLB-21
"Modern Style" (1857), by Cockburn Thomson [excerpt] DLB-57
The Modernists (1932), by Joseph Warren Beach DLB-36
Modiano, Patrick 1945- DLB-83
Moffat, Yard and Company DLB-46
Moffet, Thomas 1553-1604 . . . . DLB-136
Mohr, Nicholasa 1938- DLB-145
Moix, Ana María 1947- DLB-134
Molesworth, Louisa 1839-1921 . . . . DLB-135
Möllhausen, Balduin 1825-1905 . . . . DLB-129
Molnár, Ferenc 1878-1952 . . . . DLB-215
Momaday, N. Scott 1934- DLB-143, 175
Monkhouse, Allan 1858-1936 . . . . DLB-10
Monro, Harold 1879-1932 . . . . DLB-19
Monroe, Harriet 1860-1936 . . . . DLB-54, 91
Monsarrat, Nicholas 1910-1979 . . . . DLB-15
Montagu, Lady Mary Wortley 1689-1762 . . . . DLB-95, 101
Montague, C. E. 1867-1928 . . . . DLB-197
Montague, John 1929- DLB-40
Montale, Eugenio 1896-1981 . . . . DLB-114
Montalvo, José 1946-1994 . . . . DLB-209

Monterroso, Augusto 1921- DLB-145
Montgomerie, Alexander circa 1550?-1598 . . . . DLB-167
Montgomery, James 1771-1854 . . . . . . DLB-93, 158
Montgomery, John 1919- DLB-16
Montgomery, Lucy Maud 1874-1942 . . . . DLB-92; DS-14
Montgomery, Marion 1925- DLB-6
Montgomery, Robert Bruce (see Crispin, Edmund)
Montherlant, Henry de 1896-1972 . . . . . . DLB-72
The Monthly Review 1749-1844 . . . . DLB-110
Montigny, Louvigny de 1876-1955 . . . . . . DLB-92
Montoya, José 1932- DLB-122
Moodie, John Wedderburn Dunbar 1797-1869 . . . . DLB-99
Moodie, Susanna 1803-1885 . . . . DLB-99
Moody, Joshua circa 1633-1697 . . . . DLB-24
Moody, William Vaughn 1869-1910 . . . . DLB-7, 54
Moorcock, Michael 1939- DLB-14
Moore, Catherine L. 1911- DLB-8
Moore, Clement Clarke 1779-1863 . . . . . . DLB-42
Moore, Dora Mavor 1888-1979 . . . . DLB-92
Moore, George 1852-1933 . . . . DLB-10, 18, 57, 135
Moore, Marianne 1887-1972 . . . . DLB-45; DS-7
Moore, Mavor 1919- DLB-88
Moore, Richard 1927- DLB-105
Moore, T. Sturge 1870-1944 . . . . DLB-19
Moore, Thomas 1779-1852 . . . . DLB-96, 144
Moore, Ward 1903-1978 . . . . DLB-8
Moore, Wilstach, Keys and Company DLB-49
Moorehead, Alan 1901-1983 . . . . DLB-204
Moorhouse, Geoffrey 1931- DLB-204
The Moorland-Spingarn Research Center DLB-76
Moorman, Mary C. 1905-1994 . . . . DLB-155
Mora, Pat 1942- DLB-209
Moraga, Cherríe 1952- DLB-82
Morales, Alejandro 1944- DLB-82
Morales, Mario Roberto 1947- DLB-145
Morales, Rafael 1919- DLB-108
Morality Plays: *Mankind* circa 1450-1500 and *Everyman* circa 1500 . . . . DLB-146
Morante, Elsa 1912-1985 . . . . DLB-177
Morata, Olympia Fulvia 1526-1555 . . . . . DLB-179
Moravia, Alberto 1907-1990 . . . . DLB-177
Mordaunt, Elinor 1872-1942 . . . . DLB-174
More, Hannah 1745-1833 . . . . DLB-107, 109, 116, 158
More, Henry 1614-1687 . . . . DLB-126
More, Sir Thomas 1477 or 1478-1535 . . . . DLB-136
Moreno, Dorinda 1939- DLB-122
Morency, Pierre 1942- DLB-60
Moretti, Marino 1885-1979 . . . . DLB-114
Morgan, Berry 1919- DLB-6
Morgan, Charles 1894-1958 . . . . DLB-34, 100

Morgan, Edmund S. 1916- DLB-17
Morgan, Edwin 1920- DLB-27
Morgan, John Pierpont 1837-1913 ...... DLB-140
Morgan, John Pierpont, Jr. 1867-1943 ... DLB-140
Morgan, Robert 1944- DLB-120
Morgan, Sydney Owenson, Lady
   1776?-1859 .... DLB-116, 158
Morgner, Irmtraud 1933- DLB-75
Morhof, Daniel Georg 1639-1691 ...... DLB-164
Mori, Ōgai 1862-1922 .... DLB-180
Morier, James Justinian
   1782 or 1783?-1849 .... DLB-116
Mörike, Eduard 1804-1875 .... DLB-133
Morin, Paul 1889-1963 .... DLB-92
Morison, Richard 1514?-1556 .... DLB-136
Morison, Samuel Eliot 1887-1976 ...... DLB-17
Morison, Stanley 1889-1967 .... DLB-201
Moritz, Karl Philipp 1756-1793 .... DLB-94
Moriz von Craûn circa 1220-1230 .... DLB-138
Morley, Christopher 1890-1957 .... DLB-9
Morley, John 1838-1923 .... DLB-57, 144, 190
Morris, George Pope 1802-1864 .... DLB-73
Morris, James Humphrey (see Morris, Jan)
Morris, Jan 1926- DLB-204
Morris, Lewis 1833-1907 .... DLB-35
Morris, Margaret 1737-1816 .... DLB-200
Morris, Richard B. 1904-1989 .... DLB-17
Morris, William
   1834-1896 ..... DLB-18, 35, 57, 156, 178, 184
Morris, Willie 1934- Y-80
Morris, Wright 1910-1998 ...... DLB-2, 206; Y-81
Morrison, Arthur 1863-1945 .... DLB-70, 135, 197
Morrison, Charles Clayton 1874-1966 .... DLB-91
Morrison, Toni
   1931- DLB-6, 33, 143; Y-81, Y-93
Morrow, William, and Company DLB-46
Morse, James Herbert 1841-1923 .... DLB-71
Morse, Jedidiah 1761-1826 .... DLB-37
Morse, John T., Jr. 1840-1937 .... DLB-47
Morselli, Guido 1912-1973 .... DLB-177
Mortimer, Favell Lee 1802-1878 .... DLB-163
Mortimer, John 1923- DLB-13
Morton, Carlos 1942- DLB-122
Morton, H. V. 1892-1979 .... DLB-195
Morton, John P., and Company DLB-49
Morton, Nathaniel 1613-1685 .... DLB-24
Morton, Sarah Wentworth 1759-1846 .... DLB-37
Morton, Thomas circa 1579-circa 1647 ... DLB-24
Moscherosch, Johann Michael
   1601-1669 .... DLB-164
Moseley, Humphrey
   [publishing house] DLB-170
Möser, Justus 1720-1794 .... DLB-97
Mosley, Nicholas 1923- DLB-14, 207
Moss, Arthur 1889-1969 .... DLB-4
Moss, Howard 1922-1987 .... DLB-5

Moss, Thylias 1954- DLB-120
The Most Powerful Book Review in America
   [*New York Times Book Review*] Y-82
Motion, Andrew 1952- DLB-40
Motley, John Lothrop 1814-1877 ... DLB-1, 30, 59
Motley, Willard 1909-1965 .... DLB-76, 143
Motte, Benjamin Jr. [publishing house] ... DLB-154
Motteux, Peter Anthony 1663-1718 ...... DLB-80
Mottram, R. H. 1883-1971 .... DLB-36
Mouré, Erin 1955- DLB-60
Mourning Dove (Humishuma)
   between 1882 and 1888?-1936 ...... DLB-175
Movies from Books, 1920-1974 .... DLB-9
Mowat, Farley 1921- DLB-68
Mowbray, A. R., and Company,
   Limited DLB-106
Mowrer, Edgar Ansel 1892-1977 .... DLB-29
Mowrer, Paul Scott 1887-1971 .... DLB-29
Moxon, Edward [publishing house] DLB-106
Moxon, Joseph [publishing house] DLB-170
Móricz, Zsigmond 1879-1942 .... DLB-215
Mphahlele, Es'kia (Ezekiel) 1919- DLB-125
Mtshali, Oswald Mbuyiseni 1940- DLB-125
Mucedorus DLB-62
Mudford, William 1782-1848 .... DLB-159
Mueller, Lisel 1924- DLB-105
Muhajir, El (see Marvin X)
Muhajir, Nazzam Al Fitnah (see Marvin X)
Mühlbach, Luise 1814-1873 .... DLB-133
Muir, Edwin 1887-1959 .... DLB-20, 100, 191
Muir, Helen 1937- DLB-14
Muir, John 1838-1914 .... DLB-186
Muir, Percy 1894-1979 .... DLB-201
Mujū Ichien 1226-1312 .... DLB-203
Mukherjee, Bharati 1940- DLB-60
Mulcaster, Richard
   1531 or 1532-1611 .... DLB-167
Muldoon, Paul 1951- DLB-40
Müller, Friedrich (see Müller, Maler)
Müller, Heiner 1929- DLB-124
Müller, Maler 1749-1825 .... DLB-94
Müller, Wilhelm 1794-1827 .... DLB-90
Mumford, Lewis 1895-1990 .... DLB-63
Munby, A. N. L. 1913-1974 .... DLB-201
Munby, Arthur Joseph 1828-1910 .... DLB-35
Munday, Anthony 1560-1633 ...... DLB-62, 172
Mundt, Clara (see Mühlbach, Luise)
Mundt, Theodore 1808-1861 .... DLB-133
Munford, Robert circa 1737-1783 .... DLB-31
Mungoshi, Charles 1947- DLB-157
Munk, Kaj 1898-1944 .... DLB-214
Munonye, John 1929- DLB-117
Munro, Alice 1931- DLB-53
Munro, H. H. 1870-1916 .... DLB-34, 162
Munro, Neil 1864-1930 .... DLB-156

Munro, George [publishing house] DLB-49
Munro, Norman L. [publishing house] ... DLB-49
Munroe, James, and Company DLB-49
Munroe, Kirk 1850-1930 .... DLB-42
Munroe and Francis DLB-49
Munsell, Joel [publishing house] DLB-49
Munsey, Frank A. 1854-1925 .... DLB-25, 91
Munsey, Frank A., and Company DLB-49
Murakami Haruki 1949- DLB-182
Murav'ev, Mikhail Nikitich
   1757-1807 .... DLB-150
Murdoch, Iris 1919- DLB-14, 194
Murdoch, Rupert 1931- DLB-127
Murfree, Mary N. 1850-1922 .... DLB-12, 74
Murger, Henry 1822-1861 .... DLB-119
Murger, Louis-Henri (see Murger, Henry)
Murner, Thomas 1475-1537 .... DLB-179
Muro, Amado 1915-1971 .... DLB-82
Murphy, Arthur 1727-1805 .... DLB-89, 142
Murphy, Beatrice M. 1908- DLB-76
Murphy, Dervla 1931- DLB-204
Murphy, Emily 1868-1933 .... DLB-99
Murphy, John H., III 1916- DLB-127
Murphy, John, and Company DLB-49
Murphy, Richard 1927-1993 .... DLB-40
Murray, Albert L. 1916- DLB-38
Murray, Gilbert 1866-1957 .... DLB-10
Murray, Judith Sargent 1751-1820 ... DLB-37, 200
Murray, Pauli 1910-1985 .... DLB-41
Murray, John [publishing house] DLB-154
Murry, John Middleton 1889-1957 ...... DLB-149
Musäus, Johann Karl August
   1735-1787 .... DLB-97
Muschg, Adolf 1934- DLB-75
The Music of *Minnesang* DLB-138
Musil, Robert 1880-1942 .... DLB-81, 124
Muspilli circa 790-circa 850 .... DLB-148
Musset, Alfred de 1810-1857 .... DLB-192
Mussey, Benjamin B., and Company DLB-49
Mutafchieva, Vera 1929- DLB-181
Mwangi, Meja 1948- DLB-125
Myers, Frederic W. H. 1843-1901 ...... DLB-190
Myers, Gustavus 1872-1942 .... DLB-47
Myers, L. H. 1881-1944 .... DLB-15
Myers, Walter Dean 1937- DLB-33
Myles, Eileen 1949- DLB-193

N

Na Prous Boneta circa 1296-1328 ...... DLB-208
Nabl, Franz 1883-1974 .... DLB-81
Nabokov, Vladimir
   1899-1977 .... DLB-2; Y-80, Y-91; DS-3
Nabokov Festival at Cornell Y-83
The Vladimir Nabokov Archive
   in the Berg Collection Y-91

Nádaši, Ladislav (see Jégé)
Naden, Constance 1858-1889 . . . . DLB-199
Nadezhdin, Nikolai Ivanovich
   1804-1856 . . . . DLB-198
Naevius circa 265 B.C.-201 B.C. DLB-211
Nafis and Cornish DLB-49
Nagai, Kafū 1879-1959 . . . . DLB-180
Naipaul, Shiva 1945-1985 . . . . DLB-157; Y-85
Naipaul, V. S. 1932- . . . DLB-125, 204, 207; Y-85
Nakagami Kenji 1946-1992 . . . . DLB-182
Nakano-in Masatada no Musume (see Nijō, Lady)
Nałkowska, Zofia 1884-1954 . . . . DLB-215
Nancrede, Joseph [publishing house] DLB-49
Naranjo, Carmen 1930- DLB-145
Narezhny, Vasilii Trofimovich
   1780-1825 . . . . DLB-198
Narrache, Jean 1893-1970 . . . . DLB-92
Nasby, Petroleum Vesuvius (see Locke, David Ross)
Nash, Ogden 1902-1971 . . . . DLB-11
Nash, Eveleigh [publishing house] DLB-112
Nashe, Thomas 1567-1601? DLB-167
Nast, Conde 1873-1942 . . . . DLB-91
Nast, Thomas 1840-1902 . . . . DLB-188
Nastasijević, Momčilo 1894-1938 . . . . DLB-147
Nathan, George Jean 1882-1958 . . . . DLB-137
Nathan, Robert 1894-1985 . . . . DLB-9
The National Jewish Book Awards Y-85
The National Theatre and the Royal
   Shakespeare Company: The
   National Companies DLB-13
Natsume, Sōseki 1867-1916 . . . . DLB-180
Naughton, Bill 1910- DLB-13
Navarro, Joe 1953- DLB-209
Naylor, Gloria 1950- DLB-173
Nazor, Vladimir 1876-1949 . . . . DLB-147
Ndebele, Njabulo 1948- DLB-157
Neagoe, Peter 1881-1960 . . . . DLB-4
Neal, John 1793-1876 . . . . DLB-1, 59
Neal, Joseph C. 1807-1847 . . . . DLB-11
Neal, Larry 1937-1981 . . . . DLB-38
The Neale Publishing Company DLB-49
Neely, F. Tennyson [publishing house] DLB-49
Negri, Ada 1870-1945 . . . . DLB-114
"The Negro as a Writer," by
   G. M. McClellan DLB-50
"Negro Poets and Their Poetry," by
   Wallace Thurman DLB-50
Neidhart von Reuental
   circa 1185-circa 1240 . . . . DLB-138
Neihardt, John G. 1881-1973 . . . . DLB-9, 54
Neledinsky-Meletsky, Iurii Aleksandrovich
   1752-1828 . . . . DLB-150
Nelligan, Emile 1879-1941 . . . . DLB-92
Nelson, Alice Moore Dunbar 1875-1935 . . . DLB-50
Nelson, Thomas, and Sons [U.S.] DLB-49
Nelson, Thomas, and Sons [U.K.] DLB-106
Nelson, William 1908-1978 . . . . DLB-103

Nelson, William Rockhill 1841-1915 . . . . . . DLB-23
Nemerov, Howard 1920-1991 . . . . . DLB-5, 6; Y-83
Nepos circa 100 B.C.-post 27 B.C. DLB-211
Nesbit, E. 1858-1924 . . . . DLB-141, 153, 178
Ness, Evaline 1911-1986 . . . . DLB-61
Nestroy, Johann 1801-1862 . . . . DLB-133
Neukirch, Benjamin 1655-1729 . . . . DLB-168
Neugeboren, Jay 1938- DLB-28
Neumann, Alfred 1895-1952 . . . . DLB-56
Neumann, Ferenc (see Molnár, Ferenc)
Neumark, Georg 1621-1681 . . . . DLB-164
Neumeister, Erdmann 1671-1756 . . . . DLB-168
Nevins, Allan 1890-1971 . . . . DLB-17; DS-17
Nevinson, Henry Woodd 1856-1941 . . . . DLB-135
The New American Library DLB-46
New Approaches to Biography: Challenges
   from Critical Theory, USC Conference
   on Literary Studies, 1990 . . . . Y-90
New Directions Publishing
   Corporation DLB-46
A New Edition of *Huck Finn* Y-85
New Forces at Work in the American Theatre:
   1915-1925 . . . . DLB-7
New Literary Periodicals:
   A Report for 1987 . . . . Y-87
New Literary Periodicals:
   A Report for 1988 . . . . Y-88
New Literary Periodicals:
   A Report for 1989 . . . . Y-89
New Literary Periodicals:
   A Report for 1990 . . . . Y-90
New Literary Periodicals:
   A Report for 1991 . . . . Y-91
New Literary Periodicals:
   A Report for 1992 . . . . Y-92
New Literary Periodicals:
   A Report for 1993 . . . . Y-93
The New Monthly Magazine
   1814-1884 . . . . DLB-110
The New Ulysses Y-84
The New Variorum Shakespeare Y-85
A New Voice: The Center for the Book's First
   Five Years Y-83
The New Wave [Science Fiction] DLB-8
New York City Bookshops in the 1930s and 1940s:
   The Recollections of Walter Goldwater . . Y-93
Newbery, John [publishing house] DLB-154
Newbolt, Henry 1862-1938 . . . . DLB-19
Newbound, Bernard Slade (see Slade, Bernard)
Newby, Eric 1919- DLB-204
Newby, P. H. 1918- DLB-15
Newby, Thomas Cautley
   [publishing house] DLB-106
Newcomb, Charles King 1820-1894 . . . . DLB-1
Newell, Peter 1862-1924 . . . . DLB-42
Newell, Robert Henry 1836-1901 . . . . DLB-11
Newhouse, Samuel I. 1895-1979 . . . . DLB-127
Newman, Cecil Earl 1903-1976 . . . . DLB-127
Newman, David (see Benton, Robert)

Newman, Frances 1883-1928 . . . . Y-80
Newman, Francis William 1805-1897 . . . . DLB-190
Newman, John Henry
   1801-1890 . . . . DLB-18, 32, 55
Newman, Mark [publishing house] DLB-49
Newnes, George, Limited DLB-112
Newsome, Effie Lee 1885-1979 . . . . DLB-76
Newspaper Syndication of American
   Humor DLB-11
Newton, A. Edward 1864-1940 . . . . DLB-140
Nexø, Martin Andersen 1869-1954 . . . . . . DLB-214
Nezval, Vítěslav 1900-1958 . . . . DLB-215
Németh, László 1901-1975 . . . . DLB-215
Ngugi wa Thiong'o 1938- DLB-125
Niatum, Duane 1938- DLB-175
The *Nibelungenlied* and the *Klage*
   circa 1200 . . . . DLB-138
Nichol, B. P. 1944- DLB-53
Nicholas of Cusa 1401-1464 . . . . DLB-115
Nichols, Beverly 1898-1983 . . . . DLB-191
Nichols, Dudley 1895-1960 . . . . DLB-26
Nichols, Grace 1950- DLB-157
Nichols, John 1940- Y-82
Nichols, Mary Sargeant (Neal) Gove
   1810-1884 . . . . DLB-1
Nichols, Peter 1927- DLB-13
Nichols, Roy F. 1896-1973 . . . . DLB-17
Nichols, Ruth 1948- DLB-60
Nicholson, Edward Williams Byron
   1849-1912 . . . . DLB-184
Nicholson, Norman 1914- DLB-27
Nicholson, William 1872-1949 . . . . DLB-141
Ní Chuilleanáin, Eiléan 1942- DLB-40
Nicol, Eric 1919- DLB-68
Nicolai, Friedrich 1733-1811 . . . . DLB-97
Nicolas de Clamanges circa 1363-1437 . . . DLB-208
Nicolay, John G. 1832-1901 and
   Hay, John 1838-1905 . . . . DLB-47
Nicolson, Harold 1886-1968 . . . . DLB-100, 149
Nicolson, Nigel 1917- DLB-155
Niebuhr, Reinhold 1892-1971 . . . . . DLB-17; DS-17
Niedecker, Lorine 1903-1970 . . . . DLB-48
Nieman, Lucius W. 1857-1935 . . . . DLB-25
Nietzsche, Friedrich 1844-1900 . . . . DLB-129
Nievo, Stanislao 1928- DLB-196
Niggli, Josefina 1910- Y-80
Nightingale, Florence 1820-1910 . . . . DLB-166
Nijō, Lady (Nakano-in Masatada no Musume)
   1258-after 1306 . . . . DLB-203
Nijō, Yoshimoto 1320-1388 . . . . DLB-203
Nikolev, Nikolai Petrovich
   1758-1815 . . . . DLB-150
Niles, Hezekiah 1777-1839 . . . . DLB-43
Nims, John Frederick 1913- DLB-5
Nin, Anaïs 1903-1977 . . . . DLB-2, 4, 152
1985: The Year of the Mystery:
   A Symposium Y-85

The 1997 Booker Prize................... Y-97	Noone, John 1936- DLB-14	Noyes, Crosby S. 1825-1908 .... DLB-23
The 1998 Booker Prize................... Y-98	Nora, Eugenio de 1923- DLB-134	Noyes, Nicholas 1647-1717 .... DLB-24
Niño, Raúl 1961- DLB-209	Nordbrandt, Henrik 1945- DLB-214	Noyes, Theodore W. 1858-1946 .... DLB-29
Nissenson, Hugh 1933- DLB-28	Nordhoff, Charles 1887-1947 .... DLB-9	N-Town Plays circa 1468 to early sixteenth century................. DLB-146
Niven, Frederick John 1878-1944 .... DLB-92	Norman, Charles 1904- DLB-111	Nugent, Frank 1908-1965............. DLB-44
Niven, Larry 1938- DLB-8	Norman, Marsha 1947- Y-84	Nugent, Richard Bruce 1906- DLB-151
Nixon, Howard M. 1909-1983 .... DLB-201	Norris, Charles G. 1881-1945 .... DLB-9	Nušić, Branislav 1864-1938 .... DLB-147
Nizan, Paul 1905-1940 .... DLB-72	Norris, Frank 1870-1902........ DLB-12, 71, 186	Nutt, David [publishing house]........ DLB-106
Njegoš, Petar II Petrović 1813-1851 ..... DLB-147	Norris, Leslie 1921- DLB-27	Nwapa, Flora 1931- DLB-125
Nkosi, Lewis 1936- DLB-157	Norse, Harold 1916- DLB-16	Nye, Bill 1850-1896 .... DLB-186
"The No Self, the Little Self, and the Poets," by Richard Moore DLB-105	Norte, Marisela 1955- DLB-209	Nye, Edgar Wilson (Bill) 1850-1896 .. DLB-11, 23
Nobel Peace Prize	North, Marianne 1830-1890............DLB-174	Nye, Naomi Shihab 1952- DLB-120
The 1986 Nobel Peace Prize: Elie Wiesel..... Y-86	North Point Press DLB-46	Nye, Robert 1939- DLB-14
The Nobel Prize and Literary Politics Y-86	Nortje, Arthur 1942-1970 .... DLB-125	
Nobel Prize in Literature	Norton, Alice Mary (see Norton, Andre)	## O
The 1982 Nobel Prize in Literature: Gabriel García Márquez............Y-82	Norton, Andre 1912- DLB-8, 52	Oakes, Urian circa 1631-1681 .... DLB-24
The 1983 Nobel Prize in Literature: William Golding Y-83	Norton, Andrews 1786-1853............. DLB-1	Oakley, Violet 1874-1961............. DLB-188
The 1984 Nobel Prize in Literature: Jaroslav Seifert....................Y-84	Norton, Caroline 1808-1877 ... DLB-21, 159, 199	Oates, Joyce Carol 1938- ...DLB-2, 5, 130; Y-81
The 1985 Nobel Prize in Literature: Claude Simon....................Y-85	Norton, Charles Eliot 1827-1908 ...... DLB-1, 64	Ōba Minako 1930- DLB-182
The 1986 Nobel Prize in Literature: Wole Soyinka.....................Y-86	Norton, John 1606-1663................. DLB-24	Ober, Frederick Albion 1849-1913...... DLB-189
The 1987 Nobel Prize in Literature: Joseph Brodsky Y-87	Norton, Mary 1903-1992 .... DLB-160	Ober, William 1920-1993 .... Y-93
The 1988 Nobel Prize in Literature: Najīb Mahfūz....................Y-88	Norton, Thomas (see Sackville, Thomas)	Oberholtzer, Ellis Paxson 1868-1936 ..... DLB-47
The 1989 Nobel Prize in Literature: Camilo José Cela Y-89	Norton, W. W., and Company DLB-46	Obradović, Dositej 1740?-1811........DLB-147
The 1990 Nobel Prize in Literature: Octavio Paz....................Y-90	Norwood, Robert 1874-1932 .... DLB-92	O'Brien, Edna 1932- DLB-14
The 1991 Nobel Prize in Literature: Nadine Gordimer..................Y-91	Nosaka Akiyuki 1930- DLB-182	O'Brien, Fitz-James 1828-1862 .... DLB-74
The 1992 Nobel Prize in Literature: Derek Walcott Y-92	Nossack, Hans Erich 1901-1977 .... DLB-69	O'Brien, Kate 1897-1974............. DLB-15
The 1993 Nobel Prize in Literature: Toni Morrison....................Y-93	A Note on Technique (1926), by Elizabeth A. Drew [excerpts] DLB-36	O'Brien, Tim 1946- DLB-152; Y-80; DS-9
The 1994 Nobel Prize in Literature: Kenzaburō Ōe Y-94	Notker Balbulus circa 840-912 .... DLB-148	O'Casey, Sean 1880-1964............... DLB-10
The 1995 Nobel Prize in Literature: Seamus Heaney Y-95	Notker III of Saint Gall circa 950-1022 .... DLB-148	Occom, Samson 1723-1792............DLB-175
The 1996 Nobel Prize in Literature: Wisława Szymborsha................Y-96	Notker von Zweifalten ?-1095 .... DLB-148	Ochs, Adolph S. 1858-1935 .... DLB-25
The 1997 Nobel Prize in Literature: Dario Fo........................Y-97	Nourse, Alan E. 1928- DLB-8	Ochs-Oakes, George Washington 1861-1931 ....DLB-137
The 1998 Nobel Prize in Literature José Saramago Y-98	Novak, Slobodan 1924- DLB-181	O'Connor, Flannery 1925-1964 ....DLB-2, 152; Y-80; DS-12
Nodier, Charles 1780-1844............ DLB-119	Novak, Vjenceslav 1859-1905 .... DLB-147	O'Connor, Frank 1903-1966 .... DLB-162
Noel, Roden 1834-1894 .... DLB-35	Novalis 1772-1801 .... DLB-90	Octopus Publishing Group............ DLB-112
Nogami, Yaeko 1885-1985............. DLB-180	Novaro, Mario 1868-1944 .... DLB-114	Oda Sakunosuke 1913-1947............ DLB-182
Nogo, Rajko Petrov 1945- DLB-181	Novás Calvo, Lino 1903-1983 .... DLB-145	Odell, Jonathan 1737-1818 .... DLB-31, 99
Nolan, William F. 1928- DLB-8	"The Novel in [Robert Browning's] 'The Ring and the Book' " (1912), by Henry James DLB-32	O'Dell, Scott 1903-1989 .... DLB-52
Noland, C. F. M. 1810?-1858 .... DLB-11	The Novel of Impressionism, by Jethro Bithell................. DLB-66	Odets, Clifford 1906-1963 ....DLB-7, 26
Noma Hiroshi 1915-1991 .... DLB-182	Novel-Reading: *The Works of Charles Dickens, The Works of W. Makepeace Thackeray* (1879), by Anthony Trollope DLB-21	Odhams Press Limited DLB-112
Nonesuch Press DLB-112	Novels for Grown-Ups................... Y-97	Odoevsky, Aleksandr Ivanovich 1802-1839 .... DLB-205
Noonan, Robert Phillipe (see Tressell, Robert)	The Novels of Dorothy Richardson (1918), by May Sinclair................. DLB-36	Odoevsky, Vladimir Fedorovich 1804 or 1803-1869 .... DLB-198
Noonday Press DLB-46	Novels with a Purpose (1864), by Justin M'Carthy DLB-21	O'Donnell, Peter 1920- DLB-87
	Noventa, Giacomo 1898-1960 .... DLB-114	O'Donovan, Michael (see O'Connor, Frank)
	Novikov, Nikolai Ivanovich 1744-1818................. DLB-150	Ōe Kenzaburō 1935- DLB-182; Y-94
	Novomeský, Laco 1904-1976 .... DLB-215	O'Faolain, Julia 1932- DLB-14
	Nowlan, Alden 1933-1983 .... DLB-53	O'Faolain, Sean 1900- DLB-15, 162
	Noyes, Alfred 1880-1958 .... DLB-20	Off Broadway and Off-Off Broadway DLB-7
		Off-Loop Theatres DLB-7
		Offord, Carl Ruthven 1910- DLB-76
		O'Flaherty, Liam 1896-1984 ...DLB-36, 162; Y-84
		Ogilvie, J. S., and Company DLB-49

Ogilvy, Eliza 1822-1912 ....DLB-199	Ondaatje, Michael 1943- DLB-60	Otis, James, Jr. 1725-1783 ....DLB-31
Ogot, Grace 1930- DLB-125	O'Neill, Eugene 1888-1953 ....DLB-7	Otis, Broaders and Company DLB-49
O'Grady, Desmond 1935- DLB-40	Onetti, Juan Carlos 1909-1994 ......DLB-113	Ottaway, James 1911- DLB-127
Ogunyemi, Wale 1939- DLB-157	Onions, George Oliver 1872-1961 ...DLB-153	Ottendorfer, Oswald 1826-1900 ....DLB-23
O'Hagan, Howard 1902-1982 ....DLB-68	Onofri, Arturo 1885-1928 ....DLB-114	Ottieri, Ottiero 1924- DLB-177
O'Hara, Frank 1926-1966 ......DLB-5, 16, 193	Opie, Amelia 1769-1853 ....DLB-116, 159	Otto-Peters, Louise 1819-1895........DLB-129
O'Hara, John 1905-1970 ....DLB-9, 86; DS-2	Opitz, Martin 1597-1639 ....DLB-164	Otway, Thomas 1652-1685 ....DLB-80
O'Hegarty, P. S. 1879-1955 ....DLB-201	Oppen, George 1908-1984 ....DLB-5, 165	Ouellette, Fernand 1930- DLB-60
Okara, Gabriel 1921- DLB-125	Oppenheim, E. Phillips 1866-1946 ....DLB-70	Ouida 1839-1908 ....DLB-18, 156
O'Keeffe, John 1747-1833 ....DLB-89	Oppenheim, James 1882-1932 ....DLB-28	Outing Publishing Company...........DLB-46
Okes, Nicholas [publishing house] DLB-170	Oppenheimer, Joel 1930-1988 .....DLB-5, 193	Outlaw Days, by Joyce Johnson DLB-16
Okigbo, Christopher 1930-1967 ......DLB-125	Optic, Oliver (see Adams, William Taylor)	Overbury, Sir Thomas circa 1581-1613..................DLB-151
Okot p'Bitek 1931-1982................DLB-125	Oral History Interview with Donald S. Klopfer Y-97	The Overlook Press....................DLB-46
Okpewho, Isidore 1941- DLB-157	Orczy, Emma, Baroness 1865-1947......DLB-70	Overview of U.S. Book Publishing, 1910-1945 ....DLB-9
Okri, Ben 1959- DLB-157	Origo, Iris 1902-1988................DLB-155	Ovid 43 B.C.-A.D. 17 ....DLB-211
Olaudah Equiano and Unfinished Journeys: The Slave-Narrative Tradition and Twentieth-Century Continuities, by Paul Edwards and Pauline T. Wangman DLB-117	Orlovitz, Gil 1918-1973 ....DLB-2, 5	Owen, Guy 1925- DLB-5
	Orlovsky, Peter 1933- DLB-16	Owen, John 1564-1622 ....DLB-121
	Ormond, John 1923- DLB-27	Owen, John [publishing house] DLB-49
	Ornitz, Samuel 1890-1957 ....DLB-28, 44	Owen, Robert 1771-1858.........DLB-107, 158
	O'Rourke, P. J. 1947- DLB-185	Owen, Wilfred 1893-1918........DLB-20; DS-18
Old English Literature: An Introduction..................DLB-146	Orten, Jiří 1919-1941.................DLB-215	Owen, Peter, Limited.................DLB-112
Old English Riddles eighth to tenth centuries DLB-146	Ortese, Anna Maria 1914- DLB-177	The Owl and the Nightingale circa 1189-1199..................DLB-146
Old Franklin Publishing House DLB-49	Ortiz, Simon J. 1941- DLB-120, 175	Owsley, Frank L. 1890-1956 ....DLB-17
Old German Genesis and Old German Exodus circa 1050-circa 1130..............DLB-148	Ortnit and Wolfdietrich circa 1225-1250 ....DLB-138	Oxford, Seventeenth Earl of, Edward de Vere 1550-1604 ....DLB-172
Old High German Charms and Blessings DLB-148	Orton, Joe 1933-1967.................DLB-13	Ozerov, Vladislav Aleksandrovich 1769-1816 ....DLB-150
	Orwell, George 1903-1950........DLB-15, 98, 195	
The Old High German Isidor circa 790-800 ....DLB-148	The Orwell Year Y-84	Ozick, Cynthia 1928- DLB-28, 152; Y-82
Older, Fremont 1856-1935 ....DLB-25	Ory, Carlos Edmundo de 1923- DLB-134	**P**
Oldham, John 1653-1683..............DLB-131	Osbey, Brenda Marie 1957- DLB-120	
Oldman, C. B. 1894-1969 ....DLB-201	Osbon, B. S. 1827-1912 ....DLB-43	Pace, Richard 1482?-1536.............DLB-167
Olds, Sharon 1942- DLB-120	Osborn, Sarah 1714-1796 ....DLB-200	Pacey, Desmond 1917-1975 ....DLB-88
Olearius, Adam 1599-1671.............DLB-164	Osborne, John 1929-1994 ....DLB-13	Pack, Robert 1929- DLB-5
Oliphant, Laurence 1829?-1888......DLB-18, 166	Osgood, Herbert L. 1855-1918 ....DLB-47	Packaging Papa: The Garden of Eden.........Y-86
Oliphant, Margaret 1828-1897......DLB-18, 190	Osgood, James R., and Company DLB-49	Padell Publishing Company DLB-46
Oliver, Chad 1928- DLB-8	Osgood, McIlvaine and Company....DLB-112	Padgett, Ron 1942- DLB-5
Oliver, Mary 1935- DLB-5, 193	O'Shaughnessy, Arthur 1844-1881 ....DLB-35	Padilla, Ernesto Chávez 1944- DLB-122
Ollier, Claude 1922- DLB-83	O'Shea, Patrick [publishing house] DLB-49	Page, L. C., and Company DLB-49
Olsen, Tillie 1912 or 1913- DLB-28, 206; Y-80	Osipov, Nikolai Petrovich 1751-1799.....DLB-150	Page, P. K. 1916- DLB-68
	Oskison, John Milton 1879-1947 ....DLB-175	Page, Thomas Nelson 1853-1922 ....DLB-12, 78; DS-13
Olson, Charles 1910-1970 .....DLB-5, 16, 193	Osler, Sir William 1849-1919 ....DLB-184	
Olson, Elder 1909- DLB-48, 63	Osofisan, Femi 1946- DLB-125	Page, Walter Hines 1855-1918 ......DLB-71, 91
Omotoso, Kole 1943- DLB-125	Ostenso, Martha 1900-1963 ....DLB-92	Paget, Francis Edward 1806-1882 ....DLB-163
"On Art in Fiction "(1838), by Edward Bulwer DLB-21	Ostriker, Alicia 1937- DLB-120	Paget, Violet (see Lee, Vernon)
	Osundare, Niyi 1947- DLB-157	Pagliarani, Elio 1927- DLB-128
On Learning to Write Y-88	Oswald, Eleazer 1755-1795 ....DLB-43	Pain, Barry 1864-1928............DLB-135, 197
On Some of the Characteristics of Modern Poetry and On the Lyrical Poems of Alfred Tennyson (1831), by Arthur Henry Hallam..................DLB-32	Oswald von Wolkenstein 1376 or 1377-1445 ....DLB-179	Pain, Philip ?-circa 1666................DLB-24
	Otero, Blas de 1916-1979 ....DLB-134	Paine, Robert Treat, Jr. 1773-1811 .....DLB-37
	Otero, Miguel Antonio 1859-1944 .....DLB-82	Paine, Thomas 1737-1809 ....DLB-31, 43, 73, 158
"On Style in English Prose" (1898), by Frederic Harrison DLB-57	Otero, Nina 1881-1965 ....DLB-209	Painter, George D. 1914- DLB-155
	Otero Silva, Miguel 1908-1985 ....DLB-145	Painter, William 1540?-1594 ....DLB-136
"On Style in Literature: Its Technical Elements" (1885), by Robert Louis Stevenson DLB-57	Otfried von Weißenburg circa 800-circa 875? DLB-148	Palazzeschi, Aldo 1885-1974 ....DLB-114
"On the Writing of Essays" (1862), by Alexander Smith................DLB-57	Otis, James (see Kaler, James Otis)	Paley, Grace 1922- DLB-28

363

Palfrey, John Gorham 1796-1881 . . . . . DLB-1, 30
Palgrave, Francis Turner 1824-1897. . . . . . DLB-35
Palmer, Joe H. 1904-1952. . . . . DLB-171
Palmer, Michael 1943- DLB-169
Paltock, Robert 1697-1767. . . . . DLB-39
Paludan, Jacob 1896-1975. . . . . DLB-214
Pan Books Limited DLB-112
Panama, Norman 1914- and Frank, Melvin 1913-1988. . . . . DLB-26
Panaev, Ivan Ivanovich 1812-1862. . . . . . DLB-198
Pancake, Breece D'J 1952-1979. . . . . DLB-130
Panduro, Leif 1923-1977. . . . . DLB-214
Panero, Leopoldo 1909-1962 . . . . DLB-108
Pangborn, Edgar 1909-1976 . . . . DLB-8
"Panic Among the Philistines": A Postscript, An Interview with Bryan Griffin Y-81
Panizzi, Sir Anthony 1797-1879. . . . . DLB-184
Panneton, Philippe (see Ringuet)
Panshin, Alexei 1940- DLB-8
Pansy (see Alden, Isabella)
Pantheon Books DLB-46
Papantonio, Michael (see Kohn, John S. Van E.)
Paperback Library DLB-46
Paperback Science Fiction. DLB-8
Paquet, Alfons 1881-1944. . . . . DLB-66
Paracelsus 1493-1541 . . . . DLB-179
Paradis, Suzanne 1936- DLB-53
Pardoe, Julia 1804-1862 . . . . DLB-166
Paredes, Américo 1915- DLB-209
Pareja Diezcanseco, Alfredo 1908-1993 . . . . DLB-145
Parents' Magazine Press DLB-46
Parise, Goffredo 1929-1986 . . . . DLB-177
Parisian Theater, Fall 1984: Toward A New Baroque Y-85
Parizeau, Alice 1930- DLB-60
Parke, John 1754-1789 . . . . DLB-31
Parker, Dorothy 1893-1967 . . . . . DLB-11, 45, 86
Parker, Gilbert 1860-1932 . . . . DLB-99
Parker, James 1714-1770 . . . . DLB-43
Parker, Matthew 1504-1575 . . . . DLB-213
Parker, Theodore 1810-1860 . . . . DLB-1
Parker, William Riley 1906-1968 . . . . DLB-103
Parker, J. H. [publishing house] DLB-106
Parker, John [publishing house] DLB-106
Parkman, Francis, Jr. 1823-1893 . . . . DLB-1, 30, 183, 186
Parks, Gordon 1912- DLB-33
Parks, William 1698-1750. . . . . DLB-43
Parks, William [publishing house] DLB-49
Parley, Peter (see Goodrich, Samuel Griswold)
Parmenides late sixth-fifth century B.C.
. . . . DLB-176
Parnell, Thomas 1679-1718. . . . . DLB-95
Parnicki, Teodor 1908-1988. . . . . DLB-215
Parr, Catherine 1513?-1548 . . . . DLB-136

Parrington, Vernon L. 1871-1929. . . . . . DLB-17, 63
Parrish, Maxfield 1870-1966. . . . . DLB-188
Parronchi, Alessandro 1914- DLB-128
Partridge, S. W., and Company DLB-106
Parton, James 1822-1891 . . . . DLB-30
Parton, Sara Payson Willis 1811-1872. . . . . DLB-43, 74
Parun, Vesna 1922- DLB-181
Pasinetti, Pier Maria 1913- DLB-177
Pasolini, Pier Paolo 1922- DLB-128, 177
Pastan, Linda 1932- DLB-5
Paston, George (Emily Morse Symonds) 1860-1936 . . . . DLB-149, 197
The Paston Letters 1422-1509 . . . . DLB-146
Pastorius, Francis Daniel 1651-circa 1720 . . . . DLB-24
Patchen, Kenneth 1911-1972 . . . . DLB-16, 48
Pater, Walter 1839-1894. . . . . DLB-57, 156
Paterson, Katherine 1932- DLB-52
Patmore, Coventry 1823-1896 . . . . . DLB-35, 98
Paton, Alan 1903-1988 . . . . DS-17
Paton, Joseph Noel 1821-1901 . . . . DLB-35
Paton Walsh, Jill 1937- DLB-161
Patrick, Edwin Hill ("Ted") 1901-1964 . . DLB-137
Patrick, John 1906- DLB-7
Pattee, Fred Lewis 1863-1950. . . . . DLB-71
Pattern and Paradigm: History as Design, by Judith Ryan DLB-75
Patterson, Alicia 1906-1963 . . . . DLB-127
Patterson, Eleanor Medill 1881-1948 . . . . . DLB-29
Patterson, Eugene 1923- DLB-127
Patterson, Joseph Medill 1879-1946 . . . . . . DLB-29
Pattillo, Henry 1726-1801 . . . . DLB-37
Paul, Elliot 1891-1958 . . . . DLB-4
Paul, Jean (see Richter, Johann Paul Friedrich)
Paul, Kegan, Trench, Trubner and Company Limited. DLB-106
Paul, Peter, Book Company DLB-49
Paul, Stanley, and Company Limited. . . . DLB-112
Paulding, James Kirke 1778-1860 . . . . DLB-3, 59, 74
Paulin, Tom 1949- DLB-40
Pauper, Peter, Press DLB-46
Pavese, Cesare 1908-1950 . . . . DLB-128, 177
Pavlova, Karolina Karlovna 1807-1893. DLB-205
Pavić, Milorad 1929- DLB-181
Pavlov, Konstantin 1933- DLB-181
Pavlov, Nikolai Filippovich 1803-1864 . . . . DLB-198
Pavlova, Karolina Karlovna 1807-1893. . . . DLB-205
Pavlović, Miodrag 1928- DLB-181
Paxton, John 1911-1985 . . . . DLB-44
Payn, James 1830-1898. . . . . DLB-18
Payne, John 1842-1916. . . . . DLB-35
Payne, John Howard 1791-1852. . . . . DLB-37
Payson and Clarke DLB-46
Paz, Octavio 1914-1998 . . . . Y-90, Y-98

Pazzi, Roberto 1946- DLB-196
Peabody, Elizabeth Palmer 1804-1894 . . . . . DLB-1
Peabody, Elizabeth Palmer [publishing house] DLB-49
Peabody, Oliver William Bourn 1799-1848. . . . . DLB-59
Peace, Roger 1899-1968 . . . . DLB-127
Peacham, Henry 1578-1644? DLB-151
Peacham, Henry, the Elder 1547-1634 . . . DLB-172
Peachtree Publishers, Limited. DLB-46
Peacock, Molly 1947- DLB-120
Peacock, Thomas Love 1785-1866 . . . DLB-96, 116
Pead, Deuel ?-1727 . . . . DLB-24
Peake, Mervyn 1911-1968 . . . . DLB-15, 160
Peale, Rembrandt 1778-1860 . . . . DLB-183
Pear Tree Press DLB-112
Pearce, Philippa 1920- DLB-161
Pearson, H. B. [publishing house]. DLB-49
Pearson, Hesketh 1887-1964. . . . . DLB-149
Peck, George W. 1840-1916. . . . . DLB-23, 42
Peck, H. C., and Theo. Bliss [publishing house] DLB-49
Peck, Harry Thurston 1856-1914. . . . . . DLB-71, 91
Peele, George 1556-1596 . . . . DLB-62, 167
Pegler, Westbrook 1894-1969 . . . . DLB-171
Pekić, Borislav 1930-1992 . . . . DLB-181
Pellegrini and Cudahy DLB-46
Pelletier, Aimé (see Vac, Bertrand)
Pemberton, Sir Max 1863-1950 . . . . DLB-70
de la Peña, Terri 1947- DLB-209
Penfield, Edward 1866-1925 . . . . DLB-188
Penguin Books [U.S.] DLB-46
Penguin Books [U.K.] DLB-112
Penn Publishing Company. DLB-49
Penn, William 1644-1718 . . . . DLB-24
Penna, Sandro 1906-1977 . . . . DLB-114
Pennell, Joseph 1857-1926 . . . . DLB-188
Penner, Jonathan 1940- Y-83
Pennington, Lee 1939- Y-82
Pepys, Samuel 1633-1703 . . . . DLB-101, 213
Percy, Thomas 1729-1811 . . . . DLB-104
Percy, Walker 1916-1990 . . . . . . DLB-2; Y-80, Y-90
Percy, William 1575-1648 . . . . DLB-172
Perec, Georges 1936-1982 . . . . DLB-83
Perelman, Bob 1947- DLB-193
Perelman, S. J. 1904-1979 . . . . DLB-11, 44
Perez, Raymundo "Tigre" 1946- DLB-122
Peri Rossi, Cristina 1941- DLB-145
Periodicals of the Beat Generation DLB-16
Perkins, Eugene 1932- DLB-41
Perkoff, Stuart Z. 1930-1974. . . . . DLB-16
Perley, Moses Henry 1804-1862 . . . . DLB-99
Permabooks DLB-46
Perovsky, Aleksei Alekseevich (Antonii Pogorel'sky) 1787-1836 . . . . DLB-198

Perrin, Alice 1867-1934 ....DLB-156	Phillips, Robert 1938- DLB-105	Pix, Mary 1666-1709 ....DLB-80
Perry, Bliss 1860-1954..................DLB-71	Phillips, Stephen 1864-1915............DLB-10	Pixerécourt, René Charles Guilbert de 1773-1844 ....DLB-192
Perry, Eleanor 1915-1981 ....DLB-44	Phillips, Ulrich B. 1877-1934 ....DLB-17	
Perry, Matthew 1794-1858............DLB-183	Phillips, Willard 1784-1873 ....DLB-59	Plaatje, Sol T. 1876-1932...............DLB-125
Perry, Sampson 1747-1823 ....DLB-158	Phillips, William 1907- DLB-137	The Place of Realism in Fiction (1895), by George Gissing DLB-18
Persius A.D. 34-A.D. 62 ....DLB-211	Phillips, Sampson and Company........DLB-49	
"Personal Style" (1890), by John Addington Symonds DLB-57	Phillpotts, Adelaide Eden (Adelaide Ross) 1896-1993 ....DLB-191	Plante, David 1940- Y-83
		Platen, August von 1796-1835..........DLB-90
Perutz, Leo 1882-1957 ....DLB-81	Phillpotts, Eden 1862-1960 ....DLB-10, 70, 135, 153	Plath, Sylvia 1932-1963..........DLB-5, 6, 152
Pesetsky, Bette 1932- DLB-130		Plato circa 428 B.C.-348-347 B.C. DLB-176
Pestalozzi, Johann Heinrich 1746-1827.....DLB-94	Philo circa 20-15 B.C.-circa A.D. 50 ....DLB-176	
Peter, Laurence J. 1919-1990...........DLB-53		Platon 1737-1812 ....DLB-150
Peter of Spain circa 1205-1277 ....DLB-115	Philosophical Library..................DLB-46	Platt and Munk Company.............DLB-46
Peterkin, Julia 1880-1961 ....DLB-9	"The Philosophy of Style" (1852), by Herbert Spencer DLB-57	Plautus circa 254 B.C.-184 B.C. DLB-211
Peters, Lenrie 1932- DLB-117		Playboy Press DLB-46
Peters, Robert 1924- DLB-105	Phinney, Elihu [publishing house].......DLB-49	Playford, John [publishing house] DLB-170
Petersham, Maud 1889-1971 and Petersham, Miska 1888-1960 ....DLB-22	Phoenix, John (see Derby, George Horatio)	Plays, Playwrights, and Playgoers DLB-84
	PHYLON (Fourth Quarter, 1950), The Negro in Literature: The Current Scene DLB-76	Playwrights and Professors, by Tom Stoppard....................DLB-13
Peterson, Charles Jacobs 1819-1887.......DLB-79		
Peterson, Len 1917- DLB-88		Playwrights on the Theater DLB-80
Peterson, Levi S. 1933- DLB-206	Physiologus circa 1070-circa 1150 ....DLB-148	Der Pleier flourished circa 1250 ....DLB-138
Peterson, Louis 1922- DLB-76	Piccolo, Lucio 1903-1969..............DLB-114	Plenzdorf, Ulrich 1934- DLB-75
Peterson, T. B., and Brothers DLB-49	Pickard, Tom 1946- DLB-40	Plessen, Elizabeth 1944- DLB-75
Petitclair, Pierre 1813-1860 ....DLB-99	Pickering, William [publishing house]....DLB-106	Pletnev, Petr Aleksandrovich 1792-1865 ....DLB-205
Petronius circa A.D. 20-A.D. 66 ....DLB-211	Pickthall, Marjorie 1883-1922 ....DLB-92	
Petrov, Aleksandar 1938- DLB-181	Pictorial Printing Company DLB-49	Plievier, Theodor 1892-1955...........DLB-69
Petrov, Gavriil 1730-1801 ....DLB-150	Piercy, Marge 1936- DLB-120	Plimpton, George 1927- DLB-185
Petrov, Vasilii Petrovich 1736-1799 ......DLB-150	Pierro, Albino 1916- DLB-128	Pliny the Elder A.D. 23/24-A.D. 79......DLB-211
Petrov, Valeri 1920- DLB-181	Pignotti, Lamberto 1926- DLB-128	Pliny the Younger circa A.D. 61-A.D. 112 ....DLB-211
Petrović, Rastko 1898-1949............DLB-147	Pike, Albert 1809-1891 ....DLB-74	
Petruslied circa 854?..................DLB-148	Pike, Zebulon Montgomery 1779-1813 ....DLB-183	Plomer, William 1903-1973.....DLB-20, 162, 191
Petry, Ann 1908- DLB-76		Plotinus 204-270 ....DLB-176
Pettie, George circa 1548-1589 ....DLB-136	Pilon, Jean-Guy 1930- DLB-60	Plume, Thomas 1630-1704 ....DLB-213
Peyton, K. M. 1929- DLB-161	Pinckney, Eliza Lucas 1722-1793 ....DLB-200	Plumly, Stanley 1939- DLB-5, 193
Pfaffe Konrad flourished circa 1172......DLB-148	Pinckney, Josephine 1895-1957 ....DLB-6	Plumpp, Sterling D. 1940- DLB-41
Pfaffe Lamprecht flourished circa 1150...DLB-148	Pindar circa 518 B.C.-circa 438 B.C. DLB-176	Plunkett, James 1920- DLB-14
Pfeiffer, Emily 1827-1890...............DLB-199		Plutarch circa 46-circa 120............DLB-176
Pforzheimer, Carl H. 1879-1957 ....DLB-140	Pindar, Peter (see Wolcot, John)	Plymell, Charles 1935- DLB-16
Phaedrus circa 18 B.C.-circa A.D. 50.....DLB-211	Pineda, Cecile 1942- DLB-209	Pocket Books......................DLB-46
Phaer, Thomas 1510?-1560............DLB-167	Pinero, Arthur Wing 1855-1934 ....DLB-10	Poe, Edgar Allan 1809-1849 ....DLB-3, 59, 73, 74
Phaidon Press Limited................DLB-112	Pinget, Robert 1919- DLB-83	Poe, James 1921-1980 ....DLB-44
Pharr, Robert Deane 1916-1992 ....DLB-33	Pinnacle Books......................DLB-46	The Poet Laureate of the United States Statements from Former Consultants in Poetry Y-86
Phelps, Elizabeth Stuart 1815-1852 ......DLB-202	Piñon, Nélida 1935- DLB-145	
Phelps, Elizabeth Stuart 1844-1911 ....DLB-74	Pinsky, Robert 1940- Y-82	
Philander von der Linde (see Mencke, Johann Burckhard)	Pinter, Harold 1930- DLB-13	"The Poet's Kaleidoscope: The Element of Surprise in the Making of the Poem," by Madeline DeFrees DLB-105
	Piontek, Heinz 1925- DLB-75	
Philby, H. St. John B. 1885-1960........DLB-195	Piozzi, Hester Lynch [Thrale] 1741-1821 ....DLB-104, 142	
Philip, Marlene Nourbese 1947- DLB-157		"The Poetry File," by Edward Field DLB-105
Philippe, Charles-Louis 1874-1909........DLB-65	Piper, H. Beam 1904-1964...............DLB-8	Pogodin, Mikhail Petrovich 1800-1875 ....DLB-198
Philips, John 1676-1708 ....DLB-95	Piper, Watty DLB-22	
Philips, Katherine 1632-1664 ....DLB-131	Pirckheimer, Caritas 1467-1532.........DLB-179	Pogorel'sky, Antonii (see Perovsky, Aleksei Alekseevich)
Phillipps, Sir Thomas 1792-1872 ....DLB-184	Pirckheimer, Willibald 1470-1530 ....DLB-179	
Phillips, Caryl 1958- DLB-157	Pisar, Samuel 1929- Y-83	Pohl, Frederik 1919- DLB-8
Phillips, David Graham 1867-1911 .....DLB-9, 12	Pitkin, Timothy 1766-1847 ....DLB-30	Poirier, Louis (see Gracq, Julien)
Phillips, Jayne Anne 1952- Y-80	The Pitt Poetry Series: Poetry Publishing Today Y-85	Polanyi, Michael 1891-1976............DLB-100
		Poláček, Karel 1892-1945 ....DLB-215
	Pitter, Ruth 1897- DLB-20	Pole, Reginald 1500-1558 ....DLB-132

Cumulative Index   DLB 216

Polevoi, Nikolai Alekseevich 1796-1846 .... DLB-198

Polezhaev, Aleksandr Ivanovich 1804-1838 .... DLB-205

Poliakoff, Stephen 1952- DLB-13

Polidori, John William 1795-1821 .... DLB-116

Polite, Carlene Hatcher 1932- DLB-33

Pollard, Alfred W. 1859-1944 .... DLB-201

Pollard, Edward A. 1832-1872 .... DLB-30

Pollard, Graham 1903-1976 .... DLB-201

Pollard, Percival 1869-1911 .... DLB-71

Pollard and Moss DLB-49

Pollock, Sharon 1936- DLB-60

Polonsky, Abraham 1910- DLB-26

Polotsky, Simeon 1629-1680 .... DLB-150

Polybius circa 200 B.C.-118 B.C. DLB-176

Pomilio, Mario 1921-1990 .... DLB-177

Ponce, Mary Helen 1938- DLB-122

Ponce-Montoya, Juanita 1949- DLB-122

Ponet, John 1516?-1556 .... DLB-132

Poniatowski, Elena 1933- DLB-113

Ponsard, François 1814-1867 .... DLB-192

Ponsonby, William [publishing house] DLB-170

Pontiggia, Giuseppe 1934- DLB-196

Pony Stories DLB-160

Poole, Ernest 1880-1950 .... DLB-9

Poole, Sophia 1804-1891 .... DLB-166

Poore, Benjamin Perley 1820-1887 .... DLB-23

Popa, Vasko 1922-1991 .... DLB-181

Pope, Abbie Hanscom 1858-1894 .... DLB-140

Pope, Alexander 1688-1744 .... DLB-95, 101, 213

Popov, Mikhail Ivanovich 1742-circa 1790 .... DLB-150

Popović, Aleksandar 1929-1996 .... DLB-181

Popular Library DLB-46

Porete, Marguerite ?-1310 .... DLB-208

Porlock, Martin (see MacDonald, Philip)

Porpoise Press DLB-112

Porta, Antonio 1935-1989 .... DLB-128

Porter, Anna Maria 1780-1832 ..... DLB-116, 159

Porter, David 1780-1843 .... DLB-183

Porter, Eleanor H. 1868-1920 .... DLB-9

Porter, Gene Stratton (see Stratton-Porter, Gene)

Porter, Henry ?-? DLB-62

Porter, Jane 1776-1850 .... DLB-116, 159

Porter, Katherine Anne 1890-1980 .... DLB-4, 9, 102; Y-80; DS-12

Porter, Peter 1929- DLB-40

Porter, William Sydney 1862-1910 .... DLB-12, 78, 79

Porter, William T. 1809-1858 .... DLB-3, 43

Porter and Coates DLB-49

Portillo Trambley, Estela 1927-1998 ..... DLB-209

Portis, Charles 1933- DLB-6

Posey, Alexander 1873-1908 .... DLB-175

Postans, Marianne circa 1810-1865 ..... DLB-166

Postl, Carl (see Sealsfield, Carl)

Poston, Ted 1906-1974 .... DLB-51

Postscript to [the Third Edition of] *Clarissa* (1751), by Samuel Richardson DLB-39

Potok, Chaim 1929- DLB-28, 152; Y-84

Potter, Beatrix 1866-1943 .... DLB-141

Potter, David M. 1910-1971 .... DLB-17

Potter, John E., and Company DLB-49

Pottle, Frederick A. 1897-1987 ..... DLB-103; Y-87

Poulin, Jacques 1937- DLB-60

Pound, Ezra 1885-1972 ..... DLB-4, 45, 63; DS-15

Povich, Shirley 1905- DLB-171

Powell, Anthony 1905- DLB-15

Powell, John Wesley 1834-1902 .... DLB-186

Powers, J. F. 1917- DLB-130

Pownall, David 1938- DLB-14

Powys, John Cowper 1872-1963 .... DLB-15

Powys, Llewelyn 1884-1939 .... DLB-98

Powys, T. F. 1875-1953 .... DLB-36, 162

Poynter, Nelson 1903-1978 .... DLB-127

The Practice of Biography: An Interview with Stanley Weintraub Y-82

The Practice of Biography II: An Interview with B. L. Reid Y-83

The Practice of Biography III: An Interview with Humphrey Carpenter Y-84

The Practice of Biography IV: An Interview with William Manchester Y-85

The Practice of Biography V: An Interview with Justin Kaplan Y-86

The Practice of Biography VI: An Interview with David Herbert Donald Y-87

The Practice of Biography VII: An Interview with John Caldwell Guilds Y-92

The Practice of Biography VIII: An Interview with Joan Mellen Y-94

The Practice of Biography IX: An Interview with Michael Reynolds Y-95

Prados, Emilio 1899-1962 .... DLB-134

Praed, Winthrop Mackworth 1802-1839 .... DLB-96

Praeger Publishers DLB-46

Praetorius, Johannes 1630-1680 .... DLB-168

Pratolini, Vasco 1913-1991 .... DLB-177

Pratt, E. J. 1882-1964 .... DLB-92

Pratt, Samuel Jackson 1749-1814 .... DLB-39

Preciado Martin, Patricia 1939- DLB-209

Preface to *Alwyn* (1780), by Thomas Holcroft DLB-39

Preface to *Colonel Jack* (1722), by Daniel Defoe DLB-39

Preface to *Evelina* (1778), by Fanny Burney DLB-39

Preface to *Ferdinand Count Fathom* (1753), by Tobias Smollett DLB-39

Preface to *Incognita* (1692), by William Congreve DLB-39

Preface to *Joseph Andrews* (1742), by Henry Fielding DLB-39

Preface to *Moll Flanders* (1722), by Daniel Defoe DLB-39

Preface to *Poems* (1853), by Matthew Arnold DLB-32

Preface to *Robinson Crusoe* (1719), by Daniel Defoe DLB-39

Preface to *Roderick Random* (1748), by Tobias Smollett DLB-39

Preface to *Roxana* (1724), by Daniel Defoe DLB-39

Preface to *St. Leon* (1799), by William Godwin DLB-39

Preface to Sarah Fielding's *Familiar Letters* (1747), by Henry Fielding [excerpt] ... DLB-39

Preface to Sarah Fielding's *The Adventures of David Simple* (1744), by Henry Fielding DLB-39

Preface to *The Cry* (1754), by Sarah Fielding DLB-39

Preface to *The Delicate Distress* (1769), by Elizabeth Griffin DLB-39

Preface to *The Disguis'd Prince* (1733), by Eliza Haywood [excerpt] DLB-39

Preface to *The Farther Adventures of Robinson Crusoe* (1719), by Daniel Defoe DLB-39

Preface to the First Edition of *Pamela* (1740), by Samuel Richardson DLB-39

Preface to the First Edition of *The Castle of Otranto* (1764), by Horace Walpole DLB-39

Preface to *The History of Romances* (1715), by Pierre Daniel Huet [excerpts] DLB-39

Preface to *The Life of Charlotta du Pont* (1723), by Penelope Aubin DLB-39

Preface to *The Old English Baron* (1778), by Clara Reeve DLB-39

Preface to the Second Edition of *The Castle of Otranto* (1765), by Horace Walpole DLB-39

Preface to *The Secret History, of Queen Zarah, and the Zarazians* (1705), by Delariviere Manley DLB-39

Preface to the Third Edition of *Clarissa* (1751), by Samuel Richardson [excerpt] DLB-39

Preface to *The Works of Mrs. Davys* (1725), by Mary Davys DLB-39

Preface to Volume 1 of *Clarissa* (1747), by Samuel Richardson DLB-39

Preface to Volume 3 of *Clarissa* (1748), by Samuel Richardson DLB-39

Préfontaine, Yves 1937- DLB-53

Prelutsky, Jack 1940- DLB-61

Premisses, by Michael Hamburger DLB-66

Prentice, George D. 1802-1870 .... DLB-43

Prentice-Hall DLB-46

Prescott, Orville 1906-1996 .... Y-96

Prescott, William Hickling 1796-1859 .... DLB-1, 30, 59

The Present State of the English Novel (1892), by George Saintsbury DLB-18

Prešeren, Francn 1800-1849 .... DLB-147

Preston, May Wilson 1873-1949 .... DLB-188

Preston, Thomas 1537-1598 .... DLB-62

Price, Reynolds 1933- DLB-2

Price, Richard 1723-1791 .... DLB-158

366

DLB 216 — Cumulative Index

Price, Richard 1949- Y-81
Priest, Christopher 1943- DLB-14, 207
Priestley, J. B. 1894-1984
.... DLB-10, 34, 77, 100, 139; Y-84
Primary Bibliography: A Retrospective Y-95
Prime, Benjamin Young 1733-1791 .... DLB-31
Primrose, Diana floruit circa 1630 .... DLB-126
Prince, F. T. 1912- DLB-20
Prince, Thomas 1687-1758 .... DLB-24, 140
The Principles of Success in Literature (1865), by
   George Henry Lewes [excerpt] DLB-57
Printz, Wolfgang Casper 1641-1717 ...... DLB-168
Prior, Matthew 1664-1721 .... DLB-95
Prisco, Michele 1920- DLB-177
Pritchard, William H. 1932- DLB-111
Pritchett, V. S. 1900- DLB-15, 139
Probyn, May 1856 or 1857-1909 .... DLB-199
Procter, Adelaide Anne 1825-1864 ... DLB-32, 199
Procter, Bryan Waller 1787-1874 ..... DLB-96, 144
Proctor, Robert 1868-1903 .... DLB-184
*Producing Dear Bunny, Dear Volodya: The Friendship
   and the Feud* Y-97
The Profession of Authorship:
   Scribblers for Bread Y-89
The Progress of Romance (1785), by Clara Reeve
   [excerpt] DLB-39
Prokopovich, Feofan 1681?-1736 ...... DLB-150
Prokosch, Frederic 1906-1989 .... DLB-48
The Proletarian Novel DLB-9
Propertius circa 50 B.C.-post 16 B.C. DLB-211
Propper, Dan 1937- DLB-16
The Prospect of Peace (1778),
   by Joel Barlow DLB-37
Protagoras circa 490 B.C.-420 B.C.
   .... DLB-176
Proud, Robert 1728-1813 .... DLB-30
Proust, Marcel 1871-1922 .... DLB-65
Prynne, J. H. 1936- DLB-40
Przybyszewski, Stanislaw 1868-1927 ..... DLB-66
Pseudo-Dionysius the Areopagite floruit
   circa 500 .... DLB-115
Public Domain and the Violation of Texts ... Y-97
The Public Lending Right in America
   Statement by Sen. Charles McC.
   Mathias, Jr. PLR and the Meaning
   of Literary Property Statements on
   PLR by American Writers Y-83
The Public Lending Right in the United Kingdom
   Public Lending Right: The First Year in the
   United Kingdom Y-83
The Publication of English
   Renaissance Plays DLB-62
Publications and Social Movements
   [Transcendentalism] DLB-1
Publishers and Agents: The Columbia
   Connection Y-87
A Publisher's Archives: G. P. Putnam Y-92
Publishing Fiction at LSU Press Y-87
The Publishing Industry in 1998:
   Sturm-und-drang.com Y-98

Pückler-Muskau, Hermann von
   1785-1871 .... DLB-133
Pufendorf, Samuel von 1632-1694 ..... DLB-168
Pugh, Edwin William 1874-1930 .... DLB-135
Pugin, A. Welby 1812-1852 .... DLB-55
Puig, Manuel 1932-1990 .... DLB-113
Pulitzer, Joseph 1847-1911 .... DLB-23
Pulitzer, Joseph, Jr. 1885-1955 .... DLB-29
Pulitzer Prizes for the Novel, 1917-1945 .... DLB-9
Pulliam, Eugene 1889-1975 .... DLB-127
Purchas, Samuel 1577?-1626 .... DLB-151
Purdy, Al 1918- DLB-88
Purdy, James 1923- DLB-2
Purdy, Ken W. 1913-1972 .... DLB-137
Pusey, Edward Bouverie 1800-1882 ..... DLB-55
Pushkin, Aleksandr Sergeevich
   1799-1837 .... DLB-205
Pushkin, Vasilii L'vovich 1766-1830 ..... DLB-205
Putnam, George Palmer 1814-1872 .... DLB-3, 79
Putnam, Samuel 1892-1950 .... DLB-4
G. P. Putnam's Sons [U.S.] DLB-49
G. P. Putnam's Sons [U.K.] DLB-106
Puzo, Mario 1920- DLB-6
Pyle, Ernie 1900-1945 .... DLB-29
Pyle, Howard 1853-1911 ..... DLB-42, 188; DS-13
Pym, Barbara 1913-1980 ...... DLB-14, 207; Y-87
Pynchon, Thomas 1937- DLB-2, 173
Pyramid Books DLB-46
Pyrnelle, Louise-Clarke 1850-1907 ..... DLB-42
Pythagoras circa 570 B.C.-? DLB-176

Q

Quad, M. (see Lewis, Charles B.)
Quaritch, Bernard 1819-1899 .... DLB-184
Quarles, Francis 1592-1644 .... DLB-126
The Quarterly Review 1809-1967 .... DLB-110
Quasimodo, Salvatore 1901-1968 ..... DLB-114
Queen, Ellery (see Dannay, Frederic, and
   Manfred B. Lee)
The Queen City Publishing House DLB-49
Queneau, Raymond 1903-1976 .... DLB-72
Quennell, Sir Peter 1905-1993 ..... DLB-155, 195
Quesnel, Joseph 1746-1809 .... DLB-99
The Question of American Copyright
   in the Nineteenth Century Headnote
   Preface, by George Haven Putnam
   The Evolution of Copyright, by Brander
      Matthews
   Summary of Copyright Legislation in
      the United States, by R. R. Bowker
   Analysis oæ the Provisions of the
      Copyright Law of 1891, by
      George Haven Putnam
   The Contest for International Copyright,
      by George Haven Putnam
   Cheap Books and Good Books,
      by Brander Matthews DLB-49
Quiller-Couch, Sir Arthur Thomas
   1863-1944 .... DLB-135, 153, 190
Quin, Ann 1936-1973 .... DLB-14

Quincy, Samuel, of Georgia ?-? DLB-31
Quincy, Samuel, of Massachusetts
   1734-1789 .... DLB-31
Quinn, Anthony 1915- DLB-122
Quinn, John 1870-1924 .... DLB-187
Quiñónez, Naomi 1951- DLB-209
Quintana, Leroy V. 1944- DLB-82
Quintana, Miguel de 1671-1748
   A Forerunner of Chicano
   Literature DLB-122
Quintillian circa A.D. 40-circa A.D. 96 ... DLB-211
Quist, Harlin, Books DLB-46
Quoirez, Françoise (see Sagan, Françoise)

R

R-va, Zeneida (see Gan, Elena Andreevna)
Raabe, Wilhelm 1831-1910 .... DLB-129
Raban, Jonathan 1942- DLB-204
Rabe, David 1940- DLB-7
Raboni, Giovanni 1932- DLB-128
Rachilde 1860-1953 .... DLB-123, 192
Racin, Kočo 1908-1943 .... DLB-147
Rackham, Arthur 1867-1939 .... DLB-141
Radcliffe, Ann 1764-1823 .... DLB-39, 178
Raddall, Thomas 1903- DLB-68
Radichkov, Yordan 1929- DLB-181
Radiguet, Raymond 1903-1923 .... DLB-65
Radishchev, Aleksandr Nikolaevich
   1749-1802 .... DLB-150
Radnóti, Miklós 1909-1944 .... DLB-215
Radványi, Netty Reiling (see Seghers, Anna)
Rahv, Philip 1908-1973 .... DLB-137
Raich, Semen Egorovich 1792-1855 ..... DLB-205
Raičković, Stevan 1928- DLB-181
Raimund, Ferdinand Jakob 1790-1836 ..... DLB-90
Raine, Craig 1944- DLB-40
Raine, Kathleen 1908- DLB-20
Rainolde, Richard
   circa 1530-1606 .... DLB-136
Rakić, Milan 1876-1938 .... DLB-147
Rakosi, Carl 1903- DLB-193
Ralegh, Sir Walter 1554?-1618 .... DLB-172
Ralin, Radoy 1923- DLB-181
Ralph, Julian 1853-1903 .... DLB-23
Ralph Waldo Emerson in 1982 .... Y-82
Ramat, Silvio 1939- DLB-128
Rambler, no. 4 (1750), by Samuel Johnson
   [excerpt] DLB-39
Ramée, Marie Louise de la (see Ouida)
Ramírez, Sergío 1942- DLB-145
Ramke, Bin 1947- DLB-120
Ramler, Karl Wilhelm 1725-1798 .... DLB-97
Ramon Ribeyro, Julio 1929- DLB-145
Ramos, Manuel 1948- DLB-209
Ramous, Mario 1924- DLB-128
Rampersad, Arnold 1941- DLB-111

Ramsay, Allan 1684 or 1685-1758 .... DLB-95	Rèbora, Clemente 1885-1957 .... DLB-114	Rendell, Ruth 1930- DLB-87
Ramsay, David 1749-1815 .... DLB-30	Rechy, John 1934- DLB-122; Y-82	Rensselaer, Maria van Cortlandt van 1645-1689 .... DLB-200
Ramsay, Martha Laurens 1759-1811 .... DLB-200	The Recovery of Literature: Criticism in the 1990s: A Symposium...................... Y-91	
Ranck, Katherine Quintana 1942- DLB-122	Redding, J. Saunders 1906-1988...... DLB-63, 76	Representative Men and Women: A Historical Perspective on the British Novel, 1930-1960 .... DLB-15
Rand, Avery and Company DLB-49		
Rand McNally and Company DLB-49	Redfield, J. S. [publishing house] DLB-49	
Randall, David Anton 1905-1975 ...... DLB-140	Redgrove, Peter 1932- DLB-40	(Re-)Publishing Orwell................... Y-86
Randall, Dudley 1914- DLB-41	Redmon, Anne 1943- Y-86	Research in the American Antiquarian Book Trade Y-97
Randall, Henry S. 1811-1876 .... DLB-30	Redmond, Eugene B. 1937- DLB-41	
Randall, James G. 1881-1953 .... DLB-17	Redpath, James [publishing house]...... DLB-49	Responses to Ken Auletta............... Y-97
The Randall Jarrell Symposium: A Small Collection of Randall Jarrells Excerpts From Papers Delivered at the Randall Jarrel Symposium Y-86	Reed, Henry 1808-1854 .... DLB-59	Rettenbacher, Simon 1634-1706 .... DLB-168
	Reed, Henry 1914- DLB-27	Reuchlin, Johannes 1455-1522 ....DLB-179
	Reed, Ishmael 1938- ... DLB-2, 5, 33, 169; DS-8	Reuter, Christian 1665-after 1712....... DLB-168
	Reed, Rex 1938- DLB-185	Reuter, Fritz 1810-1874................ DLB-129
Randolph, A. Philip 1889-1979.......... DLB-91	Reed, Sampson 1800-1880 .... DLB-1	Reuter, Gabriele 1859-1941 .... DLB-66
Randolph, Anson D. F. [publishing house] DLB-49	Reed, Talbot Baines 1852-1893 .... DLB-141	Revell, Fleming H., Company DLB-49
	Reedy, William Marion 1862-1920 ...... DLB-91	Reventlow, Franziska Gräfin zu 1871-1918.................... DLB-66
Randolph, Thomas 1605-1635...... DLB-58, 126	Reese, Lizette Woodworth 1856-1935 .... DLB-54	
Random House.................... DLB-46	Reese, Thomas 1742-1796 .... DLB-37	Review of Reviews Office............. DLB-112
Ranlet, Henry [publishing house]........ DLB-49	Reeve, Clara 1729-1807 .... DLB-39	Review of [Samuel Richardson's] Clarissa (1748), by Henry Fielding................... DLB-39
Ransom, Harry 1908-1976 .... DLB-187	Reeves, James 1909-1978 .... DLB-161	
Ransom, John Crowe 1888-1974 ..... DLB-45, 63	Reeves, John 1926- DLB-88	The Revolt (1937), by Mary Colum [excerpts] DLB-36
Ransome, Arthur 1884-1967 .... DLB-160	"Reflections: After a Tornado," by Judson Jerome................. DLB-105	
Raphael, Frederic 1931- DLB-14		Rexroth, Kenneth 1905-1982 ....DLB-16, 48, 165, 212; Y-82
Raphaelson, Samson 1896-1983......... DLB-44	Regnery, Henry, Company DLB-46	
Rashi circa 1040-1105................. DLB-208	Rehberg, Hans 1901-1963 .... DLB-124	Rey, H. A. 1898-1977................. DLB-22
Raskin, Ellen 1928-1984................ DLB-52	Rehfisch, Hans José 1891-1960 .... DLB-124	Reynal and Hitchcock DLB-46
Rastell, John 1475?-1536..........DLB-136, 170	Reich, Ebbe Kløvedal 1940- DLB-214	Reynolds, G. W. M. 1814-1879 .... DLB-21
Rattigan, Terence 1911-1977 .... DLB-13	Reid, Alastair 1926- DLB-27	Reynolds, John Hamilton 1794-1852 ..... DLB-96
Rawlings, Marjorie Kinnan 1896-1953 ....DLB-9, 22, 102; DS-17	Reid, B. L. 1918-1990................ DLB-111	Reynolds, Mack 1917- DLB-8
	Reid, Christopher 1949- DLB-40	Reynolds, Sir Joshua 1723-1792 .... DLB-104
Rawlinson, Richard 1690-1755 .... DLB-213	Reid, Forrest 1875-1947 .... DLB-153	Reznikoff, Charles 1894-1976......... DLB-28, 45
Rawlinson, Thomas 1681-1725 .... DLB-213	Reid, Helen Rogers 1882-1970 .... DLB-29	"Rhetoric" (1828; revised, 1859), by Thomas de Quincey [excerpt] DLB-57
Raworth, Tom 1938- DLB-40	Reid, James ?-? DLB-31	
Ray, David 1932- DLB-5	Reid, Mayne 1818-1883 .... DLB-21, 163	Rhett, Robert Barnwell 1800-1876 .... DLB-43
Ray, Gordon Norton 1915-1986 ... DLB-103, 140	Reid, Thomas 1710-1796 .... DLB-31	Rhode, John 1884-1964 .... DLB-77
Ray, Henrietta Cordelia 1849-1916 ...... DLB-50		Rhodes, James Ford 1848-1927 .... DLB-47
Raymond, Ernest 1888-1974........... DLB-191	Reid, V. S. (Vic) 1913-1987 .... DLB-125	Rhodes, Richard 1937- DLB-185
Raymond, Henry J. 1820-1869....... DLB-43, 79	Reid, Whitelaw 1837-1912 .... DLB-23	Rhys, Jean 1890-1979......... DLB-36, 117, 162
Raymond Chandler Centenary Tributes from Michael Avallone, James Elroy, Joe Gores, and William F. Nolan................. Y-88	Reilly and Lee Publishing Company DLB-46	Ricardo, David 1772-1823 ....DLB-107, 158
	Reimann, Brigitte 1933-1973 .... DLB-75	Ricardou, Jean 1932- DLB-83
	Reinmar der Alte circa 1165-circa 1205 .... DLB-138	Rice, Elmer 1892-1967 .... DLB-4, 7
Reach, Angus 1821-1856 .... DLB-70		Rice, Grantland 1880-1954...........DLB-29, 171
Read, Herbert 1893-1968 .... DLB-20, 149	Reinmar von Zweter circa 1200-circa 1250 .... DLB-138	Rich, Adrienne 1929- DLB-5, 67
Read, Herbert, "The Practice of Biography," in The English Sense of Humour and Other Essays DLB-149		Richard de Fournival 1201-1259 or 1260................ DLB-208
	Reisch, Walter 1903-1983 .... DLB-44	
	Reizei Family DLB-203	Richards, David Adams 1950- DLB-53
Read, Martha Meredith DLB-200	Remarks at the Opening of "The Biographical Part of Literature" Exhibition, by William R. Cagle..................... Y-98	Richards, George circa 1760-1814 .... DLB-37
Read, Opie 1852-1939 .... DLB-23		Richards, I. A. 1893-1979 .... DLB-27
Read, Piers Paul 1941- DLB-14		Richards, Laura E. 1850-1943 .... DLB-42
Reade, Charles 1814-1884 .... DLB-21		Richards, William Carey 1818-1892 ...... DLB-73
Reader's Digest Condensed Books....... DLB-46	Remarque, Erich Maria 1898-1970....... DLB-56	Richards, Grant [publishing house] DLB-112
Readers Ulysses Symposium Y-97	"Re-meeting of Old Friends": The Jack Kerouac Conference Y-82	Richardson, Charles F. 1851-1913 .... DLB-71
Reading, Peter 1946- DLB-40	Reminiscences, by Charles Scribner Jr. DS-17	Richardson, Dorothy M. 1873-1957...... DLB-36
Reading Series in New York City........... Y-96	Remington, Frederic 1861-1909 ....DLB-12, 186, 188	Richardson, Henry Handel (Ethel Florence Lindesay) 1870-1946 ....DLB-197
Reaney, James 1926- DLB-68		
Rebhun, Paul 1500?-1546.............DLB-179	Renaud, Jacques 1943- DLB-60	Richardson, Jack 1935- DLB-7
	Renault, Mary 1905-1983 .... Y-83	Richardson, John 1796-1852........... DLB-99

Richardson, Samuel 1689-1761 ......DLB-39, 154
Richardson, Willis 1889-1977 ....DLB-51
Riche, Barnabe 1542-1617 ....DLB-136
Richepin, Jean 1849-1926 ....DLB-192
Richler, Mordecai 1931- DLB-53
Richter, Conrad 1890-1968 ....DLB-9, 212
Richter, Hans Werner 1908- DLB-69
Richter, Johann Paul Friedrich
  1763-1825 ....DLB-94
Rickerby, Joseph [publishing house] DLB-106
Rickword, Edgell 1898-1982 ....DLB-20
Riddell, Charlotte 1832-1906..........DLB-156
Riddell, John (see Ford, Corey)
Ridge, John Rollin 1827-1867...........DLB-175
Ridge, Lola 1873-1941 ....DLB-54
Ridge, William Pett 1859-1930 ....DLB-135
Riding, Laura (see Jackson, Laura Riding)
Ridler, Anne 1912- DLB-27
Ridruego, Dionisio 1912-1975 ....DLB-108
Riel, Louis 1844-1885 ....DLB-99
Riemer, Johannes 1648-1714 ....DLB-168
Rifbjerg, Klaus 1931- DLB-214
Riffaterre, Michael 1924- DLB-67
Riggs, Lynn 1899-1954 ....DLB-175
Riis, Jacob 1849-1914...................DLB-23
Riker, John C. [publishing house] DLB-49
Riley, James 1777-1840.................DLB-183
Riley, John 1938-1978 ....DLB-40
Rilke, Rainer Maria 1875-1926 ....DLB-81
Rimanelli, Giose 1926- DLB-177
Rinehart and Company..................DLB-46
Ringuet 1895-1960.......................DLB-68
Ringwood, Gwen Pharis 1910-1984.......DLB-88
Rinser, Luise 1911- DLB-69
Ríos, Alberto 1952- DLB-122
Ríos, Isabella 1948- DLB-82
Ripley, Arthur 1895-1961 ....DLB-44
Ripley, George 1802-1880 ....DLB-1, 64, 73
The Rising Glory of America:
  Three Poems.......................DLB-37
The Rising Glory of America: Written in 1771
  (1786), by Hugh Henry Brackenridge and
  Philip Freneau....................DLB-37
Riskin, Robert 1897-1955................DLB-26
Risse, Heinz 1898- DLB-69
Rist, Johann 1607-1667.................DLB-164
Ritchie, Anna Mowatt 1819-1870.........DLB-3
Ritchie, Anne Thackeray 1837-1919 ......DLB-18
Ritchie, Thomas 1778-1854 ....DLB-43
Rites of Passage [on William Saroyan].......Y-83
The Ritz Paris Hemingway Award Y-85
Rivard, Adjutor 1868-1945 ....DLB-92
Rive, Richard 1931-1989................DLB-125
Rivera, Marina 1942- DLB-122
Rivera, Tomás 1935-1984 ....DLB-82

Rivers, Conrad Kent 1933-1968 ....DLB-41
Riverside Press.........................DLB-49
Rivington, James circa 1724-1802 ......DLB-43
Rivington, Charles [publishing house]....DLB-154
Rivkin, Allen 1903-1990 ....DLB-26
Roa Bastos, Augusto 1917- DLB-113
Robbe-Grillet, Alain 1922- DLB-83
Robbins, Tom 1936- Y-80
Robert Pinsky Reappointed Poet Laureate ...Y-98
Roberts, Charles G. D. 1860-1943........DLB-92
Roberts, Dorothy 1906-1993 ....DLB-88
Roberts, Elizabeth Madox
  1881-1941 ....DLB-9, 54, 102
Roberts, Kenneth 1885-1957 ....DLB-9
Roberts, William 1767-1849............DLB-142
Roberts Brothers DLB-49
Roberts, James [publishing house]......DLB-154
Robertson, A. M., and Company DLB-49
Robertson, William 1721-1793 ....DLB-104
Robins, Elizabeth 1862-1952 ....DLB-197
Robinson, Casey 1903-1979..............DLB-44
Robinson, Edwin Arlington 1869-1935....DLB-54
Robinson, Henry Crabb 1775-1867.......DLB-107
Robinson, James Harvey 1863-1936.......DLB-47
Robinson, Lennox 1886-1958 ....DLB-10
Robinson, Mabel Louise 1874-1962.......DLB-22
Robinson, Marilynne 1943- DLB-206
Robinson, Mary 1758-1800 ....DLB-158
Robinson, Richard circa 1545-1607......DLB-167
Robinson, Therese 1797-1870........DLB-59, 133
Robison, Mary 1949- DLB-130
Roblès, Emmanuel 1914- DLB-83
Roccatagliata Ceccardi, Ceccardo
  1871-1919 ....DLB-114
Rochester, John Wilmot, Earl of
  1647-1680 ....DLB-131
Rock, Howard 1911-1976 ....DLB-127
Rockwell, Norman Perceval
  1894-1978 ....DLB-188
Rodgers, Carolyn M. 1945- DLB-41
Rodgers, W. R. 1909-1969 ....DLB-20
Rodríguez, Claudio 1934- DLB-134
Rodríguez, Joe D. 1943- DLB-209
Rodríguez, Luis J. 1954- DLB-209
Rodriguez, Richard 1944- DLB-82
Rodríguez Julia, Edgardo 1946- DLB-145
Roe, E. P. 1838-1888....................DLB-202
Roethke, Theodore 1908-1963 ....DLB-5, 206
Rogers, Jane 1952- DLB-194
Rogers, Pattiann 1940- DLB-105
Rogers, Samuel 1763-1855...............DLB-93
Rogers, Will 1879-1935 ....DLB-11
Rohmer, Sax 1883-1959 ....DLB-70
Roiphe, Anne 1935- Y-80
Rojas, Arnold R. 1896-1988 ....DLB-82

Rolfe, Frederick William
  1860-1913 ....DLB-34, 156
Rolland, Romain 1866-1944 ....DLB-65
Rolle, Richard circa 1290-1300 - 1340....DLB-146
Rölvaag, O. E. 1876-1931 ....DLB-9, 212
Romains, Jules 1885-1972 ....DLB-65
Roman, A., and Company...............DLB-49
Roman de la Rose: Guillaume de Lorris
  1200 to 1205-circa 1230, Jean de Meun
  1235-1240-circa 1305 ....DLB-208
Romano, Lalla 1906- DLB-177
Romano, Octavio 1923- DLB-122
Romero, Leo 1950- DLB-122
Romero, Lin 1947- DLB-122
Romero, Orlando 1945- DLB-82
Rook, Clarence 1863-1915 ....DLB-135
Roosevelt, Theodore 1858-1919 .....DLB-47, 186
Root, Waverley 1903-1982 ....DLB-4
Root, William Pitt 1941- DLB-120
Roquebrune, Robert de 1889-1978 .....DLB-68
Rosa, João Guimarāres 1908-1967 .....DLB-113
Rosales, Luis 1910-1992 ....DLB-134
Roscoe, William 1753-1831..............DLB-163
Rose, Reginald 1920- DLB-26
Rose, Wendy 1948- DLB-175
Rosegger, Peter 1843-1918 ....DLB-129
Rosei, Peter 1946- DLB-85
Rosen, Norma 1925- DLB-28
Rosenbach, A. S. W. 1876-1952 ....DLB-140
Rosenbaum, Ron 1946- DLB-185
Rosenberg, Isaac 1890-1918 ....DLB-20, 216
Rosenfeld, Isaac 1918-1956 ....DLB-28
Rosenthal, M. L. 1917- DLB-5
Rosenwald, Lessing J. 1891-1979 ......DLB-187
Ross, Alexander 1591-1654 ....DLB-151
Ross, Harold 1892-1951 ....DLB-137
Ross, Leonard Q. (see Rosten, Leo)
Ross, Lillian 1927- DLB-185
Ross, Martin 1862-1915................DLB-135
Ross, Sinclair 1908- DLB-88
Ross, W. W. E. 1894-1966 ....DLB-88
Rosselli, Amelia 1930- DLB-128
Rossen, Robert 1908-1966..............DLB-26
Rossetti, Christina Georgina
  1830-1894 ....DLB-35, 163
Rossetti, Dante Gabriel 1828-1882 ....DLB-35
Rossner, Judith 1935- DLB-6
Rostand, Edmond 1868-1918 ....DLB-192
Rosten, Leo 1908- DLB-11
Rostenberg, Leona 1908- DLB-140
Rostopchina, Evdokiia Petrovna
  1811-1858 ....DLB-205
Rostovsky, Dimitrii 1651-1709 ....DLB-150
Rota, Bertram 1903-1966 ....DLB-201
Bertram Rota and His Bookshop...........Y-91
Roth, Gerhard 1942- DLB-85, 124

Cumulative Index DLB 216

Roth, Henry 1906?- DLB-28
Roth, Joseph 1894-1939 . . . . DLB-85
Roth, Philip 1933- DLB-2, 28, 173; Y-82
Rothenberg, Jerome 1931- DLB-5, 193
Rothschild Family DLB-184
Rotimi, Ola 1938- DLB-125
Routhier, Adolphe-Basile 1839-1920 . . . . . DLB-99
Routier, Simone 1901-1987 . . . . DLB-88
Routledge, George, and Sons DLB-106
Roversi, Roberto 1923- DLB-128
Rowe, Elizabeth Singer 1674-1737 . . . . DLB-39, 95
Rowe, Nicholas 1674-1718 . . . . DLB-84
Rowlands, Samuel circa 1570-1630 . . . . . DLB-121
Rowlandson, Mary
 circa 1637-circa 1711 . . . . DLB-24, 200
Rowley, William circa 1585-1626 . . . . DLB-58
Rowse, A. L. 1903- DLB-155
Rowson, Susanna Haswell
 circa 1762-1824 . . . . DLB-37, 200
Roy, Camille 1870-1943 . . . . DLB-92
Roy, Gabrielle 1909-1983 . . . . DLB-68
Roy, Jules 1907- DLB-83
The Royal Court Theatre and the English
 Stage Company DLB-13
The Royal Court Theatre and the New
 Drama DLB-10
The Royal Shakespeare Company
 at the Swan Y-88
Royall, Anne 1769-1854 . . . . DLB-43
The Roycroft Printing Shop DLB-49
Royde-Smith, Naomi 1875-1964 . . . . DLB-191
Royster, Vermont 1914- DLB-127
Royston, Richard [publishing house] DLB-170
Ruark, Gibbons 1941- DLB-120
Ruban, Vasilii Grigorevich 1742-1795 . . . DLB-150
Rubens, Bernice 1928- DLB-14, 207
Rudd and Carleton DLB-49
Rudkin, David 1936- DLB-13
Rudolf von Ems
 circa 1200-circa 1254 . . . . DLB-138
Ruffin, Josephine St. Pierre
 1842-1924 . . . . DLB-79
Ruganda, John 1941- DLB-157
Ruggles, Henry Joseph 1813-1906 . . . . . . DLB-64
Ruiz de Burton, María Amparo
 1832?-1895 . . . . DLB-209
Rukeyser, Muriel 1913-1980 . . . . DLB-48
Rule, Jane 1931- DLB-60
Rulfo, Juan 1918-1986 . . . . DLB-113
Rumaker, Michael 1932- DLB-16
Rumens, Carol 1944- DLB-40
Runyon, Damon 1880-1946 . . . . . . DLB-11, 86, 171
Ruodlieb circa 1050-1075 . . . . DLB-148
Rush, Benjamin 1746-1813 . . . . DLB-37
Rush, Rebecca 1779-? DLB-200
Rushdie, Salman 1947- DLB-194
Rusk, Ralph L. 1888-1962 . . . . DLB-103

Ruskin, John 1819-1900 . . . . DLB-55, 163, 190
Russ, Joanna 1937- DLB-8
Russell, B. B., and Company DLB-49
Russell, Benjamin 1761-1845 . . . . DLB-43
Russell, Bertrand 1872-1970 . . . . DLB-100
Russell, Charles Edward 1860-1941 . . . . . . DLB-25
Russell, Charles M. 1864-1926 . . . . DLB-188
Russell, Countess Mary Annette Beauchamp
 (see Arnim, Elizabeth von)
Russell, George William (see AE)
Russell, R. H., and Son DLB-49
Rutebeuf flourished 1249-1277 . . . . DLB-208
Rutherford, Mark 1831-1913 . . . . DLB-18
Ruxton, George Frederick 1821-1848 . . . DLB-186
Ryan, Michael 1946- Y-82
Ryan, Oscar 1904- DLB-68
Ryga, George 1932- DLB-60
Rylands, Enriqueta Augustina Tennant
 1843-1908 . . . . DLB-184
Rylands, John 1801-1888 . . . . DLB-184
Ryleev, Kondratii Fedorovich
 1795-1826 . . . . DLB-205
Rymer, Thomas 1643?-1713 . . . . DLB-101
Ryskind, Morrie 1895-1985 . . . . DLB-26
Rzhevsky, Aleksei Andreevich
 1737-1804 . . . . DLB-150

S

The Saalfield Publishing Company DLB-46
Saba, Umberto 1883-1957 . . . . DLB-114
Sábato, Ernesto 1911- DLB-145
Saberhagen, Fred 1930- DLB-8
Sabin, Joseph 1821-1881 . . . . DLB-187
Sacer, Gottfried Wilhelm 1635-1699 . . . . DLB-168
Sachs, Hans 1494-1576 . . . . DLB-179
Sack, John 1930- DLB-185
Sackler, Howard 1929-1982 . . . . DLB-7
Sackville, Thomas 1536-1608 . . . . DLB-132
Sackville, Thomas 1536-1608
 and Norton, Thomas
 1532-1584 . . . . DLB-62
Sackville-West, Edward 1901-1965 . . . . . DLB-191
Sackville-West, V. 1892-1962 . . . . DLB-34, 195
Sadlier, D. and J., and Company DLB-49
Sadlier, Mary Anne 1820-1903 . . . . DLB-99
Sadoff, Ira 1945- DLB-120
Sáenz, Benjamin Alire 1954- DLB-209
Saenz, Jaime 1921-1986 . . . . DLB-145
Saffin, John circa 1626-1710 . . . . DLB-24
Sagan, Françoise 1935- DLB-83
Sage, Robert 1899-1962 . . . . DLB-4
Sagel, Jim 1947- DLB-82
Sagendorph, Robb Hansell 1900-1970 . . . DLB-137
Sahagún, Carlos 1938- DLB-108
Sahkomaapii, Piitai (see Highwater, Jamake)
Sahl, Hans 1902- DLB-69

Said, Edward W. 1935- DLB-67
Saigyō 1118-1190 . . . . DLB-203
Saiko, George 1892-1962 . . . . DLB-85
St. Dominic's Press DLB-112
Saint-Exupéry, Antoine de 1900-1944 . . . . DLB-72
St. John, J. Allen 1872-1957 . . . . DLB-188
St. Johns, Adela Rogers 1894-1988 . . . . . . DLB-29
The St. John's College Robert Graves Trust . . Y-96
St. Martin's Press DLB-46
St. Omer, Garth 1931- DLB-117
Saint Pierre, Michel de 1916-1987 . . . . . . DLB-83
Saints' Lives DLB-208
Saintsbury, George 1845-1933 . . . . . . DLB-57, 149
Saiokuken Sōchō 1448-1532 . . . . DLB-203
Saki (see Munro, H. H.)
Salaam, Kalamu ya 1947- DLB-38
Šalamun, Tomaž 1941- DLB-181
Salas, Floyd 1931- DLB-82
Sálaz-Marquez, Rubén 1935- DLB-122
Salemson, Harold J. 1910-1988 . . . . DLB-4
Salinas, Luis Omar 1937- DLB-82
Salinas, Pedro 1891-1951 . . . . DLB-134
Salinger, J. D. 1919- DLB-2, 102, 173
Salkey, Andrew 1928- DLB-125
Sallust circa 86 B.C.-35 B.C. DLB-211
Salt, Waldo 1914- DLB-44
Salter, James 1925- DLB-130
Salter, Mary Jo 1954- DLB-120
Saltus, Edgar 1855-1921 . . . . DLB-202
Salustri, Carlo Alberto (see Trilussa)
Salverson, Laura Goodman 1890-1970 . . . DLB-92
Sampson, Richard Henry (see Hull, Richard)
Samuels, Ernest 1903- DLB-111
Sanborn, Franklin Benjamin 1831-1917 . . . DLB-1
Sánchez, Luis Rafael 1936- DLB-145
Sánchez, Philomeno "Phil" 1917- DLB-122
Sánchez, Ricardo 1941- DLB-82
Sánchez, Saúl 1943- DLB-209
Sanchez, Sonia 1934- DLB-41; DS-8
Sand, George 1804-1876 . . . . DLB-119, 192
Sandburg, Carl 1878-1967 . . . . DLB-17, 54
Sanders, Ed 1939- DLB-16
Sandoz, Mari 1896-1966 . . . . DLB-9, 212
Sandwell, B. K. 1876-1954 . . . . DLB-92
Sandy, Stephen 1934- DLB-165
Sandys, George 1578-1644 . . . . DLB-24, 121
Sangster, Charles 1822-1893 . . . . DLB-99
Sanguineti, Edoardo 1930- DLB-128
Sanjōnishi Sanetaka 1455-1537 . . . . DLB-203
Sansay, Leonora ?-after 1823 . . . . DLB-200
Sansom, William 1912-1976 . . . . DLB-139
Santayana, George
 1863-1952 . . . . DLB-54, 71; DS-13
Santiago, Danny 1911-1988 . . . . DLB-122

Santmyer, Helen Hooven 1895-1986........ Y-84
Sanvitale, Francesca 1928- DLB-196
Sapidus, Joannes 1490-1561............ DLB-179
Sapir, Edward 1884-1939...............DLB-92
Sapper (see McNeile, Herman Cyril)
Sappho circa 620 B.C.-circa 550 B.C.
 ....DLB-176
Saramago, José 1922- Y-98
Sardou, Victorien 1831-1908...........DLB-192
Sarduy, Severo 1937- DLB-113
Sargent, Pamela 1948- DLB-8
Saro-Wiwa, Ken 1941- DLB-157
Saroyan, William 1908-1981 ... DLB-7, 9, 86; Y-81
Sarraute, Nathalie 1900- DLB-83
Sarrazin, Albertine 1937-1967............DLB-83
Sarris, Greg 1952- DLB-175
Sarton, May 1912- DLB-48; Y-81
Sartre, Jean-Paul 1905-1980............DLB-72
Sassoon, Siegfried
 1886-1967 ....DLB-20, 191; DS-18
Sata, Ineko 1904- DLB-180
Saturday Review Press.................DLB-46
Saunders, James 1925- DLB-13
Saunders, John Monk 1897-1940 ....DLB-26
Saunders, Margaret Marshall
 1861-1947 ....DLB-92
Saunders and Otley DLB-106
Savage, James 1784-1873 ....DLB-30
Savage, Marmion W. 1803?-1872 ....DLB-21
Savage, Richard 1697?-1743............DLB-95
Savard, Félix-Antoine 1896-1982.........DLB-68
Saville, (Leonard) Malcolm 1901-1982 ...DLB-160
Sawyer, Ruth 1880-1970 ....DLB-22
Sayers, Dorothy L.
 1893-1957 .... DLB-10, 36, 77, 100
Sayle, Charles Edward 1864-1924.......DLB-184
Sayles, John Thomas 1950- DLB-44
Sbarbaro, Camillo 1888-1967 ....DLB-114
Scalapino, Leslie 1947- DLB-193
Scannell, Vernon 1922- DLB-27
Scarry, Richard 1919-1994 ....DLB-61
Schaefer, Jack 1907-1991 ....DLB-212
Schaeffer, Albrecht 1885-1950..........DLB-66
Schaeffer, Susan Fromberg 1941- DLB-28
Schaff, Philip 1819-1893 ....DS-13
Schaper, Edzard 1908-1984 ....DLB-69
Scharf, J. Thomas 1843-1898............DLB-47
Schede, Paul Melissus 1539-1602 ....DLB-179
Scheffel, Joseph Viktor von 1826-1886 ...DLB-129
Scheffler, Johann 1624-1677............DLB-164
Schelling, Friedrich Wilhelm Joseph von
 1775-1854 ....DLB-90
Scherer, Wilhelm 1841-1886............DLB-129
Scherfig, Hans 1905-1979..............DLB-214
Schickele, René 1883-1940..............DLB-66
Schiff, Dorothy 1903-1989.............DLB-127

Schiller, Friedrich 1759-1805 ....DLB-94
Schirmer, David 1623-1687............DLB-164
Schlaf, Johannes 1862-1941............DLB-118
Schlegel, August Wilhelm 1767-1845 ......DLB-94
Schlegel, Dorothea 1763-1839 ....DLB-90
Schlegel, Friedrich 1772-1829...........DLB-90
Schleiermacher, Friedrich 1768-1834 .....DLB-90
Schlesinger, Arthur M., Jr. 1917- DLB-17
Schlumberger, Jean 1877-1968 ....DLB-65
Schmid, Eduard Hermann Wilhelm (see
 Edschmid, Kasimir)
Schmidt, Arno 1914-1979...............DLB-69
Schmidt, Johann Kaspar (see Stirner, Max)
Schmidt, Michael 1947- DLB-40
Schmidtbonn, Wilhelm August
 1876-1952 ....DLB-118
Schmitz, James H. 1911- DLB-8
Schnabel, Johann Gottfried
 1692-1760 ....DLB-168
Schnackenberg, Gjertrud 1953- DLB-120
Schnitzler, Arthur 1862-1931.........DLB-81, 118
Schnurre, Wolfdietrich 1920-1989........DLB-69
Schocken Books.....................DLB-46
Scholartis Press DLB-112
Scholderer, Victor 1880-1971..........DLB-201
The Schomburg Center for Research
 in Black Culture DLB-76
Schönbeck, Virgilio (see Giotti, Virgilio)
Schönherr, Karl 1867-1943 ....DLB-118
Schoolcraft, Jane Johnston 1800-1841 ....DLB-175
School Stories, 1914-1960 ....DLB-160
Schopenhauer, Arthur 1788-1860 ....DLB-90
Schopenhauer, Johanna 1766-1838 ....DLB-90
Schorer, Mark 1908-1977...............DLB-103
Schottelius, Justus Georg 1612-1676 ....DLB-164
Schouler, James 1839-1920 ....DLB-47
Schrader, Paul 1946- DLB-44
Schreiner, Olive 1855-1920 ......DLB-18, 156, 190
Schroeder, Andreas 1946- DLB-53
Schubart, Christian Friedrich Daniel
 1739-1791 ....DLB-97
Schubert, Gotthilf Heinrich 1780-1860 ....DLB-90
Schücking, Levin 1814-1883 ....DLB-133
Schulberg, Budd 1914- DLB-6, 26, 28; Y-81
Schulte, F. J., and Company..............DLB-49
Schulz, Bruno 1892-1942 ....DLB-215
Schulze, Hans (see Praetorius, Johannes)
Schupp, Johann Balthasar 1610-1661.....DLB-164
Schurz, Carl 1829-1906 ....DLB-23
Schuyler, George S. 1895-1977 ....DLB-29, 51
Schuyler, James 1923-1991 ....DLB-5, 169
Schwartz, Delmore 1913-1966........DLB-28, 48
Schwartz, Jonathan 1938- Y-82
Schwarz, Sibylle 1621-1638 ....DLB-164
Schwerner, Armand 1927- DLB-165
Schwob, Marcel 1867-1905 ....DLB-123

Sciascia, Leonardo 1921-1989 ....DLB-177
Science Fantasy DLB-8
Science-Fiction Fandom and Conventions ...DLB-8
Science-Fiction Fanzines: The Time
 Binders DLB-8
Science-Fiction Films DLB-8
Science Fiction Writers of America and the
 Nebula Awards DLB-8
Scot, Reginald circa 1538-1599 ....DLB-136
Scotellaro, Rocco 1923-1953 ....DLB-128
Scott, Dennis 1939-1991 ....DLB-125
Scott, Dixon 1881-1915................DLB-98
Scott, Duncan Campbell 1862-1947.......DLB-92
Scott, Evelyn 1893-1963 ....DLB-9, 48
Scott, F. R. 1899-1985 ....DLB-88
Scott, Frederick George 1861-1944 ......DLB-92
Scott, Geoffrey 1884-1929 ....DLB-149
Scott, Harvey W. 1838-1910 ....DLB-23
Scott, Paul 1920-1978...............DLB-14, 207
Scott, Sarah 1723-1795 ....DLB-39
Scott, Tom 1918- DLB-27
Scott, Sir Walter
 1771-1832 ....DLB-93, 107, 116, 144, 159
Scott, William Bell 1811-1890 ....DLB-32
Scott, Walter, Publishing
 Company Limited................DLB-112
Scott, William R. [publishing house] DLB-46
Scott-Heron, Gil 1949- DLB-41
Scribe, Eugene 1791-1861 ....DLB-192
Scribner, Arthur Hawley 1859-1932 ... DS-13, 16
Scribner, Charles 1854-1930 .... DS-13, 16
Scribner, Charles, Jr. 1921-1995 .... Y-95
Charles Scribner's Sons DLB-49; DS-13, 16, 17
Scripps, E. W. 1854-1926 ....DLB-25
Scudder, Horace Elisha 1838-1902 ....DLB-42, 71
Scudder, Vida Dutton 1861-1954 ....DLB-71
Scupham, Peter 1933- DLB-40
Seabrook, William 1886-1945 ....DLB-4
Seabury, Samuel 1729-1796 ....DLB-31
Seacole, Mary Jane Grant 1805-1881 ....DLB-166
The Seafarer circa 970 ....DLB-146
Sealsfield, Charles (Carl Postl)
 1793-1864 ....DLB-133, 186
Sears, Edward I. 1819?-1876 ....DLB-79
Sears Publishing Company DLB-46
Seaton, George 1911-1979 ....DLB-44
Seaton, William Winston 1785-1866......DLB-43
Secker, Martin, and Warburg Limited ...DLB-112
Secker, Martin [publishing house] DLB-112
Second-Generation Minor Poets of the
 Seventeenth Century DLB-126
Second International Hemingway Colloquium:
 Cuba............................. Y-98
Sedgwick, Arthur George 1844-1915......DLB-64
Sedgwick, Catharine Maria
 1789-1867 ....DLB-1, 74, 183
Sedgwick, Ellery 1872-1930 ....DLB-91

Sedley, Sir Charles 1639-1701..........DLB-131
Seeberg, Peter 1925-1999.............DLB-214
Seeger, Alan 1888-1916...............DLB-45
Seers, Eugene (see Dantin, Louis)
Segal, Erich 1937-....................Y-86
Šegedin, Petar 1909-................DLB-181
Seghers, Anna 1900-1983.............DLB-69
Seid, Ruth (see Sinclair, Jo)
Seidel, Frederick Lewis 1936-..........Y-84
Seidel, Ina 1885-1974................DLB-56
Seifert, Jaroslav 1901-1986........DLB-215; Y-84
Seigenthaler, John 1927-.............DLB-127
Seizin Press........................DLB-112
Séjour, Victor 1817-1874.............DLB-50
Séjour Marcou et Ferrand, Juan Victor (see Séjour, Victor)
Sekowski, Jósef-Julian, Baron Brambeus (see Senkovsky, Osip Ivanovich)
Selby, Bettina 1934-.................DLB-204
Selby, Hubert, Jr. 1928-..............DLB-2
Selden, George 1929-1989.............DLB-52
Selden, John 1584-1654...............DLB-213
Selected English-Language Little Magazines and Newspapers [France, 1920-1939]...DLB-4
Selected Humorous Magazines (1820-1950)....................DLB-11
Selected Science-Fiction Magazines and Anthologies......................DLB-8
Selenić, Slobodan 1933-1995..........DLB-181
Self, Edwin F. 1920-.................DLB-137
Self, Will 1961-....................DLB-207
Seligman, Edwin R. A. 1861-1939......DLB-47
Selimović, Meša 1910-1982............DLB-181
Selous, Frederick Courteney 1851-1917.....................DLB-174
Seltzer, Chester E. (see Muro, Amado)
Seltzer, Thomas [publishing house].....DLB-46
Selvon, Sam 1923-1994...............DLB-125
Semmes, Raphael 1809-1877...........DLB-189
Senancour, Etienne de 1770-1846.....DLB-119
Sendak, Maurice 1928-................DLB-61
Seneca the Elder circa 54 B.C.-circa A.D. 40........DLB-211
Seneca the Younger circa 1 B.C.-A.D. 65..............DLB-211
Senécal, Eva 1905-...................DLB-92
Sengstacke, John 1912-...............DLB-127
Senior, Olive 1941-..................DLB-157
Senkovsky, Osip Ivanovich (Józef-Julian Sekowski, Baron Brambeus) 1800-1858......DLB-198
Šenoa, August 1838-1881.............DLB-147
"Sensation Novels" (1863), by H. L. Manse....................DLB-21
Sepamla, Sipho 1932-................DLB-157
Seredy, Kate 1899-1975...............DLB-22
Sereni, Vittorio 1913-1983...........DLB-128
Seres, William [publishing house].....DLB-170

Serling, Rod 1924-1975...............DLB-26
Serote, Mongane Wally 1944-.........DLB-125
Serraillier, Ian 1912-1994...........DLB-161
Serrano, Nina 1934-..................DLB-122
Service, Robert 1874-1958............DLB-92
Sessler, Charles 1854-1935...........DLB-187
Seth, Vikram 1952-..................DLB-120
Seton, Elizabeth Ann 1774-1821.......DLB-200
Seton, Ernest Thompson 1860-1942..............DLB-92; DS-13
Setouchi Harumi 1922-...............DLB-182
Settle, Mary Lee 1918-................DLB-6
Seume, Johann Gottfried 1763-1810....DLB-94
Seuse, Heinrich 1295?-1366..........DLB-179
Seuss, Dr. (see Geisel, Theodor Seuss)
The Seventy-fifth Anniversary of the Armistice: The Wilfred Owen Centenary and the Great War Exhibit at the University of Virginia.....Y-93
Severin, Timothy 1940-..............DLB-204
Sewall, Joseph 1688-1769.............DLB-24
Sewall, Richard B. 1908-.............DLB-111
Sewell, Anna 1820-1878..............DLB-163
Sewell, Samuel 1652-1730............DLB-24
Sex, Class, Politics, and Religion [in the British Novel, 1930-1959]..........DLB-15
Sexton, Anne 1928-1974............DLB-5, 169
Seymour-Smith, Martin 1928-.........DLB-155
Sgorlon, Carlo 1930-.................DLB-196
Shaara, Michael 1929-1988............Y-83
Shadwell, Thomas 1641?-1692.........DLB-80
Shaffer, Anthony 1926-...............DLB-13
Shaffer, Peter 1926-.................DLB-13
Shaftesbury, Anthony Ashley Cooper, Third Earl of 1671-1713..........DLB-101
Shairp, Mordaunt 1887-1939..........DLB-10
Shakespeare, William 1564-1616...DLB-62, 172
The Shakespeare Globe Trust..........Y-93
Shakespeare Head Press..............DLB-112
Shakhovskoi, Aleksandr Aleksandrovich 1777-1846.....................DLB-150
Shange, Ntozake 1948-...............DLB-38
Shapiro, Karl 1913-..................DLB-48
Sharon Publications.................DLB-46
Sharp, Margery 1905-1991............DLB-161
Sharp, William 1855-1905............DLB-156
Sharpe, Tom 1928-....................DLB-14
Shaw, Albert 1857-1947...............DLB-91
Shaw, George Bernard 1856-1950................DLB-10, 57, 190
Shaw, Henry Wheeler 1818-1885.......DLB-11
Shaw, Joseph T. 1874-1952...........DLB-137
Shaw, Irwin 1913-1984..........DLB-6, 102; Y-84
Shaw, Robert 1927-1978............DLB-13, 14
Shaw, Robert B. 1947-................DLB-120
Shawn, William 1907-1992............DLB-137
Shay, Frank [publishing house].......DLB-46

Shea, John Gilmary 1824-1892.........DLB-30
Sheaffer, Louis 1912-1993...........DLB-103
Shearing, Joseph 1886-1952...........DLB-70
Shebbeare, John 1709-1788...........DLB-39
Sheckley, Robert 1928-................DLB-8
Shedd, William G. T. 1820-1894......DLB-64
Sheed, Wilfred 1930-..................DLB-6
Sheed and Ward [U.S.]...............DLB-46
Sheed and Ward Limited [U.K.].......DLB-112
Sheldon, Alice B. (see Tiptree, James, Jr.)
Sheldon, Edward 1886-1946............DLB-7
Sheldon and Company.................DLB-49
Shelley, Mary Wollstonecraft 1797-1851..........DLB-110, 116, 159, 178
Shelley, Percy Bysshe 1792-1822..................DLB-96, 110, 158
Shelnutt, Eve 1941-..................DLB-130
Shenstone, William 1714-1763.........DLB-95
Shepard, Ernest Howard 1879-1976....DLB-160
Shepard, Sam 1943-................DLB-7, 212
Shepard, Thomas I, 1604 or 1605-1649...DLB-24
Shepard, Thomas II, 1635-1677.......DLB-24
Shepard, Clark and Brown.............DLB-49
Shepherd, Luke flourished 1547-1554.............DLB-136
Sherburne, Edward 1616-1702.........DLB-131
Sheridan, Frances 1724-1766........DLB-39, 84
Sheridan, Richard Brinsley 1751-1816....DLB-89
Sherman, Francis 1871-1926...........DLB-92
Sherriff, R. C. 1896-1975..........DLB-10, 191
Sherry, Norman 1935-................DLB-155
Sherwood, Mary Martha 1775-1851....DLB-163
Sherwood, Robert 1896-1955.........DLB-7, 26
Shevyrev, Stepan Petrovich 1806-1864....................DLB-205
Shiel, M. P. 1865-1947...............DLB-153
Shiels, George 1886-1949.............DLB-10
Shiga, Naoya 1883-1971..............DLB-180
Shiina Rinzō 1911-1973...............DLB-182
Shikishi Naishinnō 1153?-1201.......DLB-203
Shillaber, B.[enjamin] P.[enhallow] 1814-1890.....................DLB-1, 11
Shimao Toshio 1917-1986.............DLB-182
Shimazaki, Tōson 1872-1943..........DLB-180
Shine, Ted 1931-....................DLB-38
Shinkei 1406-1475....................DLB-203
Ship, Reuben 1915-1975...............DLB-88
Shirer, William L. 1904-1993..........DLB-4
Shirinsky-Shikhmatov, Sergii Aleksandrovich 1783-1837....................DLB-150
Shirley, James 1596-1666.............DLB-58
Shishkov, Aleksandr Semenovich 1753-1841.....................DLB-150
Shockley, Ann Allen 1927-............DLB-33
Shōno Junzō 1921-..................DLB-182
Shore, Arabella 1820?-1901 and Shore, Louisa 1824-1895..........DLB-199

Short, Peter [publishing house] DLB-170
Shorthouse, Joseph Henry 1834-1903 . . . . . DLB-18
Shōtetsu 1381-1459 . . . . DLB-203
Showalter, Elaine 1941- DLB-67
Shulevitz, Uri 1935- DLB-61
Shulman, Max 1919-1988 . . . . DLB-11
Shute, Henry A. 1856-1943 . . . . DLB-9
Shuttle, Penelope 1947- DLB-14, 40
Sibbes, Richard 1577-1635 . . . . DLB-151
Siddal, Elizabeth Eleanor 1829-1862 . . . . . DLB-199
Sidgwick, Ethel 1877-1970 . . . . DLB-197
Sidgwick and Jackson Limited DLB-112
Sidney, Margaret (see Lothrop, Harriet M.)
Sidney, Mary 1561-1621 . . . . DLB-167
Sidney, Sir Philip 1554-1586 . . . . DLB-167
Sidney's Press DLB-49
Siegfried Loraine Sassoon: A Centenary Essay
 Tributes from Vivien F. Clarke and
 Michael Thorpe. Y-86
Sierra, Rubén 1946- DLB-122
Sierra Club Books DLB-49
Siger of Brabant
 circa 1240-circa 1284. . . . . DLB-115
Sigourney, Lydia Howard (Huntley)
 1791-1865 . . . . DLB-1, 42, 73, 183
Silkin, Jon 1930- DLB-27
Silko, Leslie Marmon 1948- DLB-143, 175
Silliman, Benjamin 1779-1864 . . . . DLB-183
Silliman, Ron 1946- DLB-169
Silliphant, Stirling 1918- DLB-26
Sillitoe, Alan 1928- DLB-14, 139
Silman, Roberta 1934- DLB-28
Silva, Beverly 1930- DLB-122
Silverberg, Robert 1935- DLB-8
Silverman, Kenneth 1936- DLB-111
Simak, Clifford D. 1904-1988 . . . . DLB-8
Simcoe, Elizabeth 1762-1850 . . . . DLB-99
Simcox, Edith Jemima 1844-1901 . . . . DLB-190
Simcox, George Augustus 1841-1905 . . . . . DLB-35
Sime, Jessie Georgina 1868-1958 . . . . DLB-92
Simenon, Georges 1903-1989 . . . . . . DLB-72; Y-89
Simic, Charles 1938- DLB-105
Simmel, Johannes Mario 1924- DLB-69
Simmes, Valentine [publishing house] DLB-170
Simmons, Ernest J. 1903-1972 . . . . DLB-103
Simmons, Herbert Alfred 1930- DLB-33
Simmons, James 1933- DLB-40
Simms, William Gilmore
 1806-1870 . . . . DLB-3, 30, 59, 73
Simms and M'Intyre DLB-106
Simon, Claude 1913- DLB-83; Y-85
Simon, Neil 1927- DLB-7
Simon and Schuster DLB-46
Simons, Katherine Drayton Mayrant
 1890-1969 . . . . Y-83
Simović, Ljubomir 1935- DLB-181

Simpkin and Marshall
 [publishing house] DLB-154
Simpson, Helen 1897-1940. . . . . DLB-77
Simpson, Louis 1923- DLB-5
Simpson, N. F. 1919- DLB-13
Sims, George 1923- DLB-87
Sims, George Robert
 1847-1922 . . . . DLB-35, 70, 135
Sinán, Rogelio 1904- DLB-145
Sinclair, Andrew 1935- DLB-14
Sinclair, Bertrand William 1881-1972 . . . . . DLB-92
Sinclair, Catherine 1800-1864 . . . . DLB-163
Sinclair, Jo 1913- DLB-28
Sinclair Lewis Centennial Conference Y-85
Sinclair, Lister 1921- DLB-88
Sinclair, May 1863-1946 . . . . DLB-36, 135
Sinclair, Upton 1878-1968 . . . . DLB-9
Sinclair, Upton [publishing house] DLB-46
Singer, Isaac Bashevis
 1904-1991 . . . . DLB-6, 28, 52; Y-91
Singer, Mark 1950- DLB-185
Singmaster, Elsie 1879-1958 . . . . DLB-9
Sinisgalli, Leonardo 1908-1981 . . . . DLB-114
Siodmak, Curt 1902- DLB-44
Siringo, Charles A. 1855-1928 . . . . DLB-186
Sissman, L. E. 1928-1976 . . . . DLB-5
Sisson, C. H. 1914- DLB-27
Sitwell, Edith 1887-1964 . . . . DLB-20
Sitwell, Osbert 1892-1969 . . . . DLB-100, 195
Skármeta, Antonio 1940- DLB-145
Skeat, Walter W. 1835-1912 . . . . DLB-184
Skeffington, William [publishing house] . . DLB-106
Skelton, John 1463-1529 . . . . DLB-136
Skelton, Robin 1925- DLB-27, 53
Skinner, Constance Lindsay
 1877-1939 . . . . DLB-92
Skinner, John Stuart 1788-1851 . . . . DLB-73
Skipsey, Joseph 1832-1903 . . . . DLB-35
Skou-Hansen, Tage 1925- DLB-214
Slade, Bernard 1930- DLB-53
Slamnig, Ivan 1930- DLB-181
Slančeková, Božena (see Timrava)
Slater, Patrick 1880-1951 . . . . DLB-68
Slaveykov, Pencho 1866-1912 . . . . DLB-147
Slaviček, Milivoj 1929- DLB-181
Slavitt, David 1935- DLB-5, 6
Sleigh, Burrows Willcocks Arthur
 1821-1869 . . . . DLB-99
A Slender Thread of Hope: The Kennedy
 Center Black Theatre Project DLB-38
Slesinger, Tess 1905-1945 . . . . DLB-102
Slick, Sam (see Haliburton, Thomas Chandler)
Sloan, John 1871-1951 . . . . DLB-188
Sloane, William, Associates DLB-46
Small, Maynard and Company DLB-49

Small Presses in Great Britain and Ireland,
 1960-1985 . . . . DLB-40
Small Presses I: Jargon Society Y-84
Small Presses II: The Spirit That Moves
 Us Press Y-85
Small Presses III: Pushcart Press Y-87
Smart, Christopher 1722-1771 . . . . DLB-109
Smart, David A. 1892-1957 . . . . DLB-137
Smart, Elizabeth 1913-1986 . . . . DLB-88
Smedley, Menella Bute 1820?-1877 . . . . . . DLB-199
Smellie, William [publishing house] DLB-154
Smiles, Samuel 1812-1904 . . . . DLB-55
Smith, A. J. M. 1902-1980 . . . . DLB-88
Smith, Adam 1723-1790 . . . . DLB-104
Smith, Adam (George Jerome Waldo Goodman)
 1930- DLB-185
Smith, Alexander 1829-1867 . . . . DLB-32, 55
Smith, Betty 1896-1972 . . . . Y-82
Smith, Carol Sturm 1938- Y-81
Smith, Charles Henry 1826-1903 . . . . DLB-11
Smith, Charlotte 1749-1806 . . . . DLB-39, 109
Smith, Chet 1899-1973 . . . . DLB-171
Smith, Cordwainer 1913-1966 . . . . DLB-8
Smith, Dave 1942- DLB-5
Smith, Dodie 1896- DLB-10
Smith, Doris Buchanan 1934- DLB-52
Smith, E. E. 1890-1965 . . . . DLB-8
Smith, Elihu Hubbard 1771-1798 . . . . DLB-37
Smith, Elizabeth Oakes (Prince)
 1806-1893 . . . . DLB-1
Smith, Eunice 1757-1823 . . . . DLB-200
Smith, F. Hopkinson 1838-1915 . . . . DS-13
Smith, George D. 1870-1920 . . . . DLB-140
Smith, George O. 1911-1981 . . . . DLB-8
Smith, Goldwin 1823-1910 . . . . DLB-99
Smith, H. Allen 1907-1976 . . . . DLB-11, 29
Smith, Harry B. 1860-1936 . . . . DLB-187
Smith, Hazel Brannon 1914- DLB-127
Smith, Henry circa 1560-circa 1591 . . . . . . DLB-136
Smith, Horatio (Horace) 1779-1849 . . . . . DLB-116
Smith, Horatio (Horace) 1779-1849 and
 James Smith 1775-1839 . . . . DLB-96
Smith, Iain Crichton 1928- DLB-40, 139
Smith, J. Allen 1860-1924 . . . . DLB-47
Smith, Jessie Willcox 1863-1935 . . . . DLB-188
Smith, John 1580-1631 . . . . DLB-24, 30
Smith, Josiah 1704-1781 . . . . DLB-24
Smith, Ken 1938- DLB-40
Smith, Lee 1944- DLB-143; Y-83
Smith, Logan Pearsall 1865-1946 . . . . DLB-98
Smith, Mark 1935- Y-82
Smith, Michael 1698-circa 1771 . . . . DLB-31
Smith, Red 1905-1982 . . . . DLB-29, 171
Smith, Roswell 1829-1892 . . . . DLB-79
Smith, Samuel Harrison 1772-1845 . . . . DLB-43
Smith, Samuel Stanhope 1751-1819 . . . . . . DLB-37

Smith, Sarah (see Stretton, Hesba)	Sorensen, Virginia 1912-1991 . . . . DLB-206	Spener, Philipp Jakob 1635-1705 . . . . DLB-164
Smith, Sarah Pogson 1774-1870 . . . . DLB-200	Sorge, Reinhard Johannes 1892-1916. . . . DLB-118	Spenser, Edmund circa 1552-1599 . . . . . . DLB-167
Smith, Seba 1792-1868 . . . . DLB-1, 11	Sorrentino, Gilbert 1929- DLB-5, 173; Y-80	Sperr, Martin 1944- DLB-124
Smith, Sir Thomas 1513-1577 . . . . DLB-132	Sotheby, James 1682-1742 . . . . DLB-213	Spicer, Jack 1925-1965 . . . . .DLB-5, 16, 193
Smith, Stevie 1902-1971 . . . . DLB-20	Sotheby, John 1740-1807 . . . . DLB-213	Spielberg, Peter 1929- Y-81
Smith, Sydney 1771-1845 . . . . DLB-107	Sotheby, Samuel 1771-1842 . . . . DLB-213	Spielhagen, Friedrich 1829-1911. . . . . . . DLB-129
Smith, Sydney Goodsir 1915-1975 . . . . . . DLB-27	Sotheby, Samuel Leigh 1805-1861 . . . . . . DLB-213	"*Spielmannsepen*"
Smith, Wendell 1914-1972 . . . . .DLB-171	Sotheby, William 1757-1833 . . . . DLB-93, 213	(circa 1152-circa 1500) DLB-148
Smith, William flourished 1595-1597 . . . . DLB-136	Soto, Gary 1952- DLB-82	Spier, Peter 1927- DLB-61
Smith, William 1727-1803 . . . . DLB-31	Sources for the Study of Tudor and Stuart Drama DLB-62	Spinrad, Norman 1940- DLB-8
Smith, William 1728-1793 . . . . DLB-30		Spires, Elizabeth 1952- DLB-120
Smith, William Gardner 1927-1974 . . . . . . DLB-76	Souster, Raymond 1921- DLB-88	Spitteler, Carl 1845-1924 . . . . DLB-129
Smith, William Henry 1808-1872 . . . . DLB-159	The *South English Legendary* circa thirteenth-fifteenth centuries DLB-146	Spivak, Lawrence E. 1900- DLB-137
Smith, William Jay 1918- DLB-5		Spofford, Harriet Prescott
Smith, Elder and Company DLB-154	Southerland, Ellease 1943- DLB-33	1835-1921 . . . . DLB-74
Smith, Harrison, and Robert Haas [publishing house] DLB-46	Southern Illinois University Press Y-95	Spring, Howard 1889-1965 . . . . DLB-191
	Southern, Terry 1924- DLB-2	Squier, E. G. 1821-1888 . . . . DLB-189
Smith, J. Stilman, and Company. DLB-49	Southern Writers Between the Wars DLB-9	Squibob (see Derby, George Horatio)
Smith, W. B., and Company DLB-49	Southerne, Thomas 1659-1746 . . . . DLB-80	Stacpoole, H. de Vere 1863-1951 . . . . DLB-153
Smith, W. H., and Son DLB-106	Southey, Caroline Anne Bowles 1786-1854 . . . . DLB-116	Staël, Germaine de 1766-1817 . . . . . . .DLB-119, 192
Smithers, Leonard [publishing house]. . . . DLB-112		Staël-Holstein, Anne-Louise Germaine de (see Staël, Germaine de)
Smollett, Tobias 1721-1771 . . . . DLB-39, 104	Southey, Robert 1774-1843 . . . . . . DLB-93, 107, 142	
Smythe, Francis Sydney 1900-1949 . . . . . DLB-195	Southwell, Robert 1561?-1595 . . . . DLB-167	Stafford, Jean 1915-1979 . . . . .DLB-2, 173
Snelling, William Joseph 1804-1848 . . . . . DLB-202	Sowande, Bode 1948- DLB-157	Stafford, William 1914-1993. . . . . DLB-5, 206
Snellings, Rolland (see Touré, Askia Muhammad)	Sowle, Tace [publishing house] DLB-170	Stage Censorship: "The Rejected Statement" (1911), by Bernard Shaw [excerpts] . . . DLB-10
Snodgrass, W. D. 1926- DLB-5	Soyfer, Jura 1912-1939 . . . . DLB-124	Stallings, Laurence 1894-1968 . . . . .DLB-7, 44
Snow, C. P. 1905-1980 . . . . .DLB-15, 77; DS-17	Soyinka, Wole 1934- DLB-125; Y-86, Y-87	Stallworthy, Jon 1935- DLB-40
Snyder, Gary 1930- DLB-5, 16, 165, 212	Spacks, Barry 1931- DLB-105	Stampp, Kenneth M. 1912- DLB-17
Sobiloff, Hy 1912-1970 . . . . DLB-48	Spalding, Frances 1950- DLB-155	Stanev, Emiliyan 1907-1979 . . . . DLB-181
The Society for Textual Scholarship and *TEXT* Y-87	Spark, Muriel 1918- DLB-15, 139	Stanford, Ann 1916- DLB-5
	Sparke, Michael [publishing house] DLB-170	Stangerup, Henrik 1937-1998 . . . . DLB-214
The Society for the History of Authorship, Reading and Publishing Y-92	Sparks, Jared 1789-1866 . . . . DLB-1, 30	Stankevich, Nikolai Vladimirovich 1813-1840 . . . . DLB-198
	Sparshott, Francis 1926- DLB-60	
Sønderby, Knud 1909-1966 . . . . DLB-214	Späth, Gerold 1939- DLB-75	Stanković, Borisav ("Bora") 1876-1927. . . . . .DLB-147
Sørensen, Villy 1929- DLB-214	Spatola, Adriano 1941-1988 . . . . DLB-128	
Soffici, Ardengo 1879-1964 . . . . DLB-114	Spaziani, Maria Luisa 1924- DLB-128	Stanley, Henry M. 1841-1904 . . . DLB-189; DS-13
Sofola, 'Zulu 1938- DLB-157	Special Collections at the University of Colorado at Boulder Y-98	Stanley, Thomas 1625-1678 . . . . DLB-131
Solano, Solita 1888-1975 . . . . DLB-4		Stannard, Martin 1947- DLB-155
Soldati, Mario 1906- DLB-177	The Spectator 1828- DLB-110	Stansby, William [publishing house] DLB-170
Šoljan, Antun 1932-1993 . . . . DLB-181	Spedding, James 1808-1881 . . . . DLB-144	Stanton, Elizabeth Cady 1815-1902 . . . . . . DLB-79
Sollers, Philippe 1936- DLB-83	Spee von Langenfeld, Friedrich 1591-1635 . . . . DLB-164	Stanton, Frank L. 1857-1927 . . . . DLB-25
Sollogub, Vladimir Aleksandrovich 1813-1882. . . . . DLB-198		Stanton, Maura 1946- DLB-120
	Speght, Rachel 1597-after 1630 . . . . DLB-126	Stapledon, Olaf 1886-1950 . . . . DLB-15
Solmi, Sergio 1899-1981 . . . . DLB-114	Speke, John Hanning 1827-1864 . . . . DLB-166	Star Spangled Banner Office DLB-49
Solomon, Carl 1928- DLB-16	Spellman, A. B. 1935- DLB-41	Stark, Freya 1893-1993 . . . . DLB-195
Solway, David 1941- DLB-53	Spence, Thomas 1750-1814 . . . . DLB-158	Starkey, Thomas circa 1499-1538 . . . . . . DLB-132
Solzhenitsyn and America. Y-85	Spencer, Anne 1882-1975 . . . . DLB-51, 54	Starkie, Walter 1894-1976 . . . . DLB-195
Somerville, Edith Œnone 1858-1949 . . . . DLB-135	Spencer, Charles, third Earl of Sunderland 1674-1722 . . . . DLB-213	Starkweather, David 1935- DLB-7
Somov, Orest Mikhailovich 1793-1833. . . . . DLB-198		Starrett, Vincent 1886-1974 . . . . .DLB-187
	Spencer, Elizabeth 1921- DLB-6	Statements on the Art of Poetry DLB-54
Song, Cathy 1955- DLB-169	Spencer, George John, Second Earl Spencer 1758-1834. . . . . DLB-184	The State of Publishing Y-97
Sono Ayako 1931- DLB-182		Stationers' Company of London, The DLB-170
Sontag, Susan 1933- DLB-2, 67	Spencer, Herbert 1820-1903 . . . . DLB-57	Statius circa A.D. 45-A.D. 96 . . . . DLB-211
Sophocles 497/496 B.C.-406/405 B.C. DLB-176	Spencer, Scott 1945- Y-86	Stead, Robert J. C. 1880-1959 . . . . DLB-92
	Spender, J. A. 1862-1942 . . . . DLB-98	
Šopov, Aco 1923-1982 . . . . DLB-181	Spender, Stephen 1909- DLB-20	Steadman, Mark 1930- DLB-6

374

The Stealthy School of Criticism (1871), by
 Dante Gabriel Rossetti DLB-35

Stearns, Harold E. 1891-1943 . . . . .DLB-4

Stedman, Edmund Clarence 1833-1908 . . .DLB-64

Steegmuller, Francis 1906-1994 . . . . .DLB-111

Steel, Flora Annie 1847-1929 . . . . . . .DLB-153, 156

Steele, Max 1922- Y-80

Steele, Richard 1672-1729 . . . . .DLB-84, 101

Steele, Timothy 1948- DLB-120

Steele, Wilbur Daniel 1886-1970 . . . . .DLB-86

Steere, Richard circa 1643-1721 . . . . .DLB-24

Stefanovski, Goran 1952- DLB-181

Stegner, Wallace 1909-1993 . . . . .DLB-9, 206; Y-93

Stehr, Hermann 1864-1940 . . . . .DLB-66

Steig, William 1907- DLB-61

Stein, Gertrude
 1874-1946 . . . . .DLB-4, 54, 86; DS-15

Stein, Leo 1872-1947 . . . . .DLB-4

Stein and Day Publishers DLB-46

Steinbeck, John 1902-1968 . . . . DLB-7, 9, 212; DS-2

Steiner, George 1929- DLB-67

Steinhoewel, Heinrich 1411/1412-1479 . . .DLB-179

Steloff, Ida Frances 1887-1989 . . . . .DLB-187

Stendhal 1783-1842 . . . . .DLB-119

Stephen Crane: A Revaluation Virginia
 Tech Conference, 1989 . . . . .Y-89

Stephen, Leslie 1832-1904 . . . . . . DLB-57, 144, 190

Stephen Vincent Benét Centenary Y-97

Stephens, Alexander H. 1812-1883 . . . . . . .DLB-47

Stephens, Alice Barber 1858-1932 . . . . . . .DLB-188

Stephens, Ann 1810-1886 . . . . .DLB-3, 73

Stephens, Charles Asbury 1844?-1931 . . . . .DLB-42

Stephens, James 1882?-1950 . . . .DLB-19, 153, 162

Stephens, John Lloyd 1805-1852 . . . . .DLB-183

Sterling, George 1869-1926 . . . . .DLB-54

Sterling, James 1701-1763 . . . . .DLB-24

Sterling, John 1806-1844 . . . . .DLB-116

Stern, Gerald 1925- DLB-105

Stern, Gladys B. 1890-1973 . . . . .DLB-197

Stern, Madeleine B. 1912- DLB-111, 140

Stern, Richard 1928- Y-87

Stern, Stewart 1922- DLB-26

Sterne, Laurence 1713-1768 . . . . .DLB-39

Sternheim, Carl 1878-1942 . . . . .DLB-56, 118

Sternhold, Thomas ?-1549 and
 John Hopkins ?-1570 . . . . .DLB-132

Steuart, David 1747-1824 . . . . .DLB-213

Stevens, Henry 1819-1886 . . . . .DLB-140

Stevens, Wallace 1879-1955 . . . . .DLB-54

Stevenson, Anne 1933- DLB-40

Stevenson, D. E. 1892-1973 . . . . .DLB-191

Stevenson, Lionel 1902-1973 . . . . .DLB-155

Stevenson, Robert Louis 1850-1894
 . . . . .DLB-18, 57, 141, 156, 174; DS-13

Stewart, Donald Ogden
 1894-1980 . . . . .DLB-4, 11, 26

Stewart, Dugald 1753-1828 . . . . .DLB-31

Stewart, George, Jr. 1848-1906 . . . . .DLB-99

Stewart, George R. 1895-1980 . . . . .DLB-8

Stewart and Kidd Company DLB-46

Stewart, Randall 1896-1964 . . . . .DLB-103

Stickney, Trumbull 1874-1904 . . . . .DLB-54

Stieler, Caspar 1632-1707 . . . . .DLB-164

Stifter, Adalbert 1805-1868 . . . . .DLB-133

Stiles, Ezra 1727-1795 . . . . .DLB-31

Still, James 1906- .DLB-9

Stirner, Max 1806-1856 . . . . .DLB-129

Stith, William 1707-1755 . . . . .DLB-31

Stock, Elliot [publishing house] DLB-106

Stockton, Frank R.
 1834-1902 . . . . .DLB-42, 74; DS-13

Stoddard, Ashbel [publishing house] DLB-49

Stoddard, Charles Warren
 1843-1909 . . . . .DLB-186

Stoddard, Elizabeth 1823-1902 . . . . .DLB-202

Stoddard, Richard Henry
 1825-1903 . . . . .DLB-3, 64; DS-13

Stoddard, Solomon 1643-1729 . . . . .DLB-24

Stoker, Bram 1847-1912 . . . . .DLB-36, 70, 178

Stokes, Frederick A., Company DLB-49

Stokes, Thomas L. 1898-1958 . . . . .DLB-29

Stokesbury, Leon 1945- DLB-120

Stolberg, Christian Graf zu 1748-1821 . . . . .DLB-94

Stolberg, Friedrich Leopold Graf zu
 1750-1819 . . . . .DLB-94

Stone, Herbert S., and Company DLB-49

Stone, Lucy 1818-1893 . . . . .DLB-79

Stone, Melville 1848-1929 . . . . .DLB-25

Stone, Robert 1937- DLB-152

Stone, Ruth 1915- DLB-105

Stone, Samuel 1602-1663 . . . . .DLB-24

Stone, William Leete 1792-1844 . . . . .DLB-202

Stone and Kimball .DLB-49

Stoppard, Tom 1937- DLB-13; Y-85

Storey, Anthony 1928- DLB-14

Storey, David 1933- DLB-13, 14, 207

Storm, Theodor 1817-1888 . . . . .DLB-129

Story, Thomas circa 1670-1742 . . . . .DLB-31

Story, William Wetmore 1819-1895 . . . . . . .DLB-1

Storytelling: A Contemporary Renaissance . . . Y-84

Stoughton, William 1631-1701 . . . . .DLB-24

Stow, John 1525-1605 . . . . .DLB-132

Stowe, Harriet Beecher
 1811-1896 . . . . .DLB-1, 12, 42, 74, 189

Stowe, Leland 1899- DLB-29

Stoyanov, Dimitr Ivanov (see Elin Pelin)

Strabo 64 or 63 B.C.-circa A.D. 25
 . . . . .DLB-176

Strachey, Lytton
 1880-1932 . . . . .DLB-149; DS-10

Strachey, Lytton, Preface to Eminent
 Victorians DLB-149

Strahan and Company DLB-106

Strahan, William [publishing house] DLB-154

Strand, Mark 1934- DLB-5

The Strasbourg Oaths 842 . . . . .DLB-148

Stratemeyer, Edward 1862-1930 . . . . .DLB-42

Strati, Saverio 1924- DLB-177

Stratton and Barnard DLB-49

Stratton-Porter, Gene 1863-1924 . . . . DS-14

Straub, Peter 1943- Y-84

Strauß, Botho 1944- DLB-124

Strauß, David Friedrich 1808-1874 . . . . . .DLB-133

The Strawberry Hill Press DLB-154

Streatfeild, Noel 1895-1986 . . . . .DLB-160

Street, Cecil John Charles (see Rhode, John)

Street, G. S. 1867-1936 . . . . .DLB-135

Street and Smith DLB-49

Streeter, Edward 1891-1976 . . . . .DLB-11

Streeter, Thomas Winthrop
 1883-1965 . . . . .DLB-140

Stretton, Hesba 1832-1911 . . . . .DLB-163, 190

Stribling, T. S. 1881-1965 . . . . .DLB-9

Der Stricker circa 1190-circa 1250 . . . . . . .DLB-138

Strickland, Samuel 1804-1867 . . . . .DLB-99

Stringer and Townsend DLB-49

Stringer, Arthur 1874-1950 . . . . .DLB-92

Strittmatter, Erwin 1912- DLB-69

Strniša, Gregor 1930-1987 . . . . .DLB-181

Strode, William 1630-1645 . . . . .DLB-126

Strong, L. A. G. 1896-1958 . . . . .DLB-191

Strother, David Hunter 1816-1888 . . . . .DLB-3

Strouse, Jean 1945- DLB-111

Stuart, Dabney 1937- DLB-105

Stuart, Jesse 1906-1984 . . . . . DLB-9, 48, 102; Y-84

Stuart, Ruth McEnery 1849?-1917 . . . . . . .DLB-202

Stuart, Lyle [publishing house] DLB-46

Stubbs, Harry Clement (see Clement, Hal)

Stubenberg, Johann Wilhelm von
 1619-1663 . . . . .DLB-164

Studio DLB-112

The Study of Poetry (1880), by
 Matthew Arnold DLB-35

Sturgeon, Theodore 1918-1985 . . . . . .DLB-8; Y-85

Sturges, Preston 1898-1959 . . . . .DLB-26

"Style" (1840; revised, 1859), by
 Thomas de Quincey [excerpt] DLB-57

"Style" (1888), by Walter Pater DLB-57

Style (1897), by Walter Raleigh
 [excerpt] DLB-57

"Style" (1877), by T. H. Wright
 [excerpt] DLB-57

"Le Style c'est l'homme" (1892), by
 W. H. Mallock DLB-57

Styron, William 1925- DLB-2, 143; Y-80

Suárez, Mario 1925- DLB-82

Such, Peter 1939- DLB-60

Suckling, Sir John 1609-1641? DLB-58, 126

Suckow, Ruth 1892-1960 . . . . .DLB-9, 102

Sudermann, Hermann 1857-1928 . . . . DLB-118	Swados, Harvey 1920-1972 . . . . DLB-2	Talese, Gay 1932- DLB-185
Sue, Eugène 1804-1857 . . . . DLB-119	Swain, Charles 1801-1874 . . . . DLB-32	Talev, Dimitr 1898-1966 . . . . DLB-181
Sue, Marie-Joseph (see Sue, Eugène)	Swallow Press DLB-46	Taliaferro, H. E. 1811-1875 . . . . DLB-202
Suetonius circa A.D. 69-post A.D. 122 . . . DLB-211	Swan Sonnenschein Limited DLB-106	Tallent, Elizabeth 1954- DLB-130
Suggs, Simon (see Hooper, Johnson Jones)	Swanberg, W. A. 1907- DLB-103	TallMountain, Mary 1918-1994 . . . . DLB-193
Sukenick, Ronald 1932- DLB-173; Y-81	Swenson, May 1919-1989 . . . . DLB-5	Talvj 1797-1870 . . . . DLB-59, 133
Suknaski, Andrew 1942- DLB-53	Swerling, Jo 1897- DLB-44	Tamási, Áron 1897-1966 . . . . DLB-215
Sullivan, Alan 1868-1947 . . . . DLB-92	Swift, Graham 1949- DLB-194	Tan, Amy 1952- DLB-173
Sullivan, C. Gardner 1886-1965 . . . . DLB-26	Swift, Jonathan 1667-1745 . . . . DLB-39, 95, 101	Tanner, Thomas 1673/1674-1735 . . . . DLB-213
Sullivan, Frank 1892-1976 . . . . DLB-11	Swinburne, A. C. 1837-1909 . . . . DLB-35, 57	Tanizaki, Jun'ichirō 1886-1965 . . . . DLB-180
Sulte, Benjamin 1841-1923 . . . . DLB-99	Swineshead, Richard floruit circa 1350 . . . . DLB-115	Tapahonso, Luci 1953- DLB-175
Sulzberger, Arthur Hays 1891-1968 . . . . . DLB-127	Swinnerton, Frank 1884-1982 . . . . DLB-34	Taradash, Daniel 1913- DLB-44
Sulzberger, Arthur Ochs 1926- DLB-127	Swisshelm, Jane Grey 1815-1884 . . . . DLB-43	Tarbell, Ida M. 1857-1944 . . . . DLB-47
Sulzer, Johann Georg 1720-1779 . . . . DLB-97	Swope, Herbert Bayard 1882-1958 . . . . DLB-25	Tardivel, Jules-Paul 1851-1905 . . . . DLB-99
Sumarokov, Aleksandr Petrovich 1717-1777 . . . . DLB-150	Swords, T. and J., and Company DLB-49	Targan, Barry 1932- DLB-130
Summers, Hollis 1916- DLB-6	Swords, Thomas 1763-1843 and Swords, James ?-1844 . . . . DLB-73	Tarkington, Booth 1869-1946 . . . . DLB-9, 102
Sumner, Henry A. [publishing house] DLB-49	Sykes, Ella C. ?-1939 . . . . DLB-174	Tashlin, Frank 1913-1972 . . . . DLB-44
Surtees, Robert Smith 1803-1864 . . . . DLB-21	Sylvester, Josuah 1562 or 1563 - 1618 . . . . DLB-121	Tate, Allen 1899-1979 . . . . DLB-4, 45, 63; DS-17
Surveys: Japanese Literature, 1987-1995 . . . . DLB-182	Symonds, Emily Morse (see Paston, George)	Tate, James 1943- DLB-5, 169
A Survey of Poetry Anthologies, 1879-1960 . . . . DLB-54	Symonds, John Addington 1840-1893 . . . . DLB-57, 144	Tate, Nahum circa 1652-1715 . . . . DLB-80
Surveys of the Year's Biographies	Symons, A. J. A. 1900-1941 . . . . DLB-149	Tatian circa 830 . . . . DLB-148
A Transit of Poets and Others: American Biography in 1982 . . . . Y-82	Symons, Arthur 1865-1945 . . . . . DLB-19, 57, 149	Taufer, Veno 1933- DLB-181
The Year in Literary Biography Y-83–Y-98	Symons, Julian 1912-1994 . . . . . DLB-87, 155; Y-92	Tauler, Johannes circa 1300-1361 . . . . . . DLB-179
Survey of the Year's Book Publishing	Symons, Scott 1933- DLB-53	Tavčar, Ivan 1851-1923 . . . . DLB-147
The Year in Book Publishing Y-86	A Symposium on *The Columbia History of the Novel* Y-92	Taylor, Ann 1782-1866 . . . . DLB-163
Survey of the Year's Book Reviewing	Synge, John Millington 1871-1909 . . . . DLB-10, 19	Taylor, Bayard 1825-1878 . . . . DLB-3, 189
The Year in Book Reviewing and the Literary Situation Y-98	Synge Summer School: J. M. Synge and the Irish Theater, Rathdrum, County Wiclow, Ireland Y-93	Taylor, Bert Leston 1866-1921 . . . . DLB-25
Survey of the Year's Children's Books		Taylor, Charles H. 1846-1921 . . . . DLB-25
The Year in Children's Books Y-92–Y-96, Y-98	Syrett, Netta 1865-1943 . . . . DLB-135, 197	Taylor, Edward circa 1642-1729 . . . . DLB-24
The Year in Children's Literature Y-97	Szabó, Lőrinc 1900-1957 . . . . DLB-215	Taylor, Elizabeth 1912-1975 . . . . DLB-139
Surveys of the Year's Drama	Szabó, Magda 1917- DLB-215	Taylor, Henry 1942- DLB-5
The Year in Drama Y-82–Y-85, Y-87–Y-96	Szymborska, Wisława 1923- Y-96	Taylor, Sir Henry 1800-1886 . . . . DLB-32
The Year in London Theatre Y-92	**T**	Taylor, Jane 1783-1824 . . . . DLB-163
Surveys of the Year's Fiction		Taylor, Jeremy circa 1613-1667 . . . . DLB-151
The Year's Work in Fiction: A Survey Y-82	Taban lo Liyong 1939?- DLB-125	Taylor, John 1577 or 1578 - 1653 . . . . . . DLB-121
The Year in Fiction: A Biased View Y-83	Tabucchi, Antonio 1943- DLB-196	Taylor, Mildred D. ?- DLB-52
The Year in Fiction . . . Y-84–Y-86, Y-89, Y-94–Y-98	Taché, Joseph-Charles 1820-1894 . . . . DLB-99	Taylor, Peter 1917-1994 . . . . Y-81, Y-94
The Year in the Novel Y-87, Y-88, Y-90–Y-93	Tachihara Masaaki 1926-1980 . . . . DLB-182	Taylor, William, and Company DLB-49
The Year in Short Stories Y-87	Tacitus circa A.D. 55-circa A.D. 117 . . . . DLB-211	Taylor-Made Shakespeare? Or Is "Shall I Die?" the Long-Lost Text of Bottom's Dream? Y-85
The Year in the Short Story Y-88, Y-90–Y-93	Tadijanović, Dragutin 1905- DLB-181	Teasdale, Sara 1884-1933 . . . . DLB-45
Surveys of the Year's Literary Theory	Tafdrup, Pia 1952- DLB-214	*The Tea-Table* (1725), by Eliza Haywood [excerpt] DLB-39
The Year in Literary Theory Y-92–Y-93	Tafolla, Carmen 1951- DLB-82	Telles, Lygia Fagundes 1924- DLB-113
Survey of the Year's Literature	Taggard, Genevieve 1894-1948 . . . . DLB-45	Temple, Sir William 1628-1699 . . . . DLB-101
The Year in Texas Literature Y-98	Taggart, John 1942- DLB-193	Tenn, William 1919- DLB-8
Surveys of the Year's Poetry	Tagger, Theodor (see Bruckner, Ferdinand)	Tennant, Emma 1937- DLB-14
The Year's Work in American Poetry Y-82	Taiheiki late fourteenth century DLB-203	Tenney, Tabitha Gilman 1762-1837 . . . . DLB-37, 200
The Year in Poetry Y-83–Y-92, Y-94–Y-98	Tait, J. Selwin, and Sons DLB-49	Tennyson, Alfred 1809-1892 . . . . DLB-32
Sutherland, Efua Theodora 1924- DLB-117	*Tait's Edinburgh Magazine* 1832-1861 . . . . DLB-110	Tennyson, Frederick 1807-1898 . . . . DLB-32
Sutherland, John 1919-1956 . . . . DLB-68	The Takarazaka Revue Company Y-91	Tenorio, Arthur 1924- DLB-209
Sutro, Alfred 1863-1933 . . . . DLB-10	Talander (see Bohse, August)	Tepliakov, Viktor Grigor'evich 1804-1842 . . . . DLB-205
Svendsen, Hanne Marie 1933- DLB-214		

Terence circa 184 B.C.-159 B.C. or after DLB-211

Terhune, Albert Payson 1872-1942 ....DLB-9

Terhune, Mary Virginia 1830-1922 .... DS-13, DS-16

Terry, Megan 1932- DLB-7

Terson, Peter 1932- DLB-13

Tesich, Steve 1943- Y-83

Tessa, Delio 1886-1939 ....DLB-114

Testori, Giovanni 1923-1993....... DLB-128, 177

Tey, Josephine 1896?-1952 ....DLB-77

Thacher, James 1754-1844...............DLB-37

Thackeray, William Makepeace 1811-1863 .... DLB-21, 55, 159, 163

Thames and Hudson Limited DLB-112

Thanet, Octave (see French, Alice)

Thatcher, John Boyd 1847-1909 ....DLB-187

Thayer, Caroline Matilda Warren 1785-1844 ....DLB-200

The Theater in Shakespeare's Time DLB-62

The Theatre Guild.....................DLB-7

Thegan and the Astronomer flourished circa 850.............DLB-148

Thelwall, John 1764-1834 ....DLB-93, 158

Theocritus circa 300 B.C.-260 B.C. DLB-176

Theodulf circa 760-circa 821 ....DLB-148

Theophrastus circa 371 B.C.-287 B.C. DLB-176

Theriault, Yves 1915-1983..............DLB-88

Thério, Adrien 1925- DLB-53

Theroux, Paul 1941- DLB-2

Thesiger, Wilfred 1910- DLB-204

They All Came to Paris................. DS-16

Thibaudeau, Colleen 1925- DLB-88

Thielen, Benedict 1903-1965 ....DLB-102

Thiong'o Ngugi wa (see Ngugi wa Thiong'o)

Third-Generation Minor Poets of the Seventeenth Century...............DLB-131

This Quarter 1925-1927, 1929-1932 .... DS-15

Thoma, Ludwig 1867-1921 ....DLB-66

Thoma, Richard 1902- DLB-4

Thomas, Audrey 1935- DLB-60

Thomas, D. M. 1935- DLB-40, 207

Thomas, Dylan 1914-1953 ...... DLB-13, 20, 139

Thomas, Edward 1878-1917 ....DLB-19, 98, 156, 216

Thomas, Frederick William 1806-1866 ....DLB-202

Thomas, Gwyn 1913-1981 ....DLB-15

Thomas, Isaiah 1750-1831....... DLB-43, 73, 187

Thomas, Isaiah [publishing house]........DLB-49

Thomas, Johann 1624-1679 ....DLB-168

Thomas, John 1900-1932................DLB-4

Thomas, Joyce Carol 1938- DLB-33

Thomas, Lorenzo 1944- DLB-41

Thomas, R. S. 1915- DLB-27

The Thomas Wolfe Collection at the University of North Carolina at Chapel Hill Y-97

The Thomas Wolfe Society...............Y-97

Thomasîn von Zerclære circa 1186-circa 1259..............DLB-138

Thomasius, Christian 1655-1728........DLB-168

Thompson, David 1770-1857..............DLB-99

Thompson, Daniel Pierce 1795-1868.....DLB-202

Thompson, Dorothy 1893-1961 ....DLB-29

Thompson, Francis 1859-1907..........DLB-19

Thompson, George Selden (see Selden, George)

Thompson, Henry Yates 1838-1928 .....DLB-184

Thompson, Hunter S. 1939- DLB-185

Thompson, John 1938-1976..............DLB-60

Thompson, John R. 1823-1873 ....DLB-3, 73

Thompson, Lawrance 1906-1973 ....DLB-103

Thompson, Maurice 1844-1901 ...... DLB-71, 74

Thompson, Ruth Plumly 1891-1976 ......DLB-22

Thompson, Thomas Phillips 1843-1933 ...DLB-99

Thompson, William 1775-1833 ....DLB-158

Thompson, William Tappan 1812-1882 ....DLB-3, 11

Thomson, Edward William 1849-1924....DLB-92

Thomson, James 1700-1748 ....DLB-95

Thomson, James 1834-1882 ....DLB-35

Thomson, Joseph 1858-1895 .... DLB-174

Thomson, Mortimer 1831-1875...........DLB-11

Thoreau, Henry David 1817-1862..... DLB-1, 183

Thornton Wilder Centenary at Yale Y-97

Thorpe, Thomas Bangs 1815-1878 ..... DLB-3, 11

Thorup, Kirsten 1942- DLB-214

Thoughts on Poetry and Its Varieties (1833), by John Stuart Mill DLB-32

Thrale, Hester Lynch (see Piozzi, Hester Lynch [Thrale])

Thubron, Colin 1939- DLB-204

Thucydides circa 455 B.C.-circa 395 B.C. DLB-176

Thulstrup, Thure de 1848-1930 ....DLB-188

Thümmel, Moritz August von 1738-1817 ....DLB-97

Thurber, James 1894-1961 .... DLB-4, 11, 22, 102

Thurman, Wallace 1902-1934...........DLB-51

Thwaite, Anthony 1930- DLB-40

Thwaites, Reuben Gold 1853-1913 ....DLB-47

Tibullus circa 54 B.C.-circa 19 B.C. DLB-211

Ticknor, George 1791-1871 .... DLB-1, 59, 140

Ticknor and Fields....................DLB-49

Ticknor and Fields (revived) DLB-46

Tieck, Ludwig 1773-1853................DLB-90

Tietjens, Eunice 1884-1944 ....DLB-54

Tilney, Edmund circa 1536-1610........DLB-136

Tilt, Charles [publishing house]........DLB-106

Tilton, J. E., and Company DLB-49

Time and Western Man (1927), by Wyndham Lewis [excerpts]..................DLB-36

Time-Life Books DLB-46

Times Books DLB-46

Timothy, Peter circa 1725-1782 ....DLB-43

Timrava 1867-1951 ....DLB-215

Timrod, Henry 1828-1867 ....DLB-3

Tindal, Henrietta 1818?-1879 ....DLB-199

Tinker, Chauncey Brewster 1876-1963 ....DLB-140

Tinsley Brothers DLB-106

Tiptree, James, Jr. 1915-1987............DLB-8

Tišma, Aleksandar 1924- DLB-181

Titus, Edward William 1870-1952 ....DLB-4; DS-15

Tiutchev, Fedor Ivanovich 1803-1873 ....DLB-205

Tlali, Miriam 1933- DLB-157

Todd, Barbara Euphan 1890-1976.......DLB-160

Tofte, Robert 1561 or 1562-1619 or 1620.........DLB-172

Toklas, Alice B. 1877-1967................DLB-4

Tokuda, Shūsei 1872-1943.............DLB-180

Tolkien, J. R. R. 1892-1973 .... DLB-15, 160

Toller, Ernst 1893-1939...............DLB-124

Tollet, Elizabeth 1694-1754 ....DLB-95

Tolson, Melvin B. 1898-1966 .... DLB-48, 76

Tom Jones (1749), by Henry Fielding [excerpt] DLB-39

Tomalin, Claire 1933- DLB-155

Tomasi di Lampedusa, Giuseppe 1896-1957 ....DLB-177

Tomlinson, Charles 1927- DLB-40

Tomlinson, H. M. 1873-1958 .... DLB-36, 100, 195

Tompkins, Abel [publishing house].......DLB-49

Tompson, Benjamin 1642-1714..........DLB-24

Ton'a 1289-1372 ....DLB-203

Tondelli, Pier Vittorio 1955-1991 ......DLB-196

Tonks, Rosemary 1932- DLB-14, 207

Tonna, Charlotte Elizabeth 1790-1846 ....DLB-163

Tonson, Jacob the Elder [publishing house] DLB-170

Toole, John Kennedy 1937-1969 .... Y-81

Toomer, Jean 1894-1967 ....DLB-45, 51

Tor Books DLB-46

Torberg, Friedrich 1908-1979 ....DLB-85

Torrence, Ridgely 1874-1950............DLB-54

Torres-Metzger, Joseph V. 1933- DLB-122

Toth, Susan Allen 1940- Y-86

Tottell, Richard [publishing house] DLB-170

Tough-Guy Literature..................DLB-9

Touré, Askia Muhammad 1938- DLB-41

Tourgée, Albion W. 1838-1905..........DLB-79

Tourneur, Cyril circa 1580-1626..........DLB-58

Tournier, Michel 1924- DLB-83

Tousey, Frank [publishing house] DLB-49

Tower Publications DLB-46

Towne, Benjamin circa 1740-1793 ....DLB-43

Cumulative Index DLB 216

Towne, Robert 1936- DLB-44

The Townely Plays fifteenth and sixteenth centuries DLB-146

Townshend, Aurelian by 1583 - circa 1651.............. DLB-121

Toy, Barbara 1908- DLB-204

Tracy, Honor 1913- DLB-15

Traherne, Thomas 1637?-1674......... DLB-131

Traill, Catharine Parr 1802-1899 .... DLB-99

Train, Arthur 1875-1945......... DLB-86; DS-16

The Transatlantic Publishing Company... DLB-49

The Transatlantic Review 1924-1925 .... DS-15

Transcendentalists, American.............. DS-5

transition 1927-1938 .... DS-15

Translators of the Twelfth Century: Literary Issues Raised and Impact Created DLB-115

Travel Writing, 1837-1875 .... DLB-166

Travel Writing, 1876-1909 .... DLB-174

Traven, B. 1882? or 1890?-1969? DLB-9, 56

Travers, Ben 1886-1980 .... DLB-10

Travers, P. L. (Pamela Lyndon) 1899- DLB-160

Trediakovsky, Vasilii Kirillovich 1703-1769 .... DLB-150

Treece, Henry 1911-1966............. DLB-160

Trejo, Ernesto 1950- DLB-122

Trelawny, Edward John 1792-1881................DLB-110, 116, 144

Tremain, Rose 1943- DLB-14

Tremblay, Michel 1942- DLB-60

Trends in Twentieth-Century Mass Market Publishing........... DLB-46

Trent, William P. 1862-1939 .... DLB-47

Trescot, William Henry 1822-1898 ...... DLB-30

Tressell, Robert (Robert Phillipe Noonan) 1870-1911..................... DLB-197

Trevelyan, Sir George Otto 1838-1928 .... DLB-144

Trevisa, John circa 1342-circa 1402 ..... DLB-146

Trevor, William 1928- DLB-14, 139

Trierer Floyris circa 1170-1180 .... DLB-138

Trillin, Calvin 1935- DLB-185

Trilling, Lionel 1905-1975 .... DLB-28, 63

Trilussa 1871-1950 .... DLB-114

Trimmer, Sarah 1741-1810............ DLB-158

Triolet, Elsa 1896-1970............... DLB-72

Tripp, John 1927- DLB-40

Trocchi, Alexander 1925- DLB-15

Troisi, Dante 1920-1989............. DLB-196

Trollope, Anthony 1815-1882 ....DLB-21, 57, 159

Trollope, Frances 1779-1863 .... DLB-21, 166

Trollope, Joanna 1943- DLB-207

Troop, Elizabeth 1931- DLB-14

Trotter, Catharine 1679-1749 .... DLB-84

Trotti, Lamar 1898-1952 .... DLB-44

Trottier, Pierre 1925- DLB-60

Troubadours, *Trobaíritz,* and Trouvères DLB-208

Troupe, Quincy Thomas, Jr. 1943- DLB-41

Trow, John F., and Company.......... DLB-49

Trowbridge, John Townsend 1827-1916 .... DLB-202

Truillier-Lacombe, Joseph-Patrice 1807-1863..................... DLB-99

Trumbo, Dalton 1905-1976 .... DLB-26

Trumbull, Benjamin 1735-1820 .... DLB-30

Trumbull, John 1750-1831 .... DLB-31

Trumbull, John 1756-1843 .... DLB-183

Tscherning, Andreas 1611-1659...... DLB-164

T. S. Eliot Centennial Y-88

Tsubouchi, Shōyō 1859-1935.......... DLB-180

Tucholsky, Kurt 1890-1935 .... DLB-56

Tucker, Charlotte Maria 1821-1893 .... DLB-163, 190

Tucker, George 1775-1861 .... DLB-3, 30

Tucker, Nathaniel Beverley 1784-1851..... DLB-3

Tucker, St. George 1752-1827 .... DLB-37

Tuckerman, Henry Theodore 1813-1871.. DLB-64

Tunis, John R. 1889-1975.........DLB-22, 171

Tunstall, Cuthbert 1474-1559......... DLB-132

Tuohy, Frank 1925- DLB-14, 139

Tupper, Martin F. 1810-1889 .... DLB-32

Turbyfill, Mark 1896- DLB-45

Turco, Lewis 1934- Y-84

Turgenev, Aleksandr Ivanovich 1784-1845..................... DLB-198

Turnball, Alexander H. 1868-1918 .... DLB-184

Turnbull, Andrew 1921-1970.......... DLB-103

Turnbull, Gael 1928- DLB-40

Turner, Arlin 1909-1980 .... DLB-103

Turner, Charles (Tennyson) 1808-1879..................... DLB-32

Turner, Frederick 1943- DLB-40

Turner, Frederick Jackson 1861-1932 .DLB-17, 186

Turner, Joseph Addison 1826-1868 ...... DLB-79

Turpin, Waters Edward 1910-1968...... DLB-51

Turrini, Peter 1944- DLB-124

Tutuola, Amos 1920- DLB-125

Twain, Mark (see Clemens, Samuel Langhorne)

Tweedie, Ethel Brilliana circa 1860-1940 .... DLB-174

The 'Twenties and Berlin, by Alex Natan DLB-66

Twysden, Sir Roger 1597-1672......... DLB-213

Tyler, Anne 1941- DLB-6, 143; Y-82

Tyler, Mary Palmer 1775-1866......... DLB-200

Tyler, Moses Coit 1835-1900.........DLB-47, 64

Tyler, Royall 1757-1826 .... DLB-37

Tylor, Edward Burnett 1832-1917 ...... DLB-57

Tynan, Katharine 1861-1931 .... DLB-153

Tyndale, William circa 1494-1536 .... DLB-132

U

Udall, Nicholas 1504-1556............ DLB-62

Ugrešić, Dubravka 1949- DLB-181

Uhland, Ludwig 1787-1862............ DLB-90

Uhse, Bodo 1904-1963............... DLB-69

Ujević, Augustin ("Tin") 1891-1955......DLB-147

Ulenhart, Niclas flourished circa 1600 ... DLB-164

Ulibarrí, Sabine R. 1919- DLB-82

Ulica, Jorge 1870-1926 .... DLB-82

Ulivi, Ferruccio 1912- DLB-196

Ulizio, B. George 1889-1969 .... DLB-140

Ulrich von Liechtenstein circa 1200-circa 1275 .... DLB-138

Ulrich von Zatzikhoven before 1194-after 1214 .... DLB-138

Ulysses, Reader's Edition................. Y-97

Unamuno, Miguel de 1864-1936 .... DLB-108

Under the Microscope (1872), by A. C. Swinburne DLB-35

Unger, Friederike Helene 1741-1813 ..... DLB-94

Ungaretti, Giuseppe 1888-1970 .... DLB-114

United States Book Company DLB-49

Universal Publishing and Distributing Corporation DLB-46

The University of Iowa Writers' Workshop Golden Jubilee Y-86

The University of South Carolina Press...... Y-94

University of Wales Press DLB-112

University Press of Kansas................. Y-98

"The Unknown Public" (1858), by Wilkie Collins [excerpt]........... DLB-57

Uno, Chiyo 1897-1996............... DLB-180

Unruh, Fritz von 1885-1970 .... DLB-56, 118

Unspeakable Practices II: The Festival of Vanguard Narrative at BrownUniversity .Y-93

Unsworth, Barry 1930- DLB-194

The Unterberg Poetry Center of the 92nd Street Y....................... Y-98

Unwin, T. Fisher [publishing house] DLB-106

Upchurch, Boyd B. (see Boyd, John)

Updike, John 1932- DLB-2, 5, 143; Y-80, Y-82; DS-3

Upton, Bertha 1849-1912............. DLB-141

Upton, Charles 1948- DLB-16

Upton, Florence K. 1873-1922 .... DLB-141

Upward, Allen 1863-1926 .... DLB-36

Urban, Milo 1904-1982 .... DLB-215

Urista, Alberto Baltazar (see Alurista)

Urrea, Luis Alberto 1955- DLB-209

Urzidil, Johannes 1896-1976............ DLB-85

Urquhart, Fred 1912- DLB-139

The Uses of Facsimile.................... Y-90

Usk, Thomas died 1388.............. DLB-146

Uslar Pietri, Arturo 1906- DLB-113

Ussher, James 1581-1656 .... DLB-213

Ustinov, Peter 1921- DLB-13

Uttley, Alison 1884-1976 . . . . DLB-160
Uz, Johann Peter 1720-1796 . . . . DLB-97

V

Vac, Bertrand 1914- DLB-88
Vail, Laurence 1891-1968 . . . . DLB-4
Vailland, Roger 1907-1965 . . . . DLB-83
Vajda, Ernest 1887-1954 . . . . DLB-44
Valdés, Gina 1943- DLB-122
Valdez, Luis Miguel 1940- DLB-122
Valduga, Patrizia 1953- DLB-128
Valente, José Angel 1929- DLB-108
Valenzuela, Luisa 1938- DLB-113
Valeri, Diego 1887-1976 . . . . DLB-128
Valerius Flaccus fl. circa A.D. 92 . . . . DLB-211
Valerius Maximus fl. circa A.D. 31 . . . . . . DLB-211
Valesio, Paolo 1939- DLB-196
Valgardson, W. D. 1939- DLB-60
Valle, Víctor Manuel 1950- DLB-122
Valle-Inclán, Ramón del 1866-1936 . . . . . DLB-134
Vallejo, Armando 1949- DLB-122
Vallès, Jules 1832-1885 . . . . DLB-123
Vallette, Marguerite Eymery (see Rachilde)
Valverde, José María 1926- DLB-108
Van Allsburg, Chris 1949- DLB-61
Van Anda, Carr 1864-1945 . . . . DLB-25
van der Post, Laurens 1906-1996 . . . . DLB-204
Van Dine, S. S. (see Wright, Williard Huntington)
Van Doren, Mark 1894-1972 . . . . DLB-45
van Druten, John 1901-1957 . . . . DLB-10
Van Duyn, Mona 1921- DLB-5
Van Dyke, Henry 1852-1933 . . . . . DLB-71; DS-13
Van Dyke, John C. 1856-1932 . . . . DLB-186
Van Dyke, Henry 1928- DLB-33
van Gulik, Robert Hans 1910-1967 . . . . DS-17
van Itallie, Jean-Claude 1936- DLB-7
Van Loan, Charles E. 1876-1919 . . . . DLB-171
Van Rensselaer, Mariana Griswold
  1851-1934 . . . . DLB-47
Van Rensselaer, Mrs. Schuyler (see Van
  Rensselaer, Mariana Griswold)
Van Vechten, Carl 1880-1964 . . . . DLB-4, 9
van Vogt, A. E. 1912- DLB-8
Vanbrugh, Sir John 1664-1726 . . . . DLB-80
Vance, Jack 1916?- DLB-8
Vančura, Vladislav 1891-1942 . . . . DLB-215
Vane, Sutton 1888-1963 . . . . DLB-10
Vanguard Press DLB-46
Vann, Robert L. 1879-1940 . . . . DLB-29
Vargas, Llosa, Mario 1936- DLB-145
Varley, John 1947- Y-81
Varnhagen von Ense, Karl August
  1785-1858 . . . . DLB-90
Varro 116 B.C.-27 B.C. DLB-211
Vásquez, Richard 1928- DLB-209

Varnhagen von Ense, Rahel
  1771-1833 . . . . DLB-90
Vásquez Montalbán, Manuel
  1939- DLB-134
Vassa, Gustavus (see Equiano, Olaudah)
Vassalli, Sebastiano 1941- DLB-128, 196
Vaughan, Henry 1621-1695 . . . . DLB-131
Vaughn, Robert 1592?-1667 . . . . DLB-213
Vaughan, Thomas 1621-1666 . . . . DLB-131
Vaux, Thomas, Lord 1509-1556 . . . . DLB-132
Vazov, Ivan 1850-1921 . . . . DLB-147
Véa Jr., Alfredo 1950- DLB-209
Vega, Janine Pommy 1942- DLB-16
Veiller, Anthony 1903-1965 . . . . DLB-44
Velásquez-Trevino, Gloria 1949- DLB-122
Veley, Margaret 1843-1887 . . . . DLB-199
Velleius Paterculus
  circa 20 B.C.-circa A.D. 30 . . . . DLB-211
Veloz Maggiolo, Marcio 1936- DLB-145
Vel'tman Aleksandr Fomich
  1800-1870 . . . . DLB-198
Venegas, Daniel ?-? DLB-82
Venevitinov, Dmitrii Vladimirovich
  1805-1827 . . . . DLB-205
Vergil, Polydore circa 1470-1555 . . . . DLB-132
Veríssimo, Erico 1905-1975 . . . . DLB-145
Verne, Jules 1828-1905 . . . . DLB-123
Verplanck, Gulian C. 1786-1870 . . . . DLB-59
Very, Jones 1813-1880 . . . . DLB-1
Vian, Boris 1920-1959 . . . . DLB-72
Viazemsky, Petr Andreevich 1792-1878 . . . DLB-205
Vickers, Roy 1888?-1965 . . . . DLB-77
Vickery, Sukey 1779-1821 . . . . DLB-200
Victoria 1819-1901 . . . . DLB-55
Victoria Press DLB-106
Vidal, Gore 1925- DLB-6, 152
Viebig, Clara 1860-1952 . . . . DLB-66
Viereck, George Sylvester 1884-1962 . . . . . DLB-54
Viereck, Peter 1916- DLB-5
Viets, Roger 1738-1811 . . . . DLB-99
Viewpoint: Politics and Performance, by
  David Edgar DLB-13
Vigil-Piñon, Evangelina 1949- DLB-122
Vigneault, Gilles 1928- DLB-60
Vigny, Alfred de 1797-1863 . . . . DLB-119, 192
Vigolo, Giorgio 1894-1983 . . . . DLB-114
The Viking Press DLB-46
Villanueva, Alma Luz 1944- DLB-122
Villanueva, Tino 1941- DLB-82
Villard, Henry 1835-1900 . . . . DLB-23
Villard, Oswald Garrison 1872-1949 . . . DLB-25, 91
Villarreal, Edit 1944- DLB-209
Villarreal, José Antonio 1924- DLB-82
Villaseñor, Victor 1940- DLB-209
Villegas de Magnón, Leonor
  1876-1955 . . . . DLB-122

Villehardouin, Geoffroi de
  circa 1150-1215 . . . . DLB-208
Villemaire, Yolande 1949- DLB-60
Villena, Luis Antonio de 1951- DLB-134
Villiers de l'Isle-Adam, Jean-Marie
  Mathias Philippe-Auguste, Comte de
  1838-1889 . . . . DLB-123, 192
Villiers, George, Second Duke
  of Buckingham 1628-1687 . . . . DLB-80
Villon, François 1431-circa 1463? DLB-208
Vine Press DLB-112
Viorst, Judith ?- DLB-52
Vipont, Elfrida (Elfrida Vipont Foulds,
  Charles Vipont) 1902-1992 . . . . DLB-160
Viramontes, Helena María 1954- DLB-122
Virgil 70 B.C.-19 B.C. DLB-211
Vischer, Friedrich Theodor
  1807-1887 . . . . DLB-133
Vitruvius circa 85 B.C.-circa 15 B.C. DLB-211
Vitry, Philippe de 1291-1361 . . . . DLB-208
Vivanco, Luis Felipe 1907-1975 . . . . DLB-108
Viviani, Cesare 1947- DLB-128
Vizenor, Gerald 1934- DLB-175
Vizetelly and Company DLB-106
Voaden, Herman 1903- DLB-88
Voigt, Ellen Bryant 1943- DLB-120
Vojnović, Ivo 1857-1929 . . . . DLB-147
Volkoff, Vladimir 1932- DLB-83
Volland, P. F., Company DLB-46
Vollbehr, Otto H. F. 1872?-
  1945 or 1946 . . . . DLB-187
Volponi, Paolo 1924- DLB-177
von der Grün, Max 1926- DLB-75
Vonnegut, Kurt
  1922- DLB-2, 8, 152; Y-80; DS-3
Voranc, Prežihov 1893-1950 . . . . DLB-147
Voß, Johann Heinrich 1751-1826 . . . . DLB-90
Voynich, E. L. 1864-1960 . . . . DLB-197
Vroman, Mary Elizabeth
  circa 1924-1967 . . . . DLB-33

W

Wace, Robert ("Maistre")
  circa 1100-circa 1175 . . . . DLB-146
Wackenroder, Wilhelm Heinrich
  1773-1798 . . . . DLB-90
Wackernagel, Wilhelm 1806-1869 . . . . . . DLB-133
Waddington, Miriam 1917- DLB-68
Wade, Henry 1887-1969 . . . . DLB-77
Wagenknecht, Edward 1900- DLB-103
Wagner, Heinrich Leopold 1747-1779 . . . . DLB-94
Wagner, Henry R. 1862-1957 . . . . DLB-140
Wagner, Richard 1813-1883 . . . . DLB-129
Wagoner, David 1926- DLB-5
Wah, Fred 1939- DLB-60
Waiblinger, Wilhelm 1804-1830 . . . . DLB-90
Wain, John 1925-1994 . . . . . DLB-15, 27, 139, 155
Wainwright, Jeffrey 1944- DLB-40

Cumulative Index

Waite, Peirce and Company............ DLB-49
Wakeman, Stephen H. 1859-1924...... DLB-187
Wakoski, Diane 1937-................ DLB-5
Walahfrid Strabo circa 808-849........ DLB-148
Walck, Henry Z..................... DLB-46
Walcott, Derek 1930-..... DLB-117; Y-81, Y-92
Waldegrave, Robert [publishing house]...DLB-170
Waldman, Anne 1945-............... DLB-16
Waldrop, Rosmarie 1935-........... DLB-169
Walker, Alice 1900-1982 .... DLB-201
Walker, Alice 1944-......... DLB-6, 33, 143
Walker, George F. 1947-............. DLB-60
Walker, Joseph A. 1935-............. DLB-38
Walker, Margaret 1915-......... DLB-76, 152
Walker, Ted 1934-................ DLB-40
Walker and Company DLB-49
Walker, Evans and Cogswell
  Company...................... DLB-49
Walker, John Brisben 1847-1931....... DLB-79
Wallace, Alfred Russel 1823-1913...... DLB-190
Wallace, Dewitt 1889-1981 and
  Lila Acheson Wallace
  1889-1984 .... DLB-137
Wallace, Edgar 1875-1932 .... DLB-70
Wallace, Lew 1827-1905 .... DLB-202
Wallace, Lila Acheson (see Wallace, Dewitt,
  and Lila Acheson Wallace)
Wallant, Edward Lewis
  1926-1962 .... DLB-2, 28, 143
Waller, Edmund 1606-1687 .... DLB-126
Walpole, Horace 1717-1797..... DLB-39, 104, 213
Walpole, Hugh 1884-1941 .... DLB-34
Walrond, Eric 1898-1966 .... DLB-51
Walser, Martin 1927-......... DLB-75, 124
Walser, Robert 1878-1956 .... DLB-66
Walsh, Ernest 1895-1926 .... DLB-4, 45
Walsh, Robert 1784-1859............. DLB-59
Waltharius circa 825................ DLB-148
Walters, Henry 1848-1931............ DLB-140
Walther von der Vogelweide
  circa 1170-circa 1230 .... DLB-138
Walton, Izaak 1593-1683......... DLB-151, 213
Wambaugh, Joseph 1937-....... DLB-6; Y-83
Waniek, Marilyn Nelson 1946-...... DLB-120
Wanley, Humphrey 1672-1726......... DLB-213
Warburton, William 1698-1779....... DLB-104
Ward, Aileen 1919-................ DLB-111
Ward, Artemus (see Browne, Charles Farrar)
Ward, Arthur Henry Sarsfield
  (see Rohmer, Sax)
Ward, Douglas Turner 1930-........DLB-7, 38
Ward, Lynd 1905-1985 .... DLB-22
Ward, Lock and Company DLB-106
Ward, Mrs. Humphry 1851-1920 ...... DLB-18
Ward, Nathaniel circa 1578-1652 ..... DLB-24
Ward, Theodore 1902-1983 .... DLB-76

Wardle, Ralph 1909-1988 .... DLB-103
Ware, William 1797-1852............... DLB-1
Warne, Frederick, and Company [U.S.]... DLB-49
Warne, Frederick, and
  Company [U.K.] DLB-106
Warner, Anne 1869-1913........... DLB-202
Warner, Charles Dudley 1829-1900 ..... DLB-64
Warner, Marina 1946-............. DLB-194
Warner, Rex 1905-................ DLB-15
Warner, Susan Bogert 1819-1885...... DLB-3, 42
Warner, Sylvia Townsend
  1893-1978.................. DLB-34, 139
Warner, William 1558-1609............DLB-172
Warner Books DLB-46
Warr, Bertram 1917-1943 .... DLB-88
Warren, John Byrne Leicester
  (see De Tabley, Lord)
Warren, Lella 1899-1982 ....Y-83
Warren, Mercy Otis 1728-1814...... DLB-31, 200
Warren, Robert Penn
  1905-1989 .... DLB-2, 48, 152; Y-80, Y-89
Warren, Samuel 1807-1877............ DLB-190
Die Wartburgkrieg
  circa 1230-circa 1280 .... DLB-138
Warton, Joseph 1722-1800.........DLB-104, 109
Warton, Thomas 1728-1790........DLB-104, 109
Washington, George 1732-1799 .... DLB-31
Wassermann, Jakob 1873-1934 .... DLB-66
Wasson, David Atwood 1823-1887....... DLB-1
Waterhouse, Keith 1929-......... DLB-13, 15
Waterman, Andrew 1940-........... DLB-40
Waters, Frank 1902-...........DLB-212; Y-86
Waters, Michael 1949-............. DLB-120
Watkins, Tobias 1780-1855 .... DLB-73
Watkins, Vernon 1906-1967 .... DLB-20
Watmough, David 1926-............ DLB-53
Watson, James Wreford (see Wreford, James)
Watson, John 1850-1907............. DLB-156
Watson, Sheila 1909-............... DLB-60
Watson, Thomas 1545?-1592.......... DLB-132
Watson, Wilfred 1911-.............. DLB-60
Watt, W. J., and Company DLB-46
Watten, Barrett 1948-.............. DLB-193
Watterson, Henry 1840-1921........... DLB-25
Watts, Alan 1915-1973 .... DLB-16
Watts, Franklin [publishing house]....... DLB-46
Watts, Isaac 1674-1748 .... DLB-95
Wand, Alfred Rudolph 1828-1891...... DLB-188
Waugh, Alec 1898-1981............. DLB-191
Waugh, Auberon 1939-......... DLB-14, 194
Waugh, Evelyn 1903-1966......DLB-15, 162, 195
Way and Williams DLB-49
Wayman, Tom 1945-............... DLB-53
Weatherly, Tom 1942-.............. DLB-41
Weaver, Gordon 1937-............. DLB-130
Weaver, Robert 1921-............... DLB-88

Webb, Beatrice 1858-1943 and
  Webb, Sidney 1859-1947......... DLB-190
Webb, Frank J. ?-?.................... DLB-50
Webb, James Watson 1802-1884........ DLB-43
Webb, Mary 1881-1927............. DLB-34
Webb, Phyllis 1927-............... DLB-53
Webb, Walter Prescott 1888-1963........DLB-17
Webbe, William ?-1591............. DLB-132
Webber, Charles Wilkins 1819-1856?... DLB-202
Webster, Augusta 1837-1894........... DLB-35
Webster, Charles L., and Company...... DLB-49
Webster, John
  1579 or 1580-1634?.............. DLB-58
Webster, Noah 1758-1843 ... DLB-1, 37, 42, 43, 73
Weckherlin, Georg Rodolf 1584-1653... DLB-164
Wedekind, Frank 1864-1918 .... DLB-118
Weeks, Edward Augustus, Jr.
  1898-1989 ....DLB-137
Weeks, Stephen B. 1865-1918 ....DLB-187
Weems, Mason Locke
  1759-1825.................DLB-30, 37, 42
Weerth, Georg 1822-1856 .... DLB-129
Weidenfeld and Nicolson............. DLB-112
Weidman, Jerome 1913-............ DLB-28
Weigl, Bruce 1949-................ DLB-120
Weinbaum, Stanley Grauman
  1902-1935 .... DLB-8
Weintraub, Stanley 1929-........... DLB-111
Weise, Christian 1642-1708 .... DLB-168
Weisenborn, Gunther 1902-1969.... DLB-69, 124
Weiß, Ernst 1882-1940............... DLB-81
Weiss, John 1818-1879............... DLB-1
Weiss, Peter 1916-1982 .... DLB-69, 124
Weiss, Theodore 1916-............... DLB-5
Weisse, Christian Felix 1726-1804 ...... DLB-97
Weitling, Wilhelm 1808-1871.......... DLB-129
Welch, James 1940-.................DLB-175
Welch, Lew 1926-1971?.............. DLB-16
Weldon, Fay 1931-............. DLB-14, 194
Wellek, René 1903-................ DLB-63
Wells, Carolyn 1862-1942 .... DLB-11
Wells, Charles Jeremiah
  circa 1800-1879 .... DLB-32
Wells, Gabriel 1862-1946............. DLB-140
Wells, H. G. 1866-1946 ..... DLB-34, 70, 156, 178
Wells, Helena 1758?-1824 .... DLB-200
Wells, Robert 1947-................ DLB-40
Wells-Barnett, Ida B. 1862-1931......... DLB-23
Welty, Eudora
  1909-........ DLB-2, 102, 143; Y-87; DS-12
Wendell, Barrett 1855-1921 .... DLB-71
Wentworth, Patricia 1878-1961 .... DLB-77
Werder, Diederich von dem
  1584-1657 .... DLB-164
Werfel, Franz 1890-1945 .... DLB-81, 124
The Werner Company................ DLB-49
Werner, Zacharias 1768-1823.......... DLB-94

Wersba, Barbara 1932- DLB-52	White, Edgar B. 1947- DLB-38	Wilbrandt, Adolf 1837-1911 ....DLB-129
Wescott, Glenway 1901- DLB-4, 9, 102	White, Ethel Lina 1887-1944............DLB-77	Wilbur, Richard 1921- DLB-5, 169
We See the Editor at Work..............Y-97	White, Henry Kirke 1785-1806..........DLB-96	Wild, Peter 1940- DLB-5
Wesker, Arnold 1932- DLB-13	White, Horace 1834-1916 ....DLB-23	Wilde, Lady Jane Francesca Elgee
Wesley, Charles 1707-1788............DLB-95	White, Phyllis Dorothy James (see James, P. D.)	1821?-1896 ....DLB-199
Wesley, John 1703-1791...............DLB-104	White, Richard Grant 1821-1885 ....DLB-64	Wilde, Oscar 1854-1900
Wesley, Richard 1945- DLB-38	White, T. H. 1906-1964 ....DLB-160	..........DLB-10, 19, 34, 57, 141, 156, 190
Wessels, A., and Company DLB-46	White, Walter 1893-1955 ....DLB-51	Wilde, Richard Henry 1789-1847 ....DLB-3, 59
Wessobrunner Gebet circa 787-815 ....DLB-148	White, William, and Company DLB-49	Wilde, W. A., Company DLB-49
West, Anthony 1914-1988...............DLB-15	White, William Allen 1868-1944.......DLB-9, 25	Wilder, Billy 1906- DLB-26
West, Dorothy 1907-1998 ....DLB-76	White, William Anthony Parker	Wilder, Laura Ingalls 1867-1957 ....DLB-22
West, Jessamyn 1902-1984 ....DLB-6; Y-84	(see Boucher, Anthony)	Wilder, Thornton 1897-1975 ....DLB-4, 7, 9
West, Mae 1892-1980 ....DLB-44	White, William Hale (see Rutherford, Mark)	Wildgans, Anton 1881-1932 ....DLB-118
West, Nathanael 1903-1940.........DLB-4, 9, 28	Whitechurch, Victor L. 1868-1933 ....DLB-70	Wiley, Bell Irvin 1906-1980..............DLB-17
West, Paul 1930- DLB-14	Whitehead, Alfred North 1861-1947.....DLB-100	Wiley, John, and Sons................DLB-49
West, Rebecca 1892-1983 ....DLB-36; Y-83	Whitehead, James 1936- Y-81	Wilhelm, Kate 1928- DLB-8
West, Richard 1941- DLB-185	Whitehead, William 1715-1785 ......DLB-84, 109	Wilkes, Charles 1798-1877..............DLB-183
Westcott, Edward Noyes 1846-1898 .....DLB-202	Whitfield, James Monroe 1822-1871 .....DLB-50	Wilkes, George 1817-1885 ....DLB-79
West and Johnson DLB-49	Whitgift, John circa 1533-1604 ....DLB-132	Wilkinson, Anne 1910-1961 ....DLB-88
Western Publishing Company..........DLB-46	Whiting, John 1917-1963...............DLB-13	Wilkinson, Eliza Yonge
The Westminster Review 1824-1914 ....DLB-110	Whiting, Samuel 1597-1679 ....DLB-24	1757-circa 1813 ....DLB-200
Weston, Elizabeth Jane	Whitlock, Brand 1869-1934.............DLB-12	Wilkinson, Sylvia 1940- Y-86
circa 1582-1612..................DLB-172	Whitman, Albert, and Company........DLB-46	Wilkinson, William Cleaver
Wetherald, Agnes Ethelwyn 1857-1940....DLB-99	Whitman, Albery Allson 1851-1901 ......DLB-50	1833-1920.....................DLB-71
Wetherell, Elizabeth (see Warner, Susan Bogert)	Whitman, Alden 1913-1990..............Y-91	Willard, Barbara 1909-1994 ....DLB-161
Wetzel, Friedrich Gottlob 1779-1819 ....DLB-90	Whitman, Sarah Helen (Power)	Willard, L. [publishing house] DLB-49
Weyman, Stanley J. 1855-1928 .....DLB-141, 156	1803-1878 ....DLB-1	Willard, Nancy 1936- DLB-5, 52
Wezel, Johann Karl 1747-1819 ....DLB-94	Whitman, Walt 1819-1892 ....DLB-3, 64	Willard, Samuel 1640-1707 ....DLB-24
Whalen, Philip 1923- DLB-16	Whitman Publishing Company..........DLB-46	William of Auvergne 1190-1249 ....DLB-115
Whalley, George 1915-1983 ....DLB-88	Whitney, Geoffrey	William of Conches
Wharton, Edith	1548 or 1552?-1601 ....DLB-136	circa 1090-circa 1154................DLB-115
1862-1937 ...... DLB-4, 9, 12, 78, 189; DS-13	Whitney, Isabella	William of Ockham
Wharton, William 1920s?- Y-80	flourished 1566-1573..............DLB-136	circa 1285-1347 ....DLB-115
Whately, Mary Louisa 1824-1889.......DLB-166	Whitney, John Hay 1904-1982 ....DLB-127	William of Sherwood
Whately, Richard 1787-1863 ....DLB-190	Whittemore, Reed 1919- DLB-5	1200/1205 - 1266/1271 ....DLB-115
What's Really Wrong With Bestseller Lists ..Y-84	Whittlesey House DLB-46	The William Chavrat American Fiction
Wheatley, Dennis Yates 1897-1977 ....DLB-77	Whittier, John Greenleaf 1807-1892........DLB-1	Collection at the Ohio State University
Wheatley, Phillis circa 1754-1784......DLB-31, 50	Who Runs American Literature? Y-94	Libraries Y-92
Wheeler, Anna Doyle 1785-1848?.......DLB-158	Whose *Ulysses*? The Function of	William Faulkner Centenary..............Y-97
Wheeler, Charles Stearns 1816-1843 .....DLB-1	Editing.........................Y-97	Williams, A., and Company DLB-49
Wheeler, Monroe 1900-1988..............DLB-4	Wideman, John Edgar 1941- DLB-33, 143	Williams, Ben Ames 1889-1953.........DLB-102
Wheelock, John Hall 1886-1978 ....DLB-45	Widener, Harry Elkins 1885-1912.......DLB-140	Williams, C. K. 1936- DLB-5
Wheelwright, John circa 1592-1679.......DLB-24	Wiebe, Rudy 1934- DLB-60	Williams, Chancellor 1905- DLB-76
Wheelwright, J. B. 1897-1940..........DLB-45	Wiechert, Ernst 1887-1950..............DLB-56	Williams, Charles 1886-1945....... DLB-100, 153
Whetstone, Colonel Pete (see Noland, C. F. M.)	Wied, Martina 1882-1957 ....DLB-85	Williams, Denis 1923- DLB-117
Whetstone, George 1550-1587..........DLB-136	Wiehe, Evelyn May Clowes (see Mordaunt,	Williams, Emlyn 1905- DLB-10, 77
Whicher, Stephen E. 1915-1961 ....DLB-111	Elinor)	Williams, Garth 1912- DLB-22
Whipple, Edwin Percy 1819-1886......DLB-1, 64	Wieland, Christoph Martin	Williams, George Washington
Whitaker, Alexander 1585-1617 ....DLB-24	1733-1813 ....DLB-97	1849-1891.....................DLB-47
Whitaker, Daniel K. 1801-1881..........DLB-73	Wienbarg, Ludolf 1802-1872..........DLB-133	Williams, Heathcote 1941- DLB-13
Whitcher, Frances Miriam	Wieners, John 1934- DLB-16	Williams, Helen Maria 1761-1827 ....DLB-158
1812-1852 ....DLB-11, 202	Wier, Ester 1910- DLB-52	Williams, Hugo 1942- DLB-40
White, Andrew 1579-1656..............DLB-24	Wiesel, Elie 1928- DLB-83; Y-86, Y-87	Williams, Isaac 1802-1865..............DLB-32
White, Andrew Dickson 1832-1918 ......DLB-47	Wiggin, Kate Douglas 1856-1923 ....DLB-42	Williams, Joan 1928- DLB-6
White, E. B. 1899-1985 ....DLB-11, 22	Wigglesworth, Michael 1631-1705........DLB-24	Williams, John A. 1925- DLB-2, 33
	Wilberforce, William 1759-1833 ....DLB-158	Williams, John E. 1922-1994 ....DLB-6
		Williams, Jonathan 1929- DLB-5

Williams, Miller 1930-	DLB-105
Williams, Raymond 1921-	DLB-14
Williams, Roger circa 1603-1683	DLB-24
Williams, Rowland 1817-1870	DLB-184
Williams, Samm-Art 1946-	DLB-38
Williams, Sherley Anne 1944-	DLB-41
Williams, T. Harry 1909-1979	DLB-17
Williams, Tennessee 1911-1983	DLB-7; Y-83; DS-4
Williams, Terry Tempest 1955-	DLB-206
Williams, Ursula Moray 1911-	DLB-160
Williams, Valentine 1883-1946	DLB-77
Williams, William Appleman 1921-	DLB-17
Williams, William Carlos 1883-1963	DLB-4, 16, 54, 86
Williams, Wirt 1921-	DLB-6
Williams Brothers	DLB-49
Williamson, Henry 1895-1977	DLB-191
Williamson, Jack 1908-	DLB-8
Willingham, Calder Baynard, Jr. 1922-	DLB-2, 44
Williram of Ebersberg circa 1020-1085	DLB-148
Willis, Nathaniel Parker 1806-1867	DLB-3, 59, 73, 74, 183; DS-13
Willkomm, Ernst 1810-1886	DLB-133
Willumsen, Dorrit 1940-	DLB-214
Wilmer, Clive 1945-	DLB-40
Wilson, A. N. 1950-	DLB-14, 155, 194
Wilson, Angus 1913-1991	DLB-15, 139, 155
Wilson, Arthur 1595-1652	DLB-58
Wilson, Augusta Jane Evans 1835-1909	DLB-42
Wilson, Colin 1931-	DLB-14, 194
Wilson, Edmund 1895-1972	DLB-63
Wilson, Ethel 1888-1980	DLB-68
Wilson, F. P. 1889-1963	DLB-201
Wilson, Harriet E. Adams 1828?-1863?	DLB-50
Wilson, Harry Leon 1867-1939	DLB-9
Wilson, John 1588-1667	DLB-24
Wilson, John 1785-1854	DLB-110
Wilson, John Dover 1881-1969	DLB-201
Wilson, Lanford 1937-	DLB-7
Wilson, Margaret 1882-1973	DLB-9
Wilson, Michael 1914-1978	DLB-44
Wilson, Mona 1872-1954	DLB-149
Wilson, Romer 1891-1930	DLB-191
Wilson, Thomas 1523 or 1524-1581	DLB-132
Wilson, Woodrow 1856-1924	DLB-47
Wilson, Effingham [publishing house]	DLB-154
Wimsatt, William K., Jr. 1907-1975	DLB-63
Winchell, Walter 1897-1972	DLB-29
Winchester, J. [publishing house]	DLB-49
Winckelmann, Johann Joachim 1717-1768	DLB-97
Winckler, Paul 1630-1686	DLB-164
Wind, Herbert Warren 1916-	DLB-171
Windet, John [publishing house]	DLB-170
Windham, Donald 1920-	DLB-6
Wing, Donald Goddard 1904-1972	DLB-187
Wing, John M. 1844-1917	DLB-187
Wingate, Allan [publishing house]	DLB-112
Winnemucca, Sarah 1844-1921	DLB-175
Winnifrith, Tom 1938-	DLB-155
Winning an Edgar	Y-98
Winsloe, Christa 1888-1944	DLB-124
Winslow, Anna Green 1759-1780	DLB-200
Winsor, Justin 1831-1897	DLB-47
John C. Winston Company	DLB-49
Winters, Yvor 1900-1968	DLB-48
Winterson, Jeanette 1959-	DLB-207
Winthrop, John 1588-1649	DLB-24, 30
Winthrop, John, Jr. 1606-1676	DLB-24
Winthrop, Margaret Tyndal 1591-1647	DLB-200
Winthrop, Theodore 1828-1861	DLB-202
Wirt, William 1772-1834	DLB-37
Wise, John 1652-1725	DLB-24
Wise, Thomas James 1859-1937	DLB-184
Wiseman, Adele 1928-	DLB-88
Wishart and Company	DLB-112
Wisner, George 1812-1849	DLB-43
Wister, Owen 1860-1938	DLB-9, 78, 186
Wister, Sarah 1761-1804	DLB-200
Wither, George 1588-1667	DLB-121
Witherspoon, John 1723-1794	DLB-31
Withrow, William Henry 1839-1908	DLB-99
Witkacy (see Witkiewicz, Stanisław Ignacy)
Witkiewicz, Stanisław Ignacy 1885-1939	DLB-215
Wittig, Monique 1935-	DLB-83
Wodehouse, P. G. 1881-1975	DLB-34, 162
Wohmann, Gabriele 1932-	DLB-75
Woiwode, Larry 1941-	DLB-6
Wolcot, John 1738-1819	DLB-109
Wolcott, Roger 1679-1767	DLB-24
Wolf, Christa 1929-	DLB-75
Wolf, Friedrich 1888-1953	DLB-124
Wolfe, Gene 1931-	DLB-8
Wolfe, John [publishing house]	DLB-170
Wolfe, Reyner (Reginald) [publishing house]	DLB-170
Wolfe, Thomas 1900-1938	DLB-9, 102; Y-85; DS-2, DS-16
Wolfe, Tom 1931-	DLB-152, 185
Wolff, Helen 1906-1994	Y-94
Wolff, Tobias 1945-	DLB-130
Wolfram von Eschenbach circa 1170-after 1220	DLB-138
Wolfram von Eschenbach's *Parzival:* Prologue and Book 3	DLB-138
Wollstonecraft, Mary 1759-1797	DLB-39, 104, 158
Wolker, Jiří 1900-1924	DLB-215
Wondratschek, Wolf 1943-	DLB-75
Wood, Anthony à 1632-1695	DLB-213
Wood, Benjamin 1820-1900	DLB-23
Wood, Charles 1932-	DLB-13
Wood, Mrs. Henry 1814-1887	DLB-18
Wood, Joanna E. 1867-1927	DLB-92
Wood, Sally Sayward Barrell Keating 1759-1855	DLB-200
Wood, Samuel [publishing house]	DLB-49
Wood, William ?-?	DLB-24
Woodberry, George Edward 1855-1930	DLB-71, 103
Woodbridge, Benjamin 1622-1684	DLB-24
Woodcock, George 1912-	DLB-88
Woodhull, Victoria C. 1838-1927	DLB-79
Woodmason, Charles circa 1720-?	DLB-31
Woodress, Jr., James Leslie 1916-	DLB-111
Woodson, Carter G. 1875-1950	DLB-17
Woodward, C. Vann 1908-	DLB-17
Woodward, Stanley 1895-1965	DLB-171
Wooler, Thomas 1785 or 1786-1853	DLB-158
Woolf, David (see Maddow, Ben)
Woolf, Leonard 1880-1969	DLB-100; DS-10
Woolf, Virginia 1882-1941	DLB-36, 100, 162; DS-10
Woolf, Virginia, "The New Biography," *New York Herald Tribune,* 30 October 1927	DLB-149
Woollcott, Alexander 1887-1943	DLB-29
Woolman, John 1720-1772	DLB-31
Woolner, Thomas 1825-1892	DLB-35
Woolsey, Sarah Chauncy 1835-1905	DLB-42
Woolson, Constance Fenimore 1840-1894	DLB-12, 74, 189
Worcester, Joseph Emerson 1784-1865	DLB-1
Worde, Wynkyn de [publishing house]	DLB-170
Wordsworth, Christopher 1807-1885	DLB-166
Wordsworth, Dorothy 1771-1855	DLB-107
Wordsworth, Elizabeth 1840-1932	DLB-98
Wordsworth, William 1770-1850	DLB-93, 107
Workman, Fanny Bullock 1859-1925	DLB-189
The Works of the Rev. John Witherspoon (1800-1801) [excerpts]	DLB-31
A World Chronology of Important Science Fiction Works (1818-1979)	DLB-8
World Publishing Company	DLB-46
World War II Writers Symposium at the University of South Carolina, 12–14 April 1995	Y-95
Worthington, R., and Company	DLB-49
Wotton, Sir Henry 1568-1639	DLB-121
Wouk, Herman 1915-	Y-82
Wreford, James 1915-	DLB-88
Wren, Sir Christopher 1632-1723	DLB-213

Wren, Percival Christopher 1885-1941 .... DLB-153
Wrenn, John Henry 1841-1911 .... DLB-140
Wright, C. D. 1949- DLB-120
Wright, Charles 1935- DLB-165; Y-82
Wright, Charles Stevenson 1932- DLB-33
Wright, Frances 1795-1852 .... DLB-73
Wright, Harold Bell 1872-1944 .... DLB-9
Wright, James 1927-1980 .... DLB-5, 169
Wright, Jay 1935- DLB-41
Wright, Louis B. 1899-1984 .... DLB-17
Wright, Richard 1908-1960 .... DLB-76, 102; DS-2
Wright, Richard B. 1937- DLB-53
Wright, Sarah Elizabeth 1928- DLB-33
Wright, Willard Huntington ("S. S. Van Dine") 1888-1939 .... DS-16
Writers and Politics: 1871-1918, by Ronald Gray DLB-66
Writers and their Copyright Holders: the WATCH Project Y-94
Writers' Forum Y-85
Writing for the Theatre, by Harold Pinter DLB-13
Wroth, Lady Mary 1587-1653 .... DLB-121
Wroth, Lawrence C. 1884-1970 .... DLB-187
Wurlitzer, Rudolph 1937- DLB-173
Wyatt, Sir Thomas circa 1503-1542 .... DLB-132
Wycherley, William 1641-1715 .... DLB-80
Wyclif, John circa 1335-31 December 1384 .... DLB-146
Wyeth, N. C. 1882-1945 .... DLB-188; DS-16
Wylie, Elinor 1885-1928 .... DLB-9, 45
Wylie, Philip 1902-1971 .... DLB-9
Wyllie, John Cook 1908-1968 .... DLB-140
Wyman, Lillie Buffum Chace 1847-1929 .... DLB-202
Wynne-Tyson, Esmé 1898-1972 .... DLB-191

X

Xenophon circa 430 B.C.-circa 356 B.C. DLB-176

Y

Yasuoka Shōtarō 1920- DLB-182
Yates, Dornford 1885-1960 .... DLB-77, 153
Yates, J. Michael 1938- DLB-60
Yates, Richard 1926-1992 .... DLB-2; Y-81, Y-92
Yavorov, Peyo 1878-1914 .... DLB-147
Yearsley, Ann 1753-1806 .... DLB-109
Yeats, William Butler 1865-1939 .... DLB-10, 19, 98, 156
Yep, Laurence 1948- DLB-52
Yerby, Frank 1916-1991 .... DLB-76
Yezierska, Anzia 1885-1970 .... DLB-28
Yolen, Jane 1939- DLB-52
Yonge, Charlotte Mary 1823-1901 .... DLB-18, 163
The York Cycle circa 1376-circa 1569 .... DLB-146
A Yorkshire Tragedy DLB-58
Yoseloff, Thomas [publishing house] DLB-46
Young, Al 1939- DLB-33
Young, Arthur 1741-1820 .... DLB-158
Young, Dick 1917 or 1918 - 1987 .... DLB-171
Young, Edward 1683-1765 .... DLB-95
Young, Francis Brett 1884-1954 .... DLB-191
Young, Gavin 1928- DLB-204
Young, Stark 1881-1963 .... DLB-9, 102; DS-16
Young, Waldeman 1880-1938 .... DLB-26
Young, William [publishing house] DLB-49
Young Bear, Ray A. 1950- DLB-175
Yourcenar, Marguerite 1903-1987 .... DLB-72; Y-88
"You've Never Had It So Good," Gusted by "Winds of Change": British Fiction in the 1950s, 1960s, and After DLB-14
Yovkov, Yordan 1880-1937 .... DLB-147

Z

Zachariä, Friedrich Wilhelm 1726-1777 .... DLB-97
Zagoskin, Mikhail Nikolaevich 1789-1852 .... DLB-198
Zajc, Dane 1929- DLB-181
Zamora, Bernice 1938- DLB-82
Zand, Herbert 1923-1970 .... DLB-85
Zangwill, Israel 1864-1926 .... DLB-10, 135, 197
Zanzotto, Andrea 1921- DLB-128
Zapata Olivella, Manuel 1920- DLB-113
Zebra Books DLB-46
Zebrowski, George 1945- DLB-8
Zech, Paul 1881-1946 .... DLB-56
Zeimi (Kanze Motokiyo) 1363-1443 .... DLB-203
Zepheria DLB-172
Zeidner, Lisa 1955- DLB-120
Zelazny, Roger 1937-1995 .... DLB-8
Zenger, John Peter 1697-1746 .... DLB-24, 43
Zesen, Philipp von 1619-1689 .... DLB-164
Zhukovsky, Vasilii Andreevich 1783-1852 .... DLB-205
Zieber, G. B., and Company DLB-49
Zieroth, Dale 1946- DLB-60
Zigler und Kliphausen, Heinrich Anshelm von 1663-1697 .... DLB-168
Zimmer, Paul 1934- DLB-5
Zingref, Julius Wilhelm 1591-1635 .... DLB-164
Zindel, Paul 1936- DLB-7, 52
Zinnes, Harriet 1919- DLB-193
Zinzendorf, Nikolaus Ludwig von 1700-1760 .... DLB-168
Zitkala-Ša 1876-1938 .... DLB-175
Zola, Emile 1840-1902 .... DLB-123
Zolla, Elémire 1926- DLB-196
Zolotow, Charlotte 1915- DLB-52
Zschokke, Heinrich 1771-1848 .... DLB-94
Zubly, John Joachim 1724-1781 .... DLB-31
Zu-Bolton II, Ahmos 1936- DLB-41
Zuckmayer, Carl 1896-1977 .... DLB-56, 124
Zukofsky, Louis 1904-1978 .... DLB-5, 165
Zupan, Vitomil 1914-1987 .... DLB-181
Župančič, Oton 1878-1949 .... DLB-147
zur Mühlen, Hermynia 1883-1951 .... DLB-56
Zweig, Arnold 1887-1968 .... DLB-66
Zweig, Stefan 1881-1942 .... DLB-81, 118

ISBN 0-7876-3125-6

90000